WI THD RAWN

W9-ABZ-525

WITHDRAWN

PERSONALITY DEVELOPMENT AND ADJUSTMENT IN ADOLESCENCE

PERSONALITY
DEVELOPMENT
AND
ADJUSTMENT
IN ADOLESCENCE

Alexander A. Schneiders, Ph.D.

**PROFESSOR OF PSYCHOLOGY AND DIRECTOR OF
PSYCHOLOGICAL SERVICES, FORDHAM UNIVERSITY**

THE BRUCE PUBLISHING COMPANY   MILWAUKEE

Library of Congress Catalog Card Number: 60–14397
© 1960 Alexander A. Schneiders
Made in the United States of America

To my seven Children who made this revision
necessary by becoming adolescents.

PREFACE TO REVISED EDITION

This book is a revised edition of the author's *Psychology of Adolescence*, which originally appeared in 1951. But what started out as an ordinary revision led, in the course of time and after considerable reflection, to a complete reorganization and reshaping of the original text. The reader will note from the Table of Contents that the "Psychology of Adolescence," which was the original title, is now only one of the essential parts of the book, and therefore would no longer be appropriate as a general title. However, the spirit of the book is the same as that which guided the writing of the original volume, which was to develop a thoroughgoing interpretation of the conduct and personality of young people between the ages of 14 and 21. High school teachers, parents, students in psychology, and counselors of youth need to know as much as possible about the thinking and behavior, the needs, feelings, and goals of the teen-age boy or girl, if they are to understand them, guide them, and help them cope with the conflicts and difficulties of the adolescent period. This is particularly true today, when youth is faced with the breakdown of basic values, the disintegration of the family, the constant threat of global war, and the demands of military service. The principal aim of this book, therefore, is to provide such information, and to define the principles and the techniques whereby the problems of youth can be effectively controlled.

To achieve this over-all aim, the author has structured the text around certain major emphases. First of all, as the reader will quickly observe, the text is *problem-oriented*, which means that the development of the material is directed always toward the problems encountered by young people. Second, it is *research-oriented*, so that the opinions and interpretations of the author are substantiated whenever possible by empirical data. Third, the viewpoint presented is *motivation-oriented*, with the result that considerable stress is put upon the dynamics underlying adolescent behavior and personality development. Because of long experience in dealing with adolescent problems, the author feels that a thorough understanding of the needs, motives, and goals of the teen-ager is a prerequisite to understanding and coping with adolescent problems. And finally, the text may be described as *counseling-oriented*, in the sense that the requirements for effective counseling have been kept constantly in mind in the presentation of the material and in the interpretation of adolescent behavior. The author believes that these four emphases, which permeate the entire structure of the book, give it a coherence that is not always too easily achieved.

The structure and coherence of the text are strengthened by certain other characteristics that should interest the reader. As he may note from the Table of Contents, the text is organized into three essential parts, all of which are closely interrelated. These three parts are called the *Physiology of Adolescence*, the *Psychology of Adolescence*, and the *Sociology of Adolescence*. This organization not only promotes coherence, but it also emphasizes the fact that adolescent development and personality are determined by physical factors, by social and cultural determinants, and by the unique psychology of the individual. This arrangement, moreover, falls directly in line with the tendency in contemporary psychology to recognize the important influence on personality of both physical and sociocultural determinants.

A second characteristic that should interest the reader is the attempt throughout the text to develop *basic principles* of adolescent behavior and personality; principles that not only serve to crystallize central ideas about adolescence, but that also form a basis for applying knowledge to the business of coping with adolescent problems. Thus, the final chapter should be of particular interest because it includes a statement of principles that emerge throughout the text and defines a pattern of counseling that can be used with teen-agers.

The text is further characterized by a serious effort to cover *all areas* of adolescent personality and development, and to bring to the reader's attention an extensive group of selected references that can be used for further study, research, or the satisfaction of particular interests. This aid to a better understanding of the adolescent problem is complemented by a fairly extensive glossary and a film bibliography that should be of particular interest to teachers and to students of the adolescent problem.

In putting together a textbook of this type, there are many unseen hands whose skill is just as important and just as necessary as that of the author's. And to all of the persons who had a hand in the production of this volume, the author expresses his most sincere gratitude. To the many authors and publishers who so generously granted permission to use material from many different sources, the author is especially grateful because of the added strength which this material gives to the book. Thanks are also due to the author's publisher for unremitting support and encouragement, and for the skillful productive talents that are so clearly exemplified in the structure and format of the text. To all of his colleagues, and particularly to Dr. John P. Treacy of Marquette University, who offered many suggestions and constructive criticisms, the author is deeply grateful. To the two artists, Matthias C. and Ronald F. Schneiders, the author wishes to express particular gratitude for their skill and their cooperation in bringing the author's ideas to life throughout the text. To the many persons who supplied the author with photographs, and to his secretary, Mrs. Josephine Murphy, the author is deeply grateful; and finally, as always, it is a privilege to express publicly his grateful thanks to his wife whose encouragement and effort shine forth from every page.

June, 1960   A. A. S.

CONTENTS

PART IV

The Sociology of Adolescence

PART V

Principles and Practices

PART I

Introduction

The meaning and significance of adolescence

The American adolescent — his problems and whereabouts

Key concepts for the student of youth

CHAPTER I

THE MEANING AND SIGNIFICANCE OF ADOLESCENCE

When we think of youth, many questions come to mind. What is the meaning of adolescence? Why does it seem to have particular significance? Are the adolescents today different from those of a generation ago? What do we mean by the "psychology of adolescence"? What can we do to understand the adolescent and his problems better?

ADOLESCENCE, A PERIOD OF TRANSITION

The Teen-Ager, the Adolescent, and Youth. Teen-ager is a term which obviously applies to the years of growth and development extending from thirteen to nineteen years of age. It corresponds generally to the period of development known as *adolescence* and also to the period of *youth*.[1] This correspondence, however, is only general, since adolescence may begin before or after the age of thirteen, and may well extend beyond the age of nineteen. Parents and counselors of youth would be wise to keep this fact in mind. Adolescence actually begins with the physical changes of *puberty*, during which the child matures physically and becomes capable of re-

production, and then terminates at some indefinite point called maturity or adulthood. It is common practice nowadays to refer to a transitional period between adolescence and adulthood with the term "young adult." This distinction is not too important for our purposes but is worth noting because the term appears in the literature. The boundaries of adolescence, then, are pubescence on the one side and adulthood on the other.

The most important fact about adolescence, especially where parents are concerned, is that it is essentially a *period of transition*, during which the teen-ager is neither child nor adult but is judged by the standards of both, and treated accordingly. This itself confuses the youngster in his teens, and gives rise to a number of problems. Transition also involves constant and sometimes confusing and bewildering change, which tends to throw the adolescent off balance. These changes are profound and pervasive, and reach into every area of personality — the emotional, sexual, so-

[1] Horrocks lists five factors common to adolescence: physical development and growth, intellectual expansion and development, formation of values, development of individuality, and growth of group relationships. J. E. Horrocks, "What Is Adolescence?" *Education*, 1955, 76, 218–221.

Transition during adolescence means a continuous striving of the teen-ager for adult status.

cial, moral, and religious. Transition means also the gradual conversion of child into adult, and thus implies a continuous striving of the teen-ager for adult status. For the young boy or girl this adult status means independence, freedom, and responsibility, and these aspects of the approaching and desired adulthood cause additional consternation in the life of the teen-ager. Conflicts within themselves, and conflicts between the teen-ager on the one hand and parents and society on the other, are common experiences, and are prolific sources of problems that the adolescent encounters.

Adolescence, Childhood, and Adulthood. Because the adolescent is judged and guided according to the concepts and the expectations of the adults in his life,

it is important to distinguish this period as clearly as we can from other developmental periods. If the adolescent is no longer a child we should certainly know the difference between the two, since it is obvious that to treat the adolescent as a child could lead to a number of difficulties.[2] Similarly, if it is important for the adolescent to reach adulthood, and particularly if society insists on his doing so, then we should know what adulthood is. Knowing what an adult is, we may become less prone to judge the adolescent in terms of adult standards.

[2] J. R. Gallagher, "Various aspects of adolescence," *J. Pediat.*, 1951, 39, 532–543. Gallagher argues that the adolescent should be handled and interpreted in terms of his own age group; therefore, as many facts should be known about the adolescent as possible.

It is well known that parents often react to adolescents in terms of both sets of standards, those adopted for childhood and those supposedly characteristic of adulthood, and the adolescent therefore is caught between these two sets of values. How often we hear parents say, "Why don't you stop acting like a child?" or, "Remember, Johnny, just because you're getting older and bigger doesn't mean that you can do just as you please. You are still a child, and children must obey their parents." In these two phrases the implications of adolescence as a period of transition are dramatically illustrated. Characteristically, parents insist that the young boy or girl assume adult responsibilities, and at the same time insist that they have no rights in the matter.

What is a child as compared with an adolescent? Typically, of course, the child is smaller and weaker than the adolescent; he is somewhat more restricted in his activities; he is in grade school rather than in high school; he has less freedom in the choice of clothes, places he will go, friends with whom he may associate, or how late he may stay up to watch television; he is somewhat less sure of himself, and more dependent on authority of some kind; he is more interested in his gang than in girls; and he is more impulse-dominated than self-controlled.[3]

In other words, there are *psychological* and *social* as well as physical distinctions between the child and the adolescent. However, it is possible to go beyond these somewhat vague criteria of distinction and identify a more precise line of demarcation between the two periods of human development. This does not mean that there is an abrupt break between childhood and adolescence, but rather that certain clear-cut physical changes do take place which help convert the child into the adolescent and pave the way for eventual adulthood. These changes are known collectively as *puberty*.

Puberty or pubescence is the period during which the growing organism becomes capable of reproduction and thus of assuming the role of father or mother. These changes, as we shall see more fully in Chapter V, are signified by the emergence of primary and secondary sex characteristics which alter the physical condition and picture of the developing organism to an important extent. Puberty therefore may be regarded as the *early boundary* of adolescence. It is the first stage in a complex process by which the boy or girl changes deeply and fundamentally in every department of personality, and moves by imperceptible degrees toward the goal of adulthood.

The line of demarcation between adolescence and adulthood, on the other hand, is not at all as clear. Even where physical qualities are concerned, there are no precise criteria that we can use to determine the attainment of adulthood, although we know that the curve of physical growth and development, based on such factors as size, weight, height, and strength, reaches a plateau toward the end of the teen-age period and in early adulthood. In other words, as the adolescent moves into the third decade of life, the boy *looks* more and more like a man, and the girl like a woman.[4]

---

[3] See the interesting study by Tryon in which adolescents evaluate themselves. C. M. Tryon, "Evaluations of Adolescent Personality by Adolescents," *Soc. Child Develpm.*, Monogr. No. 4, Vol. 4 (Washington, D. C.: National Research Council, 1939).

[4] Some authors extend the boundaries of youth past the adolescent period. Landis, for example, distinguishes adolescence and youth on

The trouble here, of course, is that looks are often deceiving; it might well be that a very immature psychic structure or social personality is encased within a powerful and imposing physical frame. It is this developmental paradox that lies at the basis of many severe problems encountered by the young adult. We need, then, to define and to apply other criteria in order to identify true adulthood. Later on (Chapter III) we shall deal at greater length with the concept of *maturity*, which is a more precise term than adulthood, and one that is more meaningful for the psychology of adolescence. Here, however, in the interest of determining the boundaries of adolescence, we can identify several basic criteria that will be helpful to us in achieving a more thorough understanding of adolescence and its goals. Leaving aside physical maturity, adulthood can be thought of as dependent on the following factors: (1) *emotional and economic independence*, (2) *willing acceptance of personal and social responsibility*, (3) *self-identity and self-control*, and (4) *goal-directedness and a realistic attitude regarding the future*. There can be no doubt that any person in whom these qualities are realized has every right to regard himself as a mature adult.

The Goal of Adolescence. The identification of these basic qualities of the adult personality serves to remind us that the transitional period to which we refer loosely as teen-age, youth, or ado-

lescence, *is dominated throughout by its own intrinsic goal.*[5] This goal is defined simply as *adulthood*. We are not referring here to the obvious fact that if the adolescent lives long enough he will become an adult, but rather to the much more basic fact that the whole business of maturing, of changing over from child into adult, of striving for selfhood and self-identity, of shaking oneself loose from the emotional bondage of childhood, and of reaching for independence and responsibility, is dominated by the need to become an adult. The achievement of adulthood, therefore, is not so much a historical fact as it is a *psychological experience*. It is less an evolution than it is a revolution. It does not represent simply a passive transition from an earlier to a later period of development but a continuous, dynamic striving for a higher and more responsible level of human action. Fundamentally, "adolescence represents an effort of the young person to emancipate himself from the constricting bonds of his own family and to establish a basis for normal heterosexual relations." In other words, the primary goal of the adolescent is the attainment of manhood, to be or not to be a man. "Where social institutions fail to satisfy this need, youth will develop behavior patterns which appear to be psychologically satisfying substitutes for adult status. . . . The gang provides a 'custom-built' answer to the adolescent's strivings for adult fulfillment." The fascinating paradox of American culture "is that mature people want to remain perpetually young, while youngsters yearn to leave youth behind and become adult as rapidly as possible. This tendency is,

---

an age basis. Adolescence extends from 12 to 19 years of age, youth from 20 to 24 years of age, and young adults from 25 to 34 years of age. P. H. Landis, *Adolescence and Youth*, 2 ed. (New York: McGraw-Hill, 1952), p. 23. See also B. S. Gottlieb, *Understanding Your Adolescent* (New York: Rinehart, 1957), pp. 213–214.

---

[5] See B. S. Gottlieb, *op. cit.*, pp. 235–244, for a more thorough discussion of the intrinsic goal of adolescent development.

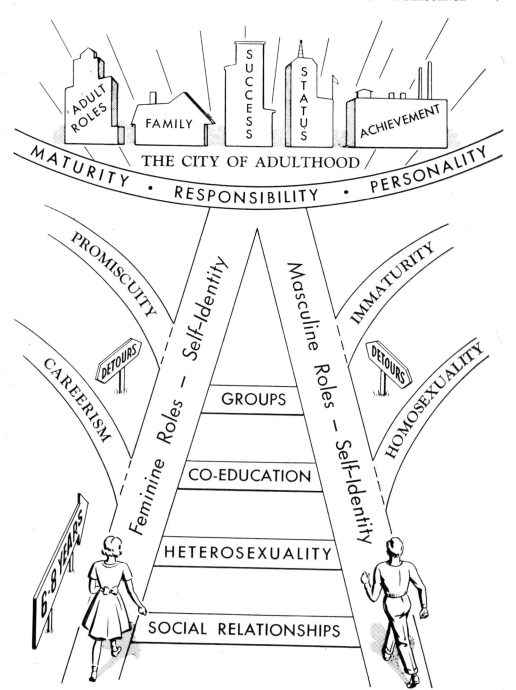

Fig. 1. The paths to adulthood are beset with many difficulties and detours.

upon occasion, almost obsessive. Thus, the need of the adolescent boy to become a man may be added to an already imposing catalog of needs."[6]

We parents, counselors, and teachers often lose sight of the fact that adolescence is intrinsically goal-directed. We are prone to fall back on such bromides as "Oh, she will grow out of it" or "Adolescents are just impossible!" without realizing the dynamic imperativeness of the needs and wants that influence the adolescent's behavior. Or sometimes we just give up in a despair of ignorance and confusion as to what is going on. These are attitudes that parents and counselors cannot afford because the adolescent needs a great deal of understanding, support, and sympathetic guidance.

Negative attitudes often stem from, or may in turn foster, false notions regarding adolescence. It is customary, for example, to think of the youths of today as presenting many more problems than those of a generation ago. Parents and public officials tend to regard youth as generally more wayward, less disciplined, more rebellious, or more promiscuous in matters of sex than when they themselves were adolescents. Or they may regard the trials and tribulations of youth as something that the youngster simply has to live through, and about which little can be done. Some of these notions may be at least partially correct; but we must recognize the fact that ignorance of the dynamics of adolescent behavior is often substituted for an effort to help youth with their problems. Adults should recognize the tendency to repress the memo-

ries of their own adolescence, especially those aspects that were disagreeable or traumatic in nature. Adults often have only a hazy recollection of what went on in their own youth, and thus their comparisons often suffer from a very faulty memory. We shall see later on that the so-called conflict of generations is an important factor in understanding today's youth. But we must exercise extreme caution in the matter of judging modern youth falsely.

ADOLESCENCE, A DEVELOPMENTAL PHENOMENON

The Physiology of Adolescence. To characterize adolescence as a period of transition, marked by pervasive change, conflict, and uncertainty, is only to underscore the fact that adolescence is essentially a developmental phenomenon. It involves, therefore, *continuous* growth and *continuous* unfolding of capacities, and *continuous* change in interpersonal relationships. This is a fact of which adults must be constantly aware. There is nothing static about the adolescent period. Interests change, likes and dislikes change, relationships change, moods and feelings change, and these often change from day to day, from month to month, and certainly from year to year. The changes are real and pervasive, and are necessary, because adolescence is always pointed toward the goal of maturity. Thus, the girl who was so deeply interested in doll play disdains such childish behavior. The boy who could think of nothing more wonderful than to follow in his father's footsteps suddenly veers in a totally different direction. The youngster who was indifferent to sex suddenly becomes very conscious of sex reali-

---

[6] H. Bloch and A. Niederhoffer, *The Gang: a Study in Adolescent Behavior* (New York: Philosophical Library, 1958), pp. 11, 143. See also Irene Josselyn, "Growing to Adulthood," in Sidonie M. Gruenberg (ed.), *Our Children Today* (New York: Viking, 1955), Chap. 15

ties. In every aspect of the adolescent's life there is constant and sometimes bewildering change because the developmental process is carrying the youngster ineluctably to the stage of adulthood.

Prominent among the changes that occur during adolescence are those of a physical nature, changes that underlie to an important extent the achievement of maturity at a later date. We shall discuss these changes and their implications in much more detail in Chapters IV and V. Right now we are concerned with the fact that the adolescent picture is altered not only in respect to such obvious factors as height, weight, and size, but also with respect to deep-seated *physiological* alterations that involve particularly the glandular system. It is possible, therefore, to speak of a *physiology of adolescence* just as in other cases we use the term psychology of adolescence. The physiology of adolescence has particular reference to the deep-seated changes that occur in the glandular system, particularly the sex glands, and in the other systems of the body. For the adolescent to mature, he must mature physiologically first of all; that is, certain developmental changes must take place in the physical systems in order for him to ascend the ladder of development to adulthood. It is primarily physiological development that converts the boy into a man, and the girl into a woman, even though both might be psychologically and socially immature. Without such development, the youngster remains on an immature level and may be thrown completely off balance in his relationships with other members of his age group. Physiological development, then, sets the stage for psychological and social maturation.

The Sociology of Adolescence. If adolescence is in some respects a physiological phenomenon, it has to be argued with equal gravity that it is also a *social* phenomenon, a fact which gives rise to the term, the *sociology of adolescence.*[7] This term refers simply to the influence on adolescent personality and behavior of the total environment in which the youngster grows up. This "total environment" includes his home and family, his neighborhood, his friends and acquaintances, the peer group to which he belongs, his school, church, and community. Thus, to an important extent, the adolescent personality emerges out of the combined influence of physiological development on the one hand and social conditioning on the other.

No one will question the assertion that the behavior and personality of adolescents reflect to an important degree the social and cultural environment in which they grow up.[8] But the *extent* of this influence is a matter of considerable dispute. Anthropologists particularly like to point to the extensive variations of adolescent behavior that characterize different cultures, the implication being that adolescence, its development, and its problems are to a large extent culturally determined. The issue is not merely academic, since if the cultural determinist is correct, then the more serious problems of adolescence, such as delinquency

---

[7] See E. B. Reuter, "The Sociology of Adolescence," *Amer. J. Sociol.,* 1937, 43, 414–427; E. C. Cline, "Social implications of modern adolescent problems," *Sch. Rev.,* 1941, 49, 511–514; P. Blanchard, "Adolescent experience in relation to personality and behavior," in J. McV. Hunt (ed.), *Personality and the Behavior Disorders* (New York: Ronald Press, 1944), Vol. II, pp. 691–713.

[8] The idea of a distinct adolescent culture has been called into question by several investigators. See especially F. Elkin and W. A. Westley, "The Myth of Adolescent Culture," *Amer. Sociol. Rev.,* 1955, 20, 680–684. See also H. Bloch and A. Niederhoffer, *op. cit.,* p. xiii.

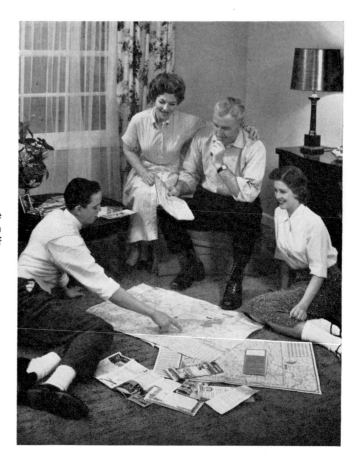

The family is one of the chief influencing factors in the total environment of the adolescent.

and mental disorder, are a reflection of cultural changes and pressures and not of factors that are intrinsic to the process of growing up. Delinquency, therefore, would have to be tackled from a social rather than from a psychological point of view. This issue is not easily resolved and we shall have to turn to the question again in several other parts of this book.

For one thing, the period of adolescence has always been regarded as one of great significance by primitive and civilized peoples alike.[9] Among primitive peoples the indulgence in some form

of pubertal rite is very common; and even at the present time there are practices in our own civilization that highlight the differences between childhood and youth. During the Middle Ages there was a sharp distinction drawn between the pages, who were singled out to attend women, and the squires, who were admitted into the company of men. In our own times certain elements of society cling to such rites as the "coming-out" party accorded young women, who are by that means rendered eligible for the attentions of suitors. The rites of Confirmation and Bar Mitzvah are the modern equivalents of ancient puberty rites also, although, as one author says, the Bar Mitzvah rite of the Jewish youth today

<hr />

[9] See Chapters I and II in J. M. Seidman (ed.), *The Adolescent: a Book of Readings* (New York: Dryden, 1953).

may mean little to the boy as a puberty rite even though he piously intones the familiar words, "Today I am a man." Significantly, too, as many publications stress, formalized rites are used widely by adolescents to initiate new members into organized gangs. In each case the particular rite, whatever its form, is in the nature of an investiture, involving the inculcation of certain rights and duties hitherto proscribed, and marking the emergence into a new mode of life.[10]

This similarity in attitudes toward adolescence among different groups should not be allowed to obscure certain fundamental differences. It is a serious error to think of adolescence (or any other period for that matter) solely in terms of individual growth and development, since it is to an important extent a reflection of a particular culture. It is true that physical development must run its course, and that the end of adolescence is not reached in the physical sense until such development is complete. Adolescent development, however, is not simply a matter of physical change; more importantly it is a matter of intellectual, emotional, and cultural development which, under normal circumstances, finally culminates in maturity. Unlike physical development, these other phases of growth are conditioned more by environmental factors, so that maturity may be as much a function of a particular culture as it is of intrinsic development. Since, therefore, adolescence is the natural prelude to maturity, it may be said also that adolescence itself is, in part at

---

[10] See the discussion of the meaning and significance of puberty rites both in primitive and in modern society in G. J. Mohr and Marian A. Despres, *The Stormy Decade: Adolescence* (New York: Random House, 1958). See also Chapters III, IV, and V of H. Bloch and A. Niederhoffer, *op. cit.*

least, a function of a particular culture.

Thus we find that the attitudes of primitive peoples toward puberty and maturity are quite different from those of more civilized people. Among certain primitive tribes the boy, on reaching puberty, is initiated into tribal secrets, laws, customs, and rites. He soon marries, and then becomes a full tribesman. The initiatory rites by which this transformation is achieved are sometimes very impressive and are always significant, for they indicate cultural attitudes that influence the whole outlook on the adolescent problem. Analysis of these primitive rites reveals that they are regarded as a means of converting the child into something like a complete adult, the period that we call adolescence being greatly foreshortened. To express it in another way, the trials and tribulations that mark the transition from childhood to adulthood are compressed into a much smaller span of time, the individual being expected to emerge from his period of trial and ordeal fully prepared to meet the demands of adult life.

These practices, incidentally, are a striking illustration of the notion that adolescence involves the birth of a new self. It is regarded as a period when the individual makes a distinct break with the past, and the various rites are regarded as a symbol of the profound change, or as a means of bringing it about. Knowing little about the processes of development, and probably caring less, the primitive tribesman in simple and direct fashion seizes upon those means which he believes will insure the maturity necessary for adequate tribal existence. "The indications are that the dramatic ordeal of primitive puberty rites and practices projects the adolescent of simpler societies rapidly into his adult world, condensing and intensifying — both for the youth and for his elders — the resolution of the conflicts that center upon his assumption of his adult role."[11]

In our own civilization, the problem of adolescence is far different from that in primitive cultures. The horizons of adulthood and maturity are being pushed back farther and farther. Where primitive youth is accorded some measure of maturity in early adolescence, the youth in our own culture does not achieve adulthood until much later. If we measure maturity in terms of independence and responsibility, we find that it is often deferred until long after the coming of physical maturity. The same is true when we use emotional stability, self-control, or self-identity as yardsticks to gauge maturity. More and more the young person of today is dependent upon others for his economic and educational welfare, and this dependence generates other forms, particularly emotional dependence. A generation ago, young men, on reaching a certain degree of physical maturity and perhaps soundness of judgment, were quickly "put on their own," that is, forced to make and to stand by their own decisions, and to live their own lives. For many young people today this situation has been greatly altered. For at least half of the adolescent population it is customary to remain in school until the ages of seventeen or eighteen, before which any real independence is almost impossible. In some instances, it is true, a degree of independence begins with the ending of the high school career; but

for many others there is the matter of additional training or education, so that dependence upon others continues well into the adult years. One result of this is the disconcerting spectacle of grown men and women who are quite adolescent in their attitudes and judgments, and adolescents who look with considerable anxiety to the responsibilities of adulthood.

To be truly adult means to have the ability to cope with all the anxieties of life without the protection and security extended to the child. This is often too much for the adolescent, who is frightened by his own impulse to free himself. If this alarm becomes too paralyzing, he feels impelled to regress to the security of childhood and again becomes the dependent child. As a result of this impulse to emancipate himself and at the same time to have the reassurance of protection, a paradoxical situation arises. While protesting his ability to take care of himself, the adolescent is actually more apprehensive and therefore more clinging than he has been since infancy. This explains why, no matter how wise a parent may be, he can never be right for any length of time.

*   *   *

The adolescent wishes to be independent, but to be so is frightening; as long as the parent gives support, it is safe to be independent. If, however, the parent permits the emancipation, the adolescent, feeling much neglected, is alarmed and regresses to a dependency relationship. As soon as the parent gratifies the adolescent's dependency needs, the adolescent feels stronger and with renewed vigor attempts to achieve independence. The retreat to dependency is a real blow to his pride. Therefore, to hide his wish to be protected, he blames the parent for what was actually a temporary regression on his own part. . . .

---

[11] G. J. Mohr and Marian A. Despres, op. cit., pp. 151–152. See the authors' discussion of the place of college rituals, including hazing and initiation rites, in relation to ancient puberty rites.

Thus the professed unconventionality of the adolescent is often simply lip service to emancipation.[12]

This situation, needless to say, brings many problems in its wake. The whole process of development points to one thing — maturity. And maturity means independence and responsibility. If, therefore, this independence and responsibility are made impossible, or deferred for too long a time, the young person will be poorly equipped to achieve the level of adjustment necessary for effective living. This is one reason why the problem of youth looms so large at the present time.

The concept of adolescence as a social phenomenon has yet another meaning, one derived in large measure from organismic psychology. In this view the phenomena of adolescence, particularly changes in attitude, the growth of social consciousness, the development of interests, and the like, are as much a product of environment as of development and maturation. The individual, to put it briefly, is a product of the culture to which he belongs. Every act, thought, and motive mirrors in some degree the traditions, mores, taboos, and customs that are part of the social structure. Thus it is argued that the nature of the part

---

[12] Irene M. Josselyn, op. cit., pp. 182, 183–184. Many writers refer to the prolongation of adolescence in our culture. See Natalie F. Joffe, "The Prolongation of Adolescence in America," Complex, 1951, No. 4, 28–33; M. E. Kirkpatrick, "The Mental Hygiene of Adolescence in the Anglo-American Culture," Ment. Hyg., N. Y., 1952, 36, 392–403; B. S. Gottlieb, op. cit., Chap. 11; and H. Bloch and A. Niederhoffer, op. cit., p. xi. See also H. H. Remmers and D. H. Radler, The American Teenager (New York: Bobbs-Merrill, 1957), pp. 151–152, for a breakdown of future problems that concern the American teen-ager.

(the person) is determined by the whole (the culture or society). There is no intent in this view to deny the process of development or the role played by factors that are relatively independent of environment; but, it is argued, the personality is so extensively conditioned by environmental and cultural determinants that the significance of intrapersonal determinants is greatly lessened. In this view, then, development can be understood only when studied in conjunction with the social framework in which it occurs.

This hypothesis has certain virtues, and most psychologists will concede that cultural determinants are much more important than was formerly realized. Certainly many of the changes of adolescence reflect the environment within which youth develops. This is particularly true with respect to attitudes, ideals, sentiments, beliefs, and interests. But it is a mistake to overemphasize the importance of cultural determination. Without physical growth and maturation, without the capacities, inclinations, and needs which the adolescent brings to the environment, the picture would be quite different. The adolescent personality, therefore, is at once an individual and a social phenomenon; and there is no way of determining in an individual case which factor has predominated in the process of development from infancy to adulthood.

The Psychology of Adolescence. The statement that the adolescent personality is an individual as well as a social phenomenon, reflecting the capacities, inclinations, and needs of the developing organism, helps to emphasize the fact that there is a third approach to the understanding of the adolescent; this approach is properly called the psy-

chology of adolescence.[13] This approach, too, has clear-cut developmental aspects and must be brought into relationship with the physiology and the sociology of adolescence. Perhaps we can clarify these interrelationships by the use of an example taken from the phenomena of adolescent development.

Everyone knows that sexual development is a prominent aspect of the transition from childhood to adulthood. That this aspect of development is basically conditioned and determined by physiological changes is a well-known fact. Similarly, it is equally well known that sexual inclinations, behavior, and relationships will be influenced to an important extent by the environment and the culture within which the youngster grows up. As we shall see more fully later on (Chapter VI), sexual behavior varies to a considerable extent with the mores, customs, and practices of different societies; thus we may say that sexual development is to some extent socially determined. But these two statements taken by themselves do not complete the picture of sexual development in adolescence. They say nothing at all about the growth of sexual impulse, sexual identity, sexual fantasy, or the development of feelings of pleasure, guilt, shame, embarrassment, and similar reactions that characteristically accompany sexual development. In other words, if we are to complete the picture of adolescent sexual development, we have to analyze and

describe what happens to the adolescent *psychologically* during the period of sexual maturation.

From this viewpoint, then, the term *psychology of adolescence* means simply the science of human mentality, behavior, and personality, as it relates to the adolescent period. As a branch of psychology it is a study of the facts, phenomena, laws, principles, and conditions that relate to and govern the psychological responses and personalities of youth. As regards subject matter, it does not differ greatly from general psychology. But there is this difference: adolescent psychology studies psychological processes from a particular viewpoint, and as they occur under certain conditions. The mentality and the behavior of youth differ considerably from those of the adult and of the child, and for this reason it can be argued, with security, that there is a distinct psychology of adolescence.

APPROACHES TO UNDERSTANDING THE ADOLESCENT

Adolescent Psychology and Related Fields of Study. Adolescent psychology differs from general psychology in another important respect: it studies personality and behavior *over a period of time.* Unlike most branches of psychology, it does not deal with cross sections of mind and behavior, but rather with these factors as they *develop* in individuals from one point of time to another. Hence it is a part of that more general and inclusive branch of psychology called *developmental,* which is the study of mental phenomena and conduct from the cradle to the grave, including the period

---

[13] Many writers have drawn a psychological picture of the typical adolescent. See, for example, Irene M. Josselyn, "Psychological Aspects of Adolescence," *Amer. J. Orthopsychiat.,* 1956, 26, 471–496; H. Joseph and G. Zern, *The Emotional Problems of Children: a Guide for Parents* (New York: Crown, 1954), pp. 54–58; H. H. Remmers and D. H. Radler, *op. cit.,* p. 50.

covered by the term "adolescent."[14] This distinction is important for the student of adolescent behavior insofar as it involves an approach quite different from that ordinarily used in psychology. The developmental psychologist is not interested in the nature of mental processes and behavior as such, but only in such processes as they occur at different stages of development and under different conditions. He is not so much concerned with what personality *is*, as with what it will *become* under the influence of certain laws of growth and development. His is a study of mind and personality in *transition*. In what way, he asks, does the adolescent differ from the child, the child from the infant, the adult from the adolescent? What are some of the characteristic features of the transition from childhood to adulthood, from adulthood to senescence? What are the conditions — physical, psychological, and social — that govern this transition? What factors within the personality, and external to it, serve to bring about the many changes that occur between birth and death? These are some of the problems with which developmental psychology is concerned, certain aspects of which come within the scope of adolescent psychology.

A distinctive feature of this viewpoint, important for the student of adolescent psychology, is its emphasis upon the *genetic* explanation of personality and conduct. Taking the stand that the course of development of the individual is determined by his previous history, the genetic psychologist argues that adequate understanding of human personality in all its aspects depends upon a knowledge of the many factors that played a part in its formation. Modern psychology, says one such writer, "is not content with the separate description of single activities; for events, however important in themselves, lose much of their meaning if considered apart from their normal surroundings and out of their natural sequence. Psychologists today are asking not only what a given form of behavior is like, but how it came to be so, and into what it is likely to develop later on."[15]

In this view, then, adolescent psychology is inseparably linked to *child psychology*. No one who has made a study of adolescence will dispute the value of a knowledge of childhood. However, from a *pedagogical* point of view, it is quite possible to consider the problems of the adolescent period by themselves. We do not mean that there is a flaw in the basic principles of genetic psychology, but only that it is a simple matter for the teacher of adolescent psychology to refer back to childhood whenever there is need to stress the developmental background of a particular fact or process. For his part, the student should learn as much as possible concerning the facts and principles of child psychology.

The relationship between adolescent and child psychology is so close that they merge into one discipline — *developmental psychology*. But what about other branches of knowledge, such as abnormal psychology, mental hygiene, physiology,

---

[14] Actually the term "developmental psychology" is broad enough to cover the study of mind and behavior from the lowest animal forms up to and including man. Perhaps a better term for this broader study would be *genetic psychology*. As ordinarily conceived, developmental psychology embraces infant, child, adolescent, adult, and senescent psychology. See J. P. Zubek and Patricia A. Solberg, *Human Development* (New York: McGraw-Hill, 1954).

[15] Florence L. Goodenough, *Developmental Psychology*, 2 ed. (New York: Appleton-Century-Crofts, 1945), p. 12.

or sociology? This question has already been partly answered in our discussion of the physiology and sociology of adolescence. If the adolescent personality grows out of and is conditioned by physiological and sociological factors, it is obvious that some knowledge of these sciences is basic to the understanding of adolescent phenomena. To physiology the psychologist must turn for an explanation of the extensive physical changes that mark the adolescent period; and to sociology he must appeal for an adequate picture of the social factors that condition the adolescent personality. These interrelationships are to be expected in view of the fact that adolescent psychology is after all a study of the *total personality*.

There are of course times, as we shall see quite often in this book, when adolescent development and personality become distorted, and the principles of normal psychology are inadequate to understand the behavior that takes place. It is then that the student of adolescence must turn to the principles of abnormal and dynamic psychology for an adequate explanation. This does not mean that undue emphasis is placed on personality disturbances among youth, since the majority of young people manage to survive the conflicts and difficulties of adolescence without permanent damage. To the contrary, a great deal more emphasis is placed on *mental hygiene*, which consists of a body of knowledge and of principles that help *prevent* the maladjustments that occur during the period of adolescent development. These and many other branches of knowledge, therefore, are important to a complete understanding of the mental life and behavior of youth. From this statement the student of youth should become aware of the

complexity and immensity of the problems with which adolescent psychology deals. It should help him to become cautious in his approach to these problems and in his judgments regarding them. He should learn to demand facts where facts are available, and he should most carefully sift the evidence, theories, and hypotheses that have been brought forth by psychologists and other scientists for the more complete understanding of adolescence.

How to Study the Adolescent. There are many approaches to the study of human personality no matter what developmental level we are dealing with, and the psychologist interested in adolescent phenomena is likely to use all of them on one occasion or another.[16] What approach we use in scientific investigation is determined always by what we want to know. In adolescent psychology, for example, we are interested in the *mental life* of the teen-ager — what he feels, his needs and impulses, his fantasy life, his level of aspiration, his ideals, attitudes, and goals, his wishes, dreams, conflicts, and frustrations. In other words, we are interested in every phase of his psychic life, including the cognitive, the emotional, and the motivational. These are realities not easily studied with scientific precision. Yet a great deal of scientific data regarding the psychic life of the

---

[16] There are many excellent treatises on methods of studying the adolescent. See H. Lane and Mary Beauchamp, *Understanding Human Development* (Englewood Cliffs: Prentice-Hall, 1959), especially Section 3; L. D. Crow and Alice Crow, *Adolescent Development and Adjustment* (New York: McGraw-Hill, 1956), Chap. 3; R. J. Havighurst and Hilda Taba, *Adolescent Character and Personality* (New York: Wiley, 1949), especially Part 5; E. S. Gollin, "Some Research Problems for Developmental Psychology," *Child Develpm.*, 1956, 27, 223–235.

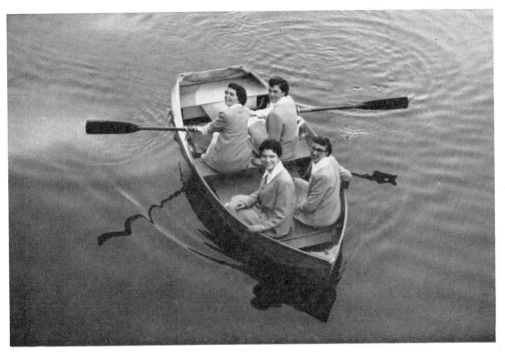

Leisure activities of adolescents can reveal much about their personality adjustment.

adolescent is available and we will make use of these data many times throughout this volume.

In order to gather such material, the investigator will use techniques ranging all the way from personal diaries and essays to carefully devised questionnaire studies and projective techniques.[17] Not all of these approaches have the same validity, and in trying to get a true picture of what adolescents are like, what they believe in, and why they behave as they do, we must be very cautious in

our interpretation of the data gathered by different investigators. As a glaring example of what can happen in the gathering of scientific data, we may cite the famous Kinsey reports on sexual behavior in American men and women. These are unquestionably the most extensive and scientifically organized studies that have been made of sexual behavior in our culture, and they are regarded by many observers as the prototypes of careful investigation. Yet they have been severely criticized by psychologists, psychoanalysts, and statisticians for their methodological errors and their unwarranted inferences, pitfalls that Kinsey very carefully set out to avoid. If such be the case with the carefully organized study, think how careful we must be with other studies that are not half as good from a scientific point of view.

[17] A. Al-Meligui, "Psychology of Adolescence Through Diaries," Egypt. J. Psychol., 1950–1951, 6, 173–184. The author contends that diaries provide an excellent source for understanding the adolescent and his conflicts. See also N. Kiell, The Adolescent Through Fiction: a Psychological Approach (New York: International Universities Press, 1959), and Ruth Strang, The Adolescent Views Himself (New York: McGraw-Hill, 1957).

The study of behavior exemplified in the Kinsey reports can be pursued quite successfully by objective means, since behavior itself is directly observable. Thus, in the realm of adolescent behavior, it is possible to study the structure, the formation, and the characteristics of city gangs as they make their appearance in different parts of the country. It is also possible to observe leisure-time activities, group functions, team play, and other forms of behavior in which adolescents engage. These studies of behavior not only reveal what the adolescent does, but enable us to draw fairly reliable conclusions regarding the character of the psychic processes to which the behavior is related. If a boy quits school at sixteen we may safely infer that his level of aspiration is different from and probably not as high as that of the boy who forges ahead into college and graduate work. The girl who is promiscuous in her relationships with boys certainly reveals a great deal about her inner psychic life, particularly basic needs. The youngster who engages consistently in bullying tactics, mugging, or the use of switch blades to settle an argument, gives more than an inkling of his antisocial attitudes and the strength of his aggressive tendencies.

Behavior analysis has to be complemented by other methods of study if we are to get a complete picture of the adolescent personality in our culture. In the past, much emphasis was laid upon documentary evidence in the form of anecdotes, biographies, fictionized youth stories, diaries, and the like. Such documents now are regarded by psychologists with considerable skepticism, because they fail to fulfill the requirements of scientific observation. Many of them represent casual observation at its worst.

All of them suffer from the same bad features: lack of control, the influence of mental stereotypes, faulty memory, sentimentality, and similar handicaps. Scientific observation means controlled observation, carried on independently of preconceived theories, mental stereotypes, or romantic ideals. To achieve this ideal of scientific observation, the psychologist, whenever possible, uses techniques and instruments that have established validity.

The serious student of adolescent behavior follows the same rule. During the past thirty years or more, hundreds of studies of adolescent behavior have been made in which these stricter methods have been employed. Tests of intelligence, achievement, aptitude, and other factors have been administered by the tens of thousands, and accurate records kept for careful study. Research on adolescent attitudes, interests, and values has produced valuable data. Careful studies of the physical and physiological changes of the adolescent are available. Many of these studies have been made possible by the use of questionnaires and inventories, and by projective techniques, with variable results and sometimes questionable validity. However, in many instances results have been subjected to the analytical tools of statistics, which has helped to increase the reliability of the investigations.

Needless to say, the student of adolescence must also depend upon his own observations of adolescent behavior, upon the observation of others who have studied the adolescent at close range, and upon such knowledge as may be gleaned from the writings, conversations, and expressive behavior of youths. These more casual observations have their shortcomings, but often provide valuable insights into the nature of adolescent phenomena.

In this analysis of approaches to the study of adolescent phenomena we must not forget that adolescent psychology is primarily developmental in its approach, and is less concerned with cross-sectional analyses than are other branches of psychology. Thus, over and above the methods already described, we must take note of the *genetic approach*, which is indispensable to the understanding of adolescent development.[18] Let us recall what we emphasized earlier, that adolescent psychology is the study of the mind in transition, a longitudinal investigation of personality and development rather than a cross-sectional one. The aim here is to know what the adolescent is like at all age levels, from the beginning of adolescence to adulthood. It is possible of course to join the cross-sectional method to the genetic approach, as Terman has done so successfully in his studies of genius; but the difficulties of such a combination are formidable. The same group of individuals has to be studied over a long period of time, which of course is not easy to do. Despite these limitations, the genetic method is indispensable to the study of adolescence, since good results can be obtained by studying different groups at different stages of growth and development. The results obtained in this way are not as reliable as when the same persons are studied over a period of time, but they have proved of great value to the understanding of adolescent development. Many of the conclusions in this text have been drawn from such studies.

Some Cautions Regarding the Study of Adolescents. Our aim in a book of this kind is primarily to paint a portrait of what the adolescent today is like — what he thinks and feels, what he does, why he does it, and how he gets that way. This is not an easy task, and all writers in the field would probably "flunk" if their efforts were graded by the adolescent himself. The difficulty of the task, and our own human limitations, should make us doubly cautious in accepting and interpreting the data and the theories on adolescent conduct that have been offered by different investigators. More theories about adolescents have been scrapped in the past fifty years than are at present advocated; this fact alone should make us cautious about going overboard for any particular approach, and even in those viewpoints that survive today there are at times such wide gaps as to make them irreconcilable.[19] No one has as yet managed to integrate the psychology, the anthropology, and the psychoanalysis of adolescence, at least not to the extent that the result would be acceptable to all concerned. Other gaps would have to be filled in also before our portrait of the adolescent would assume the clarity of detail all would like. In the area of motivation, for example, a great deal of careful research remains to be done, and the best that we can do at the present time is to make cautious inferences as to the dynamics underlying adolescent conduct.

[18] See A. A. Stone and Gloria C. Onqué, *Longitudinal Studies of Child Personality* (Cambridge, Mass.: Harvard University Press, 1959); L. H. Stott, *The Longitudinal Study of Individual Development* (Detroit: Merrill-Palmer School, 1955); D. Kodlin and D. J. Thompson, "An Appraisal of the Longitudinal Approach to Studies of Growth and Development," *Monogr. Soc. Res. Child Develpm.*, 1958, 23, No. 1.

[19] For a brief discussion of various theories of adolescence, see C. M. Fleming, *Adolescence* (New York: International Universities Press, 1949), Chap. 4.

Moreover, as we have seen already, the methods used to study the adolescent personality and its development are not always too satisfactory. In many instances studies are limited to an extremely small sample of youth, and even this sample is biased because it involves a selected population. In other instances, the tools used in the investigation have doubtful validity. In questionnaire studies on religious beliefs it is not at all uncommon for the youngster to answer as he thinks he is expected to, with the result that we get a completely distorted picture of what he really believes. In still other instances we find that youngsters are not particularly adept at analyzing or expressing their own ideas, feelings, and aspirations, as the counselor of youth well knows; and therefore, any data gathered by means of essays, themes, or autobiographies must be subjected to the most careful scrutiny. Even projective devices, such as the Rorschach Test, the Thematic Apperception Test, and similar instruments leave a great deal to be desired in the way of scientific validity and reliability. All of this does not mean that empirical studies of adolescent phenomena should be ignored or scrapped; on the contrary, such techniques and results are very important in our efforts to paint the adolescent portrait. But where the human mind and personality are concerned, scientific caution is the noblest of virtues and should be used constantly to guide our steps in traversing this field where there are so many pitfalls and booby traps.

SELECTED READINGS

Ausubel, D. P., *Theory and Problems of Adolescent Development* (New York: Grune & Stratton, 1954).

Bernard, H. W., *Adolescent Development in American Culture* (New York: World Book, 1957).

Gesell, A., Ilg, Frances L., and Ames, Louise B., *Youth: the Years From Ten to Sixteen* (New York: Harper and Bros., 1956).

Goodenough, Florence L., and Tyler, Leona E., *Developmental Psychology*, 3 ed. (New York: Appleton-Century-Crofts, 1959).

Gruenberg, Sidonie M. (ed.), *Our Children Today: a Guide to Their Needs From Infancy Through Adolescence* (New York: Viking Press, 1952).

Kuhlen, R. G., *The Psychology of Adolescent Development* (New York: Harpers, 1952).

Landis, P. H., *Adolescence and Youth; the Process of Maturing*, 2 ed. (New York: McGraw-Hill, 1952).

Mohr, G. J., and Despres, Marian A., *The Stormy Decade: Adolescence* (New York: Random House, 1958).

Pearson, G. H. J., *Adolescence and the Conflict of Generations* (New York: Norton, 1958).

Remmers, H. H., and Radler, D. H., *The American Teenager* (New York: Bobbs-Merrill Co., 1957).

Seidman, J. M. (ed.), *The Adolescent: a Book of Readings* (New York: Dryden, 1953).

Strang, Ruth, *The Adolescent Views Himself: a Psychology of Adolescence* (New York: McGraw-Hill, 1957).

CHAPTER II

THE AMERICAN ADOLESCENT: PROBLEMS AND WHEREABOUTS

Where is the adolescent? What is he doing? Do most adolescents graduate from high school? How many go on to college? Is there an adolescent problem as such? What are the main problems of American adolescents? Where do these problems come from? These and many other questions must be answered if we are to understand the American adolescent.

PERSPECTIVES ON THE ADOLESCENT AND HIS PROBLEMS

The Adolescent's View of His Own Problems. There are few areas of human behavior or of psychological research so rich in literature, or so stimulating and challenging to human thought, as the period of adolescence. Each year hundreds of professional and popular articles, and scores of technical and nontechnical books and pamphlets concerning adolescence appear on the literary scene. And the great majority of them deal to some extent with the problems of adolescence. There must be some reason for this voluminous output other than a passionate desire on the part of psychologists, psychiatrists, and free-lance writers to inform interested parties as to what is going on currently in the adolescent world. The desire for profit will account for some of this intellectual outpouring, but certainly not for the professional journal articles, or for many of the textbooks that appear. No, there is a deeper reason for this continually growing wealth of material, and the reason lies in adolescence itself.

There are those hardy souls, especially the cultural anthropologists, who would shake their heads vigorously at the suggestion that there is a specific adolescent problem. There is nothing, they would say, inherent in the adolescent make-up or in his development that causes any particular difficulty; rather, it is the cultural or environmental framework in which the adolescent develops that is the real culprit.[1] Surprisingly enough, there are probably a great many adoles-

---

[1] P. Rube, "Adolescence: I. Is There a Problem of Adolescence?" *Amer. J. Psychother.*, 1955, 9, 503–509. Rube argues that there is no single problem of adolescence, but rather a series of very complex, intricate problems. The so-called adolescent problem comes from the reorganization of the child's emotionality under the influence of puberty and leaving the parental milieu, both of which occur in adolescence. See also A. A. Luchins, "On the Theories and Problems of Adolescence," *J. Genet. Psychol.*, 1954, 85, 47–63.

If a child can understand and talk over his problems with a parent, many of the problems of adolescence can be obviated.

cents who would agree substantially with this viewpoint. Counselors will attest to the fact that many seriously confused or disturbed teen-agers will report in counseling interviews that "Everything is just fine." They are not aware of any particular problem, and it sometimes takes a great deal of skill and coaching to lay bare the conflicts, frustrations, and difficulties that the individual is facing.[2]

This is one of the most serious aspects of the adolescent problem, because very often the unresolved difficulty keeps eating away at the stability of the adolescent until his whole personality begins to fall apart. Quite often the teen-ager doesn't know what you mean when you ask him if he has any problems. The word "problem" suggests quite different things to the

---

[2] See Miriam Holman, "Adolescent Attitudes Toward Seeking Help With Personal Problems," *Smith Coll. Stud. Soc. Wk.*, 1955, 25, 1–31. This investigator found also that adolescents are least inclined to seek help for more personal problems regarding adjustment with the opposite sex and with family relations. Adolescents do not like to be considered different in a maladjustive way which is often the reason why they do not seek help. See also A. M. Rose, "Attitudes of Youth Toward Mental Health Problems," *Sociol. Soc. Res.*, 1957, 41, 343–348.

youthful mind and to a parent, or counselor, or teacher. When the adolescent thinks of problems he thinks of the difficulties of getting home in time from school, economic difficulties in financing a date, finding a job in the summer, and similar vexing and perplexing difficulties. If such problems do not exist at the moment, he might deny that he has any problems even though he is torn apart by conflict, doubt, or indecision. Incidentally, parents very often indicate the same myopic view of adolescent problems. As long as Johnny or Mary has spending money, enough dates to fill in Saturday evenings, and is getting at least a 75 average in school, what is there to worry about?

Let us probe a bit into the reason for this blind spot. First of all, where parents are concerned, we have already noted the tendency to repress the unpleasant aspects of their own adolescent struggles. As they look back, they tend to remember only the more obvious and superficial difficulties that they ran into, and thus project this memory viewpoint on to their own adolescent youngsters. Also, parents are loath to face the reality of deeper and more disturbing problems in their children, and thus close their eyes in the hope that the problems will go away. Moreover, some of these deeper problems, particularly those in the sexual area, would if recognized involve the parents' own anxieties, conflicts, and frustrations, and thus present a threat to the parent when he gets a glimmering of their existence in the son or daughter. Finally, there is always the ubiquitous fact of sheer ignorance on the part of parents regarding deeper personality problems. If the father himself managed to muddle through adolescence without any deep-seated sexual, moral, or social conflicts, at least none that he remembers, he may demonstrate a startling ignorance about adolescent difficulties. Or it may be that he has never taken the trouble to find out what he should know about adolescent problems.

As for the adolescent himself, there are several reasons why the "adolescent problem" has little meaning for him. The basic reason is the one we have already suggested, that he has not generalized the concept of problem to include many troubling experiences that characterize this developmental period. In addition, he is often so confused by the kaleidoscopic changes that are occurring that he finds it impossible to formulate his ideas concerning these experiences, or to put them into words.[3] Very often,

too, he is frightened by what is happening, or he feels extremely self-conscious and ashamed of his impulses and behavior, so that he will deny the existence of a problem, and believe his own denial. Speaking of the need of all adolescents to adjust their feelings about sex and their relationships to their parents, and to meet the confusions which school, religion, death, and a host of other matters may bring, Gallagher and Harris state:

> . . . that all of these often constitute problems does not mean that adolescents do not solve them quite adequately. Most of them do, and the period during which confusion and worry are handicapping is usually quite brief. However, for one reason or another, some problems are more troublesome for some adolescents than for others, and they either cause, or act as the "last straw" in, the development of an "anxiety state." This is no more than to say that for the time being this young person's problems are more than he can handle: they, to a certain extent, are running him, are keeping him from working and living as happily and efficiently as he should.[4]

We must not expect adolescents to have insight into their own psychological difficulties, nor should we expect them to be able to verbalize about these problems in the way that most adults can. There is the added fact, of course, that many problems have unconscious origins which leave the adolescent in the dark as to why he feels and why he behaves in certain ways that may be very disturbing to him as well as to the people around him. All of this tells us why it is so important for adolescents to be accepted by the significant people in their environment, particularly the par-

---

[3] J. P. Finn, A Study of the Problems of Certain Catholic High-School Boys as Told by Themselves and Their Teachers (Washington, D. C.: The Catholic University of America Press, 1950): "Some of the adolescents whose responses were classified in this category, hardly seem to know what are their problems and can hardly express them in words. Perhaps an increasing awareness of the wide world around them, and their small part in its affairs may stir within their natures a vague feeling of uneasiness and dissatisfaction with their lives as they are" (p. 40).

[4] J. R. Gallagher and H. I. Harris, Emotional Problems of Adolescence (New York: Oxford University Press, 1958), p. 76.

ents, so that they may turn in confidence to someone when a problem at any level begins to interfere with their successful progress toward maturity.

The Adolescent Problem and the Problems of Adolescents. Before taking up the typical problems of the adolescent period, we should consider first whether there is an adolescent problem in and of itself, or whether the anthropologist is right in insisting that the trouble lies within society. Remmers, for example, on the basis of his extensive research, states bluntly that "the teenager finds his years of transition from little boy or girl to grown-up man or woman a time of tension. There is no doubt that *inherently* these years of major change and adaptation are difficult ones. In most societies and in all ages, adults have noticed and reacted to troubled teens."[5] But what about youngsters who seem to glide through the teen-age years with considerable poise, self-confidence, and contentment? Are we going to be ultrapsychological and insist that they have a problem whether they like it or not?

Certainly not. Undoubtedly, there are numerous young people who pass

---

[5] H. H. Remmers and D. H. Radler, *The American Teenager* (New York: Bobbs-Merrill Co., 1957), p. 35 (italics mine). See also "The Emergence of the Adolescence-Youth Problem" in P. H. Landis, *Adolescence and Youth: the Process of Maturing*, 2 ed. (New York: McGraw-Hill, 1952), pp. 24–25. Landis constantly uses the term "youth problem" in much the same way as it is used in this text. Similarly Josselyn: "The problems of adolescence are thus in part the inevitable struggles of growing from childhood to adulthood. The difficulties presented here are to a certain degree inevitable during this transitional phase" — Irene M. Josselyn, "Growing to Adulthood," in Sidonie M. Gruenberg (ed.), *Our Children Today* (New York: Viking, 1955), p. 186. See also the much earlier article by W. H. McHugh, "The Ameircan Youth Problem," *Cath. Educ. Rev.*, 1938, 36, 257–267.

through adolescence without the need of intensive parental guidance or counseling or extensive support. Indeed, if this were not the case, there would be so many neurotic, delinquent, and socially disturbed adolescents that the normal youth would constitute the exception, and clinical agencies would be swamped with demands many times as great as they are today. In the adolescent's reaction to his adolescence, he is influenced by many different factors, including such important things as the quality and happiness of his childhood, family relationships, experiences with success, intellectual level and insight, and wise and understanding parents. For all we know, the majority of adolescents have a background approximating this ideal, and thus do not exemplify in their behavior or their relationships the so-called "adolescent problem." These more fortunate youngsters will of course, like everyone else, have some problems, since the only people without problems are those who have already gone to their eternal reward.

Despite the fact that the majority of youngsters in the teen-age category escape the deeper ravages of the adolescent problem, it is well to remind ourselves at this point that there are hundreds of thousands who do not. The number of teen-agers who are unhappy, neurotic, academically maladjusted, socially disjointed, vocationally disoriented, or experiencing deep-seated moral and religious conflicts runs into the millions. If to this large number we add the constantly growing list of those who fall prey to crime and delinquency, the resulting figure is staggering in its implications. Even if all youths were happy and well adjusted it would still be important for parents and teachers to develop a thorough and precise understanding of adolescent phenomena because it is their responsibility to help young people reach mature adulthood, and they cannot fulfill this responsibility without adequate knowledge. If to this general responsibility we add the demand created by the several millions of unhappy and disturbed youth, it is not difficult to see why the adolescent problem has gained so much attention.

We have not yet defined what we mean by the "adolescent problem" as distinct from the problems of adolescence. What we indicate by this term is that, despite the acknowledged influence of environmental and cultural factors and interpersonal relationships, the adolescent period contains within itself the seeds of its own disruption. We have already indicated this by characterizing adolescence as a period of profound and pervasive change, transition, and unceasing struggle for adulthood. This is the basic determinant of the adolescent problem because out of it grows the instability, the uncertainty, and the confusion of the adolescent. There are no comparable periods in life, except perhaps the menopause, where again the effects are differential, and the declining years of advanced age, when senescence brings in its wake many complicating problems.

It is clear from this analysis that the adolescent problem is essentially *intrapersonal* in nature, a situation that stems from the very nature of adolescence.[6] In this sense there is always something of an adolescent problem for all teen-agers. The changes and the transition that take place would of themselves be enough to cause the youngster some trouble, but we must note that there are other intrapersonal factors that help to complicate the problem. These include the developing needs of adolescents, and the internal conflicts, frustrations, tensions, and anxieties to which the expression of such needs often give rise. In addition, the adolescent experiences basic perceptual reorganizations and intellectual reorientations that complicate the problem of growing up (see Chapter XVII).

All these factors are of course functionally interdependent in such a way that transitional features determine instability, changes affect needs, needs determine perceptual reorganization, and intellectual growth conditions conflicts and frustrations. All such things taken together, with their interdependencies, constitute the *adolescent problem*. On the border line between the basic intrapersonal determinants of the adolescent problem and those factors in the environment that nurture the seeds of conflict and frustration are the fundamental needs and wants of the adolescent. For it is these needs that often come into conflict with the demands of the environment, and thus bring about some disorder in the youngster's life. In a later chapter (Chapter VIII) we shall have a great deal more to say about the motivations of youth, whereas at this point we wish merely to relate these needs to the adolescent problem.

Perhaps the most important thing that

---

[6] This is the view taken by Bloch and Niederhoffer who refer to "the impressive similarity of adolescent crisis in all cultures and in all times." Similarities "were found in all societies and on all social levels, resulting not so much from the physiological changes of adolescence itself, but from the social necessity to confront the demands of the new adult status" — H. Bloch and A. Niederhoffer, *The Gang: a Study in Adolescent Behavior* (New York: Philosophical Library, 1958), p. xiii. See also page 124, where the authors state: "The movement from childhood to adulthood invariably appears to be fraught with some peril. It appears highly unlikely that a certain degree of strain and anxiety is not present."

the teen-ager wants is *independence*, a chance to make his own decisions, to think for himself, and to begin in a really important way to work out his own destiny. This craving for independence, as we all know, can cause a great many difficulties. At the same time, however, because of his deep roots in the dependencies of childhood, plus his own uncertainties, the adolescent needs *affection* and *security*, experiences and feelings that help to secure him against the threats and hostilities of the world he does not yet clearly understand. It is because of these contradictory cravings that the adolescent is confused and at odds with himself and with his world. In much the same way that he craves affection, the teen-ager also needs *acceptance* and the conviction of *belonging*, conditions that are very important to the feeling of security and to the conviction that he is loved and respected.

The gratification of these basic adolescent needs is of great importance to *identification* and the achievement of *self-identity*, both of which are required for stability, adjustment, and the achievement of independent maturity. Of importance also in the struggle for self-identity are the needs for *achievement*, *status*, and *recognition*, each one of which the adolescent constantly seeks in his upward struggle to adulthood. And finally, there is the need for *conformity* and for *new experiences*, experiences that will add to the zest of living, rupture the monotony of ordinary events, and add to the meaning of life itself.

These are some of the more important things that adolescents want, and which they often try with considerable effort to wrest from their environment. This brief cataloguing of needs does not complete the motivational picture by any means, but it helps us to understand better the basic ingredients of the adolescent problem. We are not suggesting of course that these motivations are peculiar to the adolescent period; but they are often more dynamic and more intense during this particular period than during others. It is not too important whether such needs *characterize* adolescence, but only whether, and the extent to which, they *influence* adolescent behavior and relationships.

The Adolescent Problem and the World of the Adolescent. The adolescents of every generation, we may suppose, have many common characteristics since human nature is fairly constant. Although human nature does not change fundamentally, the environment and culture of people do. And since human personality — including motives, feelings, thoughts, and attitudes — is to an important extent influenced by these *extra-personal* factors, any important changes in these can be of considerable significance. It is at this point that the problem of adolescence, which has characteristic intrapersonal features, begins to reflect the influence of factors outside the adolescent himself. Thus the interplay between these extrapersonal determinants and the demands of youth itself gives rise to numerous instances of conflict, instability, and maladjustment. As Peck and Bellsmith point out:

> Socially acceptable behavior by the adolescent requires a high degree of frustration tolerance. He is expected to accept and adjust to values which are not only insubstantial but which bear little relation to the powerful psychological and biological pressures he is trying to control. He can no longer function adequately by dependence on parental identification since normal development

in adolescence is characterized by movement away from parents.[7]

The obvious factor of change in both civilization and in culture has never been more clearly exemplified than in the present era.[8] With the many inventions of recent years that have radically changed our modes of transportation, our leisure-time activities, and our work habits; with the progress in social reform, the development of mass education, and the emancipation of women, there has been something like a complete break with previous modes of life. Contemporary civilization is characterized by new viewpoints and new ways of doing things that have profound significance for the behavior and the well-being of youth. Wheelis points out, "Many persons these days find no firm footing; and if everything is open to question, no question can be answered. The past half century has encompassed enormous gains in understanding and in mastery; but many of the old fixed points of reference have been lost, and have not been replaced."[9] And later on he says:

_____

[7] H. V. Peck and Virginia Bellsmith, _Treatment of the Delinquent Adolescent_ (New York: Family Service Association of America, 1954), p. 10.

[8] The terms _culture_ and _civilization_ should not be confused, although they are closely related. The culture of a people is the system of concepts, values, laws, and traditions which gradually, over a period of centuries, crystallizes out of the formation and development of a particular society. Civilization, on the other hand, signifies the degree of progress or advancement achieved with respect to standards of living and acting. Both England and America, for example, are civilized, but each possesses its own distinctive culture. Furthermore, culture is independent of civilization, as is exemplified in China, whose culture is far ahead of its civilization. It is well to remember this in assessing the value of any society.

[9] A. Wheelis, _The Quest for Identity_ (New York: Norton, 1958), pp. 19–20.

The immediate causes of the characterological change are to be found in the secondary effects of technological change: the loss of the eternal varieties and the fixed order, the weakening of traditions and institutions, the shifting values, the altered patterns of personal relationships. These changes directly mold character, and these changes occur with a continuity that is traceable to the continuity of the instrumental process.[10]

The youth of today finds himself in a society that is in constant flux, in which the concepts and values of past eras are seemingly inadequate for modern life. He searches for a scale of values that will give meaning to life and is offered a materialistic philosophy that promises little more than pleasure, bodily comfort, and the accumulation of money. The simple pleasures of a previous age have been replaced by sexy movies or the dubious excitements of a dim-lit cocktail bar. The natural desire for marriage and a home is chilled by the spectacle of the family threatened with disruption by widespread divorce, desertions, and almost childless marriages. Ideals and values, formerly derived from the home, the school, and the church, are determined in many instances by Hollywood script writers. Everywhere youth turns, he runs headlong into values and practices that grow less satisfactory day by day in a world of bewildering change and complexity.

_____

[10] _Ibid._, p. 83. See Chapter 3 of this remarkable book for an intensive study of the relationship between character and culture, particularly the changes that occur in the culture. See also J. Stumpf, "Atomic-Age Youth," _Group_, 1951, _13_, 3–6. Stumpf outlines some of the potential sociological trends in the United States inherent in the present age of atomic power and international tension, and the psychological implication of these as they impinge on the adolescent and the young adult.

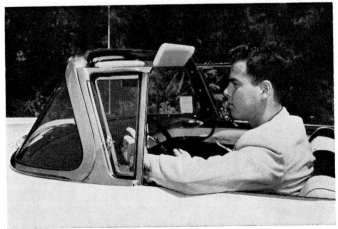

Much of the life of the modern teen-ager revolves around the automobile.

In this growingly puzzling world, where everything changes quickly, and nothing seems stable and fixed, the young look for firm guidance and counsel. What do they find? A world of adults as puzzled and uncertain as they are themselves. So much has changed, so much has been proved wrong, everythings seems so different; old ideas and conventions are no longer respectable simply because they are old or widely accepted. Should the rights of private property always be considered sacred? Are extra-marital relations always wrong? Is absolute freedom to be desired above all? Can one believe stories of miracles? Should one accept the dogmas of religion? Is the profit motive a morally acceptable one? The list of questions could be extended indefinitely and no easy and assured answer can be given to any of them — or at least, few would dare to give it, or would be listened to if they did. Fixed standards, it seems, have gone; the barriers to thought, speculation, doubt, and heresy are down. It is in this world of shifting, changing values that the child and the adolescent of today has to build his spiritual habitation.[11]

But even this is not the whole story of the impact of society on youth, and of the problems this impact engenders. Any single teen-ager might withstand the onslaughts of distorted and spurious values, but might react with extreme cynicism or bitterness to the *double standard* often imposed by adults.[12] Characteristically, the young person is enjoined and even commanded to obey duly enacted laws only to witness the breaking of these laws by his own parents whenever the occasion permits. "Don't exceed the speed limit" is often an injunction applied to the teen-ager but not to the parent himself. Sexual behavior and intimacies among adolescents are severely frowned on by adults as being immoral, whereas every teen-ager knows that sexual misconduct among adults is rampant, winked at, and

Amer. J. Orthopsychiat., 1957, 27, 508–517. Gardner points out in this article that we are thrusting our adolescents into a group of social situations which are beset with the same conflicts that they face.

[12] See Irene M. Josselyn, "Social Pressures in Adolescence," *Social Casewk.*, 1952, 33, 187–193; J. R. Seeley, R. A. Sim, and Elizabeth W. Loosley, *Crestwood Heights* (New York: Basic Books, 1956), pp. 102, 112; A. B. Hollingshead, *Elmtown's Youth* (New York: Wiley, 1949), pp. 149–152.

[11] Editors, "Education and Morals," in *The Yearbook of Education*, 1951 (London: Evans Bros., Ltd., 1951), p. 4. See also G. E. Gardner, "Present-Day Society and the Adolescent,"

often condoned. The ban on teen-age drinking is matched by alcoholic bouts among the adults who protest the loudest whenever a violation of this ban occurs. Adults recoil from the aggression and savagery of teen-age gang fights and killings, and yet will look with disdain on the youths who rebel at military service wherein brutality and killing have been developed into a fine art.[13] The local clergyman who preaches the exalted virtues of self-discipline and poverty may drive around in a Thunderbird. Teachers are held up to youth as the paragons of correct and dignified behavior and are sometimes arrested for molesting and prostitution. Small wonder that many adolescents look upon adults and the adult world as a sham and a hypocrisy that provides little in the way of worthwhile values. Small wonder that in their consternation, confusion, and resentment at a world that offers nothing but contradictions they often break with society and try to find values and security within the structure of the peer group, which is often no more than a street gang.

It is because of the demoralization of social, spiritual, and religious values, and the double standards imposed on the young by adults, that conflicts with society have become a common characteristic of the modern teen-ager. In the area of sexual behavior, we often witness a complete rejection of the moral standards offered by parents and clergy as a means of controlling immoral behavior. In the area of discipline, especially parental discipline, we witness the outbreak of hostility and aggression, and the development of independence that reaches far beyond the capacity of youth to control. Even in the matter of school attendance, youth tends to reject the ideals and admonitions of adults and to strike out on his own rather than create a world in the image of his parents. It is for all of these reasons that he inclines strongly toward breaking family ties, sometimes much too early, and to find his gratifications and identifications within the peer group. Our social structure, our behavior, and our standards do not make it easy for adolescents to accept the world created by adults, and therefore it is not easy for them to grow up in the manner prescribed by tradition.

Not only are teen-agers subjected to unstable and contradictory social and moral values, to demands unfortified by example, and the spectacle of practices that are often different from what adults preach, but they are also the unwilling and unwitting victims of questionable parental and social *expectations*.[14] The

---

[13] In the article quoted previously by the editors of *The Yearbook of Education*, the authors state, "In brief, the experiences, at first or second hand, of fighting, of war, and of enemy occupation, produce widespread apathy towards moral values and spiritual ideals. They accustom everyone to brutality and cruelty, they weaken respect for law and right . . ." (p. 8). In an interesting study of happiness and unhappiness of girls in different cultures Barschak found that only 48 per cent of girls in Berlin reported happiness as against 84 per cent for Americans, 92 per cent for Swiss, 82 per cent for English, and 74 per cent for German girls in a city not much affected by the war — Erna Barschak, "A Study of Happiness and Unhappiness in the Childhood and Adolescence of Girls in Different Cultures," *J. Psychol.*, 1951, 32, 173–215.

[14] "The stress of adolescence can be explained partly by the discontinuities in cultural institutions every child encounters just by growing older. As he grows, he finds social expectations of him change regardless of whether he has been prepared and trained for the change. The middle-class child in the American culture has been forbidden even elementary knowledge about many aspects of sex relations, yet as an adult he must deal with them in mature fashion. In our society it is understood that children should play and adults should work. The play of child-

term "victims" is chosen quite deliberately, because there is nothing that will victimize a person more quickly than expectations to which he cannot or perhaps will not conform. There is the case, for example, of the freshman in college whose parents always expected him to be on the honor roll. The idea that their son should fail to achieve this distinction was unthinkable. Bill was a good student, and applied himself diligently, and was earning respectable grades. But he became so anxious and self-deprecatory about his failure to meet the parental expectations that it began to interfere seriously with his academic work. When it was pointed out to him that the only important thing for him was to set reasonable goals for himself and to strive diligently to achieve these goals, irrespective of the irrational demands of others, his grades did take an upward turn and it wasn't long before his name again appeared on the honor roll.

This of course is a fairly common and relatively mild example of parental expectation influencing behavior. There are other instances that have a much deeper and a more lasting effect on young people. For example, parents often expect their teen-agers to be wiser, more controlled, and more mature than is possible at their level of development. As a result, adult standards are applied as a criterion against the behavior of youngsters who are still closely tied to the patterns of childhood. This is particularly true in the areas of responsibility, emotional control,

and social behavior. In the matter of the adolescent measuring up to moral standards, too, it is very easy for expectations to outrun potentiality or performance. To expect a teen-ager always to appreciate the importance of punctuality, the immorality of cheating, or the sacredness of purity may not only be unrealistic but thoughtless and unkind, and therefore damaging. Nor should we as parents or teachers indulge the privilege of expecting the older teen-ager to know what he wants, the direction his efforts should take, or to what ideal he wishes to devote his life. Expectations of this kind are adult inventions for the control of adolescent behavior which they little understand or are too impatient to cope with. To *help* the teen-ager achieve the important goal of maturity is a privilege. To *demand* wisdom, responsibility, or maturity by means of constantly imposed expectations that outrun developmental level is an unwarranted imposition. In all situations, one must always be careful not to project his image of what is correct, good, and acceptable onto the behavior of others.

The Range of Adolescent Problems. Having defined the adolescent problem and its sources, we can now turn our attention to the range and the variety of problems that the teen-ager is likely to encounter. Some of these problems, stemming as they do directly from the central problem we have been considering, are for the most part intrapersonal in character. These are generally of deeper concern to the adolescent and his adjustment than other problems that are more external in nature. Prominent among this group of difficulties are the more serious conflicts, frustrations, and anxieties that adolescents characteristically experience. In addition are the feel-

hood does not prepare the child for his adult role" — From *The Stormy Decade: Adolescence,* by George J. Mohr and Marian A. Despres. © Copyright 1958 by George J. Mohr and Marian A. Despres. Reprinted by permission of Random House, Inc., p. 146. See also H. Bloch and A. Niederhoffer, *op. cit.,* pp. 108 and 154.

ings of insecurity, inadequacy, uncertainty, confusion, inferiority, and guilt — any one or all of which are likely to plague the teen-ager in his upward climb to maturity. At the same time, the youngster will undergo deep-seated changes in his feelings and attitudes toward himself, and may often experience an intense lack of self-identity. All of these stumbling blocks to adjustment, peace of mind, and happiness, it will be noted, are basically psychological in character, and thus may be categorized even more precisely as the *emotional problems of adolescents*.[15] In fact, it is just because they generate so much emotional turmoil and disruption that they stand out as the most serious group of problems that adolescents encounter.[16]

---

[15] G. S. Stevenson, "Mental-Hygiene Problems of Youth Today," *Ment. Hyg.*, 1941, *25*, 539–551; J. R. Gallagher and H. I. Harris, op. cit., p. 8 f.; H. Joseph and G. Zern, *The Emotional Problems of Children: a Guide for Parents* (New York: Crown, 1954), Chap. 4. See also P. M. Symonds, "Life Problems and Interests of Adolescents," *Sch. Rev.*, 1936, *44*, 506–519; Sr. Helen De Sales Forrest, "The Actual Incidence of Moral and Emotional Problems of College Girls and High School Boys and Girls, unpublished master's thesis, The Catholic University, 1937; Caroline B. Zachry, "Problems of Adolescents," *Bull. Menninger Clin.*, 1940, *4*, 63–73; Ada Lent, "A Survey of the Problems of Adolescent High School Girls Fourteen to Eighteen Years of Age," *Alberta J. Educ. Res.*, 1957, *3*, 127–137; B. M. Wedge, *Psychosocial Problems of College Men* (New Haven, Conn.: Yale University Press, 1958).

[16] The relative importance of different problems is interpreted differently by various investigators. In his study of the problems of Catholic high school boys, Finn lists moral, school life, and vocational problems as being the most important, followed by a low incidence for family and personality adjustment problems. Boy-girl problems also rank very low in number — J. P. Finn, op. cit., p. 46. By contrast, Remmers and Radler found that not having dates is one of the most frequent problems encountered by adolescents. For a comprehensive picture of adolescent problems, see H. H. Remmers and D. H. Radler, op. cit., pp. 80–85.

TABLE 1

TOTALS FOR EACH CATEGORY OF PROBLEMS ENCOUNTERED BY 1840 CATHOLIC HIGH SCHOOL BOYS*

Category of Problem	Total Numbers	Per Cent
Moral	647	29.82
School life	578	26.65
Vocational	378	17.44
Family	184	8.48
Personality adjustment	164	7.57
Boy-girl	120	5.53
Financial	72	3.32
Health	14	.64
Unusual	12	.55
Totals	2169	100.00

*From J. P. Finn, *A Study of the Problems of Certain Catholic High School Boys as Told by Themselves and Their Teachers* (Washington, D. C.: The Catholic University of America Press, 1950), p. 46.

These more intrinsic difficulties are very likely to spread into other areas of adjustment and thus create additional problems for the adolescent. All of them taken together may be thought of simply as problems of adjustment, arising from the attempts of the adolescent to understand himself and his world, and to cope effectively with both (see Tables 1 and 2). Many of them, also, may be characterized as *explorations in adjustment*, the goal of which is the eventual achievement of maturity and a completely integrated and efficiently functioning personality. Grouped into categories, the most commonly encountered problems include the following:

1. *Home Adjustments.* Many of the adolescent's problems arise from conflict with parental rules, demands, and restrictions, other children in the family, family traditions, and the like. Often he is torn between family loyalties on the one hand and a strong desire for independence and peer group loyalty on the other, a situation that is fraught with considerable tension.

2. *Social Problems.* These include difficulties that the adolescent meets in trying to establish himself with the group and to achieve group identification. Peer group membership is the essential feature of this phase of development. Learning how to get along with others, social acceptance, group participation, dating, and similar behaviors are some of the situations encountered in this area.

3. *Psychosexual Problems.* These are among the most serious and disturbing problems that the adolescent encounters. Few adolescents are equipped by knowledge, experience, or temperament to cope adequately with the various aspects of psychosexual development that characterize adolescent growth. These problems can reach deeply into those we have characterized as intrapersonal, and will just as readily complicate social, academic, family, and moral adjustments.

4. *Moral and Religious Problems.* Many adolescents experience difficulty in living up to standards of obedience, sex behavior, veracity, and other phases of moral conduct, out of which deep-seated conflicts and tensions often arise. Similarly, they often develop religious doubts and scruples, uncertainty regarding religious beliefs or practices, and a religious reorientation that lead to feelings of insecurity, guilt, or shame.

5. *Academic and Vocational Problems.* Difficulties with school work, study habits, meeting the demands of individual teachers, developing interests in school subjects, and school failures are so common among adolescents that they require little emphasis. More difficult to cope with, actually, is the necessity which faces the adolescent of making a vocational choice, deciding on whether he wants to go on to college, and determining what curriculum he should follow.

TABLE 2

PERCENTAGE OF 5500 HIGH-SCHOOL SENIORS
WHO CHECKED CERTAIN PERSONALITY PROBLEMS*

Personality Problem	Boys	Girls
Being able to talk to people	27.9	33.3
How to develop self-confidence	21.1	34.4
Daydream too much	20.6	28.3
Having a desirable personality	23.7	25.4
Losing my temper	16.3	26.2
Wanting people to like me	16.8	25.5
Worrying too much	14.7	23.5
Being too nervous	13.1	21.3
Worried about my appearance	15.9	17.8
Being overweight or underweight	11.0	21.3
Want to learn to dance	23.7	10.3
Having an inferiority complex	14.9	17.0
Not enough sleep	14.4	12.7
Shyness	13.8	12.9
Poor complexion	10.0	15.4
Controlling my emotions	8.8	14.7
Understanding myself	9.7	13.5
Having the blues a lot	7.9	13.4
Being left out of things	10.3	10.8
Getting along with people	11.5	9.8
Not very attractive	8.0	12.2
Too short or too tall	7.4	11.1

*Adapted from L. J. Elias, *High School Youths Look at Their Problems* (Pullman, Wash.: State College of Washington Book Store, State Board of Education, 1949), p. 34.

This problem is a particularly stubborn one for the adolescent, and he needs all the help that parents and counselors can give him in reaching a solution.

6. *Problems Arising From Leisure-Time Activities.* The adequate and wholesome use of leisure time also constitutes a serious problem for many adolescents. Excessive interests in movies or television, cheap and sexy literature, gang activities, lack of worthwhile hobbies, and lack of adequate facilities for play and recreation are some of the typical problems that arise in this area.[17]

[17] For other descriptions of adolescent problems, see A. A. Steinbach, "A Survey of Adjustment Difficulties in Children and Youth Drawn From Normal Population," *Elem. School J.*, 1933, 34, 122–129; E. McC. Howard, "An Analysis of Adolescent Adjustment Problems," *Ment. Hyg.*, 1941, 25, 363–391; W. Griffiths, *Behavior Difficulties of Children as Perceived*

A Problem-Oriented Approach. The problems of the teen-ager, as we have seen, begin with the sweeping physical, intellectual, and social changes that occur in the normal course of development. Physically he no longer appears to himself or to others as the same little boy or girl who only recently was attending grade school. Intellectually his horizons are pushed farther and farther back, with new and sometimes disturbing ideas being encountered for the first time. The acquisition of knowledge takes on a different aspect, and he finds himself empowered to think and to express himself in a fashion resembling more closely the adult. But it is in the social sphere particularly that development brings out the greatest changes. The world and the people in it are not quite the same as they were. The parents, the family, male and female companions, teachers, spiritual advisers, the neighborhood, social organizations — all of them are viewed differently, because the adolescent is motivated by newer interests and wants, because he is growing up, because his self-concept is continually changing, and because of newer concepts and ideals.

It is problems such as these that challenge the student of adolescent phenomena and that give rise to a problem-oriented approach. This approach is not determined by a myopic and distorted

and *Judged by Parents, Teachers, and Children Themselves* (Minneapolis: University of Minn. Press, 1952); U. H. Fleege, *Self-Revelation of the Adolescent Boy* (Milwaukee: Bruce, 1945), Chaps. 1, 2, 16, 17; C. M. Fleming, *Adolescence* (New York: International University Press, 1949), Chap. XVII; J. W. M. Rothney, *Guidance Practices and Results* (New York: Harper, 1958); B. S. Gottlieb, *Understanding Your Adolescent* (New York: Rinehart, 1957), Part 2; and J. M. Seidman (ed.), *The Adolescent: a Book of Readings* (New York: Dryden, 1953), Chap. 3.

view of the modern teen-ager. We are quite aware, as we have said already, that many youngsters grow up successfully despite conflicts, frustrations, anxieties, and stresses. The important point is that every adolescent encounters some problems which need understanding and guidance, and there are thousands of adolescents who run headlong into very serious and complicated problems for which they are ill-equipped. It is this latter group that demands our special attention and the best skills we have to offer, whereas all of us could afford to understand even the most normal adolescent a great deal better.

WHERE ARE THE ADOLESCENTS?

Some General Facts About Teen-Agers. The number of youth will depend of course on where we set the limits for adolescence. If we take the usually accepted age range of 14 to 21, there were as of 1957 a little more than 19,000,000 boys and girls in this group. In the early adolescent years, 14 to 17, there were 10.2 million teen-agers, representing an increase of 21 per cent since 1950. This number is expected to increase to 14.3 million by 1965. In the 18-to-21-year-old group, there were 8.9 million youngsters, which is about the same as it was in 1950. Surprisingly enough, while there are only 98 males for every 100 females in the general population in this country, there are more than 103 males for every 100 females in the under-25 group.

Some Facts About School Attendance. Contrary to widespread opinion, the majority of adolescents are not in school, since statistics show that approximately 50 per cent of 16-year-olds leave school before the tenth grade. This would involve, therefore, close to ten million teen-

TABLE 3

SCHOOL ENROLLMENT, IN PUBLIC AND PRIVATE SCHOOLS OF PERSONS 5 TO 34 YEARS OLD: 1957*
(Expressed in thousands, and based on Current Population Survey.)

Type	Number Enrolled				Per Cent Enrolled			
	Kinder-garten	Elementary School	High School	College or Professional School	Kinder-garten	Elementary School	High School	College or Professional School
Total	1,824	27,248	8,956	3,138	100.0	100.0	100.0	100.0
Public	1,471	23,076	8,059	2,054	80.6	84.7	90.0	65.5
Private	353	4,172	897	1,084	19.4	15.3	10.0	34.5

*From U. S. Department of Commerce: Statistical Abstract of the United States, 1958 (Washington, D. C.: United States Government Printing Office, 1958), p. 109.

agers. The majority of this group are employed in one capacity or another. While this picture looks a little bleak from the educational point of view, we might keep in mind that in 1900 only 11 per cent of teen-agers in the 14-to-17 age bracket were in school. And, as we shall see, a substantial portion of high school graduates do go on to college (see Table 3).

Youth and College. The large number of dropouts in high school has a serious effect not only on the general college population but also on the number of men and women who become available for positions of leadership and responsibility in politics and statesmanship, in the arts and the professions, since among the dropouts are thousands of youths with great potentiality who never acquire the education that would make it possible to utilize these abilities. We will get to that point in just a moment. Looking at the over-all picture of college attendance, in the fall of 1958 well over 3,000,000 students were enrolled in college, and it is estimated that this figure would rise to 3½ million before the end of the school year. It is predicted that in another ten years the total college enrollment will be well over 6,000,000 youths. This picture certainly is encouraging,

but it is not at all as it could be if we had some means of educationally exploiting all of youths' potentialities. The statistics here are somewhat discouraging in view of the ever increasing demands for highly qualified people to fill our important jobs. For example, according to a study made by the Educational Testing Service of Princeton, New Jersey, one half of the *top 30 per cent* of the nation's high school graduates do not go to college. The number who end their education with high school diplomas is estimated to be between 120,000 and 200,000. The study, conducted under a grant from The National Science Foundation, was based on returns of a questionnaire from approximately 60,000 high school seniors and juniors in 478 representative high schools in the spring of 1955. In another study by the same agency, involving 10,000 high school seniors, also in the top 30 per cent of academic aptitude, it was found that 80 per cent of the boys and 70 per cent of girls reported that they would *like* to go to college.

Similar results are reported by the Office of Education which conducted a nationwide study for the period 1950 to 1954. This study indicated that approximately 325,000 high school graduates during this four-year period who were in the top 30 per cent of their class academically did not go on to college. In addition, 315,000, also in the top 30 per cent, attended only night school or took irregular college classes. Other studies show substantially the same results.

Even more disturbing is the fact that among the students of superior ability many drop out of high school before graduation. For example, in one study it was found that of approximately 528,000 eighteen-year-olds who were in the top quarter of scholastic ability, one out of five dropped out of high school before graduation. Of the 422,000 who did graduate, 219,000 (52 per cent) went on to college. A similar survey of high school seniors in Wisconsin in the spring of 1957 showed that 44 per cent of the students in the top one fourth of their class had no chance to continue education beyond high school. Finally, we may mention the report of the Commission on Human Resources and Advanced Training which shows that every year about 52,500 students in the top 25 per cent of scholastic ability drop out of high school before graduation. From the standpoint of human resources that could be available for productive effort and leadership, this is not an encouraging picture. It is for this reason that large-scale efforts have been launched in recent years by the federal government for the education and guidance of youth.

Adolescents in Trouble. The adolescent who finishes high school, although not free of problems, is at least kept reasonably well occupied until his seventeenth or eighteenth year. This is not true, of course, of those adolescents who drop out of school just as soon as the law allows; and many of these get into trouble. It is not sheer accident that many more delinquents than nondelinquents have poor scholarship records and show a strong dislike for school in general. Poor school adjustment, in other words, is highly correlated with poor social adjustment. However, by the term "adolescents in trouble" we do not mean to signify only those who come into conflict with society or with the law; there are many more teen-agers who are in trouble academically, sexually, morally, and especially emotionally. Needless to say, the gamut of troublesome behavior runs all the way from the simplest problems and maladjustments, such as occasional fits of depression or conflict at home, to the most seriously disrupting forms of behavior manifested in crime, delinquency, and serious behavior disorders.

It is not at all an easy matter to give anything like a true picture of adolescents in trouble. In some instances, facts and figures are not available, and in others there is no sure way of telling what the figures mean. We know, for example, that thousands of teen-agers lack basic scholastic skills, or fail to apply themselves adequately, and thus become academically maladjusted. We know too that thousands of others graduate from high school without the faintest idea of a vocational goal and thus are vocationally disoriented. In addition, there are countless hundreds of adolescents who are being referred every day to psychological clinics, clinical psychologists, and psychiatrists for the treatment of emotional difficulties and mental disorder. And of course there are the hundreds of thousands of youths who come into conflict with the law. If we add all of these together, we can certainly estimate that the number of adolescents in trouble runs well into the millions.

ARE *THESE*
OUR ADOLESCENTS ?
● ● ●
OR *THESE* ?

Fig. 2. Adolescents are capable of the noblest and the basest kind of behavior.

TABLE 4

JUVENILE DELINQUENCY — POLICE ARRESTS OF
CHILDREN UNDER 18 — CASES HANDLED BY
JUVENILE COURTS, 1940 TO 1957*

(Index, 1940 = 100)

| | Children Under 18 Arrested by Police | | Juvenile Court Cases |
Year	Number	Index	Index
1940	35,332	100	100
1943	47,884	136	172
1944	46,690	132	165
1945	49,566	140	172
1946	37,833	107	148
1947	34,376	97	131
1948	31,750	90	127
1949	32,922	93	136
1950	34,599	98	140
1951	37,259	105	149
1952	86,128	. . .	166
1953	149,806	. . .	187
1954	163,666	. . .	198
1955	195,626	. . .	216
1956	234,474	. . .	260
1957	253,817	. . .	302

*Adapted from U. S. Department of Commerce: Statistical Abstract of the U. S., 1958 (Washington, D. C.: U. S. Government Printing Office, 1958), p. 143.

A more precise picture of what is happening to many adolescents can be derived from the statistics on crime and delinquency (Tables 4 and 5). In the most recent figures on youth crime released by the Federal Bureau of Investigation and published in April of 1958, Director J. Edgar Hoover noted an upsurge of youth crime, with an increase of about 55 per cent since 1952 among persons under 18 years of age. It should be noted that Mr. Hoover makes a sharp distinction between juvenile crime as reported by his bureau, and juvenile delinquency. Whatever the value of this distinction, it is a safe guess that delinquency as well as crime among youth has had a sharp upswing in the past six years. But from all available evidence it is clear that the problem of delinquent behavior is very intense and is continually growing in scope. The picture of adolescent crime is particularly disturbing. For the year 1954 alone 58 per cent of all auto thefts, 49 per cent of all burglaries, 15 per cent of all recorded rapes, 5 per cent of homicides, and 6 per cent of all assaults were committed by adolescents under 18 years of age. In addition, over 55 per cent of all crimes involving personal property were perpetrated by adolescents. These stark figures will give the reader some idea of the magnitude of the problem posed by modern youth.

Even this does not complete the picture, since the New York City Youth Board finds that juvenile delinquency is at an all-time high and is breaking through class lines, showing an ominous shift from petty and mischievous events to crimes of violence, and spreading to the towns and suburbs. Gang wars are often based on racial and religious hatreds. During 1954 the delinquency rate of New York City youth between the ages of 16 and 21 jumped 52.7 per cent, which is very similar to the national average. Among juveniles below 16 years of age there was a large increase in arrests for felonious assault, with 1141 arrests in 1956 as compared with 836 in 1955, which constitutes a rise of 36.5 per cent. Most disturbing is the fact that the group below the 16–20 age category revealed the greatest percentage increase of arrests in 1956. Arrests for possession of dangerous weapons rose 92.1 per cent, felonious assault rose 39.3 per cent, and grand larceny, automobile, rose 36 per cent. Some of these data are indicated in Table 5.

TABLE 5

ADOLESCENT CRIME IN NEW YORK CITY
DURING 1955–1957*

Type of Crime	Total Arrested of All Ages	Total of 16–20 Group Arrested	Position of 16–20 Group
Destruction of Property	950	288	1
Robbery	2,195	721	1
Grand Larceny From Highway, Vehicle, etc.	2,384	1,371	1
Burglary	2,772	1,175	1
Petit Larceny From Highway, Vehicle, etc.	762	344	1
General Criminality Felonies	838	238	1
Homicide Unclassified	107	26	1
Homicide by Shooting	63	17	1
Assault on Officer Felony	768	177	1
Kidnapping	53	13	2
Rape, Age of Female Not Reported	76	18	2
Rape, Female Under 18	560	144	2
Abduction	32	19	1
Sodomy	176	26	3
Impairing Morals of Children, Misdemeanor	263	45	1
Arson	74	15	2
Malicious Mischief Felony	41	15	1
Misdemeanor	835	258	1
Extortion, Felony	74	12	2
Larceny of Auto	1,894	1,262	1
Dangerous Weapons	693	204	1
Burglars, Tools	117	28	2

*Adapted from H. Bloch, and A. Niederhoffer, *The Gang: a Study in Adolescent Behavior* (New York: Philosophical Library, 1958), p. 147.

In addition to these distressing statistics, other facts show that adolescent misbehavior is increasing at an alarming rate. For example, over half the VD (venereal-disease) case loads in our public clinics throughout the country are teen-agers and young adults, and in 1957 14 states and 19 cities noted a rise in VD among the age group 11–19. Also, one out of every three arrested for rape in 18 cities throughout the United States reporting sex offenses by age in 1956 was a teen-ager. And one out of every thirty persons arrested for prostitution was a teen-ager. These figures on sexual delinquency are complemented by a notable increase in illegitimate pregnancies among high school youth. All in all, therefore, the youth problem is certainly growing in proportion throughout the United States, and is spreading at an alarming rate from the urban to the rural areas. Girls as well as boys are involved in many of these delinquencies, and these facts make it imperative for parents, teachers, and counselors to understand the adolescent problem as completely as possible.[18]

[18] See the informative article by Leona Baumgartner, "A Look at Children in the U. S. A.," in Sidonie M. Gruenberg (ed.), op. cit., Chap. 2.

SELECTED READINGS

Bell, H. M., *Youth Tell Their Story* (Washington, D. C.: American Council on Education, 1938).

Benjamin, Zoe, *The Emotional Problems of Childhood: a Book for Parents and Teachers*, 2 ed. (London: University of London Press, 1951).

Edelston, H., *Problems of Adolescents* (New York: Philosophical Library, 1956).

English, O. S., and Finch, S. M., *Emotional Problems of Growing Up* (Chicago: Science Research Associates, 1951)

Farnham, Marynia F., *The Adolescent* (New York: Harper, 1951).

Finn, J. P., *A Study of the Problems of Certain Catholic High School Boys as Told by Themselves and Their Teachers* (Washington, D. C.: The Catholic University of America Press, 1950).

Fleege, U. H., *Self-Revelation of the Adolescent Boy* (Milwaukee: Bruce, 1945).

Gallagher, J. R., and Harris, H. I., *Emotional Problems of Adolescence* (New York: Oxford University Press, 1958).

Joseph, H., and Zern, G., *The Emotional Problems of Children* (New York: Crown Publishers, 1954).

Knoebber, Sister M., *The Self-Revelation of the Adolescent Girl* (Milwaukee: Bruce, 1936).

Landis, P. H., *Understanding Teen-Agers* (New York: Appleton-Century-Crofts, 1955).

McKinney, F., *Counseling for Personal Adjustment in Schools and Colleges* (Boston: Houghton Mifflin, 1958).

Pearson, G. H. J., *Adolescence and the Conflict of Generations* (New York: Norton, 1958).

CHAPTER III

KEY CONCEPTS
FOR THE STUDENT OF YOUTH

Every branch of study employs certain basic concepts which are particularly important to it. These are the "key" concepts. In adolescent psychology, we open many doors with the concepts of development and adjustment, conflict and frustration, personality and individual variation, and the like. Let us open a few of these doors in this chapter.

THE CONCEPT OF DEVELOPMENT

Development and Maturation. One of the terms most frequently encountered in the study of adolescence is *development*, and yet it is a term that is not always clearly understood. Certainly it is used with different meanings by different writers. When we say, for example, that intelligence undergoes development during the adolescent years, exactly what do we mean? Do we mean that intelligence "grows"? Do we mean only that it increases in power? Are we always using the term development to mean the same thing? Or do we sometimes use it analogously, intending it to mean partly the same thing and partly something else when used in different connections? Unless, of course, such terms are used to mean the same thing at all times, there is bound to be a great deal of confusion;

and confusion is a first step toward misunderstanding and error.[1]

One dictionary says that "to develop" means "to bring out the capabilities or possibilities of; bring to a more advanced or effective state; cause to grow or expand; elaborate." Thus development means essentially *progress*, but a progression that is "upward." It signifies progression toward a goal, something in the nature of an achievement. We say, of course, that a person "develops" a disease, but actually this is not development, it is regression. Development involves in living things a gradual emergence or realization of capacities, powers, and attri-

---

[1] H. W. Bérnard, *Adolescent Development in American Culture* (New York: World Book, 1957), Chap. 2; Nancy Bayley, "Individual Patterns of Development," *Child Develpm.*, 1956, 27, 45–74; Nancy Bayley, "Normal Growth and Development," in P. H. Hoch and J. Zubin (eds.), *Psychopathology of Childhood* (New York: Grune & Stratton, 1955), pp. 1–14.

butes. Thus we say, correctly, that the child *develops* the language function, that the adolescent *develops* intellectually, that the adult *develops* music appreciation. In each of these instances there is achievement, or progression toward a particular aim. Development applies also, of course, to physiological functions. They too unfold, and in many cases their development underlies the development of nonphysiological capacities and attributes.

This is generally the meaning of the term *development* in the fields of child and adolescent psychology. In the latter instance, the term is used specifically to signify *progression toward maturity*, a concept that corresponds exactly with the preceding definitions of development. Maturity is a goal, it is something to be achieved; and the mature person is one in whom has occurred the development of those capacities and attributes required for adulthood.

Closely allied to development is the concept of *maturation*. These two ideas are so much alike that they are often used interchangeably. To mature means, of course, to develop, as when we say that the sex drive matures at puberty; and this maturation certainly involves the gradual emergence that is characteristic of development. Regarded in this sense, maturation may be thought of as a special phase of the broader process of development. However, it is at this point that we can discern a difference between the two ideas. Development begins at the very moment of conception and continues until that indefinite period in life when maturity is achieved, at which time regression or deterioration becomes the characteristic feature of the life process. Maturation is something different. Since the individual organism *matures* along

certain lines only at specific times, we cannot apply the concept of maturation until the conditions requisite for such maturation are fulfilled. Thus the maturing of the sex function takes place only after the individual has developed physiologically to the point where such maturation is possible, normally between the ages of twelve and fourteen. Therefore, development is a general characteristic that pervades the life process, whereas maturation is a specific characteristic of certain processes that develop at certain times in the life cycle.[2]

An Essential Feature of Development. An essential feature of the developmental process is its *continuous and gradual* character. Development is a gradual unfolding, one period or phase shading off into another by imperceptible degrees. We can never therefore witness the actual process of development, we can only see its effects and reason back to the facts involved. It is like watching the hands of a clock; we know they are moving simply because they *have* moved from one point to another, but we cannot observe the actual movement. The movements are so gradual, the distance covered at any one moment so infinitesimal, that they escape our powers of observation; but the fact of movement is undeniable. So it is with development. We know the child before us is developing from moment to moment; but it is only after an interval of time, when the *accumulated* effects of development are apparent, that we can conclude that the process of development has been at work.

This basic quality of development enables the student of adolescent behavior

2 W. M. Krogman, "The Concept of Maturity From a Morphological Viewpoint," *Child Develpm.*, 1950, 21, 25–32; Charlotte Buhler, "Maturation and Motivation," *Personal.*, 1951, 1, 184–211.

to understand why the psychologist is impatient of theories which attempt to explain phenomena in terms of sudden or cataclysmic changes. Keeping this point in mind will help parents and teachers to realize the importance of giving the young boy or girl a chance to manifest more mature traits and abilities, and will put them on their guard against rash attempts to "speed up" the process of development, which so often causes unhappiness and maladjustment. The problems and the characteristics of youth require a great deal of patience, tolerance, and understanding.

THE CONCEPT OF MATURITY

The Many Meanings of Maturity. The word *maturity*, like its closely related term *adjustment*, wears many faces. It is not an easy concept to define, certainly not to the satisfaction of everyone interested in the problems of human development. We can, of course, easily discern its various parts, and thus we speak almost glibly of physical and intellectual, social and emotional, moral and psychosexual maturity. Naming these different facets does not really tell us what maturity is, but it does provide a starting point for the definition of maturity.[3]

We have said that maturity is the natural, intrinsic goal of adolescent development, meaning that it is something

---

[3] The literature in this area is very extensive. See L. K. Frank, "Introduction: Concept of Maturity," *Child Develpm.*, 1950, 21, 21–24; C. Binger, "What Is Maturity?" *Harpers Mag.*, 1951, 202, 70–79; Louise T. Welch, "The Meaning of Maturity," *Bull. Maritime Psychol. Assoc.*, 1954 (Dec.), 40–46. See also B. S. Gottlieb, *Understanding Your Adolescent* (New York: Rinehart, 1957), pp. 235–244. This book contains also an excellent chapter on "Escape Into Immaturity."

to be achieved within the foreseeable future of the adolescent. And we do see at least one aspect of this goal actually realized, and that is *physical maturity.* Somewhere in the late teens or early twenties, the young person will achieve the physical proportions, the height, the muscular development and strength, and the physical appearance that, taken together, denote physical maturity. The boy now *looks* like a man, and the girl like a woman, even though they may *act* like infants. This physical maturity is rather easy to identify because we are sure of the *criteria* that we want to use. These are the qualities just mentioned. Thus, the baby-faced youth of 25 looks like a child and therefore immature; similarly the small, hipless and breastless woman of 30 looks immature. We are often unwilling to entrust such persons with the responsibilities of adulthood. They just don't look the part. These judgments and misgivings arise of course because we unconsciously apply the criteria of physical maturity in such a way as to form a judgment of general immaturity.[4]

Now that we have made a start, it will be easier to define the other meanings of maturity. It so happens that those aspects of maturity that are most closely allied to physical growth and maturation are also more easily defined; that is, the criteria are more readily identified. For example, it is obvious that economic maturity is dependent to an important extent on physical maturity, and we all know that to be economically mature a person must be reasonably financially in-

---

[4] See the general criteria of behavior maturity and immaturity in B. R. Sappenfield, *Personality Dynamics* (New York: Knopf, 1954), pp. 232–237; also J. M. Seidman (ed.), *The Adolescent; a Book of Readings* (New York: Dryden Press, 1953), pp. 762–768.

dependent, self-supporting, and capable of assuming normal economic obligations. Thus the boy who depends too much on his parents for his college education, or on a dowry when he gets married, or on a loan to "get started" is economically immature. This economic dependence on parents is one of the basic reasons that many young adults are woefully immature despite their graduation from college.

Social Maturity. The achievement of physical maturity is a great step forward in the young person's efforts to adjust to the social situations in the world about him. We see this fact clearly illustrated in boy-girl relationships, since the boy who is physically mature feels much more secure in this relationship than the one who is physically inadequate or undersized. There is of course a great deal more to social maturity than the forging of adequate heterosexual relationships, but such relationships are often the starting point of broader social adjustments. The concept of social maturity embraces all such relationships and adjustments, and may be described as the degree to which a person can react adequately to varying social situations and relationships. Thus a girl gives evidence of being socially mature if she knows how to "handle" a date; a boy is socially mature if he can react to group situations, peculiarities, and demands without excessive shyness, withdrawal, panic, or other emotional reactions that would disrupt his relationship to the group. Adolescents develop social maturity if they learn to handle a group situation with confidence, ease, and skill. The socially mature person is at ease in a group situation and reacts favorably to bids for friendship, invitations to participate in social activities, and opportunities for social experience and expression.

Intellectual and Volitional Maturity. As the adolescent progresses toward adulthood, he develops intellectually as well as physically and socially, and thus eventually reaches a level of intellectual maturity. This aspect of maturity is reflected in the increase and better use of knowledge, the refinement of concepts, increased capacity for critical evaluation, independence of judgment, and more precise reasoning. The intellectually mature person knows what he is talking about before he ventures an opinion, knows when to keep quiet, avoids rash and unsubstantiated statements, and cautiously evaluates new opinions and ideas rather than accepting them on the basis of flimsy evidence or inadequate authority. The mature person knows how to think and to evaluate carefully, when to venture an opinion, and what to say; and he refuses to stick out his neck for the sake of getting into a conversation, or because someone asks his opinion concerning something of which he knows very little. Intellectual maturity has a profound influence on all important phases of a person's life. Without it, moral, religious, and social maturity are impossible.

The intellectual development of adolescents, as we shall see more fully later on (Chapter XVII), is a natural forerunner of *volitional development*. Volition is essentially the capacity for *self-direction*. It is the rational aspect of man's striving which is reflected in his more significant interests, attitudes, values, ideals, and goals. Volition, then, furnishes the groundwork for self-realization and self-determination. To the degree, therefore, that the adolescent achieves independence in making decisions, striving for goals, and determining for himself his basic values and ideals, he is said to be *volitionally mature*. Thus,

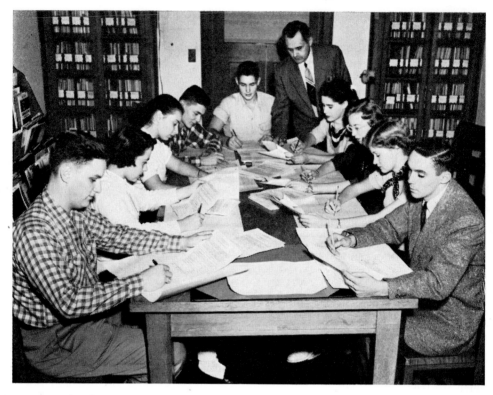

Intellectual maturity has many ingredients.

volitional maturity puts the finishing touches on the process of self-development made possible by intellectual maturity.

Psychological-Emotional Maturity. Despite the deep significance of intellectual and volitional maturity, the most important facet of adolescent striving is *psychological-emotional maturity*. The reasons for this statement are not hard to find. First of all, this area of maturity is so fundamental to development, integration, and adjustment, and therefore to the demands and stresses of adult living, that without it other aspects of maturity are impossible to achieve or are quickly disrupted. Without emotional maturity, for example, a young man or a young woman can't think straight, will often make unwise decisions, and perhaps seek the wrong values or goals. Emotional immaturity has a disorganizing and disruptive effect on all aspects of human behavior and human relationships.[5]

The basic ingredients of psychological-emotional maturity are: (1) emotional independence, (2) internal control, (3) self-identity, (4) a sense of responsibility, and (5) goal-directedness. All of this means that the adolescent must develop *psychologically* to the point where he has a clear conception of what he is and

[5] See E. C. Glanz and E. D. Walston, *An Introduction to Personal Adjustment* (Boston: Allyn & Bacon, 1958), Part 2; and J. M. Seidman, *op. cit.*, pp. 754–762. See also the article by Mary L. Northway, "In Defense of Immaturity," *Bull. Inst. Child Stud.*, Toronto, 1955, 17, 1–4.

what he should become, where behavior and relationships are no longer dominated by impulses or needs, and where the demands of daily life are not only dealt with efficiently but are freely accepted. The psychologically mature person accepts the responsibilities of life as a challenge rather than as a burden or as a threat. Possessing self-identity, independence, emotional stability (control), and a high degree of integration, he wades into the conflicts, frustrations, and demands of adult life with a vigor and a self-assurance that make good adjustment a foregone conclusion. That is why the mature person is self-confident and self-reliant, and can be depended upon to fulfill his responsibilities at any level of action in a secure and acceptable manner.

If then, we put together the physical, the social, the intellectual, the volitional, the psychological, and the emotional aspects of maturity, we end up with a *fundamental* quality of human personality that is indispensable to effective adulthood. It is for this reason that we said earlier that the goal of adolescent striving, and of our education and guidance of the adolescent, is the mature personality. Maturity is the core of effective adult life.

THE CONCEPT OF ADJUSTMENT

Adjustment and Maturity. The analysis of maturity is a natural prelude to the study of adjustment because the two concepts and the conditions which they represent are inseparably linked. Certainly adjustment at the adult level requires a high degree of maturity, and even at earlier levels of development successful adjustment will vary with maturity level.

The reason for this close relationship is easy to see. Each age level brings with it new demands — physical, intellectual, social, and economic; and maturity is the quality that enables the organism to meet these demands in an adequate manner, in other words, to adjust adequately to the situation. The adult world does not readily tolerate behavior of a childish kind in a person who is supposed to be grown up.

There is, of course, a similar relationship between development and adjustment, since the achievement of maturity hinges upon adequate development. Development is in a very real sense a prerequisite of good adjustment. For if development along a certain line fails to occur, or does not take place in normal fashion, the organism is quite likely to become maladjusted. The child, for example, who does not develop certain everyday skills such as walking, climbing, speaking, and writing is severely handicapped in his efforts to meet the demands imposed upon him by the environment. Needless to say, such development must be complemented at every stage of the process by *learning*, so that these factors constitute two of the most important determinants of adequate adjustment.

The concept of adjustment itself is not easy to define, partly because it has several meanings and partly because of the difficulty in determining the criteria for evaluating it. Also, adjustment and maladjustment have common boundaries, which means that human behavior can be arranged on a continuum extending from the extreme of good adjustment to the other extreme of the most serious maladjustment. We may illustrate these points by reference to two contrasting cases of teen-age adjustment that came to the author's attention. We will call them Bill and Mary. These youngsters are about the same age, 15 and 16 respectively, and from much the same social and economic backgrounds. But there the similarity ends. Bill is a happy, carefree young man, who has done well in school, has many friends, is spoken of highly by his teachers, has a wide interest in sports, and has already decided what he wants to be when he finishes high school. Mary is just the opposite. She is a moody youngster, hostile toward her parents, uninterested in schoolwork or extracurricular activities, and seemingly without any close friends. She is showing definite signs of failure in her schoolwork. Bill, of course, is obviously a well-adjusted adolescent who will probably sail right into adulthood with a minimum of conflict, frustration, or confusion, while Mary is emotionally disturbed, poorly adjusted to several aspects of her environment, and, in a word, maladjusted.

From the standpoint of adjustment, what is the difference between these two teen-agers? Why do we say that one has achieved good adjustment and the other is maladjusted? Is it in the relationship between them and their environments? Is it the state of their own personal feelings? Is it the range and depth of their interests and goals that determine the level of adjustment? Is it how well they get along with others? One can see that there are many questions to answer before adjustment can be defined. Perhaps the most important fact to note is that the behavior of both Bill and Mary is adjustive in nature. Mary's hostility, jealousies, and the like are her way of coping with difficult situations, just as Bill's are. Admittedly some responses are not wholesome or desirable, but they are no less adjustive for that reason. "From the biological standpoint all modes of response — direct or indirect, adequate or inadequate — are adjustive in aim. They represent the best of which the organism is capable under the total existing conditions. Presumably an attempt is being made in every case to preserve integrated functioning by the restoration of equilibrium."[6] This is an important lesson to learn in the study of human adjustment. It is "not the kind of behavior that determines whether we are dealing with adjustment processes, but the way in which behavior is used. Whether inner demands or environment or stresses are met by prayer, delinquency, neurotic symptoms, psychotic episodes, laughter, joyousness, or fraternizing with club members — to mention just a few of thousands of possibilities — the concept of adjustment is applicable as long as the response serves to reduce or to mitigate the demands made of the person. When such responses are inefficient, unwholesome (that is, detrimental to personal well-being), or pathological, they are designated as 'maladjustment.'"[7]

Adjustment, Maladjustment, and Mental Health. The reference to maladjustment raises the question as to whether the maladjusted person is mentally unhealthy, and suggests other questions about the relationships between mental health and adjustment. The concept of mental health is useful in emphasizing one of the most important facets of human adjustment. We can certainly argue that mental health is a necessary

---

[6] S. Rosenzweig, "An Outline of Frustration Theory," in J. McV. Hunt (ed.), *Personality and the Behavior Disorders* (New York: Ronald, 1944), Vol. I, p. 384.

[7] A. A. Schneiders, *Personal Adjustment and Mental Health* (New York: Rinehart, 1955), p. 47. See the whole of Chapter 3 of this text for a thorough discussion of adjustment and related concepts.

condition of good adjustment, and to go one step further, we can say that when a person is mentally healthy there is little likelihood of serious maladjustment. Mental health, therefore, may be regarded *as the key to wholesome adjustment.*

However, the two concepts are not synonymous. A person may be academically, vocationally, or maritally maladjusted even though he is quite sound mentally. To be vocationally disoriented, or to be lacking in job satisfaction, is certainly not of itself indicative of mental ill-health or breakdown. It is only when maladjustments lead to chronic frustration, unhappiness, depression, hostility, or delusions of persecution that we have a problem in mental health. This relationship is clearly illustrated in many counseling cases where interference with good adjustment leads to mental difficulties. One boy, for example, had planned all through high school to go into teaching, but his father insisted that he take a business course in college. As a result, Johnny was disinterested in his schoolwork and transferred his resentment to his father, who had interfered with what he really wanted to do. As a result, Johnny failed in his schoolwork, and became a bitter and disappointed young man. Bitterness, hostility, envy, and the like are mental symptoms of deep-seated conflicts and frustrations that can lead to mental ill-health. Mental health, therefore, means freedom from disabling and disturbing symptoms that lead to emotional disability, intellectual disturbances, and indecision.

Mental health is, of course, more than the absence of disturbing symptoms. It includes the ability to utilize our potentialities effectively, co-ordination of effort, and control. In the mentally healthy person there is integration as well as peace of mind. Clearly, such qualities are of fundamental importance to good adjustment. The adolescent's reactions to his schoolwork, to his family, and to other individuals are constantly influenced by his state of mind. The unhappy, depressed, or anxious boy or girl cannot study or learn efficiently, he cannot enjoy leisure activities, nor can he cope effectively with his problems. Mental health (or ill-health) *permeates* the adjustment process and may be regarded therefore both as a condition and as an integral part of adjustment.

Adjustment and Morality in Adolescence. From examples that we have already used it is clear that good adjustment is similar at times to being *morally* good. We must be careful, however, not to regard maladjustive behavior as morally bad; nor is the well-adjusted person necessarily an exemplar of virtue. Good adjustment is not identical with virtue, nor is maladjustment the same thing as sinfulness. Yet morality and adjustment are closely related, and it often happens that immorality lies at the basis of maladjustment. Taken in its widest meaning, wholesome adjustment must include moral soundness, and chronic immorality must eventually lead to maladjustment. This problem is likely to arise in the sexual area during adolescence, so that sinfulness (masturbation, impure thoughts, petting, and the like) is often correlated with mental anguish or poor adjustment.[8]

But we must emphasize the fact that morality and adjustment are not identi-

---

[8] See A. A. Schneiders, "Psychology as a Normative Science," in Magda B. Arnold and J. A. Gasson (eds.), *The Human Person: an Approach to an Integral Theory of Personality* (New York: Ronald, 1954), pp. 373–394.

cal. Sin is primarily a moral evil and is only secondarily maladjustive, whereas maladjustment is primarily a psychological evil and is morally bad only when the response involved is a moral act. Youngsters particularly need to know something about these distinctions so that they do not confuse sinful behavior with mental derangement.

Adjustment and Normality in Adolescence. Commonly recurring questions regarding youth are: "What is a normal adolescent?" or "Are all adolescents to some extent abnormal?"[9] We do not want to get into a long and complicated discussion of what the word *normal* means, but it is helpful to the student of adolescence to develop an adequate concept of normality. To be normal means, of course, to be or to act according to some standard or norm, and it is at this point that confusion begins to arise. What standard? What norm? Are we normal when we think and act according to the standards of the group? Is social behavior of others a norm? Is the commonly accepted code of conduct the criterion for normality? To answer yes to any one of these questions would lead to a number of difficulties. If large numbers of teen-agers go wild over rock and roll, wear red vests or sweaters, or indulge in necking and petting, this doesn't make these actions normal. All one could say about such behavior is that, looked at statistically, the majority of a certain age group in a particular culture engage in certain patterns of behavior. This sort of approach gives us the picture of the "average" man, the "average" teen-ager, or the "average" housewife. The statisti-

cal norm is of course valid for certain purposes *but not for determining psychological normality.*

Nor can we look to medicine, to ethics, or to theology for an answer to the question of what it means to be normal. Each one of these disciplines supplies us with norms and standards that are necessary for the evaluation of certain conditions or actions, but none of them can be used to determine adjustive normality. In this case, we have to go to psychology itself to determine what the norms of behavior should be. For example, we can say quite positively that regardless of what the average person is like, or what the group does, or what society accepts, it is *psychologically* normal to be mentally healthy, emotionally stable, well integrated, and adequately adjusted to the demands of self and of reality.

Anything, therefore, such as rock and roll or ducktail haircuts or sexual misbehavior that militates against these qualities, and tends to undermine them in the course of development, is contrary to normality. This explains why certain attitudes on the part of adults toward teen-age behavior can be dangerous. We often hear such remarks as "Oh, they're just kids," "Oh, teen-agers have to sow some wild oats," or "He'll snap out of it — all teen-agers go through this at some time or other." Such attitudes imply that certain forms of behavior are normal and thus to be expected. In many such cases the behavior is "normal" only in the sense that it is common, tolerated, or accepted by society. In itself it may be degrading and, psychologically, very abnormal. In the nature of the case we cannot expect teen-agers to be perfectly normal in our sense of the term, but certainly we should

---

[9] G. A. Gardner, "The Mental Health of Normal Adolescents," *Ment. Hyg.,* 1947, 31, 524–540. See also A. A. Schneiders, *Personal Adjustment and Mental Health,* Chap. 10.

know what normality is, and do what we can to help teen-agers reach this goal.

The Definition of Adjustment. To be normal and well adjusted, therefore, means to get along with other people, to express legitimate wants and aspirations in a wholesome and healthy manner, and to achieve worthwhile goals. Particularly, it means to be mentally at peace with oneself, and with the world in which one lives. The boy or girl, therefore, troubled with sex problems, the youth who has no friends or who "can't make the grade," the young person tortured with religious scruples or subject to uncontrollable fits of temper — these and others like them are the maladjusted individuals. For them peace of mind seems an ideal that can never be achieved. For them the environment holds a thousand perils, a thousand petty annoyances from which there is no escape. They are constantly at war with two worlds — the one that is made up of people, laws, and customs that we call the environment; the other is the self, with its thoughts, desires, and feelings that so readily get out of hand. From these various ideas we can say that adjustment itself, whether good or bad, *is a process involving mental and behavioral responses, by which an individual strives to cope with inner needs, tensions, frustrations, and conflicts, and to effect a degree of harmony between these inner demands and those imposed on him by the objective world in which he lives.* Good adjustment occurs when the individual, within the limitations imposed by his own capacities and traits, learns to react to himself and his environment in a mature, responsible, and satisfying manner. Being mature and responsible, such a person can resolve mental conflicts, frustrations, and prob-

lems without developing a host of defense mechanisms, symptoms, or behavior peculiarities.

Adjustment and Normality as Relative. The achievement of adjustment is not an easy task, and there is no such thing as a perfectly adjusted person. We must therefore think of adjustment in terms of degrees. We must try to realize the complexity of the two factors that must be brought into effective relationship — personality and environment. If we take the latter as our starting point, we see that it comprises a multitude of objects, stimuli, and situations to which the individual responds and to which he must make adjustments. There are other persons — parents, siblings, teachers, friends — all of whom possess certain rights which must be respected, and who make certain demands which must be met. One must adapt himself also to the physical aspects of the environment; but of greater importance are the socioeconomic aspects — the laws and customs, folkways, mores, and manners to which one is expected to conform. Moreover, the situation is complicated further by the fact that this complex environment is constantly changing, so that the individual is required to make ever new adjustments beyond those already achieved.

If against these multifarious demands of a continually changing environment, we stack the equally multifarious needs of the individual personality, we see how limitless are the possibilities of friction and disharmony. There are desires, attitudes, and actions which are proscribed by law, custom, or precept; there are the beliefs that conflict with what is socially acceptable. Whichever way the individual turns he runs headlong into one or another barrier. He may even create the barrier himself, as in the case of the overscrupulous person. But whatever the nature of the barrier, the person often finds it impossible to gear his thoughts, desires, and feelings to the demands that are imposed by an unyielding environment. It is then that mental conflict results, ending at times in serious maladjustment.

Such maladjustment is essentially a compromise; it is in fact the individual's unhealthy way of resolving the conflict. And just because it is a compromise it fails to work, and brings in its wake despair or complete mental breakdown. Thus the teen-ager, unable to bring his own growing needs in line with parental demands and restrictions, or with the rules of society, or with morality, finds himself caught in the throes of anxiety, shame, or intolerable guilt. This condition is fertile soil for the development of disabling mechanisms or symptomatic behavior which serves only to further complicate the situation. In the interplay between personality and environment, compromises of this sort are maladjustive and abnormal. The adolescent's needs and aspirations must be patterned to the demands of the environment in such a way that conflicts and frustrations can be either avoided or effectively resolved.

Adjustment Is a Continuum. Adjustive behavior runs the gamut from very good to very poor; that is, it ranges from the extreme of healthy adjustment to severe maladjustment. But this is not the whole story, since adjustment like maturity assumes different forms. The human personality is many-sided, and it is not uncommon that adjustment in one area may be counterbalanced by maladjustment in others. How often we hear it said of teen-agers that they are well liked,

accepted, and even popular with the peer group, at the same time that they are experiencing raging conflicts at home. Similarly, the young lady who is sought after by half of the boys in her class may be an academic misfit. The number of these forms of adjustment will vary somewhat with different groups of individuals. For adolescents it is possible to distinguish the following types: (1) personal adjustment which includes emotional, moral, and religious aspects of the teen-ager's life; (2) adjustment to home and family; (3) social adjustment; and (4) academic and vocational adjustment.

Each one of these forms of adjustment has its own special significance for the well-being of the adolescent, but perhaps the most important fact about them is their *mutual dependence*. In most cases of maladjustment it is found that difficulties in one sphere will be related to difficulties in another. Thus if a boy is emotionally disturbed the chances are that he will be socially and scholastically maladjusted, and will be having difficulties at home. Similarly, if he is socially maladjusted — that is, if he has no friends, cannot get along with his peer group, or comes into conflict with civil authority — he will likely manifest difficulties in his academic life, and even more so in his attitudes toward himself. We should keep in mind that the human personality, while many-sided, is also a unity. Because it has many facets it is involved in several kinds of adjustment; because it is also a unity, because it is one *thing* embracing many aspects, we may expect that what happens in one area is almost certain to be reflected in others. To be unhappy at home is the surest way for a teen-ager to become unhappy at school; to do poorly in school is the surest road to emotional unrest. *Adequate adjustment requires that there be harmony within oneself, and harmony between oneself and the persons, things, and events that constitute the environment.*

ADJUSTMENT AND RELATED CONCEPTS

The Adolescent Problem and Adjustment. The psychology of adjustment is of particular significance to the study of adolescence because of the adolescent problem that we described in Chapter II. The myriad and deep-seated changes of the adolescent period, its transitional character, and the resulting confusion, uncertainty, and instability are fertile soil for maladjustive responses, and call upon all the resources the youth can muster to cope with the situation. At any period of life, adjustment becomes increasingly difficult as changes become rapid, bewildering, or widespread. Thus a young child, torn from his home and environment by war, disaster, death of parents, or divorce, may show unmistakable signs of psychological disorder. The much older person, forced to retire because of age, might find it equally impossible to adjust adequately to the situation. In all such instances, including adolescence, the individual is caught without the resources necessary to cope with the frustrations, demands, and threats that the changing situation imposes. Here again we see the importance of understanding the adolescent problem in relation to the difficulties that young people encounter. If to this problem we add the demands of family, school, church, and society, it is not hard to see why the adjustive behavior of the teen-ager is often inadequate.

Conflict and Frustration in the Life of the Teen-Ager. The adolescent problem, family influences, peer group membership, and the like may be considered as the more remote determinants of the adolescent's adjustive behavior. More immediate determinants of such behavior are the *conflicts* and *frustrations* that all teen-agers experience.[10] Concepts like these must be studied closely because it is easy to get the wrong impression of them. Are conflicts and frustrations always bad? Do they always lead to maladjustment? Should adolescents learn to avoid them as much as possible? These are some of the questions that come to mind in studying the background of adolescent behavior, and they are questions that we should answer very carefully.

First of all, the reader is aware from his own experience that conflicts and frustrations are a part of daily experience. We cannot escape them, and it is doubtful whether we would want to get rid of all such experiences. The idea of conflict refers here to *psychological conflict* by which is meant a mental struggle between opposed motivations. It is a battle between what a person wants and what he can have, between the cravings of human nature and the stern impositions of the environment. Often the conflict begins when actions fail to correspond to ideals, when the individual is torn between the pleasures and satisfactions of behavior and the more spiritual satisfaction that comes from following the dictates of principle. Thus we often find teen-agers torn between the thrill of acting independently and the ideal of fol-

---

[10] B. R. Sappenfield, *op. cit.*, Chap. IV; L. D. Crow and Alice Crow, *Adolescent Development and Adjustment* (New York: McGraw-Hill, 1956), Chap. 11.

lowing the admonitions of the parents. This type of situation is fertile ground for the development of conflict and often results in poor adjustment.

While it may seem that conflict is of necessity psychologically bad, such a view is incorrect. What is bad is not the conflict itself, but the failure to resolve the conflict. In fact, a certain amount of conflict is essential to complete development. *Mental growth and synthesis are achieved in large measure through the media of conflicts,* and very often in proportion to the number and seriousness of one's mental crises. The all-important fact is that *this synthesis is achieved only through resolution of the conflicts experienced.* Moreover, this resolution must be personally, morally, and socially acceptable. One might solve a problem or avoid a crisis by simply acceding to one or another impulse or desire; but this course is unacceptable in many instances, because it is contrary to one's ideals and principles or to the customs and laws of society. Thus the "solution," if it may be so called, would only lead to further and perhaps more serious difficulties.

In its highest form the resolving of conflict involves an appreciation of the issues at stake, a decision that results in banishing one of the conflicting factors, and conduct in accordance with the stand finally taken. We cannot, of course, expect the adolescent to manifest this type of resolution very often, since he does not possess the psychological means for such decisive action; but he can be helped in formulating important decisions. By bringing the experience and wisdom of older persons to bear on the situation, he can be taught how to deal effectively with conflicts. He can be fur-

nished with the concepts, principles, and ideals that will enable him to evaluate his desires and his conduct and will make it possible for him to achieve that synthesis of impulses, experiences, and conduct that characterizes the integrated personality. With such help, conflicts may well become steppingstones to adjustment; without this help they often become barriers. Let us recall that the teen-age is one of extremes — when the individual is torn between the loftiest ideals and the basest of impulses; between periods of great joy and pleasure and those of melancholy and despondency; between periods of unbounded energy and others of inexplicable lassitude. It is small wonder therefore that it offers so many possibilities for conflict and maladjustment.

The effect of conflict on behavior and adjustment will depend to an important extent on the nature of the conflict itself. *Conscious* conflict normally engenders deliberation or reflection, or perhaps some verbal discussion, by which we are able to evaluate the good and bad points of different courses of action, and thus determine which course we should choose. Here we have a clear instance of the application of reason to a problem of adjustment. The use of deliberation enables us to resolve the conflict by accepting one of the possibilities and rejecting others. The disposition of conflicts in this manner is a great step toward mental health and adjustment. On the other hand, *unconscious* conflicts cannot be disposed of in this way because they are unknown to the person himself. There are many persons who are paragons of moral virtue at the conscious level and raging beasts at the unconscious level. The kind, considerate person may be unconsciously very hostile, or the altruistic individual may be deeply selfish.[11]

Such conflicts function unconsciously and are expressed as symptoms, defensive mechanisms, or disturbing dreams. Normally they cannot be resolved without the help of counseling or psychotherapy. Whenever mental conflicts cannot be resolved because they are inaccessible to deliberation, or because of personality factors, they are likely to affect adjustment and mental stability in an adverse manner. They seriously disrupt emotional balance and peace of mind, and thus interfere with the efficient control of emotional reactions and with mental efficiency. They also work against the organization and direction of behavior and personality integration. In addition, unresolved conflicts tend toward a state of continuous frustration since they interfere with the normal expression of needs and motives. Finally, as we have already suggested, they lead often to the development of disabling symptoms which in actuality are symbolic efforts to reduce the tension produced by the conflict. It is for these reasons that psychotherapy is often necessary.

Conflict is closely related to *frustration*, which plays an equally important role in determining the teen-ager's adjustment to his environment. Whereas conflict involves a struggle between motivational opposites, frustration results from the *blocking* of motivation or behavior. Thus the youngster who is striving for academic achievement and fails to get good grades may experience a deep sense of frustration which often leads to emotional tension, to the development of psychological mechanisms like compensation or rationalization, or to behavior difficulties. What happens in any particular case will be determined by a number of factors, but most particularly by what the frustration *means* to the young person. Thus if being on the honor role or being president of the class or captain of the basketball team is regarded by the adolescent as almost indispensable to his happiness, the frustration will be felt very deeply and may cause widespread emotional reactions and a disruption of behavior. Similarly, the young girl who can never get a date will feel deeply frustrated and will show unmistakable signs of frustration.[12]

The effect of frustrations will be determined to an important extent by the manner in which they originate. Some frustrations originate in the environment and are often quite temporary and unimportant. The poor teacher may block the youngster's efforts to achieve, or lack of finances may stand in the way of attending a school dance. The more serious frustrations are those that arise from *personal* deficiency, especially those that have particular significance for the adolescent. Physical inferiority, lack of athletic prowess, intellectual deficiency, feelings of inferiority, or a family background of which the adolescent is ashamed, often stand in the way of achieving personal goals; and such frustrations can cause serious disruptions in adjustment. What the teen-ager needs to know or

---

[11] See the article by D. R. Miller and G. E. Swanson, "The Study of Conflict," in M. R. Jones (ed.), *Nebraska Symposium on Motivation*, 1956 (Lincoln, Nebr.: University of Nebraska Press, 1956), pp. 137–174.

[12] See A. A. Schneiders, *Personal Adjustment and Mental Health*, Chap. 9. See also the article by M. H. Marx, "Some Relations Between Frustration and Drive," in M. R. Jones (ed.), *op. cit.*, pp. 92–130.

to learn is that frustration like conflict is to some extent unavoidable, and therefore he must develop a degree of *frustration tolerance*. Everyone must learn how to defer the gratification of needs and desires at different times in his life, and the ability to do this is dependent to an important degree on frustration tolerance. This is one way in which the adolescent can learn how to deal efficiently and healthfully with the frustrations that arise in the course of his experience. Thus the youngster who because of defective vision cannot participate in certain sports must learn to tolerate the situation and find an acceptable substitute; whereas the person who is frustrated in his aims because of lack of effort or of application should be taught how to meet the demands of the situation so that the frustrating element is eliminated.

Typical Conflicts and Frustrations in Adolescence. The more significant conflicts and frustrations of adolescence occur in the same areas of adjustment as the problems we discussed in a previous section. This is to be expected since problems grow out of conflicts and frustrations. Thus we may expect that many adolescents will experience severe and sometimes damaging conflict in the area of sexual adjustment.[13] In other words, the young boy or girl of fifteen and sixteen is torn between what he *ought* to

do and what his impulses urge him to do. This is a good example of an *intrapsychic* conflict. Typical conflicts also arise in the *interpersonal* area of adjustments whenever the adolescent's need for independence and self-assertion runs counter to the demands and restrictions of parents or other persons in authority. In the school situation, too, conflicts often occur between recreational and social interests on the one hand, and academic demands on the other; or between the desire for an education and the call to economic independence. Such conflicts are often resolved, as we have already seen, by the inadequate expedient of quitting school. Finally, in the religious area, there are a number of opportunities for conflict. With the general reshaping of ideals and values, under the influence of sexual conflicts and the effects of peer group membership, the adolescent often finds his earlier religious orientation inadequate, and thus experiences considerable conflict before a new solution is worked out.

The frustrations of adolescence are of course closely related to the conflicts and problems that characterize this period of development. As compared with the child, there is noticeable in the adolescent a partial shift from *external* to *internal* frustrations, which are generally more difficult to cope with. The child may experience little or no frustration in the area of sex behavior, whereas the adolescent may experience all kinds of frustration of this type, since both society and morality frown on sexual expression. In general, therefore, we note some increase in frustration because of motivational changes that occur in adolescence. The teen-ager's need for new experience, his greater awareness of moral principles and social expectations, and

---

[13] L. G. Lowrey, "Adolescent Frustrations and Evasions," in P. H. Hoch and J. Zubin (eds.), *Psychopathology of Childhood* (New York: Grune & Stratton, 1955), pp. 267–284; D. Segel, *Frustration in Adolescent Youth*, Bull. 1951, No. 1 (Washington: U. S. Office of Education). This author sees frustration as the greatest threat to psychological development. The effects of frustration both on psychosocial development and on education are indicated. The author pulls together the literature relating to frustration and integrates it with other relevant material.

the increased need for conformity, recognition, and social approval may all set the stage for frustrating experiences. Moreover, the teen-ager is much more conscious of his personal limitations, especially those that have any social implications, and he takes achievement and status more seriously. The older he gets the closer he comes to adult responsibilities, and yet he is denied the privileges of voting, joining the armed forces, living away from home, quitting school, steady dating, or getting married. It is for these reasons that adolescence stands out as a period when both internal and external frustrations reach their peak.

What is worse, because he is immature and lacking in experience, the average teen-ager is not well equipped to deal effectively with these frustrating situations. Here too the groundwork is often laid for maladjustments, such as marital and economic difficulties that appear later on in adulthood. We must always keep in mind that while behavior is ultimately determined by needs and motives, frustration has its own dynamic quality and will play an important part in patterning the adjustments of the individual. As we have pointed out in another place, frustration

> is often the springboard for the development of maladjustive behavior. The child frustrated by school adopts the simple expedient of truancy; the adolescent who is denied recognition or status turns to delinquency; the adult frustrated in the realization of personal ambitions drifts from one job to another until there are no jobs left for him. Aggression, antisocial behavior, destructiveness, escape or defense mechanisms, hostility, crime, and similar symptomatic responses are often outcomes of the frustration of basic needs, motives, and goals. One can see the importance and the necessity of understanding the phenomenon of frus-

tration in all its different aspects. It can tip the scale toward normality or abnormality, adjustment or maladjustment.[14]

Outcomes of Conflict and Frustration in Adolescence. From the above statement it is clear that the experiences of conflict and frustration play an impressive role in determining adolescent adjustments to the world in which they live. What happens in any given instance will be determined by a number of factors such as level of maturity, frustration tolerance, personality integration, emotional stability, and availability of substitute responses. This means of course that individual adolescents will vary a great deal in their response to conflict and frustration. But in every case an effort will be made to cope with the conflicting or frustrating situation by the adoption of some objective or symbolic response. The appropriateness of this response will determine whether it is adjustive or maladjustive in character. To illustrate this principle, let us take a typical case of adolescent frustration:

> Terry is sixteen years old. She is an attractive girl, well developed and well proportioned for her age, and popular with boys and with her peer group. Terry has many invitations to dances, parties, picnics and outings, and the like. These attentions and invitations flatter her ego and give her a keen sense of acceptance and belonging. Her mother, however, feels that Terry is getting a bit out of hand, is neglecting her studies, is developing an egoistic and snobbish attitude, and is staying out late at night too often for a sixteen-year-old. Terry herself secretly believes her mother is right and wants parental control, but is sensitive to the opinions of her classmates and acquaintances about old-fashioned parents, and strongly desires their approval. As a result, Terry is in constant conflict with

14 A. A. Schneiders, op. cit., p. 252.

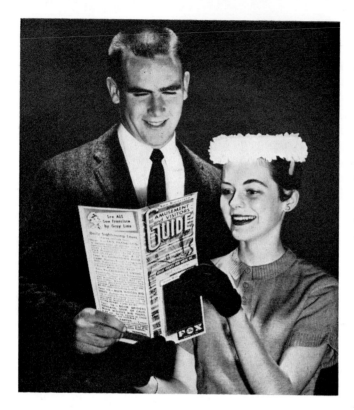

The well-adjusted adult personality is the result of proper personality development in childhood and adolescence.

her conscience and with her mother, and feels deeply frustrated whenever her mother enforces certain rules and restrictions. Not knowing how to handle this situation, she often sulks and pouts and argues with her mother, talks about leaving home as soon as she is 18, and bursts into tears whenever frustration tolerance reaches the breaking point. Her mother is equally at a loss to know what to do with this "impossible" child.

Here is a typical example of an adolescent problem built around conflict and frustration. Terry's response to these conditions is quite inappropriate and therefore unadjustive because it tends to heighten rather than to reduce tension, and is fertile soil for the development of symptomatic behavior. If Terry were a little older, a little wiser, and more mature, she would probably be able to bring her own needs and longings in line with her mother's ideas on appropriate be-

havior. She could, for example, understand better why her mother is anxious about her behavior. She could more effectively balance the demands of school life with the craving for social experience and pleasure. She could sit down with her mother and arrive at some compromise that would be satisfactory to both. She could see that prolonged anger, manifested in sulking and pouting, is disruptive of personal well-being and her relationships with others. If Terry could do these things she could then react more adjustively to the situations that involve conflict and frustration. Of course, as we have seen, the reason for their failure to do so is that adolescents do not have the experience, the wisdom, and the maturity required for adequately coping with situations which often loom very large in their own eyes as well as in the eyes of parents.

THE CONCEPT OF PERSONALITY

Personality and Adjustive Response. When we analyze the conditions of adjustment and the response that a person makes to conflict and frustration, we find that his personality and its level of development and integration are the most important single determinants of the outcome. This alone makes the study of personality important. But even apart from its intrinsic relationship to adjustment, the concept of personality is basic to the study of all aspects of adolescent development. The psychology of adolescence, like other branches of psychology, is more than a study of physical changes, needs, interests, goals, and other aspects of the psychic life and behavior of youth. In its broader and deeper meaning, it is *a study of the nature, organization, and development of the adolescent personality.* Too often in our investigation of the motivations and behavior of people we lose sight of the whole in our preoccupation with the parts, and this mistake can be avoided by an early definition of the concept of personality and its characteristics.

The Nature and Characteristics of Personality. There are as many meanings associated with the term *personality* as there are viewpoints in psychology. But underlying this diversity of viewpoints is the fact that the word *personality* refers to an abstraction rather than to a real, self-existing thing. What really exists, if we wish to be exact, are not personalities but persons, and it is these persons — individual, living human beings — whose traits, capacities, and peculiarities we abstract and bring under the heading of personality. Personality in this sense, therefore, is the person as conceived or

known by an observer, in which case the concept of personality in general, as well as the impression of a particular personality, will depend in part upon the viewpoint, experiences, ideas, and attitudes of the observer.

The term itself comes from "person," and a person is the whole human being made up of body and mind. Both of these aspects, therefore, must be subsumed by the general concept of personality. What we are looking for is a definition that will embrace all human characteristics, including those that are not so obvious in our day-to-day observations of persons. Stated briefly, the concept of personality signifies *an emergent, unique organization of physical and psychological traits, capacities, dispositions, habits, and mannerisms which, peculiar to an individual human being, determine his reactions to himself and to others and his impressions on the environment of persons, things, and customs in which he lives.*

Let us take a close look at this definition in order to pick out features that are important to adolescent psychology. First of all, the definition indicates that personality is not merely a group of traits but a *unique organization,* which implies distinctiveness, cohesion, and integration — all of which are significant features of the total personality. Second, physical as well as psychological features are included since they are integral parts of the total person; this fact is quite important for the physiology of adolescence, which we shall study in the next section. Third, the concept is not limited to traits since it embraces those other factors, such as capacities, mannerisms, and dispositions that play so important a role in the estimation and evaluation of personality by one's self as well as by others. Finally, this unique organization is socially as well as individually significant, which implies that personality is a social as well as an individual phenomenon.

From the standpoint of adolescent psychology it is important to emphasize also the *emergent* and *fluid* quality of personality. During childhood and adolescence especially, personality is kaleidoscopic in character, changing by minute degrees from day to day and from year to year. Sometimes the changes occur fairly rapidly, sometimes sporadically, and at other times suddenly, and without apparent cause. This idea is directly in line with the concept of development. Since development involves a progressive unfolding of capacities, plus certain changes in structures and functions, it must be that personality changes continuously, at least as long as the process of development goes on.

This fact suggests an important addition to our concept of personality when applied to the study of youth. Because of the continuous development during adolescence, we are forced to think of personality not as a relatively permanent organization but *as something to be achieved*, in the same manner that maturity, adjustment, and integration are achieved. For the teen-ager, therefore, personality may be regarded *as a goal* to be attained through the rigorous conditioning imposed by experience, development, education, and self-discipline. This is what certain writers have in mind when they characterize personality as a *value*, a concept that is particularly appropriate to and useful in the study of adolescence.

As adolescence merges into mature adulthood, personality becomes more and more stable, although this stability is never absolute. Between personality and environment *there is a dynamic relationship* which makes absolute stability impossible. This fact is clearly exemplified during periods of great social or economic upheaval, such as war or depression, when deep-seated changes are likely to occur in ideals, attitudes, and beliefs. Under more normal circumstances, smaller and more subtle changes occur within the framework of the person-environment relationship. In all persons, and at all age levels, these changes continue to take place under the rule that the relationship between personality and environment is a dynamic and therefore constantly changing thing.

Personality Integration and Goal-Directedness. The mature personality, as we intimated earlier, is characterized by *integration and goal-directedness*. This is an important point because the entire span of youth is characterized to a greater or less extent by *lack of integration.* The inconsistencies in behavior, the confusion, the emotional stability, the conflicts, and the tendencies toward maladjustment are all indicative of failure in integrative control, and thus integration and integrative control become a dominant aim of adolescent development.[15]

Integration means essentially *unity*. It signifies harmony *within* the mind and personality of the individual — a harmony among wishes, thoughts, ambitions, desires, and purposes; between attitudes and traits; between impulses and behavior. It is reflected in a unity of purpose as well as in a unity of action; in the ability to make and adhere to decisions and

[15] J. S. Plant, *The Envelope: a Study of the Impact of the World Upon a Child* (New York: Commonwealth Fund, 1950), Chaps. 7 and 8. See the article by J. Seeman, "Toward a Concept of Personality Integration," *Amer. Psychologist,* 1959, *14,* pp. 633–637.

resolutions regardless of difficulties or opposition. In the well-integrated personality there often is conflict, but such conflict does not result in maladjustment or neurotic behavior. What occurs instead is a resolution of the conflict in such a manner that unity is preserved and harmony among conflicting tendencies is re-established. It is this integral unity which, though conspicuous by its absence in many instances, is the common goal of all adolescents. Without it maturity and adjustment become impossible.

Integration is an essential feature of the developmental process; and in the absence of disruptive influences integration is achieved normally as the organism matures. These disruptive influences must be controlled or suppressed if integration is to be achieved; and here intellectual development is of particular significance because it enables the adolescent to acquire the values, ideals, and principles by which he can create future goals which will give meaning and purpose to his existence and to his style of life. He becomes, so to speak, goal-directed; and this goal-directedness is reinforced by a growing appreciation of values in terms of which he can estimate the intrinsic worth of some things and the superficial character of others.

In the process of achieving integration, factors such as these act as synthesizing forces. They bring unity and direction to the adolescent's experiences and aspirations. They are the nucleus around which attitudes, traits, and tendencies become organized into an efficiently functioning whole. These goals and values make it possible to resolve the difficulties and conflicts that often threaten to disrupt the unstable personality of the adolescent. When there is something of value

in life, and a definite goal to strive for, it is not so difficult. to bring harmony into the many conflicting tendencies of personality.

Personality and Self-Discipline. Good adjustment, integration, and goal-directedness imply the capacity for *self-direction*. Concepts like maturity and responsibility are meaningless if normal persons are incapable of self-discipline. In the absence of the concept of self-discipline, it would be necessary to revamp our social structure and abandon most of what now passes for sound educational practice, psychotherapy, and counseling. The inculcation of ideals, the setting of examples, the teaching of precepts, and the giving of advice are all predicated on the assumption that the individual can act in accordance with them. Certainly, the firm conviction that the person under our guidance cannot control his impulses, emotions, or conduct, or that his adjustments are inevitably predetermined by previous events, would lead to complete discouragement if not despair on the part of parents, teachers, or counselors.

The concept of self-control is somewhat ambiguous. Actually, if we wish to be exact, we would say that it is not the self that *is* controlled, *but that which does the controlling*. What is controlled are those many modifications of self that take the form of desires, impulses, thoughts, and habits. In this sense *self-control means self-discipline* — the *ordering* of mental life and conduct in a way that will promote the happiness and well-being of the individual. Human nature being what it is, there is bound to be conflict between ideals and basic needs, between impulses and the demands of morality, and between what we know to be right and what is pleasurable; and it is then that self-discipline is necessary if we are to secure mental stability and adjustment. To abandon oneself to impulse, or to indulge in the uncontrolled pursuit of pleasure, is the surest road to maladjustment. Whether the teen-ager likes it or not, he cannot escape the fact that he is bound to live according to certain standards and laws, imposed on man either by himself or by some external agent. And this means that he must exercise self-control since it is certain that some of his wishes, needs, ambitions, or desires would sooner or later come into conflict with those restrictions.

We may thus broaden the concept of self-control to mean the regulation of our tendencies and habits so as to achieve harmony within ourselves, and harmony between ourselves and the demands of the world in which we live. This is self-discipline, without which the personality tends toward disintegration and maladjustment. Without it the integration of personality so necessary to effective living is impossible. There is little need to stress the significance of this factor for adolescent development. Is there anyone who has not witnessed the moral, social, and emotional havoc wrought in those personalities that lack self-discipline? The adolescent personality is by its nature unstable, and thus tends toward disharmony; and the only effective antidote to these tendencies is the imposition of self-discipline through which the adolescent finally achieves character. Character is what a person makes of himself; and it is character above all which every adolescent should realize as the crowning achievement of his attempts to master himself and his environment on the difficult road to maturity and adulthood. As Karen Horney says so pointedly, man by his very nature and of his own accord

... strives toward self-realization, and ... his set of values evolves from such striving. Apparently he cannot, for example, develop his full human potentialities unless he is truthful to himself; unless he is active and productive; unless he relates himself to others in the spirit of mutuality. Apparently he cannot grow if he indulges in a "dark idolatry of himself" (Shelley) and consistently attributes all his own shortcomings to the deficiencies of others. He can grow, in the true sense, *only if he assumes responsibility for himself.*[16]

INDIVIDUAL AND SEX DIFFERENCES

Adolescents — Alike or Different? One big problem that parents and others face is trying to understand and cope with variations among teen-agers.[17] This occurs with distressing frequency even in the same family. Mary is quiet, demure, and likes to read a great deal. Joan is spritely, passionately devoted to television, and is constantly engaged in an effort to entertain others with comical remarks and funny faces. Joe is the athlete of the family, starring in every major event at school. Pete is studious and research-minded. This is the phenomenon of *individual differences*, the phenomenon that sets precise and sometimes irritating limits to any effort to build an exact science around the concept of personality. As we have seen, the very concept of personality, with its emphasis on uniqueness, contains in itself the idea of variation — that people differ

---

[16] Karen Horney, *Neurosis and Human Growth* (New York: Norton, 1950), p. 15 (italics mine). See also G. H. J. Pearson, *Adolescence and the Conflict of Generations* (New York: Norton, 1958), p. 154.

[17] See A. H. Washburn, "Why Be Interested in Child Growth and Development?" *Child*, 1951, *16*, 50–54.

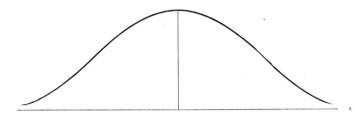

Fig. 3. The normal curve. Such a curve would result from plotting the I.Q.'s of a large, unselected group of people.

markedly from one another in traits, behavior, and personality organization.

Thus, against the idea of sameness, the differential psychologist argues that the distribution of individuals in terms of any one factor (such as intelligence) will follow the curve of normal probability (Fig. 3) the majority (roughly 60 per cent) clustering around a mid-point, and the remainder shading off to the extremes of the distribution. This interpretation is applied to all human characteristics, including capacities as well as traits, and emphasizes *quantitative* rather than *qualitative* variations. In other words, Mary is more intelligent than John, and John is more introverted than Lucille. This emphasis should not blind us to the fact that people also differ qualitatively from one another; in fact, it is these qualitative differences to which we are generally more sensitive. Thus if Helen is timid and retiring, and Jane is bold and aggressive, we have more than a difference in amount. Here we have a real trait differ-

ence and the distribution is exemplified in Figure 4.

Trait Differences vs. Capacities. In order to understand better the problem of individual variation, it is useful to distinguish capacities and functions, such as intelligence or memory, from traits. Capacities are not qualitatively distinguishing features since everyone has them in greater or lesser degree. Thus, the only distinction that can be made in terms of such factors is quantitative: John has little intelligence, James has a great deal; Gloria has a good memory, Anne a poor one. The distinction between a moron and a genius is not qualitative, since the difference between them is one of degree and not of *kind*.

Personality and character traits, on the other hand, are qualitatively distinguishing features, so that possession of one trait leads to the exclusion of its opposite. We cannot say, for example, that cowardice is only a small amount of courage, or that dishonesty is only honesty in a

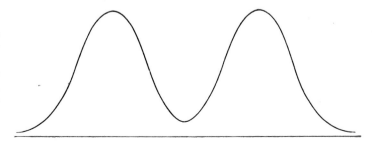

Fig. 4. A bimodal distribution. Such a curve would result from plotting two dissimilar features, indicating that selection had occurred. In this distribution two distinct groups of people are represented.

```
0   50   100   120   150   200
```
Intelligence

Fig. 5. A difference in capacity is not qualitative.

```
110   50   0   50   100
```
Introversion — Extroversion

Fig. 6. Character trait differences are qualitative.

small degree. Thus, whereas intelligence or any other *function* can be ranged on a continuum from zero to some indefinite maximum, paired personality traits cannot be so arranged. This distinction is illustrated in Figures 5 and 6.

It will be seen from these figures that the progression for intelligence is continuous, whereas that for introversion-extroversion is discontinuous; that is, the progression from introversion to extroversion passes through a zero point at which, theoretically, neither the one nor the other exists. When we say that the one excludes the other we are not unmindful of the fact that both aspects may be manifested in the same person under different conditions: the dishonest person, for example, is not without his honest moments. But these aspects are manifested under different conditions. The important fact is that the trait is *characteristic* of the individual, and as such will serve to distinguish him from those persons possessing other tendencies or attitudes.

More important for the study of adolescence is the fact that people do differ both quantitatively and qualitatively, and in the *distinctive organization* of their individual personalities. It is this fact that parents and teachers must always keep in mind in trying to understand and to guide young people. In all fairness to teen-agers we cannot afford to develop

iron-clad rules and set expectations to which the young person must conform. Each son and daughter and each student and counselee are different from all others, and this difference must be respected. It is both foolish and dangerous to expect all high school graduates to go to college or to think of future vocations for our youngsters only in terms of the professions, or to expect the same degree of obedience, of love, or of respect from each one of the young individuals with whom we come in contact. It is the prerogative of each person to be different, and we can only understand people and learn to live with them when we take this difference into account.

Where Do Differences Come From? The individual differences that we observe in people have many sources, and the whole problem is much too complex to discuss adequately at this point.[18] There are, however, a few facts of practical significance that we can mention here. Undoubtedly, many traits and capacities are related to hereditary background, whereas others are environmentally influenced. One practical principle that we can use safely is that the less any factor is related to or dependent upon physical structure (the body) the more susceptible it is to environmental influences and training, and the less likely it is to be determined genetically. Thus qualitative differences, such as social and character traits, are more amenable to nongenetic influences than are the vari-

---

[18] See J. S. Plant, *op. cit.*, Chap. 4. Plant discusses individual differences under the heading of the feeling of difference, and this feeling of difference is as important as individuation itself. Regarding the origin of differences, see Anne Anastasi, "Heredity, Environment, and the Question 'How,'" *Psychol. Rev.*, 1958, 65, 197–208.

ous capacities and functions of the individual such as memory and imagination. Numerous studies, especially those on identical twins reared apart, bear this out. In these studies it was found generally that differences in personality were much greater than differences in intelligence or physical make-up. In general we may say that the influence of heredity diminishes as we pass from purely physical traits, through those capacities and functions that are dependent upon physical constitution, to those traits and characteristics that are more distinctly social and psychological in nature.

This fact is of great practical significance. While such functions as memory, learning, and even intelligence can be significantly affected by environment and training, it is incontestable that nature imposes certain limitations which may hinder our best efforts. We cannot, for example, make a college student out of a moron. The situation is somewhat brighter in respect to social, moral, and religious traits, since the limitations imposed by heredity or by innate constitution are much less restrictive. These aspects of personality are to a large extent what conditioning, training, example, and education make out of the individual; and character is what he makes of himself. If, therefore, we employ sound training, provide the right kind of environment, and encourage the development of self-discipline in children and adolescents, there is little to fear concerning heredity. This interpretation supposes that other factors, such as physical make-up and mental capacity, are at least normally developed, in which case there is practically no limit to what can be accomplished in the shaping of personality.

Boys and Girls Are Different Too.

The concept of individual variation spans all groups, whereas the concept of *group differences* applies to certain individuals who, while different in themselves, are grouped together because of certain similarities. Thus we have sex differences, race differences, nationality differences, and religious differences. Here we are interested in sex differences only because of the importance of these differences for the understanding of adolescents.

Anyone who has worked or lived with young people has noted the real differences between boys and girls, particularly during the adolescent period.[19] What are these differences, and just how significant are they? The differences between boys and girls are significant because they deeply affect our reactions to adolescents and to their problems. Adjustment difficulties are not always the same for the two sexes, and if we are to understand these difficulties and guide the teen-ager toward his goals, we must have an intelligent awareness of how boys and girls differ from each other.

While the die-hards of feminine equality and emancipation have tried desperately to minimize the differences between men and women, the effort has met with a conspicuous lack of success, for the simple reason that nature will not be denied. Boys and girls are different in almost every aspect of personality, and these differences have a great deal to do with the manner in which they face their

---

[19] In this connection see Loretta M. Sheehy, *A Study of Preadolescents by Means of a Personality Inventory* (Washington, D. C.: Catholic University, 1938); L. M. Terman and Leona E. Tyler, "Psychological Sex Differences," in L. Carmichael (ed.), *Manual of Child Psychology*, 2 ed. (New York: Wiley, 1954), Chap. 17; C. G. Moser, *Understanding Girls* (New York: Association Press, 1957), Chap. 3.

parents, their problems, or reality. First of all, boys are *physically* different from girls, and this physical difference is of deep significance for personality development, for psychosexual attitudes and behavior, for the formation of the self-concept, and for the achievement of self-identity. It is significant also for economic independence and maturity.

Boys and girls are also different *psychosexually*, and this difference conditions their behavior, their attitudes toward the opposite sex, the control of sexual impulse and feeling, and their respective moral development. In general, girls are not as strongly oriented toward sexual fantasy or behavior, and this fact changes the sexual problem to an important degree. Boys and girls are different *psychologically* and *emotionally*, and thus react to their own development and to the demands of self and of reality in a distinctive manner. Girls generally are more sensitive, more docile, more emotional, and more idealistic than boys, and are thus more amenable to training and discipline. Boys and girls are different *morally* and *spiritually*, since girls are generally more sensitive to moral and spiritual values than are boys. Thus we can expect moral and religious developments to take different directions in the two sexes. There are even some educative differences between the two sexes, as girls incline more toward the literary fields and boys more toward the mathematical and scientific areas of learning.[20]

While there are many sex differences that must be kept in mind, there are also basic similarities that are important to an understanding of the adolescent. This is particularly true where innate factors are concerned, including especially needs and instincts, capacities, feelings, and emotions. It is these basic similarities that make it possible for us to develop a coherent psychology of adolescence for both boys and girls.

These, then, are some of the basic concepts for the study of adolescents. We will meet them as well as many other concepts many times in the course of our investigation. We should study them carefully because they will open many doors to our understanding of the mind and personality of youth.

[20] See D. W. Armstrong, "The Adolescent Boy," *J. Hum. Rela.*, 1955, 3, 41–57; Vera C. Edwards, "The Adolescent Girl," *J. Hum. Rela.*, 1955, 3, 26–40; M. Powell, "Age and Sex Differences in Degree of Conflict Within Certain Areas of Psychological Adjustment," *Psychol. Monogr.*, 1955, 69, No. 387. See also F. J. J. Buitendijk, "Femininity and Existential Psychology," in H. T. David and H. von Bracken (eds.), *Perspectives in Personality Theory* (New York: Basic Books, 1957), pp. 197–211.

SELECTED READINGS

Allport, G. W., *Personality, a Psychological Interpretation* (New York: Holt, 1937).

Anastasi, Anne, *Differential Psychology*, 3 ed. (New York: Macmillan, 1958).

Connell, W. A., and McGannon, J. D., *The Adolescent Boy* (Chicago: Fides, 1958).

Dollard, J., *et al.*, *Frustration and Aggression* (New Haven: Yale University Press, 1939).

English, O. W., and Pearson, G. H. J., *Emotional Problems of Living*, rev. ed. (New York: Norton, 1955).

Harris, D. B. (ed.), *The Concept of Development: an Issue in the Study of Human Behavior* (Minneapolis: University of Minnesota Press, 1957).

Horney, Karen, *Our Inner Conflicts* (New York: Norton, 1945).

King, F. W., *Emotional Maturity: Its Nature and Measurement* (unpublished doctor's dissertation, Harvard University, 1951).

Maier, N. R. F., *Frustration: the Study of Behavior Without a Goal* (New York: McGraw-Hill, 1949).

Moser, C. G., *Understanding Girls* (New York: Association Press, 1957).

Overstreet, H. A., *The Mature Mind* (New York: Norton, 1949).

Saul, L. J., *Emotional Maturity* (Philadelphia: Lippincott, 1947).

Schneiders, A. A., *Personal Adjustment and Mental Health* (New York: Rinehart, 1955).

Sherman, M., *Mental Conflicts and Personality* (New York: Longmans, Green, 1938).

Valentine, C. W., *The Normal Child and Some of His Abnormalities* (Baltimore, Md.: Penguin Books, 1956).

PART II

The Physiology of Adolescence

Implications of physical development
Physical changes during adolescence
Psychosexual development and problems of youth

CHAPTER IV

IMPLICATIONS
OF PHYSICAL DEVELOPMENT

The physiology of adolescence has many important implications for the growing boy and girl. Some of these implications are psychological, some are economic, some are social, and some are even moral, but all of them are important and we must study them carefully.

DEVELOPMENT AND GROWTH

Some Important Facts and Distinctions. The most obvious features of adolescent development are the changes in physical growth and in physiological development. These changes impress themselves more directly on the attention of the observer than do the more subtle alterations in psychic life. While organic changes are interesting in themselves, and constitute an absorbing chapter in developmental *morphology*, to the psychologist, concerned always with problems of mind and behavior, their significance lies mainly in the fact that they have important psychological and social implications. The psychologist therefore is interested not so much in the question "What physical changes occur during adolescence?" as in the deeper question of the *meaning* that these changes have for the adolescent, and for the student of the adolescent period.[1]

[1] W. M. Krogman, "Biological Growth as It May Affect Pupil's Success," *Merrill-Palmer Quart.*, 1955, 1 (Spring), 90–98.

The period of adolescence is characterized by changes both in *growth* and in *development* of the physical organism. Before we study the psychological implications of these changes, therefore, we may profitably consider the manner in which these two factors are related. In Chapter III we saw that development signifies progression toward maturity. The term *growth*, on the other hand, refers to the minute and gross changes *in structure* that characterize the development of the organism from the moment of conception to complete physical maturity. It is correct, therefore, to speak of the growth of the brain, the limbs, the trunk, or the head, wherein the term refers to *increase in size* of these organs and structures. It would be incorrect, however, to designate such changes as development, even though growth is an important factor in achieving maturity. Similarly, it is equally incorrect to refer to the changes that occur in certain capacities and functions as growth. It is meaningless to speak of the "growth" of such functions or capacities as intellect, memory, or perception. By the same rule, the various physiological functions such as sex, respiration, and digestion develop, but certainly do not grow. Functions or capacities of any kind *develop*; that is, they increase in scope or in power; they do not grow since growth means increase in size or quantity.

This distinction grows in importance when we realize that changes in growth and in development do not occur in a one-to-one ratio. We cannot therefore predict the one from the other. A boy or girl may grow very rapidly, and approach full stature so far as different bodily organs and structures are concerned; yet development may lag far behind, presenting the anomalous and somewhat disturbing picture of the overgrown youth. It is this discrepancy, coupled with the failure to distinguish between growth and development, that often leads to unfair judgment of adolescents, and to the use of ill-fitting criteria in dealing with their problems. To judge in terms of growth independently of the rate and level of development is certain to lead to misunderstanding. Changes in size may at any one point be the poorest criterion to use in the evaluation of personality or maturity.

Nor may we forget that the converse of this situation can occur. Development often outdistances growth, as in the case of the precocious child; and this precociousness may be sexual, intellectual, social, or emotional — or it may be all of them together. Such early and rapid development is most likely to occur within those functions that are relatively independent of physical structures and functions, and which are conditioned to an important extent by environment and culture. Thus an adolescent may be socially mature long before physical or emotional maturity is achieved, since social development depends less upon the maturation of physical factors. In such situations we are again faced with an anomaly, and are likely to use the wrong concepts and standards in judging adolescent behavior. But the harm done, if any, will not be as serious as when too advanced criteria are used.

Similarities in Growth and Development. These discrepancies between growth and development must not be allowed to obscure the fact of *general* correspondence that obtains in the majority of instances. The growth of sex organs, for example, presages the development of the sexual function; the increase in size of the trunk and limbs foreshadows the development of motor capacities and skills; and growth in general, plus the vague realization of this growth by the adolescent, play a part in the development of many social concepts and attitudes. When the adolescent boy complains to the overanxious parent, "Aw, Mom, I'm not a kid any more," he bases his assertion on the incontrovertible fact of increase in size, even though other changes may also prompt such an attitude. It is this *realization* of growth, as much as actual growth changes, that profoundly affects the pattern of development.

Relationships Among Developmental Processes. In this connection we should bear in mind that growth and development are not the only covariables. It is well known that development of one kind may profoundly affect other phases of development, independently of changes in growth, or in conjunction with such changes. This is reflected clearly in the relationship between physical and mental development, but it is no less true of other forms. The development of the glandular functions, for instance, may condition intellectual, emotional, and social changes. Development of intelligence is reflected in social, moral, and emotional development. And motivational development affects nearly all other forms. It is partly these interrelationships among the various phases of development that induces a separate consideration of the psychological implications of organic changes, to which we now direct our attention.

THE PSYCHOLOGIST'S VIEW OF ADOLESCENT PHYSICAL DEVELOPMENT

The Unity of the Personality. There are two distinct ways of looking at the implications of physical growth and development during adolescence. One is from the standpoint of the psychologist (or student), and the other is from the standpoint of the adolescent himself. Of course, the implications of these changes for the psychologist derive from their importance to the adolescent; yet it is profitable to consider them from the two separate viewpoints. For the psychologist, then, the central fact in the study of the physical and physiological changes of adolescents is the unity of the human personality. In other words, the growing adolescent is not a mind and a body, a psyche and a soma, but a mind-body entity. Were it not for this unity the changes we are studying would be of interest and significance to the physiologist only. Were psychology still regarded as nothing more than the study of mind or consciousness, as was true many years ago, such changes would be largely ignored, and the emphasis put upon those phases of development that are more clearly psychic in character.

In more recent years, however, psychologists have rediscovered a fact that was known to many of the ancients — that man is a psychophysical unit, a totality in which mind and body are substantially united to form a human person. This concept is basic to the understanding of most of the problems with which psychology deals. The separation of the mental and physical is in one sense an artifact of logical distinction, and has done more to distort and confuse the thinking of students of human nature than has any other single hypothesis. This statement should not be taken to mean that we cannot distinguish mental from physical processes. An idea or an attitude is still something quite different from a muscle twitch or a glandular secretion. But the significant fact is that these different processes occur within a unity, and should not be thought of as modifications of, or changes in, two things — a mind and a body.

Mutual Influence of Mental and Physical Processes. The significance of this fact is brought into sharp relief by considering the interrelationships that exist among physical and mental phenomena. To some extent everyone is aware of this connection. We all know, for example, that physical fatigue can cause depression or irritability, that emotional excitement can result in digestive disturbances, that thoughts tend to express themselves in action, and so on. What we are not so keenly aware of, and in fact what we often forget, are the relationships that exist between the sensory and the intellectual functions, the intellectual and the volitional, the volitional and the emotional. Nor are we so likely to credit mind with exercising any noticeable influence over physical processes. Yet these relationships are just as real as the more obvious ones. Intellectual functions, such as judging and reasoning, are intimately dependent upon sensory and imaginative processes, and can be influenced also by volitional factors. Volitions in their turn are dependent upon intellective functioning, since they are aroused only by the formation of motives. And the whole pattern of our thinking and willing is shot through with feeling and emotion. In brief, therefore, the mental life is like a mosaic, each feature distinguishable in itself, yet each one contributing something to the other, and all of them contributing something to the whole.

Conceding the influence of physical on mental functions, is the reverse true? Can mental and emotional processes influence physical conditions? The answer is very clear. Neurasthenics, for example, develop pains, headaches, lassitude, fatigue, etc., for which there is no assignable physical basis. Hysterical patients become anesthetic or paralyzed when it suits their particular (subconscious) purpose. The anxious person will often manifest his anxiety in the form of stuttering. Children are known to develop actual pain when there is a desirable end to be achieved. These influences are tacitly admitted in the use of such expressions as "it's just your imagination." And they are only a few among many that can be cited in evidence of this relationship, which is so important to an understanding of adolescent phenomena.

Physical Basis of Psychic Life. Another fact that commands attention in this connection is that much of our behavior and experience has its origin in or is conditioned by physical processes. Emotions and drives, which play a significant role in all stages of development, are intimately bound up with physical structures and functions. We know that the glands of internal secretion and the autonomic nervous system are quite important in determining emotional response. Any alteration or dysfunction in these systems may upset the intricate balance that exists among the various facets of personality.

What is true of emotions is true also of other psychological factors that influence adolescent behavior. Many of the basic needs have their origin in organic conditions, a relationship that is clearly exemplified in the sex drive. Needs such as food, liquid, rest, and activity are also conditioned by the structure and development of the physical mechanism. We have no way of knowing the extent to which many other needs are determined by physical factors but we may be sure that the general condition of the organism will play an important part in the functioning of fundamental human drives.

Nor can we afford to neglect the relationship between the central nervous system and psychological functions. By means of this system experiences are originally received thus making possible and influencing the processes of perception, imagination, memory, and learning. Thus any deficiency, injury, or malfunction of the nervous system may well be reflected in corresponding alterations of the psychic life or of personality. Even intellectual functions are conditioned by the state of the brain, a fact clearly exemplified in pathological states such as paresis, aphasia, and alcoholism.

In this connection we are reminded also of the significant relationship between the central nervous system and the *organization* of personality. The integration toward which the organism strives during adolescence has its prototype in the integration of the nervous system. There is no clearer instance of the unity and organization necessary to integration than that found in this highly developed structure. The nervous system is the integrating force of the physical mechanism, so that its impairment will threaten the entire system of co-ordination within the organism. Without this integration the harmony and unity sought for the entire personality would be quite impossible of achievement. All of this is only another way of reiterating the basic fact mentioned at the beginning of this discussion, namely, that the mind-body entity is a unity, and this unity is the fundamental reason why the relationship between mental and physical functions is of primary importance.

Implications of Mind-Body Relationships. For the student of adolescent phenomena these facts are of particular significance, not only because they are important in themselves, but especially because of their relationship to the entire process of development. The physical development and growth that occur during adolescence are the foundations on which the stones of maturity may be securely laid. Other forms of maturity — intellectual, emotional, economic, and social — are in part dependent upon adequate physical development. The reality of this fact will be more clearly appreciated if we keep in mind the interdependence and mutual influence of the several phases of maturation. For one thing, increase in size during the adolescent years can have considerable social significance.[2] The adolescent's attitude

toward the group, and the attitude of the group toward him, will be conditioned by such changes. To be small is to be like a child; to be tall and big is to be like an adult; and the realization of this smallness or bigness reflects itself in the attitudes of the growing boy or girl. Physical growth will not insure social maturity, since too many other factors are also necessary; but these changes are a long step toward it. Of importance to social maturation also is physical development, particularly development of the sex function, since it is the maturation of this factor that leads to heterosexual attitudes and behavior, and heterosexuality is an important aspect of social development.

The achievement of economic status may also be affected by the growth and development of the physical organism. The boy or girl who develops normally in size and weight, and who is able to reach and maintain a satisfactory level of physical health and appearance, has a distinct advantage where vocational aims are concerned. Social development will also contribute to this achievement, so that economic adjustment is favored both directly and indirectly by physical maturation.

In general, therefore, there are few aspects of adolescent personality and behavior that are wholly independent of physical growth and development. It is for this reason that these changes, while in themselves nonpsychological in char-

---

[2] H. E. Jones, "Physical Ability as a Factor in Social Adjustment in Adolescence," *J. Educ. Res.*, 1946, 40, 387–401. The weak boys in the study showed later maturation, poor health, social difficulties, lack of status, and inferiority feelings, whereas the social ratings for the strong group were consistently favorable and showed an apparent upward trend in popularity. See also Mary C. Jones and Nancy Bayley, "Physical Maturing Among Boys as Related to Behavior," *Jour. Educ. Psychol.*, 1950, 41, 129–148; Mary C. Jones, "The Later Careers of Boys Who Were Early- or Late-Maturing," *Child Develpm.*, 1957, 28, 113–128; P. H. Mussen and Mary C. Jones, "Self-Conceptions, Motivations, and Interpersonal Attitudes of Late- and Early-Maturing Boys," *Child Develpm.*, 1957, 28, 243–256; A. J. Latham, "The Relationship Between Pubertal Status and Leadership in Junior High School Boys," *J. genet. Psychol.*, 1951, 78, 185–194.

acter, are of considerable importance to the student of adolescent psychology. As Gallagher and Harris point out, the adolescent feels different than does the child about physical characteristics:

Height, weight, and state of sexual maturity all mean a great deal to him. The adolescent who is not maturing as rapidly as his or her companions, the boy who is shorter, or the girl who is taller or more obese than usual, dislike being different and may become emotionally upset fearing that they will keep on getting taller or fatter or that they will never mature. . . . Few adolescents are aware that wide variation from the average is compatible with normality: to most of them to vary from what is average is to be abnormal. They need to understand the fact that a variety of different states and rates of growth and development are normal.[3]

IMPLICATIONS OF PHYSICAL DEVELOPMENT TO THE ADOLESCENT HIMSELF

Experiences as Physical. The attitude of the psychologist regarding physical development during adolescence will of course be different from that of the adolescent himself. From his objective standpoint the psychologist can observe these changes and surmise their implications, but it is the youngster himself in whom these changes occur and who reacts to them favorably or unfavorably, or perhaps at times with considerable indifference. It is our task here to study these reactions and to define their implications for adolescent development.

The first fact to take account of in this connection is that some of the most important experiences that children have, especially in the early phases of development, are "physical." Certainly the first years of life are marked by sedulous attention to physical needs, such as hunger, rest, comfort, thirst, and activity. Muscular activity is predominant in this stage, so that for the young child running, eating, sleeping, playing, jumping, and climbing are the more essential forms of behavior. These activities and the experiences associated with them enhance the reality of the body, and possibly its worth; and they help a great deal also in bringing the physical organism within the framework of the self-concept.

Just how long this emphasis on physical experience lasts is hard to say, but we can be sure that such experiences leave a lasting impression, and that this impression is reinforced during the adolescent period, as the widespread changes of puberty again enhance the reality of the physical system. Here, too, physical experiences stand out in sharp relief, although not the same kind of experience that characterizes early childhood, but experiences that often cause an acute or even painful awareness of the adolescent's own body. If, of course, the teenager realized that these changes and experiences are largely transitory in nature they would be far less important to him; but to the adolescent the present is very important and the future is a somewhat vague unreality, so that every item of experience and every defect in appearance or conduct can be quite significant. Only when such experiences are modified by the deeper insights of a later maturity do they begin to lose their significance.[4]

---

[3] J. R. Gallagher and H. I. Harris, *Emotional Problems of Adolescents* (New York: Oxford University Press, 1958), pp. 5–6.

[4] Speaking of the adolescent girl, Pearson says, she "cannot wait for the future; therefore she does not believe that in the future she will be different. In order to make the future present she begins to indulge in much magical action —

Physical Development, Maturity, and Independence. We have already noted the implications of physical growth and development for the achievement of maturity; but these changes, when looked at from the standpoint of the adolescent himself, take on added significance. The point we want to note is that this growth and development not only contribute to maturity, but, in addition, they enforce a *realization of approaching adulthood* in the mind of the adolescent. The increase in size and the maturation of physical structures and functions are the first and most concrete, tangible signs that adulthood is within reach.[5] Thus a certain *measure of equality* with adults is first realized through the growth and development of the physical organism. To the adolescent this is of great importance since the status of adulthood is his primary goal. There is perhaps nothing that the adolescent prizes more highly than the recognition of this equality; and almost from the very onset of puberty he strains toward its realization. Consciously or unconsciously, therefore, the adolescent will place considerable emphasis on these changes as he realizes their contribution to the achievement of maturity.

Physical development also contributes

to the *achievement of independence.* Independence of course requires a great deal more than physical growth and maturation, as evidenced by the fact that many full-grown men and women are clearly lacking in this quality. Yet without physical maturity independence can be very elusive. The growing adolescent boy realizes that more and more is he capable of doing a man's work; the girl, that she can bear children and endure the physical strain of motherhood; and this realization stems directly from the fact of physical maturation. Recognizing that this kind of development is only one of several factors contributing to independence, we can express the relationship most succinctly by emphasizing that while independence has its *beginning* in physical development it is *completed* by the achievement of intellectual, emotional, and social maturity.

Physical Development and Sexual Identity. One of the most significant aspects of this complex problem is the role of the physical organism in the *realization of sex differences.* There are of course many factors that contribute to the distinction between maleness and femaleness, but there is none that outranks in importance the structure of the body itself. It may be in any single case that before the child becomes aware of structural differences between the sexes he is brought to a realization that some kind of difference exists. The attitudes of parents, relatives, and playmates; methods of segregation that are used to prohibit familiarity; differences in toys and dress; injunctions with respect to privacy in dressing and matters of toilet; the use of boy names and girl names — all of these and numerous other experiences serve to enforce the distinction between the sexes almost from infancy. Yet it is doubtful

the use of diets, cosmetic aids, and so on — or the boy begins to place excessive importance on exercise, or weight lifting" — G. H. J. Pearson, *Adolescence and the Conflict of Generations* (New York: Norton, 1958), pp. 35–36. See also H. H. Remmers and D. H. Radler, *The American Teenager* (New York: Bobbs-Merrill, 1957), pp. 40–42.

[5] See J. W. McFarlane, "Some Findings From a Ten-Year Guidance Research Program," *Progressive Educ.*, 1938, 15, 529–535; also Helen G. Davidson and Lucille S. Gottlieb, "The Emotional Maturity of Pre- and Post-Menarcheal Girls," *J. Genet. Psychol.*, 1955, 86, 261–266; P. H. Mussen and Mary C. Jones, "The Behavior-Inferred Motivations of Late- and Early-Maturing Boys," *Child Develpm.*, 1958, 29, 61–67.

whether all of these experiences taken together would exert as much influence on the growing boy and girl as the knowledge of actual physical differences. Cultural practices regarding names, toys, or clothes bear no intrinsic relation to the actual fact of maleness or femaleness. To treat a boy like a girl will not make a girl out of him even though it may make him "girlish" in his attitudes and reactions. But it is definitely known that physical structure can have a decided effect on sexual status.[6]

The awareness of basic physical differences between the sexes may come as a shock, as a pleasant surprise, or with little feeling, depending upon how the knowledge is acquired. But whatever the experience that accompanies this realization, we can be sure that the fact itself profoundly affects the *development of the self-concept*. The reason is that the self-concept *hinges to an important extent on sexual identity*; and sexual identity is dependent on adequate physical development and the clear realization of physical maleness or femaleness. In this way the self-concept, sexual identity, and self-identity become closely interwoven and interdependent, and form the most solid groundwork for later maturity.

There is perhaps no surer way to distort self-concept development than by masking or obscuring the differences between the sexes. This is true of the childhood period, and it is even more true of adolescence. A knowledge of this difference is *essential* for the adequate growth of the child's or adolescent's idea of what he is and of what he should be. To deny this difference, or even to obscure it, is

to encourage ignorance and superstition. The child should be allowed to discover this physical difference early in life, and in a wholly natural manner, in order that later consternation and the development of unhealthy attitudes may be avoided. Similarly, the adolescent should be made aware of the physical differences between the growing boy and girl. Knowledge correctly imparted is the only secure antidote to the uncertainty that is bred by ignorance of these facts. *The conviction of maleness is the prerogative of every man; the conviction of femaleness is the prerogative of every woman.* And the sooner this conviction comes the more likely will the development of the self-concept progress in a normal and healthy manner, free of distortions that are caused by ignorance and half-truths.[7]

With this realization the *life style* of the individual takes on a different aspect. The *future role* of the boy or girl as an adult, what he or she wants to be when he "grows up," is thoroughly conditioned by this realization. The boy wants to be an aviator or a garage mechanic; the girl wants to be a nurse or a teacher. That this is not mere imagination or child's play, but is actually based upon a realiza-

[7] "The deeper determinants of the boy's reaction to the problems of vocation and work are his feelings about his independent masculine role. A free approach to vocational choice and activity require successful masculine identifications. . . . The complaints of the adolescent — that he 'cannot find himself,' that he has no well-defined purpose, that he does not know where he is heading — are the surface manifestations of the incompleteness of his mastery of feeling about himself, his sexual orientation, and his social role" — from *The Stormy Decade: Adolescence*, by George J. Mohr and Marian A. Despres. © Copyright 1958 by George J. Mohr and Marian A. Despres. Reprinted by permission of Random House, Inc., pp. 135–136.

[6] J. H. Conn, "Children's Reactions to the Discovery of Genital Differences," *Amer. J. Orthopsychiat.*, 1940, 10, 747–755.

tion of physical differences, is evidenced by the fact that physical differences are often mentioned by children as reasons why they chose a certain goal. The differences mentioned by children are often quite superficial, but the fact that differences are noticed at all shows a readiness in children for the realization and acceptance of more basic sexual distinctions.

In adolescence, of course, the future roles of male and female are more clearly envisioned. Terms such as "father," "mother," "wife," "husband," and "sweetheart" take on added significance. Perhaps for the first time the youngster becomes aware of what these terms really mean. The girl begins to envision the possibility of becoming a wife and mother, the boy a husband and father. And these projections of the individual into adult roles are to a very important extent predicated on the physical differences that distinguish men and women.

Needless to say, this projection does not end here. There are many other roles that can be played in adult life which involve physical differences. A boy of good physical constitution begins to dream of college sports, and of professional football or baseball as a career. The anemic youngster tends to drift in his thinking to the more sedentary occupations. The attractive girl dreams occasionally of a career in motion pictures or on the stage. Gracefulness, precision of movement, beauty, physical charm, athletic prowess, strength, and a host of other physical qualities suggest to adolescents the roles they ought to assume. Whether or not they ever actually realize such aspirations makes little difference. The important thing is that these physical factors play a significant part in determining the character of their thinking

and in the development of their self-concept.[8]

Body-Image and Self-Concept. In the gradual emergence of this male and female ego and of self-identification, the *body-image* plays a distinctive and significant role. This psychic reality, which is the innermost core of the self-concept, is simply the adolescent's *mental picture of his physical self.* It is what the adolescent pictures himself to be along physical dimensions — his height and weight, his walk, his gestures, his smile, his verility and general manliness, his energy, his posture, the condition of his skin, his attractiveness or ugliness, his physical contours, the quality of his voice, his prowess or clumsiness, and so on. These are the factors that are organized into the body image, and it is this image or mental picture of himself that constitutes the center of his self-concept. The self-concept, however, is broader in scope since it includes many things besides the physical aspect of personality — one's attitudes, past experiences, hopes, ambitions, and failures, remembrances of things done and things left undone, of accomplishments and mistakes, all those things that affect the individual personality and its relationship to others. The self-concept subsumes personal values, ideals and principles, loves, hatreds, and joys. At all times it is a tenuous, shifting phenomenon, forming the background against which experiences are cast, and the criterion in terms of which actions are contemplated or evaluated. Only occasionally does it come to the foreground of attention, at which time it gives rise to the experience of *self-consciousness.*

---

[8] W. M. Cruickshank, "The Impact of Physical Disability on Personal Aspiration," *Quart. J. Child Behav.*, 1951, III, 323–333.

Good grooming is important to one's self-concept.

A. Devaney, Inc., N. Y.

Whether in the foreground or background of consciousness, the concept of self is always present, determining our responses to self and to others. As Moser says about young girls:

> A large measure of her self-acceptance centers around the acceptance of her body. This is a symbol of the self. It has a realism beyond other aspects of personality. It represents the impression of her which is held by others. Her own concept of self is well-nigh impossible apart from her body. All these factors concentrate on the importance of the body and establish it as one of the keys to her self-acceptance. To have a body which conforms to her idea of what it should be is a tremendous advantage. Such a body will support her desire to be attractive, to be popular, to be sought.

The girl who is short, tall, fat, or skinny — who feels outside the desired type — will face a greater struggle to accept herself, and will need the help which clothes styling, beauticians, and medical authorities can give. Girls with a physical deformity need special help, for this self-acceptance at adolescence often becomes very difficult.[9]

The significance of this image and idea may be derived from the meaning of the term *self*. The self is the whole person constituted of both body and mind. The concept of self, therefore, naturally embraces physical as well as psychological

[9] C. G. Moser, *Understanding Girls* (New York: Association Press, 1957), p. 193. See also Ruth Strang, *The Adolescent Views Himself* (New York: McGraw-Hill, 1957), Chap. 6.

qualities of personality, and the one is no less important than the other. In fact, the first impression of self is in the form of a perception and an image of one's own body, physical characteristics, and bodily movements, and only later does the notion become expanded to include psychological features. After all, in the early stages of development the body is much more real than the mind. It is something tangible, something that can be seen and felt, perceived as well as imagined, something that casts a reflection when we stand in front of a mirror. Since it is always in terms of the material and the concrete that we tend to formulate our ideas, it is only natural that the image of the body should become an integral part of the concept of self.

The realism of the body is reflected in the inviolability with which it is regarded by its owner. Children and adolescents, and even adults, will readily submit to the influence of ideas, opinions, and values that threaten their personal integrity; but it is the rare individual who will not rebel violently against physical attack or punishment. Admittedly, mental integrity is more important than physical inviolability, but physical attack is often much more real to the experiencing person than such things as advertising or propaganda that may undermine his beliefs or loyalties.

Physical Deficiencies and Body-Image. These facts alone are sufficient to underscore the importance of physical development to the adolescent. But there are many other facts to support this hypothesis. Anyone who has had close contact with teen-agers knows that physical deficiencies or advantages will play a prominent role in the development of the adolescent's idea of self. The mere existence of a deficiency, or what is *thought* by the youngster to be a deficiency, such as acne in the boy or lack of feminine contours in the girl, is enough to distort the self-concept. If in addition attention is called to the defect by the attitudes or remarks of others, the distortion may assume serious proportions. Adler, in his development of the theory of inferiority, called attention to the close relationship between physical and psychic inferiority; and his hypothesis is well substantiated from clinical sources by the high incidence of feelings of inferiority among neurotics in particular. Such inferiority is as often imagined as real, or it may be grounded in a psychological rather than a physical deficiency; but whatever its origin, it constitutes a widespread problem.

Instances of physical deficiencies are very numerous among adolescents. Some are of such a minor character as to escape the attention of all but the most careful observers. Others are of a much more obvious and serious kind. The seriousness, however, is determined not by the actual deficiency, but *by the adolescent's attitude toward it*. Even the very existence of a defect is partly dependent upon the attitude that is assumed, since what is a defect to one person may not be regarded as such by another. It is always the *implication* of the deficiency that is important, not the deficiency itself.[10]

[10] See R. C. Kammerer, "An Exploratory Psychological Study of Crippled Children," *Psychol. Rec.*, 1940, 4, 47–100. Kammerer argues that crippling has no unique influence on the child's behavior. He reports that whether maladjustment occurs seems to be dependent upon the number and severity of problems with which the child is confronted and not alone the presence of crippling. He found evidence of overprotection, indulgence, and spoiling in 64 per cent of his cases. This viewpoint is shared by other investigators who also find that treatment that crippled children often receive causes maladjustment. False sympathy, indulgence, severity, and neglect

These deficiencies range from minor conditions like skin eruptions to the major structural defects caused by ravaging diseases like infantile paralysis. Visual and auditory defects, especially those necessitating corrective devices, undue shortness or tallness, deformities of all kinds, mismated eyes, poor complexion, thinness or obesity, chronic illness — all of these and many other deficiencies like them can be the cause of mental anguish to the adolescent.

Body-Image and Sex Roles.   What the adolescent conceives himself to be is to an important extent a reflection of the opinions and attitudes of the group to which he belongs, particularly the peer group. This is to be expected during adolescence since social values, under the influence of social needs, begin to take more definite form. In itself a poor complexion is unimportant, but if it means social disapproval or rejection it can be very important. And the greater the defect in the eyes of the adolescent, the deeper are the implications.[11] Moreover, there is always the possibility that the attitude toward one's physical self is a carry-over from previous conditions that no longer exist. Feelings of inferiority may be generated in childhood by some organic deficiency and carried over into the adolescent period as a residual effect. Here again we see that it is not what the person is physically but what he conceives himself to be that is important. Physically handicapped persons have often rid themselves of feelings of inadequacy by the simple discovery that their handicap was more apparent than real. In many such instances the handicap has actually become the means to greater achievement. As regards our physical make-up particularly, therefore, the attitude we assume toward it may be much more significant for our welfare than is our actual physical condition. A knowledge of this fact can be of great help to anyone concerned with human problems.

The social implications of physical characteristics, whether good or bad, are most clearly exemplified in the relationship between such characteristics and sex roles. In this area physical deficiencies and advantages can be of the utmost significance. The young girl who fails to develop a bustline and other typical feminine contours finds it difficult to establish a clear-cut sex role. Her body-image prevents her from feeling attractive to the opposite sex, even though she may have a pleasing personality and a high moral character. Similarly, the boy who is physically puny, lacking in muscular development, shallow-chested, or effeminate in facial appearance or voice finds it difficult to feel strongly masculine. What is worse, this lack of sex-role identification will be projected into relationships with the opposite sex and in the development of healthy interpersonal relationships.[12] A girl must learn gradually to feel that she is a woman in the

---

are all frequent and unfortunate. An important factor here that influences adjustments is the extent of the disparity between goals and ability to achieve them. See also R. G. Barker, et al., *Adjustment to Physical Handicap and Illness: A Survey of the Social Psychology of Physique and Disability*, Bull. No. 55, rev. (New York: Soc. Sci. Res. Council, 1953).

[11] F. J. Curran and J. Frosch, "The Body Image in Adolescent Boys," *J. Genet. Psychol.*, 1942, 60, 37–60.

[12] On the development of sexual identification, see M. Rabban, "Sex-Role Identification in Young Children in Two Diverse Social Groups," *Genet. Psychol. Monogr.*, 1950, 42, 81–158; D. G. Brown, "Masculinity-Femininity Development in Children," *J. Consult. Psychol.*, 1957, 21, 197–202; D. Riesman, "Permissiveness and Sex Roles," *Marr. & Fam. Liv.*, 1959, 21, 211–217.

fullest sense of the term, and the boy that he is a man. Only then will personal and sexual identity be assured.

Influence of Physical Advantages on the Body-Image. It is obvious of course that physical excellences play just as notable a part in the development of the body-image and of the self-concept. Such factors often serve as a bulwark against the feelings of inadequacy and worthlessness which often develop during adolescence. Many an academic failure in high school has managed to avoid discouragement by the constant reminder of his physical prowess on the athletic field. Many a high school girl has rescued her self-ideal from complete wreckage by the realization of her own physical attractiveness. Such a feat is possible even in the face of moral turpitude or academic disaster, so highly valued is the possession of certain physical traits. The problem here, of course, is how to prevent physical excellence from distorting the self-concept in the direction of superiority or unjust pride.

Physical attractiveness for both boys and girls — beauty of face and figure for the girls, vigor and power for the boys — is essential to the concept of an acceptable individuality toward which they strive. The healthy adolescent girl takes pride in the physical evidence of her developing femininity. For the younger adolescent, older girls will often serve as models; her standard may be the current movie queen. Her concerns about her person are oriented chiefly toward her need to feel accepted and admired by her own group. . . . The adolescent boy's interest in his growing physical powers also has meaning, both in relation to his status in his group and — of even more importance — to his inner concept of himself. The handsome, athletic young man obviously enjoys his powers and the esteem they bring him. When he feels physically well endowed, it becomes easier for him to conceive of himself as an effective man and to cope with the normal inner uncertainties of adolescent life. These physical attributes of themselves do not necessarily assure him successful surmounting of the problems of adolescence, but they may help tip the scale in the right direction.[13]

In evaluating the role of the physical apparatus in the development of the self-concept we must not forget the influence of less obvious factors. Physical deficiencies are not always apparent. There may be glandular disturbances, digestive inadequacies, heart ailments, or incipient pathological conditions which also exert their influence. And the danger here is that the less obvious the difficulty the more insidious the influence. It is in fact this kind of inferiority that Adler had in mind in developing his theory. In such cases the deficiency is not known to the person, but the reaction is no less certain and pervasive. Feelings of inadequacy and inferiority often have their origins in such deficiencies; and feelings of this kind are sure to work their way into the structure of the self-concept. What the adolescent thinks of himself may therefore be in part a reflection of how well or how poorly he assimilates his food, or how rapidly he becomes fatigued!

Extension of the Self-Concept. The boundaries of the self-concept are not limited to natural endowments. Often the concept of self is projected to include many things only accidentally related to personality. Among these extrinsic items

[13] From *The Stormy Decade: Adolescence*, by George J. Mohr and Marian A. Despres. © Copyright 1958 by George J. Mohr and Marian A. Despres. Reprinted by permission of Random House, Inc., pp. 181–182. See also H. E. Jones, "Physical Ability as a Factor in Social Adjustment in Adolescence," *J. Educ. Res.*, 1946, 40, 287–301; C. Hanley, "Physique and Reputation of Junior High School Boys," *Child Develpm.*, 1951, 22, 247–260.

a person's clothes, his home, and his material possessions may, by a process of introjection, become a part of the self-concept, even though they have no intrinsic relation to personality. Thus the adolescent may experience shame or embarrassment if his clothes are ill-fitting or out of style, especially the style created by the peer group; and he will experience pride when his clothes are neat and correctly styled, in much the same manner that he feels shame or pride with respect to personal qualities that are an intrinsic part of the self.

In some instances, extension of the self-concept and introjection of external factors like family characteristics are so pronounced as to distort ego development completely. Jane, for example, a young girl just starting college, has parents who are immigrants from Southeastern Europe. Jane has incorporated within her self-concept an image of her parents as loud, uneducated, illiterate, poorly dressed, and thoroughly objectionable "peasants," whom she got away from as soon as she possibly could, and whom she visits only when it is absolutely necessary. Despite this negative attitude, it is obvious that Jane has identified herself with her parents and family, and thus she is totally rejecting of herself. Although an unusually bright girl with a straight A record in high school, she regards herself as stupid, possessed of very little ability, and also as unattractive and socially undesirable. Here, then, we have a clear instance of how introjection and extension of the self-concept can have a damaging effect on the attitude one assumes toward himself.

Similarly, feelings of inferiority, pride, embarrassment, or shame are engendered by the condition of one's home, one's neighborhood, or the family car. These extrinsic items become important because they are reflections of personal judgments and values; like expressive movements, they are one of the ways in which the self is externalized. Everyone realizes, consciously or subconsciously, that judgments of other persons or of ourselves are as often made in terms of these external assets or liabilities as they are in terms of the more basic intra-personal qualities of personality. Moreover, these extrinsic factors are objective and easily observed, and it is well known that impressions are more readily formed on the basis of objective aspects of personality.

The implications of these facts are clear. For the adolescent, to whom the opinions and attitudes of other persons are very important, and who likes to think of himself as excellent in all things, these extrinsic extensions of self may take on more significance than many subjective factors which in themselves are much more valuable. To be constrained to wear hand-me-downs or to be dressed in a style not in conformity with that set by the group or to live in a shabby neighborhood can be a very painful thing to the young person whose value system is still a very shaky thing. These unfavorable experiences and negative feelings constitute a direct frustration of the adolescent's desires for social approval and conformity, and will thus tend to impair his estimation of his worth in his own eyes and in the eyes of others.

Physical Change and the Body-Image. In the gradual emergence of the body-image, the *continuous change* in function, size, and appearance of the bodily apparatus during adolescence has deep-seated psychological implications. The facial mask undergoes readjustment and may appear for a time as distorted or even ugly to the uncertain mind of the adolescent. Movement becomes awkward because of the rapid growth of the skeletal and muscular systems. Increased height may give the impression of undue leanness in appearance — and so on. At no one point can the adolescent be sure of his physical status, and this uncertainty is disturbing because of the effect on the self-concept, and also because of the social implications physical status is thought to have. The adolescent literally does not know what to think of himself, and he is at the same time plagued by the fear of what others may think of him. The stability which he ardently desires — especially in view of the uncertainty of his feelings, experiences, and values — is made even more impossible by the constantly changing physical structure, the one thing in his self-concept that was at all certain and tangible. At a time when he wants above all the approbation of the group, he finds himself to be unattractive and clumsy, with a skin that no one loves to touch, a facial mask that is anything but handsome, and a voice that insists on squeaking at just the wrong time. This fact of continuous change lies at the basis of much of the instability and inconsistency noted by all students of the adolescent period.

Body-Image, Self-Concept, and Self-Expression. The implications of adolescent physical development are further extended by reason of the role which the bodily mechanism plays in *expressive movement.* Through this medium we express our thoughts and attitudes, our feelings and desires, our likes and dislikes. Thus we smile or laugh, frown or cry, nod our head, shake hands, or utter a curse, depending upon our feelings and thoughts of the moment. The facility with which such expressions are executed, the smoothness or clumsiness of the performance, the gracefulness of our movements — all of these tend to make us keenly aware of our physical organism, its assets and its liabilities. To be "all thumbs" when the situation calls for delicate manipulation; to trip and fall headlong when we wish to walk gracefully, or to develop a vocal squeak at a time when full-throated resonance is demanded, can be very disturbing. Of course disaffections such as these do not reflect on integrity or character. These remain intact, no matter how poorly we express ourselves. But such experiences are disturbing because the self-concept embraces an image of the body and what it should and should not do. While the social implications of situations such as these are quite obvious, it is also true that even in the absence of witnesses such experiences are annoying. At no time do we like to admit clumsiness or lack of graceful physical expression. And certainly this problem is greatest during the adolescent period when expressive movements are at a distinctly low ebb of efficiency. Here again we are reminded of the fact that the more objective any personality factor is, the more significant it is when evaluated in terms of the attitude or opinion of an observer. Expressive movement is the mode par excellence by which the self is externalized, and for that reason it plays a leading role in the development of the self-concept.

Other Outcomes of Body-Image Formation. As we discussed the formation of the body-image, its relation to the self-concept, and its various social and psychological implications, we had occasion to note some of the effects these developments can have on the adolescent personality. Let us examine these effects or outcomes in more detail. First of all, there are the effects produced on the adolescent's *feelings*, particularly, of course, feelings about himself. The healthy, well-built, good-looking teen-ager is very likely to experience feelings of acceptance, self-confidence, well-being, and even superiority. Moreover, he is likely to express these feelings in his relationships to others, in his attitudes toward his work, and in the definition of his future goals.[14] The physically handicapped teen-ager, on the other hand, is just as likely to develop feelings of inadequacy and inferiority, and to reflect these feelings in his attitudes toward himself, toward his peer group, and his ambitions.

Such feelings and attitudes, based upon a negative self-concept, can lead to a great deal of frustration. The handicapped adolescent, regardless of the nature of his handicap, is always to some extent frustrated in the achievement of needs and goals, and this frustration will deeply affect his behavior and adjustment. Feelings of inadequacy and inferiority, or of nonacceptance, coupled with frustration, tend strongly toward the development of defensive reactions of one kind or another. Among the adolescents who are physically inferior, or imagine themselves to be so, one may expect to find typical reactions of overcompensation, superiority, and egocentrism, rationalization, and sour grapes. Negative feelings and attitudes always tend to undermine the structure of the

ego, and for that reason defensive reactions become psychologically necessary.[15] Thus we encounter the adolescent who rationalizes his failure to get a date, who boasts about nonexistent accomplishments, or who argues that the goal is not worth the effort. In many such instances a poorly developed or damaged self-concept is the basic cause.

The simple process of physical growth produces much worry and unhappiness for the adolescent. His conflicts turn around the disparity between his physical ability and his ideal of what that ability should be, and are reinforced by comparisons made by the adolescent between himself and his peers. Consequently, the adolescent's problems center consciously about his feelings of self-esteem and self-confidence.

* * *

These comparisons reactivate the old feelings of shame about body size, but these are now felt consciously as feelings of inadequacy and inferiority.[16]

---

[14] I. D. Steiner, "Self-Perception and Goal-Setting Behavior," *J. Personality*, 1957, *25*, 344–355; F. M. Jervis, "The Meaning of a Positive Self-Concept.," *J. Clin. Psychol.*, 1959, *15*, 370–372; Nancy Bayley, "Some Psychological Correlates of Somatic Androgyny," *Child Develpm.*, 1951, *22*, 47–60. See also H. F. Faterson, "Organic Inferiority and the Inferiority Attitude," *J. Soc. Psychol.*, 1931, *2*, 87–101.

[15] A. Christie, "Physical Defects in Adolescent Boys," *J. Juven. Res.*, 1934, *18*, 13–22; J. Levi and Barbara Michelson, "Emotional Problems of Physically Handicapped Adolescents — A Study of Ten Adolescent Boys," *Exceptional Children*, 1952, *18*, 200–206; W. M. Cruickshank, "The Impact of Physical Disability on Social Adjustment," *J. Soc. Issues*, 1948, *4*, 78–83. In this and other articles Cruickshank suggests that handicapped adolescents often have difficulty in effecting happy social and emotional adjustments. They seem less able to evaluate the interpersonal relationships and thus develop ambivalent or neutral responses. They indicate a definite tendency to withdraw from social contacts and relations, show fewer normal adolescent interests than do normal children and indicate a tendency to seek substitute gratifications in fantasy. Adjustments seem to be on a more mature level than that observed among nonhandicapped children of the same age and sex. Investigators find evidence of sensitivity and self-consciousness stemming from physical handicap in a substantial proportion of adolescents, and a need to compensate for limits on behavior imposed on them by their physical disability.

[16] G. H. J. Pearson, *Adolescence and the Conflict of Generations* (New York: Norton, 1958), pp. 25, 28.

To these feelings the adolescent will react with withdrawal, compensation, and other mechanisms. However:

> . . . the logical compensation — better grooming, more attention to clothes — is never used. This may be because the adolescent's self-pride is so deeply hurt by the comparison.

Or, in order to assuage his feelings of shame:

> . . . he may attempt to get sympathy from his environment by being constantly unhappy. . . . The whole process results from the comparison between himself and his peers made by the adolescent himself; but his shame is vastly increased when the adults whom he respects actually let him know that they consider him inferior. . . .[17]

SELF-CONCEPT AND SELF-IDENTITY

The Emergence of the Self or Ego. The portrait of the developing personality of the adolescent is not complete until we fit the self or the ego into the total picture. While much of the story of development is filled in by studying the evolution and the maturation of physical characteristics, social and moral traits, psychosexual development and other aspects of the growing personality, we have to take into account that at the core of all of these changes *is the growing self of the teen-ager.*[18] It is not an easy task to define this concept be-

cause the ego or self is not a sharply defined, concrete reality that can be easily forced into a verbal mold like a definition. Yet it is a very real thing that plays a fundamental role in the adolescent's effort to cope with reality and achieve satisfactory adjustments.

The psychoanalysts have provided us with the most satisfactory concept of the ego and have brought it into clear relationship with other aspects of the human psyche. In this view, the Ego is conceived as that "part" of the total psyche which mediates between the experiencing person and reality. In contrast with the Id, it is the conscious aspect of the psyche whereas the Id and in some respects the Superego are unconscious. In the language of the adolescent, the ego is the all-important "I" of conversation, interpersonal relationships, secret ambitions, or the precious diary. The adolescent is expressing the reality of his ego when he says: "*I* want to go to college," "*I* cannot agree with my parents," "*I* was kissed by my boy friend last night," "*I* hope to become an actor," and the like. Let us note that while the theorists may be confused as to the meaning or the reality of the ego, there is no confusion in the mind of the adolescent when he breaks out with these positive statements. The "I" of the teenagers is very real and very important.

This ego or self emerges and crystallizes in the course of human development beginning in the earliest years of the child's growth.[19] It is not something that emerges in adolescence. It is true that the infant does not distinguish himself from objective reality, but it is not

---

[17] G. H. J. Pearson, *op. cit.*, pp. 28, 29–30.

[18] See the article by P. M. Symonds in J. M. Seidman (ed.), *The Adolescent: a Book of Readings* (New York: Dryden, 1953), pp. 222–227. See also F. McKinney, *Counseling for Personal Adjustment in Schools and Colleges* (Boston: Houghton Mifflin, 1958), Chap. 6; G. H. J. Pearson, *op. cit.*, p. 169; M. Sherif and H. Cantril, *The Psychology of Ego-involvements* (New York: Wiley, 1947), Chaps. 7, 8, 9.

[19] For an interesting discussion of this point, see H. Joseph and G. Zern, *The Emotional Problems of Children: a Guide for Parents* (New York: Crown, 1954), pp. 54–56.

long before the young child begins to use the pronoun "I" with unmistakable reference to himself, and in distinguishing between himself and objective reality. However, the adolescent period, with all of its trials and tribulations, is a crucible in which the ego is pounded and eventually forged into a more sharply defined reality. The adolescent, as distinct from the child, must come to grips with reality more firmly, and this forces a sharper delineation of the boundaries of the ego. The adolescent is literally more *self-conscious*, which means not only that he may be sensitive to his own shortcomings or the critical evaluation of others, but that he is naturally *more conscious of the self*. During adolescence the self becomes a more adequate tool for holding off or for coping with the demands of reality.

Ego and Superego Formation. With the formation of the conscious ego, there is also the gradual emergence of the *superego*, which is another concept provided by the psychoanalyst.[20] In simplest language, the superego is the internalized image, usually of the parents, conceived as the source of morality, rules, demands, and restrictions. In early childhood the superego is the individual's conscience, since the child accepts what the parents say about right and wrong, good and bad, and acts accordingly. This superego continues to function in adolescence and in adult life, and in many instances is the only conscience that the person can lay claim to. If development is normal and adequate, the superego is gradually replaced in adolescence by *conscience*, which represents the development of an internal, self-disciplined morality. This

aspect of ego and superego development is particularly important for adolescent adjustment, because of the fact that superego domination can lead to pervasive personality disorders. This is most clearly evidenced in *scrupulosity* which is a common ailment during adolescence, and also is reflected in the obsessive-compulsive neurosis. The task of the parent and teacher in this regard is clear: to help the adolescent develop a well-ordered conscience and thus reduce the influence of the superego.

Self-Concept and Self-Ideal. As the ego or self emerges more clearly during adolescence, there is continued growth of the *self-concept*, an element of personality formation that has come to be recognized as one of the most important determinants of adequate adjustment and mental health. The self-concept is *the adolescent's perception of himself* as a person and as a focal point of interpersonal relationships. It is the idea that a person has of himself — his meaning and worth, his particular identity, his feelings, attitudes, values, beliefs, experiences, goals, and aspirations. The self-concept is not always a clearly defined entity; in any single person it may be quite nebulous and shifting; but it is always in the center of the adolescent's striving for identity and for adequate adjustment.

During adolescence particularly, the self-concept supplies the groundwork for the development of the *self-ideal*, which as the term suggests is the idealized perception of self.[21] Whereas the self-concept is the adolescent's idea of *what he is*,

---

[20] For a thorough discussion of superego formation, see P. M. Symonds, *Dynamic Psychology* (New York: Appleton-Century-Crofts, 1949), Chap. XI.

[21] R. J. Havighurst, M. Z. Robinson, and M. Dorr, "The Development of the Ideal Self in Childhood and Adolescence," *J. Educ. Res.*, 1946, 40, 241–257; Eva M. Shippee-Blum, "The Young Rebel: Self-Regard and Ego-Ideal." *J. Consult. Psychol.*, 1959, 23, 44–50.

the self-ideal is the adolescent's concept of *what he wants to be or what he ought to be*. The self-ideal then is in the nature of a goal toward which the adolescent strives.

The relationship of these two concepts to mental health and adjustment is both clear and fundamental. If the self-concept is healthy and realistic, the adolescent's reactions to himself and to objective reality (especially to other persons in his environment) will likely be wholesome and stable. If on the other hand the self-concept is distorted, if the adolescent thinks of himself as inadequate or inferior, as worthless and depraved, or as inordinately superior to other people, these ideas will twist his reactions to himself and to other persons. The self-depreciating teen-ager will experience a great deal of shame and guilt whenever he fails to live up to expectancies, and will thus reject himself; whereas the self-aggrandizing youngster will alienate everyone with whom he comes in contact and will tend toward the development of defensive mechanisms, particularly rationalization, to support his egocentrism.

The self-ideal will affect the mental health and adjustment of the adolescent for good or ill depending on its structure. Teen-agers tend to be idealistic and demanding of self, and incline strongly toward the development of a *perfectionistic self-ideal*. Perfectionism, like the demands of the superego, can cause the adolescent a great deal of trouble. Because he is young, immature, and lacking in wisdom, the teen-ager does not realize that perfection is a lifelong goal and is never achieved on this earth. As a result, he demands perfection of himself here and now. This overdevelopment of the self-ideal can lead to scrupulosity,

pervasive guilt, and self-rejection, and will tend to distort interpersonal relationships. The perfectionistic adolescent often projects his perfectionism into his relationships with other people who of course do not measure up to his standards. Thus girl friends, boy friends, teachers, and parents come in for their share of criticism and rejection. Parents and counselors must see to it that this overdevelopment of the self-ideal is toned down to a point where the ideal becomes realistic and realizable.

The Emergence of Self-Identity. The gradual emergence of the ego, and the development of the self-concept and self-ideal, are closely correlated with the *development of self-identity*. This process begins in childhood, is continued throughout adolescence, and normally is achieved with the realization of maturity. Self-identity is a quality of personal experience that is linked to the growth of the self-concept and the self-ideal, and just as profoundly influences mental stability and adjustment. In simple terms, self-identity means a *clear awareness of one's role and status* in life, one's goals and purposes, and one's relationships to reality, to society, and to a Supreme Being. The person with self-identity knows the answers to such questions as: "What am I?" "Who am I?" "What am I supposed to be or to become?" "Where am I going?" The person lacking self-identity, on the other hand, is confused and uncertain as to what he is supposed to be and where he is going. This state of affairs is clearly exemplified in the deeply neurotic person and in the homosexual, neither one of whom has a clear awareness of what he is supposed to be. Adolescents often manifest lack of self-identity, and this is one of the reasons why they are often uncertain, confused, and extremely vacillating in their opinions, behavior, or goals. The core of self-identity is the body-image which grows out of physical development, and this phenomenon we have already discussed in preceding pages.[22]

What Determines Self-Identity? We have already noted that in the growth of the self-concept and of self-identity the body-image plays a very important part, and that this factor in turn is closely related to sexual identity. And thus *the body-image and sexual identity may be regarded as the core of self-identity*. Without the conviction of masculinity or of femininity it is impossible for any growing boy or girl to achieve adequate self-identity.[23] However, we must

recognize that there are other developmental factors that enter into the growth of self-identity. For example, the growing boy tends to identify with his father and the girl with her mother, and this process of identification is very helpful in establishing the conviction of masculinity or femininity, and therefore of self-identity. The youngster also identifies with other important facets of his daily life, such as his family, his nationality, his religion, his community, and his school; and from all of these identifications he derives some measure of self-identity.[24] Later on in adulthood, some of these identifications will have to be broken up, as when the individual leaves the community, graduates from school, or establishes a home of his own. But in the normal course of events this does not happen until the individual has forged his own personal self-identity out of the many identifications he has formed during the process of growing up.

Here then we have the story of what it means to the adolescent to grow up physically. To the parent, growing up physically may mean nothing much more than that the adolescent is getting taller and heavier, is developing a voracious and sometimes peculiar appetite, and is always growing out of recently purchased suits or dresses. But to the teen-ager, growing up physically means much more than this, and it is this meaning that we have tried to capture and interpret in the foregoing pages.

---

[22] For more studied discussions of this central problem of adolescence, see A. Wheelis, *The Quest for Identity* (New York: Norton, 1958), especially Chap. 5; E. H. Erikson, *Childhood and Society* (New York: Norton, 1950), Part Four, "Youth and the Evolution of Identity." Erikson states categorically, "the study of identity, then, becomes as strategic in our time as the study of sexuality was in Freud's time" (p. 242). See also G. J. Mohr and Marian A. Despres, *The Stormy Decade: Adolescence* (New York: Random House, 1958), Chap. XI; Evelyn Deno, "Self-Identification Among Adolescent Boys," *Child Develpm.*, 1953, 24, 269–273; E. H. Erickson, "Adolescence and Identity," paper read at the Fifth Annual Symposium, Committee on Youth Development, University of Chicago, February 6, 1954; and E. H. Erickson, *Identity and the Life Cycle* (New York: International Universities Press, 1959).

[23] Gardner ranks identification with biologically determined sex role as one of the four basic developmental tasks of adolescents. G. E. Gardner, "Present-Day Society and the Adolescent," *Amer. J. Orthopsychiat.*, 1957, 27, 508–517. See also G. J. Mohr and Marian A. Despres, *op. cit.*, p. 143: "The boy's identification with his father or the girl's with her mother provides the basis for acceptance of his or her sexual identity. Later identifications with new adults permit the ego to modify basic feelings about adult functioning, including sexual functioning . . . his very later relationships also contribute to this conception of himself as a person in action in his social environment." Holmes makes

the same point in his article on identification — M. H. Holmes, "The Child's Need for Identification," *Ment. Hlth. Lond.*, 1951, 10, 64–65. An excellent discussion of the mechanism of identification will be found in P. M. Symonds, *op. cit.*, Chap. XIII. See especially pp. 243–246.

[24] See G. H. J. Pearson, *op. cit.*, pp. 95–98; A. Wheelis, *op. cit.*, Chap. I; G. J. Mohr and Marian A. Despres, *op. cit.*, p. 155.

SELECTED READINGS

Barker, R. G., et al., *Adjustment to Physical Handicap and Illness: a Survey of the Social Psychology of Physique and Disability*, Bull. No. 55, rev. ed. (New York: Soc. Science Res. Council, 1953).

Fisher, S., and Cleveland, S. E., *Body Image and Personality* (Princeton: Van Nostrand, 1958).

Garrett, J. F. (ed.), *Psychological Aspects of Physical Disability* (Washington, D. C.: U. S. Office of Vocational Rehabilitation, Bull. No. 210, n.d.).

Gottlieb, B. S., *Understanding Your Adolescent* (New York: Rinehart, 1957), Chap. 6.

May, R., *Man's Search for Himself* (New York: Norton, 1953).

Merry, Frieda K., and Merry, R. V., *The First Two Decades of Life* (New York: Harper, 1950), pp. 81–127.

Mohr, G. J., and Despres, Marian A., *The Stormy Decade: Adolescence* (New York: Random House, 1958), Chap. XIII.

Seidman, J. M. (ed.), *The Adolescent: a Book of Readings* (New York: Dryden, 1953), Chap. 5.

Strang, Ruth, *The Adolescent Views Himself* (New York: McGraw-Hill, 1957), Chaps. 3, 5, 6.

Tanner, J. M., *Growth and Adolescence* (Springfield, Ill.: C. C. Thomas, 1955).

Wheelis, A., *The Quest for Identity* (New York: Norton, 1958).

CHAPTER V

PHYSICAL CHANGES
DURING ADOLESCENCE

Physical changes during adolescence have many social and psychological implications. This we have already seen. Now it is our task to see what these changes are, what systems of the body are affected by adolescent development, and to what extent. These changes are obvious and observable, but they are also numerous and complex, and we must study them carefully.

CHARACTERISTICS OF PHYSICAL GROWTH AND DEVELOPMENT

Many of the developmental changes of adolescence are shrouded in doubt and obscurity, partly because they must be teased out of the matrix of changes that take place, and partly because they are not easily measured and quantified. But there is little difficulty in observing physical development. These changes are objective, quantitative, and measurable. They can be directly observed, and they are among the most striking, if not always the most important, of the changes that characterize the period of youth. They set the pace, as it were, for other developmental processes; and it is our task, therefore, to determine the characteristics and the extent of this physical transformation.[1]

[1] For a thorough study of research in physical growth and development, see the article by K. Jensen, "Physical Growth and Physiological Aspects of Development," *Rev. Educ. Res.*, 1950, 20, 390–410.

Developmental Charges in Man and Animals. It is interesting to note the sharp contrast between human and animal development on the purely physical plane. Man is the only mammal with a prolonged period of physical development. All primates have a lengthened childhood; but on reaching what corresponds to the six-year-old phase of man's history, they progress very rapidly, so that within the space of one year they reach man's twelve-and-one-half-year stage. In the subsequent twelve-month period they reach a point of development that takes man twenty years to complete. Man, like the anthropoids, develops in spurts, but it takes him fourteen years to complete what the latter achieves in the brief period of two years. This long period of physical immaturity makes the developmental history of man far different from that of the lower animals, for physical maturity is ordinarily a prerequisite to the achievement of other forms of maturity. The child is dependent upon others not only in matters of intellect and emotion, but he is physically dependent for a great many years, reaching full physical status only after many transformations within his physical make-up. This contrast serves to indicate quite clearly the limitations inherent in a comparative developmental psychology of man and animals, and to highlight the significance of the long period of human physical development.

Individual Differences in Development. Another important fact about physical development is that, although the general curve of physical growth is typical of the individual changes that occur, there are wide variations that must always be taken into account.[2] This is only a particular instance of the general law of variation described in Chapter III, but it requires emphasis because the psychological and social implications of physical development vary as development itself varies. It makes a considerable difference, for example, if sexual maturation occurs at age twelve instead of fourteen or fifteen, and this maturity (or lack of it) must be considered carefully by those dealing with any particular adolescent. Also the rate of growth and maturation varies to some extent from person to person; and the exact level of physical development must be known if the psychological and social implications are to be understood.

Sex Differences in Development. This principle applies with even greater force to the differences in development that distinguish the two sexes, because

these differences are still more pronounced, and more significant psychologically and socially. At birth the two sexes are quite similar in level of physical development, but boys begin to lag behind at the end of the first year, causing a difference that tends to become intensified during the first few years of postnatal existence. At about the age of five, however, the boy and girl are again nearly equal in physical development. This similarity is again disrupted at six years when most girls progress more rapidly than boys; but at the age of nine the differences have again largely disappeared. From the ages of ten to twelve years there occurs in boys the typical preadolescent slump, so that in physical development the twelve-year-old girl is normally from one to two years ahead of her male counterpart. These differences tend to shade off during the teen-age, until at seventeen years there is little difference, and by the age of twenty all differences have disappeared.

The *implications* of these differences between the sexes in physical development are obvious. The earlier physical maturity of girls heralds important changes in social outlook, in emotionality, and in the intellectual, moral, and religious spheres. These differences give rise to many situations that require the most tactful and intelligent handling. The lumping of boys and girls into an adolescent age bracket that covers, let us say, the period between twelve and eighteen years of age can be the source of serious mistakes. It must be realized also that these differences in physical development are conditioned by the factor of *individual* variation, so that in a final analysis it is always the *individual* whose developmental pattern must be studied. General laws and growth curves

---

[2] For an intensive study of individual differences in growth patterns, see H. R. Stolz and Lois M. Stolz, *Somatic Development of Adolescent Boys* (New York: Macmillan, 1951). See also E. L. Reynolds and Janet V. Wines, "Individual Differences and Physical Changes Associated With Adolescence in Girls," *Amer. J. Dis. Child.*, 1948, 75, 329–350.

serve merely as the background in terms of which the development of the individual can be better understood.

Sporadic Nature of Physical Development. As we noted earlier, development is of its nature a gradual process that involves a continuous and biologically logical change from one stage of growth to another. This gradualness, however, merely excludes sudden or cataclysmic alterations; it does not preclude *saltation*, by which is meant periods of slower and more rapid growth and change. Actually, development takes place in spurts of relatively great velocity, preceded and followed by periods of slower progress. For example, it is not uncommon for a girl, once menstruation begins, to complete what amounts to three years' skeletal development in a span of six to nine months. These spurts in development occur between the ages of six and nine, and again at puberty.

> The outstanding phenomenon of somatic growth during the period between childhood and adulthood is the puberal sequence of rapid increase followed by rapid decrease in the growth rate. In almost all velocity profiles the apex between acceleration and deceleration is an easily recognizable feature and has been used very generally as a reference point for estimating maturity. . . . As our profiles of growth velocity were extended from six month period to six month period during the seven year accumulative study, it became evident that the pattern of each profile was unique, but it also became evident that for many measurements in many individuals there was a strong tendency toward a systematic sequence of rise and fall in growth rate.[3]

---

[3] Reprinted with permission of the Macmillan Company from H. R. Stolz and Lois M. Stolz, *op. cit.*, p. 395.

Here again the implications are clear. These spurts mean that at certain stages of growth the organism reaches a level of development considerably advanced over previous levels and in a relatively short time. In common parlance, the youngster "shoots up like a weed," attaining a physical structure that materially alters the relationship between himself and his environment. These rather sudden changes do not necessarily signify greater maturity; but they may well be interpreted by the adolescent himself as a sign of approaching manhood or womanhood, and give rise to changes in attitudes, interests, and the concept of self, and to alterations in the relationships between self and other aspects of the environment. They may also give rise to uncertainty and confusion in the mind of the growing boy or girl. One might say that for a while their mentality lags behind their physical growth, and a certain period of adjustment to these changes is required. This peculiarity of physical development, while not as marked or as important as formerly thought, should be taken into account by parents and teachers, so that necessary adjustments may be made easier by their help and counsel.

Imbalance Among Various Growth Factors. One other characteristic of physical development is the lack of correspondence in development between various physical structures. Each structure has its own rate of development, with a resulting imbalance among the skeletal, muscular, glandular, nervous, and other physical organs which lasts until development is completed (see Fig. 7). This imbalance can at times be the source of considerable anguish for the growing child, who must learn that this condition is purely temporary; and

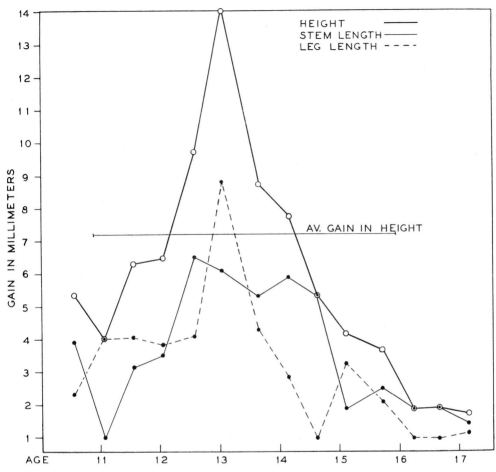

Fig. 7. Velocity curves for a boy, illustrating leg-length apex synchronous with and stem-length apex prior to height apex. Used with the permission of the Macmillan Company. From H. R. Stolz, and Lois M. Stolz, **Somatic Development of Adolescent Boys** (New York: Macmillan, 1951), p. 219.

that the gangling arms, spindly legs, distorted facial mask, etc., will before long assume more respectable proportions. An understanding of the facts concerning physical growth and development can be of immense value to the youngster to whom, as we have seen, the image of the body is a most important element in the development of the self-ideal. It is the prevention of distortion of this con-

cept, with the resulting feelings of inadequacy and inferiority, that makes guidance necessary.[4]

THE ONSET OF PUBERTY

Puberty and Its Determinants. The changes involved in the transition from

[4] See H. R. Stolz and Lois M. Stolz, op. cit., Chap. 18, where somatic changes are brought into relationship with other developmental characteristics, including effect of discrepancies, cul-

childhood to adolescence are identified as *puberty*, a transitional period marked by physical growth, and a corresponding development of physiological functions. In girls this period can be fairly easily identified, since it begins with the first menstrual flow, which marks the onset of the adolescent period proper. The boundary line between pubescence and adolescence is not so clearly marked in boys, although there are certain physical signs such as change in voice, and growth and distribution of pubic hair, which indicate quite clearly that the transition has occurred.

Of some importance is the fact that there are considerable variations in pubescence due to sex, race, climate, locality, social status, intelligence, and physical condition of the organism.[5] Variations such as these have some important implications, since the time of onset of pubescence always is an important factor in the adolescent's striving toward the goal of maturity. It will affect in part his readiness to mature socially, emotionally, and economically. It will influence his attitudes toward himself and others, and others' attitudes toward him. One can readily imagine the difference between two girls if one matures physically at the age of 11, and thereby is initiated into some of the secrets of womanhood, while another matures at the age of fifteen. The social "distance" between two such persons can be very great.

One of the most significant variations among adolescents are the *sex differences* in pubescence. On the average, girls mature from one to two years earlier than boys, although the range is very wide. For girls the onset of puberty can occur any time between the ages of 9 and 18, the largest number maturing between 12 and 14. The range for boys, however, extends from age 11 to age 17, the average age of puberty being around 14 years. These sex differences will, of course, be conditioned by all of the other factors mentioned as influencing pubescent variation, and it is thus impossible to determine what to expect in a given case.

Various studies indicate also that *racial factors* affect the onset of puberty. In general, children from the southern parts of Europe mature earlier than those from the north; Latins mature earlier than Celts; and American colored children mature sooner than whites. In a country like the United States, where there is considerable contact among different racial groups, particularly in the northern schools, this fact can be of some significance socially. In line with this racial peculiarity is the finding that children living in tropical climates tend to mature earlier than those in either the temperate or the arctic zones. This fact undoubtedly is closely connected with the differences due to race, since racial and national groups are fairly well distributed climatically.

Of interest, too, is the fact that the onset of pubescence varies both with locality and with social status. In one study it was found that the mode of pubescence for country boys is 13½, with the range extending from 9½ to 15½ years; for boys living in the city the mode was 14 years, and the range 10 to 18 years. Terman and others found that

tural expectations, maturational readiness, and the like. See also S. Fisher and S. E. Cleveland, *Body Image and Personality* (Princeton: Van Nostrand, 1958).

[5] D. M. More, "Developmental Concordance and Discordance During Puberty and Early Adolescence," *Monogr. Soc. Res. Child Develpm.*, 1953, 18 (1); R. W. B. Ellis, "Age of Puberty in the Tropics," *Brit. Med. J.*, 1950, 1, 85–89.

pubescence varies also with *social status*, children from the "upper" social levels tending to reach puberty slightly ahead of those from "lower" social strata. Intelligence also seems to be related to the maturation process. On the average, those with high intelligence reach puberty somewhere earlier than those with lower I.Q.'s, a fact that applies particularly to persons in the feeble-minded group. Exactly how or why these factors influence pubescence is not known, but it may be discerned that on the whole it is the more favored groups that tend toward earlier maturation. All these factors may in turn be conditioned by the *physical status* of the developing organism. Insufficient rest or sleep, disease, inadequate diet, heredity, and other factors may cause either retardation or acceleration of pubertal evolution. In general, these gross differences are important only insofar as they affect the individual. National, racial, climatic, and other variations are of little importance until they are reflected in the mentality and behavior of the individual, or until they affect the conduct of the group to which he belongs.

Extent of Growth and Development. The significance of physical development during adolescence is reflected in the fact that there is no structure, function, or system within the organism that is unaffected by the pattern of development. Some of these changes are unmistakable, some are barely noticeable, while still others are known only by inference. We shall see, for example, that there is a great difference between the amount of growth in the skeletal and muscular systems and that which occurs in the nervous system; and it is such differences, as well as the actual changes themselves, that enforce a separate consideration of

each of the several structures and systems of the body.[6]

SKELETAL AND MUSCULAR GROWTH

Changes in Height and Weight. Changes in height and weight are, of course, the most obvious alterations of a physical nature that occur during adolescence, and are among the first signs of physical maturation. These gross changes are clearly illustrated in Figure 8. During early adolescence the long bones of the arms and legs lengthen considerably, and there are instances of increase of six inches in height during a single year. There are noticeable increases in weight also, and during the first five or six years of the adolescent period the increase in weight is approximately equal to that of the ten preceding years. However, increase in weight may not keep pace with that of height at first, with the result that the adolescent presents the typical appearance of the gangling youth who seems to be all arms and legs. The greatest increase occurs during pubescence, after which there is a gradual deceleration in skeletal growth until the end of adolescence. The greater height is caused to a large extent by growth in the bones of the legs, although in later adolescence the trunk also increases in length

---

[6] There are a number of excellent studies relating to physical growth. See, for example, J. M. W. Rothney, "Recent Findings in the Study of Physical Growth of Children," *J. Educ. Res.*, 1941, 35, 161–182; F. K. Shuttleworth, *The Physical and Mental Growth of Girls and Boys, Age Six to Nineteen in Relation to Age at Maximum Growth* (Washington, D. C.: Nat. Res. Council, 1939); J. P. Zubek and Patricia A. Solberg, *Human Development* (New York: McGraw-Hill, 1954), Chap. 5; Ruth Strang, *The Adolescent Views Himself* (New York: McGraw-Hill, 1957), Chap. 6.

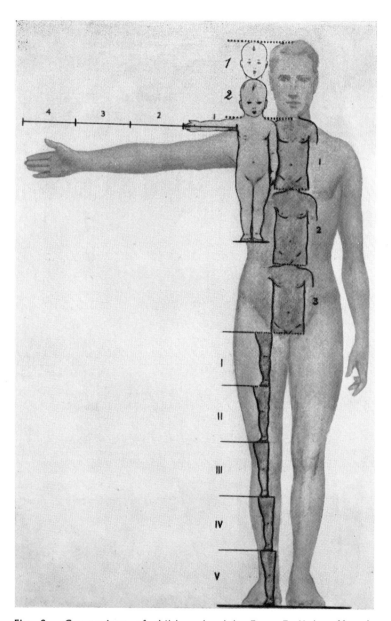

Fig. 8. Comparison of child and adult. From F. Kahn, **Man in Structure and Function**, 2 vols., trans. and ed. by G. Rosen (New York: Knopf, 1943), p. 77. It is readily apparent that the proportions of the child are very different from those of the adult. During growth the head doubles its size, the trunk triples its original size, the arms grow four times as long and the legs five times as long.

and gives the body its proper proportions. The changes in weight are traceable in part to the increase in height, to lengthening of the arms, and also to muscular development and to increase in adipose tissue. All these changes should, of course, be related to the development that occurs during childhood, particularly that of the preadolescent stage, since many of the changes that occur have their beginnings in this period.[7]

Sex Differences. There are interesting and sometimes striking sex differences in skeletal and muscular growth. From the ages of 6 to 12 the average weight of boys and girls is about the same. At pubescence the girls' weight surpasses that of boys, and this obtains for a period of several years, when the weight curve for girls flattens out and the curve for boys passes above it. Height changes closely parallel those of weight. A crossing of curves for height occurs between the ages of 10 and 11 in favor of girls, and between 13 and 14 in favor of boys. In boys the velocity of growth in stature diminishes from birth to the age of 10 or 11, rises rapidly during the next four years, and reaches a peak at about 14½ years, after which it falls rapidly until full height is reached. In girls, on the other hand, the velocity of growth declines only until about the ninth year, reaches its maximum at 12½ years, and then diminishes rather rapidly until the eighteenth year. These differences are relatively unimportant except in extreme cases. The very tall girls are usually taller than boys of the same age which may have social or psychological implications for both sexes when they come together in situations where such differences are too readily apparent.

Muscular development occurs in both sexes during the pubescent and later adolescent periods, but is usually more apparent in boys, probably because throughout childhood and adolescence boys are generally given greater opportunities for such development. One cannot escape the impression that innate differences in muscular development between the sexes do exist, but these differences are being reduced considerably by the fact that the modern girl is afforded much greater opportunity for muscular development. During adolescence there is a rapid increase also in muscular strength; but there is nevertheless an important difference between muscular size and strength, since strength in males continues to develop into the early years of adulthood, whereas muscular size does not. Girls generally reach adult strength by the time they are 17 or 18 years old. Brooks cites one study of college men in which it was found that increase in muscular power during three and one half years of college was 24.9 per cent as against an increase of 1.3 per cent for bone structure and 4.47 per cent for muscular size. Brooks suggests that the difference between muscular strength and size is probably due to a development of muscle fibers, which is itself traceable to exercise and use.[8] A consideration of the ratio of strength to height and weight indicates that from the age of 7 to the end of the adolescent period strength increases more rapidly than height, especially during the teen years. Strength is

_____

[7] See H. R. Stolz and Lois M. Stolz, op. cit., Chaps. IV, V, VIII, XII, and XIII. See also W. M. Krogman, "A Handbook of the Measurement and Interpretation of Height and Weight in a Growing Child," Monogr. Soc. Res. Child. Develpm., 1948. 13 (No. 3); A. Sutcliffe and J. W. Canham, The Height and Weight of Boys and Girls (London: John Murray, 1950).

[8] F. D. Brooks, The Psychology of Adolescence (Boston: Houghton Mifflin, 1959), pp. 48–49.

somewhat more closely correlated with weight than with height, especially in boys, which is to be expected, since weight is closely related to muscular growth. With these changes in weight, height, and strength there is a corresponding decrease in the amount of fatigue. In general there is greater endurance during the adolescent period than before, and there are smaller losses in physical efficiency. It is these facts, dimly realized by the adolescent himself, that lead him to the impression that he is capable of any exertion, which in some instances leads to overexertion with undue strain on and permanent damage to the muscles of the heart.

Pelvic Changes. At the same time that the above changes are taking place there occurs corresponding alterations in the thickness, size, and angle of the pelvis, changes that are among the clearest signs of approaching maturity. These changes are more noticeable in the female, in whom they are very necessary to the role of motherhood the girl is to play later on. This, at least, is nature's intention. The significance of this phase of development is brought out clearly by Kahn:

> By far the most characteristic structure of the human skeleton is the pelvis, and in no part of the skeleton is man so far removed from the animals as in this. . . . Woman has surpassed man in the evolution of the pelvis. In this matter she is more "human" than man. Man has surpassed woman, however, in the size and shape of the skull. Man is a "skull" creature, woman a "pelvis" organism. In the human species, as in all other animal groups, nature has instituted a division of labor between the sexes. Woman's chief biological function is the bearing of children, while man is

destined by nature for intellectual activities.[9]

It is because of this "division of labor," therefore, that there are the characteristic differences in development noted above. This phase of physical development also contributes to the distinctive female form, which plays an indirect but nonetheless important role in the psychosexual development of both male and female (see Chapter VI).

Head Growth. Because the head develops to a maximum extent before and shortly after birth, changes in its size are among the least noticeable structural changes of adolescence. Studies indicate that by the age of six the head is 93 per cent as large as it will ever be, and by the beginning of adolescence it is 98 per cent of its final size. This corresponds, as we shall see later on, to changes in the size of the brain. It is, therefore, not in the size of the head that significant alterations occur, but rather in facial make-up and proportion, owing to eruption of the permanent teeth and the development of the jawbone, which enforce a readjustment of the facial mask to adult proportions. These changes are clearly illustrated in Figure 9. The nose increases in length, and the bridge widens until finally the typical rounded childish face is replaced by the equally typical adult profile and contours that are characteristically aquiline and oval. As the face becomes more oval, there is almost twice as much added to its length as in the seven years prior to adolescence. The face grows in height, width, and depth, and the entire facial

---

[9] F. Kahn, *Man in Structure and Function* (New York: Knopf, 1943), Vol. I, pp. 92–93. See C. Landis, et al., *Sex in Development* (New York: Hoeber, 1940), pp. 104–106.

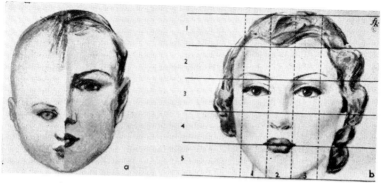

Fig. 9. Head and facial proportions. From F. Kahn, **Man in Structure and Function,** Vol. I, p. 76. In the process of development and growth the various parts of the head shift their relative positions. The intervals 1–5 of the child and 1–3 of the adult are equal.

mask becomes readjusted until the typical adult contours are achieved.

Changes in Bodily Proportions. It is not so much the actual changes described that are a source of difficulty for adolescent adjustment as it is the lack of proper bodily and facial proportions. In the early period of adolescence particularly, the legs seem too long, the arms too thin, the hands and feet unusually big and clumsy, the wrists and ankles far too fragile, and the facial mask almost completely distorted. The psychological implications of these facts were indicated in Chapter IV; here we wish merely to re-emphasize their importance for adolescent development and adjustment. At times there may be actual pain and discomfort, when the muscles are too big for the bones, or the bones too long for the muscles. These temporary inconveniences, however, would be of little importance were it not for the adolescent's reaction to his own physical image, which may be a source of considerable worry and anguish.

It is interesting and instructive to note in this connection the differences in bodily proportions between the child and the adult. The child is not only smaller

but he is differently constructed than the adult. Proportional differences are clearly seen in the relatively large size of the child's head and in the shortness of his legs. In the adult the proportions are much more exact: the span of the extended arms corresponds to the height of the body, the trunk is three times the height of the head, the arm three times as long as the hand, and the leg three times as long as the foot. These proportional relationships are carried out also in the adult human face. "The proportions of the human body," says Kahn, "prove to us that profound internal laws of harmony regulate the formation of the body. They also reveal to us the mystery of human beauty. We regard as beautiful those individuals in whom these proportions are embodied as purely as possible. . . ."[10]

PHYSIOLOGICAL DEVELOPMENT[11]

The Respiratory System. All systems

[10] F. Kahn, op. cit., I, pp. 75–76.
[11] For various research studies of physiological development, see K. Jensen, "Physical Growth and Physiological Aspects of Development," Rev. Educ. Res. 1950, 20, 390–410. See also J. P. Zubek and Patricia A. Solberg, op. cit., Chap. 4.

of the body undergo some development during adolescence, although there is little to relate regarding the respiratory system. The lungs continue to grow throughout the period, keeping pace with the increases in width and depth of the chest cavity. Boys' development in this respect is greater than that of girls throughout childhood, and especially during adolescence; the girls' curve of growth reaches a stable level at the age of 16, while the boys' continues to rise until late adolescence, subject, of course, to individual variation. These changes are in themselves of little significance for the psychologist, although we may note that proper exercise should be encouraged in order that maximal respiratory development may be achieved.

The Digestive System. The organs of digestion undergo marked development during adolescence, resulting in increased appetite, the appearance of new cravings, and a variety of digestive disturbances. The capacity of the stomach increases considerably, and much more nourishment is required. This change manifests itself in a greater craving for food, and the consumption of much more food than is required by the normal adult. Because of vague and unlocalized disturbances, peculiar notions regarding food may develop, and digestive difficulties resulting from overeating or from dietary indiscretions are not uncommon. Skin troubles are often a reflection of digestive disturbances during adolescence. Of greater import from the standpoint of health adjustment are the dietary deficiencies that may result from inadequate diet. Care should be taken that the peculiar cravings of the youngster do not lead to the ingestion of foods that are low in necessary vitamins or other elements, or to the avoidance of those which are necessary for vigorous health.

The Circulatory System. There are no striking changes in the blood-vascular system during adolescence, at least none that has direct psychological significance. Needless to say, the changes that do occur are important physically, and must be considered as a phase of the whole process of physical development.

Perhaps the most significant fact here is the difference between the growth of the heart and that of the arteries. During adolescence the size of the heart increases greatly, so that the size ratio between heart and arteries is 5:1 as against 5:4 in childhood. Thus, a certain amount of strain on the heart is unavoidable until such time as a corresponding growth of arteries re-establishes a proper ratio. This temporary disparity is paralleled by considerable irregularities in blood pressure. At age 11 the average is 109, at age 15 it is 125, and at age 18 it is back to 112. The changes that occur in the size of the heart are coincidental with increases in the amount of blood, another fact that tends to increase heart strain. At birth the amount of blood driven into the aorta each second is 20 grams; at age 3, 63 grams; and at age 14 it is 141 grams. This last figure represents an amount that is many times greater than in early childhood, whereas the heart is only 30 per cent larger, and the aorta only 10 per cent larger.

It is not surprising, therefore, that during adolescence there are spells of dizziness, palpitation, headaches, faintness, and the like. The seriousness of these symptoms depends, of course, upon their severity, but in minor form they are normal occurrences. Adequate rest, proper diet, and a reasonable amount of exercise are prescribed. All forms of undue physical exertion — sports, dancing, late hours, or overwork — should be rigidly excluded, since any one of them can lead to permanent impairment of the heart. To this class belong also those activities like drinking, smoking, and excessive emotional excitement, which tend to contribute to physical maladjustment. Moderation in all things is a rule which applies with particular force to adolescents, just because they are in a period of physical transition, when irreparable harm can be done to the physical organism by faulty control and foolish expenditure of physical energy.

The Nervous System. From a general developmental standpoint, one of the most significant changes that take place in the physical organism is the growth and development of the nervous system; but it is significant also, from our present viewpoint, that most of these changes occur prenatally, or shortly after birth, rather than at puberty. If we turn for a moment to a consideration of the development of the nervous system in its earliest stages, we find that this development is the most conspicuous feature of intrauterine life. The enormous size of the embryo's head, as compared with the rest of the body, is almost entirely due to the development of the brain, and particularly the cerebral hemispheres. The significance of this fact is enlarged by the circumstance that the most important difference between the brains of humans and those of the lower animals is found in the much greater development of these parts. From the very start of embryonic development the nervous system leads in growth over the other parts of the body.[12]

However, it is noteworthy that no

new cells form in either the cerebrum — the largest portion of the brain — or in the brain stem after birth. Whatever increase in size occurs is the result of an increase in the size of the cells already existing, and of the growth of fibers and auxiliary structures. In the cerebellum, too, the major portion (about 95 per cent) of all cells are formed prenatally, while in the spinal cord some new cells are formed for several years after birth. The brain continues to grow in size quite rapidly during the first four years of life, more slowly during the next four years, and by puberty has reached almost its full adult weight. The ratio of brain weight to body weight is clearly illustrated by the fact that at birth the brain constitutes nearly 10 per cent of the body weight, whereas at maturity it makes up only one fiftieth of the total weight. There is, of course, much more growth in the spinal cord and nerves than in the brain, since these structures necessarily become elongated with skeletal growth.

The fact that there is no change in brain size during adolescence should not be construed to mean that no development takes place. Growth and development, as we pointed out earlier, are not convertible terms. If we compare the brain of a four-months-old fetus with that of a newborn child, we see that the most conspicuous feature is the change in the appearance of the surface of the brain, since the relatively smooth surface of the earlier brain has become indented with fissures and convolutions that increase considerably the surface and complexity of the brain. This is an effect of development rather than of growth, and is one of the outstanding differences between the human and lower-animal brains. While there is no definite evi-

[12] For a good discussion of the development of the nervous system, see J. P. Zubek and Patricia A. Solberg, op. cit., Chap. 3.

dence to indicate similar development during adolescence, it may be surmised that some such development does occur. Changes such as these are very difficult to determine, and it may be a long time before we have any certain answer to this problem. But we can be fairly certain at present that the brain develops, in complexity at least, insofar as new connections are established through experience and learning. At any rate, there is no evidence to indicate that the brain does not develop during adolescence, and from several sources we are led to presume that a certain amount of development does occur.[13]

Any changes in the nervous system have obvious implications for adolescent development, since it is the physical basis of conscious life, including sensory, perceptual, imaginal, learning, and other psychological functions. However, the most significant feature of the nervous system from the standpoint of development is its integrative function. It is well known that the nervous system is the co-ordinator of living activities, the medium through which the physical organism achieves unity of function; and it may be here that the most important development occurs. While integrative control seems to be a fundamental characteristic of the nervous system, this quality can be conditioned by factors like experience, training, and habit formation; and it is not unlikely that it can be influenced indirectly by ideals, purposes, and goals. Certainly the inducement, through rigorous training, of voluntary control over basic functions and needs in the young child will con-

tribute to integrative control. This process extends into adolescence, where ever-increasing control of impulses, desires, and habits becomes (or should become) a leading feature of development. In this way the nervous system, itself an integrating factor, becomes a more integrated, unified, and highly developed mechanism. In other words, the integration toward which the adolescent strives is not a part process; it involves the whole organism, the nervous system being a primary component.

The Glandular System. So much has been written during the past quarter century concerning the glands of internal secretion and their influence on behavior and personality that a great deal of what we have to say is already common knowledge. Everyone is aware of the relationship between glands and emotional life; of how the thyroids influence feeling and action, of the impórtance of a proper development of the sex glands, and so on. Unfortunately, however, some of this knowledge has been distorted and overemphasized to the point where it is often held that a knowledge of the endocrine system is the key to an understanding of human personality. No one at the present time seriously questions the pervasive influence of these structures and their functions; but it is a serious error to regard endocrinology as the open sesame to a knowledge of psychological processes and behavior. That dysfunction of any glandular factor can upset the delicate balance of the human mind is well known; but this is true of other factors as well, both physical and psychological. It is well to keep in mind the fundamental principle that the particular effects produced by any factor are determined always by conditions that already

---

[13] See H. C. Solomon, S. Cobb, and W. Penfield (eds.), *The Brain and Human Behavior* (Baltimore: Williams & Wilkins, 1958).

obtain. If, for example, the nervous system is poorly integrated, or there is an existing predisposition to neurosis or psychosis, then certainly glandular dysfunction will have its effects; but there may be little or no effect if these or similar conditions do not already exist. The apologists for the primacy of glandular control (e.g., Berman) write always as though there were no other factors within the personality worth mentioning; whereas the fact is that the glands, like any other intraorganic factor, are always and necessarily conditioned by the "environment" in which they function.

There are, nevertheless, certain characteristics of the endocrine system that make it stand out as one of the most important physical factors to be considered. There is, first of all, the fact that the endocrines (the ductless glands) pour their secretions *directly* into the blood, so that their effects become pervasive through the medium of the blood stream. The brain itself, for example, is bathed in blood; and Steinach for one has given excellent experimental demonstrations of what this means for the development of various characteristics in his experimental animals. Thus, there is practically no part of the body that is entirely impervious to the influence of these glands. Second, the endocrine system is so closely integrated with other systems of the organism that its functions are bound to influence whatever processes are controlled by these systems. We have already noted its close connection with the blood-vascular system; it is functionally integrated also with the autonomic nervous system, and, though less directly, with the central nervous mechanism. These three great systems of the human body — the glandular, nervous, and blood-vascular — form an interlocking triumvirate that directs, controls, or in some manner conditions all human conduct.[14]

There is one other characteristic that calls for attention, and that is the interdependence of the various glands themselves. The endocrine system is an interlocking hierarchy, so organized that the function of one structure is likely to produce some effect on or condition the functioning of others. This fact puts added importance on glandular activity, and gives to the consideration of each gland a double significance.

It is, of course, only the endocrine glands that have an important bearing on development. These are the thyroids, parathyroids, adrenals, pituitary, pineal, thymus, and sex glands or gonads. All of these, except the gonads, exhibit fairly regular development from birth to maturity; whereas the gonads, which in childhood remain constant in size, develop rapidly in adolescence. It is, therefore, this phase of glandular development that is of the greatest importance to adolescent psychology. It must not be thought, however, that the sex glands are the all-important factor, for many conditions in adolescence are traceable to dysfunction of the other glands. As far as is known the gonads, adrenals, pituitary, and to some extent the pineal and thymus glands have the most direct effect on pubertal evolution; whereas the thyroids, parathyroids, the endocrine portions of the liver and pancreas function in adolescence much as before.

---

[14] See F. A. Beach, *Hormones and Behavior* (New York: Hoeber, 1949) and C. H. Lawrence, "The Endocrine Factor in Personality Development," *Educ. Rec.*, 1942, 23. Suppl. 15, 83–94.

Limitations of space preclude a detailed account of all these various structures and their effects. We shall, therefore, mention only the outstanding facts that should be known. The *thyroids* are two maroon-colored organs situated on either side of the windpipe, adjacent to the larynx. They secrete a substance that plays a part in the regulation of metabolism; hyperactivity or hypoactivity of these glands produces readily observable effects. Thyroid abnormalities of all kinds may appear during adolescence, particularly in girls. Underactivity of this gland (hypothyroidism) produces sluggishness, overweight, sleepiness, and slowness of reaction generally — conditions that are particularly prevalent in certain portions of the midwestern United States. Hyperthyroidism (overactivity), on the other hand, causes irritability, excitability, fainting spells, hysterical symptoms, rapid pulse, and other conditions that require immediate attention, and that are amenable to medical treatment.

The *parathyroids* are four small glands attached to the thyroids but differing in function; they are involved in the regulation of calcium metabolism. Psychological effects caused by dysfunction of these glands resemble those produced by the thyroids. Parathyroid deficiency may cause a child to be nervous, tense, overly sensitive, and disobedient. With oversecretion of the parathyroid hormone, the individual may exhibit an unusual lassitude, muscular relaxation, and lack of enthusiasm for activities of all kinds.

The *pineal* gland, a small structure located in the brain, is more active in childhood, and becomes less important after the beginning of adolescence. In this it is similar to the *thymus*, a gland that continues to grow throughout childhood, and begins to atrophy at the onset of puberty. It is thought that these two together affect the maturation of the reproductive system. Continued activity of either of these structures may cause perseverance of childish characteristics, and the primary and secondary sex characteristics may fail to develop. Pineal tumors result in precocious development of both the soma and genitalia. As early as age five, the subject is a Hercules in miniature, with low voice and beard, and the genital structures of an adult. In several cases studied there occurred also precocious mental development. In all, the evidence strongly suggests that the pineal and thymus play an indirect but significant role in the somatic, sexual, and mental development of the organism.

The *pituitary* gland, sometimes referred to as the "motor of the endocrine system," is a small structure lying in a bony recess at the base of the brain. It secretes a number of hormones, and seems to have a bearing on several aspects of development. Extirpation of the pituitary results in failure of growth, adiposity, genital infantilism, and sometimes a condition of pathological somnolence. Characteristic pituitary diseases include gigantism, acromegaly, and dwarfism, resulting from disturbance of the anterior lobe. If the condition occurs in earlier years, dwarfism results, with arrested development of sexual structures and functions and of the secondary sex characteristics. Pituitary deficiency at puberty results in mixed normality and infantilism. The secondary sex characteristics are imperfectly developed and late in appearance, menstruation begins later than usual, and other signs of arrested sexual development are common, since the hormone from the anterior lobe is necessary for the sex glands to begin functioning. The posterior lobe is known to affect metabolism, and the enormously fat child who fails to mature sexually and is lazy is probably a victim of underactivity of this part of the pituitary.

The *adrenal* glands are small structures located on the upper part of the kidneys. While their effect on behavior is well known, the exact part they play in pubertal development is obscure, although the evidence indicates that they are capable of greatly modifying the picture. Excessive activity of the cortex of the adrenals may result in precocious maturation of the entire body, and particularly the gonads. In certain cases of marked masculinity the cortex has been observed to be relatively large. The most striking evidence of their relation to development is suprarenal virilism, which may appear in either sex from infancy to childhood, and is marked by accentuation of masculine attributes in the male and masculinization in the female. Subjects of adrenal deficiency are underweight, manifesting a reduced basal metabolism which predisposes to fatigue and increases susceptibility to colds.

From the strictly psychological viewpoint the most outstanding feature of adrenal activity is its effect on the emotional life. The adrenals are the major factor in the bodily concomitants of such reactions as anger, fear, and embarrassment, and are the immediate cause of the physical manifestations of blushing, paling, and sweating that result from these emotional seizures. It should be noted also that while the adrenals play a causative role in emotional reactions, they themselves can be influenced by emotional reactions, so that overactivity may be a result of psychic as well as physical factors. In all such instances, therefore, it is as important to regulate the emotional life so as to insure the

physical well-being of the individual.

The Sex Glands or Gonads. Of all the physical alterations at puberty there is none that ranks in importance with the development of the sex glands, not only because of their bearing on physical development, but also because of the psychological and social implications of these changes. The hormones of the gonads determine and regulate the development of the reproductive system and the secondary sex characteristics. The sexual organs of the male grow rapidly in size, and in the female there is the beginning of the menstrual cycle. These are the two most prominent features of sexual maturation, and both are laden with possibilities for disturbing the mental equanimity of youth. The boy may become acutely conscious of the size of the sexual organs, believing them to be apparent to everyone, and he may be disturbed by involuntary erections, nocturnal emissions, and the erotic dreams and desires that attend the process of becoming sexually mature. As for the young girl, she may experience considerable emotional shock from the first menstruation, especially when not adequately prepared for its onset. It has been determined that some women never quite recover from the shock of the first menstrual period, and always associate it with feelings of fear, anxiety, or disgust. Sometimes, of course, there is actual pain, which may lead to ideas of illness or to incapacity for the period of the menstrual flow. It must be remembered that this is an entirely new experience for the young girl, and one not without its frightening, embarrassing, and unpleasant aspects.[15]

---

[15] See C. Landis, *et al.*, *op. cit.*, pp. 43, 44, 126, 209; also F. K. Shuttleworth, *Sexual Maturation and the Physical Growth of Girls Age Six to Nineteen* (Washington, D. C.: Nat. Res. Council, 1937).

That much of this reaction could be mitigated by proper instruction and development of the right attitudes in such matters is unquestionable, but there are, unfortunately, too few parents willing to undertake this serious responsibility. Feelings of guilt, shame, or embarrassment on the part of youth with respect to such natural functions are an indictment of parents and others whose ignorance and prudishness stand in the way of developing the right attitudes in youth. Self-control, proper instruction, avoidance of sexually stimulating situations, modesty, and cleanliness are the factors required to deal sanely with psychosexual development. Above all, youth should be protected from the effects produced by old wives' tales relating to sexual maturation — such tales, for example, as that the loss of semen is physically and mentally dangerous, that menstruation prevents strenuous activity of any kind, that to experience sexual dreams is a shameful thing, and so on. One would think that in this day of widespread education these ideas would have been ridiculed out of existence; but the fact is that education often stops at the door of sexual matters, and children are left to get what information they can in the worst possible ways. Later on we shall deal more fully with the problems of psychosexual development not touched upon in this section (Chapter VI).

More prominent in some respects than these primary changes of sexual maturation is the appearance of the secondary sex characteristics. Kahn calls them the advertising department of the firm called "man." They are the external signs of the fact that sex cells have become mature within the body. In the boy these include the growth and characteristic distribution of pubic hair, growth of hair on

the face, arms, and legs, and under the armpits, and the changes in quality of voice due to enlarging of the larynx. These changes may or may not be the source of emotional difficulties, depending upon the individual's reaction to them and upon the attitudes of others. The tricks played on the boy by his own voice, which for a while seems beyond his control, may be the source of some embarrassment; and any ridicule by others regarding his appearance or his attempts to cope with these changes by the development of new habits, such as shaving, will certainly aggravate matters. This situation requires understanding and tact until the youngster has adjusted to his new manhood.[16]

In the female the chief secondary sex characteristics include development of the breasts, the widening of the hips, growth and characteristic distribution of pubic hair, appearance of hair under the armpits, and a moderate change of voice. In addition, the hair on the head grows long, and there is a deposit of fat on shoulders and hips which, with the growth of the breasts, causes the typically rounded contours of the sexually mature woman. The development of the breasts is the one change likely to cause any difficulties, since it is the only prominent one. Depending upon their size and weight, some girls become acutely conscious of these structures, especially when attention is called to them by the meaningful glances of others. In both appearance and movement they can be unusually conspicuous; and since their development is always coincident with

---

[16] See P. Blanchard, "Adolescent Experience in Relation to Personality and Behavior," in J. McV. Hunt (ed.), *Personality and the Behavior Disorders* (New York: Ronald, 1944), Vol. II, p. 694.

sexual maturation, it is very likely to have some sexual connotation of which the young girl may become acutely aware. Perhaps of greater significance, however, is the failure of the breasts to develop, due to lateness of puberty or gonadal deficiency. This failure marks the individual as different from other girls, and may lead to feelings of inferiority or insecurity regarding sexual status. The development of the breasts is one of the most conspicuous signs of womanhood and potential motherhood. Therefore, any inadequacy relating to those goals may well have some effect on personality. In any event, here again the right attitudes and the right kind of instruction can be of inestimable value to the growing girl.

Considerable insight into the possible significance of these sexual developments may be derived from a study of the effects that follow from failure of or interference with the process of sexual maturation. Experimental studies of ovarian deficiency in animals demonstrates that prepuberal gonadectomy (surgical removal of gonads) results in sexual neutrality with absence of secondary characteristics. In human subjects, when ovarian extirpation is undertaken postpuberally, the breasts and uterus atrophy, and sexual desire is frequently lessened. The condition of ovarian deficiency is not an uncommon occurrence, and is characterized by a delay in appearance or a lessening of the sexual functions, and a depression of the secondary sex characteristics. Psychologically, this condition often results in socially conditioned inferiority feelings, and a failure of normal erotization during the pubescent period, a condition which has its own psychic effects. Little is known of hypergonadism in the female, although precocious puberty appears quite often, and

it is well known that some girls and women are highly erotic and tend toward the perversion of nymphomania. Whether this latter condition is socially determined or due to hyperactivity of the sex glands is not always certain.

Male hypogonadism is a well-known condition resulting from castration, or from such diseases as gonorrhea. Surgical removal of the testes before puberty results in persistence of juvenile characteristics. The skin is delicate, sallow, and wrinkled. Fat accumulates in the breast region and buttocks, giving a pseudofeminine configuration. The beard and body hair are very scanty, or lacking altogether. The pubic hair has the horizontal demarcation characteristic of the female, and the sexual structures retain their infantile appearance. Intelligence seems unaffected, but there may be personality effects. The results of postpubertal removal of the gonads are variable, but there is a tendency toward reduction of the typical sex characteristics. Precocious puberty has also been observed very often in the male, sometimes appearing extremely early. In such cases the sexual structures grow rapidly and soon reach adult size, and the secondary characteristics resemble those of the adult. Skeletal development is almost always affected, and there may be some development of intelligence. The psychological situation is quite complex, the subject being mentally immature but with well-defined sex impulses. To what extent hypergonadism is a factor in such development is not known, although it is likely that there is a definite physical basis. It is a significant fact that the symptoms caused by hormonal deficiency may often be relieved by the administration of sex hormones.

From all of these data it may be

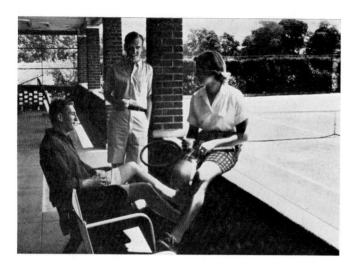

Sports are important to development.

safely concluded that the sex organs of the male and female produce hormones that have a masculinizing or a feminizing effect, and that they play a dominant role in the development of the individual into a man or a woman in the full sense of those terms. Any unusual deviations from the average in sexual maturation may in many instances be traced to inadequate or arrested development of the sexual structures.

ADOLESCENT PHYSICAL HYGIENE

This brief review of the physical alterations of the adolescent period should serve to indicate clearly the necessity of an adequate physical hygiene program for the growing boy and girl. Hygiene is always an important factor in healthful living and in complete adjustment; but it is doubly important during adolescence, because of the continuous changes through which the organism is passing. It is just because the organism is in a state of transition that hygienic care is an absolute requirement. Serious and sometimes permanent damage can be done through lack of adequate rest, proper diet, and exercise, or through bad physical habits. Undue strain on the heart, as the result of extreme exertion, should be carefully avoided. Vitamin deficiencies should be excluded through the development of a carefully arranged diet; and there should be provided abundance of opportunity for the right kind of exercise in the open, in order adequately to cope with such changes as take place in the respiratory and muscular systems. These means should be supplemented by intelligent instruction in the basic principles of physical hygiene. Only by understanding something of the nature of the changes that are occurring in him can the adolescent be expected to grasp fully the necessity of hygienic practices, and to co-operate in the achievement of a reasonable degree of physical efficiency. In such a program the schools can be expected to take a leading role; but this does not excuse the parents from the obligation of contributing what they can to the healthful physical development of the boys and girls entrusted to their care.

SELECTED READINGS

Beach, F. A., *Hormones and Behavior* (New York: Hoeber [Harper], 1949).

Billett, R. O., and Yeo, J. W., *Growing Up* (Boston: Heath, 1951).

Fields, M. R., Goldberg, J. A., and Kilander, H. F., *Youth Grows Into Adulthood* (New York: Chartwell House, 1950).

Krogman, W. M., "A Handbook of the Measurement and Interpretation of Height and Weight in the Growing Child," *Monogr. Soc. Res. Child Develpm.*, 1948, *13*, (No. 3).

Kuhlen, R. G., and Thompson, T. G. (eds.), *Psychological Studies of Human Development* (New York: Appleton-Century-Crofts, 1952), pp. 34–43.

Seidman, J. M. (ed.), *The Adolescent: a Book of Readings* (New York: Dryden, 1953), Chap. 4.

Sherrington, C. S., *The Integrative Action of the Nervous System* (New Haven: Yale University Press, 1906).

Shuttleworth, F. K., *The Physical and Mental Growth of Girls and Boys Age Six to Nineteen in Relation to Age at Maximum Growth* (Washington, D. C.: Nat. Res. Council, 1939).

———— "The Adolescent Period: a Graphic Atlas," *Monogr. Soc. Res. Child Develpm.*, 1949, *14* (No. 1).

———— "The Adolescent Period: a Pictorial Atlas," *Monogr. Soc. Res. Child Develpm.*, 1949, *14* (No. 2).

Stolz, H. R., and Stolz, Lois M., *Somatic Development of Adolescent Boys* (New York: Macmillan, 1951).

Sutcliffe, A., and Canham, J. W., *The Height and Weight of Boys and Girls* (London: John Murray, 1950).

Zachry, Caroline B., *Emotion and Conduct in Adolescence* (New York: Appleton-Century-Crofts, 1940), Chap. 2.

CHAPTER VI

PSYCHOSEXUAL DEVELOPMENT AND PROBLEMS OF YOUTH

The physiology of youth's development heralds deep and significant changes in the psyche as well as the soma of the growing boy and girl. Among these changes the most significant are those that transform the sexual life of the individual. Let us open the door of psychosexual development, too often tightly closed, and see what is going on inside.

YOUTH AND THE SEX PROBLEM

Sex as One Aspect of Adjustment. The striving of youth toward the goal of maturity has many facets, all of which are related in one way or another to the process of adjustment. In school the teen-ager tries to meet the demands of the academic situation; in the home he strives to cope with family demands, conflicts, and responsibilities; in society he wrestles with the demands and problems created by the peer group to which he belongs. In these and similar situations the adolescent tries to meet and cope with the requirements and frustrations of daily living, and to do so in an acceptable, reasonably efficient, and wholesome manner. In other words, he strives to effect some measure of adjustment. Each of these ways of adjusting, or, more precisely, these attempts at adjustment, has its own significance for adolescent development, and all are

closely interrelated. But there is no aspect of adjustment more difficult, more pervasive, or more significant than those that occur in the area of sexual development.[1] There are many reasons for this, as we shall see; and we shall have to examine these reasons carefully in order to understand the process of psychosexual development and adjustment

The somewhat hazardous situation of civilized youth who, on achieving sexual maturation, are required by social and moral rules to forego sexual expression is a well-known fact. Parents, educators, and youth counselors know that adjustment to the sex problem is one of the most difficult and complex demands that the growing boy or girl faces. The urge toward sexual behavior, and toward heterosexual relationships of one kind and another, is a basic human need that

[1] U. H. Fleege, *Self-Revelation of the Adolescent Boy* (Milwaukee: Bruce, 1945), pp. 262–263, 296; D. J. Mohr and Marian A. Despres, *The Stormy Decade: Adolescence* (New York: Random House, 1958), Chap. 7.

is itself very dynamic, and often influenced by other personality needs. If, therefore, we are to help youth deal effectively with sexual problems and relationships we must know a great deal about this phase of adolescent development, its special characteristics, and the types of behavior that may be associated with it. The simple fact that at puberty the boy and girl become sexually mature is at best a starting point. This fact must be studied in the light of its implications for the social, emotional, and moral development of youth. Only in this way will we understand the real character of psychosexual development.

Let us clarify a point before plunging into this complex problem. Psychosexual development has its roots in the physiology of the adolescent period, and thus we have brought it into relationship with the implications and the facts of physical development during adolescence. Without such development the psychosexual growth of the youngster would not even occur. But we must emphasize that the concept of psychosexual development is much broader than the biology of sexual growth. This is why we use the term *psychosexual development* in place of the simpler term *sexual maturation*. Sex has many facets to it, reaching into the psychic life of the individual, into his feelings and emotions, into his moral, social, and religious developments and problems. It is this pervasive quality of sex that makes it so important, apart from the fact that sexual problems in our society have a way of assuming much greater proportions than the dynamics of the sex drive would seem to justify.

Sex and Society. Is it true that modern society causes sexual development to be psychologically hazardous by requiring youth to defer sexual expression?[2] There is little doubt that it may be better for some young people to marry earlier than is ordinarily the case in order to reduce sexual frustration. But we should remember that it is just because sexual urges are so dynamic in quality that their control may contribute important elements to the development of character and personality. Earlier (Chapter III) we pointed out that psychological conflict and frustration are not necessarily bad; in fact, through the efficient handling of conflict individuals often achieve a higher level of integration and self-control. While early marriages would put a stop to some forms of undesirable sex behavior, it is more important to stress the *psychological value of self-control*, since self-control is necessary for many aspects of adjustment. It is victory over impulses, rather than surrender to them, that leads to personal integration.

Sex adjustment and problems associated with it should be regarded as parts of a much larger problem having to do with the development of adequate interpersonal relationships during adolescence. When, for example, we refer in this chapter to heterosexual orientation, we are not limiting ourselves to intersexual behavior. What we are referring to is the development of attitudes, feelings, and relationships which bring the two sexes together in a normal, wholesome way so that they can enjoy each other's company, have fun together, relate easily to each other, and eventually form those relationships that lead to lasting friendship, marriage, and the building of families. Thus, because of these broad ramifications, psychosexual development must be studied in terms of its implications

[2] P. H. Landis, *Adolescence and Youth*, 2 ed. (New York: McGraw-Hill, 1952), pp. 249–255.

for other forms of development, particularly the moral and social. As the teen-ager moves toward maturity he must learn not only how to cope with sex problems that arise, but also how to achieve healthy social relationships with the opposite sex, how to handle the problem of dating, puppy love, and similar experiences. The adolescent must also become oriented toward future roles as husband and father, or wife and mother. Instruction and guidance in this area therefore should be directed not only toward adequate sex information but also toward the responsibilities of dating, courtship, and marriage.

How Widespread Are Sex Problems Among Youths? That sexual drives and experiences and healthy heterosexual development are among the more serious problems of adolescents is attested daily by clinical experience, and by numerous empirical studies. Such investigators as Howard, Fry, Ramsey, Kinsey, and Fleege, to mention only a few, all report a high incidence of problems of various types associated with psychosexual development. These problems range all the way from behavior difficulties like masturbation and premarital intercourse to the more distinctively emotional problems associated with sexual response such as anxiety, shame, and guilt.[3] In the author's own extensive experience with the problems of youth, he has found that guilt, shame, anxiety, and a sense of personal debasement associated with sex

---

[3] For typical statements regarding adolescent sex problems, see J. R. Gallagher and H. I. Harris, *Emotional Problems of Adolescents* (New York: Oxford University Press, 1958), Chap. 3; also J. P. Finn, *A Study of the Problems of Certain Catholic High School Boys as Told by Themselves and Their Teachers* (Washington, D. C.: The Catholic University of America Press, 1950), Chap. 3.

problems are among the most common complaints of adolescents, and that many youths are wholly incapable of developing adequate heterosexual relationships. There are also many youngsters who experience problems in sexual identity and are thus ill-equipped to project themselves into future roles of husband or wife, father or mother. Thus many young people at the ages of 15, 16, and 17 are extremely lonely, incapable of establishing firm interpersonal relationships, and feel isolated and rejected by their peers. Regardless, therefore, of the statistical picture of adolescent sexual difficulties, the important fact is that *some* teen-agers run headlong into these problems, and that *all* of them undergo psychosexual and heterosexual development. For all of these reasons the course of such development must be carefully studied.

SOME CHARACTERISTICS OF PSYCHOSEXUAL DEVELOPMENT

Preadolescent Sexual Development. Puberty and adolescence, as we have seen, are characterized by pervasive physical and physiological changes that underlie psychosexual development. It is important to know what these changes are and the implications they have for different aspects of development; but of even greater importance are the psychological and social effects of these changes. To understand the teen-ager we must know a great deal about the impulses, feelings, frustrations, and conflicts that develop in the transition from childhood to adulthood. What bearing do such factors have on the behavior of adolescents and on their mutual relationships? Is there a sexual consciousness in childhood, or does this emerge only after the physical maturation at puberty? What is it in development that brings about the distinctive reorientation of youth? These are just a few of the questions suggested by the term *psychosexual development*, which Landis and his co-authors define as "the growth and changes in the biological, psychological, and sociological aspects of sex in the course of the life history of the individual."[4] This definition indicates that the term is much broader in meaning than ordinarily supposed.

It is well known that according to psychoanalytic theory, which is certainly the most comprehensive and most useful interpretation of sexual developments, sexual experience and behavior have their beginnings in the earliest years of childhood. According to this viewpoint, at about the age of five or six, the child enters a latency period during which the sexual activity is reduced to a minimum and then emerges in full strength at puberty.[5] This interpretation is of considerable practical as well as theoretical importance because of its implications for later sexual development. If the latency period is overrun by sexual impulses and behavior, psychosexual development during adolescence is likely to be seriously distorted.

Larry is a young man, twenty years of age, who was referred for counseling because of extreme anxiety during examinations. Despite good intellectual potential as indicated by objective tests, and a satisfactory high school record, Larry had run into numerous academic difficulties because of his "examination anxiety."

During the course of interview, it became apparent that Larry had a serious personal problem. His anxieties stemmed from deep-seated feelings of insecurity about himself, lack of personal self-identity, and deficient interpersonal relationships especially where the opposite sex is concerned. Larry complained of incessant homosexual fantasies which led to and were associated with compulsive masturbation which extended back to the first year of high school. However, sexual behavior of an exploratory and masturbatory kind dated back as far as Larry could remember. He cited instances of sexual exploration and self-stimulation at the ages of four and five, and this pattern of behavior continued right through the latency period. At the present time, Larry is sexually confused, disoriented in relations with the opposite sex, and extremely anxious about his inability to control masturbation.

This case illustrates with forceful clarity the effect of precocious sexuality on later psychosexual development.[6] During the latency period, according to Freudian theory, ego development should take precedence over sexual development, so that by the time the individual encounters the conflicts and frustrations of adolescence the ego has gained sufficient strength to cope with them. If the latency period is overrun by precocious sexual impulses and behavior, ego development is severely restricted and psychosexual development is likely to take a pathological turn. Thus, during this period the groundwork of homosexuality is most often laid.

---

[4] C. Landis, et al., *Sex and Development* (New York: Hoeber, 1940), p. 2.

[5] See *ibid.*, pp. 5–8, for a brief survey and critical analysis of the Freudian interpretation. For an empirical answer to this question of sexual development in children, see E. H. Campbell, "The Social-Sex Development of Children," *Genet. Psychol. Monogr.*, 1939, 21, 463–552.

[6] See Lauretta Bender and A. E. Grugett, "A Follow-Up Report on Children Who Had Atypical Sexual Experience," *Amer. J. Orthopsychiat.*, 1952, 22, 825–837. Some writers interpret childhood sexuality as definitely secondary to other problems. See P. H. Hoch and J. Zubin (eds.), *Psychosexual Development* (New York: Grune & Stratton, 1949).

Apart from precocious or pathological sex development in childhood, there is abundant evidence to indicate that psychosexual development begins long before the onset of puberty. This may take the form of sexual exploration or play, self-stimulation, and particularly curiosity. One author, for example, made a study of the questions of young children concerning sex in 981 homes with 1797 children.[7] In all, 1763 questions were reported and of these 49.1 per cent were asked by preschool children. Children of early school age, 6 to 10 years, asked 40.1 per cent, and the 10 to 13 age group asked 10.8 per cent of the questions. Figures such as these indicate that young children are certainly aware of sex realities, but we may expect that this awareness will vary to an important degree with cultural factors. In any event, these data indicate clearly that psychosexuality is not a phenomenon peculiar to the sexually mature person. Here we see again that the distinctions between childhood and adolescence are obscured by the gradualness of all development, and that changes in youth have clearly defined antecedents in childhood.

Emergence of Sexual Feelings, Attitudes, and Interests. Numerous studies of psychosexual development indicate that adolescence only intensifies behavior which is probably controlled by an endocrine readjustment. Sexual and heterosexual impulses seem to appear spontaneously; only the forms of gratification are acquired, and these are conditioned to an important extent by cultural factors. Questionnaire studies suggest that the age of first sex impression varies considerably from one group to another, the average age for one group for example, being 9.6 and for another 12.5. In the former group, 64 per cent reported first sex impressions before age 11, and 88 per cent before age 13. Another investigator found that the age at which a group of 969 boys first became conscious of sex realities in conversation ranged from 9 to 19, the average age again being 12.5. In this study, the awareness of sex factors was brought about in 70 per cent of the cases by *conversation.*[8] There is no way of telling, then, whether first sex impression is always due to spontaneous development or to environmental factors. According to Fry, sexual awakening at this point seems to be "a vague, undifferentiated response to many stimuli. The individual reacting to these experiences is excited, often without realizing fully what is happening to him. Mixed feelings accompany the new sensations which he likes and does not like. They please, but they are disturbing because he feels that they are forbidden. Pervading these responses and his activity is a fundamental bewilderment."[9]

The nature of sexual awakening is revealed by the mental factors and the behavior that accompany sex development. Feelings, desires, curiosity, fantasies, and dreams are all signposts of sexual ripening. In a study of 295 normal and abnormal women, Landis found first sex curiosity to occur between the ages

[7] K. W. Hattendorf, "A Study of the Questions of Young Children Concerning Sex: a Phase of an Experimental Approach to Parent Education," *J. Soc. Psychol.,* 1932, 3, 37–65. By the same author, "Parents' Answers to Children's Sex Questions," *Child Welfare Pamphlets* of the State University of Iowa, 1933, No. 710.

[8] R. R. Willoughby, "Sexuality in the Second Decade," *Monogr. Soc. Res. Child Develpm.,* 1937, 2, No. 3. See also J. H. Conn, "Sexual Curiosity in Children," *Amer. J. Dis. Child,* 1940, 60, 1110–1119.

[9] C. C. Fry, *Mental Health in College* (New York: The Commonwealth Fund, 1942), p. 104.

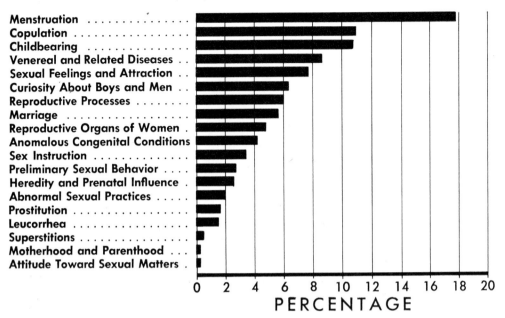

Menstruation ....
Copulation ....
Childbearing ....
Venereal and Related Diseases ..
Sexual Feelings and Attraction ..
Curiosity About Boys and Men ..
Reproductive Processes ....
Marriage ....
Reproductive Organs of Women .
Anomalous Congenital Conditions
Sex Instruction ....
Preliminary Sexual Behavior ....
Heredity and Prenatal Influence .
Abnormal Sexual Practices .....
Prostitution ....
Leucorrhea ....
Superstitions ....
Motherhood and Parenthood ...
Attitude Toward Sexual Matters .

0   2   4   6   8   10 12 14 16 18 20

PERCENTAGE

Fig. 10.   Percentage distribution by major classes of 880 spontaneous questions asked by 160 women, ages 17 to 23, in a training school for teachers prior to a course in sex instruction which they had requested. Based on data of F. I. Davenport, "Adolescent Interests, a Study of the Sexual Interests and Knowledge of Young Women," **Arch. Psychol.**, 1923, No. 66.

of 6 and 9, followed by a latent period in which sex interest decreased, only to occur again at the ages of 11 and 12. As remembered by these women, this curiosity was stimulated by such events as the birth of children, but not to any great extent by such factors as a knowledge of physical differences between the sexes.[10] Willoughby, on the other hand, gives a much higher age for the first appearance of curiosity, generally between the ages of 12 and 18. This difference may be due to the way in which the term *curiosity* is used in different studies. In his study of Catholic high-school boys, Fleege found definite psychosexual changes with age. Thus, 37.8 per cent of freshmen reported worry over problems of purity, whereas 59 per

cent of seniors said that they had such worries. Results such as these indicate that sexual phenomena, like other forms of behavior, are influenced by developmental processes.[11]

Another instance of this is exemplified by the fact that sex awareness, expressed most often in curiosity, precedes desire and conduct by many years in the majority of instances. Whereas general sex awareness may occur as early as the preschool age, the onset of desire may not occur until 16 or 18 years of age. Most studies indicate a later awakening for girls. Such awakening can occur spontaneously, but is more often excited by companions, reading, and so on.

Sexual awareness is manifested also in

---

[10] C. Landis, et al., op. cit., p. 209.

[11] U. H. Fleege, op. cit., p. 297.

the appearance of *sexual fantasy.* In one study, 40 per cent of the men and 26 per cent of the women reported such fantasies before there was any conscious intellectual content to explain it. Moreover, nearly 39 per cent of the men and 25 per cent of the women indicated that such fantasies occurred *before puberty.*[12] As may be expected, postpubescent fantasies were more realistic and vivid than the earlier ones. These findings are similar to those dealing with erotic dreams, except that in our culture such dreams seem to be characteristic largely of males. The great majority of boys in various studies report the occurrence of sex dreams, the incidence ranging from 60 to 100 per cent by the age of 20. These experiences are often accompanied by sexual reactions of one kind or another which may lead to fear, anxiety, or guilt.

Psychosexual Development in Relation to Other Factors. Facts such as these should serve to remind us that psychosexual development is *integral* in character, and cannot be adequately understood apart from other changes that occur between birth and maturity. As Fry states, "The development of maturity involves the individual's entire personality, and achieving sexual maturity is an integral part of the process." "It is apparent throughout that sexual growth cannot be considered alone; it is connected at many points with other departments of life, and the absence of satisfactory adjustment elsewhere apparently impedes the achievement of sexual maturity."[13] Such factors as childhood illness, the presence or absence of brothers and sisters in the family, opportunities for healthy contacts between the sexes, identification with the like-sex parent, and many other factors will play a part in determining the course of psychosexual development.

These facts should be correlated with the influence of cultural and environmental determinants on this phase of development. "Psychosexual development can be understood only against the background of other experiences, attitudes, and feelings of the individual and the restrictions, prescriptions, and proscriptions of the culture as transmitted by parents, associates, and school authorities."[14] This opinion is supported by anthropological studies of sex behavior. Mead's data indicate that in Samoa opportunity for sexual expression greatly reduces adolescent conflict; but it also produces unimaginative personalities without much drive.[15] For the anthropologist, man's native sexual tendencies

> are molded by a system of cultural rules which vary from one society to another. The end product of individual sexual development, adjustment and practice depends upon the interaction of innate drives, emotions, and social factors, and religious ideals which are impressed upon the sexual inclination of men and women. These either include or exclude certain general types of reactions and determine the particular habit responses that are incorporated into the adult personality. . . . In this way are created the categories of decent and indecent, the avoidance of forbidden relationships, the orientation toward certain other groups, and subtler tones of feelings toward the mother, father, sister, and brother.[16]

More immediate environmental determinants, particularly family relation-

---

[12] R. R. Willoughby, *op. cit.* See also R. Allers, "Daydreams and sexuality," *Hom. and Past. Rev.,* 1939, 39, 469–475, and G. V. Ramsey, *Factors in the Sex Life of 291 Boys* (Ann Arbor, Mich.: Edwards, 1950).

[13] C. C. Fry, *op. cit.,* pp. 94, 134.

[14] C. Landis, *et al., op. cit.,* p. 2.

[15] Margaret Mead, *Coming of Age in Samoa* (New York: William Morrow, 1928).

[16] Reprinted with permission of Harper and Brothers from C. Landis, *et al., op. cit.,* pp. 3–4.

ships, are known to influence the course of psychosexual and heterosexual development. Thus in the study by Landis, a significant difference was found between the normal and abnormal women with respect to the resolution of family difficulties. More of the abnormal than of the normal women gave evidence of still being closely tied emotionally to their families, and no adequate love attachments outside the family had ever been developed by those closely tied to the parents. Similarly, a lack of interest in sex, or a lack of sex feelings, was found more frequently in those women who, in adult life, were still emotionally bound to their families.[17] It may be safely assumed that other environmental factors, particularly religious, moral, and social influences, also have a distinct bearing on the pattern of psychosexual development.[18]

In relatively normal persons, this pattern is characterized by a transition from sexual immaturity to psychosexual maturity, from asexual disinterest to heterosexual interest, from an amorphous personal identity to a clear-cut and well-defined sexual identity. In the same way that the youngster is striving toward intellectual, social, and emotional maturity, so also is he groping toward sexual maturity which involves predominantly a satisfactory heterosexual orientation, along with the self-control and the self-identity that always marks the mature individual. An adequate orientation to the opposite sex may be regarded as one of the primary goals of psychosexual development, a fact of considerable importance to understanding the implications of the conflicts, experiences, and behavior of the adolescent. In the last analysis, many of the sexual problems of adolescence are nothing more than symptoms of sexual immaturity.

✓ SEXUAL ATTITUDES AND PROBLEMS OF YOUTH

Attitudes of Youths Toward Sex. Further insight into the nature and trend of psychosexual development may be had by studying the sexual viewpoints and problems of young people. Needless to say, the nature of such attitudes will depend partly upon the object of reference. The phenomena of sexual maturation, for example, evoke different attitudes in different subjects. Some youngsters react with pleasure or excitement, and others experience shame, disgust, bashfulness, and similar attitudes. On the basis of data gathered by Achilles, Willoughby indicates in graphic form definite changes in attitudes and emotional reactions of youths regarding the phenomena of maturation (see Fig. 1).

This investigator also found that worry differs according to sex, girls being more worried than boys, and this attitude, like others, increases with age. These data indicate clearly that there are significant changes in attitudes associated with maturation, attitudes that influence later experience and conduct. In 1939, Stone made a study of the attitudes and interests of premenarchial and post-menarchial girls and found clear-cut differences. For example, the postmenarchial group favored responses indicating heterosexual interests more often than the other group, and showed also a greater interest in adornment and personal dis-

---

[17] *Ibid.*, pp. 47, 48, 49.

[18] For the influence on sex attitude of such factors as class and family, social attitudes, group participation and group status, see P. H. Hoch and J. Zubin, *op. cit.*, pp. 245–254; G. E. Seward, *Sex and the Social Order* (New York: McGraw-Hill, 1946).

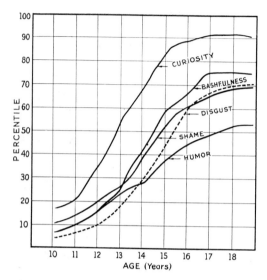

Fig. 11. Age of occurrence of sex attitudes in men. From R. R. Willoughby, "Sexuality in the Second Decade," **Monogr. Soc. Res. Child Develpm.**, Lafayette, Ind., Child Development Publications, 1937, **2**, No. 3.

play, less interest in active or vigorous games, and more interest in imaginative or daydreaming activities.[19] Such studies bring out clearly the relationship between sexual development and changes in attitudes and interests.

Of greater significance are the attitudes of youths toward sex practices. In some studies it has been found that attitudes toward sexual behavior are very liberal and contrary to moral and social restrictions; but it should be kept in mind that attitudes vary to a considerable extent with the character of the group being studied. Thus, Fry, on the basis of extensive clinical experience with students at Yale University, says, "Undergraduates, especially, are not radicals about sex. Their attitude — contrary to popular belief — seems to be conservative, embodying respect for virginity and disapproval of promiscuity."[20]

These different and sometimes contradictory findings can be explained only in terms of the groups studied and in terms of the determinants of the attitudes themselves. If the environment is such as to favor the development of liberal attitudes regarding sex matters, then we can expect one thing; if, on the other hand, youngsters grow up in an environment free of liberalism and promiscuity, we can expect totally different attitudes. As Fry remarks, "It is apparent from the cases that community and family sex standards are important among the factors which shape student attitudes toward sex. . . . The force of these influences is such that, despite an increase in the circulation of books on sex and a seemingly greater frankness about it in speech and press, student patients in general were ignorant or misinformed about sex and unable to consider the sexual impulse properly, as a natural biological force." And again, "Case histories under discussion are evidence of the effectiveness with which community attitudes toward sex are perpetuated. The community limits the dissemination of

---

[19] C. P. Stone, "The Attitudes and Interests of Premenarchial and Postmenarchial Girls," *J. Genet. Psychol.*, 1939, 57, 393–414. See also J. C. Whitehorn, "Sex Behavior and Sex Attitudes in Relation to Emotional Health," *Stanford Med. Bull.*, 1949, 7, 45–60.

[20] C. C. Fry, *op. cit.*, p. 100.

proper information, tolerates the spread of false notions, and inculcates a fear of sex. And as a result, the student's view of sex is compounded of misinformation and taboo."[21] The author's own experience with high-school and college youths thoroughly confirms these viewpoints.

These interpretations may be generalized to include the majority of youth. It is well known that, owing to social and educational trends in the past quarter century, attitudes toward sex and sex behavior have tended to become more liberal, and thus sex is not as taboo as formerly. However, it is doubtful whether this has resulted in greater freedom in sexual relations among youth, which is after all the criterion of the significance of changed attitudes. Moreover, family influences, cultural traditions, and environments vary so much that it is dangerous to generalize too broadly regarding either sex attitudes or behavior. In any individual, or in any homogeneous group of individuals, attitudes and conduct may be expected to reflect the social and cultural milieu which provides the framework for psychosexual development. Religious and moral principles, ideals, parental attitudes, early experiences, parent-child relationships, cultural traditions, and sex instruction will all play a part in determining attitudes and conduct. Any consideration of trends in psychosexual development apart from these factors, therefore, will lead to misunderstanding.[22]

---

[21] *Ibid.*, pp. 101, 107.

[22] The influence of religious affiliation and home background on sex attitudes is brought out clearly in Fleege's study of 2000 Catholic boys. See U. H. Fleege, *op. cit.*, pp. 284–286. See also the thorough study of this problem by A. B. Hollingshead, *Elmtown's Youth* (New York: Wiley, 1949).

Some Psychosexual Problems of Youths. Our understanding of the psychosexual experiences and behavior of teen-agers can be furthered a great deal by a study of the problems that youngsters encounter in this area. The changing character of these problems, incidentally, reflects the pattern of psychosexual maturation to an appreciable extent as the youngster moves toward maturity and adulthood. Needless to say, these problems are significant in themselves since they stand directly in the path of complete adjustment and integration. Thus a careful study of these difficulties, their incidence, their origin, and their general characteristics promises a much broader perspective on the youth problem in America.

The first question that arises in this connection has to do with the factors, in the adolescent himself or in the environment, that cause psychosexual difficulties. The first part of the answer to this question is very subtle, since it is development itself that sets the stage for many of the difficulties that occur. The growth of sex urges, the stimulation of sexual feeling and desire, and the increased capacity for such behavior are the first links in the chain of difficulties. These changes bring about a different orientation in the individual's thinking and feeling about himself, about the opposite sex, and about his future role, all of which may cause confusion, anxiety, or guilt. Clearly, in the absence of such development, there would not be much of a sex problem.

In this connection we must recognize that the sex drive is one of the most dynamic forces in the personality, and can act during adolescence to disrupt all the defenses erected by the ego during the latency period for its own security. The youngster, impelled by his impulses to sexual fantasy, dreams, masturbation, and other sexual practices, often finds that his ideals, principles, and other superego restrictions are of small avail in the face of his dynamic impulses. As Pearson points out:[23]

> With the onset of puberty, the individual finds that the increase in the force of the sexual drives inundates all his defenses; and he feels overwhelmed, because his ego, aided by his superego, no longer seems capable of remaining in control. The ego has to call in supplies of the energy which during the latency period it had used for exploring the external world to reinforce the defense mechanisms. . . . The energy mobilized by the ego which is directed to supplementing its defenses is, however, barely enough to maintain some equilibrium; and the ego consequently feels quite helpless. The main fear in early adolescence is the fear of the strength of the instincts — the fear, itself, being lest the individual fly to pieces. The adolescent, therefore, faces the same frightening experience that the individual who is becoming psychotic does.

This overwhelming of the adolescent ego by instinctual drives is basic to understanding the adolescent problem and some of the characteristic developments of the period. Under the avalanche of instinctual urges, the adolescent's ego feels weak and helpless, and he tries to strengthen it by forming close relationships with one or more people, or by having a best friend. These persons are not love objects but rather objects for identification by which the ego can be strengthened. Here we have one of the most striking instances of the intimate relationship between psychosexual development and social changes of the adolescent period.

Psychosexual Problems and the Culture of the Adolescent. In emphasizing the primacy of sex development in setting the stage for various problems, we must not lose sight of the strong influence of environmental and cultural factors. We referred to this fact briefly when discussing the cultural determinants of psychosexual development. Here we will use the same argument with respect to sexual problems. Naturally, the attitudes and restrictions of society regarding sexual expression and heterosexual relationships may be expected to play a leading role in creating problems for the adolescent. Wile points up this relationship in discussing the origin of such problems: "The philosophy of naturalness has taken the place of a philosophy of self-control for all generations of men. There has been a general release of sexual activity and a decline of inhibitions. . . . The absolute morality has lost regulative power and the new generation finds itself floundering in the restless sea of relative morality without great certainty as to the course to pursue to a safe haven."[24]

Wile discusses various cultural changes in Western civilization that have complicated the sex problems of youth. Perhaps the most important of these changes is the profound change in the status of modern woman, which has helped to destroy the old ideal of chastity. This change of status is not common to all societies, and is probably most strongly reflected in the American attitude toward women. Nevertheless, the idea of sex equality, feminine independence, the right to work outside the home, and

---

[23] G. H. J. Pearson, *Adolescence and the Conflict of Generations* (New York: Norton, 1958), p. 38.

[24] I. S. Wile, "The Sex Problems of Youth," *J. Soc. Hyg.*, 1930, 16, 421.

similar notions which are part of the philosophy of feminine emancipation, have spread to far corners of the earth. And along with this freedom comes greater freedom in all areas of behavior. Moreover, the changing role of women in modern society can have a profound effect on the relations between the sexes both at the adolescent and at the adult level. The growing boy's conception of womanhood cannot remain unaffected by this change. Such effects are often subtle, but no less profound and pervasive, as they affect heterosexual development.

Several other aspects of contemporary society are important in determining adolescent sexual problems. The more intimate biological knowledge regarding sex, greater familiarity with the art of manipulating sex behavior and relationships, and misinformation regarding the mental effects of sexual restraint, have led to less clandestine behavior, even though it is probable that modern youth is no more promiscuous than his counterpart of a generation ago. There is also increased stimulation of sexual tendencies, by reason of changes in style of clothing, lusty literature, sexy movies, and what amounts to pornographic art. In other words, the realities and secrets of sex are more openly flaunted today than they were a generation ago.

Finally, we may note that recent social and economic changes facilitate much greater contact between the sexes than was formerly the case, and often under conditions that offer a great deal of opportunity and temptation. In general, therefore, sex problems continue to reflect changes in the social order — greater freedom of expression, emphasis on hedonistic philosophy, emancipation of women, greater contact between the sexes, style of dress, literature, the break-down of tradition, disruption of family life, loss of parental authority, and particularly the loss of a moral and spiritual anchorage. All these cultural changes have seriously influenced the nature and the extent of psychosexual problems reflected in the thinking and behavior of modern youth.

Variety of Psychosexual Problems in Adolescence. Problems in this area may be studied from several viewpoints. Wile, for example, lists four categories of such problems: (1) those having to do with autoeroticism or masturbation; (2) those arising out of homosexual inclinations and practices; (3) those coincident with heterosexual practices; and (4) those deriving from sexual perversions of one kind or another.[25] This classification has considerable merit, especially in view of its similarity to recognizable stages of psychosexual development, but it is somewhat oversimplified. There are some sex problems that do not fit into this scheme, such as emotional conflicts or feelings of guilt that arise in connection with erotic dreams and nocturnal emissions — experiences that can lead to difficulties just as surely as do the more obvious sexual inclinations and practices. However, it is sexual behavior that occasions the greater number of emotional conflicts in adolescence, and it is to such behavior that we will give special attention. Major emphasis will be put on heterosexual problems, because these problems are of transcendent importance in the healthy development and the adequate adjustment of youth. We shall also study the problem of sex education because this is the best means of preventing psychosexual problems during the adolescent period.

---

[25] *Ibid.* See also O. M. Butterfield, *Love Problems of Adolescence* (New York: Teachers College, Columbia University, 1939).

HETEROSEXUAL DEVELOPMENT DURING ADOLESCENCE

The Beginnings of Love. The very young child is predominantly narcissistic and ego-centered rather than other-centered. It is not that the child is incapable of love; rather, he is more interested in his own pleasures, impulses, and need-gratifications than he is in the needs or welfare of other persons who constitute his social world. This is natural, because it takes time and development for the child to break away from his egocentricity and learn about the needs and rights of others. He loves his parents, his grandparents, his brothers and sisters; but he loves them less for themselves and more as they reflect the projection of his own egoistic needs. It should be understood that love relationships, although founded in a natural human need and capacity for affection, must nevertheless be learned.[26] That is why many rejected and unwanted children have a great deal of difficulty in establishing wholesome interpersonal relationships when they reach adulthood. *They have not learned how to love,* and therefore they do not know how to relate effectively to other persons in their environment. Inevitably, their records will show that during adolescence they formed very few and inadequate friendships, and often turned to perverse relationships like homosexuality for the gratification of basic needs. During the period of childhood, the groundwork for wholesome interpersonal relationships should be formed by loving and accepting parents who, in their relationship to the child, teach him how to love, how to be accepted, and how to accept others.

Adolescent Love Relationships. The normal psychosexual development of the adolescent period brings with it a pervasive social (heterosexual) reorientation of the individual teen-ager. This, again, does not mean that the preadolescent is *asocial,* since it is clear that in play activities, gang membership, etc., he is definitely involved in social relationships. However, these relationships are more peripheral and temporary than those of a later period. The child's orientation is still predominantly egocentric, and thus he is less likely to establish lasting social relationships.

The situation is different with the normal adolescent. His increasingly pervasive heterosexual orientation leads to the development of feelings, attitudes, interests, and relationships that put him in closer emotional contact with others, particularly persons of the opposite sex, and set the stage for the gradual emergence of *bona fide* love relationships. Thus, typically, the 15- or 16-year-old adolescent may actually fall in love, whereas this phenomenon is not observed in the young child. This early "puppy love" is the forerunner of more adequate love relationships which eventuate in courtship and marriage. It should be further observed that the same sort of heterosexual orientation leads to other social relationships manifested in play activities and games, the formation of cliques, memberships in various organizations both in and out of school, dating, partying, and social dancing. It is this orientation that is so completely distorted in cases where homosexual development supersedes heterosexual interests.

---

[26] See the booklet by Edith G. Neisser, *When Children Start Dating* (Chicago: Science Research Associates, 1954); also C. G. Moser, *Understanding Girls* (New York: Association Press, 1957), pp. 194–199; Mary C. Jones, "Guiding the Adolescent," *Progr. Educ.,* 1938, 15, 605–609.

The Phenomenon of Crushes. In the early stages of adolescence, the transition to a heterosexual outlook often involves what has been called a *homoerotic* phase, in which the youngster establishes a temporary but deep-seated relationship with some important person of the same sex. It cannot be said that this phenomenon is universal, since there are many instances in which such tendencies have not been experienced. The term *homo-eroticism* as used here is borrowed from Landis and his associates who define it as *"the tendency for persons of one sex to have strong libidinal attachment to members of their own sex."*[27] The most striking and probably the most common example of this kind of attachment is the phenomenon of *adolescent crushes.*[28]

So-called crushes occur typically in situations where some important person in the youngster's life, such as a well-liked teacher, counselor, or friend, embodies in more or less ideal form those qualities of mind and personality which the youngster regards as being most important or desirable. This hero worship leads to strong feelings of attachment and a reaction that the adolescent often interprets as love. The incidence of this homoerotic tendency seems to be quite high, as reported by different investigators, at least in the American culture. Landis and his co-workers report that crushes on chums or adults were very common in early adolescence among the 295 women studied. Of the entire group only 22

women reported that they had never experienced this emotional relationship in childhood or adolescence. According to these writers, "The homoerotic phase in personality development, as evidenced by strong emotional (libidinal) attachments to members of the same sex, was found to be a characteristic of the usual psychological status at certain ages. The frequency of intense crushes on chums and superiors during early adolescence showed that such attachments cannot be conceived as a deviation in the course of psychosexual development."[29]

Considerable support for the argument that crushes constitute a normal phase of psychosexual development is supplied by several investigations. In one study, questionnaires were submitted to one group of adolescents and postadolescents, and to a second group of teachers and counselors who in the course of their experience had been the objects of such attachments. Subjects included students in boys' and girls' high schools, in coeducational high schools, in men's and women's colleges, and in coeducational colleges and universities. The majority of the subjects were between 17 and 21 years of age. Results indicated that crushes were regarded by both teachers and counselors as very common, and the frequency of crushes reported by the students was very high. There was much less evidence of crushes among students in coeducational institutions, suggesting that environmental situations condition the development to an important extent.[30]

Crushes seem to occur most often between 16 and 20 years of age in boys, and between 14 and 18 in girls. Most of them are reported as lasting only from one to

---

[27] C. Landis, et al., op. cit., p. 51.
[28] See Elizabeth B. Hurlock and E. R. Klein, "Adolescent 'Crushes,'" *Child Develpm.*, 1934, 5, 63–80; G. H. J. Pearson, op. cit., p. 71; J. S. Plant, *The Envelope* (New York: Commonwealth Fund, 1950), Chap. 18; Irene M. Josselyn, "Growing to Adulthood," in Sidonie M. Gruenberg (ed.), *Our Children Today* (New York: Viking, 1955), pp. 179–180.

[29] C. Landis, et al., op. cit., p. 55.
[30] Elizabeth B. Hurlock and E. R. Klein, op. cit.

six months, although some last much longer. Boys seem to base the attraction on physical, or on both physical and mental qualities of the "loved object," whereas the attraction for girls seems to depend largely on mental qualities. Identification with the "loved object" probably lies at the basis of the crush since ideas and mannerisms of the idealized person are copied. In some instances the sex urge becomes involved in the crush relationship. Although men and women teachers reported a comparatively small percentage of youngsters as attempting physical advances, camp counselors reported a higher percentage of those who did than those who did not. As for the youngsters themselves, they were alike in craving affection, being affectionate themselves, making friends easily, and being sentimental.

These findings suggest that crushes are not universal since their development depends upon the personality of the individuals involved and on the environmental setting. In the Landis study it was found that subjects who had no homoerotic experiences reported equal fondness for both parents whereas homoerotics tended to record a marked preference for one of the parents. More of the latter group also recorded prepuberal sex explorations or aggression, a fact that is in line with our statement earlier regarding sexual behavior during the latency period. The development of homoerotic tendencies in youth, therefore, depends upon both intrinsic and extrinsic factors.

Adolescence is a period of idealism and of strong group tendencies, when complete heterosexual orientation has not yet been achieved; therefore, it is not surprising that homoerotic attachments should develop temporarily. That these relationships do not normally cause serious dis-

tortions in psychosexual development is attested by the fact that the majority of individuals studied are found to have made successful heterosexual adjustments in later life. "Our data secured from 295 women clearly showed that such crushes occurred so frequently and were so much a part of normal development that they could not be considered the differentiating factor between those who were homoerotic in adult life and those who were not. A continuation of crushes up to the age of 16 seemed to be of no importance in the final outcome of emotional or libidinal attachments. Most individuals who had such crushes did establish heterosexual attachments later without difficulty."[31] Perhaps the most important feature about these phenomena is that they presage the early beginnings of more adequate love relationships that occur later on. They indicate a swing away from the egocentricity of the child and a corresponding investment of affection and interest in other persons. Perhaps something like this is more or less necessary to effect the transition from the limited relationships of childhood to the more adult relationships of later adolescence.

The Adolescent Homosexual. The crush phenomenon is not the same thing as true homosexuality in which libidinal attachment to members of the same sex is deep, pervasive, and often irreversible. This is one of the most serious and most difficult problems that the counselor of youth encounters in his work. Unfortunately, while the incidence of homosexuality among adolescents is distressingly high, little is actually known regarding the causes of the phenomenon, and even less about effective treatment. True homosexuality is the kind of problem that

---

[31] C. Landis, et al., op. cit., p. 53.

the parent, the teacher, or the counselor should refer immediately for expert psychiatric treatment. It is not accessible to ordinary counseling, nor to the moral and spiritual principles and practices that may be used effectively with other types of adolescent problems. It is essentially a psychological problem rather than a moral one, and therefore the method of treatment should itself be psychological.[32]

Further Heterosexual Developments in Adolescence. The orientation of the adolescent toward sexual experience and activity is the most significant phase of psychosexual development. Temporary lapses into autoerotic behavior or crushes are after all merely instances of sexual exploration and transition even though they may constitute a serious problem themselves.

The development of the sexual impulse and its eruption during adolescence alters the nature of human experience and conduct in many ways. Just as we may refer to a social, moral, or religious consciousness, so too can we identify a heterosexual consciousness after puberty. Consciousness becomes as it were sexualized with the development of sexual impulses, curiosity, emotions, desires, and fantasy. Perceptions, images and thought are influenced by this process. For the first time members of the opposite sex become truly sexual objects. Feelings of shame, remorse, guilt, disgust, and embarrassment take on new meanings, or may be actually experienced for the first time. New interests and attitudes begin

to take shape, and basic needs like affection, experience, approval, and participation begin to function in terms of this new orientation. This pervasive character of psychosexual development often causes confusion in the minds of youth, because such desires, feelings, and thoughts are novel; they are to a great extent mentally inarticulate and the average youngster is not well equipped to deal with them.[33] This circumstance clearly defines the need for sympathetic understanding and instruction. Now more than ever the adolescent needs someone to whom he may turn for sound advice and counsel which, unfortunately, are not always available.

Of perhaps greater significance are the *social implications* of heterosexual development, since it is this change that brings members of the opposite sex within the orbit of social interests and activities. The gang activities of an earlier age are gradually replaced by those in which members of the other sex take an active role. Distinctly heterosexual interests, such as dating and social dancing, make their appearance. Boys and girls alike are no longer entirely satisfied with the company of members of their own sex. They begin to think and to act in terms of new-found relationships with persons of the opposite sex. Old friendships may be disrupted and new ones formed. Homoerotic inclinations are abandoned in favor of the more exciting experiences coincident with "puppy love." Then, as youth approaches the end of the adolescent period, there is a growing realization of the part he is to

[32] See Lauretta Bender and S. Paster, "Homosexual Trends in Children," *Amer. J. Orthopsychiat.*, 1941, 11, 730–744; J. S. Plant, *op. cit.*, Chap. 18; E. Bergler, *Homosexuality: Disease or Way of Life?* (New York: Hill & Wang, 1957); W. C. Bier and A. A. Schneiders (eds.), *Proceedings, Second Institute for the Clergy on Problems in Pastoral Psychology* (New York: Fordham University, 1958), pp. 140–191.

[33] See R. G. Kuhlen and B. Lee, "Personality Characteristics and Social Acceptability in Adolescence," *J. Educ. Psychol.*, 1943, 34, 321–340; E. H. Campbell, "The Social-Sex Development in Children," *Genet. Psychol. Monogr.*, 1939, 21, 463–552; J. S. Plant, *op. cit.*, Chap. 19; Ruth Strang, *The Adolescent Views Himself* (New York: McGraw-Hill, 1957), Chap. 9.

play later on in the social scheme as father or husband, mother or wife.

These changes, in turn, alter the youth's relationship to the home and parents. Confidence once reserved for family members may now be invested in the boy or girl singled out for special attention. Thoughts of marriage, of a home, and of a desirable vocation begin to enter the youngster's mind. As a result of the newer outlooks, there is something of a complete social reorientation, the social and sex consciousness of youth interacting at numerous points. Parents and counselors must understand these changes and realize that this development is an inevitable sequel to all that has gone before. How natural and significant such development is may be realized, however tragically, from those instances in which normal heterosexual development fails to take place, where the pattern of development takes an asexual or homosexual turn. It is these youngsters who constitute a serious problem in development, not those who seek the company or attention of members of the opposite sex. The effeminate boy who is ill at ease in the presence of other boys his own age, or the masculine girl who fails to see what the other girls find interesting in boys, are *the real problems*.

There are also moral and religious implications in heterosexual development, but these are more indirect in character. These aspects of adolescent life are affected only to the extent that hetero-sexual behavior *interferes with* or *complicates* moral and religious adjustment. It is conceivable that sexual development would run its course without affecting either the moral or the religious life of the individual, although this is not likely to happen. It is inconceivable, however, that the personal or social life of the individual should remain unaffected. This distinction is important to a fuller understanding of the implications of this problem.

Heterosexual Behavior in Adolescence. To trace accurately the course of psycho-sexual development it is important to distinguish between heterosexual *interest* and heterosexual *behavior*. The former is practically universal, whereas the extent of the latter depends upon individual background, environment, or culture. Many studies have been made in recent years of sex practices in certain societies, the best known in America being the Kinsey reports.[34] Nearly all these studies indicate that mild heterosexual practices are quite extensive among modern youth,

[34] A. C. Kinsey, W. B. Pomeroy, and C. E. Martin, *Sexual Behavior in the Human Male* (Philadelphia: Saunders, 1948); A. C. Kinsey, W. B. Pomeroy, C. E. Martin, and P. H. Gebhard, *Sexual Behavior in the Human Female* (Philadelphia: Saunders, 1953). A summary account of the earlier report is M. L. Ernst and D. Loth, *American Sexual Behavior and the Kinsey Report* (New York: Greystone, 1948). Other excellent studies of sexual behavior will be found in C. Landis, et al., *Sex in Development* (New York: Hoeber, 1940); P. H. Hoch and J. Zubin (eds.), *Psychosexual Development in Health and Disease* (New York: Grune & Stratton, 1949); C. S. Ford and F. A. Beach, *Patterns of Sexual Behavior* (New York: Harper, 1951).

Evaluations of the Kinsey studies will be found in A. Deutsch (ed.), *Sex Habits of American Men: a Symposium on the Kinsey Report* (New York: Prentice-Hall, 1948); L. M. Terman, "Kinsey's 'Sexual Behavior in the Human Male': Some Comments and Criticisms," *Psychol. Bull.*, 1948, *45*, 443–459; H. Hyman and J. E. Barmack, "Special Review: Sexual Behavior in the Human Female," *Psychol. Bull.*, 1954, *51*, 418–427; S. Hiltner, *Sex Ethics and the Kinsey Reports* (New York: Association, 1953); A. Ellis (ed.), *Sex Life of the American Woman and the Kinsey Report* (New York: Greenberg, 1954); E. Bergler and W. S. Kroger, *Kinsey's Myth of Female Sexuality* (New York: Grune & Stratton, 1954).

although no conclusions can be drawn for any single group. For example, in a study of 3000 Catholic high school girls, Knoebber found that only 10.4 per cent considered necking or petting a routine part of their relationship with boys.[35] These results might well be expected in view of the strong attitude the Church assumes toward such practices, and they indicate clearly how behavior is conditioned by group factors. In other studies, where the subjects were largely non-Catholic, the data indicate that limited heterosexual behavior is very extensive, running as high as 90 to 100 per cent. The beginning age of such practices is fairly constant for the different groups studied — around the ages of 15 and 16.

More important than the extent of heterosexual behavior are its *psychological implications*, which will vary with the kind of behavior involved. From the *moral* standpoint, we may presume that the majority of heterosexual practices are unacceptable; but from the standpoint of heterosexual and even postmarital adjustment, it can be argued that some of this behavior is in the nature of heterosexual exploration through which the individual becomes oriented more fully to the demands and characteristics of the opposite sex. For example, the Landis group found that significantly more of their normal than abnormal women had their first

date before the age of 16, and that more of the abnormals had never had a date with a boy. Also, 27 per cent of the abnormal single group had had no physical intimacies with men, whereas this was not reported by a single member of the normal group![36] These figures certainly suggest a relationship between adjustment and premarital behavior. However, we must also point out that the abnormal married women in the Landis group had had definitely more premarital experience than had either the normal groups, single or married, or the abnormal single group, which suggests that premarital sex experiences may also have *negative* effects on marital adjustment.

In his studies of male college students, Fry found definite *negative psychological effects* associated with all types of sex behavior. Even mild behavior, when practiced frequently, often leads to anxiety attacks, and the more overtly the individual acts contrary to sex taboos the higher is the emotional tension. Also, the more the behavior departs from accepted norms the greater the degree of tension. It should be noted that the psychological effects produced by these practices will vary with the dynamics of the behavior. If, for example, such behavior is an escape from the guilt of autosexuality, or is a means of expressing one's independence, or is used to establish sex status, the chances are that deep emotional conflicts and anxiety or guilt will result. On the other hand, if the behavior is simply a form of heterosexual exploration, negative effects may be definitely minimized.[37]

The psychological effects of heterosexual relationships will vary also with the

---

[35] Sister M. Knoebber, *Self-Revelation of the Adolescent Girl* (Milwaukee: Bruce, 1936). However, it should be noted that the findings in this study are not at all representative of data obtained from other groups. For example, in his study of 2000 Catholic boys, Fleege reports that less than half replied "No" to the question "Do you think it is part of the routine of going out with a girl to pet and neck?" Hollingshead also indicates high incidence of heterosexual behavior in his group — A. B. Hollingshead, *Elmtown's Youth* (New York: Wiley, 1949), pp. 419–424.

[36] C. Landis, *et al., op. cit.*

[37] M. J. Exner, *The Question of Petting* (New York: Association Press, 1933).

background of the individual and with the culture in which he lives. If such relationships and contacts are constantly portrayed as morally wrong, dangerous, or contrary to religious and social mores, then certainly the young person will experience remorse, fear, guilt, anxiety, and conflict whenever he becomes involved in this type of situation. Here especially understanding, instruction, wholesome ideals, and right attitudes are of great importance in helping youth to adjust adequately to these problems. Youngsters should from the very beginning of adolescence be guided toward healthy attitudes concerning marriage, their prospective role as husband or wife, and the right relationships between men and women. They must learn that the control and proper channeling of sex urges are an excellent investment in self-discipline and personal integration, and that growth of character and wholesome adjustment comes not from self-indulgence but from self-control.[38]

The Problem of Dating. Heterosexual relationships and behavior are exemplified most clearly perhaps in the practice of dating, a problem that has received a great deal of attention in recent years. Obviously, dating in itself is no problem since it may occur only once or twice in a year, and it may involve nothing more than a great deal of enjoyment for the youngsters and a quick "good night" when the episode is ended. It is only when dating begins too early in the youngster's life, occurs too frequently, and leads to intimacies, early love relationships, or outright sex behavior that it

looms as a serious problem. Unfortunately, the available evidence on dating indicates that this is exactly the situation among many youth, and therefore dating has become a serious problem for parents who have the responsibility of guiding their children toward a wholesome, mature, and well-adjusted adulthood. One can readily see that the adequate handling of the dating situation during adolescence can have profound implications for courtship and marriage, and this fact more than any other requires us to set up acceptable standards of dating behavior.[39]

Dating is, of course, a special instance of heterosexual orientation. It is a form of behavior that grows quite naturally out of the new-found interest of one sex in the other. It is a special type of socializing that has its counterpart in parties, picnics, outings, and other affairs in which the sexes come together for recreation, fun, and social participation. While initiated by the changes that are a part of psychosexual development, it is also dynamically influenced and channeled by the needs for affection, status, experience, and participation.

There is also of course a strong element of conformity, since the business of dating is patterned to an important extent by the social group or class to which one belongs. Important to note, therefore,

---

[38] On this point see R. Allers, Sex Psychology in Education, trans. by S. A. Raemers (St. Louis: Herder, 1937); J. A. O'Brien, Sex-Character Education (New York: Macmillan, 1953); T. F. Tucker, Sex Problems in Youth (London: Allen & Unwin, 1941).

[39] For patterns of dating behavior, see S. H. Lowrie, "Sex Differences and Age of Initial Dating," Soc. Forces, 1952, 30, 456–461; J. M. Seidman (ed.), The Adolescent: a Book of Readings (New York: Dryden, 1953), pp. 502–511. For differences in dating patterns, see the article by Helen Zotos, "How European Teen-Agers Date," The American Weekly, September 14, 1958. The author points out that dating among 14-year-olds is unknown and would be considered shocking. European teen-agers seldom pair off before they reach a mature 17 or 18 years of age, and then only with parental permission.

is the fact that while dating behavior is initiated by psychosexual development, it derives a great deal of its motivation from *other dynamic factors* in personality. Even *role expectations* may play a part in luring youth into the habit of dating. Therefore, when we combine all these factors into one motivational pattern we can see that dating is more or less an inevitable part of the adolescent's striving toward maturity.[40]

But dating behavior, when compared with other phases of social development, has unique characteristics of its own that may lead to difficulties. For one thing, unlike social parties or outings, dating is more or less a private affair, bringing together two persons in a more or less intimate relationship, and under circumstances that may be conducive to experiences or behavioral explorations detrimental to good adjustment. Moreover, dating has an *intrinsic purpose* that goes beyond the socializing effects of other social relationships. Dating is obviously the remote antecedent of courtship behavior, and thus is different in aim as compared with social dancing, group activities, and other behavior common to the adolescent period. For both of these reasons, dating as a form of social be-

havior must be more carefully evaluated and controlled.[41]

For purposes of evaluation, we should therefore distinguish between *occasional* and *steady* dating. Occasional dating, as when for example a boy takes a girl to a movie or to a school dance, cannot be regarded seriously, and certainly affords youngsters an opportunity for developing the social graces and skills that are necessary to adapt to the opposite sex. Even in such instances, however, it is better that the dating be controlled as to time and circumstances, and if possible the situation should be so arranged that several couples date together. Steady dating, on the other hand, is another matter. This form of dating is the immediate prelude to courtship, and therefore should not be encouraged or allowed *unless the probability of courtship actually exists*. There can be no justification for steady dating in the absence of a possible or actual love relationship that will lead to courtship; and certainly many adolescents interested in "going steady" are much too young to entertain the idea of love or courtship. Allowing young people to be together frequently, and often under circumstances that favor temptation and sexual excitement, can lead to serious difficulties.

We must always keep in mind that the adolescent is in a state of constant

---

[40] G. J. Mohr and Marian A. Despres, *The Stormy Decade: Adolescence* (New York: Random House, 1958): "Orientation toward the sexual role shifts during the course of adolescence. The early adolescent makes initial approaches to the opposite sex through dating and preliminary experimentation in petting, not because of impelling sexual feelings, but because of social expectations in his peer group" (pp. 143–144). See also W. W. Ehrmann, "Dating Behavior of College Students," *Marr. & Fam. Liv.*, 1952, 14, 322–326, and *Premarital Dating Behavior* (New York: Holt, 1959); J. R. Crist, "High School Dating as a Behavior System," *Marr. & Fam. Liv.*, 1953, 15, 23–28.

[41] For a moral evaluation of dating, see the comments in *Theology Digest* (Autumn, 1958), 6, No. 3. For suggestions on correct dating behavior, see Edith G. Neisser, *When Children Start Dating* (Chicago: Science Research Associates, 1951); and J. M. Seidman (ed.), *op. cit.*, pp. 499–502. See also J. R. Connery, "Steady Dating Among Adolescents," *Theol. Stud.*, 1958, 19, 73–80; G. Hagmaier, "The Other Side of Going Steady," *Information*, 1959, 73, 2–9, and R. H. Springer, "Adolescent Steady Dating: Is Marriage the Sole Justification?" *Hom. & Past. Rev.*, 1959, 59, 333–338.

David W. Corson from A. Devaney, N. Y.

Going steady is typical of teen-agers.

change, vacillation, and emotional uncertainty, and may find it difficult to
control his impulses and emotions. It is
certainly not wise, then, to create or to
tolerate situations that will strain the
little self-control the youth has. For these
reasons, dating at a very early age, say
between the ages of 10 and 15, should be
discouraged. As a prelude to courtship,
dating has no place in the life of a young
man or woman when the possibilities of
courtship and marriage are almost totally
excluded. When evaluating the probable
outcomes of adolescent behavior, it is always the better part of wisdom to give
the youngster time to reach a level of
stability and maturity which will enable
him to cope with behavioral situations.
We do not allow youngsters to vote, to
drink, to drive high-powered cars, or to

hold office until we feel that *they are
ready* for such responsibilities. Similarly,
where any form of heterosexual behavior
is concerned, we should be sure that
the person is ready to handle the
responsibility.

**Heterosexual Development and Role
Expectations.** The phenomenon of dating is in its own way a special aspect of
the adolescent's striving toward maturity,
and all that this means to him. Maturity
means the stability and privilege of socializing with the opposite sex, knowing how
to act in heterosexual situations, finding
the girl one wants to marry, and accepting the responsibilities of adulthood.
These aspirations may be interpreted as
role expectations, since the adolescent
often thinks about what he would like to
be when he grows up, his possible role

as a husband and father, and his role in the social and vocational world of which he expects to be a part. Dating, therefore, is a type of behavior that gives him a small opportunity to project himself into one of these roles; and in its own way it is a limited exploration in the area of love relationships. Dating, as well as social dancing, parties, and other heterosexual activities, are opportunities for teen-agers to sample these different roles. They need experience in socializing, in learning to relate adequately to the opposite sex, how to develop friendships, and how to interpret and react to the behavior of others. Without such experiences, the adolescent is only half mature, and will be confused with regard to his role expectations. Such behavior, therefore, should not be excluded or discouraged; rather, it should be controlled in such a way that the adolescent *gradually* learns the attitudes, skills, and mannerisms necessary to step into more mature roles.

Heterosexual Development and Sex Identity. Perhaps the most important aspect of psychosexual development, and one closely related to the adolescent's role expectations, is the achievement of sex identity to which reference has already been made in Chapter IV. In the absence of this identity, there is psychosexual confusion, insecurity with respect to future roles, and a generalized anxiety with respect to all types of sex realities and relationships. It is manifestly impossible for a person to relate adequately to others, particularly members of the opposite sex, unless he is sure in his own mind of *his own sex status.* Sex identity is the core of the total self-identity manifested by the mature, well-adjusted adult.

Thus, any serious doubt regarding one's masculinity or femininity creates a great deal of uncertainty. Masculinity is the natural prerogative of every man, and femininity the prerogative of every woman. Without this prerogative, a person feels lost and uncertain regarding his own status, and finds it impossible to relate adequately to members of the same sex as well as to those of the opposite sex. An effeminate boy will not be accepted by his classmates, and may be just as rudely rejected by girls, or show a decided lack of interest in them. A masculine girl is similarly handicapped in her relationships. Too often, such persons tend to develop relationships with members of the same sex that are decidedly unhealthy and destructive of personal integrity.

Sex identity, as we have already seen, comes from many sources. It has its beginning in the physical morphology of the person, since the boy is obviously different physically from the girl. It is also furthered to an important extent by the early identification of the child with important people in his life — the boy with the father and the girl with the mother. If, on the other hand, the boy identifies with the mother, or the girl with the father, the soil is prepared for failure in sex identification. This process of identification is continued into and through the adolescent period and is strongly reinforced by the morphological and physiological changes that occur at this time.

Normally, the boy develops morphological characteristics that clearly identify him as a male, and the girl even more strikingly develops physical characteristics that set her off as a female. When these physical differences are clearly marked, as they are in the normal person, the youngster is likely to develop a strong conviction of sex identity. A girl with a well-developed bust, or well-rounded hips, and the other contours that distinguish the female form, is not likely to think of herself as being masculine. The boy who can develop a beard, or the depth of voice that goes with masculinity, or the strength and skill that are characteristic of males, is not likely to feel insecure regarding his masculinity.

But more important than these physical developments are the psychological and social changes that occur in adolescence. If the boy is attractive to girls, and has opportunities to develop secure relationships with them, and to establish the fact of his prowess where girls are concerned, he is likely to achieve strong sex identity. If the young girl has numerous dates, is sought after by boys, and has a good share of distinctively heterosexual experiences, then certainly there is little likelihood of failure of sex identity. In this development, parents and teachers can play a very important role, insofar as they can foster proper identification, reassure the adolescent of his sex status, and provide the kind of experiences that are necessary for adequate psychosexual and heterosexual development. This is a most important responsibility, because the entire psychosexual picture can be seriously distorted whenever clear-cut sex identity is not achieved.

AUTOSEXUAL BEHAVIOR IN ADOLESCENTS

The Problem of Masturbation. One of the more serious sex problems, both in childhood and adolescence, is that of masturbation, not only because of its unusually high incidence, but more importantly because of its psychological effects. This fact is well known to counselors and clinicians, and is one of the reasons that the problem has received

such wide attention. Fortunately, because of these extensive investigations, attitudes toward this behavior have changed considerably in recent years. The older notion, still prevalent but gradually dying out, that masturbation leads to every form of physical and mental deterioration is being replaced by a more enlightened viewpoint of the true character of the problem, and by serious efforts to deal with it in an intelligent and scientific manner. This newer attitude does not signify a condoning of masturbation, but is based upon an objective appraisal of the actual physical and mental effects it produces.[42]

The need for the radical change of attitude toward masturbation is brought out clearly in a number of studies. In one such study, reported by Huschka, a group of 75 college freshmen were questioned regarding their beliefs as to the effects of masturbation. Of the group, 72 per cent had been told it would cause serious physical damage, 69 per cent that it would cause mental damage, and 52 per cent that it was a direct cause of insanity! Of the entire group only 5 per cent believed no serious damage would result. These results are confirmed by the findings of other investigators. Fry states that his college patients seemed uniformly to believe that masturbation was bad, that it devitalized the entire physical

---

[42] See R. J. Campbell, "Sexual Development and Pathology in the Second Decade," in W. C. Bier and A. A. Schneiders (eds.), *Proceedings of the Second Institute for the Clergy on Problems in Pastoral Psychology* (New York: Fordham University, 1958), pp. 99–113. See also pages 192–214 of these *Proceedings* for important distinctions between impulsive and habitual masturbation and its moral aspects. One of the most thorough studies of this problem is F. von Gagern, *The Problem of Onanism* (Westminster, Md: Newman, 1955), especially pp. 56–58, and Part III.

system, and caused mental deterioration. This was found to be the case particularly with those who practiced masturbation, in whom indulgence was usually accompanied by feelings of anxiety and by an intense preoccupation with the problem. These attitudes may be contrasted with those of the large majority of investigators of the problem who also universally agree that, whatever the negative moral and psychological effects of masturbation, it certainly does not lead to physical and mental deterioration.[43]

Incidence of Masturbation. If masturbation were an incidental and temporary event in the psychosexual development of the child or adolescent, it would probably receive scant attention. There are many persons, for example, who experience mild crushes or an isolated homosexual incident who are none the worse psychologically or physically for the experience and who have long since forgotten about it. Incidental experiences of this kind are not likely to be traumatic. This is not the case with masturbation. The incidence is extremely high and the practice generally continues for long periods of time, bringing in its wake many negative psychological effects.

The incidence of masturbation ranges from as low as 40 per cent to as high as 99 per cent, depending upon the group studied. Huschka, for example, reports an incidence of 44.4 per cent for 320 problem children. For the adolescent period, the figures are much higher. Ramsey reports an incidence of 98 per cent by age 15, and von Gagern cites data from vari-

ous investigators in the United States and Europe in which the incidence runs from 71 to 100 per cent. Fry subscribes to the notion that masturbation is practically universal, and argues on this basis that it cannot be regarded as abnormal. Willoughby, in his thorough study of the literature on sexuality in the second decade, also states that the practice is all but universal among boys, especially where sexual intercourse is prohibited by moral or social taboos. He cites the studies of Hamilton, Exner, and Mano, who report figures of 91 per cent, 79 per cent, and 84 per cent respectively for boys. Data on girls show much lower figures, percentages ranging from 26 to 59, the practice being more common among unmarried girls. In the Landis study of normal and abnormal women it was found that the practice was fairly widespread, although some of the subjects could not recall any masturbatory practice, and seemed completely unaware that such practices existed among women.[44]

Of some significance also is the time of onset for masturbation. Huschka reports that of the 142 children who had indulged the practice of masturbation, 54.3 per cent were known to have done so before the age of five years.[45] These, of course, were problem children for whom the incidence of masturbation usually runs much higher than for normals. In Helmon's study, 35 per cent of women and 9 per cent of men began before the tenth year, and 39 per cent and 31 per

---

[43] M. Huschka, "The Incidence and Character of Masturbation Threats in a Group of Problem Children," in F. S. Tompkins (ed.), Contemporary Psychopathology (Cambridge: Harvard University Press, 1943), pp. 49–62; C. C. Fry, Mental Health in College (New York: Commonwealth Fund, 1942), p. 99.

[44] M. Huschka, op. cit., p. 55; G. V. Ramsey, "The Sexual Development of Boys," Amer. J. Psychol., 1943, 56, 217–233, and Factors in the Sex Life of 291 Boys (Ann Arbor: Edwards, 1950), pp. 59–71; F. von Gagern, op. cit., pp. 65–68; C. C. Fry, op. cit., p. 116; R. R. Willoughby, "Sexuality in the Second Decade," Monogr. Soc. Res. Child Develpm., 1937, 2, No. 3; and C. Landis, et al., op. cit.

[45] M. Huschka, op. cit., p. 55.

cent of men between the eleventh and twelfth year.[46] Kinsey finds the peak at ten to twelve years, but most other writers would put it somewhat later. Before the age of thirteen, more girls than boys indulge the practice, but after thirteen the percentage of boys increases sharply. As far as can be determined, the act sometimes precedes sex feelings, at other times occurs simultaneously with them, or it may follow the first sexual stirrings. According to various reports, masturbation is learned most often accidentally, although it is also known to begin through example and instruction. Local irritation, accidental pressure of sex organs, and curiosity are mentioned as being the principal occasions for the start of the practice.

Psychological and Social Effects of Masturbation. The high incidence, early onset, and rapid habituation of the practice of masturbation poses serious problems for the parents and counselors of youths. This situation is complicated by the fact that masturbation is most often secret and solitary, and is securely established as a habit before the problem comes to anyone's attention. Moreover, masturbation produces serious psychological and social aftereffects that can be very damaging to healthy development and wholesome adjustment. As Campbell points out:

> While masturbation can be considered normal in certain situations, this is not to say that it is a simple alternative equivalent to proper sex relations, nor do we mean to imply that it can be put on the same level with involuntary nocturnal emissions as a form of natural activity. For we must recognize

that masturbation is not a fully adequate substitute — in contrast to sexual gratification with a love object, masturbation gives no feeling except for the self, physical pleasure becomes an end in itself, and the senses become dull and sated giving rise to a hunger for stimulation which seeks ever new ways of gratification but never leads to complete satisfaction. The easy access to satisfaction leads to an overdevelopment of fantasy life and an independence from the real object, with a resultant flight from reality into egocentricity and a moving away from object relationships.[47]

Thus, apart from the morality of the behavior, masturbation cannot be tolerated even from a strictly psychological point of view. Investigators find that there is a definite connection between masturbation and maladjustment. Fry remarks that when masturbation persists much beyond puberty, it assumes a disproportionate place and becomes the focus of physical and emotional disturbances. He found that the fear and guilt reactions to masturbation led to moodiness, depression, and anxiety; and these in turn gave rise on occasion to physical distress, such as fatigue, insomnia, or gastrointestinal upset.

> Preoccupation with the problem consumes much energy and practically every hour of the day it interferes with the ability to concentrate, and is frequently a factor in scholastic failure. Loss of memory is a common complaint. Shyness, inferiority feelings, and self-consciousness also accompany the student's concern with masturbation, coloring his social life and weakening his effectiveness as a member of the group. Guilty about his behavior, he is often embarrassed in the company of his fellow students. If he has a tendency to withdraw himself, his feelings of guilt reinforce the reaction. . . . The drain on his emo-

---

[46] As reported by R. R. Willoughby, op. cit. See also F. von Gagern, op. cit., pp. 70–76, who places the time of onset between 12 and 15 years of age normally.

[47] R. J. Campbell, op. cit., p. 107.

tional energy, his time, and his thought results in his being cut off from many activities and his feeling lonely and rejected by his environment.[48]

Moreover, immature sexual behavior of this kind interferes seriously with normal psychosexual development, and may cause or contribute to other forms of maladjustment, often perpetuating a dependent and immature relation between the individual and his family. It is effects such as these that cause masturbation to become a serious psychological problem. Perhaps its worst feature, psychologically, is that it is a decidedly *immature* response, and will if continued render an adequate psychosexual orientation and adjustment difficult to achieve. It is probable that in the majority of cases masturbation is discontinued or greatly lessened once a complete heterosexual orientation is achieved. As one writer remarks, "when satisfactory emotional and physical outlets are available the child who experiments with masturbation does not usually carry it to extremes and repeats it only occasionally."[49] In the meantime, however, the adolescent may need a great deal of understanding and guidance in order to cope with his sexual aberration.

Practical Hints in the Treatment of Masturbation. There is, of course, no sure "cure" for masturbation, but certain measures have proved helpful. One of these is *instruction* or *informative treatment.* Fry reports that many of his cases benefited from a more informed attitude toward sex, which is not surprising since it is often ignorance of the true character of sexuality that leads to inadequate adjustments in this area. Of importance also is training for adequate heterosexual adjustment, which is directly opposed to autosexuality. This principle is best understood in terms of the integral character of psychosexual adjustment. In other words, the more complete the adjustment of the individual along heterosexual lines, and the higher his developmental level, the less likely is the problem of masturbation to persist.

Finally, the problem of masturbation can be attacked from the standpoint of motivation. The sex drive can be sublimated into other channels of physical and mental activity that are socially and morally acceptable. Children whose time and energies are consumed in healthful recreational activities, or in chores of one kind or another, are partly guarded against autoerotic practices. Such measures may in turn be supplemented by the employment of principles, ideals, and religious practices which serve to strengthen protective resolutions. The effectiveness of this method will depend upon such factors as the age of the child, the manner in which motivational appeals are used, and their dynamic properties. Taken together these methods will ordinarily lead to success in the treatment of masturbation. If, however, the habit is of long standing, is symptomatic rather than habitual in nature,

---

[48] C. C. Fry, *Mental Health in College,* The Commonwealth Fund, p. 119. The negative effects of masturbation, particularly anxiety, guilt, and shame, have been observed by many investigators. For example, while Pearson argues that the adolescent boy in American culture who does not masturbate already suffers from a serious neurosis, he nevertheless feels that the feelings of fear and of sinfulness are inevitable concomitants of masturbation. He even argues that this fear is innate. G. H. J. Pearson, *Adolescence and the Conflict of Generations,* pp. 55–66. Hollingshead also remarks that the boys of his study "showed more evidence of guilt over their confessions of masturbation than they did over their sex relations with girls" (*op. cit.,* p. 417).

[49] C. Landis, *et al., op. cit.,* p. 210.

or is compulsive in character, psychotherapy may be the only effective remedy.[50]

PSYCHOSEXUAL DEVELOPMENT AND THE PROBLEM OF SEX INSTRUCTION

Significance of Sex Instruction. Although the right kind of knowledge, correctly imparted, is not enough to insure satisfactory psychosexual development, there is abundant and conclusive evidence to indicate that it is a significant contributing factor. Many investigators have reported the negative influence of false ideas on sexual behavior and experience, and that in many instances the better handling of sexual problems was encouraged by instruction regarding sex, and especially by the development of healthy attitudes toward it. Empirical studies indicate that attitudes toward sex are often fashioned haphazardly as are the patterns of sexual behavior; and that in all such cases the emotional responses related to sex behavior, such as feelings of guilt, shame, depression, and anxiety, are intensified by ignorance — often with serious consequences. Fry reports that in several instances students not well informed about sex were so ashamed and emotionally depressed by sexual experiences that they had attempted suicide.[51] Many such studies show that there is a direct relationship between adequacy of sex instruction and psychosexual adjustment. In promoting healthy development of youth, there is no substitute known that can take the place of knowledge and correct attitudes, imparted gradually at the right time and by the right persons.[52]

Inadequacy of Sex Information. Even more important than the lack of sex information are its inadequacy and the manner in which most of it is secured. Bell, for example, found that only 3 out of every 10 youths interviewed in the Maryland Youth Survey received most of their sex knowledge from parents or relatives, the chief source of such information for youth of all ages and religious groups being youths' contemporaries. Sixty-six per cent of the boys and 40 per cent of the girls in this study of 1300 youths reported that what they knew about sex was more or less limited to what friends of their own age had told them. Only a small percentage reported the school, books, or movies as sources of sex information. These data agree closely with those of many other studies.[53] Ramsey, studying the sex information of younger boys on nine specific items, found that approximately 90 per cent of first information is acquired from male companions or from experience. Even

---

[50] Excellent suggestions for the treatment of masturbation will be found in H. Joseph and G. Zern, *The Emotional Problems of Children: a Guide to Parents* (New York: Crown, 1954), Chap. 7; P. H. Hoch and J. Zubin (eds.), *Psychosexual Development* (New York: Grune and Stratton, 1949), pp. 151–152; J. R. Gallagher and H. I. Harris, *Emotional Problems of Adolescence* (New York: Oxford University Press, 1958), Chap. 3; F. von Gagern, *The Problem of Onanism*, pp. 102–108. Von Gagern flatly asserts that "the root of the matter is a healthy, positive education in sex, capable of imparting to the victim of self-abuse an affirmative attitude toward physical life" (p. 108). See A. A. Schneiders, "Masturbation," *Marriage* (September., 1959), pp. 38–43.

[51] C. C. Fry, *op. cit.*, pp. 106–107.

[52] See A. A. Schneiders, "The Problem of Sex Education: the Role of the Parent," in W. C. Bier and A. A. Schneiders (eds.), *op. cit.*, pp. 114–124; B. Y. Glassburg, "Educators Fear Sexuality — Not Sex," *Marr. & Fam. Liv.*, 1959, 21, 233–234.

[53] H. M. Bell, *Youth Tell Their Story* (Washington, D. C.: Amer. Council on Educ., 1938), pp. 40–42.

on less personal matters, such as the origin of babies, menstruation, etc., companions ranked first, although other sources became increasingly more important. Parents were rarely reported by this group as a source of information on sex matters. Ramsey also found that the school, movies, radio, printed materials, and adults other than the parents rarely were mentioned as sources of sex information.[54]

The complete inadequacy of sex information is brought out clearly in Fleege's extensive study of 2000 Catholic high school boys. As usual the results indicated that companions, books, and magazines were much more prolific sources of information than were parents, teachers, or priests. The results are indicated in Table 6.

TABLE 6

SOURCES FROM WHICH 2000 BOYS OBTAINED THEIR INFORMATION ON SEX*

Source of First Information				Source of Later Information		
Rank	Number	Per Cent	Source	Rank	Number	Per Cent
1	1098	54.9	Companions	1	995	49.8
2	692	34.6	The street	5	455	22.8
3	668	33.4	Books	2	777	38.9
4	497	24.9	Magazines	3	646	32.3
5	365	18.2	Priests	4	525	26.3
6	348	17.4	Father	9	346	17.3
7	308	15.4	Mother	10	313	15.7
8	298	14.9	Teachers	6	443	22.2
9	295	14.8	Movies	8	347	17.4
10	289	14.5	Newspapers	7	376	18.8
11	195	9.8	Older people	11	294	14.7
12	154	5.0	My brothers	12	149	7.5
13	101	4.0	Relatives	13	137	6.8
14	67	3.4	Doctor	14	129	6.5
15	40	2.0	My sisters	15	45	2.3
			Girl friends	16	24	1.7

* From U. H. Fleege, *Self-Revelation of the Adolescent Boy*, p. 272.

[54] G. V. Ramsey, "The Sex Information of Younger Boys," *Amer. J. Orthopsychiat.*, 1943, 13, 347–352.

TABLE 7

BOYS' RATINGS OF PARENTS' CONTRIBUTION TO SEX EDUCATION*

Source	None	Little	Fair	Adequate
Mother	60%	29%	10%	1%
Father	82	13	4	1
Either parent	55	32	12	1

*From G. V. Ramsey, "The Sex Information of Younger Boys," *Amer. J. Orthopsychiat.*, 350.[55]

These figures correspond generally with other published data which show that about 50 per cent of families make no attempt to give sex instruction to children. In the Ramsey study, 55 per cent of the boys questioned stated that neither parent had contributed anything whatever to their sex education. The results are indicated more fully in Table 7. These results agree with the report of the White House Conference Study of Adolescence, where the figure given for family instruction is 50 per cent.

Not only is the source of sex information generally poor, but the information itself is very inadequate. In the Landis study, nearly all of the 295 women reported that their early sex information was inadequate, and in the study by Peck and Wells, 57 per cent of the subjects felt that their sex information was poor.[56] This situation, bad as it is, is complicated by the fact that young persons possess a limited vocabulary of standard sex terms, although often acquainted with the phenomena to which the terms refer. This means that even if good printed material on sex were available, many youngsters would find it difficult to profit from it.[57]

[55] See also G. V. Ramsey, *Factors in the Sex Life of 291 Boys*, pp. 24–32.

[56] See also P. H. Hoch and J. Zubin, op. cit., p. 253.

[57] See "The Language Values of Sexual Expression," in J. S. Plant, *The Envelope*, Chap. 10. See also the responses of seventh and eighth

Age of Sex Information. Of importance also, especially from the standpoint of a good sex education program, is the age at which sex information is and should be obtained. In the Hattendorf study of the questions of young children concerning sex, it was found that 49.1 per cent of the 1763 questions were asked by preschool children between 2 and 5 years of age, whereas children between 6 and 10 years asked 40.1 per cent.[58] These data indicate that whether or not they are ready for such information, there is a great deal of curiosity regarding sex in young children.

Judging by the data of many studies in this area, information on sex and psychosexual development is obtained from as early as age 5 to adulthood. In Exner's study, 5 per cent of the subjects who had received instruction had it before the age of 12, 28 per cent between 12 and 15, and the remainder after the age of 15. In the Hughes study, boys were conscious of sex in conversation between the ages of 9 and 16, the average age being 12.6. Achilles reports that the men as well as the women in his study learned about sex intercourse at about the age of 13. Bromley and Britton found that two thirds of their 1364 college students had obtained their information concerning sex matters before leaving high school; and Terman found that 68 per cent of 678 men had knowledge of the

origin of babies by age 11.[59] These studies indicate that many items of sex information, whether obtained through instruction or other less desirable means, are often acquired before puberty or in the first years of the adolescent period, a fact which must be taken into account in developing an adequate program of sex instruction.

Effects of Sex Information. At what age sex instruction should begin, and what items of knowledge should be imparted at different age levels, depend upon the effects of early or late sex instruction. Opinions among different investigators vary considerably on this point. In any event, curiosity seems to be the most frequent effect encountered, and this itself may have negative effects. In one study, bad effects were reported by 21 per cent of the group between the ages of 5 and 15, and by 8 per cent of the 15 to 19 year olds, for whom a temptation effect was prominent. In still another study, bad effects of sex information were reported by 79 per cent of the group. In some instances the information led to sex practices and in others it created curiosity. For a sizable percentage (26 per cent) it gave rise to distorted notions regarding sex, or to vulgar sex thoughts.[60] Fleege, in his study of 2000 Catholic boys, found bad effects in a large number of cases, but these effects were found to vary a good deal with the source of sex information (see Figure 12). Where the information was predominantly wholesome, the effect was predominantly good, and vice versa. However, even unwholesome information seemed to produce some good effects, whereas wholesome information had practically no bad effects.

---

grade boys to a sexual vocabulary checklist in G. V. Ramsey, *Factors in the Sex Life of 291 Boys*, p. 17. For example, 93 per cent did not know the term *copulate*, 96 per cent were ignorant of the term *masturbation*, 72 per cent were unfamiliar with *intercourse*, and 79 per cent did not know what *semen* means.

[58] K. W. Hattendorf, "A Study of the Questions of Young Children Concerning Sex: a Phase of an Experimental Approach to Parent Education," *J. Soc. Psychol.*, 1932, 3, 37–65.

[59] As reported by R. R. Willoughby, *op. cit.*
[60] *Ibid.*

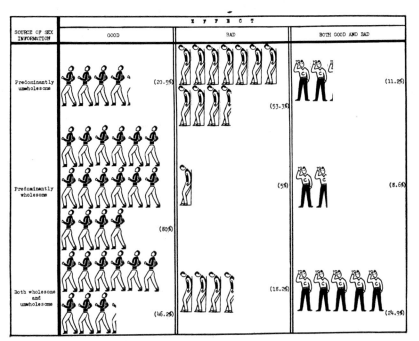

Fig. 12.   Comparison of source of sex information with effects. Each figure represents 5 per cent of the group supplying information. From U. H. Fleege, **Self-Revelation of the Adolescent Boy,** p. 281.

Sex Information Versus Sex Instruction. These data make it clear that sex information must be carefully distinguished from sex instruction, since effects vary considerably with the manner in which knowledge is acquired. When knowledge and attitudes are derived from parents or other responsible sources as part of a program of intelligent sex instruction, the effects are more often favorable. For example, of 102 subjects in the Exner group who denied sexual practices, 90 per cent had received instruction in sex matters; and of 401 who had received instruction, 60 per cent had begun sex habits before receiving the instructions, and only 10 per cent after receiving it. Moreover, 15 per cent of the subjects were led to stop the practices and 8 per cent tried to break off the habit after receiving instruction.[61] In other words, sex *information*, especially when acquired from such sources as companions, books, and movies, is likely to have bad effects, whereas with sex instruction the effects are likely to be good, especially when the information is imparted by the parents.

General Principles of Sex Instruction. From the results of empirical studies, and from the author's experience in training parents how to give sex instruction, several basic principles emerge that can be utilized effectively with the majority of children. These principles revolve around the questions When, What, and By Whom? An interesting set of sug-

[61] M. J. Exner, *Problems and Principles of Sex Education: a Study of 948 College Men* (New York: Association Press, 1915).

gestions is offered by Willoughby. On the basis of many studies of sex instruction he concludes that for adequate sex adjustment it is more favorable for girls: (a) to receive information regarding sex from the mother than from companions; (b) to learn about the mother's role in marriage before learning about the relationships between the parents, (c) to be repelled by such information than to experience a pleasant or neutral reaction, (d) to be encouraged rather than rebuffed by the parents or others when seeking sex knowledge, and (e) to learn sex facts early rather than late. Also, children should be taught the facts of sex physiology as soon as they show an interest in it. This knowledge should be acquired in proportion to their interest, it should be imparted by the parents, and instruction should be given in an entirely matter-of-fact manner.[62]

To these principles should be added the important rule that children should be carefully guarded against securing sex information from doubtful sources like companions, books, and movies. By intelligent instruction, geared to his interests, background, and capacities, the child should be trained in the formation of healthy attitudes and emotional reactions regarding the fundamental facts of sex development and the various problems to which such development is likely to give rise. The boy or girl should possess all the knowledge that is needed for adequate heterosexual adjustment — knowledge of the nature of psychosexual development, reproduction, the causes and effects of sexual practices, heterosexual relationships, and the like — imparted at an age when such knowledge becomes necessary and meaningful, and by persons who can be relied upon to

develop in youngsters the right attitudes regarding sex realities. By the same rule, imparting of knowledge too early or in the wrong amount, or the imparting of information for which the child is not yet prepared, should be carefully avoided.

Wile believes that knowledge of birth-control measures has led to a greater willingness among youths to experiment with sexual practices, and that modern ideas of marriage and divorce have given youths a greater freedom in the solving of sex problems. "Each sex dares now to view marriage as a means of sexual satisfaction with divorce available when sexual gratification diminishes or when some new sex enthusiasm hampers the successfull evolution of personality." This in turn has "a profound effect upon the ideas of youth concerning the necessity of fidelity and loyalty and the personal or social values of monogamy." Because of the ease of divorce, too many youths "see marriage as a house with exits open rather than a place of comfort, satisfaction and mutual development in terms not wholly sexual."[63] In the development of a program of sex instruction, these impressions might well be taken into account. The aim here must always be to develop wholesome attitudes and habits regarding sex behavior through the method of instruction rather than to correct faulty ones.[64]

Sex Adjustment in Adolescence. Sex adjustment, as we have noted in this chapter, is a complicated process. Many conflicts and difficulties can arise in this area to hamper the youth's efforts

---

[62] M. M. Willoughby, op. cit., pp. 7–9.

[63] I. S. Wile, "The Sex Problems of Youth," J. Soc. Hyg., 1930, 16, 413–427.

[64] See J. R. Cavanagh, Fundamental Marriage Counseling (Milwaukee: Bruce, 1957), Chap. 10, especially the principles on pp. 133–134; Sidonie M. Gruenberg (ed.), Our Children Today (New York: Viking, 1955), pp. 223–252.

to achieve maturity and adjustment. Through the medium of parental instruction and discipline, youths should be protected against experiences and situations such as pornographic literature, companions, movies, and parties that are the source of dangerous temptation and that make self-control extremely difficult. On the more positive side, the inculcation of moral and religious ideals, the development of wholesome religious practices, provision of adequate leisure facilities, the development of worthwhile ideals and attitudes regarding sex, marriage, and members of the opposite sex, and the development of a dynamic, healthy attitude toward self will go a long way toward solving the sex problems of youth. Above all, understanding on the part of parents and teachers is necessary, not only understanding of the nature of psychosexual development, but also of the problems with which youth is inevitably faced. Young people must be able to turn to the parents particularly with full confidence that they will get the advice and encouragement so sorely needed whenever such problems arise.

SELECTED READINGS

Davis, Maxine, Sex and the Adolescent (New York: Dial Press, 1958).

Deutsch, A. (ed.), Sex Habits of American Men (Englewood Cliffs, N. J.: Prentice-Hall, 1948).

Edelston, H., Problems of Adolescence (New York: Philosophical Library, 1956), Chaps. 3, 5, 6.

Farnham, Marynia F., The Adolescent (New York: Harper, 1951), Chaps. VIII and X.

Gallagher, J. R., and Harris, H. I., Emotional Problems of Adolescents (New York: Oxford University Press, 1958), Chap. III.

Himelhoch, J., and Fava, Sylvia (eds.), Sexual Behavior in American Society: an Appraisal of the First Two Kinsey Reports (New York: Norton, 1955).

Hoch, P. H., and Zubin, J., Psychosexual Development in Health and Disease (New York: Grune & Stratton, 1949).

Kirkendall, L. A., Sex Education as Human Relations (New York: Inor, 1950).

Landis, C., et al., Sex in Development (New York: Hoeber, 1940).

Pearson, G. H. J., Adolescence and the Conflict of Generations (New York: Norton, 1958), Chap. III.

Sattler, H. V., Parents, Children, and the Facts of Life (Patterson, N. J.: St. Anthony Guild Press, 1952).

Seidman, J. M. (ed.), The Adolescent: a Book of Readings (New York: Dryden, 1953), Chap. 15.

Seward, G. H., Sex and the Social Order (New York: McGraw-Hill, 1946).

von Gagern, F., The Problem of Onanism (Westminster, Md.: Newman Press, 1955).

PART III

The Psychology of Adolescence

Basic determinants of human conduct

Adolescent needs and motives

Feelings and emotions in adolescence

Motivational development during adolescence

Adolescence and the problem of discipline

Interests and activities of adolescents

Adolescent attitudes

Values, ideals, and goals in adolescence

Moral and religious development in adolescence

The emergence of character

CHAPTER VII

BASIC DETERMINANTS
OF HUMAN CONDUCT

*Human beings — husbands, wives, children, teen-agers, de-
linquents — are hard to understand, and mainly because we
cannot figure out why they act as they do. What is it that
the adolescent needs? Why? What is it that he wants?
Why? How does he get that way? If we can answer these
questions at all satisfactorily we will know a great deal more
about the modern teen-ager.*

MOTIVATION AND
HUMAN CONDUCT

Importance of Dynamic Psychology.
Mary Smith was a very attractive girl
and one of the most popular in her high-
school class. She never lacked a date
when she wanted one, and she was very
active in her school affairs. One would
be tempted to say that Mary was a
happy, well adjusted, and typical American girl. But there was one striking weakness in her personality — she had a great
deal of trouble in getting along with
people in authority. To her parents and
teachers she seemed hostile and rebellious, whereas to her peers she seemed
warm and accepting. She became particularly hostile whenever she was repri-
manded or frustrated in any way. Mary
didn't like this quality in her make-up
but she just couldn't seem to help herself
whenever authority figures "got in her
way." Why does Mary behave this way
in certain circumstances? What is the
origin of her hostility? These are the
kinds of questions to which *dynamic psy-*

chology addresses itself. It is a scientific
effort to determine the whys and where-
fores of human behavior. For every bit
of conduct there is a cause or reason of
some kind, no matter how unintelligible
it may seem at the time. Teen-agers
squeal with delight when their popular
singer turns on his charm, a boy runs
away from home, a gang member stabs
a rival gangster, a high-school graduate
decides to enter nursing, a student works
all summer to help with his tuition —
all of these behaviors and countless
others like them are instances of *motivated* conduct. They reflect basic human
needs, wants, desires, ideals, or goals; and
these *dynamic* factors explain why the
Marys and Joes, the Toms and Annes
of the teen-age world behave as they
do. This fact bears witness to the importance of dynamic psychology.[1]

Dynamic factors make human conduct
intelligible. When these factors are ob-

---

[1] For a thorough study of the relationship be-
tween dynamic factors and behavior, see H. S.
Tuttle, *Dynamic Psychology and Conduct* (New
York: Harper, 1949), especially Chapter 18.

145

scured, as in unconscious motivation, the actions stemming from them seem queer and unintelligible, as is true of many abnormal behavior patterns. The person who lies when he does not wish to, the boy who sets fires "just for fun," the homicidal "maniac" — these are persons whose actions are incomprehensible because we cannot discover an acceptable motive for their conduct. This essential relationship between conduct and motivation makes the study of motivational factors imperative for an understanding of human nature. In the absence of such knowledge the development of a practical psychology is impossible. To realize these aims, therefore, we must determine the basic needs and motives of human beings, the extent to which they are innate or acquired, what it is that makes them dynamic, the extent to which they are conditioned by the environment, and how they are related to each other. Because many of the questions of dynamic psychology remain unanswered, we shall undertake a more general discussion of motivation than would otherwise be necessary in a textbook on adolescent development.

Motivational Theories. The explanation of human behavior is complicated to some extent by the existence of different theories of motivation that have evolved in connection with the development of different schools of psychological thought. Theories can complicate the explanation of behavior because of their divergence, and because, at the same time, there is some truth in each one of them. These elements of course must be assimilated to any adequate theory of human motivation.

Take, for example, the stimulus-response and the physiological *hypotheses* of motivation, both of which are closely related in meaning. According to the physiological theory, all conduct is to be explained by reference to physiological drives or tensions, whereas the former hypothesis argues that behavior can be explained in terms of simple stimulus-response connections.[2] Both viewpoints suffer from the common fault of oversimplification. There are physiological drives, but to assert that *all* motivation is physiological in nature is simply contrary to fact. Needs like hunger and thirst are easily explained in terms of this theory; but it is stretching the point to say that the desire for knowledge or the quest for happiness is physical in nature. This theory, like so many others, is philosophically inadequate because it assumes that man's nature is exclusively physical, and thus it ignores the obvious facts regarding man's rational and spiritual characteristics.

The same arguments can be applied to the stimulus-response hypothesis. Everyone recognizes that certain responses can be explained in terms of a simple stimulus or stimulus-situation; and that behavior can be conditioned and reconditioned in complex ways so that many originally ineffective stimuli become effective in causing responses. It may well be that reactions which allegedly have their origin in an instinct

[2] The student interested in theories of motivation should consult M. R. Jones (ed.), *Nebraska Symposium on Motivation* (Lincoln: University of Nebraska Press, 1958); R. S. Woodworth, *Dynamics of Behavior* (New York: Holt, 1958), especially Chapter 5. For criticisms of motivation, see R. S. Peters, *The Concept of Motivation* (New York: Humanities Press, 1958); Magda B. Arnold, "Motivation and the Desire to Know," *Educ.*, 1956, 77, 220–226. See also the article, "A Neurological Approach to Motivation," by J. P. Stewart in M. R. Jones (ed.), *Nebraska Symposium on Motivation* (Lincoln: University of Nebraska Press, 1956), pp. 180–208.

or drive are actually the result of an intricate pattern of conditioning, the beginnings of which are obscured by the passage of time. Many social responses and personal habits seem to arise in this way. To just what extent conditioning determines human conduct one cannot say, because the boundaries between simple conditioning and more complex learning are not clearly marked. But it is certain that conditioning is not adequate as a principle of explanation for all human behavior. Conditioning is external, mechanical, and to some extent fortuitous; whereas the development of human motivation and conduct is based in large part on internal factors, and is autonomous and orderly. When the organism reaches a certain level of intellectual, emotional, and social development, some motivations become possible, but not before. Then one can motivate by appealing to reason, to "social consciousness," or to feelings, and no amount or degree of extraneous conditioning can be expected to achieve the same result. The principle of conditioning applies rather well to simpler organisms like infants and animals, but it fails completely to account for the more intricate pattern of motivation that characterizes adolescents and adults.

Of broader significance to dynamic psychology is the *instinct hypothesis*, which in one form or another has dominated human thought for centuries. In recent years this viewpoint is associated with the hormic psychology of McDougall, and with the hedonistic doctrine of Freud. Both of these outstanding theorists used the concept of instinct, but tailored it to fit their own ideas of human nature and motivation.

The instinct hypothesis supposes that living organisms are *innately* endowed with well-defined propensities or drives which initiate, influence, or determine the responses of the organism. These drives, or instincts, are antecedent to experience and learning. They are universal to the species and involve a fairly invariable mode of expression, which can be modified by external factors. At the core of each instinct is an impulse to activity of a specific kind, which is expressed by means of an innately determined psychophysical mechanism. This mechanism is activated by predetermined stimuli or situations, or in conjunction with some emotional response. On the basis of these criteria, and depending on the particular theory used, different instincts have been identified as the dynamic basis for human response.

These postulates have been called before the bar of psychological opinion and experimentation, with the result that the essential foundations of the instinct theory have been shaken.[3] What we accept in this case will depend on how rigidly we apply the criteria of instinctive behavior, and also on our interpretation of similarities and differences between human and animal life. In the case of the lower animals, for example, the criteria would seem to apply. Thus no one would argue against the instincts of sex, mating, food-seeking, exploration, and rest among the simpler organisms. And even in man one can discern patterns of behavior that fulfill the criteria of instinct. These facts led the evolutionary psychologists to apply the hypothesis without distinction to human behavior, since they view man as a direct descendant of infrahuman organisms.

[3] For a criticism of the instinct hypothesis from a sociological point of view, see P. H. Furfey, "The Group Life of the Adolescent," *J. Educ. Sociol.*, 1940, *14*, 195–204.

The reasoning here is good, but the metaphysics is bad. No matter what theory requires, the fact is that man is *essentially different* from the lower animals, since he possesses capacities and functions which transcend the capabilities of simple organisms. Understanding, judgment, reasoning, and language are activities that cannot be blinked away for the sake of a particular theory. This distinction between man and animal limits the application of the instinct hypothesis to human behavior. There are some human instincts like sex, hunger, thirst, rest, and comfort, but even these are influenced a great deal by man's rational nature. Because human beings possess understanding and can determine for themselves what they want to do and to become, the rigidity of instincts makes them unsuitable for explaining human responses. Man's ability to think, his capacity to chart his own destiny, the variability of his responses and their modifiability by experience, training, and self-discipline, rob the instinct hypothesis of its value *in re* human conduct.

We must take note, however, of one form of the instinct hypothesis which has been developed by Freud. Eventually, in the course of his theorizing, Freud advanced the view that human behavior is dominated by two basic drives — sex and *aggression*. The aim of sex is pleasure and to some extent self-fulfillment, whereas the aim of aggression is destruction. Both drives are subject to a great deal of distortion in the course of development, and these distortions help to explain neurotic, psychopathic, and other forms of abnormal behavior. Without losing sight of the facts of human nature just referred to, it can be argued that this simpler theory of human instincts is extremely useful in explaining human behavior. Freud's ideas about infantile sexuality, oral fixation, the latency period, the oedipal relationship, the development of hostility and hatred, and the combination of sex and aggression in sadism and masochism are repeatedly borne out by clinical experience. Admittedly, such a hypothesis may be better suited to the explanation of abnormal behavior than to normal responses, but the important point is that it is very helpful in understanding the troubled, confused, and perplexed adolescent. Such things as failure of sexual identity, homosexuality, and hostility toward one or another of the parents can be better explained in terms of Freudian theory than in terms of the other hypotheses available.

Freudian theory also makes extensive use of the concept of *unconscious motivation*, according to which many responses are determined or at least strongly influenced by psychic factors of which the individual himself is unaware. Bill may intensely dislike his biology teacher because he unconsciously identifies him with a rejecting father. Nancy may get emotionally involved with a young man because of strong oedipal attachments to her own father. Jim may find the company of girls distasteful because of unconscious homosexual tendencies based upon strong identification with his mother. And so on for numerous other motivational possibilities. Here we can see a close link between the sex-aggression theories of psychoanalysis and the concept of unconscious determinism. It is true too that in most of these instances the behavior tends toward the abnormal. Nevertheless, it must be admitted that without the concept of unconscious motivation a great deal of adolescent behavior and personality development could not be explained.

Opposed to the above hypotheses is the idea that human motivation is predominantly rational, that human beings for the most part act from reason. This may be called the *voluntaristic hypothesis*. Now while it is true that *many* of man's actions are the result of rational motives and volitional deliberation, it is poor psychology to contend that most of them are. An adequate dynamic psychology must take strict account of human needs, drives, instincts, and unconscious motivations which cannot be brought within the scope of a rigid voluntarism. It is a mistake to play down the fact of rational motivation; but it is just as serious a mistake to overemphasize it.

Our analysis of these several theories makes clear that all of them have some basis in actual fact. Perhaps their worst feature is oversimplification. Human motivation is extremely complex, and there is no simple pattern into which all of the facts will fit. No matter what level of development we are working with, any adequate theory of motivation must embrace all the facts and should avail itself of any theoretical formulations that promote a better understanding and a more thorough explanation of human behavior.

RANGE AND CLASSIFICATION OF MOTIVATIONAL FACTORS

The Meaning of Motivation.[4] Unfortunately, the term *motivation* has certain

[4] See the interesting article by R. A. Littman, "Motives, History and Causes," in M. R. Jones (ed.), *Nebraska Symposium on Motivation* (Lincoln: University of Nebraska Press, 1958), pp. 114–168; See also D. Bindra, *Motivation: a Systematic Reinterpretation* (New York: Ronald, 1959), especially Chap. 2. See also R. S. Harper, *Introductory Psychology* (Boston: Allyn & Bacon, 1958), Chap. 2.

implications that tend to prejudice one's thinking in favor of the voluntaristic hypothesis. The reason for this is that the term itself is derived from the word *motive* which is another name for *reason*, suggesting therefore that motivated conduct is always reasonable. In its strictest sense a motive is some thing or action, apprehended as valuable, that *moves* (or influences) a person to act in a certain manner. In this precise sense, therefore, motives are *values* which appeal to the will and make a rational decision possible. Thus education is a true motive since it is regarded intellectually as valuable; it is not something that satisfies an organic need in the manner that food satisfies hunger. To refer then to sensory or organic motives, as some writers do, is likely to lead to confusion. Yet needs and drives are like motives insofar as they influence the person to act; and since the terms *motivational* and *motivating*, used in the general sense to signify all dynamic tendencies, are already in common use, it would seem appropriate to bring all dynamic factors under the heading of *motivating factors*. In this way needs, impulses, tendencies, drives, desires, and motives come under one heading, even though the differences between them are clearly recognized.

Classification of Motivating Factors. Our understanding of the dynamics of behavior can be helped a great deal by a systematic classification of all motivating factors.[5] Such a classification should be as simple as possible yet embrace all of the known facts. This we have tried to do in Figure 13.

As this figure suggests, the dynamics of human conduct can be reduced to

[5] See the classification of motives in B. R. Sappenfield, *Personality Dynamics: an Integrative Psychology of Adjustment* (New York: Knopf, 1954), pp. 34–41.

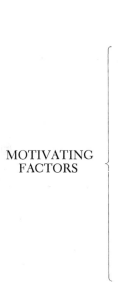

1. NEEDS

a) *Physiological needs:* hunger, thirst, elimination, rest, sex, activity, comfort, etc. (These are generally referred to as *instincts.*)

b) *Psychological and psychosocial needs:* security, status, achievement, self-identity, belonging, affection, independence, experience, social approval, recognition, conformity, psychological integrity, participation. (These needs may be classed as *desires* when the object or quality is consciously known.)

MOTIVATING FACTORS

2. MOTIVES

a) *Initiating motives:* ordinary reasons or values.

b) *Sustaining motives:* interests, attitudes, intentions, purposes, resolutions, aims, ambitions, principles, sentiments. (These may be called *determining tendencies.*)

3. GOALS AND IDEALS

a) *Immediate or remote*

b) *Personal and impersonal*

Fig. 13. Classification of motivating factors.

three basic types of motivating factors: (1) those which function independently of rational deliberation — the basic human *needs*; (2) those that are distinctively human insofar as they involve rational deliberation — the human *motives*; and (3) the *goals* and *ideals* that derive from the needs and motives. In addition, each of the three fundamental types of motivation is further subdivided so as to bring together into one group those factors that have common and distinguishing characteristics. Indicated also are certain relationships between the basic types of motivation and other dynamic factors such as instincts, desires, and determining tendencies.

HUMAN NEEDS: THEIR NATURE AND FUNCTION

Human Needs and Adjustment. The term *need* is familiar to both layman and psychologist, and may be defined as a *tension aroused within the organism by the absence of some thing or quality that is required for the welfare of the organism.* Needs may be organic or sensory, innate or acquired, conscious or unconscious. Thus the organism needs vitamins; it needs food and rest; it needs affection, security, and recognition. Because these things are required the satisfaction of needs is *basic to the process of adjustment;* and when needs are not satisfied in some way the organism tends toward illness or maladjustment.[6]

[6] For an interesting example of this principle, see the study of 200 overweight children by H. Bruch, "Obesity in Childhood and Personality Development," *Amer. J. Orthopsych*'*t.*, 1941, 11, 467–474. See also H. W. Bernard, *Mental Hygiene for Classroom Teachers* (New York: McGraw-Hill, 1952), Chap. 2; G. A. Gardner, "The Mental Health of Normal Adolescents," *Ment. Hyg.*, 1947, 31, 524–540; A. F. Bronner, "Emotional Problems of Adolescents," in *The*

A need, as distinguished from a motive therefore, is prior to and in part independent of knowledge. It originates not in the perception of an object as valuable, as does a motive or a desire, but in the *disequilibrium* caused by the absence of some *required* thing, such as food, rest, or affection. It is *intraorganic* — a physical or psychological tension that results when the organism does not possess some thing that it must have. A need, therefore, does not ordinarily begin with knowledge; it is merely the psychic equivalent of organic tension.

Needs always refer to *objects, qualities,* or *experiences.* As the organism develops, and sensory experiences become more sharply defined, the need that in infancy is only a vague tension or longing becomes in the adult a clearly felt *impulse.* An impulse, therefore, is a conscious tendency, not toward some thing but *toward some form of action or conduct* which leads to securing the thing needed. Impulses are typically conscious, whereas there may be no awareness of a functioning need. Thus a child may need vitamins or an adolescent may need security, as is evidenced by their behavior, but they may be unaware of the existence of the need. Hence, even at higher developmental levels, a need is not generated by cognition but by organic or psychological tension. This quality clearly distinguishes needs from motives and desires. Moreover, at the childhood and adolescent stages especially, needs are *mentally inarticulate*, a fact of considerable importance in understanding adolescent motivation and conduct.

In some instances needs develop into conscious impulses or desires, a process that is clearly developmental in character. Thus the inarticulate longing for affection noted in childhood crystallizes into a conscious experience or desire as familiarity with one's own experiences and longings increases. Satisfaction of this need through appropriate reactions on the part of others will also serve to make it more articulate. And if, in addition, the experience is given a definite label, as when parents remark that "All you want is attention," the need is brought into still clearer focus.

When needs become mentally articulate or clearly identified by others, as we may expect of needs like hunger, thirst, and rest, their gratification is usually more direct and certain. But when the impulse generated by a need is experienced as a vague and indescribable longing or want, the need may express itself in the form of *behavior explorations*, such as we often see in compulsive behavior. If the impulse were clearly identified, the unusual or bizarre behavior would be unnecessary, since the person would then seek the true object of the impulse. There would be no gain in utilizing random behavior for the gratification of the impulse. This concept of need in relation to impulse should enable us to understand more clearly the inexplicable conduct that often characterizes youth.

Needs in Relation to Other Dynamic Tendencies. When an impulse is universal in character, always aroused by the same stimulus or situation, and manifests itself independently of prior training or experience, it may be classed as an *instinct*. These criteria can be applied without exception to the physiological needs, but not as readily to the class of psychological or psychosocial needs.

Child's Emotions (Chicago: University of Chicago Press, 1930), pp. 222–223; Esther Lloyd-Jones and Ruth Fedder, *Coming of Age* (New York: McGraw-Hill, 1941), Chap. 2.

In the normal course of events, impulses are often frustrated by moral or social restrictions, or by some condition in the environment which prohibits their expression. It is then that *desire* or *want* is experienced, which may be described as a *mental tendency toward some object perceived as good but not actually possessed*. There is thus a close connection between needs, impulses, and desires.[7] But whereas basic needs must be gratified for the sake of adjustment, desires often refer to things one may or may not require, and therefore failure to satisfy them does not necessarily lead to maladjustment. This implies, of course, that desires do not always reflect needs since they can result from experience or cognition. The desire for food, for example, since it is based on a real need, can cause difficulties if not realized. The desire for money, on the other hand, in itself is of no serious import to adjustment. This fact, that we can apprehend something as good that is not actually necessary, lies at the basis of free choice. A motive or desire representing a thing not necessary can always be rejected.[8]

The Physiological Needs. Some dynamic tendencies are clearly rooted in physical structures and functions, and for this reason they are called *biogenic* or *physiological needs*.[9] This group includes such obvious requirements as hunger, thirst, rest, activity, comfort, elimination, and sex — all of which are known to originate in physiological changes or imbalances. We have added sex to this list because it has an unmistakable physiological basis, but we must recognize that it is different from other needs in its relationship to adjustment. Sex is like hunger, thirst, or rest in its dynamic properties; but it is unlike them insofar as its gratification can be deferred without impairing the adjustment of the individual. We know, of course, that sexual frustration and conflict cause a great deal of difficulty in the lives of many adolescents; but the point still remains that many persons are able to defer sexual gratification for indefinite periods of time without developing symptomatic or maladjustive behavior.

> Sexual activity is not, in the biological sense, essential to the well-being of the individual. Despite the fact that arguments to the contrary often provide a convenient rationalization during certain stages of life, no one ever died for the lack of sex. Sexual activity, of course, has an indispensable function, but it is indispensable to the species rather than to the individual.[10]

Moreover, unlike other physiological needs, sex impulses can be *sublimated* into other channels of activity that are socially and morally acceptable. The reason for this peculiar relation to adjustment is that the sex impulse is essentially directed toward the preservation of the species, whereas other physiological needs are directed toward preservation of the *individual*. Therefore, when these latter needs are not gratified,

---

[7] Desires may be *sensory* or *rational*, since a volitional impulse may be blocked or thwarted in the same way that a sensory or organic impulse is. Volitional impulses, however, are initiated by intellectual evaluation and not by the arousal of a need.

[8] See G. H. J. Pearson, *Adolescents and the Conflict of Generations* (New York: Norton, 1958), p. 165, for a discussion of the difference between wants and needs.

[9] See the list of biogenic and psychogenic motives, based on Murray's classification, in B. R. Sappenfield, *op. cit.*, pp. 38–41. Murray lists 13 biogenic and 22 psychogenic motives, some of which are subdivided into more specific needs.

[10] F. A. Beach, "Characteristics of Masculine 'Sex Drive,'" in M. R. Jones (ed.), *Nebraska Symposium on Motivation* (Lincoln: University of Nebraska Press, 1956), p. 3.

serious maladjustment or death will result.

The physiological needs, excluding sex and activity, do not play as dominant a role in the adjustive behavior of persons as do other personality needs. However, this should not lead to the conclusion that they are relatively unimportant. Physical needs are related to physical adjustment in exactly the same way that psychological needs are related to behavioral adjustment. And the physical well-being of the individual lays the groundwork for mental health. In interpreting the behavior of adolescents, therefore, all determinants of behavior should be taken into consideration.

The Psychological and Psychosocial Needs. The *psychological needs*, which include the most important dynamic factors in the human personality, offer the greatest challenge to dynamic psychology. For one thing, it is difficult to determine their precise nature and thus specify whether we are dealing with universal, instinctive urges or drives, or whether they are the residues of experience, conditioning, and development. For another, they are intrinsically related to psychological adjustment and mental health, and it is well known in clinical psychology and psychiatry that frustration of these basic needs can lead to serious maladjustment and disorganization of personality. This is particularly true of needs like security, affection, status, belonging, independence, and self-identity. But in some degree it is true of all psychological needs. The behavior of persons at all levels of development attests unmistakably to the adjustive significance of these drives.

Somewhat the same interpretation can be given to the *psychosocial needs*, which include four fundamental drives: con-

formity, recognition, social approval, and participation.[11] Other needs, such as belonging, status, and achievement are closely related to the social needs and serve to reinforce their dynamic influence on behavior. These relations will be studied more intently later on. The psychosocial needs do not ordinarily exercise the degree of influence on behavior that psychological needs do, but they are nevertheless importantly related to the social development and adjustment of individuals, particularly teen-agers.

Without going too far into the ontology of these distinctively human needs, we may ask briefly what it is in human nature that determines their existence. The answer is simple. Just as physiological needs exist because human beings have a physical nature, psychological and psychosocial needs exist because man is fundamentally psychic and social in his make-up. Real, innate needs exist whenever the nature of the organism is such as to require certain experiences, qualities, or activities. Children need affection because love is a requirement of human nature. Adolescents need independence because individuality is an essential ingredient of human nature. Adults need security because they are not totally self-sufficient and omnipotent. In other words, human nature being what it is, there are certain requirements that must be fulfilled for health, happiness, and stability; and these requirements we call needs.

[11] For an interesting variation on the concept of psychosocial needs, see the description and development of the concept of interpersonal needs in W. C. Schutz, *FIRO: a Three-Dimensional Theory of Interpersonal Behavior* (New York: Rinehart, 1958), Chaps. 2 and 3. Schutz's concept is vastly different from the simplified viewpoint presented here, but it has many fruitful suggestions for the theory of interpersonal behavior.

The Question of Intellectual and Spiritual Needs. Human beings hunger and thirst for knowledge, for immortality, for creativity, and for eternal salvation just as surely and as dynamically as they do for bread, for love, or for recognition. Their behavior attests this fact in a hundred different ways and in all societies. The question, therefore, of the existence of intellectual and spiritual needs is answered ontologically in exactly the same way as we answered the question regarding the physiological and psychological needs. If human nature includes intellectual and spiritual facets, then it is inevitable that certain requirements of this type will emerge in the course of development, requirements that have as much title to the term *need* as do other natural requirements. The child manifests such needs in his curiosity and his love of reading. The adolescent reflects similar needs in his eternal quest for an adequate religious orientation or for a stable philosophy of life. These are real human needs, and they are as closely tied in with the whole problem of human adjustment as are other fundamental requirements. The adolescent who is stifled in his creativity, or who flounders hopelessly in a sea of distorted values, will become maladjusted just as surely as one who fails to secure self-identity or another who cannot handle sex problems.

Here we have, then, a brief panorama of human needs at different levels of functioning. All of them are important to an understanding of human behavior and adjustment, and all of them play a significant role in determining the pattern of the teen-ager's life. In a later chapter we shall deal with these needs in direct relationship to adolescent conduct (Chapter VIII).

HUMAN MOTIVES: THEIR NATURE AND FUNCTION

Motives and Values. The second level of human motivation is defined in terms of *motives*, which may be described as dynamic factors that transcend human needs in the same way that intellectual knowledge transcends sensory experience. More precisely, motives may be regarded as *values*, that is, things or qualities which are desired because they are *apprehended as good*. This concept enables us to broaden the term *motive* to include other dynamic factors, such as interests, attitudes, and ideals, which are often derived through processes of deliberation and evaluation. In our earlier classification we identified these factors as *sustaining motives*. Both ordinary and sustaining motives are distinctively human tendencies which owe their development to the capacities for understanding, generalization, and evaluation characteristic of human beings. They are, therefore, the *rational* grounds of human conduct.

Such factors are of great importance at any level of development, since an appeal to reason often is the last recourse in our efforts to bring about desirable conduct; but they are of particular significance to the period of youth because the higher level of intellectual development makes rational motivation more feasible. Once this level is achieved, youth can be persuaded to act in desirable ways by pointing out the value to be derived from right conduct, and the evil that follows from wrong conduct. This capacity for insight into the rightness or wrongness of action makes truly *rational* conduct possible. Animals and young children do not act rationally because it is not within their power to discern the good (or the evil) in different experiences and actions.

To tell a very young child that he should take cod-liver oil because it is good for him is, psychologically, a waste of time. He simply does not know what you mean by "good." In the case of older children and adolescents, however, the situation is quite different. Experience, coupled with the development of intellect, has given them a concept of "goodness." Then they can be stimulated to seek and to strive after that which they perceive to be good. Older children and youth act not only from blind impulse or need, but from reason as well; and much of their behavior gradually assumes the character of rationally motivated conduct. Obviously the more dynamic these motives, and the more appealing they are, the more will they tend to supersede the influence of the nonrational motivating factors with which they often come into conflict.

The division of rational motives into *initiating* and *sustaining* can be of considerable help in understanding the dynamics of rational conduct. Initiating motives or ordinary reasons may be thought of as largely temporary in nature. They initiate action, but do not ordinarily become an integral part of the motivational system. A student in high school, for instance, may see clearly the value of a college education, and may experience a strong tendency toward this goal. Perhaps his thinking and his actions become oriented toward this end. The motive thus serves to initiate behavior and thinking, even though the goal itself is never reached. Such motives are, of course, indispensable to the dynamics of human conduct, particularly conduct of a rational kind. They may, however, be inadequate in themselves to insure action; they may not possess the power necessary to "see an action through."

Many efforts begun with great vigor have dwindled into a series of purposeless gestures because they were poorly sustained. In other words, the "goodness" of the goal may not possess the dynamic attraction necessary to complete an action or carry out a plan.

At this point sustaining motives often play a dominant role. These are motives which, through experience and habituation, have developed into relatively permanent *determining tendencies*, which become integral parts of a stable motivational system. These sustaining motives are so called because they keep an action going; they revitalize conduct when effort begins to lag. Interests, attitudes, resolutions, ideals, principles, and sentiments are typical examples of this group. While often inconspicuous, and hardly realized in consciousness at all, they form the background for numerous decisions and actions. Moreover, they are individualized, the residue of *personal* experiences, training, and self-discipline; and when one is aroused, others are likely to be stimulated also, lending their dynamic strength to the motivation of the act.

Because these motives are value-oriented, and also because they exist as habitual dispositions toward some mode of action, they often possess a great deal of motivating power. Every teacher, for example, knows that the student without an interest in his work, or without clearly defined purposes, has little chance of attaining a high academic level. Every social worker is aware of the great influence of attitudes and principles in the shaping of socially and morally acceptable conduct. These are motivating factors that make it possible for a person to achieve his goals when all ordinary motives or even basic needs fail. To some of these factors — particularly interests, attitudes, ideals, and principles — we shall return in subsequent chapters to determine more exactly the part they play in the motivation of adolescent conduct (Chapters XII–XIV).

GOALS AND IDEALS: THEIR NATURE AND FUNCTION

Goals, Ideals, and Motives. The dynamics of human needs and motives is complemented and completed by the development of goals and ideals; and among all three classes of these dynamic factors there are close interdependent relationships. Inherent in the concept of goal is the element of *futurity*. A goal is an end toward which one strives that is *not now* realizable but *may be* realized in the future. It is like a motive in that it is perceived as desirable; but it is in a sense external to the motivational system insofar as it is represented to one's self as only distantly realizable. A motive, on the other hand, is immediate and intrinsic. A high school boy, let us say, actively seeks summer employment. If we inquire into his reasons or motives for this act, we find that it is because he needs money, or that he would rather work than be idle, or that he wants to help support his family — all of which are perceived as good. But on closer examination we might also find that a goal is involved — completing a college education. All these factors may coalesce to sustain the youngster in his search for work. The motives behind the behavior are characterized by the elements of immediacy and temporariness, and the goals by the qualities of remoteness and permanence. This immediacy applies only to initiating and not to sustaining motives, the latter also having the character of permanence. Values, principles, and attitudes are not sought for as goals but act rather as spurs toward the realization of goals.

Goals are closely related to *ideals*, and there are times when the two cannot be clearly distinguished. A student in high school may have as his goal a career in medicine, and this may also be perceived as the ideal vocation. A young boy studying for the priesthood is motivated both by a goal and by an ideal which are closely interwoven with each other. The ideal in such instances may be regarded as a value or a goal *raised to a standard of excellence* or even of perfection. This does not mean that all ideals are goals, as we shall see more fully later on (Chapter XIV) but only that ideals and goals are often closely related.

Dynamic Aspects of Goals and Ideals. The dynamic quality of goals is determined as much by their relation to fundamental needs as by their value or desirability. Why, for instance, do some people seek fame or position? They do so not only because these things are desirable, but even more so because they satisfy a need for status, approval, or recognition. In such instances, in fact, it would be more correct to say that the goal is desired because it satisfies these basic drives.

This interpretation does not apply to all goals, and even less to ideals. Many goals and ideals are determined by the value they possess. In general, the "higher" the goal, and the more altruistic and unselfish it is, the more likely is its dynamic quality traceable to the factor of value. The service of humanity, the welfare of one's family, the contribution to knowledge through painstaking research, the improvement of society — these are goals whose driving power may be quite unrelated to needs. These goals are attractive not because they satisfy hunger, or because they guarantee approval, recognition, or security, but because *they are valuable in themselves*. Because of this fact goals like fame and fortune turn to ashes when possessed, whereas the altruistic and unselfish goals become ever more attractive. They never lose their appeal, and they seldom fail to sustain the person in his greatest trials and most vigorous efforts. In a functional sense, therefore, goals are similar to sustaining motives, since they serve to sustain a course of action over a period of time. Goals and ideals of this type, therefore, are in a real sense a measure of a person's character.

Goals and Incentives. We should add a word here regarding *incentives*, which, like ordinary motives, are characterized by immediacy. An incentive is the external counterpart of a motive; it is an immediately realizable aim that contributes to the achievement of more remote goals. One strives toward goals but not toward incentives; rather the incentive *reinforces* the striving toward a goal already determined upon. Incentives are in that sense extrinsic to the motivational situation. They are additional motivating factors that are brought in at a tangent to the direction which the action has already assumed. Thus, we may say that the goal of a student in high school is graduation, whereas pleasing his parents is one of his incentives.

Because incentives are generally extrinsic to the basic motivational process, they may possess little dynamic value; but the more closely they can be tied in with goals, the more dynamic they will become. Thus, if the goal of a working-man is the accumulation of money, bonuses become powerful incentives, but the reverse may be true if his goals are unrelated to the making of money. It is also true, of course, that incentives increase in power as they are made to elicit basic needs. Children strive to get their names on published honor roles in order to win recognition, status, or approval. In other words, the more that incentives can be made intrinsic through identification with needs, motives, or goals, the more dynamic will they be. In applying the principles of motivation to adolescent conduct, these relationships should be kept in mind.

Interdependence of Needs, Motives, and Goals. Before leaving this phase of dynamic psychology, we would like to emphasize the basic relationships between needs, motives, and goals. This is no more than we should expect in view of the unity of the organism, but it is a fact easily overlooked. Quite often the capacity of the human mind to conceive and formulate values beyond the immediate aim of some instinct or need causes us to overemphasize the importance of rational motivation, and to forget that these higher motives or values are in many instances a reflection of basic physiological or psychological needs. We do not mean to imply that all volition is basically need-determined, but we must keep in mind the interdependence of motivating factors.

The fact that rational motives are often rooted in some basic need enables us to understand more clearly the mechanism of *rationalization*. Thus any object or line of conduct may be conceived as valuable not so much because it is objectively so but because it satisfies some definite need in the personality. For example, the high-school girl may desire an education in nursing because she clearly perceives it as valuable, wherein the desire aroused is a true volition. Or — and this is the significant fact — she may seek such an education for reasons of status, social approval, or security, or to compensate for a feeling of inferiority, and this without a clear knowledge (if any at all) of the part these factors play in her decisions. At such times the individual, pressed for a motive, rationalizes his actions since it is natural to regard one's own conduct as being rational. Thus many seemingly rational actions and decisions have their ultimate origin in basic human needs, including at times those of a physiological nature. This reminds us of the psychoanalytic concept of *sublimation*, according to which the sex drive is diverted into channels of conduct to which the drive itself bears no essential relationship. Much the same may be said for aggression. Instances such as these do not exclude the possibility that the conduct is at the same time rationally motivated, in which case the volition is simply reinforced by the need involved.

This connection between motives and needs suggests interesting possibilities for the applied psychology of motivation. Every parent and teacher knows with what great difficulty purely rational motives are employed with children and adolescents. Too often a knowledge of what is right and good is not enough; to this knowledge must be added some other element that will make it dynamic. Various studies among delinquents and criminals indicate quite clearly that a knowledge of right and wrong of itself is no certain deterrent to wrong conduct. It is a well-known fact that many criminals outstrip the average noncriminal in moral insights and judgments. Where ethical values are in themselves inade-

quate, basic needs may often be employed to insure desired conduct. Appeals to affection, security, conformity, achievement, or recognition may be effective when all other motivation has failed. This reinforcement of rational motives by needs in no sense detracts from the quality of human volition. There is no good reason why human needs should not be utilized in activating conduct which, under different circumstances, would be entirely rational in character. In fact, this would seem to be the more effective means of eliciting the type of conduct necessary to happiness and adjustment.

PROPERTIES OF MOTIVATING FACTORS[12]

Motivating Factors Are Dynamic. A fundamental property of motivational tendencies is their dynamic quality. The term *dynamic* signifies that motivations *incline* the organism toward some object, act, or experience. Thus, interests, desires, and needs cause a reorganization of the psychological field in such a way that the organism becomes more receptive to certain stimuli, and begins actively seeking certain objects or experiences. This dynamism does not result from the creation or release of energy, as the term might suggest, but from a state of tension or disequilibrium caused by the lack of some thing or quality that is desirable, or that is required for the well-being of the organism.

This mechanism generally involves the development of a conscious tendency

---

[12] See B. R. Sappenfield, *Personality Dynamics: an Integrative Psychology of Adjustment*, pp. 41–50, for a good discussion of motivational principles.

toward some object or form of action that often leads to an overt response. This principle of dynamics does not apply with equal force to all motivation, because some tendencies are merely derivatives of more fundamental ones. Attitudes, for example, are dynamic, but probably only insofar as they are related to some basic need or value. Without such a basis the attitude only faintly resembles a true dynamic tendency.

Factors other than tension also contribute to the dynamics of motivation. For example, emotionally toned processes have more dynamic quality than those that are not emotional. Indeed, it is necessary at times to invest motivational tendencies with emotional value in order for them to become really dynamic. This is especially true with such motives as principles and ideals. The person in whom principles are bound up with intense feelings is much more strongly motivated than one in whom they are based solely upon intellectual conviction. Emotions have their own dynamic quality and are closely related to basic needs, and thus they have obvious implications for the dynamics of human conduct.

Allied to this relationship is the dynamic quality of pleasure and pain. So pervasive is the quality of pleasure in human motivation that Freud elevated it into a distinct principle of motivation. While one may not agree entirely with the concept of the "pleasure principle" as developed by Freud, it is certainly true that many impulses owe their dynamic power to the quality of pleasure. We do things which are pleasurable, and we avoid doing things which are painful, at least as a general rule. Pleasure and pain are of their nature dynamic simply because the one is agreeable and reduces

tension, whereas the other increases tension by reason of its disagreeable quality.[13]

This is a *primary law* of the dynamics of human action. In any motivational situation, despite the presence of contrary motives of a higher nature, the organism cannot escape a natural *inclination* toward the agreeable and away from the disagreeable. It is this quality, among others, that makes sex such a powerful drive; and because sexual behavior is of fundamental personal and social significance it is invested with a great deal of pleasure, making its avoidance very difficult. The need which the sex impulse represents is the primary factor in sexual motivation, but the pleasure derived from sex gratification contributes much to its dynamics.

This principle is in line with the idea that the dynamic property of motivating factors stems from organic tension. Pain causes tension and disagreeableness, whereas pleasure contributes to a state of quiescence. Both, in turn, are allied to those needs of the organism that are directed toward integrity and survival. Thus, eating, sleeping, and similar responses are pleasant experiences which induce organic equilibrium and quiescence. The ingestion of poisonous substances, on the other hand, is almost always disagreeable, as are fatigue, thirst, and other states that threaten the well-being of the organism.

What about motives and goals? Are they also dynamic? Is the mere perception of good in an object enough to

---

[13] See the article by P. T. Young, "The Role of Hedonic Processes in Motivation," in M. R. Jones (ed.), *Nebraska Symposium on Motivation* (Lincoln: University of Nebraska Press, 1955), 193–238.

stimulate action? The answers to these questions require a careful analysis of rational motivation and a thoroughgoing psychology of value. The basis of volition is the fact that human beings naturally seek values, those that are material in nature as well as those of a higher nature, like education, self-improvement, and the good of society. In other words, besides seeking pleasure man also seeks happiness, which is made possible by the achievement of his higher aims. The question is: Does the perception of good create a dynamic inclination toward behavior in the way that needs do?

The answer is: Not necessarily. Every person has two systems of values that are brought into play in a motivational situation of this kind. One of these is a purely *objective* system, the other a *subjective* one; and the dynamism of the motive will depend upon the degree to which the *latter* system is excited. The objective value-system comprises those concepts and judgments derived from instruction, reading, education, and experience in terms of which we evaluate anything and everything whose evaluation is at the moment a matter of interest or necessity. Subjective values, on the other hand, comprise those concepts that constitute a *distinctly personal frame of reference*, those values by means of which we determine whether any thing or action is good for us, and which are in large measure the residuals of experience, although influenced also by instruction, training, and example. Thus ordinarily, when we perceive a thing as good we should experience an inclination toward it, since goodness naturally attracts the will. Actually, however, as experience indicates, we may remain quite indifferent and not desire the object at all, because we have not brought it into relation

with our subjective value-system. This explanation enables us to understand the seeming perverseness of individuals who are unaffected by the highest values — why men turn their back on such things as education, religion, or profession.

What is it then that makes a motive dynamic? It is, first of all, the value of the thing itself insofar as that value is accepted as contributing to personal well-being, satisfaction, or happiness. It will be dynamic, secondly, in the degree to which it satisfies basic needs such as recognition, status, and security. Third, its dynamics will depend upon its pleasurable qualities, or the extent to which it insures pleasurable experiences. And finally it will be dynamic in the degree to which it excites emotional components. These factors condition the subjective value-system and make rational motives dynamic. This interpretation applies with equal force to such sustaining motives as ideals, principles, and interests.

This property of motivating factors is of great practical significance. Only to the extent that we are successful in making motivational tendencies dynamic can we succeed in bringing about desired patterns of response in ourselves or in others. There are many persons in whom motives are so weak that they wither before the first onslaught of unruly passion or impulse. To principles and ideals they give nothing more than lip service, because they are not dynamic, integral parts of a motivational system. If these factors were really dynamic the force of contrary tendencies would be greatly diminished. Thus, it is partly the task of the parent, the teacher, and the counselor to see that these motivating factors achieve true dynamic status. Interests, principles, ideals, and attitudes, as well as ordinary motives, must be made so forceful that in any crucial situation they will inhibit contrary tendencies — to the extent, at least, that the person can bring into play his powers of deliberation and choice. Without such development, human conduct is likely to remain on the impulsive level that characterizes early childhood or, worse still, depraved humanity.

Motivating Factors Are Often Unconscious. The dynamic quality of motivating factors is often strengthened by the fact that they function at an *unconscious* level, and are thus unknown and inaccessible to the person himself. This fact is basic to the understanding of a great deal of adolescent conduct. If a boy negatively identifies with his father on the basis of a real or imagined rejection, the hostility and hatred engendered by this relationship may be so disagreeable to him that it cannot be tolerated in consciousness. This hostility may then show itself in vandalism, stealing, excessive masturbation, running away from home, truancy at school, and in various other ways without the boy's being aware of why he does such things. Inferiority, inadequacy, aggression, insecurity, sexual impulses, feelings of rejection, and similar tendencies are the kind that are likely to function at an unconscious level and distort the behavior of the individual. Such tendencies are very dynamic, and their strength is increased by the fact that they are beyond the range of conscious control. They underlie the development of defense mechanisms like rationalization, compensation, and superiority, and break out in bizarre and distorted behavior such as we see in compulsive reactions. Delinquent and criminal behavior is also traceable in many instances to the influence of unconscious determinants.

Motivating Factors and Free Choice.

The foregoing interpretations prompt the question whether all human actions are rigidly determined by the combined strength of conscious and unconscious motivations. According to *psychological* determinism, a person's conduct is the inevitable result of his previous history plus the influence of impulses, needs, emotions, and unconscious influences. As Freud once said, "Whatever is not determined in consciousness is determined in the unconscious." Commenting on this dethronement of will, Wheelis states that strength is no longer thought to be in will, but man is now determined by forces over which he has no control, particularly the unconscious. In psychology the will has become an epiphenomenon.

> The unconscious is heir to the prestige of will. As one's fate formerly was determined by will, now it is determined by the repressed in mental life. Knowledgeable moderns put their backs to the couch, and in so doing they fail occasionally to put their shoulders to the wheel. As will has been devalued, so has courage; for courage can exist only in the service of will, and can hardly be valued higher than that which it serves. In our understanding of human nature we have gained determinism and lost determination — though these two things are neither coordinate nor incompatible.[14]

The contrary of psychological determinism is the viewpoint that, while psychological factors strongly influence human conduct, they do not rob the individual of free choice. Neither of these alternative viewpoints is wholly acceptable by itself. Such terms as "free choice," "determinism," and "self-determination" must be carefully defined before one can determine which of these positions is more correct; and any final

---

[14] A. Wheelis, *The Quest for Identity* (New York: Norton, 1958), p. 44.

judgment regarding their validity must be based upon an appeal to experience rather than to theory or prejudice. There are, of course, many actions which are *not* the result of free choice, including feelings, emotions, habits, and instinctive responses. Choice and self-determination require the setting up of alternatives and the balancing of one against the other through a process of deliberation, this process ending in a choice. In the self-determined response the agent of the action *is the person himself*, since it is he who weighs, deliberates, evaluates, and finally accepts or rejects a course of action. The motivating elements that enter the picture are also causes, but their relation to the response is only indirect because of the intervening process of deliberation.

In addition to spontaneous actions like emotions and impulses, there are many responses which are actually determined by dynamic factors. When the tension created by a need is great, or a motive highly emotionalized, the power of deliberation or choice may be *temporarily suspended*. The drugged person, the compulsive masturbator, the alcoholic, the psychopath, and the teen-ager acting under the influence of sexual passion may possess very little psychological freedom. In these instances human conduct may be wholly determined. Even decisions that seem to be free may in the end be determined by the weight of several influences working together. Theoretically, of course, there is always the possibility of acting contrary to a combination of forces, but whether this happens very often is problematical. Let us remember that our whole system of training and education is directed toward the development of habits and principles in children and adolescents so dynamic that, in a

crucial situation, their conduct will be practically determined. That this sort of determinism actually results from training is evidenced by persons who continue practices of various kinds long after the conviction of their value has disappeared. It is a safe guess that many social and religious practices belong in this category.

Let us recall, too, that, while some motivational factors have their own innate strength, many of those that really count in human conduct must be made dynamic, and in this process the individual's co-operation is often necessary. In other words, the determining power of certain motivations is at least partly the *responsibility of the person himself*. Therefore, once the motivational system is well developed, it may be that the person's conduct is largely determined; but since he had a hand in its development what he does later on will still be imputable to him.[15] In general, it may be assumed that the less an action is conditioned by basic needs, unconscious tendencies, and emotions, and the more it is based upon rational considerations, the more likely is it to be self-determined. When choosing a career, deciding which school to attend, the person we should marry, whether to have two children or five or none at all, or whether to write a book on adolescent psychology, experience testifies that we are quite free to deliberate and to choose in terms of the higher good, or at least what we think is the higher good. This principle is gaining wide acceptance today among counselors and psychotherapists because of the increasing realization that *effective treatment involves self-realization*, and de-

---

[15] On this point, see the provocative article by O. H. Mowrer, "Motivation and Neurosis," in *Current Theory and Research in Motivation: a Symposium* (Lincoln: University of Nebraska Press, 1953), pp. 162–188, especially p. 169.

pends a great deal upon the client himself. The conviction of self-determination is so deeply rooted in the human mind that not even the most astute theorizing can serve to uproot it. Experience is a stern master and it will not compromise with reason when reason pays homage to theory or prejudice.

Motivating Factors Are Interrelated. Dynamic tendencies, like other elements of personality, are woven into an integral pattern in such a way that one may inhibit, counterbalance, reinforce, or only faintly influence any other tendency within the total system. It has been demonstrated experimentally, for example, that in animals the hunger drive tends to reduce the sex drive to the point where sex behavior is largely inhibited. It is also known that under other conditions sex will inhibit hunger behavior — a clear instance of mutual *inhibition*. Other factors tend to reinforce each other. Thus racial prejudice is strongly influenced by anger and fear, the striving for wealth by the lust for power, or the desire to punish by the craving for revenge. This is called *facilitation*.

Both inhibition and facilitation are important in applying the principles of motivation. Two or more motives are generally better than one, and the strength of drives or driving forces can be reduced or even completely negated by opposing one motivation with another. This fact is important to rational self-control which is essentially the ability to minimize the influence of one motivating factor by contrasting it with another. The clear perception of and adherence to a moral principle is often the determining factor in enabling a person to do what is right and to avoid what is wrong. Where adolescents are concerned, rational deliberation has not reached a high point of

development, and thus parents and counselors should strive to instill motives that will serve to weaken or destroy tendencies which the young person finds difficult to control.

Motivating Factors Affect Other Psychic Processes. The relation between dynamic factors and behavior is quite evident, and has been exemplified many times in our analysis. No less real is the relation between these tendencies and psychic processes like perception, imagery, and thinking.[16] As we said earlier, dynamic tendencies cause a reorganization of the psychological field, which means that perceiving, fantasy, and reasoning are changed by the influence of different motivations. Shakespeare expressed this fact most succinctly when he said: "The wish is father to the thought."

There are many facts that exemplify this relationship. Under the impetus of extreme thirst a person may perceive a body of water that is nonexistent. The need for recognition stimulates the type of daydreaming by which one escapes reality and becomes a great hero or benefactor. Hunger causes thoughts or dreams of food, and the sex drive stimulates fantasy-thinking in which sexual wishes are realized in the most pleasurable manner. This capacity of motivations to influence other mental processes led to the development of Freud's *theory of wish fulfillment*.

---

[16] Typical of researches dealing with this relationship is the report by L. Postman, "The Experimental Analysis of Motivational Factors in Perception," in *Current Theory and Research in Motivation: a Symposium* (Lincoln: University of Nebraska Press, 1953), pp. 59–108. See also R. S. Woodworth, *Dynamics of Behavior*, Chaps. 7, 8; and J. R. Cautela, "The Factor of Psychological Need in Occupational Choice," *Personal & Guid., J.*, 1959, 38, 46–48.

The extent of this influence will depend upon a number of factors, such as the strength of the need, the presence of other motivations, the organism's resistance to dynamic tendencies, or inhibition. The important point is that conduct is often the direct expression of experiences, beliefs, fantasies, judgments, and inferences; and to the extent that these processes are influenced by needs, impulses, or motives, behavior often becomes inexplicable, bizarre, or distorted.

The Situation Influences Motivating Factors. The psychological stresses caused by needs and motives do not occur in a vacuum. As the Gestalt psychologists express it, the psychological field extends beyond the ordinary "boundary" of mind to embrace the situation in which psychological processes generally, and needs particularly, become operative. Research has indicated that the situation has as much to do with the functioning of the drive as do the innate dyanmics of the drive itself. This mechanism is referred to as *social facilitation*. To state the matter succinctly, *all drives become operative and dynamic partly in relation to the characteristics of the total situation in which the behavior response occurs.*[17] It is well known that the need for food and the habit of eating are affected by the presence of other persons; and that the very popular habits of smoking and drinking are socially facilitated to a great extent. The sex drive certainly is facilitated by a "sexual" environment, and greatly lessened by a "nonsexual" environment. Other motivations can also be influenced by this mechanism. This principle means that any dynamic tendency, *already operative*, is *reinforced* by other elements within the psychological field. The reaction is not *stimulated* by the situation; it is, however *facilitated* by the context in which it occurs. The total response, therefore, becomes more dynamic and tends toward overcompletion.

The practical significance of this fact is apparent. If, for example, we wish to stimulate more intensive studying, the obvious thing is to produce a studious environment, preferably one in which others are also studying. If we wish to reduce or ward off the dynamic influence of any drive at all, we will avoid the situations that tend to facilitate the expression and completion of that tendency. In the application of motivational principles to the problems of adolescence we should keep this important principle in mind.

ORIGINS OF MOTIVATING FACTORS

Are Motivating Factors Innate or Largely Acquired? For practical reasons, as well as for an adequate theory of motivation, it is important to know if the conduct of boys and girls, the things they do and the relationships they form, are the result of "original nature" or whether they are largely a reflection of the environment and culture in which teenagers grow up. The questions that arise in this connection are among the most difficult in dynamic psychology. Do people *naturally* seek affection, security, recognition, fame, or fortune? Are people *naturally* aggressive, gregarious, or idealistic? Or are these tendencies instilled in the human mind by environmental de-

[17] A thorough discussion of this point will be found in the article by J. B. Rotter, "The Role of the Psychological Situation in Determining the Direction of Human Behavior," in M. R. Jones (ed.), *Nebraska Symposium on Motivation* (Lincoln: University of Nebraska Press, 1955), pp. 245–268.

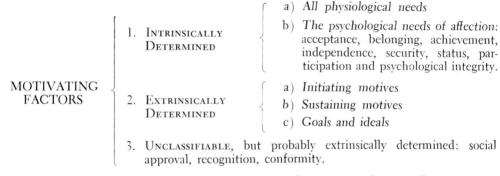

MOTIVATING FACTORS

1. INTRINSICALLY DETERMINED
   a) *All physiological needs*
   b) *The psychological needs of affection:* acceptance, belonging, achievement, independence, security, status, participation and psychological integrity.

2. EXTRINSICALLY DETERMINED
   a) *Initiating motives*
   b) *Sustaining motives*
   c) *Goals and ideals*

3. UNCLASSIFIABLE, but probably extrinsically determined: social approval, recognition, conformity.

Fig. 14. Classification of motivating factors according to the principles of intrinsic and extrinsic determination.

terminants? Will a change in culture, change human nature?[18]

Looking at our teen-agers, we see Alice striving with all her might to maintain her position at the head of the class. Every night she studies for long hours, prepares her assignments with utmost care, and burns the midnight oil whenever an examination is imminent. Is Alice expressing a need for achievement? We look at Jim who seems always to be surrounded by a group of friends. They never seem to tire of one another's company, or to run out of things to talk about. Is this a drive for participation? And then our kaleidoscope shifts to Tom who seems always on the verge of anger and irritation, especially when he is at home. His quickness to anger and his sharp, irritated replies suggest hostility. Is this sheer, natural aggression? These questions are socially and psychologically important. To answer them, we must know which motivations are innate and which acquired, and the extent human behavior is determined by extrapersonal factors.

Intrinsic Versus Extrinsic Determinants. It has been customary among psychologists to apply the heredity-environment dichotomy to questions such as these. But this can be confusing because of the limitations imposed by these terms. We propose, therefore, to use a simpler and a more meaningful terminology. For those motivating tendencies that exist prior to experience or training we shall use the term *intrinsic determination*, which means simply that the factor is determined by the nature of the organism, and is an integral part of that nature. Thus we would expect it to manifest itself in all individuals regardless of training, culture, or environment. For needs and motives that seem to be a reflection of extrapersonal factors we shall use the term *extrinsic determination*, which suggests that such tendencies will vary with environment and culture.[19]

[18] Interesting comments on this complex problem will be found in R. S. Harper, *Introductory Psychology*, pp. 66–88. See also the article by J. S. Brown, "Problems Presented by the Concept of Acquired Drives," in *Current Theory and Research in Motivation: a Symposium* (Lincoln: University of Nebraska Press, 1953), pp. 1–21.

[19] S. Koch uses a similar dichotomy in his paper, "Behavior as 'Intrinsically' Regulated: Work Notes Toward a Pre-Theory of Phenomena Called 'Motivational,'" in M. R. Jones (ed.), *Nebraska Symposium on Motivation* (Lincoln: University of Nebraska Press, 1956), pp. 42–86.

In line with these ideas, the motives, needs, and goals which we identified earlier are redistributed according to the principles of intrinsic and extrinsic determination in Figure 14. It is obvious that some of these tendencies offer no difficulty of classification. This applies particularly to the physiological needs, which are clearly intrinsic. The *expression* of such needs will of course be conditioned by environmental and cultural influences, but the needs themselves are independent of experience.

Psychological Needs Are Also Intrinsic. Physiological needs are intrinsic to the nature of the organism because they are specifically ordained to its physical welfare and integrity. These needs exist because without them the organism would languish and die. Exactly the same argument can be applied to psychological needs. Without affection, security, status, and similar needs, and their adequate gratification, the behavior of the organism tends toward distortion and maladjustment. In other words, there is serious impairment of *psychological* integrity. It may be noted that in both instances the underdevelopment or the overdevelopment of a need leads to serious difficulties, so that *adequate gratification* becomes a basic principle of healthy adjustment. Too much hunger, sex, affection, or security, or too little, inevitably leads to maladjustment.[20]

To support the interpretation that psychological needs are intrinsic, we may examine briefly several of them that stand out prominently in the background of behavior. There is, for example, the need for affection, and along with it the needs

for acceptance and belonging. Observation of children indicates unmistakably that they actively seek affection, acceptance, and belonging. They crave to be held, cuddled, hugged, and fondled; and when they are rejected they become unhappy and maladjusted just as surely as the child without food begins to show the signs of starvation.

The needs for security and for status are just as unmistakably intrinsic. Security is an integral part of the person's existence, and without it he becomes anxious, confused, and disorganized. Similarly, a person who fails to achieve status, who has a deep feeling of personal worthlessness, shows unmistakable symptoms of psychic disorganization. The need for independence, which is manifested so clearly in the adolescent period, reflects a natural requirement. Independence is a *sine qua non* of successful living and adequate adjustment, and without it the person cannot cope effectively with his environment. Finally, we may single out the need for achievement because of its important bearing on adolescent conduct. That this need is fundamental to adjustment is indicated clearly by its effect on behavior and personality. Failure and the lack of achievement are among the most serious causes of personality difficulties.[21]

---

[20] In this connection see W. Goldfarb, "Psychological Privation in Infancy and Subsequent Adjustment," *Amer. J. Orthopsychiat.*, 1945, 15, 247–255.

[21] Typical viewpoints on these various psychological needs will be found in H. H. Drewry, "Emotional Needs of Children," *Except. Child.*, 1955, 21, 178–180; J. E. Jayasuriya, "Psychological Needs of Children," *J. Educ. & Psychol.*, 1950, 8, 60–68; C. Landis, et al., *Sex in Development* (New York: Hoeber, 1950), p. 212; M. F. Grapko, "The Development of Security in Children," *Bull. Inst. Child Stud.* (Toronto, 1957), 19, 9–12; H. W. Bernard, *Mental Hygiene for Classroom Teachers*, Chap. 2; J. S. Plant, *The Envelope: a Study of the Impact of the World Upon the Child* (New York: Commonwealth Fund, 1950), Chaps. 1, 3; D. C. McClelland, "Some Social Consequences of

Social Needs Are Extrinsically Determined. While the desires for social approval, recognition, and conformity can be observed very often in the behavior of people, it would be stretching the point to say that they are intrinsically determined. Social approval, for example, is so obviously encouraged by parental attitudes, social tradition, and training that to regard it as innate or intrinsic would be to ignore the facts. Everywhere we turn, as children or as adults, we are constantly reminded of the weight of public opinion. "What will people think?" is as common an expression as "Good morning." Yet it is just as certain that many persons care little or nothing for the approval of others, and seem to be quite content without it. If this need were innate, then its frustration would lead to some form of maladjustment.[22]

The same argument can be used against the needs for recognition and conformity, even though both are common and manifest themselves at an early age. After all, the "ideal of mediocrity" is also a common phenomenon, and the writer has known scores of college students for whom mediocrity was a satisfactory standard. The people of the world who seek fame, a goal derived from recognition are very few, and they are probably influenced a great deal by cultural and environmental factors. Certainly

there are enough extrinsic events to stimulate the development of this need. In the home, in the school, and in the community at large youngsters are being constantly prodded into achievement in order that they may win some measure of acclaim. Honor rolls, class prizes, and scholarships are typical instances of such prodding. Regarding the need as extrinsic, we can account for instances in which it seems to be largely ineffective as a motivating force.

The tendency to conformity may be similarly analyzed. It involves bringing one's thoughts, attitudes, and conduct in line with those of the group in order to avoid the *stigma* attached to antisocial or extrasocial behavior. It is therefore the negative counterpart of social approval, in which *approbation* is positively sought. Conformity, then, is a means of avoiding *social disapproval*. This lure of anonymity is as general and as dynamic as the need for recognition. Allport regards conformity as fundamental. "Barring individual exceptions . . . there is a basic human tendency to temper one's opinions and conduct by deference to the opinions and conduct of others. . . . We may call this the *attitude of social conformity*."[23] However, even this writer has to recognize that there are individual exceptions.

The Principle of Interdynamic Dependency. Needs like recognition and conformity are in all probability variants of more fundamental psychological needs, and are closely bound up with the development of the self-concept. What others think of us (social approval) is

---

Achievement Motivation," in M. R. Jones (ed.), *Nebraska Symposium on Motivation* (Lincoln: University of Nebraska Press, 1955), pp. 41–65; and Pauline S. Sears, "Problems in the Investigation of Achievement and Self-Esteem Motivation," in M. R. Jones (ed.), *Nebraska Symposium on Motivation* (Lincoln: University of Nebraska Press, 1957), pp. 265–339.

[22] Hepner reports that the psychological problem most frequently mentioned by 1000 normal people is expressed in the question. "What Do People Think of Me?" See H. Hepner, *Psychology Applied to Life and Work* (New York: Prentice-Hall, 1941), p. 8.

[23] F. Allport, *Social Psychology* (Boston: Houghton Mifflin, 1924), p. 278. See also Celia B. Stendler, "The Learning of Certain Secondary Drives by Parisian and American Middle-Class Children," *Marr. Fam. Liv.*, 1954, *16*, 195–200.

always in some measure a reflection of what we think of ourselves, and this is dependent on the self-concept. Similarly, recognition is significantly related to security and status. Gaining attention and recognition is certainly one means of reducing the feelings of worthlessness and inferiority that many persons experience, feelings that may well be the result of insecure status. Watching a child go through the antics of securing attention, one cannot escape the impression that he is trying desperately to reassure himself of his own worth, which would not be necessary if he were sure of it. Recognition causes an expansion of the ego, and a bolstering of the self-concept; and these means become necessary only when there is uncertainty regarding personal status. Status-seeking also has roots in inferiority, and inferiority itself is often determined by lack of security, status, and affection. Conformity is also bound up with the same forces that generate the desire for recognition. Certainly the needs for security and status can be satisfied to some extent through conformity; and it is also true that persons seeking conformity are in many instances motivated by inferiority. They seek anonymity in the group because they are unsure of their own thoughts, feelings, and actions. They dare not risk the open stares and criticisms of some of their fellow men for fear of the repercussions these might have on their self-concept. For them the most painful of experiences is to have their weaknesses paraded before the bar of public opinion.

This reduction of certain needs to more fundamental drives is psychologically sound, and helps us to understand better the motivation of behavior. If the desire for social approval is not intrinsic, then it can best be explained by its rela-tionship to other basic needs. We may identify this relationship as the *principle of interdynamic dependency*. Whenever, therefore, some basic need cannot be aroused in the interest of stimulating respect for the opinions of others, the need for social approval does not exist. Similarly, recognition and conformity develop only on the basis of such needs as status and achievement. This principle explains the rabid individualist, the non-conformist, the underachievers, and persons who care nothing for the opinions of other people. This reduction of second order needs to more basic needs not only simplifies motivational theory but helps us to a better understanding of human motivation.

Motives, Goals, and Ideals Are Also Extrinsic. The principle of extrinsic determination is clearly applicable to motives, goals, and ideals. People are not born with values, principles, interests, or attitudes, nor do they "naturally" seek wealth, power, or position. It is customary among Adlerians to speak of a "will to power" as though it were a fundamental tendency. This is very doubtful. Undoubtedly, some persons do develop a will to power on the basis of inferiority, or in line with the "masculine protest," as Adler suggests; but at best this is only a derived tendency. Certainly there is no evidence to indicate that it is innate. Motivations of this kind are the result of training, of parental and family influences, education, and other cultural determinants. Unlike needs, they do not refer to things required; they are tendencies directed toward ends or goals that are desired because they are perceived as attractive or valuable. Their inclusion in a person's motivational system is partly the result of *introception*, a process by which the individual interiorizes the attitudes and values, the interests and ideals of his environment.

The Dynamic Organization of Motivating Factors. From time immemorial philosophers and psychologists have tried almost desperately to single out those dynamic factors that are most important in the lives and conduct of human beings. For St. Thomas it was the rational will; for Adler it was the will to power; for Freud it was sex and aggression; and for McDougall it was the parental instinct. These ideas represent sincere efforts to explain human behavior. But no one has yet come up with a fully satisfactory arrangement of motivating factors in terms of their dynamic influence or importance.[24] It is unquestionable that physiological needs are among the most powerful of all dynamic tendencies, and that they will dominate the conduct of the individual when they are denied expression for too long. Thus

[24] In connection with this problem, see A. H. Maslow, "Higher and Lower Needs," *J. Psychol.*, 1948, *25*, 433–436; C. J. Warden, "Relative Strength of the Primary Drives in the White Rat," *J. Genet. Psychol.*, 1932, *41*, 16–35; and J. R. Wittenborn, "Inferring the Strength of Drive," in M. R. Jones (ed.), *Nebraska Symposium on Motivation* (Lincoln: University of Nebraska, 1957), pp. 191–259.

they rank foremost in any hierarchy of tendencies even though at times they may be superseded by rational considerations. Thus, hunger strikes and celibacy illustrate that even the needs for food and sex can be negated by higher, non-biological motives.

Next in line would be the psychological needs because of their intimate relationship to mental health and adjustment. Affection, security, status, self-identity, achievement, and independence certainly rank foremost in influencing and determining human conduct. However, these needs may also be superseded by ideals, values, and principles. We must keep in mind that needs and motives vary in strength in the same individual over a period of time, depending upon the situation, the presence of other drives, and the level of development of the organism. It is not impossible that each person has a motivational hierarchy which he follows with fair consistency, but this fact is of limited value for a general psychology of motivation. In dealing with individual problems, however, a knowledge of those factors that are most dynamic for the individual is of great value.

SELECTED READINGS

Atkinson, J. W., *Motives in Fantasy, Action, and Society: a Method of Assessment and Study* (Princeton: Van Nostrand, 1958).

Bindra, D., *Motivation: a Systematic Reinterpretation* (New York: Ronald, 1959).

Giles, H., *Education and Human Motivation* (New York: Philosophical Library, 1957).

Jones, M. R. (ed.), *Nebraska Symposium on Motivation* (Lincoln, Nebr.: University of Nebraska Press, 1955–1958).

McClelland, D. C. (ed.), *Studies in Motivation* (New York: Appleton-Century-Crofts, 1955).

Peters, R. S., *The Concept of Motivation* (New York: Humanities Press, 1958).

Schneiders, A. A., *Personal Adjustment and Mental Health* (New York: Rinehart, 1955), Chaps. 7, 8, 9.

Stacey, C. L., and De Martini, M. F., *Understanding Human Motivation* (Cleveland: Howard Allen, 1958).

Symonds, P. M., *Dynamic Psychology* (New York: Appleton-Century-Crofts, 1949).

Tuttle, H. S., *Dynamic Psychology and Conduct* (New York: Harper, 1949).

Woodworth, R. S., *Dynamics of Behavior* (New York: Holt, 1958).

Young, P. T., *Emotion in Man and Animal* (New York: Wiley, 1943), Chap. 3.

CHAPTER VIII

ADOLESCENT NEEDS AND MOTIVES

Human motivation is basically the same at any level of development, but it is colored by the characteristics of the period in which it occurs. Adolescents want affection and security, achievement and conformity, but on their own terms. Let us see what these conditions and terms are.

A DYNAMIC PSYCHOLOGY FOR ADOLESCENCE

In the preceding chapter on the determinants of behavior we studied some of the basic principles of human motivation, and as occasion permitted drew out some of the implications of these facts for adolescent behavior. It is now time to raise the questions: To what extent is there a distinct psychology of adolescent motivation? Are there needs and motives of particular significance to the conduct of youth? In the strictest sense of the term it would be incorrect to say that there is a distinct dynamic psychology for adolescence, because of the fundamental principle that the transition from childhood to adolescence is gradual and not sudden or complete. Yet there are developmental features that cannot be ignored, and that stamp adolescent motivation with certain unique qualities. The emergence and strengthening of the sex drive, the extensive change in interests, the development of new attitudes, ideals, and goals, and the modification of certain

fundamental needs considerably alter the motivational picture. To each of these factors we shall direct our attention in subsequent chapters, in order to give a comprehensive account of adolescent behavior and personality.

For the present we shall study only the important needs and desires of adolescents, reserving for later chapters the fuller consideration of feelings and emotions, interests and attitudes, ideals and values. At this point we wish to emphasize the psychological needs because of their deep significance for adolescent adjustment. We shall begin, however, with a brief reference to physiological needs.[1]

PHYSIOLOGICAL NEEDS IN ADOLESCENCE

Apart from the sex drive, which we have already studied at considerable length, the physiological needs function in adolescence in substantially the same manner as in childhood, since they are

[1] See the article by J. E. Finesinger, "The Needs of Youth," *Psychiat.*, 1944, 7, 45–57.

171

necessary in varying degrees to the survival of the organism, regardless of developmental level. We may note, however, that the physical changes of puberty condition these drives to an important extent, especially in the matter of strength or intensity. The need for food, for example, may increase to the point where the quantity of food consumed seems incredible. Parents are often amazed at the gastronomic feats which their rapidly growing offspring manage with consummate ease. It may be, too, that qualitative changes will be manifested in the kinds of food desired. Tissue changes may reflect themselves in aberrant cravings that often, from the adult viewpoint at least, border on the nonsensical. Ordinarily, however, these changes occasion little difficulty beyond requiring admonitions from parents regarding sensible control of appetites, and regularity in eating habits.

These basic drives may be conditioned also by other than physical changes. Social factors, for example, may direct the thirst drive into peculiar and sometimes unwanted practices. This may eventuate in nothing more serious than a "Coke" habit; but it may lead also to explorations in other forms of drinking. One cannot attribute any such aberrant behavior to needs alone. Many other factors contribute to the development of these aberrations, in which the need itself plays its own particular role.

Of the physiological needs, *activity* and *rest* are the most significant for adolescent conduct and adjustment. The physical changes of puberty, including the liberation of sex hormones, the greater muscular power, and the surplus of energy, all contribute to a strengthening of the need for activity. Normal, healthy children are active enough; but where

will we find anything to correspond to the surging, ceaseless activity of youth? Hour upon hour may be filled with the most energetic dancing, handball, swimming, and other strenuous activities. While on occasion youngsters revert to a disturbing listlessness, as though suddenly deprived of the last ounce of energy, for the most part they are eager to be doing something that involves considerable expenditure of energy.

Activity of one kind or another is thus an integral part of adolescent behavior; and it is obvious that this surging need must be controlled and guided into the proper channels. All this tremendous energy must not go to waste in totally frivolous conduct. Hard work should be no more alien to the adolescent than to his hard-working parents. He should not be allowed the delusion that physical energy is to be expended solely in personal pleasures. Adolescence is a time when habits of work should be engrafted on the need for activity. Nor should we overlook the possibility that aberrations of this drive may also occur. The ever pressing need to do something may lead to forms of behavior that are socially or morally reprehensible, so that it becomes doubly important to make sure that this need has outlets in acceptable conduct.

As happens so often with human needs, the need for activity is neatly counterbalanced by the need for rest, and what we have just said about the control of activity indicates the importance of this need. The need for rest is in itself no more important than other physiological requirements, such as food or liquid, but it derives added significance from its relationship to activity. Rest *counterbalances* activity and this is what makes it particularly important for healthy adjustment. Parents should see that this balance is properly maintained in order to insure the healthy growth of the teen-ager.

PSYCHOLOGICAL NEEDS IN ADOLESCENCE

Affection, Acceptance, and Belonging. The psychological needs stand in exactly the same relationship to adjustment as do the physiological needs. This means that repeated or chronic frustration of such needs can lead to all sorts of behavior difficulties. Some of these needs, like affection and belonging, seem to be more prominent in childhood than in adolescence, whereas others, like independence, are more characteristic of the teen-age period. This fact enables us to distinguish a psychology of motivation for the adolescent period; but we must be careful not to exclude from consideration needs that may diminish during adolescence but still play an important part in the dynamics of behavior.

It could be argued, for example, that the desire for affection is more prominent in children and tends to diminish progressively with the approach of maturity, especially in normal, well-adjusted personalities.[2] However, we should not be unmindful of the possibility that, instead of actually diminishing, this need is again directed toward other goals. If we regard the transition to heterosexuality as an integral phase of adolescent development, this redirection would seem to be an expected result. What must be recog-

nized is that the need for affection is no longer manifested in the same way, nor does it have the implications for adolescent behavior and adjustment that it does for preadolescents. In some instances it becomes involved in teen-age crushes, or late adolescent "puppy love," although these manifestations can be partly explained by other motivations. A need like affection is conditioned by the urgent desire in adolescents for emancipation, and therefore tends to recede as a major driving force in adolescent conduct.

The desire for affection is complemented in adolescence by strong drives for acceptance and belonging, and it may well be that the latter needs are merely special instances of the need for affection. The important point is that adolescents have to be accepted, and they have to develop a deep sense of belonging, whether to a family, to a peer group, or to a community. Moreover, adolescents have to be accepted *as they are*, and not as parental demands or social expectations require. One of the great benefits of psychotherapy is that the client is for the first time accepted just as he is, without criticism, blame, or insidious efforts to change his personality. Acceptance and belonging, along with affection, are the *objective* counterparts of *self-acceptance*, which is a *sine qua non* of healthy-mindedness. This explains the tremendous dynamic influence of *rejection*, which is known both clinically and empirically to distort personality development and the adjustive process. It explains, too, why adolescents, consciously or unconsciously rejected by their parents, turn to the peer group for the need gratifications that are so important to peace of mind. The following newspaper article illustrates this point clearly:

---

[2] Milner found that in the absence of affection adolescents tended to experience a high level of anxiety which led to a reduction in mental efficiency. See E. Milner, "Effects of Sex Role and Social Status on the Early Adolescent Personality," *Genet. Psychol. Monogr.*, 1949, 40, 231–325.

New York, April 23, 1959. A sixteen-year-old youth swore yesterday in General Sessions that he boasted of trying to slug the murdered —— in order to curry favor with the seventeen-age old boys accused of the killing.

——, a prosecution witness under police guard in an East Side hotel, was asked whether he had told the other boys he had tried to hit —— with a stick.

"Yes, but it was not true," —— replied quietly. He said he made the empty boast in an attempt to win acceptance by the others.

The relationship between these three needs and adolescent adjustment raises the important question whether adolescents should be separated from their families during this critical period of uncertainty and confusion. Is it wise to send adolescents to boarding school, or for that matter to minor seminaries? We know from empirical studies that broken families contribute a great deal toward behavior distortion and delinquency, the reason being that the family is not available for the gratification of needs like affection and belonging. Evidently, the child away at school is in much the same predicament, and often regards his being sent to boarding school as evidence of parental rejection. What is worse is that his judgment is often correct. Boarding schools are an excellent means of escaping parental responsibilities. If the child himself shows an inclination in this direction, the probability is that he feels rejected and unwanted and is thus trying to escape an intolerable situation. The only acceptance and sense of belonging that some children experience is that provided by teachers or headmasters. One of the author's clients, whose parents were long since divorced, exclaimed during an interview: "I love this university. For the first time in my life I feel that I really belong." All the heartbreak and

tragedy of parental rejection is reflected in this one simple expression.

Clinical experience with unhappy and disturbed adolescents teaches us that it is very doubtful whether they can break away from the home successfully in the early stages of adolescence. When the teen-ager is 16 or 17 years of age, and the need for emancipation has had a chance to develop normally, the more basic needs of affection and belonging become less important. But the 13- or 14-year-old is not psychologically ready for emancipation, and can be severely damaged by a sudden disruption of his relationships with the family. Adolescence, as we have said, is a period of transition, and this transition must be given a chance to complete itself.

The Needs for Status and Achievement. Closely related to the above needs is the *desire for personal worth*, or status, which reaches its climax during the adolescent period.[3] The drive for status is similar to self-acceptance, in that it is the *subjective* counterpart of objective recognition. A person craves status in order to reassure himself of his own personal worth, and thus the status-seekers are those who are always unsure of themselves and of their position in the eyes of others. In them the need for status is overdeveloped because of deep feelings of insecurity, inferiority, or inadequacy. The need itself is a normal drive, and when not overdeveloped helps to promote the adjust-

[3] See J. S. Plant, *The Envelope: a Study of the Impact of the World Upon the Child* (New York: Commonwealth Fund, 1950), Chap. 3, especially page 49. A somewhat different and popular interpretation of this need is Vance Packard's book, *The Status Seekers* (New York: David McKay, 1959). See also W. H. Sewell and A. O. Haller, "Factors in the Relationship between Social Status and the Personality Adjustment of the Child," *Amer. Sociol. Rev.*, 1959, 24, 511–520.

Achievement is a powerful motive.

Fordham University

ment of the individual. The adolescent who seeks "political" office, the young girl who wants to be queen of the ball, and the football player who cherishes the idea of being captain of the team are all seeking status. Sometimes this need takes a wrong turn, and the youth then aspires to become the gang leader, the Big Man on campus, or the most sexually promiscuous girl in the neighborhood. These youngsters, too, are status-seekers, but the need has taken a peculiar twist because of the circumstances governing their lives.

This desire for status is complemented to an important extent by the needs for *personal integrity* and *achievement*. Integrity may be defined as a craving for inviolability which tolerates no intrusion into the domain of one's private life. Any positive threat to integrity is a threat to the self-concept and to ego-security, and there is little that will so readily disrupt the delicate pattern of personal integration as the impairment of the self-concept. Parents often violate this craving for integrity by their demands on the adolescent's trust, or by prying into his most personal thoughts and feelings, or by failing to recognize

his intrinsic worth. They may scoff at his attempts to assume adult status; they may ridicule or criticize his efforts to express himself in speech or in writing; they find fault with his sartorial selections, his choice of friends, or his meager accomplishments. These actions frustrate the need for inviolability and status, and may have the most serious negative effects on the development of personality.[4]

Achievement, of course, contributes directly to the development of personal worth or status, but it should not be regarded simply as an adjunct of status. Achievement is a need that can function independently of status, and brings its own rewards. To achieve is itself a rewarding experience that bolsters the self-

[4] See J. S. Plant, *op. cit.*, p. 46. Barron emphasizes the important relationship between status and delinquency. He says, "One conclusion concerning the relationship between status-striving and delinquency is that, despite apparent fluctuations in delinquency rates over the years, there are three basic factors underlying American social structure which are constantly conducive to delinquency: (a) inequality in status, (b) competition in school, on the playground, in the community, and for a living; and (c) aggressive individualism" — M. L. Barron, *The Juvenile in Delinquent Society* (New York: Knopf, 1954), p. 207.

concept, increases security, and tones down the negative effects of inadequacy and inferiority. Achievement, therefore, is a requirement for healthy, psychological growth, and plays a decisive role in helping the adolescent cope successfully with his environment.[5] Parents and teachers should take every opportunity to nurture this need by encouraging the youngster to utilize and to exploit his potentialities to the utmost. Adolescents need all the encouragement they can get in order to help them develop an adequate concept of themselves.

The Need for Security. The gratification of needs like affection, acceptance, and achievement can contribute a great deal to one of the most basic psychological requirements of personality, and that is *personal* security. The opposite of security is of course the feeling of insecurity, which manifests itself so clearly and unmistakably in chronic anxiety, scrupulosity, excessive timidity, social inadequacy, and perfectionistic idealism. The feeling of insecurity has the most damaging effects on ego development, and causes the person to react negatively to the most normal demands of everyday experience. For the insecure person, a

demand or a challenge becomes a *threat*, to which he reacts with anxiety, withdrawal, or defensive reactions. Getting up to recite in class, keeping an appointment, taking an examination, or going out on a date are all regarded as threatening experiences which evoke a great deal of anxiety or fear. Each such reaction is more damaging than the preceding one until the anxiety-insecurity reaction becomes deeply embedded within the personality.

The feeling or conviction of personal security has many aspects, all of which must be taken into account in explaining what security actually involves. We can distinguish economic, emotional, social, and psychological security, each one of which has different implications for different levels of development.[6] Perhaps the most common form is economic security. That the adolescent craves such security is evidenced by the characteristic fears developed during this period; and therefore the more secure the economic status of his family, the greater are his chances for developing a sense of security. However, we may assume that this type of security is far less important to the adolescent than to the adult, because the financial responsibilities coincident with adult living have not yet become a part of the teen-ager's experience. It is for this reason that the adolescent should be required to contribute in some measure to the economic well-being of the family, so that he may learn the serious lesson of financial re-

---

[5] A great deal of research has been done in recent years on the achievement motive. See, for example, D. C. McClelland, et al., The Achievement Motive (New York: Appleton-Century-Crofts, 1953); R. S. Woodworth, Dynamics of Behavior (New York: Holt, 1958), pp. 88–97; D. C. McClelland, "Some Social Consequences of Achievement Motivation," in M. R. Jones (ed.), Nebraska Symposium on Motivation (Lincoln: University of Nebraska Press, 1955), pp. 41–65; Pauline S. Sears, "Problems in the Investigation of Achievement and Self-Esteem Motivation," in M. R. Jones (ed.), Nebraska Symposium on Motivation (Lincoln: University of Nebraska Press, 1957), pp. 265–339; Elizabeth G. French and F. H. Thomas, "The Relation of Achievement Motivation to Problem-Solving Effectiveness," J. Abnorm. Soc. Psychol., 1958, 56, 45–48.

[6] See H. Meltzer, "Economic Security and Children's Attitudes to Parents," Amer. J. Orthopsychiat., 1936, 6, 590–608. See also J. S. Plant, op. cit., Chap. 1, where security is brought in relation to belongingness, parent-child relationships, racial insecurity, the influence of family tradition, the broken family, the church, and adolescence itself.

sponsibility, and indirectly contribute to his own economic security.

Personal security may be enhanced (or undermined) by the social status of the family or other group of which the adolescent is a member. Here we find a real difference between adolescent and childish reactions. The young child is little aware of the factors that cause social integration or disintegration, which is not true of the adolescent. The breakup or threatened breakup of the family, through conflict, divorce, separation, or death, will seriously affect youth's sense of security. The child will be affected also, but less so than the adolescent, because of the latter's keener appreciation of the implications of such events. The family or the state as a *social* unit is a more meaningful thing to the adolescent than to his younger brother or sister. Becoming increasingly socialized himself, events of a social nature impress themselves more deeply on his uncertain consciousness, and thus may affect his sense of security. Many adolescents react with considerable anxiety to the threat of total war, the loss of a parent, the requirements of military service, and similar events. If we keep in mind that each person is not merely a member, but *an integral part of the social unit*, that he tends to identify himself with the group and to introject the experiences of the group, we can more readily understand why he reacts so strongly when the social unit begins to disintegrate. Youth and the society in which they live cannot be understood apart from each other.

The most important aspect of this need is *psychological security*, which may be described as a feeling or conviction that one's inner and outer world will not collapse. It is akin to the feeling of safety that the young child experiences in the protective arms of its mother. In one sense all security is psychological, and such things as economic and social status merely contribute to or detract from this ego-security. The feeling of security is rooted in the individual's estimate of himself — of his abilities, his intrinsic worth, his social and moral status, his emotional balance, and his physical integrity or health. There are many persons living in a world of great economic and social security who nevertheless feel deeply insecure, and this is especially true of many adolescents. The trouble is, of course, that *they are not sure of themselves.*[7] They doubt their own personal worth, they question their own abilities, and their emotions and feelings are regarded as undependable.

This feeling of insecurity is related to *lack of integration*. That is why physical integrity, which is made difficult by the continuous changes of the bodily apparatus during adolescence, is so important to the development of security. To a person not sure of himself, whatever the causes may be, threats of social or economic insecurity can be appalling. It is bad enough not to be sure of oneself, but when in addition one cannot be sure of those things that have always endured, the psychic shock may be catastrophic. These persons often withdraw from reality to an inner world of fantasy, where the security they crave can be

---

[7] In his characterization of the shook-up generation, Salisbury remarks, "Security, security, security. This is close to the surface of almost everything the youngsters do or say. Want of security is what leads them into the gang and want of security is what keeps them in this dangerous limbo" — H. E. Salisbury, *The Shook-up Generation* (New York: Harper, 1958), p. 70. See also Jean M. Arsenian, "Young Children in an Insecure Situation," *J. Abnorm. Soc. Psychol.*, 1943, 38, 225–249.

realized. In this autistic life they need face only themselves; and their real or imagined deficiencies, not put to the test of actuality, frighten them no longer. Here we see the important link between achievement and security. The lack of achievement, or failure, is one of the most important causes of insecurity, and is a common element in the development of withdrawal reactions.[8]

Closely allied to this basic insecurity is *emotional insecurity* which may be characterized as a feeling of uncertainty regarding one's feelings and relationships. A striking instance of this is the emotion of jealousy which is an obvious confession of insecurity; the jealous person is uncertain of his emotional hold on the object of his affection.

Emotional insecurity arises most commonly from the conviction of being unwanted or unloved, and from lack of self-identity, which often results from confusion in love relationships. In adolescence particularly, emotional insecurity is likely to develop because of the uncertainty of the adolescent's emotional reactions. Torn between the desires for security, affection, and independence, his emotional life easily becomes confused. Also, he experiences vague feelings whose meaning he does not comprehend. Sexual stirrings, a "crush" on his teacher, longings for forbidden experiences, feelings of guilt, shame, and embarrassment, and exciting sensations from contact with the opposite sex — all contribute to emotional confusion. These difficulties will ordinarily be ironed out in the process of growing up, but the fact is that growing up takes a long time, and the adolescent

should be helped during this period of insecurity.[9]

The adolescent's uncertainty will lead to intellectual and volitional insecurity also. Youths often have serious misgivings about their own judgments and opinions, and they put little faith in their ability to make decisions or to select goals. It is true that they will often fight for the right to make decisions, but underlying this striving for independence is a basic uncertainty regarding themselves. This is partly due to lack of experience and knowledge, but it is in larger part a reflection of basic insecurity. There is room here for a great deal of guidance, and youth must be taught how to evaluate its own judgments and decisions.

The achievement of psychological security is of basic importance to the mental health of the growing boy and girl. The teen-ager who feels insecure is poorly equipped to deal with the many conflicts and uncertainties that beset his path to adulthood. A feeling of security, on the other hand, favors the development of courage, decisiveness, and integrity. It is the soil in which the processes of integration and maturation can best grow. One must be careful, however, not to push the development of security to an extreme, since too much security, like too much of anything, will defeat its own purpose. Security must not be bought at the expense of independence, and must not result in that emotional strangulation to which far too many adolescents are subjected by overprotective and overanxious parents.

The Need for Independence and Self-

---

[8] For a thorough discussion of the reaction of children to failure, see J. S. Plant, *op. cit.*, Chap. 12.

[9] Some writers feel that the school has a responsibility for giving a child security. See H. G. Shane, "Sense of Security," *J. Nat. Educ. Assoc.*, 1949, 38, 497–498.

Identity. It is the crowning paradox of the adolescent period that youth is motivated at the same time by two contrary tendencies: the need for security, and the *need for independence*, which involves primarily emancipation from emotional ties with the family. These two drives, along with affection, acceptance, and belonging, can cause considerable conflict and disturbance in the minds of young people. In one way or another the youngster must so reconcile these contrary tendencies that when he reaches adulthood early relationships and conflicts are completely resolved.

From the standpoint of healthy adjustment, the need for independence is one of the most important factors in the human personality. What parents especially must realize is that independence is the prerogative and the natural goal of the developing personality.[10] Without it maturity, integration, adjustment, and adequate socialization are impossible. In a very real sense a person is mature only in the degree to which he sets himself up in the business of adult living, unfettered by the demands, restrictions, prejudices, and controlling influences of other persons. He can become self-integrated only if he cuts himself

[10] Students of adolescent development are in agreement that independence and self-identity are basic to maturity and adjustment. See, for example, Elizabeth Douvan, "Independence and Identity in Adolescence," *Children*, 1957, 4, 186–190; Irene M. Josselyn, "Psychological Aspects of Adolescence," *Amer. J. Orthopsychiat.*, 1956, 26, 471–496; and J. R. Gallagher and H. I. Harris, *Emotional Problems of Adolescence* (New York: Oxford University Press, 1958), Chap. IV, especially pages 50–55. These authors argue that both boys and girls need to develop independence and individuality, and that rebellion is natural and inevitable. Parents should learn to accept it.

away from the dependency that is a necessary part of his earlier life. He can achieve adjustment only if he strikes out for himself, and learns by experience how to meet responsibilities, and how to make necessary and important decisions. The development of an adequate social life requires separation from those with whom one has become identified through affection and security, and the establishing of newer relationships with other individuals.

It is during adolescence that independence and emancipation must be achieved. In childhood there are still far too many "ties that bind." The child is not equipped to strike out for himself, and would soon founder if he tried to do so. But it is different with youth, and they should be given every opportunity to explore the realm of independent action. Like everything else, independence is a matter of learning; and if the adolescent is not given opportunities to school himself in the art of independent thinking, willing, and acting, there is little likelihood that he will achieve full maturity. Moser points out that the feeling of independence experienced by adolescents is not supported by our American culture because of the cultural delay in accepting the adolescent as an adult. Speaking of the adolescent girl, he says:

> Psychologically she feels she is an adult, socially and economically she is forced to remain a child. Her independence is not recognized. Many of the childhood controls remain in force. Girls, though more mature than boys, are subjected to more protective devices than are the boys. Through law and public opinion, she is held in school, deprived of marriage, blocked from productive labor, held under parental control. Her efforts to assert herself are suppressed. Her

possessions are limited. She is blocked from economic independence and economic status.[11]

Josselyn expresses the same idea in a more positive way:

> The adolescent wishes to be not only an individual, but an independent and grown-up one. Accepting the advice or direction of a parent is an acknowledgment of dependency, which is intolerable. The only way to be an adult is to act like one. Therefore decisions must be made, clothes must be purchased, hours must be controlled, independent of the parents, who treat him "like a child." To agree with the parent — be it on the subject of friends, the color of Mary's hair, a political situation, or the proper time to end a party — is to acknowledge one's status as a child. To disagree is to manifest one's strength as an adult. Freedom from the parent and agreement with him are incompatible.[12]

Independence means more than separate existence or economic self-sufficiency. It means, above all, emotional, volitional, and intellectual independence, and the freedom of action that this independence makes possible. There is no more crippling handicap to the achievement of maturity and adjustment than *emotional dependence* upon others. Above everything else, the adolescent must break away from the apron-string existence of childhood. He needs to establish the emotional perspective and control that will enable him to live and enjoy an existence separate from the parents. This emancipation is a prerequisite to establishing other relationships in adult life, particularly those involved in marriage. Many a boy has become seriously maladjusted through homesickness; and many a young wife (or husband) has found married life intolerable because it involved being away from "mother." Nature intended men and women to set themselves up in the business of independent living; and that is why such a strong need for it exists in the human personality.

Young people also require *volitional* independence — the opportunity to make and adhere to their own decisions. There is no way of achieving decisiveness *without practice in making decisions*. And adult life, as everyone knows, is crammed with situations in which persons are required to decide things for themselves. If experience has not provided exercise in this ability, the person will find himself at a loss as to how to go about doing it. This training should begin early in life, even before the adolescent period. Let the child learn what it means to make decisions, and what it means to make the wrong ones! He might find the results of his choice painful and embarrassing; but there is no better way to teach him the importance of intelligent deliberation.

That volitional independence is a human prerogative is attested by the fact of man's *psychological freedom*. It would be a strange thing indeed if man had the power of choice but not the opportunity to exercise it! Yet, that is exactly what many parents deny their children. *They* make the decisions, generously allowing their children the privilege of saying aye to them. *They* choose their off-

---

[11] C. G. Moser, *Understanding Girls* (New York: Association Press, 1957), pp. 199–200.

[12] Irene M. Josselyn, "Growing to Adulthood," in Sidonie M. Gruenberg (ed.), *Our Children Today: a Guide to Their Needs From Infancy Through Adolescence* (New York: Viking, 1952), p. 182. See also the article by Celia B. Stendler, "The Learning of Certain Secondary Drives by Parisian and American Middle Class Children," *Marr. Fam. Liv.*, 1954, 16, 195–200; Ruth Strang, *The Adolescent Views Himself* (New York: McGraw-Hill, 1957), Chap. 10.

spring's friends, their clothes, and their style of life. They decide whether or not the youngster should go to college, and which curriculum he will follow when he gets there. They select the boy or girl in whom the youngster should become amorously interested. While adolescents still retain the power to disagree mentally with such parental decisions, it does them little good if their own volitions cannot be translated into conduct. Parental attitudes of this kind will surely generate conflicts, emotional disturbances, and open rebellion.

Adolescents require a measure of discipline and control; but more than that they require understanding of their needs and wants, and of their prerogatives as independent human beings. More than discipline, they need guidance. With understanding guidance and wise counsel the needs for both security and independence can be adequately gratified. The adolescent in whom the desire for independence is continuously thwarted is the one in whom insecurity is most likely to develop.

The capacity to make decisions, and especially to make the right ones, is directly dependent upon the corresponding ability to think. Thus intellectual independence, by which we mean the inherent right to think for oneself, is prerequisite to volitional independence. What phrase is more annoying to the thinking child than "Mother knows best"? Admittedly, youth does not possess the experience and insight always to come to the right conclusions; but there is no denying them the right to try. Young people should acquire respect for the opinions and judgments of their elders; that is a first step toward true wisdom. But what is equally important is that parents and teachers should learn to respect, if not the opinions of youth, at least their right to form opinions. Perfection in thinking can come only from practice in thinking; and the less practice there is the poorer will the thinking be.

This principle is of particular importance for the period of adolescence since intellectual development is a characteristic feature of the maturing process, and the privilege of thinking for one's self should increase in direct proportion to this development. We are not suggesting unbridled freedom of thought, since even the adolescent is bound by first principles, logic, and authority. But we do mean that all of his thinking should not be done for him. The adolescent must be allowed exploration in the realm of ideas if he is to develop intellectually. He must learn how to think, how to form and evaluate opinions, and how to reach conclusions. This can be accomplished only by practice in the art of thinking.

Experiences like these during adolescence will eventually lead to personal, emotional, and economic independence. In the fullest sense of the term, personality and individuality are realized only to the extent that one achieves independence in all these areas. However, becoming a real person does not mean becoming antisocial or autistic. Important ties of friendship, loyalty, love, and respect must be maintained for a well-balanced adult life. The individual must not become a microcosm unto himself. He is a social as well as a personal being, and of necessity he lives within a society. Remarkably enough, it is not the persons who achieve independence who become autistic or antisocial; it is, rather, those who have not had experience in independent living and acting.

They are forced to retire to an inner world of unreality because they have not learned how to think for themselves, how to make decisions, and how to regulate their emotions. The achievement of independence *is the first step toward establishing healthy dependent relationships* with the world in which one lives.

The achievement of independence as we have described it lies at the basis of *self-identity*. We have included self-identity as a basic psychological need because it is in every sense of the word a true requirement for mental health and adjustment. The adolescent must discover himself, and come into possession of himself if he is to reach maturity and live successfully in an adult world. That is why the achievement of independence is so important to self-identity. As long as early emotional, volitional, and economic dependencies persist, then the true self of the individual is dispersed among the relationships of childhood. To find one's self means essentially to free one's self for independent and self-initiated behavior. Parents and counselors therefore should make every effort to help the teen-ager achieve self-identity, so that he can face the responsibilities of adult living with a clear knowledge of who he is, what he is, and the direction in which he is going.[13]

The Need for Experience. Complementing the drives for status, achievement, and self-identity is the need for experience, which has particular significance for adolescent conduct because experience is necessary to maturation and adjustment, and also because of the effects of experience on behavior. Sensory and intellectual, social and moral development is dependent upon the explorations which the individual makes in these areas, and often the opportunities for such exploration are seriously limited.

The need for experience can be very dynamic, and manifests itself in a variety of ways. Youth makes persistent excursions, for example, into different emotional experiences, which are usually referred to as *thrill-seeking*.[14] It is a paradox of human nature that the same emotion that drives the individual to flight, namely fear, is the very one that beckons to danger. It is admittedly a fearful thing to travel at breakneck speed in an automobile; yet such a venture may beckon youngsters with an irresistible lure. It is dangerous to break the law; but this, too, may be attractive as a means of gratifying the need for experience. A most effective advertisement for luring youngsters into the armed services is one which stresses the elements of excitement, danger, adventure, and novel experiences. Men will fight, climb mountain peaks, plunge over Niagara Falls in a barrel, scale the side of a building, go on a safari, or be a test pilot because of the experience involved.

A great deal of the erratic, unpredictable behavior of teen-agers manifested in pranks and vandalisms, joy riding and pilfering, is traceable to this same desire for experience; nor is it unlikely that

---

[13] The problem of self-identity was treated fully in Chapter IV. The reader will find excellent discussions of the development of identity in E. H. Erikson, *Childhood and Society* (New York: Norton, 1950), pp. 207–210 and 235–283; G. H. J. Pearson, *Adolescence and the Conflict of Generations* (New York: Norton, 1958), pp. 93–100.

[14] See the illustration of pyromania in H. Hepner, *Psychology Applied to Life and Work* (New York: Prentice-Hall, 1941), pp. 18–19. See also the study by W. Wattenberg, "Boys Who Run Away From Home," *J. Educ. Psychol.*, 1956, 47, 335–343. For these 575 boys, one of the most prominent causes of running away was the search for adventure.

sexual misbehavior often has its beginnings in this dynamic need. In any particular instance the sex drive itself may not be very strong; but when to this drive is added the craving for experience, unacceptable conduct is a likely result. Experiences are not always sought for their pleasurable effects, since these are often unknown. What, then, is it that leads to smoking, drinking, or petting? The answer of youth almost invariably is: "I wanted to find out what it's like." This is a layman's way of saying, "I craved the experience of doing these things."

The desire for experience is clearly manifested in the *vicarious* activities of youth, including conversation. Where one youngster seeks the actual experience, the other expresses this drive by means of a vicarious substitute. What more effective way to avoid the penalties of forbidden sex behavior than by talking about sex? There is probably more sex experience realized vicariously through the medium of conversation than through actual practice. For all we know, this sublimation of the two drives — sex and experience — by means of conversation helps prevent a great deal of sexual misbehavior, even though such conversation is itself undesirable. The writer has known more than one person who, abhorring the thought of sexual practice, never tired of talking about it!

Movies, books, radio and television programs are also prolific sources of vicarious experiences. Through identification with the characters of a story, one can experience excitement, anger, passion, fear, horror, or any other emotional quality intended by the author. These vicarious experiences may be all that a youngster needs to gratify the craving for experience. Unfortunately, however, it is often *much more* than he needs; and, forgetful of the fictional nature of the people and events encountered in these media, he tries to emulate them in actual practice.

Games and sports are also common sources of vicarious experience. The excitement derived from watching football, basketball, boxing, and wrestling is similar to the experience of the contestants themselves. Here again we find the mechanisms of identification and introjection at work; not, however, with fictionized realities, but with real-life people and events. But the result is much the same; and we actually find among adolescents a growing tendency to "engage" in these activities by symbolic participation, leaving to "professionals" the business of actual participation.

This universal need for experience is expressed also in a variety of *behavioral explorations*. Because of lack of experience with various activities, or possessing little imagination, teen-agers find it necessary at times to employ the method of "trial and error." The play of children is often in the nature of an exploration of behavior possibilities, the trying out of an activity to see what it is like; and undoubtedly many instances of erratic behavior in adolescence can be traced to these experimental tryouts. Behavior of this kind often seems inexplicable, since there is no clearly definable antecedent, and the youngster himself does not know why he acts in that manner. Vagrancies like truancy, joy riding, stealing, or burglary often begin as behavioral explorations, by which the undifferentiated need for experience finds an outlet in behavior that is alluring because it is unfamiliar.

Our examples of what the need for experience can lead to have been on the negative side, but we must remember that this drive may also lead to socially acceptable behavior. Keeping in mind that youngsters will secure experience in one way or another, parents are faced with the necessity for providing them with opportunities for experience. The behavior motivated by this need must be channeled into socially and morally acceptable ways of behaving. There are good books, movies, television, and radio programs. There are field trips, sports, games, parties, and dances that can be enjoyed without the need for censure. In short, there are many acceptable modes of conduct through which the need for experience can be gratified; but unless the means for such gratification are provided, youngsters themselves might easily choose the wrong ones.

SOCIAL NEEDS IN ADOLESCENCE

The Need for Participation.   In the behavior of adolescents one can discern a strong tendency to share and to participate actively in the experiences and behavior of other persons who constitute their social world. This twofold tendency, to share and to participate, is one of the strongest social forces in the psychological make-up of the human personality. It underlies in part the development of language, since it is by means of language that participation can be most effectively realized. There are, however, other ways in which this need is expressed, including play, sports, games, parties, clubs, and conversation. In fact, any form of group or social action involves this tendency to some degree.

While participation is expressed clearly in the social explorations of children, during adolescence it achieves fullest ex-

pression, since teen-agers are more amenable to social influences and to social growth. The need itself remains the same, but the modes of participation broaden in scope and significance during the teen-age period. Youth seems particularly eager to participate in the activities and experiences of others, to form cliques, groups, and societies of all kinds.[15] In some instances, but not all, there is noticeable a distinct change in the nature of the participation: *a transition from actual to symbolic participation*, especially in the case of activities that require strenuous exertion. Most young people by the time they reach adulthood are content to "sit on the sidelines" and watch others perform. This change involves no reduction of the need for participation. Rather, as we have seen with respect to the need for experience, it is a symbolic expression of the need through vicarious or indirect experience. For this reason activities like reading or going to the movies come to replace those that require active participation.

Participation can be a powerful socializing influence, and an important factor in social adjustment. Concepts and experiences, skills and viewpoints that are socially as well as personally valuable, can be achieved by participating in the activities and experiences of others. Some form of group action, therefore, is a prerequisite for social development. The adolescent's attitudes toward society,

---

[15] As Remmers and Radler point out, "Given the fulfillment of any one wish, most adults would, like Faust, seek fame and fortune. But the common cry of teenagers is, 'Oh, to be more popular!' " Of the group studied 54 per cent want people to like them, and more than 60 per cent "desperately want to make new friends" —H. H. Remmers and D. H. Radler, *The American Teenager* (New York: Bobbs-Merrill, 1957), p. 44.

toward members of the opposite sex, or toward religious and racial groups; his knowledge of how organizations are formed and how they function; his capacity to relate to other persons and to co-operate with them — all such developments can be greatly augmented by social participation, and all of them will contribute to social adjustment.

Parents and teachers should explore every possibility in their efforts to develop media for the expression of this need. The adolescent is by nature a social animal, and should be provided with opportunities to develop his social capacities to a healthy extent. Many opportunities are provided by family living, and by other social experiences that occur in childhood and adolescence; but the school in particular is in the best position to sponsor and encourage activities that involve participation. If the adolescent is to learn how to live in society, experience in social living is necessary; and the period of youth provides many excellent opportunities for social experience. In public and nonpublic high schools there are clubs, athletic programs, extracurricular activities, and sodalities which provide many opportunities for the healthy expression of this need. It is the responsibility of the parent and the teacher to guide youth toward wholesome and active participation in such enterprises.

Need for Recognition and Social Approval. The psychological needs of acceptance and belonging, status and achievement, are complemented by the social needs for recognition and approval. In fact, it is not unlikely that the latter needs are *developmental derivatives* of the more basic psychological requirements of the human organism. We have already explored this possibility in the preceding chapter. The important point is that recognition and social approval characterize a great deal of adolescent behavior, and have important social implications. When we observe the behavior of children in matters of dress, cleanliness, or social graces, we can see that they are not much concerned with social approval, whereas there are many indications of this desire in adolescent conduct. A great deal of the anguish experienced by adolescents because of clumsiness, irregular features, skin blemishes, overweight, or academic weakness, is traceable to the fact that they strongly desire the favorable opinion of others. Similarly, there are many instances that illustrate the desire for recognition: the competitions for scholastic honors, the hotly contested battles for class offices, the strenuous efforts to achieve athletic standing, and so on.

While such instances are admittedly the exception rather than the rule, there are many other smaller ways in which youngsters try to win recognition for themselves. Few persons are totally insensitive to acclaim, because acclaim is a public avowal of personal worth, and the conviction of worth is necessary to ego-security. This intrinsic relation to personal worth or status gives recognition and social approval their dynamic quality. This interpretation applies with particular force to adolescents, since there are many reasons why (in their minds) there is good ground for questioning their worth. Because their development and integration are still incomplete; because they so often fumble in their efforts at achievement; and because of the confusion and uncertainty they often feel with respect to themselves, adolescents are in need of the encouragement that comes from recognition and approval. They must be reassured that they and their efforts are *worthwhile*, and this reassurance contributes to a belief in themselves.

When one considers the lack of faith and the uncertainty of many *adults* who have managed to outlive the tribulations of the adolescent period — persons who have behind them the experience and wisdom that comes only with years of striving toward a goal — is it any wonder that youth is prone to question its own status? To avoid discouragement, despondency, and even despair, everyone must achieve a conviction of his own worth. Because of loss of faith in themselves, or because they have vainly sought to achieve recognition in ordinary ways, youths often turn to activities which bring recognition of the worst kind. Recognition and approval are sought in the peer group to which the adolescent belongs, but unfortunately the values and standards of the peer group may be very inadequate or even dangerous. The violence and brutality of gangs are a direct expression of this fact.

In the absence of status and achievement, acceptance and belonging, or recognition and approval, the adolescent develops feelings of inadequacy, inferiority, and worthlessness. These feelings are psychologically intolerable, and youngsters will strike out in any and every direction in an attempt to convince themselves that they are not inferior. This behavior may take any conceivable form, from greater application to studies in order to achieve academic recognition, to acts of violence and crime that insure a quick notoriety. Thus many instances of delinquent behavior are traceable to the frustration of these needs, and the feelings generated thereby.

The implications of recognition and social approval for personal worth point up the relationship between these needs and the desire for security. Since security means a great deal more than freedom from physical want or danger, the achievement of recognition and status can contribute significantly to the gratification of this need. Recognition is a boon to self-confidence; it stimulates the feeling of certainty concerning one's abilities and traits that often is achieved only by external evaluation. In children and adolescents, in whom there is a limited ability to evaluate personal capacities, efforts, and accomplishments, this external evaluation becomes doubly important. The expressed confidence of others in their achievements enhances their confidence in themselves, and this confidence in turn contributes to feelings of status and security.

The Need for Conformity. The tendency to conformity that is so strikingly expressed in certain forms of adolescent behavior is another instance of the paradoxes in motivation that characterize the American teen-ager. As many observers have noted, teen-agers are often rebellious rather than conforming. They strive for independence of thought, belief, styles, and mannerisms rather than accede to the established social pattern. They aggressively reject the codes and mores established by adult society. Such behavior, certainly, hardly indicates a need to conform. Ask any parents of teen-agers whether their sons and daughters readily conform to rules and practices and they will quickly assure you that such is not the case.

Yet the most casual observation yields evidence of the desire for conformity in adolescent behavior. In language, mannerisms, dress, habits, and strict adherence to certain behavior codes, there are numerous instances of conformity. Any teen-ager will quickly inform you how important it is to be "in the groove," and not to be a "square." Deviations from accepted patterns of appearance, behavior, and language are generally regarded with a touch of scorn. In matters of speech and dress, for example, the desire for conformity is strikingly manifested. Youth has a language of its own, containing many peculiarities of expression that are a badge of adolescent respectability. In style of dress there is a striking similarity among young people. If sweaters are the current style, then it becomes an imperative demand to wear one. If headgear has been ruled out, it becomes passé to be seen with a cap or hat of any kind. Such conformity applies to current singing idols, type of music preferred, and style of dancing.

> The inner need for group solidarity is evidenced clearly by almost everything the adolescent does. He has to dress exactly like his peers. He has to talk the way they do. His haircut has to be exactly the same. He demands the same liberties his colleagues have. He has to have the same amount of spending money, like the same music, dance the same way, express the same interests, the same prejudices, and the same fears. In short, he resembles the child of six who prefers to be governed by a consistent, rather tyrannical adult; in adolescence, however, the governing must be done by the group ideal.[16]

Obviously, then youth is both rebellious and conformist. In its striving for independence and self-identity, it reacts against the accepted standards and ways

---

[16] G. H. J. Pearson, *Adolescence and the Conflict of Generations* (New York: Norton, 1958), pp. 87–88. See also A. K. Cohen, *Delinquent Boys: the Culture of the Gang* (Glencoe, Ill.: Free Press, 1955), pp. 56–65.

of behaving characteristic of adult society. At the same time, in its desires for security, acceptance, and belonging, it turns to the peer group, wherein rebellion dissipates and conformity takes its place. The same girl who would be deeply hurt if her mother were to read her diary will confide all such intimate experiences to the selected members of the peer group. For this reason peer group influences must be studied in order to understand the development of the adolescent personality (Chapter XIX).

SPIRITUAL NEEDS IN ADOLESCENCE

Problem of Spiritual Needs. Having studied three fundamental aspects of adolescent motivation, we shall now consider whether the teen-ager strives just as hard and just as naturally for a spiritual orientation as he does for physical, psychological, or social adjustment. After all, God is as much a part of reality as are the home and school, parents and teachers, classmates and teammates. Since all human striving is directed in some measure toward an adjustive or healthy relation to reality, we cannot ignore the problem posed by the existence of spiritual realities. Above all, the teen-ager is trying to find himself, to realize his own self-identity. Adjustment and mental health require that he find his place in the scheme of things, because without this discovery he cannot achieve full maturity. He must, therefore, explore the world of values, and through them achieve an orientation to spiritual reality as well as to other aspects of reality that require adjustment.

Basic Spiritual Needs. One of the primary needs in this area is the gradual development of an adequate *philosophy* of life, compounded of those values, ideals, and principles that give meaning to human existence, and provide a rational schema for the resolution of conflicts and the adequate handling of frustrations, stresses, and anxieties. This constitutes a first step toward a wholesome spiritual orientation.[17]

Second, the adolescent needs *to define his relationship to God* as well as to his fellow man, and to strive toward a system of beliefs and practices that will activate and enrich these relationships. Because of sexual demands and difficulties, conflicts with parents, and peer group influences, many adolescents become confused and disoriented in their thinking about spiritual realities, with the result that their religious synthesis begins to break down. Also, the tendency toward independence often causes a reorganization and a re-evaluation of religious beliefs and practices. To offset these negative effects, the adolescent needs to redefine his fundamental beliefs and attitudes, and to redefine his relationship to spiritual realities.

In addition to the need to know and love God, we can distinguish the need for spiritual solace; the need for sympathy, understanding, and forgiveness, the need for purity of heart; and the need for eternal salvation. These basic cravings should make it clear why prayer, the Sacraments, confession, and a secure religious orientation can be efficacious in maintaining mental health and promoting the healthy adjustment of the adolescent. As Moser points out in reference to the adolescent girl, sound mental health requires an honest facing of one's self:

> The tears can wash away her standard of protection, and she must finally arrive at an acceptance of herself with whatever limitations and strength she has. A sound training in religion can be a powerful undergirding for this shift to reality. Here she finds a friend who will listen, who cares, yet does not expect the impossible. She can pour out her heart to Him and rise with new thoughts of herself and her place in the world. Then she can take responsibility and relate herself to others, for she has found self-acceptance.[18]

That these spiritual needs are closely allied to and often parallel psychological needs becomes evident from the most cursory analysis. The need for affection is certainly akin to the need for love of God; the craving for security finds a close parallel in the need for salvation; and the needs for acceptance and belonging are complemented by the need for sympathy, understanding, and forgiveness. But, as the child grows toward maturity,

> ... his world of reality expands, and the parents, who at one time were the primary source of affection and security, no longer play the same role. The simple pattern of relations that provided the satisfaction of basic needs gives way before a continually expanding outlook on life and reality; and thus, as the child grows older, and his spiritual needs begin to function more noticeably, the more expansive orientation to reality becomes necessary. No longer can parents, friends, and teachers provide all the answers that are necessary for effective living. Nor can wife, children, friends, and work provide the solace that is required for peace of mind. Disappointments, failures, depression, discouragement, and conflicts require something more than human relations or the joy

---

[17] See P. M. Limbert, "New Light on the Needs of Adolescents," *Relig. Educ.*, 1950, 45, 287–291. Limbert emphasizes three basic needs in adolescence: understanding of one's self and society, setting of goals, and the development of a framework of standards and convictions. See Ruth Strang, *op. cit.*, Chap. 3.

[18] C. G. Moser, *Understanding Girls* (New York: Association Press, 1957), p. 194.

of work can make available. It is then that spiritual needs are felt most strongly, and their gratification becomes as imperative as the need of a child to be loved and protected.[19]

ADOLESCENT DESIRES, WANTS, AND MOTIVES

Needs and Wants. Out of basic needs and motives springs a wide range of human *wants* — wants or desires that extend the problems of human motivation far beyond the satisfaction of basic needs. This fact can be expressed most succinctly by saying that the human mind, through abstraction and generalization, can conceive and strive after anything whatever that comes within range of experience. And because there is considerable intellectual development during adolescence, and a broadening of experience, the number and range of desires may be expected to increase considerably. Such things as a college education, a career in aviation, stardom in the movies, a trip to Europe, or graduation with honors are examples of desires rather than needs. It is apparent that while these things may be ardently desired, *they certainly are not needed.* This fact, however, does not make them any less attractive, or the desires therefore less dynamic, and it may happen that some of the more serious conflicts and difficulties of adolescence arise over the satisfaction of these wants.

But it is necessary to bear in mind two important facts. First, needs are on the whole more fundamental to the process of adjustment than are desires. Because desires are developed through a process of evaluation it is not impossible

to bring the individual to a realization that they cannot, or should not, be gratified;[20] but one cannot be "talked out" of the satisfaction of most needs, and therefore interference with the expression of these needs is likely to lead to difficulties. Second, as we have already indicated elsewhere, desires may be an *indirect expression of some need.* While one cannot question the primacy of intellectual insight in the formation of desires, we may recognize that this ability to conceive ends and goals is often utilized in the service of basic tendencies. In the example of desires mentioned previously (college education, career, etc.), the relationship to basic needs is so obvious as to make comment superfluous. No one can say that every human desire is expressive of a need, but it is unquestionable that many of them are, and that they derive a great deal of their motivating power from this relationship.[21]

Typical Adolescent Wants. Adolescent wants are an individual matter since they depend upon the person's capacities, experiences, opportunities, and environmental or cultural setting. For this reason the cataloguing of adolescent wants is impossible. Nevertheless, there are cer-

---

[19] A. A. Schneiders, *Personal Adjustment and Mental Health* (New York: Rinehart, 1955), p. 195.

[20] Pearson points out that to expand the circle of wants is to multiply temptation and thus to increase the number of sins and crime, and in this country mass media like television vie with each other in parading delectable articles for the population. "This stimulation of desires and apparent needs through propaganda could in itself account for an increase in the amount of adolescent delinquency" — G. H. J. Pearson, op. cit., p. 165.

[21] Writers in the field of adolescent psychology use the terms *need* and *want* to mean different things. For example, reference is made to the need for employment, health, recreation, a good home, or a better education. These are second order needs derived in large measure from the more basic needs like security, status, or achievement. See G. Johnson, "The Needs of Youth," *Cath. Educ. Rev.*, 1938, 36, 3–16.

tain wants that adolescents in our culture manifest with considerable consistency, and that often cause a great deal of difficulty in the handling of adolescent behavior. Shining through these typical wants are the needs of acceptance, security, independence, and the like, which reminds us that motivation is an integral process in which all factors are closely interwoven (see Fig. 15).

First of all, the teen-ager wants *to be left alone.* He doesn't like to be interfered with, told what to do, criticized as to choice of friends, or told when it is time to go to bed. This of course is independence, but independence that is culturized to an important extent by contemporary values and mores.

Second, the teen-ager wants *a place of his own.* Remember, the teen-ager is pulling away from the confines and supports of the family and is making a diligent effort to find himself. Therefore, he wants to be left alone and he wants a place where he can be alone — to dream, to think, to confide his intimate secrets to a diary, to commune with himself, to mull over the happenings of the day, or to be alone with disturbing emotions.

Third, the adolescent wants *a place to which intimate friends can be invited.* The teen-ager needs to socialize, to share new experiences, new things, feelings, conflicts, and ideas. If the home does not provide such a place the adolescent will find a place of his own, be it the corner drugstore, the "rec" room, or the closest "hangout."

Fourth, the adolescent wants to *communicate,* not so much on an intellectual level as on a personal-emotional level. Thus the youngster will spend hours on the phone expressing the most incidental and trivial things that have happened during the day.

Fifth, the adolescent wants *to go to school,* not only because of satisfaction in intellectual achievement and development, but even more so because his basic needs can be more effectively gratified in school than at home. School furnishes contact with the peer group, with persons other than the parents with whom to identify, and an opportunity to escape the demands and restrictions imposed by the family.

Sixth, the teen-ager wants *the privilege of acting like other teen-agers.* This of course reflects conformity to the peer group. The teen-ager wants to date when others do, to go to dances unescorted, to wear the latest style in clothes, to stay out as late as others, to go to postprom breakfasts, or to go on a week-end excursion "with the gang." These are the kind of wants that provide focal points for intense conflicts with parents, and that have to be handled with a great deal of understanding, tact, and wisdom.

Seventh, the teen-ager wants *to have fun.* This desire is what some writers identify as the need for recreation. Remember, the teen-ager has more responsibilities, frustrations, and conflicts than he experienced as a child, and thus it becomes important for him to work off his tensions through amusements such as listening to music, sports, dances, and recreational activities. This is very important for the emotional stability and adjustment of the teen-ager, and every opportunity should be provided by parents for adolescents to have the fun they seek.

Eighth, the typical teen-ager *wants the means to express his desires.* Thus the teen-ager wants some kind of transportation, and as soon as he reaches the legal age he will set up a clamor for the use of the family car or for a vehicle

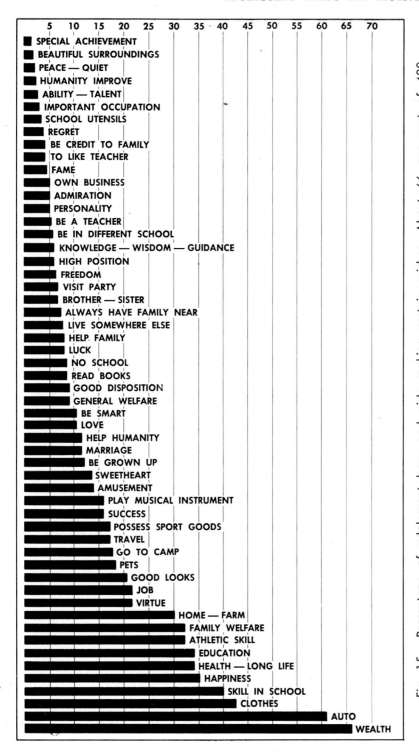

Fig. 15. Percentage of adolescent boys and girls making certain wishes. About 66 per cent of 400 adolescent boys and girls wished for wealth, 61 per cent wished for an auto, and so on. From J. N. Washburn, "The Impulsion of Adolescents as Revealed by Their Written Wishes," J. Juv. Res., 1932, 16, 193–212.

of his own. He also wants an allowance, so that he can do the things that interest him, independently of parental advice or restriction. Also, he wants a radio of his own to tune in his favorite dance bands, and a phonograph to play the records of his favorite singer. In other words, he wants the means of any kind that are necessary to fulfill needs, wants, and desires.

Finally, the teen-ager wants *understanding, help,* and *guidance.* The teen-ager is keenly aware of tendencies toward independence, emancipation, and rebellion; and he is aware that these tendencies bring him into conflict or set up barriers between him and his family. He also knows that there are many problems which he cannot solve, or even understand. He wants help in coping with these problems, and he wants guidance that will set his feet on the right path. These are some of the *normal* wants of the typical adolescent in the American culture. For parents and teachers they present the same kind of problem posed by basic needs. They are part of the mainsprings of adolescent behavior, and to understand and control such behavior effectively we must become aware of what the adolescent wants as well as what the adolescent needs.

SELECTED READINGS

Bernard, H. W., *Mental Hygiene for Classroom Teachers* (New York: McGraw-Hill, 1952), Chap. 5.

———— *Adolescent Development in American Culture* (New York: World Book, 1957), Chap. 3.

Fleming, C. M., *Adolescence* (New York: International Universities Press, 1949), Chap. V.

Mohr, G. J., and Despres, Marian A., *The Stormy Decade: Adolescence* (New York: Random House, 1958), Chap. XI.

Plant, J. S., *The Envelope: a Study of the Impact of the World Upon the Child* (New York: Commonwealth Fund, 1950), Chaps. 1, 3.

Salisbury, H. E., *The Shook-up Generation* (New York: Harper, 1958).

Shuttleworth, F. K., "The Adolescent Period: a Graphic Atlas," *Monogr. Soc. Res. & Child Develpm.,* 1949, XIV, I (336–338).

Strang, Ruth, *The Adolescent Views Himself* (New York: McGraw-Hill, 1957).

Wheelis, A., *The Quest for Identity* (New York: Norton, 1958).

CHAPTER IX

FEELINGS AND
EMOTIONS IN ADOLESCENCE

Needs and motives are not the only things that will determine what a teen-ager is going to do. He also does things just for the fun of it, or because he feels lonely or depressed, anxious, ashamed, or guilty. Here is the story of how adolescents feel, and what these feelings do to their behavior.

AFFECTIVE REACTIONS AND HUMAN BEHAVIOR

Dynamic Aspects of Affective Reactions. The needs and desires of adolescents are only a part of the reason why they behave as they do. At every moment their behavior also reflects their *feelings* and *emotions*, their *moods* and *sentiments*. When Jane says that she would like to go to the school dance but she won't because she feels so inadequate or inferior, she is unwittingly making a distinction between *dynamic* and *affective* processes, and reflecting the relative influence of both. The *desire* to do what is right is different from the *feeling* of satisfaction from having done what is right. Yet all such tendencies or experiences are closely allied to each other insofar as they motivate behavior.

In what way are feelings and emotions related to needs and motives? Do they cause or influence behavior in the same way? Part of the answer to these questions is implied in the terms used for these processes. Feelings and emotions are referred to as "affective" processes, whereas needs and motives are classified as "appetitive" or "conative." From the standpoint of experience, there is a considerable gap between felt needs like hunger, thirst, or recognition, and feelings like joy, anxiety, or guilt.

When we analyze experiences in which both needs and feelings are involved we see the reason for this distinction. Feelings and emotions are *subjective* reactions to the frustration or gratification of needs and motives. Thus, whenever a need is gratified, or an impulse expressed in appropriate action, there is generated a feeling of satisfaction, pleasantness, or joy. When, on the contrary, an impulse is inhibited or frustrated, there is a corresponding feeling of annoyance, anger, or fear. Thus the *need* for affection, when gratified, generates the *emotion* of love; the need for security, when not gratified, generates feelings of fear or inferiority.

This relationship makes it easy to see why affective processes have dynamic value. In any given response, the need or impulse is the conative element which provides the initial propulsion toward some end or goal, whereas the feeling is the affective element which serves to reinforce the tendency or behavior that results. The dynamic characteristics of the total response derive from both the satisfaction (or inhibition) of a need or desire, and from the reinforcement provided by the affective reaction. Thus, in a typical situation, the adolescent does not rebel against his parents because he is angry, but rather because he is frustrated. Frustration generates feelings of annoyance or anger, and these feelings act to reinforce whatever response occurs.

From a developmental point of view, feelings and emotions may, through learning and conditioning, become associated with certain behavior patterns in such a way that a direct connection between affective response and conduct occurs. Thus, if the feeling of sadness has come to mean "tears," the crying response will occur. Genetically, however, the response flows from a need and not from the affective component. This explains why it is possible to cry from joy as well as from sadness. If sadness generated crying of itself, then it would indeed be a paradox to cry from joy. Actually, the response is indifferent to the feeling state, so that one may cry no matter how he feels. We should note also that not all feelings or emotions are particularly dynamic. Strong emotions like anger and fear stimulate action, but feelings like awe, embarrassment, and reverence may have little effect on conduct. Even so powerful an experience as love may occasion nothing more than a deep sigh.

The Range of Affective Processes. The affective life, when fully developed in the normal person, is very broad. It includes the basic feelings of pleasantness and unpleasantness, as well as complex feelings like joy, sorrow, sadness, annoyance, and disgust. There are also the emotions which, while more complex in character, are genetically and structurally related to feelings. Outstanding among these are the reactions of fear, anger, aggression, and love. The dividing line between feelings and emotions is not at all clear, since one may think of feelings like joy, sorrow, and shame as true emotions, and of the emotions as feeling states. Genetically, it makes little difference how these affective responses are designated, as long as we understand the pattern of their development. Besides feelings and emotions there are two other affective states: moods and sentiments. These may be regarded as derivatives of the more primitive feelings and emotions.

THE DYNAMICS OF PLEASURE AND PAIN

Pleasure and Pain as Motivators of Behavior. Everyone is aware that both pleasure and pain play a major role in influencing human behavior. Pleasure was regarded by Freud as a fundamental principle of human dynamics, and his theory of the pleasure principle is one of the classic doctrines in psychoanalysis. Similarly, pain has always been regarded as dynamic, and many studies have been made to determine its role in the motivation of behavior.[1]

[1] See the article by P. T. Young, "The Role of Hedonic Processes in Motivation," in M. R. Jones (ed.), Nebraska Symposium on Motivation (Lincoln: University of Nebraska Press, 1955), pp. 193–238; T. S. Szasz, Pain and Pleasure: a Study of Bodily Feelings (New York: Basic Books, 1957), especially Parts I and IV; H. S. Tuttle, Dynamic Psychology and Conduct (New York: Harper, 1949), Chap. 7.

Where do these factors fit into the general scheme of motivation? First, let us note that pleasure and pain are not in the strict sense psychological opposites, because pleasure is essentially an affective experience whereas pain belongs to the category of sensory phenomena along with pressure, temperature, and kinesthesis. Pleasure is actually a derivative of *pleasantness*, the opposite of which is *unpleasantness*. Both qualities are "feeling tones" that condition mental processes and behavior. This dichotomy is strictly psychological and enables us to classify certain experiences in terms of their *affective value*. The term *pleasure* is less precise in meaning than pleasantness, although it denotes almost the same experience. Actually, the concept of pleasure is an abstraction that embraces all kinds of *pleasing* experiences. Pleasantness is the affective reaction to a single experience, whereas pleasure is a *diffuse* reaction involving many pleasant experiences usually stimulated in rapid succession. By abstraction, pleasure can be raised to the plane of a goal, sought after for its own sake. Both pleasant and pleasurable, therefore, refer to agreeable experiences, those things that we enjoy and want to repeat, and those that impart satisfaction.

Where the term *pain* is concerned, we must recognize that it is neither the opposite of pleasure nor of pleasantness. It is only when the term is used *analogously* to characterize an experience as extremely unpleasant that it appears as the direct opposite of pleasant. We say, for example, that music poorly rendered is "painful" to the ear of a musician, meaning that it is unpleasant, and not that it stimulates actual pain. However, the two experiences are psychologically very similar and are thus often confused.

Pleasure as a Dynamic Tendency. Pleasantness and unpleasantness pervade all areas of mental life and behavior, and in that sense are unlike other dynamic tendencies such as needs. Their dynamic function is similar to that of ideals, principles, and attitudes, insofar as they lend added strength to conduct already in process. In the course of development these factors, like the sustaining motives, acquire dynamic quality as soon as the organism learns that certain experiences are pleasant and others are unpleasant, after which they are actively sought after or avoided. In this sense we may say that an action is performed *because* of its pleasurable aspect, or another avoided *because* it is unpleasant.

Here the essential weakness of a hedonistic interpretation of behavior stands out. The pleasure principle of the psychoanalytic school is not at all adequate to account for the *beginning* of human conduct of any kind, let alone conduct that is rationally motivated. This is evident from the fact that all basic needs have the *same* affective component, namely, pleasantness. The gratification of needs like hunger, sex, affection, and security results in the experience of pleasantness, whereas frustration of these needs causes unpleasantness. If we ask why the organism seeks food or security, it is simply because the organism *requires* these things. Obviously, pleasure plays only a *secondary* role in the dynamics of such behavior. It is correct to say that the organism seeks certain experiences or objects because they are pleasant, but from the standpoint of dynamics it is more correct to say that they are sought because they are needed.

The failure to keep this fundamental distinction in mind may lead to serious behavior difficulties. When anything is sought mainly because of the pleasure it affords rather than because it is actually needed, the organism tends to over-activity in the direction of the need. Thus hunger is directed primarily to the securing of food, not to the pleasure of eating. When, therefore, the pleasure of eating is given primacy in motivation, overeating is likely to result, with physical harm to the organism an inevitable outcome. This applies with equal force to all needs, psychological as well as physiological. The reader can easily imagine the results in the case of the sex drive, of which the primary end is procreation, not pleasure. Similarly, affection, security, or conformity could be misused in the interest of gaining pleasure.

The function of pleasure, therefore, is salutary; it insures continuance of activity already begun. It serves also to stimulate behavior, but only after its connection with behavior is realized through experience. The biological and psychological serviceability of this relationship is quite clear. Not only is the organism provided with needs that are so dynamic as to insure activity directed toward its preservation, but in addition these activities are surfeited with pleasure so that the process of self-preservation is doubly insured. The teen-ager not only needs experience or status and is dynamically oriented toward it, but derives a great deal of pleasure from achieving it. Not only does he experience strong urges toward sexual exploration in the form of necking and petting, but his whole body is suffused with exciting pleasure when he kisses his girl or holds her close.

The Freudian concept of the pleasure principle is valuable in emphasizing the fact that the state of pleasantness is more natural to the organism than is unpleasantness. Unpleasantness may be likened to the state of tension or disequilibrium that characterizes the frustration of needs, whereas its opposite is similar to the condition of quiescence that results from the satisfaction of needs. Tension, especially when prolonged, is unpleasant; and the reduction of tension by appropriate activity is decidedly pleasant in character. The progression, therefore, is always *in the direction of pleasantness*, in much the same way that the direction of activity is always toward equilibrium. Thus, the experience of hunger (the need for food) is unpleasant, and this leads to the ingestion of food, which is a pleasant experience. In this way nature utilizes unpleasantness to secure pleasantness and the gratification of basic needs. The fact that these needs, when experienced in mild form, appear as pleasant experiences in nowise contradicts this interpretation. Mild hunger is pleasant because of the *anticipation* (itself a symbolic realization) of food. In infants it is quite probable that hunger is always experienced as unpleasant.

The Dynamics of Pain. The dynamics of pain is essentially the same as that of pleasantness-unpleasantness. Biologically, pain exists as a sign of disaffection or danger; psychologically, it is an adjustment sign which leads to behavior by which the cause of the pain is eliminated. In itself pain is no more dynamic than any other sensation. Its motivational properties derive from the twin circumstances that it is unpleasant, and that it exists as a threat to the satisfaction of certain basic needs, particularly security and physical integrity. The experience of pain does not lead directly to behavior as do needs and motives; rather, pain stimulates unpleasantness, and arouses needs which in turn lead to adjustive behavior. For this reason pain (especially in mild form) can be endured indefinitely. It can be endured so long as it is not too unpleasant. We should note, however, that pain plays an important part in human motivation because of its intrinsic relation to *punishment*, a problem to which we shall turn in a later section. Punishment is effective in motivating behavior only because it is painful and disagreeable, and without this quality it would have little motivational significance.[2]

The Role of Pleasure and Pain in Human Motivation. Explaining the dynamics of pleasure and pain in this way does not detract from their importance to human motivation. Pleasure does exist as a *goal* for all persons to a greater or less extent, regardless of the satisfaction of basic needs; and, similarly, many actions are a reflection of the desire *to avoid pain*. We read books, attend movies, or play ball because these activities ensure pleasure; and we put off going to the dentist or avoid a fight because of its painful consequences.

This common-sense viewpoint of pleasure and pain should be brought in line with certain developmental facts. Both pleasantness and unpleasantness exist originally as qualities of experience only; but through experience some actions and events *become associated* with pleasantness, and others with unpleasantness or pain. The former experiences are then sought out and repeated, and the latter as carefully avoided. Eventually, therefore, pleasure is elevated to the rank of a good (the *bonum delectabile* of Scholastic writers), and is then *sought for its own sake*. Thus pleasure can exist as a

goal regardless of the satisfaction of basic needs.

Also because the pleasurable aspect of experiences and activities can be abstracted and personified as a good in itself, we can speak of a distinct "pleasure goal," that is, a goal separate and distinct from the ends toward which fundamental needs are directed. Discovering through experience that an activity is pleasurable, the person seeks its repetition, whether it leads to the satisfaction of a need or not. Thus, going to the movies may be a means of gratifying the need for experience; but it may also be done for pleasure. In this sense, pleasure becomes a *motive in itself* and may thus influence activity in the same way that any other motive does. It then becomes a *reason* for acting. In other words, pleasure can be "rationalized" into a distinct motive independent of the dynamics of needs. The same is true of unpleasantness and pain.

Of greatest significance here is the *dynamic value of pleasure*. Often all we need to know about an act is that it is pleasurable; and because of the driving power of pleasure, some actions *get beyond control*, especially those determined by certain basic needs. For example, if sexual experience were divested of its pleasurable quality, the sex problems of adolescents would largely disappear. The drinking of alcoholic beverages can also be partly explained by the feeling of pleasant euphoria induced by alcohol. Other activities are similarly motivated. Experience, coupled with imaginative recall, plays an important part in the development of this motivation. When the adolescent learns through experience that a certain action is very pleasant, he tends to repeat it at the first opportunity. If to this tendency is added the recall of

[2] See T. S. Szasz, *op. cit.*, p. 86, where pain is interpreted as "a fundamental method of asking for help." Szasz also draws a clear relationship between pain and punishment.

the delectable features of the behavior, it will almost certainly be repeated. The control of such responses depends partly, therefore, on the *avoidance of the original experience*, or upon control of one's imagination.

DEVELOPMENT OF FEELINGS IN ADOLESCENCE

The Dynamic Significance of Feelings. A significant aspect of affective development in adolescence is the emergence of the more *complex feelings*, a partial list of which is indicated below. Whether such feelings are part of the innate equipment of the organism, and await the

PARTIAL LIST OF COMPLEX FEELINGS

Anxiety	Elation
Despondency	Gratitude
Despair	Scorn
Regret	Loathing
Sorrow	Envy
Shame	Jealousy
Embarrassment	Pity
Reverence	Sympathy
Awe	Confidence
Reproach	Joy
Disgust	Guilt
Wonder	Loneliness

maturation of other factors before putting in an appearance, or whether they are derived from other emotional responses, is difficult to determine. Of these two possibilities, the second seems to be the more likely. Such responses as joy, remorse, guilt, etc., seem to emerge naturally after a certain amount of maturation has occurred, and are probably related developmentally to the more

basic emotional responses, like fear and anger, that appear earlier in the course of development.[3]

Bridges worked out a theory of emotional development based on the assumption that visceral pattern reactions like any other form of behavior undergo processes of differentiation and co-ordination as a result of physiological and environmental differences. This theory assumes a primordial excitement from which during infancy three patterns are derived: distress, delight, and excitement itself, which continues unchanged into adulthood. From the infantile distress are derived fear, anger, and distress; and from delight come joy, affection, and delight. In the middle years of childhood fear becomes differentiated into shame, anxiety, and fear; anger into disappointment, anger, jealousy, and envy; and distress into disgust and distress. Delight continues into adulthood as delight, whereas joy breaks down into elation and parental affection. Further differentiation occurs throughout later childhood and adolescence.[4] This theory admittedly offers interesting possibilities for the development of the complex feelings, the only limitation being that it is based too largely upon an objective approach to emotions. It is the subjective feeling state that differentiates one affective element from another, and the development of these feeling states must be accounted for in any complete

---

[3] On the development of certain of these feelings in relation to sexual maturation, see R. R. Willoughby, "Sexuality in the Second Decade," *Monogr. Soc. Res. in Child Develpm.*, 1937, 2, No. 3.

[4] K. M. B. Bridges, "A Genetic Theory of the Emotions," *J. Genet. Psychol.*, 1930, 37, 514–527. See also K. M. B. Bridges, "Emotional Development in Early Infancy," *Child Develpm.*, 1932, 3, 324–341.

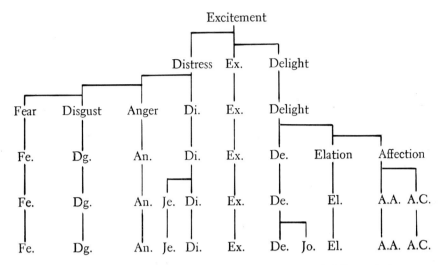

Fig. 16.   Chart showing the approximate ages of differentiation of the various emotions during the first two years of life. KEY: **A.A.** — affection for adults; **A.C.** — affection for children; **An.** — anger; **De.** — delight; **Dg.** — disgust; **Di** — distress; **El.** — elation; **Ex.** — excitement; **Fe.** — fear; **Je.** — jealousy; **Jo.** — joy. From K. M. B. Bridges, "Emotional Development in Early Infancy," **Child Develpm.** (Lafayette, Ind.: Child Development Publications), **3**, 324–341.

theory of affective development. These relationships are diagramed in Figure 16.

Exactly when these feelings develop is a matter of speculation since they are not easily identified. Reactions like shame, remorse, joy, sympathy, and wonder probably develop during the middle years of childhood; but one cannot be sure because children often admit to feelings when such feelings do not exist at all. A child may say that he is ashamed, but whether he actually experiences the feeling of shame is problematical. In some instances, such as embarrassment, sorrow, and jealousy, external signs are so clear that a safe inference may be made regarding the existence of the feeling. With respect to other reactions like reverence, pity, and despondency, it is likely that they do not develop until adolescence or even later.

Where Feelings Come From.   Some of the most important feelings of the adolescent period derive from the gratification or the frustration of basic needs, particularly those of a psychological nature. It is clear that the feeling of self-confidence is directly related to the achievement of status, acceptance, and worth; that anxiety has its origin in the blocking of security; and that feelings of joy and contentment are determined by gratifying needs for achievement, affection, and belonging. Here again, as in the case of pleasure and pain, the feelings which are generated out of basic needs serve to reinforce behavior, and thus play an important role in adolescent motivation. This intrinsic relationship between needs and feelings is fundamental to understanding the psychic development of the adolescent as well as his behavior.

Feelings are essentially a developmental phenomenon, and therefore other developments that occur during adolescence play an important role in determining their emergence. Prominent among these factors is *intellectual development*. Feelings like awe and reverence, for example, require understanding and insight, plus an awareness of the relationships between oneself and the objects of the feelings. Feelings of this kind require a concept of what the thing is, its nature, attributes, and power. A great disaster is awesome only because we understand its implications. We revere God because we grasp something of His nature and attributes, and our relationships to Him. Whether preadolescents are ordinarily capable of this kind of experience is doubtful.

Important also in the development of feelings is the growth of the self-concept, without which some of these tendencies would not appear at all. Feelings like shame, embarrassment, guilt, remorse, and loneliness are clearly based on self-awareness. In fact, the majority of these feelings depend to some extent for development on the growth of the self-concept. Affective reactions are distinctly *personal* in character; they are reactions of self to events that have significance for self; and therefore the more fully developed is the idea of self the more surely will such reactions emerge.

Affective processes may also have a distinct objective reference. They are, in the language of psychology, *adient* responses. This is certainly true of such feelings as sympathy, jealousy, and envy, and of the sentiments of friendship, patriotism, love, and loyalty. All these reactions are important to personal and social development, and some of them have serious implications for moral and religious development. Were it not for feelings like sympathy, pity, or friendliness, the individual's social consciousness would be extremely limited, and social adjustment a much more difficult task.

Conversely, social, moral, and religious development during adolescence contributes to the growth of feelings. In matters such as these it is often difficult to determine which is cause and which is effect. Nevertheless, we can be sure that many social and religious experiences help to arouse or to strengthen different feelings. Gratitude, for example, is more likely to develop in a person who is keenly aware of social relationships and responsibilities than one in whom such development has not yet taken place. Guilt will assume more precise form in the adolescent than in the child because of a more highly developed moral consciousness, just as reverence will develop more fully in the person with a deeper religious consciousness. Because of the close connections between intellectual, moral, social, and religious development and emotional growth, feelings emerge more clearly during the adolescent period. Adolescence, therefore, is the period *par excellence* for the development of the emotions and the formation of a stable temperament.

Feelings Important to Adolescent Conduct.   All feelings have some importance in the scheme of human motivation, but there are certain ones that are particularly significant for the mental health and stability of the adolescent. Take the case of a boy whom we will call Larry Smith. Larry is just fifteen years old and a sophomore in high school. He is a serious youngster who studies hard and hopes some day to follow in his father's footsteps and become a lawyer. Test records indicate that Larry has better than average ability and should be among the top 25 per cent of his class. Yet Larry doesn't do well in school, refuses to participate in out-of-class activities although he is strongly interested in writing, and keeps pretty much to himself.

What is wrong here? The answer is simple. Larry is lacking in *self-confidence*. He has deep feelings of *inadequacy* and *inferiority*, which prevent him from exploring different possibilities and utilizing his potentialities to the best advantage. As a result, Larry feels insecure in academic as well as social situations, and thus tends to keep to himself. It is not important here to ask what caused these feelings, but to recognize the deep and pervasive effect they have on behavior. In this case we see feelings of self-confidence and security undermined by feelings of inferiority and inadequacy; this leads to insecurity, and therefore to *lack* of self-confidence. This sort of thing is likely to happen in adolescence because of the uncertainty and instability of the adolescent, because of lack of self-identity, and because concepts and values are still in the formative stage. Adolescence being what it is, feelings of this kind may be much more disturbing in their effects than would be the case in adulthood.[5]

Larry expressed something else in his behavior that is important in this connection. He was something of a "loner" and therefore often experienced the feeling of *loneliness*. The teen-ager often feels lonely because he is caught between two worlds and has not yet found himself. He feels that he is not accepted, that he has little personal worth, or that he is "different," and this sets him apart from others. He may feel lonely, too, because he is unable to share his anxieties, conflicts, doubts, and uncertainties with other persons, including his parents and members of the peer group. Loneliness stems directly from rejection, and this is most likely to happen when the adolescent is rejected by his peers. Like all such negative feelings, loneliness contributes a great deal to the anguish and misery that many teen-agers experience.

Feelings like inferiority, inadequacy, and lack of self-confidence are augmented during adolescence to an important extent by the development of feelings of guilt, shame, and remorse.[6] Observing the behavior of young children we see little evidence of the influence of such feeling states. The preadolescent can feel guilty and ashamed, but it is unlikely that these feelings have any great dynamic significance for the child's behavior. This is not true of the adolescent. Because of the development of sexual impulses and behavior, the adolescent often experiences deep-seated feelings of guilt and shame which torture him incessantly, and which often express themselves in *scrupulosity*. Here again we see a reflection of the uncertainty, instability, and lack of wisdom of the teen-ager. At times guilt and scrupulosity develop out of *perfectionism*, a defensive reaction that the adolescent sets up in order to protect himself from his own inadequacy and inferiority. It is also in part a reflection

---

[5] See the excellent discussion of inadequacy and inferiority in J. S. Plant, *The Envelope: a Study of the Impact of the World Upon the Child* (New York: Commonwealth Fund, 1950), Chap. 14.

[6] In this connection see B. R. Sappenfield, *Personality Dynamics: an Integrative Psychology of Adjustment* (New York: Knopf, 1954), pp. 182–188.

of the unrealistic *idealism* characteristic of adolescence. The problem of guilt is one of the most serious difficulties that the adolescent runs into, and must be handled with utmost skill in order to prevent the development of scrupulosity or an obsessive-compulsive neurosis.[7]

Out of these feelings of inferiority, loneliness, guilt, and insecurity will develop a deep-seated and pervasive *anxiety*, certainly the most common and one of the most disturbing of all affective responses. Anxiety, like guilt and shame, is in itself a normal response and can be utilized by the organism to its own advantage. Anxiety stimulates remedial action of some sort, and guilt causes the person to seek forgiveness and perhaps avoidance of the behavior that causes guilt. However, too much anxiety and a distorted sense of guilt lead to all kinds of personality disorders. Anxiety develops its own neurosis and symptomotology, and guilt leads to self-rejection, self-debasement, feelings of worthlessness and inferiority, and to pathological scrupulosity or compulsive disorder.

Because of these possibilities, the feelings experienced by adolescents become important factors in understanding and interpreting their behavior. Feelings, like the needs to which they are closely related, can be very dynamic and cause considerable distortion in the behavior and personality patterns of young people. At the same time it must be observed that teen-agers give evidence also of positive, constructive feelings, such as joy,

---

[7] For a thorough discussion of guilt in relation to scrupulosity, see A. A. Schneiders (ed.), *Proceedings, First Institute for the Clergy on Problems in Pastoral Psychology* (New York: Fordham Univ., 1956), pp. 5–39, 53–85. See also Chapter 15 of P. M. Symonds, *Dynamic Psychology* (New York: Appleton-Century-Crofts, 1949). These same sources contain good discussions of the problem of anxiety.

elation, sympathy, self-confidence, security, and contentment. We often see adolescents in a group enjoying themselves immensely, sharing their innermost secrets and experiences with each other, cavorting gaily in a modern dance, and laughing happily with and at each other. This, of course, is as it should be, and our guidance and counseling of adolescents should be directed toward the development of more positive feelings.

The Development of Moods. There is no clear dividing line between feelings and moods. However, moods are more persistent than feelings, and they are generally pervasive in character, spreading their effect over the whole of mental life. A mood may be thought of as the *affective residue* of a prior emotional experience; or, conversely, as a *predisposition* to an affective response. In many instances the negative feelings described in the foregoing paragraphs will generate *depression*, which can become a serious emotional problem for the adolescent; whereas positive feelings tend to generate such moods as *joy* or *elation*. These relationships constitute a partial explanation of the genesis of moods. Children are seldom moody for the reason that their feelings and emotions are mostly transient in character, reactions of the moment that are quickly superseded by new experiences.

Moods are subject to the same laws of development that govern other affective experiences. As the individual grows in experience and insight, the implications of everyday happenings, of conflicts and disappointments, of accomplishments and mistakes, become clearer, and the affective life changes accordingly. Thus the adolescent may become moody because of feelings of guilt, a fancied wrong, an interminable conflict, the promise of things to come, a stirring religious experience, or a first venture into the realm of love. Or — and this we cannot afford to overlook — his mood may be a reflection of physical changes or disturbances. Like the majority of affective processes, moods are closely linked to physical functions and we may expect that with the changes in physical make-up during adolescence there will be corresponding alterations of mood. Ordinarily they are of no great significance, but on occasion they may be; for persistent moods — those that last for several days or weeks — are danger signals that herald severe disturbances of personality or undesirable conduct. Continuous anxiety, undue elation, ecstatic euphoria, despondency, jealousy, or pessimism are signs of emotional imbalance, and require adjustive procedures. Remembering that the adolescent mind is fertile soil for conflict and frustration, and keeping in mind the continuous change and lack of integration during adolescence, we should be on the lookout for the development of different moods during this period.

EMOTIONS AND
THEIR DEVELOPMENT

Nature of Emotional Development.
From the developmental point of view, the most striking characteristic of the affective life is its simplicity in infancy and early childhood. We may suppose that in infancy there are feelings of pleasantness and unpleasantness, plus an undifferentiated *emotional excitement* out of which patterns of emotional response gradually emerge. There is, however, little indication of the many feelings found in adult life, such as shame and sorrow, sympathy and joy, which can be very important to human conduct.

Nor are there any moods and sentiments, so that the affective life of the young child is quite narrow and perhaps somewhat shallow in character.[8]

This fact makes it important to define the term *emotional development*, since it may mean two different things: first, the transition from the simple affective life of the infant to the complex emotional life of the adult, involving the emergence of complex feelings, moods, and sentiments; and, second, certain changes that occur within the structure of the emotions and feelings themselves. An adequate developmental interpretation of emotional phenomena must cover both of these aspects.

What is meant by the term *emotion* as distinct from other affective processes? An emotion is an *innate, psychophysical* response to some stimulus, object, or situation, that is characterized by a *feeling quality.* Structurally, it involves a stimulus or cognitive element (perception, image, idea), certain bodily changes (rapid heartbeat, trembling, secretion of adrenalin, etc.), and an affective experience that serves to identify the emotion (the feeling of being afraid, angry, etc.). It may be noted that certain feelings can be defined in the same way. Shame and embarrassment, for example, are also psychophysical reactions, and, except for the fact that they occur later in develop-

[8] See J. E. Anderson, "Changes in Emotional Responses With Age," in M. L. Reymert (ed.), *Feelings and Emotions: the Mooseheart Symposium* (New York: McGraw-Hill, 1950), pp. 418–428; A. T. Jersild, "Emotional Development," in L. Carmichael (ed.), *Manual of Child Psychology* (New York: Wiley, 1946), pp. 752–790; L. D. Crow and Alice Crow, *Adolescent Development and Adjustment* (New York: McGraw-Hill, 1956), Chap. 6; H. W. Bernard, *Adolescent Development in American Culture* (New York: World Book, 1957), Chap. 10; and A. A. Schneiders, "Emotional Development in Children," *Educ.*, 1951, 72, 216–223.

ment, there is no way in which they can be clearly distinguished from emotion. Therefore, whatever we find regarding the development of the emotions may be applied equally to these experiences.

Emotions and Physical Correlates. Emotions are closely linked to bodily structures and functions. Whether this applies to all affective processes is debatable, but it certainly applies to the majority of them. Emotions, therefore are conditioned by the state of the physical organism, a relationship which is clearly exemplified in sexual responses. The bodily changes that occur during emotion are *integral parts of the emotion*, a fact of considerable importance to emotional development because of the pervasive physical changes that occur at different growth levels. We have already noted that the development of sexual feeling is directly related to the changes that occur at puberty in the sex glands; and considering the interrelationships among the various glands of internal secretion, it is more than likely that other emotional changes are similarly affected. The implications of such relationships are highlighted by the close tie-up between the gonads and the adrenals, since the latter structures play so significant a role in the reactions of fear and anger.

While the emotion *as a feeling state* remains essentially the same throughout the life span, developmental organic changes may have to occur before a particular feeling or emotion develops, or they may seriously influence the development of already existing emotions and feelings. Excitability, depression, and moodiness, for example, can be affected by changes in the thyroid glands. During adolescence, therefore, when the glandular system undergoes considerable altera-

tion, corresponding changes in the emotional life may be expected.

Cognitive and Behavioral Changes in Emotions. Changes coincident with physical development are not the only ones that occur. Casual observation as well as empirical studies indicate that the stimuli and cognitive experiences which arouse emotional responses change considerably throughout childhood and adolescence. Whereas the situations that evoke fear and anger in the infant, or embarrassment in the child, are very limited, in the adolescent and adult they are greatly increased. The infant fears loss of support or a sudden loud noise; whereas the adolescent may fear the dark, open or closed spaces, germs, people, snakes, crowds, death, and disease — anything in fact with which the response becomes associated by conditioning, experience, or learning.[9] The same is true of other emotions like anger, love, or hate. This fact has important implications for adequate emotional development and for adjustment. From the mental hygiene point of view, it means that many maladjustive responses could be avoided, or that such responses can be eliminated by relearning or by psychotherapy.

Various studies indicate that there are characteristic changes in the stimuli that evoke different emotional reactions during adolescence. For example, it has been found that, while the situations involving anger vary greatly, it is particularly the *behavior of others* that stimulates this response. This is especially true of girls, whereas boys experience anger more often with inanimate objects that get in

[9] See H. Angelino and C. L. Shedd, "Shifts in the Content of Fears and Worries Relative to Chronological Age," *Proc. Okla. Acad. Sci.*, 1953, 34, 180–186. See also Marie H. Means, "Fears of One Thousand College Women," *J. Abnorm. Soc. Psychol.*, 1936, 31, 291–311.

their way, or that do not work as well as they should. Thus anger experiences in youth are different from those of the child, at least so far as affective stimuli are concerned.

Similar results have been obtained in studies of fear-evoking stimuli. Whereas children are found to fear many things ranging from poison to sickness and floods, adolescents learn more and more to fear those things of which adults are typically afraid, like money, ability, and family. In other words, there is a developmental shift away from things that might be expected to induce fear in the inexperienced child to items of experience that are of especial significance for adult living. Here is an instance of how emotional changes are influenced by growing intellectual insight as well as by experience and association. It is the adult's ability to *interpret* events as dangerous or threatening to his well-being that causes them to become fearful.

On the *behavioral* side of emotion there are also significant changes that occur with development; that is, the *expression* of the feeling state is characteristically different. In the infant, anger produces writhing, crying, or screaming; in the adolescent it may generate nothing more violent than a verbal retort. In point of fact, investigations indicate a definite tendency to *verbalize* emotional responses. For example, the child expresses affection with embraces, hugs, and kisses, whereas the adolescent, stimulated by the same feeling, may write sonnets or pour out his love in words and song.

Fear, too, is behaviorally different in later stages of development. The natural reaction to fear is flight; yet in many instances there may be no evidence of this reaction in the adolescent or adult.

Here again verbalization may occur, which often takes the form of boasting or braggadocio to cover up the inner feeling state. Not infrequently, of course, among both adolescents and adults, the natural response to any one of these emotions occurs. Temper tantrums, for example, are not unknown among adolescents; and they are behaviorally very similar to the screaming, crying, and kicking reactions of small children who are frustrated or angry. The response to affection, too, is often childish in character. The cooing, murmuring, and babyish talk of persons in love are strikingly similar to the gurglings of an infant in whom affection is stimulated. These are instances of outmoded emotional behavior patterns, or regressions to a childish level; but they clearly exemplify the fact that overt emotional expression is not always outgrown.

The Conditions of Emotional Development. The four most important factors that lie at the basis of emotional changes are: (1) physical growth and development; (2) intellectual maturation; (3) social development; and (4) experience, including conditioning and learning. Other changes, particularly those involving basic motivations, are also important to emotional development in adolescence; but here we are concerned primarily with changes in the cognitive and behavioral aspects of emotion wherein the above factors play the dominant role.

The part played by physical changes in altering the pattern of emotional response has already been indicated, and these changes are most directly related to alterations in emotional behavior. Changes in the cognitive aspect of emotion, on the other hand, are due in large measure to the factor of intellectual development. Whereas in infancy emotional responses are caused by simple stimuli, in later life they are evoked by meaningful objects or situations. A flood is fearful to a child only because it means danger, and certain experiences stimulate anger in the adolescent only because of their particular meaning.

This transition from a simple stimulus-response situation to one where meaning is involved in emotional response is the result of both maturation and conditioning. As the person matures intellectually, events and objects become more meaningful; he begins to understand better their significance and their relationship to himself; and thus in time these factors become effective in stimulating the particular emotion. This process is also influenced by learning, and thus, as the child learns through experience or instruction that an object means danger, or thwarting, or affection, the emotion becomes associated with the object, and is then evoked whenever the object is present either perceptually or ideationally. Thus, as the boy or girl matures in knowledge, insight, and experience, certain events take on added emotional significance, and others begin to lose their significance. This development is indispensable to emotional adjustment, since if the adolescent carries over his childish fears, aversions, and tantrums into adulthood, emotional maladjustment is inevitable.

Emotional changes are also conditioned by social development and maturation, though less directly. As the adolescent gradually enlarges the sphere of his social activities and contacts, new relationships, experiences, and demands emerge that often change the meaning of affective stimuli. This change is especially prominent in the transition to a heterosexual outlook, during which emotional meanings undergo considerable change. Girls and boys, parties and dances, clothes and cosmetics assume a different emotional significance as the young person passes through the adolescent period. As we shall see more fully later on (Chapter XVII), meanings and perceptions are determined as much by dynamic factors within the personality as by the nature of the object or event the person is experiencing. It is for this reason that social development influences emotional meanings.

Intellectual and social maturation will also affect emotional expression. When we compare emotional responses of children with those of adolescents, we see that children's responses occur without regard for social implications. A child will indulge in temper tantrums, display affection, or turn in flight from a fearful object without the least regard for the opinions, codes, or demands of the group. With the adolescent it is different. As his social consciousness develops, his emotional expressions become more and more restricted, and he gradually brings them in line with accepted modes of conduct. Emotional behavior tends to assume the form of a reduced, inhibited response. This occurs not only because of social pressures, but also because the volitional capacity to inhibit and control responses has increased. These changes in emotional expression should not be separated from adolescent volitional developments, which often serve as the media by which intelligence affects emotional responses. As the adolescent understands more and more clearly the purpose and significance of emotional control, volition will play an even greater role in emotional adjustment.

Emotional development is also influenced by experience and training. Why do some children (or adolescents) fear the dark? Certainly not because it is emotionally meaningful or socially significant. Such fears are a product of experience or conditioning; children, in other words, *learn* to fear the dark. Meaning has little to do with such responses. Many persons fear the dark even though fully aware that their fear is groundless and unreasonable. Stage fright is of this kind.

Many persons are conditioned in childhood to respond with fear to different situations. In this way children become afraid of many things not in themselves fearful, through the simple process of arousing fear in connection with the object or situation. Many pathological fears (phobias) also develop in the same manner. The normal person does not *fear* germs; he merely avoids them as a possible source of infection whenever he can. The microphobic individual, on the other hand, actually fears contact with them, because in some manner he has associated fear with germs. These conditioned responses, of which there are very many, are independent of meaning, and many of them continue into adolescent and adult life. The remedy in such cases is *retraining* rather than insight.

Experience and training also play important roles in the development of overt emotional behavior. This is particularly true of training. The child who has been effectively trained (or conditioned) to inhibit and control emotional behavior will find the transition to more mature emotional levels a relatively easy matter. Conversely, where there has been little emphasis or insistence on the development of emotional control, adjustment difficulties are likely to arise in adolescence and adulthood. One may be sure that the emotional patterns of these later stages of development will be in large measure a reflection of the experience and training of earlier years. In the development of emotional control, we encounter a special instance of *self-discipline* which is so basic to mental health and adjustment.

Emotions Important to Adolescent Adjustment. In the same way that certain feelings are of particular significance for adolescent adjustment, so too are emotions like fear and anger, love and hate. In singling out these emotions we mean to imply nothing more than that they stand out prominently as determiners of adolescent conduct, not that they are peculiar to the adolescent period. Of these emotions, sex is one of the most important. It is important because it is much more characteristic of adolescent than of child development, because it conditions and qualifies the behavior and relationships of teen-agers to an important extent, and because it is the source of many conflicts, frustrations, damaging feelings, and adjustment problems.[10] We have already covered this problem area thoroughly in a preceding chapter, and therefore we shall limit ourselves at this point to the foregoing statement of its role in emotional development.

In the earlier discussion of sex development we took occasion also to discuss the development of love relationships during adolescence. But we reserved for the present chapter the discussion of an emotion which is the direct opposite of love, and that is *hate*. Love and hate are one of the basic *ambivalences* in the human mind, and this ambivalence will be found in all persons in some degree, adolescents included. Moreover, the love-hate ambivalence is only one of many such contradictory feelings that persons experience in relation to significant peo-

---

[10] On emotional development in relation to heterosexuality, see J. S. Plant, *op. cit.*, Chap. 19.

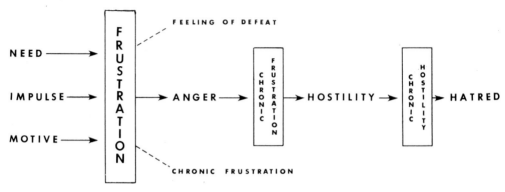

Fig. 17.   Relationships between anger, hostility, hatred, and frustration.

ple and events in their lives. Most people are ambivalent with respect to marriage, children, religion, country, politics, and many other aspects of daily life. This ambivalence is confusing, and in some instances has a disorganizing effect on behavior. This is particularly true with the love-hate dichotomy; this fact is of special significance in the study of adolescent behavior because many youngsters are strongly affected by this ambivalence.

Hate is a strong word that disturbs most people, especially when applied to themselves or to the tender and idealistic mind of the adolescent. For this reason psychologists are often accused of painting a morbid and distorted picture of the human mind. But if we examine closely the psychology of hate, and its derivation, we will see that it is quite understandable, and very likely to occur.

To understand the development of hate, we must bring it into relationship with other basic emotions, particularly anger and hostility.[11] We have diagramed these relationships in Figure 17. As the

diagram in Figure 17 indicates, anger which is itself an innate, basic emotional reaction, arises out of frustration, particularly the frusration of fundamental needs like those we discussed in the previous chapter. However, the frustration of strong desires, like use of the family car, steady dating, etc., can also provoke a great deal of anger. Repeated or prolonged frustration, and therefore prolonged anger, generate a *feeling of hostility*, and it is this chronic hostility that eventually turns into hate. Thus the teen-ager who is chronically frustrated in his striving for independence, acceptance, belonging, or a feeling of personal worth, will develop a great deal of hostility and hate toward those persons in his life who are the primary source of the frustration. Needless to say, the parents lay first claim to this dubious distinction, although hostility is often manifested toward teachers, the church, or persons in authority. Usually, such hostility represents the mechanism of *displacement* by which

---

[11] See L. J. Saul, *The Hostile Mind* (New York: Random House, 1956); B. R. Sappenfield, *Personality Dynamics*, Chap. V; A. A. Schneiders, *Personal Adjustment and Mental Health* (New York: Rinehart, 1955), Chap. 12; F. J. Curran, "Aggressive Traits in Children," *Dis.*

Nerv. Syst., 1942, 3, 114–117; and S. Ackerly, "Rebellion and Its Relation to Delinquency and Neurosis in Sixty Adolescents," *Amer. J. Ortho-psychiat.*, 1933, 3, 147–160. See also M. C. Shaw and J. Grubb, "Hostility and Able High School Underachievers," *J. Couns. Psychol.*, 1958, 5, 263–266, and P. M. Symonds, *op. cit.*, Chaps. 4 and 5.

the youngster directs his intolerable hate of the parents toward some acceptable substitute.

It is the ambivalence of the love-hate relationship, especially when it involves the parents, that causes so much anguish for the young teen-ager. Basically, the adolescent wants to love and to be loved, to accept and to be accepted, by his parents who are the most important figures in his life. But he also wants to be independent, to be left alone, to make his own decisions; and these motivations come into direct conflict with parental demands and restrictions. Hence the emergence of hostility and hate. This development will be conditioned to an important extent by the relationships that exist between the youngster and one or another of the parents. If a girl, and she is strongly identified with the mother, there may be very little hostility, or the hostility may be directed toward the father. If a boy, and he is strongly identified with an aggressive, demanding mother, hostility and hate will grow out of all proportion. The boy who is identified with the mother resents this very deeply because it interferes with his achievement of masculinity and sex-identity, and will develop unbridled hostility

toward the "offending" parent. In general, adolescent boys resent the intrusion of feminine control in their lives, and will show hostility on this ground if no other. Since the mother is often the dominant figure in the household, and exerts more control over the children, hostility is much more common among boys than among girls.

Just as sex and the emotion of love will invariably manifest themselves in behavior of one kind or another, so will anger and hostility. Sex may express itself directly in such responses as petting and necking, or, if frustrated, in fantasy and masturbation. Love expresses itself in many different ways that are too well known to require cataloguing. Anger and hostility are expressed in aggression, and this is the behavior that we witness in the adolescent's verbal lashing of the parents, in destructive behavior such as vandalism, and in various delinquent and criminal acts. We may note that in each one of these instances, if the basic emotion is thoughtlessly or chronically frustrated, behavior tends to become distorted and disorganized, with serious maladjustment as a result.

Chester is a young man, 21 years of age, and a junior in college. As a child,

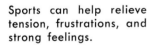

Sports can help relieve tension, frustrations, and strong feelings.

he was sickly and underweight, and prior to coming to college had undergone psychiatric treatment for a period of one year. He is an only child who resides at home with his father and mother. Presently, Chester is doing well in school, has put on considerable weight, has improved his health a great deal through proper diet and exercise, and has benefited considerably from psychiatric treatment.

However, Chester still has a serious problem in his relationship with his mother. Periodically, they get into conflict with each other in which the mother berates him with foul language and name-calling, and sometimes pummels him with her fists. Chester states that at such times he hates his mother, and that this feeling of hatred continues for weeks after the encounter. This is a typical instance of adolescent identification with the aggressive mother, in which there is a great deal of frustration, hostility, and aggression. Typically, Chester feels very depressed and guilty after each such encounter although the hostility continues underneath. Treatment would have to be directed toward resolving the basic Oedipal relationship between the boy and his mother.

Emotions, therefore, play a significant role in determining the behavior and relationships of young people. In a typical instance, they gang up, as it were, with needs and motives, feelings and desires with such dynamic force that the behavior is almost an inevitable outcome. When such behavior is unduly influenced by feelings and emotions, particularly those that are negative and damaging in character, the resulting adjustment is likely to be unhealthy, distorted, or even bizarre.

THE DEVELOPMENT OF SENTIMENTS

The Nature of Sentiment. The affective life of adolescents includes also a number of sentiments, which may be described as systems of emotional tendencies organized around some value, object, or person. They are therefore *emotional complexes* which involve several affective processes. Thus the familiar sentiment of loyalty is not a simple feeling like shame or sympathy; it is an *organized disposition* of several feelings and emotions that can be evoked at any moment depending upon the situation in which the object of loyalty is involved. Love when fully developed is also a sentiment. By way of example, then, let us consider the mother's love for her child. When the mother holds and fondles the child she experiences tenderness and affection; when the child is in danger the sentiment generates fear; when it is threatened by another person, the mother experiences anger; when the child fails to live up to expectations, she may experience shame or chagrin; and when the child accomplishes a worthwhile aim, the mother experiences pride. It is all of these potentially evocable feelings that make up the sentiment of love, and not just the feeling of tenderness that is experienced with reference to the loved object. All sentiments are like this, their particular structure in any one person depending upon his innate background and development.[12]

Sentiments and Behavior. The significance of these sentiments for the moral, social, and religious development of youth requires little emphasis. The sentiment of *self-regard*, for example, has many implications for moral and social conduct; and in its absence, any person is seriously handicapped in achieving adjustment along these lines. The nucleus of this sentiment is the self-concept, and

---

[12] See R. B. Cattell, *General Psychology* (Cambridge, Mass.: Sci-Art, 1941), Chap. IX,

it involves all those ideas, feelings, and emotions that have special reference to self. What a person thinks and feels concerning himself will condition his moral and social conduct at every turn. Where this sentiment is well developed, moral wrongs are often avoided because they come into conflict with it, and acceptable conduct is often assured because it enhances the feeling of self-regard. What others think of a person may be minimized or ignored; but one cannot ignore what he thinks and feels about himself. This is not the only factor guiding moral conduct. Personal conduct is often kept in line with moral standards by the ability to distinguish right from wrong, by the natural desire for good and by principles and ideals; but the sentiment of self-regard is a *powerful reinforcing agency.* Young people often know what should be done or avoided but find that knowledge is not enough. There must be some dynamic factor — a principle, an ideal, a sentiment — that reinforces and sustains the moral decision that results from knowledge or conscience. Social conduct is similarly influenced by self-regard.

What is true of self-regard is equally true of other sentiments. The implications of loyalty, friendship, love, and patriotism, especially for social conduct, are clear. The sentiment of loyalty binds families and social groups together when every other agency threatens them with disruption. Friendship, love, and patriotism are among the most ennobling of sentiments, contributing to the personal as well as the social development of the individual. Sentiments such as these, coupled with the needs for affection, belonging, security, and participation, can account in large measure for group coherence and social behavior.

We should consider also the significance of sentiments for religious experience and conduct. Here again the sentiments of love, loyalty, and even friendship play important roles. The object of these sentiments, when oriented toward religious values, is the Divine Being. In the truly religious person all these emotional elements are integrated into a master sentiment of adoration which is one of the most complex syntheses of affective elements, and also one of the clearest examples of sentiment formation. In its most developed form it involves the feelings of reverence, awe, wonder, and humility, the emotion of fear (in a refined form), plus the sentiments of love and loyalty, and something akin to friendship. Included also, at times, are the feelings of shame and remorse; but most of all it involves joy, an inner satisfaction and contentment that only true religious experiences can impart. While this is not the whole story of the relationship between affective and religious experiences, it is a clear illustration of how many emotional forces can be marshaled toward one thing, and how enriching such a sentiment can be when fully developed and allowed to play its ideal part in life.

How Sentiments Develop.   Sentiments are not formed to any great extent during childhood, due to a lack of intellectual and emotional maturation; nor has there been sufficient opportunity for experience of the kind that contributes to sentiment formation. The fact that such syntheses involve complex feeling states, which themselves are not developed until after a certain amount of maturation has occurred, indicates that sentiments ordinarily require a higher level of development than is characteristic of childhood. Of course one can cite instances of friendship, loyalty, and love in children; but these tendencies are in a very nascent state, and only faintly resemble the truly dynamic sentiments that are developed in adolescence and adulthood.

Sentiments, like the majority of affective elements, are the products of experience coupled with development and maturation. Through experience, feelings and emotions become associated with certain objects, and organized into a sentiment pattern. A person who never acts patriotically is not likely to develop a true sentiment of patriotism; nor will loyalty be developed until it is practiced. Like feelings, sentiments develop in direct proportion to the extent to which opportunities for their development are provided. Some persons never develop the sentiment of love simply because they never give themselves a chance to do so. Their attitude toward others is chronically one of antipathy, which precludes the development of feelings necessary to love. Other individuals never develop real moral and religious sentiments for much the same reason; and, needless to say, the antisocial person never knows the meaning of sentiments like friendship and loyalty. Everyone has the capacities for these sentiments; but capacities are not enough; they must be activated through actual experience.

This activation requires development and maturation of the emotional, intellectual, imaginative, and social capacities of the individual. We can readily see that moral sentiments cannot be formed until the person has reached a point, intellectually, where he is capable of understanding moral values, concepts, and principles. He must grasp the meaning and the function of moral law as it relates to human nature. This itself requires some understanding of the intrinsic make-up of man, that he is a rational, self-determining being capable of truly moral conduct. Obviously, such knowledge requires some degree of intellectual development.

The same criteria may be applied to social sentiments. Loyalty, for example, involves an understanding of the relationship between oneself and others, and of the duties and responsibilities of group living. Children may be loyal, but only because it is expected of them, not because loyalty as a form of conduct is actually intelligible. Thus, it is not uncommon to see loyalty thrown overboard when it comes into conflict with selfish interests, which would not be so likely to happen if its implications were clearly understood. We find the same thing in childhood friendships. They are formed and broken from day to day, with no thought of or insight into the meaning of such conduct; whereas in mature life, the breakup of a true friendship may be regarded as a real calamity.

In forming religious sentiments, too, understanding plays a basic role. Here the adolescent must grasp the relation between himself and God; he must understand how his conduct or style of life is related to his religious beliefs and aspirations. Because of the lack of such understanding much of religion, as practiced, is pure *sentimentalism*. Sentiments, unguided by reason and understanding, degenerate quickly into sentimentalism of the worst kind, exemplified in religions which are purely emotional in character, and untouched by the regulating power of understanding. The religious development of youth should be directed toward the formation of dynamic and wholesome sentiments, and away from sentimentalism.

That all these sentiments may be very dynamic is a matter of common observation. There are numerous instances of their influence on human conduct; and they are seldom exceeded in dynamic value. This is so not only because they involve dynamic affective elements, but also because they are integral in character, based upon intellectual understanding and conviction, and related in many instances to basic needs. It is in part the intellectual, moral, religious, and social developments of adolescence that make the formation of true sentiments possible; and once developed, they will contribute importantly to the achievement of maturity, the growth of character and personality, and the development of a well-integrated temperament.

THE EMERGENCE OF TEMPERAMENT IN ADOLESCENCE

What Temperament Is.   Parents and teachers often note that adolescents differ considerably from each other in their basic temperaments. One girl is moody or ill at ease in a group or pessimistic or irritable, whereas another seems always to be gay and cheerful, with a ready smile and a quick "hello" which seems to stamp her personality as entirely different from that of the first girl. Everyone recognizes that these are differences in temperament, even though we find it difficult to say exactly what temperament is.

People tend to think of temperament as the sum total of emotional traits and dispositions, but this viewpoint has serious limitations. It fails to take into account the essentially *fluid* quality of personality traits, and it does violence to the essential unity of personality. Traits are individual modes of response, whereas temperament is a single *quality*

of the person that helps to set him off from all other persons. This quality manifests itself in different traits, and by inference from these traits we arrive at a knowledge of temperament. But it is because these distinctions can be made that the traits of temperament and temperament itself should not be identified.[13]

Temperament, like character, is an *essential quality* of the total personality. It may be defined as a *disposition within the person to respond to emotional stimuli and situations, and to express himself emotionally in a unique manner.* Because of his temperament, then, a person feels and reacts in a way to distinguish himself from other persons, by reason of which temperament contributes to his uniqueness and individuality. Objectively considered, temperament is simply the emotional life of a person; but this emotional life flows from and is always conditioned by the person's *unique affective disposition.* This disposition is the *constant* element, the feelings, emotions, and moods varying from moment to moment or from day to day. It also governs the development of traits that are emotional in nature. Thus, by the term *joyous temperament* is meant a readiness to respond to situations and experiences with a feeling of joy. A person with such a temperament may on occasion feel sad or depressed or angry, but the basic disposition remains unchanged. Temperament, therefore, can only be inferred and judged on the basis of the dominant affective patterns that characterize the person over a period of time.

Of particular importance to the development of temperament are the emo-

[13] See the excellent discussion on temperament in J. S. Plant, *op. cit.*, Chap. 11. See also C. M. Fleming, *Adolescence* (New York: International Press, 1949), pp. 87–112.

tional derivatives described previously under the heading of moods and sentiments. These factors determine the pattern of temperament to a greater extent than emergency reactions like fear and anger. We must keep in mind, however, that every affective process is conditioned and colored by the disposition that constitutes the core of temperament. Sentiments, moods, feelings and emotions — all of these will in some measure reflect the constant disposition that is the real temperament of the person.

What Determines Temperament?   It has long been known that temperament and physical make-up are intimately related, a fact of considerable importance for adolescent psychology. What a person is, and what he becomes temperamentally, is determined to a large extent by what he is physically; and the principal mediums for this determination are the glands of internal secretion and the autonomic nervous system. We have already indicated the effects on behavior of hyperthyroidism, and we know also of the tremendous influence of alterations, dysfunctions, and maldevelopment of the sex glands. Because of the interlocking character of the endocrine system there are few changes in any one of the glands that may not be reflected in a changed emotionality. In normal instances, such as adolescent maturation, the emotional pattern is clearly affected. New feelings and sentiments emerge, older emotions may be more easily aroused, and moods of a different character appear. If such maturation does not occur or is delayed, or if there is malformation of sex structures, the emotional pattern may assume an entirely different aspect. Let us keep in mind also that the adolescent personality is an *integration* of all the different elements, both physical and mental, that

constitute personality. Thus any alterations or dysfunctions in other systems of the body are likely to be reflected in temperament. Pernicious anemia, digestive inadequacy, high blood pressure, constipation, and other conditions may well affect the person's emotional life and thus condition the development of temperament.

Is the relationship between bodily characteristics and temperament innate? Is what a person becomes emotionally predetermined by his physical constitution at birth? Questions such as these are not easy to answer because we have no way of determining the relationship between emotional responses in infancy and physical make-up. However, even infants manifest temperament differences, and we can safely assume that at least some of these differences are determined either genetically or prenatally. This relationship explains why heredity looms large in the list of predisposing causes of mental disorder, since it is likely that temperament is the medium for the transmission of psychotic tendencies. This argument is bolstered by the fact that affective responses are of their nature psychophysical, and therefore influenced by genetic determinants.

Developmental Aspects of Temperament.   Despite this relationship, we must recognize also the influence on temperament of nongenetic factors. We noted earlier that emotions are from infancy influenced by conditioning, training, experience, and development, and even in part by self-control. The *adult* temperament, therefore, is the product of innate endowment *plus* learning, development, and experience. However, the influence of these nongenetic factors will be rigidly conditioned by physical constitution as it exists at birth, as it develops from birth to maturity, and as it declines from maturity to old age. Physical make-up, therefore, is the *primary* factor in the determination of temperament.

Finally we may ask, to what extent is temperament affected by the physical changes of puberty and adolescence? Does the adolescent temperament undergo the same amount of change as physical constitution? We may be sure that temperament is affected by the physical changes of adolescence, but we must remember also that normal development is gradual, and that in whatever alteration does occur there will always be a residue of previously existing temperament factors. The disposition that constitutes the core of temperament is well formed by the time adolescence begins. This disposition is psychophysical; and although the physical changes that occur will deeply affect it, *its intrinsic character will not be changed* because of the *gradualness of the changes that occur*. In other words, just as the body *remains the same while changing*, so we may assume that so fundamental a disposition as temperament remains essentially the same throughout the course of development.

The emphasis on the relationship between temperament and physical make-up must not become one-sided. The adolescent, after all, is a *rational* being, and his emotions and feelings are more than glandular responses. Their development is conditioned throughout by intellectual growth, from the early years of childhood until the very end of the adolescent period. This fact underlies the growth of sentiments, and of the more refined feelings like respect, awe, reverence, joy, and sorrow. Intellectual insight gives *meaning* to emotional experiences, and extends their range far beyond the

narrow confines that limit the emotional processes of lower animals. Intellect makes possible a distinctly *human* temperament, one that can become integrated with the noblest qualities of man as they are reflected in his character. Similarly, the development of temperament is closely related to the social changes of adolescence, as we have noted in our discussion of sentiments. To the extent that any affective process is socially conditioned, temperament will be similarly affected.

Temperament and Religious Experience. The growth of temperament should also be related to religious experience and development. The church has social aspects, but its influence on developing personality is quite distinct from that of other social factors. Of course, what a person becomes religiously is determined not so much by church membership as by the quality of his personal religious experiences and practices, and by his conception of the relationship between himself and God. The development of religious attitudes, emotions, and sentiments may begin exteriorly early in childhood through religious services and similar practices. And in many instances, particularly among children for whom religious instruction is an integral part of the educational process, the process of developing a religious temperament is well on its way long before the adolescent period. This is as it should be, for the soil of religious life must be well prepared by the time the young person is beset with the trials, uncertainties, and conflicts of the adolescent period.

Yet the full flowering of religious temperament does not occur until adolescence, because then the intellectual and moral development so basic to an adequate religious synthesis occurs. Also, during adolescence the individual first experiences those deep-seated conflicts that often find their solution in the concepts and the hopes offered by religion and its practices. These conflicts enforce the development of religious concepts and attitudes, which, in turn, become part of the structure of religious sentiments. Because of these conflicts and their relation to religion, conversions are not uncommon during the adolescent period, whereas they are practically unknown during childhood. Such intense religious experiences would, in all likelihood, never occur apart from the physical, social, and moral upheavals that characterize the period of youth.

Temperament and Self-Discipline. In the development of temperament, training and discipline are also important. Parental discipline, or lack of it, in early childhood will leave an indelible impress on the child's temperament. Thus the child who has gained control of his environment by the use of temper tantrums, sulking, or aggression will in adolescence possess a temperament quite different from that of the child who has been properly disciplined.

Related to training is self-discipline or self-control. In fact, self-discipline is the outgrowth of training to which the child is subjected at a time when self-control is psychologically impossible. This fact emphasizes the importance of training in the formative years of childhood. To the extent, therefore, that the young child is taught through external discipline to discipline himself will he achieve some control over his emotional life, without which the integration of personality needed for complete adjustment is impossible. In some measure, then, temperament is attributable to the person himself. Although this control is indirect, it would be a serious error to regard temperament as being the product only of physical and environmental factors.

Temperament and the Conduct of Youth. This brief discussion of temperament indicates clearly why it plays a significant role in many phases of adolescent personality and conduct. Some of the most basic attitudes toward self, society, morality, and religion are rooted in this disposition. Everything that the adolescent thinks and does will be conditioned to some extent by the sentiments, the feelings, the moods, and the emotional attitudes that are part of his temperamental make-up. For these reasons, knowing what temperament is, how it develops, and its relationship to other personality factors is of first importance in the guidance of youth.

EMOTIONAL ADJUST-MENTS IN ADOLESCENCE

The Nature of Emotional Adjustment. The development of affective processes during adolescence is closely related to the problem of emotional adjustment. Adolescence is a period of continuous striving toward adjustment, punctuated by conflicts and frustrations that generate many feelings and disrupt emotional stability. Thus we may ask, what is emotional adjustment, and what are some of the reasons for the difficulties and conflicts that culminate in emotional maladjustment?

Emotional adjustment requires the *proper ordering* of affective experiences and behavior to the demands of human nature and to the requirements imposed by the environment. It includes three essential elements: *harmony, balance,* and *control,* all of which are important to the total integration process necessary for maturity, adjustment, and adult living. Thus the teen-ager who is chronically worried, suspicious, obsessed by morbid fears, anxious and guilty, or subject to fits of depression, is emotionally ill-balanced. So too the youngster who suppresses emotions or fails to control them is poorly adjusted emotionally. Jealousy, hatred, temper tantrums, despondency, hysterical outbursts, nervousness, night terrors, extreme excitability, migraine headaches, excessive perspiration, bed-wetting, are all signs of poor emotional adjustment or of imminent breakdown in the affective life. All these symptoms may be observed in adolescence at one time or another, but no one of them, nor any group, is peculiar to the adolescent period.[14] There is no neurosis or psychosis that is distinctively characteristic of youth, but it is true that the many conflicts, uncertainties, and instabilities of adolescence are likely to lead to emotional imbalance.

Various attempts have been made to catalogue the adjustment difficulties that are most typical of young people. In his survey of adjustment difficulties in childhood and youth, Steinbach found that nervousness, sensitiveness, stubbornness, disobedience, and temper tantrums were among the difficulties most often mentioned. There were, of course, notable

sex differences. Among boys it was found that stubbornness, disobedience, temper tantrums, fighting, selfishness, laziness, untruthfulness, indifference, and lack of interest in childhood activities were more prominent; whereas among girls it was nervousness, sensitiveness, shyness, emotional outbreaks, biting nails, desire to be alone, conceit, and playing poorly with other children that stood out as the chief sources of trouble. Other investigators approach the problem in a more general way, discussing the emotional problems of adolescents under the general headings of hysteria, neurasthenia, psychopathic personality, and similar categories.

The Causes of Emotional Maladjustment. Let us consider briefly some of the factors that are most likely to lead to emotional difficulties in adolescence. There are, first of all, the continuous *physical changes* that occur, which often give rise to emotional uncertainty and insecurity. Typically, the adolescent is unsure of his feelings. To him they may be vague and ill-defined, or confused with other feeling states. This lack of insight into and inability to clearly identify emotional experiences make control and adjustment difficult. The confusion so often manifested by adolescents in relation to different events is in part due to this emotional immaturity.

Related to immaturity is the *instability* of the adolescent, which is manifested in many ways: extreme variability of interests, desires, and ambitions; alternation between laziness and activity; conflict between values; and so on. The enthusiasms of today may become totally uninteresting tomorrow. There may be variation in mood from cheerfulness and buoyancy to the extreme of emotional depression. This lack of stability, which is traceable

---

[14] The literature on emotional problems in adolescence is very extensive. See, for example, A. F. Bronner, "Emotional Problems of Adolescence," in *The Child's Emotions* (Chicago: University of Chicago Press, 1930); G. S. Stevenson, "Mental-Hygiene Problems of Youth Today," *Ment. Hyg.*, 1941, 25, 539–551; C. M. Fleming, *op. cit.*, pp. 62–69; Freda K. Merry and R. V. Merry, *The First Two Decades of Life* (New York: Harper, 1950), pp. 318–373; G. J. Mohr and Marian A. Despres, *The Stormy Decade: Adolescence* (New York: Random House, 1958), Chap. XII.

to the continuous physical, mental, and social changes going on, can be the source of many emotional difficulties. Of importance too in causing emotional difficulties are the feelings of *insecurity, inadequacy,* and *inferiority* that young people often experience. Whatever the origin of these feelings, to which reference has already been made in an earlier section, they can be expected to cause considerable discouragement, anxiety, or depression. Failure to measure up to ideals, to achieve new goals, to win approval or recognition, to be accepted by the peer group, or to be loved and cherished are very likely to generate feelings of inadequacy, and these in turn disturb the emotional equanimity of youth.

Emotional conflicts result also from the *activation of specific needs* like sex, independence, and the desire for new experiences. These drives often conflict with the rules and demands of society, morality, and religion, leading to feelings of anxiety, resentment, anger, or guilt. Thus the sex drive is a prolific source of emotional disturbances in adolescence. Practices such as masturbation, petting, and sex conversation invariably lead to feelings of guilt and remorse, and to self-debasement, these in turn aggravating feelings of inadequacy and inferiority. Erotic dreams, nocturnal emissions, and sexual fantasies also stimulate guilt and depression. There is no more miserable teen-ager than the one who is plagued by inability to cope with his sexual desires and experiences, or with the feelings of anxiety, shame, and guilt to which sex gives rise.

The strivings of the adolescent toward *emancipation* are loaded with possibilities for emotional conflict, not only because they vie with the emotional attachment to the parents, but also because they conflict with the need for security. A great deal of the anguish and unhappiness that many youngsters manifest is traceable to this particular conflict. Finally, we may indicate the influence of the *need for experience* on emotional adjustment. This tendency often leads to dissatisfaction with the prosaic and humdrum existence of the adolescent's life. Much of the restlessness, ennui, and boredom of youth are related to this need, particularly in youngsters whose desires have been overgratified by indulgent parents. Boredom often leads a youngster to questionable sources for the satisfaction of the need for experience — to books, movies, gang activities, drinking, narcotics, and truancy — behavior that quickly leads to emotional difficulties.

When we consider the many interrelations among all of the factors that constitute human personality, the widespread developmental changes of adolescence, and the demands and limitations placed upon conduct by the environment, it is not difficult to see that the possibilities for emotional conflict, instability, and maladjustment are almost endless. In many instances the course of adolescent development is run smoothly; in many others there is almost continuous conflict. In any single case one would have to determine carefully what factors are operating in order to trace the source of the difficulty and work toward its solution.

S,ELECTED READINGS

Beebee-Center, J. G., *The Psychology of Pleasantness and Unpleasantness* (New York: Van Nostrand, 1932).

Cannon, W. B., *Bodily Changes in Pain, Hunger, Fear and Rage* (New York: D. Appleton-Century, 1929).

Diamond, S., *Personality and Temperament* (New York: Harper, 1957).

Dunbar, F., *Emotions and Bodily Changes*, 2 ed. (New York: Columbia University Press, 1938).

Gallagher, J. R., and Harris, H. I., *Emotional Problems of Adolescence* (New York: Oxford University Press, 1958).

Reymert, M. L. (ed.), *Feelings and Emotions: the Moosehart Symposium* (New York: McGraw-Hill, 1950).

Sheldon, W. H., and Stevens, S. S., *The Varieties of Temperament* (New York: Harper, 1942).

Szasz, T. S., *Pain and Pleasure: a Study of Bodily Feelings* (New York: Basic Books, 1957).

Young, P. T., *Emotion in Man and Animal* (New York: Wiley, 1943).

Zachry, Caroline B., *Emotion and Conduct in Adolescence* (New York: Appleton-Century-Crofts, 1940).

Zubek, J. P., and Solberg, Patricia A., *Human Development* (New York: McGraw-Hill, 1954), Chap. 11.

CHAPTER X

MOTIVATIONAL DEVELOPMENT DURING ADOLESCENCE

Needs and motives and feelings have a great deal to do with adolescent behavior. The big question now is: Do these motivating factors undergo any noticeable and significant changes during adolescence? If they do, we should know about it because such changes will make a lot of difference where the behavior and personality of the teen-ager are concerned.

THE CONCEPT OF MOTIVATIONAL DEVELOPMENT

Motivation and Development. Throughout these discussions we have tried to adhere consistently to a developmental viewpoint of adolescent behavior and personality. After all, adolescence is itself a phenomenon of development, and therefore such a viewpoint is necessary to understanding and solving the problems of youth. At this point we are faced with a peculiar difficulty: Does the concept of development apply to motivational tendencies, such as needs and desires, in the same manner that it does to other aspects of personality? Are there real or significant changes during childhood and/or adolescence which can be identified as motivational changes, and which therefore give meaning to the concept of motivational development? The literature on this question is surprisingly scarce; seldom do we run across any reference to characteristic changes in ado-

lescent motivation.[1] It is true that many writers have noted motivational changes in the area of values, interests, ideals, and attitudes, all of which are acquired tendencies and thus are more subject to change than basic needs or impulses. This aspect of motivational development is important; but more fundamental is the question of whether basic motivations also follow a developmental pattern.

In view of the extensive physical, psychological, and social alterations that characterize adolescence, it is highly improbable that dynamic factors of any kind would remain unaffected by development since they are so closely related to or dependent on physical and psychological factors in human personality. It is hard to think of a good reason why needs and motives should remain unaffected by the developmental process when all other aspects of personality change. Such a notion would be meaningful only if motivating factors were independent of the physical, psychologi-

[1] See Selected Readings.

220

cal, and social aspects of personality. This hypothesis is manifestly untenable. Throughout our discussion of dynamic tendencies we have emphasized repeatedly how they are grounded in and conditioned by these various factors; and thus the conclusion is inescapable, namely, that with changes in the different aspects of personality there must be corresponding changes in motivation. Whether these are changes *in degree* or *in kind* is part of the problem.

The Nature of Motivational Development. The concept of motivational development suggests four distinct possibilities. It could refer, first of all, to the disappearance of certain tendencies and the emergence of others at various stages of development, which would mean that the adolescent is at times motivated differently than is the child. Second, it could mean that new needs and motives are generated out of those already existing in childhood. Third, it could refer to the fact that some motivations, like interests and attitudes, actually undergo considerable change during the adolescent period. Or finally, the concept could suggest a shift in emphasis from one kind of motivation to another at different levels of development. No one of these possibilities necessarily excludes the others, since it is not impossible that motivational development may occur in all these directions. Our task is to determine which of these modes of development takes place during adolescence, and the extent of such development.

THE QUESTION OF EMERGING DYNAMIC FACTORS

Are There New Needs in Adolescence? The first possibility, that some tendencies disappear and others occur later in the course of development, must be studied very carefully. As far as can be determined by observation and analysis of experience, no one of the basic organic or psychological needs disappears completely in the transition from childhood to adulthood. All of the physiological needs continue to function throughout the life history of the organism, for reasons that are too obvious to require comment, although there are some external changes that occur at different stages. Nor is there evidence that any psychological needs cease to function, even though they vary considerably in their relation to behavior from one period to another. As we pointed out in our discussion of these tendencies earlier (p. 166), it is the fact that they continue to influence behavior at all levels of development that leads to the conclusion that such needs are intrinsic to human nature. Were these needs extrinsically determined, some of them would cease to function as conditions changed. But the fact is that they are *basic* needs, rooted in man's intrinsic make-up; and therefore, like their physiological counterparts, they continue to function throughout the life span of the organism.

Nevertheless, needs are to an important extent a function of development, in the sense that some of them are dependent upon the maturation of various structures and capacities. Of the physiological drives it is well known that the sexual function is inseparably linked with the maturation of physical structures, and that ordinarily it does not manifest itself as a true drive until the beginning of the adolescent period. This statement does not mean that there is *no* capacity for sexual experience prior to this time, since there are numerous instances of sexual precocity among children of nearly all ages. To what extent, however, such experiences are truly sexual is a debatable question; all that is known with certainty is that small children derive sensuous gratification from contact with sexual structures and erogenous zones before the pubescent period. The point is that the true flowering of the sex drive does not occur until the start of the adolescent period, bringing in its wake many other developmental phenomena; and this is what we are referring to when we speak of sexual development. In this sense it is not incorrect to speak of the "appearance" of a new drive in the transition from childhood to adolescence. This fact is the reason why so much emphasis is placed on sexual maturation.

Regarding other physical needs, it is clear that they, too, are affected by maturational changes. Physical growth and development certainly affect hunger, rest, and activity, which is to be expected in view of the close relationship of organic needs to physical make-up. But more important for the understanding of adolescent behavior is the significant change that occurs in the drive toward aggression. We have already studied the nature and the effects of this tendency, and we need here note only that aggression assumes a much more dynamic form in adolescence than during childhood.

Young children often manifest hostility and aggression; but it is seldom that they will act aggressively in the manner and to the degree which characterizes many teen-agers. The open defiance of parents, the rebellion against the rules and restrictions of society, the flouting of school authorities, the wanton and brutal physical attacks against rival gang members, and similar types of behavior that characterize many youngsters are rarely found in childhood. Aggression, as it were, comes into its own during the adolescent period and changes the motivational picture to a considerable extent. As with sex, the aggressive behavior of the teen-ager is one of the things that beclouds both understanding and, probably more important, adult sympathy.[2]

To what extent the psychological needs are bound up with maturation is more difficult to determine. The needs for affection and security certainly begin to function very early in life, whereas tendencies like independence, status, and conformity are more dependent on maturation and development. No one of these, so far as can be determined, is peculiar to the adolescent period, since all of them are manifested prior to the onset of puberty. Yet it is true that some of them gain full status during adolescence, in much the same manner that the sex drive does. This interpretation applies particularly to the needs for independence, status, social approval, conformity, participation, and, in lesser degree, new experiences. Affection and security also play prominent roles in adolescent conduct as we have already noted, but there is no evidence to indicate that they are any more dynamic in one period than in another. We need to remind ourselves here of the fact that all development is integrative, and that development along one line naturally tends to induce or to suppress development along others. For

[2] See R. C. Hendrickson, Youth in Danger (New York: Harcourt, Brace, 1956); H. E. Salisbury, The Shook-up Generation (New York: Harper, 1958); H. Block and A. Niederhoffer, The Gang: a Study in Adolescent Behavior (New York Philosophical Library, 1958); A. K. Cohen, Delinquent Boys: the Culture of the Gang (Glencoe, Ill.: Free Press, 1955).

this reason we may expect development of some of the basic needs during adolescence. Thus, while there are no new psychological needs in adolescence, many of those that already exist become more dynamic and more pervasive in character, playing an increasing role in the determination of human conduct. This fact in itself is no less significant than would be the emergence of new needs.[3]

The Development of Rational Motives. Of greater significance in the long run are the developmental changes that occur in rational motivation. In the sustaining motives particularly, and in goals and ideals, we can see some of the most extensive changes during the adolescent period. In the earliest stages of life there is no such thing as rational motivation. Behavior is the result of stimuli, needs, and feelings. Only as understanding and the capacity to form general concepts develop does it become possible to elicit rational motives. Motives are basically intellectual, and the human person cannot be expected to act reasonably until the intellect can be brought into play, whereby concepts and values can be successfully manipulated. This development occurs much earlier than is ordinarily supposed, and certainly long before the beginning of adolescence. But the fact remains that adolescent development alters the picture of rational motivation to a considerable degree. As intellectual ability increases, perceptions become clearer, values assume a more definite form, and understanding improves appreciably. For the adolescent, as compared with the child, education, work, and life itself are more clearly understood and thus assume deeper meaning. This change marks the beginning of dynamic developments that help convert the individual from a child into an adult.

Of particular significance are the changes that occur in the sustaining motives, including principles, ideals, interests, and attitudes. While some of these tendencies have their beginnings in childhood, the evidence indicates that they develop to a much greater degree during adolescence. Careful observation of children's behavior certainly indicates that ideals and principles play a minor role in determining their behavior. Admittedly, the experiences and training to which children are exposed will have an important bearing on the later development of these motives, but for the most part the younger child is acting on the level of needs, impulses, and feelings.

Interests also stand out prominently in the pattern of adolescent development. While some interests are developed early in childhood, the kinds and intensity of interests change measurably during adolescence. In fact, there is no area of human motivation where the changes are so clear-cut and widespread. In subsequent chapters we shall trace out in greater detail the development of these important tendencies.

The development of values, ideals, and interests is complemented to an important extent by the development of goals in later adolescence. While in a broad sense all behavior is goal-directed, in the period of youth goals begin to assume definite form for the first time. The child's goals, if such they may be called, are immediate and transitory, whereas during adolescence the more remote and

---

[3] One of the few references to this relationship between development and motivation is the article by Charlotte Buhler, "Maturation and Motivation," *Personality*, 1951, 1, 184–211. See also J. Olds, *The Growth and Structure of Motives* (Glencoe, Ill.: Free Press, 1956).

permanent goals emerge for the first time. Even these goals are often vague, tenuous, and inarticulate; but the fact remains that adolescents can and often do create important goals which give direction to their striving. Thus, as regards all of the sustaining motives, we can conclude that there is a great deal of motivational development during adolescence, and that this development changes the picture of adolescent behavior and personality to an important extent.

THE EMERGENCE OF SECONDARY NEEDS OR DESIRES

Increase in the Range of Motivations. As we pointed out earlier, the concept of motivational development includes the possibility that new "needs" and desires are generated out of those already existing. That such secondary needs do arise during the period of adolescence is a matter of common observation. These tendencies should be distinguished from other derived needs like social approval and conformity, which are immediate derivatives, and fit more closely into the general concept of need; and for that reason we shall refer to these tendencies as *desires* or *wants*. From the very earliest years of childhood, with the advent of new experiences and the continually ripening powers of perception, imagination, and intellect, the number of things wanted, as contrasted with those actually needed, grows enormously. Obviously, one is not born with the desires for clothes, books, trips into the country, fishing expeditions, reading, dancing, going to movies, or dating. These things come to be desired because through ex-

perience, imagination, or intellectual appreciation one learns that they are attractive, pleasurable, or valuable.[4]

In many instances, but not all, these new wants are rooted in fundamental needs. Some of those mentioned as examples can be traced quite readily to the needs for experience, conformity, approval, etc.; and it is important always to recognize such possible connections in order to understand the dynamics of the desires generated in this way. But this is not the whole story. Experience, development, and the capacity for rational evaluation are also important elements. In perhaps the majority of cases the growth of the particular desire is traceable to all these factors working together. In this way, when a particular need is aroused and strengthened through experience, there is added a realization that the thing wanted is attractive or valuable. Whatever the origin of these desires, the important fact is that new ones are being almost constantly elicited, so that the range of motivational tendencies becomes immensely broadened as the individual progresses from childhood to adulthood. No longer is a knowledge of basic needs adequate to account for all behavior; one must look also to the desires that follow in the wake of the process of growing up.

Desires Are Often Superficial. It is important for parents and others to recognize the superficial character of many of these desires. Often they become so dynamic, and their gratification so "necessary," that they come to be regarded as actual needs. Youth particularly is blinded to the superficiality of the things he wants. How often we hear the expression: "I've just got to have . . ."

---

[4] See A. E. Morgan, *The Needs of Youth* (New York: Oxford University Press, 1949).

this, that, or the other thing, whether it be a coat, money, a dress, or anything else which at the moment captures the interest or imagination. Young people do not possess the experience, the wisdom, or the values necessary to analyze and interpret adequately the cravings they experience. They cannot distinguish clearly the required from the superficial, the important from the unimportant and unnecessary. There is a tendency in youth to deal in absolutes. A thing is either absolutely indispensable or practically worthless. With quaint logic a youngster may regard a room of his own as the quintessence of possessions, and at the same time question the value of a college education.

Often the desires of youth are characterized by immediacy: they must be satisfied now, and there is little tolerance for future gratifications. Young people have no way of knowing, nor the means of understanding, that many of their most intense cravings are only experiences of the moment. For them the present is all-important, and the future a dim, unknown, and largely unknowable realm of pure possibility. For these reasons the guidance of adolescents in the matter of their wants is of the greatest importance. They must be brought to a realization that not all desires are equally important, and that not all of them can or should be gratified. Parents and teachers must help youth build a scale of true values. They must be given a proper perspective so that the conflicts caused by their cravings may be adequately resolved. They should not be allowed the delusion that the superficial things are the most important in life, that pleasure outstrips real happiness, or that the present is always more important than the future. They must be given insight into the true character of their wants, in a way that will insure proper evaluation.

MOTIVATIONAL GROWTH THROUGH SHIFT IN EMPHASIS

The Shift to Rational Motivation. There is a third kind of motivational development which involves a shift in emphasis from one type of motivation to another. Because it is the most important, we may note first of all the changes from nonrational to rational motivation during the adolescent period. This process is not peculiar to the adolescent level since it begins early in childhood and then reaches a climax during the teen-age. The behavior of the infant is characteristically reflexive and instinctive, the direct result of stimuli, needs, or feelings that flow uninterruptedly into different modes of behavior. The conduct of the child is admittedly less impulsive in character than that of the infant, but no one would argue that children's conduct is characteristically reasonable. Children act largely from basic needs. Their behavior is typically impulsive and only occasionally reasonable; the power of deliberate choice, while potentially present, is not actualized to any great extent.

This predilection for impulsive conduct is carried into the adolescent years, and one can witness numerous instances of purely impulsive behavior among youth. Yet the intellectual development coincident with adolescence makes possible a greater and more effective use of the capacity for deliberative conduct. Whether any adolescent actually uses this power is another matter. This will depend upon his background, training, experiences in self-control, and native capacity. From the standpoint of motivational development, the important thing is that the adolescent does possess a *greater capacity for reasoned conduct.* Much more so than the child, he can be made to understand the rightness and wrongness of actions, their value, or their purpose. One can appeal more readily to his reason, because he possesses greater insight and understanding. He may continue to act on impulse, but that may be simply because rational motives are not sufficiently attractive, or because he has not learned to discipline his impulses. Adolescence, therefore, is an excellent period for the development of rational conduct.

In line with this characteristic is the fact that teen-agers *are amenable to the inculcation of ideals and principles.* This too represents a shift in emphasis toward other and higher levels of motivation. As we remarked earlier, there is little evidence of principle-directed conduct in children. The development of principles requires more experience and greater intellectual insight than children can be expected to possess. For these same reasons, the inculcation of ideals, sentiments, attitudes, and resolutions in children offers great difficulties. Even in the matter of interests, which admittedly play a conspicuous role in the motivations of children, there are decided shifts in emphasis, those of childhood being rapidly replaced by the characteristic interests of youth.

The *greater orientation toward goals* during adolescence may be cited as another instance of this kind of motivational development. As noted earlier, the goals of children are immediate and transitory, tending to shift from day to day. But youth is approaching a period of life when goals are integral to life itself, and become an intrinsic part of the entire motivational pattern. The adolescent gradually becomes conscious of the relationships between present activities and experiences and future modes of living. He begins to question more seriously the value and worth of his experiences, and to search out the basic reasons for his activities. Much more so than the child, the teen-ager has the ability and the proclivity to project himself into the future, partly because of his greater experience and insight, but also because he is so much closer to the adult life he must soon lead.

Social Aspects of Motivational Development. Up to this point, we have urged that the leading factor underlying these shifts of emphasis in motivation is intellectual development. One is prompted to ask, therefore, if the social changes of the adolescent period do not also produce characteristic alterations in motivation. We may take as our starting point the fact that the impulsive behavior of preadolescents is of its nature *selfish* and *egocentric.* Needs are naturally self-centered tendencies; and the largely unmitigated selfishness of children has been noted by everyone. It is not that children are totally incapable of unselfish behavior — there are too many instances of this among children to justify such a contention. Rather, we should say that their behavior is *characteristically* egocentric. Because they do not clearly perceive the relationships between themselves and others, they do not readily become aware of their responsibilities to others in the matter of kindness, charity, or unselfishness. Nor are they greatly motivated by those factors, like ideals and sentiments, that often are altruistic in nature.

Conversely, the adolescent becomes increasingly aware of his relationship to society, and as a result his motivations tend to become more *sociocentric*. There is in youth a greater predilection for evaluating experiences and conduct in terms of their social implications. The individual adolescent, it is true, may not be any more altruistic than he was as a child; but there may still be the *tendency* to evaluate in terms of group relationships. Egocentricity, taken in the broad sense, tends to reign supreme at all levels of human development, simply because one's personal needs and satisfactions are much more real than are those of other people. Nevertheless, human beings are capable of great altruism, in which concern for the welfare of others, sympathy, love, generosity, and kindness are the predominant motivating factors. And this capacity for unselfish or sociocentric conduct grows in direct proportion to the individual's increasing realization of his relationship to other members of society, a realization that is fostered by social contacts and experiences, and is dependent upon intellectual development. This tendency toward sociocentric thinking and acting fosters the growth of many great ideals, of sentiments like love and patriotism, and of social attitudes that enkindle kindness to others, generosity, and sympathy. Without this shift in emphasis from egocentric to sociocentric motivation, society in its present form would not long endure.

THE GROWTH OF MOTIVATIONAL INSIGHT

Children Lack Motivational Insight. One other fact worth noting in this connection is the continually developing insight into causes underlying behavior. We may safely assume that the infant has no insight whatever into the "reasons" for his

behavior; and even if he did, we have no way of knowing of its existence or extent. Among small children one may note occasional insight, especially where reasons are involved; but in the matter of behavior motivated by needs and impulses, the answer invariably comes back, "I do not know." Does a child know anything at all of the "reasons" why he tears paper from the wall, scratches the furniture, or decorates a window with tooth paste? Does he possess any insight into the mechanisms of attention-getting, affection, security, or status? The questions answer themselves. Such insight comes only with experience, intellectual development, and ability to analyze one's own behavior. Observation of children leads us to conclude that, as they grow older, they strive more and more to tear away the veil that obscures the causes of their actions. We may note parenthetically that they never completely succeed in this effort, because some motives or needs are hidden from consciousness, repressed (to use Freudian terminology) into the unconscious; or they are so tenuous in character that the attempt to make them mentally articulate invariably results in failure.

Insight in Adolescence. But the fact remains that the insights of the adolescent and of the adult regarding motivation are much greater than those of the child; and this more extensive knowledge is favored to a large extent by a gradual increase in intellectual power. This factor is not alone in promoting insight. To it should be added the important element of experience, because experience often forces a consideration of the events leading up to a course of action. The importance of this greater insight into the causes of human conduct is well known to those who deal with the problems of adolescence. Psychologists and other counselors are well aware of the necessity of developing such insight in individuals burdened with mental conflicts, guilt feelings, neurosis, and maladjustment. Parents, too, are often aware of the significance of this factor since they are forced daily to cope with problems of motivation. To put the matter briefly, we may say that the greater the insight into the causes of behavior, the better equipped is any person to control human conduct, his own as well as that of others; conversely, of course, the less insight there is, the more difficult it becomes to regulate conduct. This greater insight, therefore, is another reason for asserting that the motivational picture in adolescence differs from that of the preadolescent period.

Motivational Development Has Many Causes. Because of facts we have already brought to light in our study of motivation in all its aspects, there is little that need be added regarding the factors that underlie motivational development. All of the various forms of development during adolescence — physiological, psychological, social, moral, and emotional — contribute to the changes that occur in the motivational picture. These relationships are important; but more important is the basic fact that motivations underlying human behavior are subject to the same laws of development that govern all other aspects of personality.

SELECTED READINGS

Bindra, D., Motivation: a Systematic Reinterpretation (New York: Ronald Press, 1959), Chap. 4.

Harper, R. S., Introductory Psychology (Boston: Allyn & Bacon, 1958), Chap. 2.

Nowlis, V., "The Development and Modification of Motivational Systems in Personality," in Current Theory and Research in Motivation: a Symposium (Lincoln: University of Nebraska Press, 1953), pp. 114–138.

Olds, J., The Growth and Structure of Motives (Glencoe, Ill.: Free Press, 1956).

Sappenfield, B. R., Personality Dynamics: an Integrative Psychology of Adjustment (New York: Knopf, 1954), Chap. 2.

Tuttle, H. S., Dynamic Psychology and Conduct (New York: Harper, 1949), Chap. VI.

CHAPTER XI

ADOLESCENCE AND
THE PROBLEM OF DISCIPLINE

Behavior can be controlled in two ways, one by appealing to basic needs, motives, and ideals, and the other by channeling behavior through the use of rules, demands, restrictions, and other disciplinary measures. The one method of control is motivation and the other discipline; and now that we have studied adolescent motivation we must turn our attention to the study of discipline in adolescence.

MOTIVATION AND DISCIPLINE

Discipline and Behavior Dynamics. The applied psychology of motivation, regardless of developmental level, is based on the assumption that an intelligent and resourceful manipulation of the dynamic factors underlying behavior will encourage or even insure the kind of conduct that everybody wants. The whole philosophy of motivational research is oriented toward this idea. Thus, the parent tries to motivate the child to obey promptly, to help with the household chores, to keep his room neat and orderly, or to get to school on time. And the teacher tries to motivate the student to successful effort by appeals to achievement, recognition, self-respect, or future goals like graduation and admission to college. In all such instances there is an attempt to manipulate and to control the behavior of persons in our charge by direct appeals to basic needs or rational motives.

This is certainly the more desirable way to control conduct. One can imagine how pleasant it would be if children always obeyed their parents because of the appeal of the Fourth Commandment, or always avoided sexual misbehavior because of the ideal of purity. If Mary always responded positively to her need for achievement, or her desire for recognition, there is little doubt that her report card would always be quite acceptable. And if John were always guided by the goals of maturity and responsibility, or by deep affection for his brothers and sisters and for his parents, there would be little doubt as to the quality of his adjustments or his relationships to others. The fact of the matter is that motivations can lead to unacceptable as well as acceptable behavior, and therefore cannot be manipulated always for the parent's or teacher's benefit. It is at this point that discipline enters the picture and becomes necessary as an adjunct to effective motivation.

The Need for Discipline. This need for discipline extends all the way back to infancy and all the way forward to adulthood. There is no period within the formative years of a person's life when discipline is unnecessary, and there is no period in life at all when some form of discipline is not needed. Discipline is needed to channel behavior and point it in the right direction; it is needed for purposes of limiting behavior; and it is needed to bring behavior in line with the requirements of society, of the environment, and of sound principles. The basic reason for this need is the fact that the individual person is part of a larger framework to which he must make certain concessions, and unless some restraint or restriction is placed on the expression of needs and motives, he is very likely to come into damaging conflict with society and its members. We see this clearly in the case of the aggressive child who teases and bullies other children, or reacts in a destructive manner toward his environment. This aggressive behavior has to be limited by some form of discipline.

Whenever there are a dozen children there are problems of discipline. In fact, wherever there are human beings of any age, living, growing, working, or playing together, there are problems of discipline. No family and no society can escape the necessity and responsibility of disciplining its members, including its children. But the inevitability of discipline does not answer our questions "when to discipline," "how to discipline," or even "why to discipline."[1]

Kirkpatrick expresses the same idea when he says,

The adolescent child needs restrictions and limitations imposed by his family. His controls are not well established, and in attempting to find out just what they should be, he gets some strength in knowing that the limitations imposed by his parents and by society will protect him. Parental control must be realistic, it must be fair, consistent and reinforced by demonstrable affection. There are few things which precipitate panic behavior so readily as to have all adult controls lifted. For many, excessive permissiveness is an indication of weakness.[2]

But the demands or requirements of society are not the only things that make discipline necessary. The health and safety, and the orderly growth and development of the individual himself, require a measure of discipline. If, for example, the young child does not learn to discipline feelings and emotions he will grow into an emotionally immature and maladjusted adult. If the need for dependence or security is not disciplined, the youngster will fail to develop self-identity or responsibility. At every stage of development, some discipline must be injected into the lives of children and of adolescents, for without it *they cannot achieve the goal of maturity.* Education, experience, and healthy relationships with peers and adults are the *basic ingredients* of mental health and adjustment, but discipline is the *essential means* by which these factors can

---

[1] Mary F. Langmuir, "Discipline: Means and Ends" in Sidonie M. Gruenberg (ed.), *Our Children Today* (New York: The Viking Press,

1955), p. 125. See also J. B. Geisel, "Discipline Viewed as a Developmental Need of the Child," *Nerv. Child,* 1951, 9, 115–121.

[2] M. E. Kirkpatrick, "The Mental Hygiene of Adolescence in the Anglo-American Culture," in A. Maillan (ed.), *Proceedings of the Fourth International Congress of Mental Health* (New York: Columbia University Press, 1952), p. 275.

be made to work for the healthy growth of the individual.[3]

Discipline and Age Level. Parents and school authorities often raise the question whether discipline in some form or other applies to the adolescent as well as to the young child. This is especially true when discipline is mistakenly equated with punishment. The idea seems to be that the adolescent outgrows the need for discipline because he is older and can be expected to assume responsibility for himself. The child must be *made to do things* that conform to parental and social demands, whereas the adolescent *should be motivated or guided* toward doing the right things — or so the reasoning goes. But this sort of reasoning is the result of an inadequate concept of the nature and the function of discipline. As we said before, discipline in some form is necessary at all stages of human life. Without discipline, personality, ideals, behavior, goals, and interpersonal relationships rapidly disintegrate. Discipline in its highest form *is necessary to real freedom;* and one basic reason why maladjusted, neurotic, psychotic, and psychopathic personalities have so much trouble is because they lack control of their own emotions and behavior. In other words, lacking control or discipline *they are also lacking in freedom.* Age level, therefore, is not a determinant of

the need for discipline, even though parents and educators must recognize that the *structure* of discipline must change with developmental progress. This is a point that we shall clarify in our discussion of the nature of discipline.

WHAT DISCIPLINE IS

The Nature of Discipline. As soon as the child emerges from his nine-month imprisonment in the mother's uterus, external forces are set in motion by which his motivations, feelings, and behavior are continuously modified, and which continue to influence him in one way or another until adulthood or beyond. These modifying influences go by different names, but they are all related in some degree to the process of discipline. One of the first things the mother does is to inaugurate a program of *training*, by which the child's bowel movements, eating habits, emotional responses, and tendencies toward soiling or uncleanliness are modified in such a way as to bring them in line with the expectations or demands of society, or her own ideas of how a child should behave. Soiling one's panties, spilling food on the floor, pinching baby sister, playing with expensive bric-a-brac, or sassing Mommy are regarded as instances of unacceptable behavior which must be brought under control, and out of which the child must be gradually trained. Later on, in the middle years of childhood, the child will be trained to brush his teeth regularly, to hang up his own clothes, to straighten his room, to make the bed, to do his homework on time, to tip his cap to a lady, or to act respectfully toward adults. Training, therefore, at any level of development and in any situation, includ-

---

[3] R. S. Stewart and A. D. Workman, *Children and Other People: Achieving Maturity Through Learning* (New York: Dryden Press, 1956), Part 5; F. S. DuBois, "The Security of Discipline," *Ment. Hyg., N. Y.*, 1952, 36, 353–372. DuBois concludes that as the parents succeed in establishing adequate discipline, the child will succeed in the attainment of a sound, healthy and secure basis for maturity. See also E. J. Simburg, "Must Our Children Be Neurotic?" *Ment. Hyg., N. Y.*, 1951, 35, 96–103, and Norma Kent and D. R. Davis, "Discipline in the Home and Intellectual Development," *Brit. J. Med. Psychol.*, 1957, 32, 27–33.

ing military service, dental school, or surgery, is a form of discipline.

This early conditioning and training of the child is supplemented in the middle years by formal education, much of which remains at the level of training. Insofar as education is the imparting of knowledge, then certainly teaching the child to read, write, draw, and spell are more in the nature of training than of education. However, this distinction is not so important as the fact that formal education itself *is a type of discipline.* In this case the process of discipline switches from the impulses and behavior habits of the child to the realm of intellect, perception, and learning, in which case it assumes the form of *mental discipline.* Education like training, therefore, is intrinsically related to the process of discipline.

From an analysis of the relationship between training, education, and discipline, we can get an idea of the broader meaning of discipline, and can understand readily why discipline cannot be equated with punishment. Discipline is essentially, or at least should be, the *proper ordering of a person's life.*[4] It means bringing a person's impulses, needs, habits, and behavior in line with the demands of his own life, with sound principles of conduct, with the requirements of health and adjustment, and with the acceptable rules and restrictions

of family and society. Looked at positively, therefore, *discipline is a process of achieving order,* and the negative features of restraint, denial, frustration, or punishment are simply necessary means by which this order is at times achieved.

The Forms of Discipline. This viewpoint of discipline helps us to understand the broadness of the concept and why it appears in different forms. We can say, for example, that logic is a discipline of the mind, that an officer disciplines his troops, that exercise is a discipline of the body, and that a parent disciplines his child. In each instance the concept is used partly in the same way and partly in a different way, but each usage is correct when we understand the essential meaning of discipline.

These meanings and relationships can be clarified by distinguishing the different forms of discipline. First of all, we should distinguish between *physical, mental,* and *moral* discipline, each one of which pertains to a different area of behavior. Education is directed toward mental discipline, exercise toward physical discipline, and such measures as motivation, advice, exhortation, command, and punishment are directed toward moral discipline. It is the latter term that we usually have in mind when we refer to the discipline of children, by which we mean to imply the regulation or control of impulses, feelings, and behavior patterns. Incidentally, the term *physical discipline* is often used to indicate the use of physical means, such as spanking, to achieve the ends of moral discipline. It is moral discipline that is most closely allied to the problems of healthy development and adjustment. Physical and mental discipline are also important in achieving these goals, but it is moral discipline that

---

[4] Havighurst argues that one of the basic functions of discipline is "to teach the child there is a moral orderliness in the world through the use of consistent discipline" — R. J. Havighurst, "The Functions of Successful Discipline," *Understanding the Child,* 1952, 21, 35–38. See also the interesting parallel between discipline and counseling in F. McKinney, *Counseling for Personal Adjustment in Schools and Colleges* (Boston: Houghton Mifflin, 1958), pp. 507–520.

will in the final analysis determine the success or failure of our efforts in this direction. The undisciplined child or adolescent will be impulsive, intractible, headstrong, stubborn, aggressive, disobedient, weak, disorderly, irresponsible, and immature. This statement indicates clearly why discipline is essential to adjustment.

A second important distinction is between *external* and *internal* discipline. *All* discipline begins with the external ordering of a person's inner life and behavior. The rules and expectations laid down by the parents are forced on the child without his having much to say about it. The infant must be *made* to do certain things, and the child must be *told* what to do. The discipline or control *comes from without.* This means simply that the child is not equipped morally or psychologically to effect control over himself, or to order the events in his life. Between the period of infancy and adulthood, a great deal of intellectual, emotional, and psychological maturation has to take place before a youngster can establish a system of *inner controls*, that is, before internal discipline takes over. Parents and teachers of young children, therefore, should not expect them to act as though such controls exist. Many youngsters do not reach the point of inner discipline until late in the adolescent period if they reach it then. As one writer says,

> Discipline is a slow process of transferring authority from without (parents, teachers, law-enforcement officers) to within the individual's own personality (self-discipline, self-control, maturity). The older the student, the greater the proportion of reason and explanation and self-participation in enforcing discipline. Without definite external standards in

the young child, self-discipline is nearly impossible in the older child.[5]

This statement brings out clearly the important relation between external and internal discipline. It is the latter form of discipline which emerges as *self-discipline, self-control,* or *"will power."*[6] The important thing for parents and educators to realize is, as Farnsworth says, that the one cannot exist without the other. External discipline is the *sine qua non* of self-control. This is how the child learns to control his impulses, his feelings, and his behavior. Overindulgent, overpermissive, and overprotective parents always fail to lay the groundwork for the emergence in adolescence of effective self-control, which puts the teenager in the position of being a victim of his own drives, feelings, and impulses, and unable to act in terms of rules, principles, and ideals. These teen-agers are apt to be in constant conflict with parents and other authorities, unable to concentrate and to study effectively, and constant prey to unbidden fantasies,

---

[5] D. L. Farnsworth, *Mental Health in College and University* (Cambridge, Mass.: Harvard University Press, 1957), pp. 206–207. Lourie advances a similar argument when he says that children must learn how to discipline from people, not from rules. In the effective use of discipline the child will eventually learn to discipline himself. N. V. Lourie, "Discipline: a Consistent, Non-Punitive Concept," *Child Welfare*, 1951, 30, 3–6. For an interesting discussion of different approaches to discipline, see the chapter on vicarious discipline in H. S. Tuttle, *Dynamic Psychology and Conduct* (New York: Harper, 1949), Chap. XIII.

[6] "And like our parents, and our parents' parents, we believe that discipline should lead to self control" — Mary F. Langmuir, *op. cit.*, p. 132. See also W. A. Connell and J. D. McGannon, *The Adolescent Boy* (Chicago: Fides, 1958), pp. 55–74; A. M. Rose, "The Role of Self-Direction in Child Development," *Sociol. Soc. Res.*, 1950, 34, 424–430.

temptations, and feelings of guilt. The adolescent who cannot discipline himself provides the typical picture of the unhappy, confused, unstable, and inconsistent teen-ager about whom parents and civil authorities worry so much.

External Discipline in Adolescence. Like all aspects of growth, discipline is a *developmental* process in which there is a gradual transition throughout infancy, childhood, and adolescence from external to internal discipline. Gradually the parents or other persons in authority should lessen the control, demands, and restrictions directed toward the child in such a way and to such a degree that the child assumes full responsibility for himself. Self-discipline, therefore, is not only the basis of maturity and adjustment but of the feeling and acceptance of *responsibility for self.* We cannot expect the youngster to achieve this high level of discipline until late adolescence or early adulthood, but it is a goal that should guide parents in the effective use of discipline.

Because the growth of effective self-discipline is a process that takes a great deal of time, and that varies considerably from one person to another, external discipline *in some degree* remains a necessity throughout most of the adolescent period. For example, obedience to reasonable demands on the part of parents is a requirement not only for effective growth but for healthy interpersonal relationships, and obedience often has to be enforced. Even in military service, which almost never occurs until age 17, a great deal of external discipline is necessary to achieve the aims of military training. Similarly, in matters of dating, staying out late, use of the family car, the spending of allowances or money earned, the performance of household chores, or style of dress, the parents often have to enforce discipline when the youngster fails to act in accordance with good sense, reasonable demands, or the rules of morality. Teachers also have to enforce discipline when students fail to discipline themselves. In every such instance, parents and teachers must fall back on external discipline when personal responsibility or self-control temporarily proves inadequate or breaks down.

The Roots of Discipline. To say that self-discipline has its beginnings in external discipline is to indicate one of the most important facts about growing up. But this is not the whole picture. There are numerous instances in which the transition from the one form of discipline to the other fails to take place. In some cases, external discipline seems to fall on poor ground so that no basis for self-discipline is established. In still others, discipline seems to go too far and turns into rigidity or extreme docility or overcontrol. In other words, the process of discipline, like all other developmental phenomena, is conditioned and altered in its progress by many different factors which are part of the child's growth picture. Discipline occurs within the context of the child's total development, his experiences, his successes and failures, and the network of relationships that bind him to parents and siblings, friends and classmates.

Starting with the most fundamental factor, good discipline and the emergence of self-discipline depend upon good health. The weak child, the chronically ill child, the hypochondriacal child, or the neurotic child who uses illness as a defense, are poor subjects for discipline. Discipline takes root only in healthy soil; and thus the happy, well-adjusted child is much easier to discipline than one who is unhappy or neurotic. By the same rule, *self*-discipline is much more readily developed in the well-adjusted child.

The effectiveness and growth of discipline hinge also on certain developmental factors, particularly adequate intellectual development and wholesome emotional development. As we have seen, discipline in its earliest stages must take the form of conditioning and training for the simple reason that the child does not possess the understanding or the knowledge necessary for more advanced forms of discipline or for self-discipline. It is obviously a waste of time to "encourage" a two-year-old child to do something because it is right, or to avoid doing something because it is wrong. It is useless to appeal to reason when reason is not yet functioning at any discernible level. Even young school children are more impulse-controlled than reasonable in their behavior, so that discipline remains at the external level for a long time. It is because the adolescent is forging ahead intellectually, acquiring more knowledge, and developing clearer values, concepts, and ideals, that discipline can assume more mature characteristics and gradually change into self-discipline.

Emotional growth and maturation are also important determiners of the progress of discipline. If the adolescent remains emotionally at an infantile or childish level, and is thus the victim of outmoded feelings and responses, discipline will also remain at a lower level of development. The adolescent who uses temper tantrums, crying, pouting, or self-pity to get what he wants is a disciplinary problem right from the start, and will show little evidence of self-discipline. By the same rule, wholesome moral development will contribute a great deal to progress in self-discipline. The youngster who develops or internalizes sound moral values, principles, and ideals, provides excellent soil for disciplinary growth, and will find little difficulty in exercising the self-control necessary to adequate adjustment. When such moral development is complemented by healthy religious growth, the problem of discipline assumes relatively small proportions.

The effectiveness of external discipline, and the growth of self-discipline, will be influenced at all levels of development by the context of interpersonal relationships within which the child develops. In the early formative years, the relationships between the child and the parents are of course the most important, and this situation continues right into adolescence. Obviously, when such relationships are permeated with love, acceptance, mutual respect and confidence, and a feeling on the part of parents for the dignity of the child, the process of discipline will progress smoothly. Conversely, the rejected, hostile, resentful, aggressive, or rebellious child is going to react very poorly to any disciplinary approach, and will experience a great deal of trouble in achieving any measure of self-discipline.

Healthy discipline flourishes also in a democratic as against an autocratic home environment. Autocracy, which usually involves an imperious and punitive father, is ill-suited to the background and mentality of the American teen-ager. The American family is surrounded by democratic ideals and principles, the basis of which is a respect for the worth and dignity of the individual. For this reason, acceptance and permissiveness are more commonly found in the American home than autocracy or punishment. When, therefore, the adolescent sees his peers treated with respect and dignity by their parents he may rebel violently against the imperiosness or autocracy of his own.

This viewpoint of discipline is supported by empirical studies and by expert opinion. Landis, for example, in a study of 1900 boys and 2410 girls, all high school seniors, found that the child from the democratic home has a big advantage in personal and social adjustment factors as compared with the child from an authoritarian family. Also, authoritarian parents were found to be more often in disagreement with their children, and in most cases the girl in these families disagreed more often than the boy.[7] As Kirkpatrick says,

> Ideally speaking, the home should tolerate a rather free expression of feelings and when it does so, there is less evidence of impulsive behaviour in the school and in the community. Where the home does not tolerate the necessary amount of freedom, then three adjustments are possible: repression with hostility, acceptance of reality and integration, or an acting out of impulses elsewhere. A large part of adolescent misbehaviour in school stems from this latter source.[8]

Similarly, Farnsworth states:

> A permissive attitude balanced with firm discipline is the quickest route to responsibility and self control, especially when discipline is applied with consistency, kindness, and thoughtfulness.
>
> Authoritarian, inflexible, and impersonal attitudes in the teacher encourage

and perpetuate rebellion, negativism, and hostility in the pupil.[9]

Of considerable importance also to the healthy growth of discipline is the development of the self-concept, particularly during adolescence. As we saw earlier (Chapter IV), the emergence of the self-concept is a particular aspect of ego development and is therefore directly related to superego formation. At this point parental attitudes toward the child and the self-concept merge to influence jointly the process of discipline. Insofar as the superego involves the internalization of parental attitudes, demands, and proscriptions, the process of discipline will be directly influenced by its formation. The stronger and the more overpowering the superego, the more will the child be subject to parental authority, and the less freedom will there be in the matter of self-discipline. Growth in freedom and in self-discipline, therefore, requires a gradual attenuation of the superego and an emancipation from parental authority. Many adolescents never achieve this emancipation, and consequently carry into adulthood a rigid, authoritative, and autocratic superego which stands *in loco parentis* for the rest of their adult lives, or at least until such time as the stranglehold of the superego is broken by counseling or psychotherapy.

The Proper Use of Discipline With Adolescents. Taking all these facts into account, it is not difficult to see what attitudes parents should adopt toward teen-agers in the matter of healthy discipline. First of all, the parents should do everything in their power to foster the transition from external to internal or self-discipline. There should be a lessen-

---

[7] P. H. Landis, "The Ordering and Forbidding Technique in Teenage Adjustment," *Sch. & Soc.*, 1954, 80, 105–106. See also R. Bakwin and H. Bakwin, "Discipline in Children," *J. Pediat.*, 1951, 39, 623–634.

[8] M. E. Kirkpatrick, op. cit., p. 275. See also F. J. Hacker and E. R. Geleerd, "Freedom and Authority in Adolescence," *Amer. J. Orthopsychiat.*, 1945, 15, 621–630.

[9] D. L. Farnsworth, *Mental Health in College and University* (Cambridge, Mass.: Harvard University Press, 1957), p. 207.

ing of punitive attitudes and practices, and a constant effort to help the youngster achieve independence in thought, feeling, and conduct. The parent should respect the worth and dignity of son or daughter, and do everything to win respect for himself. The parent should pay careful attention to the gratification of basic needs, particularly affection and independence, and should utilize positive motivations whenever possible. Rather than restrict, demand, or punish, the parent should exert maximum effort to appeal to the adolescent's knowledge of right and wrong, his respect for authority, his deepening sense of values, and his principles and ideals. Whenever restrictive discipline is necessary, the adolescent should be made aware of its purpose and justice, it should be exercised in an atmosphere of mutual trust and love, and it should be, above all, consistent.

> An adolescent wants to know where he stands. He is anxious, tense, and insecure enough anyway; and when rules always give way to exceptions, when policy vacillates between harshness and leniency, impetuosity and deliberation, and when rules are constantly changed, he becomes very confused and very annoyed. When an institution — or parent — constantly changes tactics and rules, the adolescent loses respect, learns nothing about proper behavior, and builds up tension and resentment.[10]

When these approaches to a sane and sensible discipline are brought together in the shaping of adolescent conduct, no serious problems should be encountered.

REWARD AND PUNISHMENT

The Nature of Reward.   In the exercise

---

10 J. R. Gallagher and H. I. Harris, *Emotional Problems of Adolescents* (New York: Oxford University Press, 1958), p. 168.

of discipline, whether in the home or at school, rewards and punishments are apt to play a prominent role. The significance of these factors for the motivation of conduct is reflected in the large number of investigations that have been undertaken to determine their efficacy. There are many questions that experimenters have tried to answer. What is the dynamic relationship between reward and punishment? Which one of the two motives is the more effective? Is punishment an adequate motive or is it always detrimental? How can such factors be employed most effectively? These are some of the problems which have been experimentally studied, often with gratifying results. We will note some of these results in our analysis, and indicate briefly the more important dynamic features of reward and punishment.

Rewards are of course a special form of motive or incentive. The term *reward* is used when a motive is of a kind that is offered as a special inducement for a particular task; it has a relationship to one task and to no other. Thus, we reward a child for completing a task satisfactorily; we reward a soldier for heroic action beyond the call of duty; we reward a worker for increased output beyond what is expected of him. In each case the reward is an *added* motivational factor; it is not something that the person has earned but something to which he takes title by reason of *exceptional* effort. A worker earns a wage by ordinary effort, but is rewarded with a bonus by reason of exceptional effort. For these reasons rewards, to be effective, must be novel, exceptional, something beyond and different from that which the person has earned; and always they must be adequate to the conduct involved. A child is not rewarded for meritorious conduct by a slap on the back or a promise of a fishing trip six months hence. He is rewarded by being allowed to stay up an hour longer than usual in the evening in order to see a favorite television show or by a trip to the zoo that would not ordinarily be made.

As motivational factors, rewards have the advantage of novelty; they possess a quality that makes them especially attractive and desirable. Thus they may be effective in motivating conduct when other appeals fail. Because, however, they are exceptional in character, they must never be employed with tasks that are normal duties. One does not reward an adolescent for studying, for keeping his room in order, or for being neat in appearance. These are things to which he must become habituated through practice, and for no other reason than that they are the right things to do. To reward a person for things he is *supposed* to do makes a mockery of reward and cheapens all incentives. On the other hand, to fail to reward an individual for *exceptional* and *meritorious* action tends to destroy willingness and initiative.

The Dynamics of Reward. Rewards are motives that should be prized highly. They should stimulate a person to exceptional effort and at the same time impart a keen sense of accomplishment, satisfaction, or pride in possession. It is in this that their dynamic value lies. Because they are exceptionally attractive they appeal with special force to the person's will, and the desire thus aroused is fortified by the anticipation of the pleasure and satisfaction to be derived from possession. Nor must we forget that, like ordinary motives and goals, rewards may often be made most effective by relating them to basic needs. The best reward for a soldier, for example, may be a furlough which will enable him to spend a few precious hours with loved ones. Another may be rewarded most effectively by the coveted Congressional Medal of Honor, which he may display proudly to friends and relatives. In other words, rewards that are rooted in psychological needs — affection, security, recognition, social approval, and the like — are among the most effective.

Here again we see that the dynamism of motives is often proportional to the extent to which they are rooted in fundamental tendencies. We may ask: Why is a trip to the zoo a reward for the child? Partly, at least, it is because the reward is based on the desire for experience; it gratifies the impulse of curiosity that is generated by this need. Why is a little piece of metal and ribbon regarded so highly by the soldier? Because it ministers to his feeling of worth, to his integrity, to his status in the opinion of others, or to his desire for recognition. It must be admitted that to perform meritoriously is regarded by many as a good in itself, independent of the relationship to fundamental needs. Yet it is unquestionable that the more closely the forthcoming reward is tied into such needs the more dynamic will the reward become. The dynamics of reward, therefore, are a special instance of the dynamics of motives in general, since rewards are different from ordinary motives only in being extraordinary.

The Nature of Punishment. Of equal significance is the motive of *punishment*. To punish in order to insure desired behavior is a very common and age-old means of motivation. Among all men it has been regarded as one of the most effective means of controlling the conduct of others, especially of children. This attitude is clearly exemplified in the well-known rule of thumb: Spare the rod and spoil the child.[11] Psychologists, however, have cast a critical eye at punishment as an efficacious means for motivating desirable conduct. It is of its nature a negative and (from the humanitarian viewpoint) distasteful way of securing acceptable behavior in others.[12] There is, in fact, little in the dynamics of human conduct that warrants the universally accepted notion that punishment is a *necessary* evil. The fact that it is at best a *negative* means serves to indicate that there is in all probability a more efficacious way of securing the same end. Yet we cannot disregard the fact that punishment is and always has been an integral part of individual and social motivation. Looking back over the history of human relations, one cannot easily escape the conviction that without punishment mankind would have been seriously handicapped in bringing about the kind of behavior that is both necessary and desirable.[13]

The Dynamics of Punishment. The dynamics of punishment is based upon the fact that it induces pain or unpleasantness; and, as we have seen, unpleasantness can be a strong motivating factor. Because the organism naturally abhors the unpleasant, the inducement of un-

pleasantness should be a good means of eliminating undesirable conduct. Physical, moral, or mental punishment may thus be used to persuade children to stop lying, swearing, or being disobedient — a course of action strictly parallel with the social practice of fining a driver for speeding, or putting a person in jail for burglary. That punishment of this kind actually works in some instances will not be questioned by anyone who has seen it used effectively; and certainly, at times, it seems as though no other recourse is possible.

Dynamically, then, punishment is efficacious to the extent that it causes feelings of unpleasantness by inducing pain, by privation, or by withdrawing affection, approval, and other desirable qualities. In cases where it is employed simply as a check, its usefulness will depend upon the effectiveness of previous punishments, the recency of the experience, and the imaginative ability of the child to recall its effects. For these reasons, the relationship between the *method of punishment* and its possible effects must be known in order to determine its effectiveness.

By way of example, the threat of a jail term, used to deter youngsters from delinquent or criminal acts, is often ineffective because they have had no experience of being deprived of freedom for a length of time, and perhaps do not possess the ability to imagine what loss of freedom really means. Sending a child to his room for bad behavior may be no punishment at all because the unpleasantness temporarily induced by being forced to stay indoors is soon replaced by daydreaming or other pleasant experiences during the period of confinement. A careful study by parents and teachers of this relationship between the method of punishment and its effects is well worth the effort.

---

[11] In Proverbs 22:15 we find the confirmation for this rule of thumb: "He that spareth the rod hateth his son." And in Proverbs 13:24 we find: "Folly is bound up in the heart of a child, and the rod of correction shall drive it away."

[12] See L. H. Stott, "Home Punishments of Adolescents," *J. Genet. Psychol.*, 1940, 57, 415–428; M. E. Ayer and R. G. Bernreuter, "A Study of the Relationship Between Discipline and Personality Traits in Little Children," *J. Genet. Psychol.*, 1937, 50, 165–170; H. H. Remmers and D. H. Radler, *The American Teenager* (New York: Bobbs Merrill, 1957), p. 114.

[13] See F. McKinney, *op. cit.*, p. 519, and Mary F. Langmuir, *op. cit.*, p. 133.

The Use and Abuse of Punishment. Psychologists have pointed out other relationships between punishment and conduct that are important. To be most effective, punishment must first of all "fit the crime." It must be of such a nature that there is an essential connection between the wrong act and the pain or privation induced by the punishment; and *this relationship must be realized by the recipient.* A soldier A.W.O.L. is thus correctly and effectively punished by being confined to quarters or committed to the guardhouse. A child who slaps or pinches without provocation can be punished effectively by the use of physical means which induce the same experience of pain that he causes others to experience. A student who persists in ignoring his homework should be punished by being made to do the work at a time when he would otherwise be engaged in more pleasant activities. In every situation the punishment must be selected carefully in order that it will make a lasting impression, and really will act in the future as a deterrent to unwanted conduct.

Punishment must also be *proportionate* to the misconduct. It must never be too severe or too lenient. Leniency will destroy the efficacy of the measures used, breeding disdain and contempt in the child. Undoubtedly, many instances of ineffective training of children and adolescents are traceable to this lack of sternness on the part of parents.

Worse still is punishment that is overly severe. Punishment of this kind does not breed obedience for law and authority; it breeds rebellion and harshness of spirit. It violates the fundamental needs of affection, security, and physical and psychological integrity. A child should not be punished severely (if at all) for overturning a glass of milk, dumping a bowl of cereal over its head, drawing pictures on the wall, and the thousand and one similar things that spring from a wanton imagination and the urge to activity. One must always be sure that the conduct which seemingly merits punishment is understood by the wrongdoer to be a wrong act. The youngster who takes his father's car without permission might not know that his father would regard such an act as wrong. The child who breaks an ornament that admittedly he should not have been toying with may not have seen any wrong in the act at all. In many such instances, perhaps in the majority of them, what is called for is not punishment but instruction and counsel, unless the act is persistently repeated.

Many delinquent actions should be similarly regarded. When used at all, punishment must be used *immediately*. If possible, there must be no appreciable lag between the act and the administration of punishment. The reprehensible habit of mothers whose timidity causes them to defer all punishment until it can be administered by the father has done far more harm than the punishment has done good. Punishment should be inflicted when the wrong conduct is fresh in the mind of the erring individual, when he is still clearly conscious of the act which he should have avoided. Children particularly are prone to forget such acts completely, and the administration of punishment after the occasion has passed into history may appear as a rank injustice to the child who, in any event, has little understanding of such matters.

To use this means of motivation to the best advantage it is also necessary that there be some understanding on the part of the recipient of both the *necessity* and the *justice* of the punishment. Children and adolescents must be made to see that the act done by them not only suggests punishment, but *actually demands it*. They must understand the fairness of the retribution and not be allowed the impression that punishment flows from rage, revenge, or the sadistic urge to inflict pain. For this reason, punishment seldom should be used with very young children, for they cannot be made to understand the relationship between the punishment and the act. Only when children possess the insight that comes with development and experience can punishment be used fairly and effectively. In this interpretation of the effective use of punishment we are not excluding such corrective measures as an occasional slap on the hands or an old-fashioned spanking. Even young children know that they are being spanked because they did something they should not do.

From this description it is clear that punishment may be used as an effective means of motivation and discipline. Psychologically, it can be justified because it is based on the quality of unpleasantness, and a wise nature has endowed the organism with a strong aversion to the unpleasant. There is no reason, therefore, why punishment should not be used, especially when other and more positive measures are unavailing, and when it is used in a manner to insure the desired result. Employed in this way, there is no conceivable reason why it should engender the rebellion, hostility, and fear that are often attributed to it, and that are urged as reasons why it should not be employed. The writer has known personally many children with whom punishment has been used repeatedly and yet who have shown no negative psychological reaction. In fact, it is his experience that the bonds of affection between parents and children are often much

stronger where punishment has been employed judiciously than they are in those family situations where it has been sedulously avoided. Judicious punishment breeds respect, a sense of the rightness and wrongness of conduct, and a willingness to abide by authority. It is only the wrong and vicious use of punishment that is psychologically evil. Empirical evidence on the effectiveness of punishment clearly supports this interpretation. When punishment is deserved, children accept it without the least resentment.[14]

Positive Versus Negative Motivation and Discipline. Whatever its value, we must remind ourselves that punishment is a negative form of discipline, and is dynamically rooted in a negative reaction of pain and unpleasantness. Punishment is made necessary by wrong acts, never by right ones. As a result, there is something deeply repugnant about using punishment as a means of bringing about desired conduct. No one, apart from the sadist, enjoys punishing; and, however thoroughly one may be convinced of its justification and necessity, it should be used only as a last resort. This is its psychological weakness. Because it is abhorred by both the administrator and the recipient ("This hurts me more than it does you"), it is often avoided when it should be employed, or it is employed poorly because of an overdose of leniency.

The countermeasure to this weakness of punishment is the simple expedient of motivating conduct that is desirable. If a youngster runs away from home, we may

---

[14] For an excellent discussion of the effective use of punishment, see H. Joseph and G. Zern, *The Emotional Problems of Children: a Guide for Parents* (New York: Crown, 1954), pp. 120–126, 131–141. For adolescents' reaction to punishment, see R. Strang, "What Discipline Means to Adolescents," *Nerv. Child*, 1951, 9, 139–146.

feel it necessary to inflict punishment of some sort. In such instances there may be no alternative; but that is only because it is already too late to insure the *desired* behavior. If, prior to such an episode, the home had been made attractive, not only physically but psychologically and spiritually, the unwanted behavior might not have occurred at all. The problem of truancy does not arise with youngsters who enjoy school, or who understand its advantages and merits. Lying that must be punished could be avoided by making adherence to the truth a worthwhile experience. More often than not, children are forced into lying by fear of telling the truth, or by parents who fail to trust them, or simply by the advantages gained from lying. It is more natural to tell the truth than to lie, and this fact alone can be used to great advantage in training children in the habit of sticking to the truth.

One point that seems to be often overlooked is that good conduct, like bad conduct, occurs only when it is intrinsically satisfying, enjoyable, or pleasant. If the youngster finds that the bad is immediately more attractive than the good, he will in all likelihood indulge the bad. Then punishment becomes necessary. The obvious remedy, and by far the more psychologically correct and profitable method, is to make right conduct attractive and desirable. In this we really have a special advantage because the child soon learns that good conduct is generally the more advantageous. It is approved and favored, and it is in conformity also with the dictates of his own conscience. It is these factors that should be utilized in the motivation and discipline of young people in order to get them to avoid punishable behavior. Punishment, however efficacious and at times necessary, produces a negative reaction; and for that reason it is psychologically much better to motivate behavior that is the contrary of punishable conduct.

A sound general principle that has been experimentally validated is that reward is the more effective motivational instrument.[15] We are always seeking to insure right conduct; and it has been established conclusively that such conduct is more easily motivated when positive measures are employed than when the motivation is negative. We cannot, of course, apply this principle in every situation, since it is manifestly impossible to use rewards when conduct is morally bad or socially unacceptable. But it should always be remembered by parents and educators alike that bad conduct can often be forestalled by the judicious use of rewards and other motives that have the dynamic quality necessary to stimulate desirable behavior. This important alternative to the use of punishment is too often disregarded.

---

[15] See M. E. Ayer and R. G. Bernreuter, "A Study of the Relationship Between Discipline and Personality Traits in Little Children," *J. Genet. Psychol.*, 1937, 50, 165–170. These investigators found that rewarding the child for doing the right thing rather than emphasizing punishment seemed to develop the quality of sociability with other children.

SELECTED READINGS

Baruch, Dorothy W., *New Ways in Discipline* (New York: McGraw-Hill, 1949).

Bernard, H. W., *Mental Hygiene for Classroom Teachers* (New York: McGraw-Hill, 1958), Chap. 8.

Cutts, Norma E., and Moseley, N., *Better Home Discipline* (New York: Appleton-Century-Crofts, 1952).

Langdon, Grace, and Stout, I. W., *The Discipline of Well-Adjusted Children* (New York: John Day, 1952).

Sears, R. R., Maccoby, Eleanor E., and Levin, H., *Patterns of Child Rearing* (White Plains: Row, Peterson, 1957).

Sheviakov, G. V., Redl, F., and Richardson, Sybil K., *Discipline for Today's Children and Youth*, rev. ed. (Washington, D. C.: National Education Association, 1956).

Tuttle, H. S., *Dynamic Psychology and Conduct* (New York: Harper, 1949), Chaps. XII–XV.

Wittenberg, R. M., *Adolescence and Discipline* (New York: Association Press, 1959).

CHAPTER XII

THE INTERESTS AND
ACTIVITIES OF ADOLESCENTS

Adolescents, we have seen, are motivated by many things, and the behavior resulting from these motivations must be guided and disciplined. This picture of motivation and behavior is not complete until we answer the questions: What are adolescents interested in? What do they do? How much have they changed in these respects from the time when they were grade schoolers? Let us see.

WHAT INTERESTS ARE AND WHY

Interests as Motivators. The pattern of adolescent behavior and personality is influenced and colored to an important extent by the characteristic interests and activities in which teen-agers get involved. When Johnny was in the fifth grade the names of Dick Clark, Jimmy Dean, or Elvis Presley had little or no meaning to him. But now that he is a sophomore or junior in high school he would be considered a "square" and an "egg-head" if he confessed ignorance of these important luminaries. The boy has changed into the adolescent with respect to his interests, one of the most significant and pervasive of the class of sustaining motives. These factors are of particular significance because they dynamically determine a great deal of human behavior, and they reach into many different corners of our daily lives. The *activities* so characteristic of the American teen-

ager — dancing, dating, sports, going to movies, watching television, listening to the radio, reading, conversation — are the *behavioral* counterparts of subjective interests, and thus to understand the activities of teen-agers we must understand the origin and development of their interests.

What Interests Are: a Definition. Interests, as we said, belong to the category of sustaining motives. They are more or less stable determining tendencies that support the goals and activities of individuals. They constitute a mental set or readiness of the person to respond in a certain manner when conditions are appropriate for the response. Often a complex affair, interest involves the arousal of associated attitudes, feelings, desires, past experiences, and idea complexes. It induces a receptive frame of mind which favors attention and concentration. Thus, when a person finds it easy to attend, when there is expectancy of joy or pleasure, a rapid flow of ideas, absorption in the task, and a positive attitude toward it, we identify the experience or activity as *interesting*. This descriptive account should not be taken to mean that interest is merely all of these reactions taken together. Lying behind these factors is a *mental disposition* which inclines the person to respond to a situation with interest. Interest, therefore, may be defined as a *relatively permanent and dynamic disposition to respond in a complex manner to some object, experience, or activity with which the individual tends to become temporarily identified.*

Interest characteristically has an *objective reference*. It is directed toward something outside of the individual himself, and thus involves some identification of self with the object or activity. Thus interest is different from desire, even though the one may generate the other. Desire is a mental tendency toward some object that must be possessed if the desire is to be gratified. With interest, on the other hand, even though there is a certain measure of identification, the basic distinction between self and object is always maintained. Hence, the difference between a *desire* to play football and the *interest* in watching it played. So, too, with other activities. Many persons find acting interesting to witness, but relatively few persons ever experience the desire to act.

SIGNPOSTS OF INTERESTS

Are Interests Ever Permanent? The fact that interests are important as motivators of behavior raises the question whether they are or become a *stable* part of the motivational system. If Jane, at the uncertain age of fifteen, is interested in nursing as a future career, will she be

so interested after graduation from high school? Can we suppose that Bob's absorbing interest in model airplanes will lead to a career in aeronautical engineering? Sometimes parents hope and pray that these worthwhile interests will sustain the child until he is launched successfully on a career. At other times, after listening to rock 'n roll or the ever-blaring television, they pray even more fervently for a profound change of interests. It all depends on who is interested in what. But these examples show us how important the question of interest stability can be.

The most that can be said is that *some* interests are *relatively* stable in character. That many of them are not permanent is known both from casual observation and from objective studies.[1] In fact, in the transition from childhood to maturity, interests of all kinds change to a great extent. Even in adulthood, interests that have lasted a long time often change or disappear, leaving a gaping hole in the person's motivational system and in his activities. These idiosyncrasies of the interest pattern require us to study the characteristics of interests very closely.

Many interests are of their nature *transitory* — experiences that are bound to some occasional event like an accident, a street fight, a revolution in a foreign country, or the birth of quintuplets. Such events are interesting; but the interest aroused is not a mental set, determining tendency, or sustaining motive. These interests are like hundreds of other daily experiences; they are moments in the stream-of-conscious life which last only

[1] H. C. Lehman, "The Play Activities of Persons of Different Ages," *Ped. Sem.*, 1926, 33, 250–272; H. C. Lehman and P. A. Witty, "One More Study of Permanence of Interests," *J. Educ. Psychol.*, 1931, 22, 481–492. See also the selected readings at the end of this chapter.

as long as the event itself lasts. They help to explain behavior; but from the standpoint of dynamic psychology it is more important to consider those interests that form an *integral* part of the motivational system and that tend to endure and to color the whole of experience and behavior rather than one small and relatively unimportant part. The question then arises: What factors lie at the basis of the permanence or impermanence of our educational, vocational, social, religious, and recreational interests?

The stability of any interest is determined by the factors that generate it. An interest tends to become permanent when it is bound up with capacities, needs, and experiences, and when the activity resulting from the interest leads to satisfaction and success. Thus the brilliant child is likely to show a permanent interest in learning, studying, or reading. The person for whom physical stamina or appearance is important will show interest in activities leading to physical health and vigor; and the person who possesses ability to work with his hands will often develop interests in activities involving manipulation. Also, as experience in the activity grows, as its possibilities become better known, and there is increasing success and satisfaction, the more deeply rooted will the interest become. A permanent interest is like a habit; it is in fact a habit of mind to respond in a certain manner, which is about all that the phrases "mental set" and "determining tendency" mean.

Why Do Interests Change? There are several reasons why interests change, even those that promise to be permanent. First of all, needs change in certain ways. The adolescent is more interested in different kinds of stories or movies than is the child, because of that shifting of

the motivational pattern described earlier (Chapter X). For obvious reasons we would not expect the young child to be interested in love stories, although we are not surprised when the adolescent is. Second, loss of interest is often traceable to the fact that an activity or experience no longer brings sufficient satisfaction or success, or it loses its challenging quality.

Third, a change in the social structure may bring about a change in interests. The breakup of gangs, cliques, or families destroys the pattern that favored a particular interest or activity. The tendency of some families toward upper status mobility, which results in the movement of the family from one place to another, often alters interest patterns. Finally, there is the fact of maturation. As knowledge and perspective grow with each year of adolescence, fundamental values undergo considerable change, and what was formerly regarded as of great value may lose all of its appeal; and whatever is of little value is also of little interest.[2] The young boy who was so keenly interested in becoming a cowboy, spending all his days riding the range, gradually learns that there are more valuable and worthwhile pursuits and aims in life, and thus begins to lose interest in such possibilities and the activities related to them.

_____

[2] C. P. Stone and R. G. Barker, "Aspects of Personality and Intelligence in Post-Menarchial and Pre-Menarchial Girls of the Same Chronological Age," *J. Comp. Psychol.*, 1937, 23, 439–455; "Attitudes and Interests of Pre-Menarchial and Post-Menarchial Girls," *J. Genet. Psychol.*, 1939, 57, 393–414; H. C. Lehman and P. A. Witty, "A Study of Vocational Attitudes in Relation to Pubescence," *Amer. J. Psychol.*, 1931, 43, 93–101. See also W. J. Dipboye and W. F. Anderson, "The Ordering of Occupational Values by High School Freshmen and Seniors," *Personnel Guid. J.*, 1959, 38, 121–124, and C. H. Miller, "Occupational Choice and Values," *Personnel Guid. J.*, 1956, 35, 74–80.

In similar manner the teen-ager may show a declining interest in aviation, stamp collecting, and adventure stories, because of a shift in values and a broadened perspective.

WHERE INTERESTS COME FROM

Interests Are Acquired. Interests are neither genetically determined nor are they innate. All of them are acquired in the course of personal experience, and this fact is basic to their development and to our understanding of them. However, interests are often related to and dependent upon innate factors, particularly capacities and needs. To these two may be added the factors of experience, personality traits, and temperamental qualities.

Needs and Capacities Influence Interests. Interests often stem from basic capacities like intelligence, musical aptitude, or imagination. The connection between interest and capacity stands out clearly in the case of musical protégés. We would like to say that capacity *guarantees* the development of interests, but there are too many discouraging examples to the contrary; nevertheless, unusual endowment of capacity is ordinarily correlated with a deep, persistent interest. For interests not related to specific abilities, we must search for other determinants. In terms of this relationship, it can be argued that where capacity does not exist, or where it exists in small degrees, there is little point in attempting to develop interest.[3] Parents should keep this in mind when trying to develop musical skill and other interests in children in whom there is little capacity for

such activities. Similarly, the adolescent who is poorly endowed with the capacity for intellectual learning should not be forced into a college education, because he will never develop the interest necessary to sustain his efforts.

The basic needs described in Chapters VII, VIII, and X are often found at the root of interest. The need for experience obviously stimulates interest in various types of activities, and lies at the basis of some vocational aims. Physical needs stimulate interest in sports, athletic exercises, and similar activities. And the desires for participation, acceptance, belonging, and achievement often set the pattern for interest development. In other instances, interests grow out of rational motives or values, a process which is influenced greatly by experience.

Experience Determines the Formation of Interests. Personal experience, working in conjunction with capacities and needs, has a great deal to do with the growth of interests.[4] In fact, experience with an activity is often a prerequisite for such development. Through personal experience a person acquires knowledge of an activity and a desire for it, and this desire generates interest. Thus many interests are transitory because they are built upon inadequate knowledge of the activity. When such experience results in pleasure or satisfaction, a permanent interest may be formed, depending on the extent to which the interest gratifies basic needs and conforms to the individual's capacities. As satisfying experiences accumulate, the development of interest continues at an accelerated pace. These reflections on

---

[3] In this connection see J. R. Gerberich, "The Gifted Pupils of the Iowa High School Survey," *J. Appl. Psychol.*, 1930, *14*, 566–576.

[4] This point is well developed by D. B. Harris, "How Children Learn Interests, Motives, and Attitudes," in N. B. Henry (ed.), *The Forty-ninth Yearbook of the National Society for the Study of Education*, Part I (Chicago: University of Chicago Press, 1950), pp. 129–155.

Experience often generates interest.

Fordham University *Maroon*

the relations between interest and satisfying experience help us to understand why adolescents abandon different activities. The high mortality rate in both high school and college is partly explained by this fact.

Nothing Succeeds Like Success. The hard time that many teen-agers have with the educational process is traceable not only to lack of satisfactory experience but also to failure. An interest or activity is not likely to continue under the condition of chronic or repeated failure; and conversely, a meaningful, permanent interest often develops only after some success has been experienced. Failure undermines an activity, and frustrates the basic needs or desires that generate interest. If Peter can never find any girl who will dance with him because of his clumsiness or lack of skill, he is not likely to maintain an interest in dancing. If Ruth's poems or compositions are laughed at or ridiculed, and she regards them as a failure, she is likely to lose all interest in writing. Where the teen-ager is concerned, nothing fails like failure.

Personality Traits Also Determine Interests. Everyone has observed that the quiet, retiring shy youth is interested in different activities from those of the outgoing, breezy, self-confident extrovert. Shyness and autism favor activities or interests like reading, research, or art, whereas the outgoing personality is more likely to become interested in sports, other extracurricular activities, or a career as a salesman. It is to be expected that feelings of inadequacy and inferiority, or traits like aggressiveness and dominance will affect the development of interest patterns. Similarly, basic emotional dispositions, like anxiety, hostility, or cynicism, will condition interest trends. There are few personality factors that will not in some measure influence the formation and development of interests; and therefore the more any interest can be brought into line with capacities, needs, and traits, and can be enriched by experience, satisfaction, and success, the more permanent and pervasive will it become.

Developmental Influence on Interest Patterns. While the structure of interests is most closely related to the factors just described, the *development* of interest patterns hinges to a great extent on the physical, mental, and social changes that permeate the adolescent period.

Lehman and Witty, for example, found a definite relation between pubescence and interest changes. And Sollenberger found that more sexually mature boys (those whose urine had high hormone content) had more interest in personal adornment, activities of a heterosexual character, and strenuous competitive sports than did boys who were less sexually mature. This confirms the hypothesis that maturation alone is enough to stimulate interest development.[5]

Of equal importance are the teen-ager's growing awareness of approaching maturity and greater insight into the responsibilities of adult living. Certainly the appearance of more mature vocational interests can be traced to these factors, as can interests in steady dating, marriage, or a college education. As Partridge says, many of the changes in interest "can be explained by the fact that young people are striving to establish themselves as mature individuals. Certain activities are not characteristic of grown people, hence those growing individuals who like to consider themselves as mature persons cannot be seen participating in these 'childish' activities. Examples of this kind of activity would be dolls, marbles, tops, romping for fun, playing house, and so on."[6] By implication, this statement further suggests that social pressures have a great deal to do with interest development. As youth approaches maturity he finds it necessary to "readjust his interests and to pursue

activities in keeping with what society will permit for his age, sex, or social status. A boy who did not put away childish things as he stepped onto the threshold of manhood would be ridiculed by his associates. The changing definition he has of himself requires a readjustment in interests and activities."[7] This analysis can be applied also to the differences in interests between the sexes, even though factors other than social pressures play a part in the origin of such differences, some of which are certainly innate.

Changes of interest can also be ascribed to intellectual development, heterosexual reorientation, and changes in basic needs.[8] Since interests stem from fundamental capacities, needs, and personality traits, any alterations in these factors are bound to be reflected in the emergence of new interest patterns and the dropping out of old ones. Thus all of the physical, intellectual, social, and motivational changes of the adolescent period will be mirrored to some extent in the pattern of interest development, and the more profound these changes are the greater will be the changes in interests.

Other Determiners of Interests. Finally, we may note that the formation of interests will be conditioned by such factors as sex, age, nationality, cultural milieu, home environment, the father's occupation, locality, and social facilitation. The interest of the typical American boy in playing cowboys and Indians, or in imitating Superman, is not likely to be found in areas where such traditions are unknown; nor is the avocation of

[5] H. C. Lehman and P. A. Witty, "A Study of Vocational Attitudes in Relation to Pubescence," Amer. J. Psychol., 1931, 43, 93–101; R. T. Sollenberger, "Some Relationships Between the Urinary Excretion of Male Hormone by Mature Boys and Their Expressed Interests and Attitudes," J. Psychol., 1940, 9, 179–190.

[6] E. D. Partridge, Social Psychology of Adolescence (Englewood Cliffs, N. J.: Prentice-Hall, 1939), p. 239.

[7] Ibid., p. 235.

[8] See P. A. Witty and H. C. Lehman, "A Study of the Reading and Reading Interests of Gifted Children," J. Genet. Psychol., 1932, 40, 473–485; L. M. Terman (ed.), Genetic Studies of Genius, 3 vols. (Stanford, Calif.: Stanford University Press, 1925).

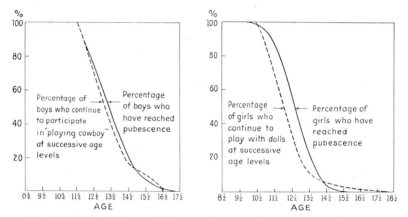

Fig. 18. Proportion of boys who continue to participate in "playing cowboy" at successive age levels versus the proportion who have reached pubescence; and proportion of girls who continue to play with dolls at successive age levels versus the proportion who have reached pubescence. — From H. C. Lehman and P. A. Witty, "A Study of Play in Relation to Pubescence," **J. Soc. Psychol.**, 1930, 1, 519, 514.

building model airplanes likely to attract the interest of the islanders of the South Pacific. Even such a limited factor as locality plays a definite part in determining interest, as revealed by Jones and Conrad in their study of rural preferences in motion pictures.[9] Experience testifies also that sex, age, and race have differential effects on interest formation, and that the home environment often plays a significant role, especially in the matter of both vocational and avocational interests. All these relationships are themselves affected by social facilitation, since interest is often aroused when other persons are already engaged in an activity, especially when they are obviously deriving enjoyment from it. Many of these factors determining interest cannot be manipulated for the betterment

[9] H. E. Jones and H. S. Conrad, "Rural Preferences in Motion Pictures," *J. Soc. Psychol.*, 1930, *1*, 419–423. See also the more recent study by M. W. Cramer, "Leisure Time Activities of Privileged Children," *Sociol. Soc. Res.*, 1950, *34*, 444–450.

or enrichment of adolescent activity. However, a knowledge of their relationship to interest development is helpful in understanding the peculiarities and changes in adolescent behavior.

THE PATTERN AND DEVELOPMENT OF INTERESTS IN ADOLESCENCE

Extent and Character of Interest Changes. Various studies indicate that throughout the adolescent period there are unmistakable and characteristic developmental changes in interest. In one such investigation of play in relation to pubescence, Lehman and Witty found a remarkable parallelism between the onset of pubescence and the waning of play interests (Fig. 18). In this study over 5000 children were asked to check from a list of 200 play activities those in which they had participated voluntarily during the preceding week. The list was checked on three separate dates in order to take account of seasonal variations. In the case of the girls, the authors point out that the relationship revealed is especially noteworthy, since the data were assembled during different decades from entirely different groups of girls living in different communities.

In a similar study of the relationship of vocational attitudes to pubescence, Lehman and Witty again found a striking parallelism. The Lehman Vocational Attitude Quiz was given to more than 25,000 school children in two different localities. The quiz consisted of a list of 200 occupations, on which the children were asked to check only those in which they would be willing to engage as a lifework. The results of this study are indicated in Tables 8 and 9. The

relationship between the changes in vocational interest and the onset of pubescence is so obvious that no comment is necessary. The authors, however, caution against drawing too many inferences from this relationship, because of the lack of children's knowledge regarding vocations and other factors that may condition such a relationship. Nevertheless it is clear, as they point out, that the onset of pubescence is intimately associated with attitude changes, and that these attitudes mature relatively rapidly after the onset of pubescence. These results are supported by many other investigations on play, reading, and similar activities.[10]

---

[10] See A. M. Jordan, "Children's Interests in Reading," *Columbia Univer. Contr. to Educ.*, No. 107; V. Elder and H. S. Carpenter, "Read-

TABLE 8

VOCATIONS TOWARD WHICH GIRLS MANIFEST A CHANGE IN ATTITUDE
THAT PARALLELS THE ONSET OF PUBESCENCE*

Vocation	Ages							
	10½	11½	12½	13½	14½	15½	16½	17½
Magician	100%	72%	45%	32%	26%	7%	8%	1%
Circus performer	100	80	56	47	32	18	11	6
Jeweler or watchmaker	100	72	44	34	24	17	20	19
Maid or servant	100	74	49	42	22	19	21	13
Movie actor or actress	100	72	57	43	32	18	15	10
Teacher in grades or rural schools	100	77	53	37	26	17	11	6
Nurse	100	72	61	48	31	15	13	8

* From H. C. Lehman and P. A. Witty, "A Study of Vocational Attitudes in Relation to Pubescene," *Amer. J. Psychol.*, 1931, *43*, 97.

TABLE 9

VOCATIONS TOWARD WHICH BOYS MANIFEST A CHANGE IN ATTITUDE
THAT PARALLELS THE ONSET OF PUBESCENCE*

Vocation	Ages						
	11½	12½	13½	14½	15½	16½	17½
Shipbuilder	100%	75%	55%	40%	38%	32%	25%
Soldier	100	80	57	34	22	19	14
Circus performer	100	75	50	25	14	12	12
Brakeman or conductor on train	100	70	68	49	32	30	23
Fireman	100	74	46	33	26	14	9
Cowboy	100	75	63	43	21	20	9
Sheriff or policeman	100	70	47	32	17	13	10

*From H. C. Lehman and P. A. Witty, *ibid.*, 99.

The Varieties of Interests. For purposes of discussion we may conveniently distinguish the following types of interests: (1) recreational, which includes both play and amusement; (2) social; and (3) vocational. Among these various types there is considerable overlapping, which is indicative of the fact that interest patterns tend toward mutual influence. Intellectual interests in adolescence will strongly condition recreational, social, and vocational interests; and vocational aspirations will influence such activities as reading, studying, and leisure-time pursuits. This fact is important since it means that new interests may be developed on the basis of those that already exist. For example, an interest in the professions could be aroused in an intelligent adolescent by an appeal to the fact that training for a profession depends upon intellectual capacity.

PLAY INTERESTS

Youth Likes to Play. In an age of tension and anxiety, the attitude we assume toward the role of recreation in our lives can be quite important. This applies particularly to play. The nature and function of play has attracted the attention of psychologists for many decades because of its importance for both physical and mental health. Play has been regarded variously as an instinct, an escape mechanism, a release of surplus energy, a preparation for the more serious activities of adult living, and an escape from conflict and inhibition.[11] Perhaps it

is all of these at one time or another. In any event, play activities assume an important role in the lives of both children and adolescents. It is a purposive form of activity, promoting gratification of basic needs, and insuring freedom from restraint, obligations, and social pressures. Play is pleasant, it enhances the feeling of well-being, and serves to lift the individual temporarily out of the morass of restraints imposed by a too-complex civilization. Even in organized play, such as football and basketball, which involve rules and regulations, the restraint imposed has only to do with the conditions necessary for the playing of the game, rather than with the activities themselves. However, it should be noted that the greater the number of rules the more restraint increases, and what begins as play may end as work.

Adolescents and Children Are Interested in Different Things. There are clearly discernible differences between the play interests of children and of adolescents, those of the latter becoming more and more like those of adults. This fact is illustrated in Figure 19, which is based on a study of 1500 boys in New York City. As the figure indicates, significant differences appear with increasing age. Tables 10 and 11, based on the study by Lehman and Witty, indicate a similar loss of interest in childhood play with increasing age.[12] In the Maryland survey, which dealt with youth sixteen years and older, individual sports,

ing Interests of High School Children," *J. Educ. Res.*, 1929, 19, 276–282; H. C. Lehman and P. A. Witty, *The Psychology of Play Activities* (New York: Barnes, 1927); P. M. Symonds, "Changes in Problems and Interests With Increasing Age," *J. Gen. Psychol.*, 1937, 50, 83–89.

[11] See S. H. Britt and S. Q. Janus, "Toward a Social Psychology of Play," *J. Soc. Psychol.*, 1941, 13, 351–384.

[12] This point is brought out by many investigators. See H. C. Lehman, "The Play Activities of Persons of Different Ages," *Ped. Sem.*, 1926, 33, 250–272; A. B. Hollingshead, *Elmtown's Youth* (New York: Wiley, 1949), Chap. 15; Ruth Strang, *The Adolescent Views Himself* (New York: McGraw-Hill, 1957), Chap. 4; J. P. Zubeck and Patricia A. Solberg, *Human Development* (New York: McGraw-Hill, 1954), Chap. 13.

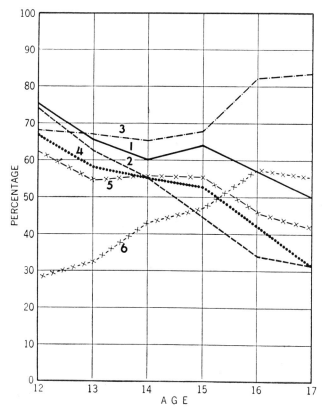

Fig. 19.   Changes of interest with age among adolescent boys:
(1) marching in a parade, (2) cowboy movies, (3) riding in an
auto, (4) making model airplanes, (5) detective stories, (6)
arguments — from E. D. Partridge, **Social Psychology of Adolescence**, p. 238.

reading, dating, dancing, team games, movies, listening to radio, and hobbies were found to be most popular.[13]

Studies such as these indicate that the adolescent evidences greater willingness to participate in team play and organized games as compared with the more random play activities of younger children, and to gravitate toward activities more social in nature. Participation in organized play reaches its peak in adolescence and then slowly declines with approaching maturity, although interest in various games and activities remains at a high level. There is also a decided shift toward activities that can be enjoyed by "inner imitation" and away from those involving actual participation.

Girls Are Interested in Different Types of Play.   Sex differences in the play interests of adolescents can be observed, but they are not as striking as ordinarily

[13] H. M. Bell, Youth Tell Their Story (Washington, D. C.: Amer. Council on Educ., 1938), p. 162. See also D. B. Van Dalen, "A Differential Analysis of the Play of Adolescent Boys," J. Educ. Res., 1947, 41, 204–213.

TABLE 10

JUVENILE PLAY ACTIVITIES THAT WANE WITH INCREASING AGE IN GIRLS*

%	Activity	Ages						
		11½	12½	13½	14½	15½	16½	17½
66	Cutting paper things with scissors	100%	80%	73%	44%	33%	27%	15%
57	Playing with dolls, etc.	100	77	44	14	7	4	2
45	Jumping rope	100	78	62	42	24	9	7
31	Jacks	100	77	48	32	19	10	3
24	London Bridge	100	67	46	29	14	4	0
17	Blindman's Bluff	100	77	65	35	24	12	6
13	Run Sheep Run	100	85	69	46	31	15	0

*Adapted from H. C. Lehman and P. A. Witty, "A Study of Play in Relation to Pubescence," *J. Soc. Psychol.*, 1930, *1*, 516.

TABLE 11

JUVENILE PLAY ACTIVITIES THAT WANE WITH INCREASING AGE IN BOYS*

%	Activity	Ages						
		10½	11½	12½	13½	14½	15½	16½
45	Climbing porches, trees, etc.	100%	91%	76%	53%	31%	16%	7%
29	Playing cowboys	100	72	42	17	10	0	0
21	Mumbly Peg	100	95	67	48	29	19	5
19	Robber and police	100	63	37	16	5	0	0
14	Digging caves or dens	100	86	79	50	36	14	0
12	Playing soldier	100	58	33	17	0	0	0
7	Blindman's Bluff	100	86	43	29	14	0	0

*From H. C. Lehman and P. A. Witty, *ibid.*, 517.

supposed. Whether from innate factors or because of environmental conditioning, girls generally gravitate less to muscular sports and activities involving competition and regulation than do boys. These differences tend to decrease with the approach of adulthood, although they do not disappear entirely. For example, at ten years of age boys prefer football, baseball, boxing, playing catch, and riding a bicycle; at fifteen years basketball, driving an automobile, and playing tennis have been added. Girls at the age of ten like to play the piano, go to the movies, look at the funnies, play with dolls, and roller skate; whereas at fifteen they are interested in reading books, dancing, and riding in an automobile in addition to some earlier activities. While these are small samples of the most popular play activities at different age levels, they indicate certain sex differences, and also the decided developmental shift that occurs during adolescence.

Play Is Important to Young People. Play activities have many important effects on development.[14] Some of them afford excellent opportunities for freedom of action and expression that a

---

[14] This relationship is pointed out in several recent articles. See, for example, J. E. Davis, "A Theoretical Formulation of Play as Life Exercise," *Ment. Hyg. N. Y.*, 1954, 38, 570–575, and L. K. Frank, "Play and Personality Development," *Amer. J. Orthopsychiat.*, 1955, 25, 576–590.

Teen-agers like to dance.

New York Times

complex civilization does not always make possible. They provide occasions for exercise of both physical and mental capacities, and they afford a temporary relief from the social pressures and conflicts characteristic of the adolescent period. This is true even for nonparticipants, since by inner imitation they experience in a smaller way all of the features of the play experience. Whether actual participation in organized play leads to the development of such traits as loyalty, courage, and perseverance, as is often thought, cannot be accurately determined. However, insofar as the development of any mental trait or habit depends upon exercise and use, it is likely that such traits will develop when they are given opportunity to do so, as they certainly are in organized games. It may be, as Conklin suggests, that these traits exist in the individual prior to his participation in these activities; but it is certain that the more they are exercised the more dynamic will they become. Moreover, apart from their influence on personality and character, many play activities provide opportunities for physical exercise, which is important to complete adjustment.

One activity of particular interest in this connection is social dancing, which generally appears during adolescence. This activity evidences all of the characteristics and advantages of play, but is also motivated by other factors like sex, the desire for participation, and experience. The psychology of dancing varies from one form to another. The social dancing of modern youth differs greatly from the religious and predominantly sexual dances of certain aboriginal tribes, where the playful characteristics disappear entirely in favor of other motives.[15] The more that dancing is tied up with social and religious factors the more its character as play tends to disappear. Certainly in later adolescence the social element in dancing is as prominent as the play interest, and it becomes difficult to determine whether the basic motivation is social or playful.

Dancing serves the heterosexual need of bringing young persons together in groups, and affords a certain amount of experience in the development of social mannerisms, gracefulness, and rhythm.

[15] See V. Robinson (ed.), *Encyclopedia Sexualis* (New York: Dingwall-Rock, 1936), pp. 165–168.

Play and amusement are important to young people.

But it may sometimes generate moral problems, not because of the activity itself necessarily, but because two different interests are merged into one activity — play and heterosexual contact. As a play activity, dancing should be free from restraints of various kinds, as is true of all forms of play, and this is actually the case in modern forms of dancing. But when freedom of expression and abandon spread to social situations there is considerable moral danger. Dancing involves physical contact which may stimulate sexual desires, and this is often a difficult control problem for the adolescent. The more, therefore, he abandons himself to complete freedom of expression the more likely are desires and emotions of a sexual nature to get out of hand. In fact, among primitive people the dance is often used for this purpose; and the thin veneer of civilization worn by modern man is not always enough of a protection against primitive tendencies.

Apart from these limited negative effects, play activities are quite important to complete development. Play provides effective and wholesome use of the adolescent's leisure time, which serves as a preparation for the more intelligent use of leisure time in adult life. It is also a means of temporary escape from restrictions imposed in the home, school, and society and thus serves to reduce tension and conflict. This is one of the most basic purposes of play activities at all levels of development, and explains why some recreation is a *sine qua non* of adequate adjustment. Play activities also promote social development and adjustment, since they often involve participation and group co-operation. Finally, play contributes to the physical, mental, and moral development of the individual involving as it does physical exercise, muscular co-ordination, and a certain amount of self-control, as well as experience in making decisions, quick thinking, and other adjustments required in various competitive games.

AMUSEMENTS IN ADOLESCENCE

Play Versus Amusement. Besides active play there are many other activities that attract youth, but which are *passively* rather than actively enjoyed. These are properly called *amusements*. Where play involves active, personal participation in some activity, amusements involve participation *through inner imitation*. Whereas play is real, amusement is imaginative in character. In play there is a projection and spending of self in some activity; in amusement, on the other hand, there is *introjection* of the experiences of others, resulting in imaginal participation. This distinction is particularly appropriate here because of the fact that amusements tend more and more to supersede the play interests of adolescents. Among the various amusements are several that are especially interesting to adolescents: leisure reading, movies, television, listening to the radio, and conversation. In discussing the needs of youth in an earlier chapter we referred to some of these activities in terms of their basic motivations. Now we wish to study them as a specific type of adolescent interest, and trace their relationship to the conduct of teen-agers.

Reading for Amusement. Of these amusements reading is one of the most important. It is important in the right use of leisure time; in forming wholesome literary tastes that will carry over into adult life; in the formation of values, principles, ideals, and attitudes; in satisfying or stimulating certain desires, and so on — all such effects depending upon the content of the material read. Experimental studies have yielded conflicting results regarding the development of reading interests in adolescence. According to some investigators reading interests reach a peak toward the end of the preadolescent period and then begin to decline; but there is so much individual variation that no general principles can be drawn. Moreover, the decline is not always due to loss of interest in reading, but to the increase of studies and participation in other activities that leave much less time for leisure reading.[16]

Studies indicate that the amount of leisure reading varies with sex, race, age, intelligence, amount of schooling, and type of youth. In their study of the reading interests of gifted children, Witty and Lehman found that the average number of books read in a two-month period by gifted children was 14, whereas for a control group of average children the number was only 6.[17] In other studies it has been found that reading ranked first

---

[16] For the extent of leisure reading, see Freida K. Merry and R. V. Merry, *The First Two Decades of Life* (New York: Harper, 1950), pp. 499–537; U. H. Fleege, *Self-Revelation of the Adolescent Boy* (Milwaukee: Bruce, 1945), pp. 238–242; G. W. Norvell, *The Reading Interests of Young People* (Boston: Heath, 1950).

[17] P. A. Witty and H. C. Lehman, "A Study of the Reading and Reading Interests of Gifted Children," *J. Genet. Psychol.*, 1932, 40, 473–485.

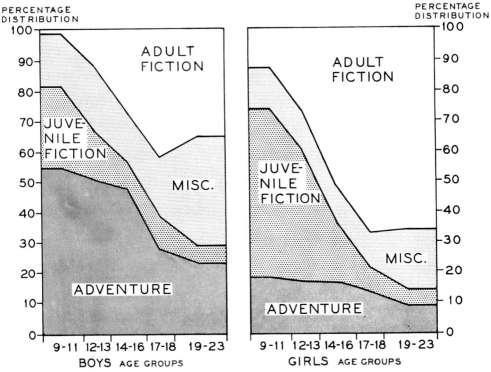

Fig. 20.   Sex and age differences in reading interests. Based on A. M. Jordan, "Children's Interests in Reading," **Teachers Coll. Contr. to Educ.,** 1921, No. 107.

for girls and second for boys, that white youth favored reading more than did Negroes, and that amount of schooling completed constituted an important determinant of reading.[18]

Studies such as these indicate, therefore, that the popularity of reading does not necessarily decrease with age, although there are decided shifts in the kind of material that is read. There is, of course, a continuous change in the direction of adult reading interest. For example, reading newspapers is often

popular among college students, whereas it is seldom found among young adolescents. Magazine reading interests also change a great deal during adolescence.

Girls' Reading Interests Versus Boys'. There are striking sex differences in reading interests. In early adolescence girls turn to fiction more readily than do boys, and seem to achieve maturity of reading interests earlier. Also, while boys seldom read girls' books, girls often show interest in books written mainly for boys. In the early teens, boys' interests incline toward books on travel, adventure, and technical subjects more than toward fiction. As might be expected, there is considerable overlapping among age groups, since development is always a gradual

18 For determinants of reading interests, see R. L. Thorndike, *Children's Reading Interests: A Study Based on a Fictitious Annotated Titles Questionnaire* (Columbia Univer.: Teachers College Bureau of Publ., 1941); G. W. Norvell, *op. cit.*, Chaps. 3, 5, 6, 7, 8, and 9.

process. Girls in the early teens like juvenile fiction, adult fiction, and adventure stories in that order, whereas in later years adult fiction takes the lead, followed by adventure stories. For boys who read fiction, adventure stories seem to be the most popular, and even at age 18 they are still in the lead, but by that time adult fiction is becoming more popular. More girls than boys are interested in popular novels and love stories.

Among other types of reading material, there is often substantial agreement between the sexes, although girls' tastes are more homogeneous than the boys'. As teen-agers move toward adulthood, reading habits continue to change, and such well-known periodicals as *Good Housekeeping, Ladies' Home Journal, Time, Reader's Digest, Saturday Evening Post,* and similar publications appear on the list of magazines that are read. Incidentally, boys and girls of all ages indicate that reading the comic strips is a most favored pastime, although it begins to lose ground after age 15, especially with girls. This widespread interest can be explained by the fact that the comics are brief, pictorial, colored, and generally amusing or exciting. Like the movies, they satisfy needs and interests with a minimum of effort.[19]

Regardless of material read, or sex differences in reading, the important point is that reading experiences can be the source of worthwhile influences on personality development, especially in view of the fact that books are readily accessible, and can be read as often as one likes. One investigator, analyzing the influence of reading on racial attitudes of adolescent girls, found definite positive effects, including better attitudes, greater consistency of opinion, and better understanding of the Negro problem. But there are dangers in reading also. Books and magazines can stimulate higher ideals, or they can be the source of extremely poor concepts of life or of false standards of conduct. Reading can be used for vicarious experiences that act as a compensation for or sublimation of inhibited tendencies. It is of great importance to the use of leisure time, although excessive reading should be discouraged since it may lead to the development of seclusive tendencies, or to withdrawal into a world of fantasy that conflicts with actual reality.[20]

Youths' Interest in Movies. When

---

[19] See P. A. Witty, "Children's Interest in Comics, Radio, Motion Pictures, and TV," *Educ. Adm. Superv.*, 1952, 38, 138–147; D. G. Burns, "Newspaper Reading in the Secondary Modern School," *Brit. J. Educ. Psychol.*, 1955, 25, 1–9; Alice P. Sterner, *Radio, Motion Picture and Reading Interests* (New York: Teachers College, Columbia University Press, 1947); M. I. Kramer, "Children's Interests in Magazines and Newspapers, I," *Cath. Educ. Rev.*, 1941, 39, 284–290; "Children's Interests in Magazines and Newspapers, II," *Cath. Educ. Rev.*, 1941, 39, 348–358; G. W. Norvell, *The Reading Interests of Young People* (Boston: Heath, 1950), Part 2; R. C. Hendrickson, *Youth in Danger* (New York: Harcourt, Brace, 1956), pp. 193–227.

[20] Good and bad effects alike are attributed to reading by various investigators. Sex crimes are often laid at the door of pornographic literature, and many bad effects are attributed to the comics. See, for example, F. Wertham, *Seduction of the Innocent* (New York: Rinehart, 1954). This is a seven-year investigation of the effects of comic books on children and the contribution of such reading to juvenile delinquency. Other writers stress the more positive aspects of reading. See, for example, N. A. Ford, "Literature as an Aid to Social Development," *Teach. Coll. Rec.*, 1957, 58, 377–381; F. B. Thornton, *How to Improve Your Personality by Reading* (Milwaukee: Bruce, 1949); Sister Mary Agnes, "Influence of Reading on the Racial Attitudes of Adolescent Girls," *Cath. Educ. Rev.*, 1947, 45, 415–420; and Alice L. Goddard and Mildred C. Widher, "Mental Health Reading for Children," *Pastoral Psychol.*, 1952, 3, June, 39–48.

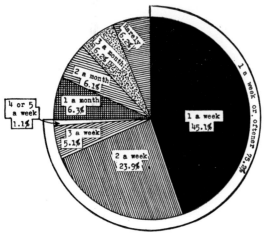

Fig. 21. Frequency with which high school boys attend movies. From U. H. Fleege, **Self-Revelation of the Adolescent Boy** (Milwaukee: Bruce, 1945), p. 246.

teen-agers are not actively engaged in some form of play or sports, or wiling away leisure hours in reading, they are often seen at the movies, or with their eyes glued to a modern substitute for the movies, the television program. There is no doubt that television has lured many people away from the movies, but this fact is not too important so far as influences on personality development are concerned.[21] However, television viewing occurs in a totally different setting from that of movies; this setting can have a lot to do with the differential effects that each one produces. Movie attendance is often used for purposes of dating, socializing with members of the peer group, hand-holding, necking and petting, or as an excuse to get away from parental control. This is not the case with television viewing, which is much more under the control of the parents.

These facts have changed the pattern of movie attendance in recent years, and therefore the significance of studies that have been made on movie attendance. For example, in one study of 500 feature pictures it was found that love stories comprised 29.6 per cent, crime stories 27.4 per cent, and sex themes 15 per cent. Obviously this is not an encouraging picture, but the effects of such movies will vary in direct proportion to the amount of attendance, and this has altered considerably in recent years.[22] Early investigators found that movies were extremely popular at nearly all age levels, but these figures would have to be revised downward for the present generation of teen-agers (see Fig. 21).

However, not all investigations agree on the amount of movie attendance, which means that this activity, like others, varies with such factors as locality, sex, and race. Thus movies seem to be less attractive to youth than to younger children, and more attractive to girls than to boys. This reflects the fact that during adolescence there are more activities to engage the interests of youth. Also, the compensatory function of movies is probably less necessary to teen-agers than to young children because

[21] See the article by P. A. Witty, "Children's Interest in Comics, Radio, Motion Pictures, and TV," *Educ. Adm. Superv.*, 1952, 38, 138–147. The studies reviewed in this article indicate that in the early years of TV it was preferred over radio at all school ages, and that movie attendance and reading were also reduced.

[22] See Alice P. Sterner, *op. cit.*

TABLE 12

PRINCIPAL LEISURE-TIME ACTIVITIES OF YOUTH ACCORDING TO SEX*

	Male Youth				Female Youth	
Rank	Activity	Percentage		Rank	Activity	Percentage
1	Individual sports	21.6		1	Reading	35.0
2	Reading	16.7		2	Dating, dancing	13.7
3	Team games	15.7		3	Handicrafts, hobbies	13.4
4	Loafing	13.1		4	Movies	12.0
5	Dating, dancing	10.9		5	Individual sports	11.1
6	Movies	9.4		6	Loafing	5.4
7	Hobbies	5.5		7	Listening to radio	2.2
8	Listening to radio	1.8		8	Team games	1.1
9	Quiet games	1.5		9	Quiet games	0.8
10	Other activities	3.8		10	Other activities	5.3
	Total	100.0			Total	100.0
	Number of Youth	6872			Number of Youth	6635

* From H. M. Bell, *Youth Tell Their Story* (Washington, D. C.: Amer. Council on Educ., 1938), p. 162.

youths' hold on reality becomes increasingly more secure. Table 12, taken from an earlier survey, brings to light some interesting facts regarding movies and other leisure-time activities, and also indicates sex differences.

Movie attendance is still important in understanding the activities of youth, but as Table 12 shows, dating, dancing, team games, reading, and sports all outranked going to movies in the case of boys, whereas for girls they are still outranked by reading, dating, and dancing. These preferences vary also with such factors as race and locality. Even the amount of schooling will have a great deal to do with determining the activities in which young people get interested. Thus, reading captivates the interest of many more youths who have completed four or more years of education beyond high school as compared with youngsters whose schooling only reached the sixth-grade level.

Teen-Agers' Preferences for Movies. Tables 13 and 14, taken from two widely different surveys covering a span of years, give a clear picture of the types of movies

TABLE 13

TYPE OF MOVIE PREFERRED BY YOUTH ACCORDING TO SEX*

	Percentage		
Type of Movie	All Youth	Male	Female
Musical comedy	21.4	19.9	23.1
Historical	21.0	19.4	22.9
Action, western	16.2	23.3	8.2
Love story	13.5	4.8	23.3
Mystery	9.2	10.1	8.2
Gangster, G-men	5.7	9.3	1.6
Comedy of manners	5.1	4.7	5.5
News, education	4.7	5.6	3.6
Other types	3.2	2.9	3.6

*Adapted from H. M. Bell, *op. cit.*, p. 172.

preferred by teen-agers. Of the 13,487 youths covered in the first survey, 72.8 per cent were on the whole favorable toward movies as a leisure-time activity — a significant proportion. The order of interest in different types of movies is indicated in both tables. A casual inspection of these data indicates some correspondence with reading interests, considerable sex differences, and decided changes of interest with age. Note, for example, the effect of age and development on western movies and those dealing with love stories, although in recent

TABLE 14

TYPES OF MOVIES PREFERRED BY 2000 CATHOLIC BOYS ON THE DIFFERENT HIGH SCHOOL LEVELS*

Types of Movie	Freshmen	Sophomores	Juniors	Seniors	All
1. Mystery	48.8%	46.6%	42.6%	38 2%	44.1%
2. Musical comedy	33.2	34.2	42.6	45.8	39.0
3. Comedy of manners	27.2	31.6	30.6	24.4	28.5
4. Historical	23.2	20.4	26.6	25.1	23.8
5. Gangster, G-men	25.2	23.2	17.6	17.0	20.9
6. Western	24.8	18.0	12.6	10.0	16.4
7. News	15.6	13.4	14.0	12.6	13.9
8. Love stories	6.4	8.8	11.8	15.2	10.6
9. Educational	10.2	7.2	10.2	11.4	9.7
10. Travel	6.0	8.0	8.4	7.6	7.5
11. "I like several"	13.4	18.2	15.8	15.6	15.8
12. No preference	1.6	2.2	3.6	3.4	2.7

*From U. H. Fleege, *Self-Revelation of the Adolescent Boy,* p. 251.

years the "adult" western has reversed this trend to a great degree, if we are to accept television ratings.

Movies, Television, and the Behavior of Teen-Agers. The Legion of Decency is testimony to the fact that a large block of the American population believes that movies can be seriously detrimental to the emotions, attitudes, and morality of young people, and that movie attendance should be carefully controlled by vigilant parents. Admittedly, movies, like reading and conversation, are a type of experience which can influence attitudes and beliefs, desires and practices. In fact, empirical studies indicate that there is hardly any aspect of personality or conduct that is of itself impervious to movie experiences, although these effects are always conditioned by other factors. Ideas, impulses, ideals, mannerisms, etiquette, ideas of love-making, delinquent behavior, sexual delinquencies, and other aspects of behavior are all affected in greater or less degree. These effects will vary a great deal with amount of movie attendance, type of movie, and personality characteristics of the movie-goer. It

has been found, for example, that the excessive movie-goer is more poorly adjusted than the youngster who attends movies only occasionally, which indicates a close relationship between movie attendance and personality. In other words, movies often have detrimental effects only because of the personality traits possessed by the movie-goer.

One of the most serious effects of experiences like movie attendance is the *emotional possession* that occurs in the viewer, which involves a partial or complete abandonment of self-control, and which seems to lessen and disappear altogether with advancing age. Research has indicated that profound mental and physiological effects of an emotional nature can be produced by movie experiences, although there are wide individual differences in all age groups. In one study, scenes of pseudo-tragedy, conflict, and danger incited responses of varying degrees of intensity in different age groups, the most intense reactions occurring under age 12. The effects tended to diminish with increasing age. Love or suggestive scenes caused varying responses. Children 9 years of age gave little response; at 10, 11, and 12 the number responding increased, and above 13 there was usually a definite response. The peak of response was reached at age 16. Sixteen seemed to be the critical age when scenes of conflict caused maximal response, and when love scenes and suggestive incidents consistently caused a maximal reaction. Adults, significantly, responded much less intensely to love and sex scenes than did adolescents, and children under 12 responded less than adults. In another study, it was found that addiction to movie horrors and radio crimes had a detrimental effect on general health, including increased nervousness, sleep disturbances, and increased fears. It was found that in homes where standards of child training are high, horror movies and radio crimes stories were limited.[23]

Movies, Attitudes, and Sex. That attitudes can be seriously influenced by movies and similar experiences is attested by causal observation as well as by careful empirical studies. Thurstone, Peterson, and other investigators have found that movies which have a definite theme or message have a strong and sometimes lasting effect on the attitudes of children.[24] Other studies indicate that sex attitudes and sex delinquencies are traceable in part to movie experiences. At a time when sexual fantasy and desires are on the upswing, and when teen-agers have little or no opportunity for the legitimate expression of such tendencies, their feelings and attitudes will be strongly influenced by witnessing lovemaking, suggestive scenes, and provocative costuming. In one group of 252 delinquent girls, it was found that 39 per cent admitted permitting men to make love to them after seeing a passionate love picture, and 25 per cent acknowledged having sexual relations after becoming sexually aroused at a movie.[25]

Movies and Delinquency. In view of the continuing increase of delinquency in America, it is of considerable importance to determine whether and to what extent certain teen-age experiences lead to delinquent behavior. We have noted already that sexual delinquencies seem at times to result from sexy movies, and in all probability from sexy novels and conversation as well; but we are always faced with the stark reality that the vast majority of teen-agers do not follow the path of delinquency, no matter what their recreational experiences are. It is true that studies of delinquent youths indicate conclusively some relation between movies and delinquent behavior, but whether this relationship is determined by the experience itself or by the delinquent pattern is impossible to determine. Three important facts stand out in this connection, and these facts must be used to guide our thinking. First, movies, television, and reading experiences have the potentiality to influence feelings, attitudes, and conduct; there-

[23] M. I. Preston, "Children's Reactions to Movie Horrors and Radio Crime," *J. Pediat.*, 1941, 19, 147–169. See also the more recent study by W. D. Wall and W. A. Simson, "The Emotional Responses of Adolescent Groups to Certain Films," Part I, *Brit. J. Educ. Psychol.*, 1950, 20, 153–163; A. B. Hollingshead, *Elmtown's Youth* (New York: Wiley, 1949), pp. 389–413; and U. H. Fleege, *op. cit.*, pp. 250–258.

[24] Partridge points out that movie attendance can be a very potent learning situation, and that the effects of movies on conduct is in large measure attributable to this fact — E. D. Partridge, *Social Psychology in Adolescence* (New York: Prentice-Hall, 1939), p. 250.

[25] H. Blumer and P. M. Houser, *Movies, Delinquency, and Crime* (New York: Macmillan, 1933), p. 86.

fore some measure of control should be exercised by parents over sexy movies, and over novels, horror films, pictures, or books that glorify crime, divorce, adultery, and sexual liberty. Such experiences might not seriously affect this or that child; but just as we do not place poison in the reach of a child in the hope that he will keep his hands off, so we should not risk exposing children to experiences that may be detrimental to moral health or adjustment.

Second, nondelinquent youngsters, with a good home background and wholesome moral and religious training, will not be affected in the same way or to the same degree as children who lack such training. Moreover, these youngsters are not as likely to seek experiences that are vulgar, degrading, or damaging to moral health. They are the ones for whom the Legion of Decency provides an acceptable code of movie attendance. Third, delinquency-prone youngsters are much more likely to seek and enjoy movies, books, and television programs that are morally degrading, and will at the same time be more deeply affected by what they experience. In any event, young people should be guided in the selection of recreational experiences and activities that will contribute to healthy development and adjustment.

While empirical evidence indicates that delinquencies, attitudes, crime, and ideas of crime can be influenced by movies and similar experiences, the effect is not always in one direction. There are many instances where no effect is produced at all, or where the effect is negative, producing an attitude unfavorable to the type of conduct depicted. In other words, while movies may act as an *exciting* cause, we must take into account existing *predisposing* causes if we are to explain the true relationship between movies and conduct. It is not *what* youngsters experience but what they *introcept* from the environment that makes a difference where conduct is concerned. Thus if the ideas and practices portrayed in movies and books are not introcepted, or if they are actively rejected, the effect produced will be entirely different. And what is introcepted will in turn be determined by the background of experience, the needs, desires, ideals, attitudes, and dispositions that already exist in the youngster. If such factors are favorable to the introception of movie content, only then will they have a pernicious (or beneficial) effect. In many instances, therefore, movies have merely a compensatory or recreational function; and as adulthood is approached there is more and more detachment, less emotional possession, and less identification of self with fictional characters and situations. As integration and self-control develop, and as the hold on reality increases, the less effect will fictionalized portrayals have on the behavior of youth.

Radio and Television Interests. Movies, television, and radio listening have many common features, but it is difficult to determine empirically how important these latter activities are as a source of recreation for young people. Results of studies on the radio-listening habits of youth are somewhat conflicting, but more recent investigations indicate that listening to the radio is one of the favored recreational pastimes of young people. This interest was temporarily interrupted by the novelty of television, but in recent years radio listening has again achieved considerable popularity. Popular music, sports programs, and disk jockeys exert the strongest appeal, but other types of programs also come within the scope of radio interests. In view of the types of programs preferred by youth, it is probable that the effects of radio listening are predominantly informational and recreational.[26]

The effects of television viewing are just about as difficult to determine. Although numerous articles regarding the effects of television on children have appeared in newspapers and popular magazines, and considerable speculation regarding its detrimental effects has been offered, there are few empirical studies on which to base a sound opinion.[27] The pattern of television interests is of course similar to that which characterizes reading and movie interests, which means that comedy, variety, western stories, and sports claim a major share of attention. Out-of-home activities, movies, reading, and homework have been adversely affected by excessive television viewing in many instances, but these effects have been lessened as television lost some of its novelty. It is likely that preadolescents are more seriously affected by television than teen-agers, whose outside interests often preclude sedentary activities like movies and television.

SOCIAL AND VOCATIONAL INTERESTS OF TEEN-AGERS

Teen-Agers Like to Converse. It is not easy to determine the conversational interests and activities of young people, and it is even more difficult to determine the effects of this pastime on personality development. However, we do know that conversation is one of the most favored recreational activities of youth. Undoubtedly much of the so-called "loafing" noted in various studies was given over to conversation, idle talk, and "bull sessions." In one early study it was found that conversation ranked among the first six avocations of male college freshmen, but that women ranked it twentieth in their list of avocations.[28] This is probably an artifact of investigation, since telephone conversations are more popular among girls than among boys. The range of topics covered in such conversations is extremely wide, including sexual experiences, religion, movies, and reading material. For both men and women it

---

[26] Reference has already been made to the survey by Witty which appeared in 1952. See also P. A. Witty, "Television and the High School Student," *Educ.*, 1951, 72, 242–251. At the time that these studies were made television tended to depress reading and movie interests, but this situation has changed somewhat in recent years.

The radio habits of young people are clearly described in several places. See W. R. Clark, "Radio Listening Habits of Children," *J. Soc. Psychol.*, 1940, 12, 131–149; Alice P. Sterner, *Radio, Motion Picture and Reading Interests* (New York: Columbia University Press, 1947); and J. Johnstone and E. Katz, "Youth and Popular Music: a Study of the Sociology of Taste," *Amer. J. Sociol.*, 1957, 62, 563–568. In the study by Johnstone and Katz it was found that musical tastes and preferences for particular songs or disk jockeys are found to be anchored in relatively small groups of friends, suggesting that personal relations play an important part in determining musical interests, fads, and fashions. For a different viewpoint on the effects of radio listening, see Alberta E. Siegel, "The Influence of Violence in the Mass Media Upon Children's Role Expectations." *Child. Develpm.*, 1958, 29, 35–56. See also the study of crime and violence on television in R. C. Hendrickson, *op. cit.*, pp. 228–254.

[27] An early report is that of T. E. Coffin, "Television's Effects on Leisure Time Activities," *J. Appl. Psychol.*, 1948, 32, 511–514. See also H. Evry, "TV Murder Causes Bad Dreams," *Film World*, 1952, 8, 247. This is a study of six-year-olds which indicated the negative effects of televiewing, and the results are comparable to the negative emotional effects produced by movies.

[28] S. M. Stoke and W. F. Clive, "The Avocations of 100 College Freshmen," *J. Appl. Psychol.*, 1929, 13, 257–263.

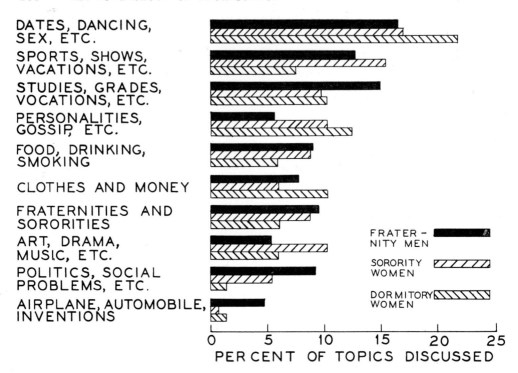

Fig. 22.   Relative importance of conversational interests as revealed by the type of topics discussed by fraternity men, sorority women, and dormitory women. Studies, grades, vocations, art, music, drama, politics, and social problems, etc., together constitute less than one fourth of the total topics discussed. Based on a regrouping of data of S. M. Stoke, and E. D. West, "Sex Differences in Conversational Interests," **J. Soc. Psychol.**, 1931, **2**, 120–126.

has been found that dates, dancing, and sex ranked first in conversational interest, followed by sports, shows, and vocations. Studies, grades, vocations, art, music, drama, politics, and social problems together constituted less than one fourth of the topics discussed by one experimental group. Men tend to discuss things and sports, whereas women incline more toward a discussion of personalities, social conventions, and cultural topics. These findings are based on studies of selected populations and cannot lead to any broad generalizations (see Fig. 22).

However, studies of adolescent conversational interests yield results similar to those obtained with college populations. In his study of 2000 adolescent boys, Fleege found that sports and girls far outranked other topics in interest at all levels of development. Hobbies, money, and future vocation claimed little attention. This investigator points out, too,

Fordham University

Youth likes to converse.

that apart from the common interest in the opposite sex, boys' and girls' conversational interests are quite divergent.[29] What the teen-ager talks about is probably of lesser interest than the distinctive and esoteric manner in which he says it. Jones, in 1946, made a functional analysis of the colloquial speech of 200 adolescents, age 13 to 17, and found a number of interesting characteristics. Adolescent language is typically colorful, highly charged, ostentatiously careless, and centered largely in personal and interpersonal relationships. Besides being used for giving or receiving information, language is also used to release tension, to bolster the ego, to channel aggression, and to establish social contacts.[30] Conversation is liberally sprinkled with esoteric terms that often leave the adult completely bewildered.

Following is a list of such terms sometimes used by American teen-agers:

Mushroom people — People who come out at night to live it up
Buzzed by germsville — Put into the hospital
A Washington — A dollar bill
Antsville — A place full of people
Like her heels were on fire — In a hurry
It's real nervous — It's good
Lid of your cave — Door of your office
Pile up the Z's — Sleep, snore
You're getting the beat — You're beginning to understand
The long and airy — An airplane ride

---

[29] U. H. Fleege, *Self-Revelation of the Adolescent Boy* (Milwaukee: Bruce, 1945), pp. 233–236.

[30] M. C. Jones, "A Functional Analysis of Colloquial Speech Among Adolescents," *Amer. Psychol.*, 1946, 1, 252–253.

As the adolescent moves closer to adulthood, references to academic and vocational interests and world affairs increase, while interest in social events, clothes, and social affairs proportionately decreases. In one study on sex differences and colloquial speech, it was found that there are many similarities between boys and girls, but in general boys were more colorful in their speech and they used language more often for aggressive purposes than did the girls.[31]

Conversational activities can have important effects on development. Attitudes are often formed or altered through discussion, and a great deal of information, whether good or bad, right or wrong, is exchanged in this manner. When youngsters discuss their ambitions, ideals, pet beliefs, sex experiences, relationships to parents, or the present state of world affairs, they are often forced to a reconsideration of their views that may lead to important changes in their attitudes. Social needs like acceptance, participation, and belonging can be partly gratified through conversational activities, and social relationship can be affected for good or ill. Conversation is a natural social function which may contribute importantly to social development.

Group Interests and Activities.   Several of the interests of youths already described in this chapter are clearly social in nature, including organized play, dancing, and conversation. But these interests are primarily recreational, and only secondarily social. There are other interests and activities that are predominantly social and rooted in needs like conformity, recognition, approval, and participation, needs which themselves are socially oriented. These needs, working in conjunction with development and experience, lead to the formation of social groups — clubs, cliques, fraternities, sororities, and other organizations. The function of such groups is in part to bring people together, and they thus

---

[31] M. C. Jones, "Differences in Adolescent Sex Roles as Revealed by Colloquial Speech," *Amer. Psychol.,* 1947, 2, 407–408.

Group activities are interesting to adolescents.

St Gabriel's High School, New Rochelle, N. Y.

play a leading role in the process of socialization.[32]

The available evidence, however, does not indicate any widespread incilination among youth toward such organizations, whatever the reason may be. Of 13,453 persons interviewed in the survey of the American Youth Commission, 74.5 per cent belonged to no club at all, participation being related in a small way to such factors as sex, race, age, and locality. In this study it was brought out that youngsters in school are more likely to belong to some organization than are those out of school; and also that schooling as an experience cultivates an enthusiasm for social activity that is carried over into the youth's social life after he leaves school.[33] In a survey of students at the University of Minnesota, it was found that most entering students belonged to two or three clubs, chiefly of a social nature.[34] Just what the reason is for the small participation in social organizations of out-of-school groups is not clear, but it is undoubtedly related to opportunities for, and experience in, organizational membership. Moreover, such groupings are not, like the family and society, natural social units, and it may well be that many persons gratify their social needs and inclinations in less artificial situations like play and conversation. Social organizations always impose certain restraints and limitations that are uncongenial to many freedom-loving youth, and for this reason club activities cannot be regarded as wholly recreational.

Nevertheless, from the standpoint of social development, the *effects* of such activities can be very important. By actively participating in social groups, individuals can acquire many of the fundamental concepts and techniques of successful social living. In some of these organizations, in and out of school, they learn such matters as how to vote, how laws are formulated and passed, and parliamentary procedures, all of which amounts to practical training in effective citizenship. Such groups provide experiences in the important business of working together toward common goals. They give members a chance to express various interests and to exercise capacities of a linguistic, scientific, artistic, or religious nature. They may therefore contribute to the development of vocational and avocational interests. And, above all, they often serve to promote healthy social relationships between members of the two sexes. Finally, but not the least important, organizational activities often provide an effective means for the worthwhile use of leisure time, which in turn may serve as an outlet for strong emotional drives and basic needs.

Drinking and Driving. Among the activities that show up prominently for the first time during the adolescent period are the drinking of alcoholic beverages and automobile driving. These activities are part of the social behavior of teenagers, and are often rooted in the same basic motivations. Both drinking and driving are related to the cravings for experience, the drive for masculinity, status, acceptance, and sex. As Bloch and Niederhoffer point out, the automobile

[32] See H. H. Moore, "The Cultivation of Social Interests Among Older High School Students," *Soc. Stud.*, 1936, 27, 28–36; H. R. Phelps and J. E. Horrocks, "Factors Influencing Informal Groups of Adolescents," *Child Develpm.*, 1958, 29, 69–87; E. D. Partridge, *Social Psychology of Adolescence* (New York: Prentice-Hall, 1939), Chaps. 5 and 7.

[33] H. M. Bell, *Youth Tell Their Story* (Washington, D. C.: Amer. Council on Educ., 1938), pp. 168, 169.

[34] R. E. Eckert, *Outcomes of General Education* (Minneapolis: University of Minnesota Press, 1943), p. 60.

The effects of participation in school-related organizations can play an important part in the social development of the adolescent.

St. Gabriel's High School, New Rochelle, N. Y.

symbolizes manhood — *sexually* by providing increased opportunity for sex experience; *age-wise*, since one must be 18 to drive legally in most states; by the *possession of material wealth*; by *development of interpersonal relations*; and by *the enhancement of status*.[35] "Our material culture has furnished a perfect solution to an otherwise inescapable dilemma. Symbolically, the automobile fulfills the demands of adolescent yearning. It represents victory in the feeling of mastery both psychological and material, which it imparts."[36]

Much the same could be said about adolescent drinking, and numerous studies of drinking among high-school and college students show conclusively that drinking increases throughout the adolescent period. McCarthy and Douglass, for example, report that occasional users increase from 26 to 40.3 per cent during the high school years, and that frequent

users increase from 2.8 to 5.1 per cent during the same period.[37] Straus and Bacon, in their study of drinking in college, reported that the incidence of drinking increases with each college year from 69 to 87 per cent among boys. Only 38 per cent of the males had never been drunk as against 82 per cent of the girls. Both boys and girls agreed that drinking leads to sexual misbehavior.[38] Considering the potential destructiveness of both drinking and driving, including both destruction of self and of others, it is obvious that these activities must be carefully controlled. The use of alcohol and the use of the family car have led to the moral debilitation and to the death and maiming of countless youth, and thus must be carefully controlled by parents and by society.

[35] H. Bloch and A. Niederhoffer, *The Gang: a Study in Adolescent Behavior* (New York: Philosophical Library, 1958), p. 183.

[36] *Ibid.*, p. 185. See also I. H. Weiland, "The Significance of Hot Rods and Automobile Driving to Adolescent Males," *Psychiat. Quart. Suppl.*, 1957, 31, 261–275.

[37] R. G. McCarthy and E. M. Douglass, "High School Driving Studies," in R. G. McCarthy (ed.), *Drinking and Intoxication: Selected Readings in Social Attitudes and Controls* (Glencoe, Ill.: Free Press, 1959).

[38] R. Straus and S. D. Bacon, *Drinking in College* (New Haven: Yale University Press, 1953). See also Maxine Davis, *Sex and the Adolescent* (New York: Dial Press, 1958), Chap. 20; and R. C. Hendrickson, *Youth in Danger* (New York: Harcourt, Brace, 1956), pp. 28–46.

Vocational Interests of Youth. The interests and activities of youth thus far considered are all *avocational* in character, and directed mainly toward leisure-time activities. Perhaps they are for that reason the most important. But in later adolescence vocational interests and goals are likely to develop, and this development is necessary for complete adjustment.[39] We have already noted the striking parallelism between pubescence and changes in vocational attitudes, illustrated in the study by Lehman and Witty. These investigators, testing the permanency of interests between the ages of 8 and 18, found that the percentage of boys expecting to enter one of forty professions increased from 25 to 47 per cent, and the girls expecting to become stenographers or typists from 3 to 30 per cent. This increase of interest and expectancy closely parallels the decline of childhood vocational aspirations.[40]

Vocational interests of adolescents are strongly influenced by factors like sex, occupation of father, and intelligence. In one study, nearly 50 per cent of girls indicated a preference for teaching, whereas only 5 per cent of the boys showed such a preference. In this study of gifted children there was an overwhelming preference for the professions, indicating the influence of intelligence level.[41] The important fact here is that such differences do exist and must be taken into account in any program of vocational guidance.

Other studies indicate just as clearly that type of environment, cultural changes, and father's occupation may influence vocational aim or choice.[42] But more important is the fact that older adolescents have definite vocational interests, and that in many instances they have formed fairly clear-cut attitudes toward the world of work. Their preferences may be based upon inadequate knowledge and experience, on parental influence, or on other questionable factors, and therefore show considerable instability. But permanency of vocational interests increases to some degree in later adolescence, and is partly correlated with intelligence, especially in boys. Studies of interest stability indicate that early preferences at the high-school level are greatly modified through experience and education, whereas at the college level stability of interests is greater. Regardless of how temporary interests are, they nevertheless influence the choice of curricula at both the high-school and college levels, a fact of importance to both educational and vocational guidance. Changes in vocational choice may have little significance in itself; much more important is the fact that the life style of the individual must often be altered to conform to the new choice. To avoid such costly mistakes, the high-school or college counselor should avail himself of the knowledge and techniques that can be used for successful vocational counseling. Regarded in this light, vocational guidance includes a great deal more than

---

[39] In this connection see A. B. Hollingshead, *Elmtown's Youth* (New York: Wiley, 1949), pp. 267–287; Ruth Strang, *The Adolescent Views Himself* (New York: McGraw-Hill, 1957), Chap. 11.

[40] H. C. Lehman and P. A. Witty, "One More Study of Permanence of Interests," *J. Educ. Psychol.*, 1931, 22, 481–492.

[41] J. R. Gerberich, "The Gifted Pupils of the Iowa High School Survey," *J. Appl. Psychol.*, 1930, 14, 566–576. See also Ruth Strang, *op. cit.*, pp. 407–410.

[42] See Elizabeth B. Hurlock and C. Jansing, "The Vocational Attitudes of Boys and Girls of High School Age," *J. Genet. Psychol.*, 1934, 44, 175–191; J. W. M. Rothney, *Guidance Practices and Results* (New York: Harper, 1958), Chap. 1.

Vocational choice is an important decision for adolescents.

direction in the choice of a vocation, since such a choice will be bound up with many other phases of adjustment.

WHAT INTERESTS MEAN TO ADOLESCENT GROWTH

Interests and Personal Growth. The importance of interests to adolescent development and adjustment requires little emphasis. If we take as our starting point the relationship between interests and intellectual development, we can readily understand the importance of activities like reading, debating, or listening to worthwhile forums on the radio. Personal and social development, on the other hand, is directly related to recreational interests and social activities.[43] As an example of the influence of recreation on teen-age behavior, we may cite the results of a study of a police district where delinquency was unusually high, made by the Baltimore Criminal Justice Commission. Here it was found that of 592 boys who were arrested, only 5 per cent had any supervised recreational activities, while 82 per cent were forced to resort to street play and corner gangs.[44] Physical well-being, attitudes, opinions, skills, personal integration, adjustment, and character are all traceable in some measure to recreational activities.

Moreover, the achievement of independence and the development of an individual life style derive in part from interests. The right use of leisure time, the interest in studies, the development of a vocational goal, and so on, have reper-

cussions in the moral and social lives of young people. This influence is often immediate and direct. There is also the indirect influence on the moral and religious development of youth of such interests and activities as movies, reading, and conversation. From the standpoint of form, an activity like conversation is a social experience; but from the standpoint of content, it may be much more of a moral (or immoral) experience. So, too, with other activities.

Interests also exert certain general effects that influence different aspects of development. First of all, they always lead to some form of activity, and thus to experiences of various kinds. Without interests, a knowledge of the activities to which they are related may never develop. A wider range of interests tends to insure broader experience, which is reflected in the corresponding development of the whole personality. Second, a wealth of interests facilitates substitution whenever there occurs frustration along one line of endeavor. This substitution is particularly important for vocational adjustment, but it has many implications for recreational and social adjustment as well. Finally, because of their dynamic qualities, interests are important for efficiency of effort, since the greater the interest the greater will be the application to whatever work or activity is necessary. As we have said before, interests are sustaining motives, and without them effort may be lacking or inefficient.

Developing Interests in Youth. Because of their important effects on behavior and development, it is necessary for parents and teachers to do everything possible to develop the right interests in youth. This fact is clearly exemplified in the answer to the question "Do you ever find your leisure time wearisome?" put to

---

[43] H. S. Tuttle, *Dynamic Psychology and Conduct* (New York: Harper, 1948), Chap. VIII.

[44] H. M. Bell, *Youth Tell Their Story* (Washington, D. C.: Amer. Council on Education, 1938), p. 160.

2000 adolescent boys. Fifty-one per cent of these boys replied in the affirmative, and more than a fourth stated that they regularly find their free time a problem on their hands.[45] To achieve the aim of interest development, several principles should be followed: (1) contact with a wide range of desirable activities should be made possible, since it is mainly through actual experience in an activity that interest develops; (2) desirable activities should lead to personal satisfaction; (3) activities should be ordered to the capacities of the individual so as to exclude discouragement and loss of interest; (4) needs, background, and traits of the person should be considered in the development of interests; and (5) activities should whenever necessary be related to future goals, so that the youngster may perceive their purpose and worth. These principles, of course, flow directly from our analysis of the nature, sources, and development of interests in the preceding paragraphs.

[45] U. H. Fleege, op. cit., p. 201.

SELECTED READINGS

Hollingshead, A. B., Elmtown's Youth (New York: Wiley, 1949), Chaps. 12, 15.

Kuhlen, R. G., and Thompson, D. G. (eds.), Psychological Studies of Human Development (New York: Appleton-Century Crofts, 1952), Chap. XIII.

Mohr, G. A., and Despres, Marian A., The Stormy Decade: Adolescence (New York: Random House, 1958), Chap. IX.

Norvell, G. W., The Reading Interests of Young People (Boston: Heath, 1950).

Partridge, E. D., Social Psychology of Adolescence (New York: Prentice-Hall, 1939), Chap. X.

Strong, E. K., Change of Interests With Age (Stanford, Calif.: Stanford University Press, 1931).

——— Vocational Interests 18 Years After College (Minneapolis: University of Minnesota Press, 1955).

Super, D. E., Psychology of Careers: an Introduction to Vocational Development (New York: Harper, 1957).

Zachry, Caroline B., Emotion and Conduct in Adolescence (New York: Appleton-Century-Crofts, 1940), Chap. 12.

Zubeck, J. P., and Solberg, Patricia A., Human Development (New York: McGraw-Hill, 1954), Chap. 13.

CHAPTER XIII

ADOLESCENT ATTITUDES

> *If Bill likes to study chemistry or to collect butterflies, we say he has an interest in such things. But if he likes his religion, his country, or the Republican party, we say he has an attitude toward them. Interests and attitudes are very similar — they are dynamic, often permanent, and always important. We have studied interests; let us now study attitudes.*

WHAT ATTITUDES ARE

Attitudes and Interests. Attitudes are complex psychic phenomena variously related to interests, traits, opinions, beliefs, and prejudices. Their close relationship to interests is recognized by Allport who lists interest along with attitude as one of the psychological concepts equivalent to, subordinate to, or partially overlapping the concept of trait.[1] Both interest and attitude are mental sets or determining tendencies, and both are dynamic in character; yet they are not identical. Thus we speak of an interest *in* some thing or event, but of an attitude *toward* it. Interest involves identification of self with some object or event; it is a readiness to respond in which there is some measure of self-projection. Attitude is also a readiness to respond, but it does not involve identification. This difference is the basic reason for the verbal distinction noted above between *having an in-*terest *in* and *adopting an attitude toward* some object. Allport identifies interest as "a special type of enduring attitude which refers, as a rule, to a *class* of objects rather than to a single object. They are dynamic attitudes, rich in ideational content, and involve a recognition and understanding of the objects which have satisfying properties. Subjective values are essentially the same as interests, except that they are more properly spoken of when the individual is mature and has reflected upon and organized his interests within a comprehensive system of thought and feeling."[2] This interpretation has a great deal in its favor, but tends to obscure the distinction between interest and attitude.

The distinction becomes clearer when we note that attitude always involves a judgment, either implicit or explicit, whereas interest involves judgment only incidentally. An attitude may in fact be regarded as a judgment or opinion that

---

[1] G. W. Allport, *Personality: a Psychological Interpretation* (New York: Holt, 1937).

[2] G. W. Allport, "Attitudes," in C. Murchison (ed.), *A Handbook of Social Psychology* (Worcester, Mass.: Clark University Press, 1935), pp. 808–809.

is habitually excitable. However, unlike ordinary judgments, it is not usually the result of intellectual deliberation or of evidence; it results rather from the *introception* of the judgments and opinions of others. Thus, as we shall see, children adopt the attitudes of parents toward the Church, communism, Negroes, and so on, with little regard for evidence or validity. These attitudes are reinforced by feelings and emotions in many instances, whereas judgment of itself is independent of such factors.

Attitudes and Personality Traits. It would be a mistake, however, to overemphasize the relationship between judgment and attitude. Attitude, as distinct from simple judgment, is of its nature dynamic, and inclines the individual toward forming judgments or toward some mode of behavior. This distinction is supported by the close relationship between attitudes and traits, which are clearly different from judgments and opinions. Allport defines this relationship very well:

> A trait is a form of readiness for response; so too is an attitude. A trait is individualized, distinctive of its possessor; so too may be an attitude. A trait guides the course of behavior, and may often become dynamic and compulsive as well; so may the attitude. . . . Are trait and attitude, therefore, equivalent concepts?[3]

Admitting a great similarity, Allport goes on to point out three distinctions:

> In the first place an attitude has a well-defined object of reference, either material or conceptual; whereas traits have no such definite reference to objects. [Secondly], attitudes may be specific as well as general; whereas a trait may be only general. [Thirdly], the term

attitude usually signifies the acceptance or rejection of the object or concept of value to which it is related. . . . Traits as a rule have no such clear-cut direction. They are often merely stylistic, and their significance often adverbial rather than prepositional.[4]

In an earlier article Allport, after reviewing 16 definitions of attitude says, "In one way or another each regards the essential feature of attitude as *a preparation or readiness for response.* The attitude is incipient and preparatory rather than overt and consummatory. It is not behavior, but the precondition of behavior."[5]

How Attitudes Function. Not only are attitudes dynamic in character, but they have the added property of rendering many experiences and responses *equivalent.* Thus, to use Allport's example, to the superpatriot a red flag, a volume by Marx, or a teacher's union are all equivalent, as are the responses that flow from his superpatriotic attitude. The constant among all of these stimuli and responses is the attitude which renders them equivalent. This feature is of considerable importance in understanding how attitudes function in everyday situations.

Attitudes may be formed with respect to almost any object or value, and therefore there are many different kinds. There are attitudes toward the Church, communism, birth control, war, divorce, religion, science, education, socialized medicine, Negroes, drinking, and so on. For the sake of discussion we may group them into moral and religious, social,

---

[3] G. W. Allport, *Personality: a Psychological Interpretation* (New York: Holt, 1937), p. 293.

[4] G. W. Allport, *ibid.*, p. 294.

[5] G. W. Allport, "Attitudes," in C. Murchison (ed.), *A Handbook of Social Psychology* (Worcester, Mass.: Clark University Press, 1935), p. 805. See also D. D. Droba, "The Nature of Attitudes," *J. Soc. Psychol.*, 1933, 4, 444–463; R. Bain, "Theory and Measurement of Attitude and Opinion," *Psych. Bull.*, 1930, 27, 357–379.

Attitudes are derived from
varied experiences.

Fordham University

vocational, and personal attitudes, the last group including those which have the self for their object. We shall not have an opportunity to discuss all these attitudes; but we shall deal generally with their origin and development, and particularly with the question of how attitudes can be successfully developed in young people.

WHERE ATTITUDES COME FROM

Attitudes Have Many Sources. Where attitudes originate, and how they finally assume the form of a dynamic motivational tendency, are problems of basic importance to the psychology of adolescence. In general, there are six primary sources of attitudes: (1) experience and conduct; (2) family influences; (3) cultural milieu, including religion; (4) psychological factors such as intelligence, motives, and feelings; (5) personality factors; and (6) instruction and prop-

aganda, including suggestion.[6] The influence of these several factors on the formation of attitudes will be conditioned by level of intellectual development, the environment in which the adolescent develops, and mechanisms like identification and introception. These latter factors are too often overlooked in attempting to explain the development of attitudes in young people. But unless we take such influences into account there is no way in which we can explain the discrepancies in attitude formation as we move from individual to individual or from group to group.

Experience Helps to Form Attitudes. Personal experience is one of the primary determinants of attitude formation. If we go back in our own experience we

---

[6] See Caroline B. Zachry, *Emotion and Conduct in Adolescence* (New York: Appleton-Century-Crofts, 1940), Chap. 8; R. L. Karen, "Some Variables Affecting Sex Attitudes, Behavior, and Inconsistency," *Marr. Fam. Liv.*, 1959, 21, 235–239. B. Lasker, *Race Attitudes in Children* (New York: Holt, 1929).

will find many instances which have contributed to the development of our attitudes toward racial groups, our religion, the part of the country from which we come, politics, God, and communism. We can well imagine how the attitudes of many Hungarians toward communism were affected by their experiences with their Russian "protectors." The attitude of the average American toward democracy is in large part an outgrowth of his experiences with it. Even a single experience may have a lasting effect, as when one witnesses motion pictures of the Nazi atrocities. If such experiences are favorable or pleasant, the attitude formed is positive and favorable; if the experiences are unpleasant, then antipathy results.[7]

The effect of experience will always be in proportion to the influence of surrounding factors. Experience may, for example, yield to the pressure of effective propaganda, and will be conditioned by education, social facilitation, and cultural milieu. Thus, given the cultural heritage of the average Southerner, it is extremely unlikely that he will develop an attitude of social equality toward the Negro. In one study it was found that only 5.5 per cent of 163 students in psychology and sociology in a Southern university were willing to accept the statement, "Negroes should be accepted now to complete social equality with white people."[8]

These results are confirmed by many similar investigations. For example, in a study of Polish boys and girls designed to find out why children developed hatred, the youngsters mentioned such experiences as explosions, cries of the wounded and dying, and the plundering tactics of the German soldiers as being the principal sources of their hatred of the enemy. Here we have a striking instance of the influence of experience on the formation of attitudes. In the survey of the American Youth Commission, it was found that the youths interviewed overwhelmingly favored government regulation of wages and labor unions as a means of raising wages, and that the majority favored government relief. Needless to say, this study was made during the depression years of the thirties. As the author remarks, "The attitudes of young people, like the attitudes of most adults, are far more likely to be based on their personal experience than upon any abstract social philosophy."[9] Other studies have shown how *lack of experience* with peoples can heighten race prejudice, suggesting that experience and tolerance often go hand in hand.

Behavior Shapes Attitudes. In a similar vein, the teen-ager who practices his religion faithfully, or goes out on dates, or participates in extracurricular activities, will develop attitudes in line with these activities. We are not likely to find an attitude favorable to the church in a person who has abandoned his religion. On the other hand, when activities are forced upon an individual — for example, requiring a boy or girl to go to Mass every morning — attitudes will also be affected but in a negative way. Young people must learn to regard such prac-

[7] See H. S. Lewin, "Changes of Attitudes Subsequent to Camp Experience," *Nerv. Child*, 1947, 6, 173–177; T. M. Newcomb, "College Experience and Attitude Development," in J. M. Seidman (ed.), *Adolescence: a Book of Readings* (New York: Dryden, 1953), pp. 397–405.

[8] K. C. Garrison and V. S. Burch, "A Study of Racial Attitudes of College Students," *J. Soc. Psychol.*, 1933, 4, 230–235. See also V. M. Sims and J. R. Patrick, "Attitude Toward the Negro of Northern and Southern College Students," *J. Soc. Psychol.*, 1936, 7, 192–204.

[9] See H. M. Bell, *op. cit.*, p. 214.

tices as valuable and desirable in themselves, so that the right attitudes may be formed through the medium of activity. Here is one reason why youth is so often antagonistic in its attitudes toward studying and school attendance. For those youngsters to whom school is interesting and profitable, right attitudes develop as a matter of course; whereas in youngsters who attend school only through force, negative attitudes just as surely develop.

Family Influences Determine Attitudes. The effects of experience and conduct will be limited in many instances by traditional family attitudes, father's employment, and the religious affiliations or practices of the family. Children's attitudes naturally reflect those of the parents and other family members. This outright adoption of family attitudes is the result of imitation, suggestion, instruction, and training, a process that is clearly exemplified in the formation of sex attitudes. Of particular importance here is the part played by *identification*. In most instances the extent to which parental attitudes influence the child varies in direct proportion to the degree to which the child identifies himself with one or another of the parents. Obviously, if the child rejects or is rejected by the parent, the likelihood of his assuming the preferences or aversions of the parent is remote. This relationship explains in part the diversification of attitude among members of the same family. Failure to identify with one of the parents may be replaced by *negative identification*, in which case the child develops attitudes and behavior patterns exactly contrary to those of the rejected parent.[10]

---

[10] On the influence of family and family relationships in the formation of attitudes, see R. E. Lane, "Fathers and Sons: the Foundations of Political Belief," *Amer. Soc. Rev.*, 1959,

What parents do in the way of training and disciplining the child will help shape basic attitudes.[11] If parents instruct the child regarding the rights of other people, the equality of all races and nationalities, or the dignity of manual labor, it is unlikely that the child will develop negative attitudes toward these things. Similarly, if the child is trained from the earliest years in self-control, he may be expected to form attitudes in line with such training. Everything that is said or done within the framework of family living may serve as an example to the child in the development of his own attitudes. In one study of the attitudes of children toward the Chinese and Japanese, it was found that parents' frequent disparagement of Chinese seemed to lower the boys' attitudes toward this racial group.[12] Where attitudes are concerned, parental responsibility is very serious.

Religious Affiliation Influences Attitudes. If you were to ask the typical Catholic boy or girl what he thinks of the Catholic Church as an influence in his life, the infallibility of the Pope, eating meat on Friday, birth control, or divorce, you

24, 502–511; H. H. Remmers and Naomi Weltman, "Attitude Interrelationships of Youth, Their Parents, and Their Teachers," in J. M. Seidman (ed.), *op. cit.*, pp. 319–327; W. L. Slocum and Carol L. Stone, "A Method for Measuring Family Images Held by Teenagers," *Marr. Fam. Liv.*, 1959, 21, 245–250; H. Meltzer, "Hostility and Tolerance in Children's Nationality and Race Attitudes," *Amer. J. Orthopsychiat.*, 1941, 11, 662–676; B. Lasker, *Race Attitudes in Children* (New York: Holt, 1929), pp. 93–114.

[11] See D. B. Harris, H. G. Gough, and W. E. Martin, "Children's Ethnic Attitudes: II. Relationship to Parental Beliefs Concerning Child Training," *Child Develpm.*, 1950, 21, 170–181.

[12] Y. I. Kashiwa and M. E. Smith, "A Study of the Attitudes of Children of Japanese Descent Toward the Chinese and Japanese," *J. Soc. Psychol.*, 1943, 18, 149–153.

would get a quite different answer from what you would get from the majority of Protestants or Jews. In other words, attitudes on certain basic life issues are determined in large measure by religious affiliation; these attitudes have been studied empirically by many investigators.[13]

Carlson, for example, studying the attitudes of 215 college seniors toward prohibition, God, pacifism, communism, and birth control, found considerable variations among different religious groups. According to Carlson, "Jewish students are most opposed to prohibition, are most sympathetic to pacifism, communism, and birth control, and believe least in the reality of God. Catholic students believe most strongly in the reality of God, and are least sympathetic to pacifism, communism, and birth control. . . . Protestant students are least opposed to prohibition, but hold a position intermediate to Jewish and Catholic students in their attitude toward God, pacifism, communism, and birth control."[14] These differences "indicate that the religious affiliation of a student is an important factor in the determination of his or her attitude on these social questions. The differences are more marked than are the differences found in regard to sex or school training. We might conclude, then, that an undergraduate's present religious affiliation, or his early religious training, may be a more important factor than the student's sex or later school training in determining his or her atti-

tude on these social questions."[15] This study also brought out, incidentally, that more liberal attitudes are favored by more intelligent students, and that attitudes are interrelated, the tendency toward radicalism or conservatism spreading from one attitude to another.

In an effort to test these conclusions, Telford investigated the attitudes of students at another university toward one social institution, the church. He found in general that Catholic students are more favorable to the church than are Protestants or Jews, that active church membership creates favorable attitudes toward the church, that sameness of church affiliation among members of the family helps create favorable attitudes, and that the mother plays a more dominant role than the father in determining religious affiliations.[16] Thus both of these studies bring out the importance of family attitudes and practices in the formation of religious attitudes in adolescence.

Church membership is also important in determining attitudes of youth toward other basic issues. In one study it was found that religious affiliation affects youths' attitude toward war. "The greatest differences show up between the responses of youth from Catholic and Jewish homes. The largest and the smallest proportions of youth who stated they would immediately volunteer came, respectively, from Catholic and Jewish homes. Of even greater significance, perhaps, is the fact that more than twice as large a proportion of Jewish youth stated they would refuse to go (28.9 per cent of the Jewish, as against 14.3 per cent of the Catholic youth)."[17] To interpret

---

[13] In this connection see A. W. Siegman, "Authoritarian Attitudes in Children: I. The Effect of Age, IQ, Anxiety and Parental Religious Attitudes," *J. Clin. Psychol.*, 1957, 13, 338–340. See also the earlier study by C. W. Telford, "An Experimental Study of Some Factors Influencing the Social Attitudes of College Students," *J. Soc. Psychol.*, 1934, 5, 421–428.

[14] H. B. Carlson, "Attitudes of Undergraduate Students," *J. Soc. Psychol.*, 1934, 5, 202–213.

[15] H. B. Carlson, *ibid.*, 207.

[16] C. W. Telford, *op. cit.*

[17] H. M. Bell, *Youth Tell Their Story* (Washington, D. C.: Amer. Council on Education, 1938), p. 244.

these results correctly, one must take into account the attitude toward country and war inherent in any particular religion. For example, the Catholic Church takes the position that its members have a serious obligation to serve one's country in time of war, and that patriotism is a noble sentiment, so that the attitudes of Catholic youth toward war are more likely to stem from religious training or affiliation than from other factors.

One's Environment Affects Attitudes. Attitudes vary considerably with environmental factors like locality and group membership.[18] In one study of individual opinion in relation to group opinion, it was found that the latter strongly inhibits disagreement, indicating the influence of social facilitation. The tendency to adopt the opinions and attitudes of the "in group" seems to be a universal and fairly dynamic tendency, although this inclination can be strongly affected by suggestibility and prestige. Urban populations seem to differ considerably from rural populations in certain basic attitudes. In the Maryland study, 53.8 per cent of farm youths felt that wages were too low, whereas 72.4 per cent of city youths held this opinion. In attitudes toward drinking, farm and city youngsters agreed fairly well, but there was a notable difference between Catholic and Protestant youths.[19] The

social and political attitudes of college students in different states throughout the country seem to vary considerably, just as vocational preferences vary with different economic and social environments. Attitudes, therefore, are sensitive to many different influences, and vary a great deal from one situation to another. That is why Protestants cannot understand Catholics, Democrats cannot fathom the minds of Republicans, and Southerners have difficulty in accepting the Supreme Court decision on desegregation.[20]

Attitudes in Relation to Race, Sex, and Age. One might expect the attitudes of teen-agers to differ considerably from those of adults on such issues as dating, or the legal age for drinking; that women would look on working mothers differently than would the majority of men; or that Negroes would regard the principle of "separate but equal education" in a different way than would the typical southern white.[21] However, while these suppositions regarding the influence of age, sex, and race are basically correct, a great deal depends upon the object of reference to which the attitude is related. Regarding the question of wage levels, both males and females, and Negroes and whites, are found to be of the same opinion. Similar results have been obtained on questions of government control of

---

[18] See, for example, R. Centers, "Children of the New Deal: Social Stratification and Adolescent Attitudes," *Int. J. Opin. Attitude Res.*, 1950, 4, 315–335; Rose Zeligs, "Children's Concepts and Stereotypes of Polish, Irish, Finn, Hungarian, Bulgarian, Dane, Czecho-Slovakian, Hindu, and Filipino," *J. Genet. Psychol.*, 1950, 77, 73–83; "Children's Concepts and Stereotypes of American, Greek, English, German and Japanese," *J. Educ. Sociol.*, 1955, 28, 360–368; D. V. McGranahan, "A Comparison of Social Attitudes Among American and German Youth," *J. Abnorm. Soc. Psychol.*, 1946, 41, 245–257.

[19] H. M. Bell, *op. cit.*, pp. 12, 238.

[20] See R. G. Kuhlen, "The Interest and Attitudes of Japanese, Chinese, and White Adolescents: a Study of Culture and Personality," *J. Soc. Psychol.*, 1945, 21, 121–133.

[21] E. A. Schuler, "Attitudes Toward Racial Segregation in Baton Rouge, La.," *J. Soc. Psychol.*, 1943, 18, 33–53. See also B. Bettleheim and M. Janowitz, "Ethnic Tolerance: a Function of Social and Personal Control," in J. M. Seidman (ed.), *op. cit.*, pp. 345–359; and Marian Radke-Yarrell and Jean S. Miller, "Children's Concepts and Attitudes About Minority and Majority American Groups," in J. M. Seidman (ed.), *op. cit.*, pp. 327–345.

wages and hours, and the problem of government relief. However, when investigation turns to questions of child labor, employment of married women, drinking, and war, significant sex and racial differences appear. On the whole, more women are opposed to drinking than are men, and this is true of youth as well as adults. Also, girls revolt against accepted religious beliefs less frequently, less profoundly, and at a later age than do boys. Women also tend to be governed by parental and public opinion in the formation of attitudes to a much greater extent than are men.[22] These differences do not hold in all cases, but there is sufficient evidence to show that race, sex, and age exert considerable influence on the formation of attitudes.

Attitudes Are Influenced by Instruction, Propaganda, and Suggestion. If all these other things determine attitude formation in youth, how much room is there for the influence of education? Educational theorists never tire of reminding us of the tremendous importance of the educational process in shaping the beliefs, attitudes, and conduct of youth, but it is not at all certain that such is actually the case.[23] Numerous studies have been made in an effort to determine the influence of education on attitudes, but with highly variable results. One student of the problem found that a semester course in criminology created more humane attitudes toward the treatment of criminals among his students, and another found that freshmen were more conservative than other college students, and that many students, especially the men, were affected in their religious views by exposure to college education.[24] A significant relationship has also been found between science instruction and decline in superstition.

Yet, formal education does not always produce the desired results. Not all Catholics educated in Catholic schools are favorable to the Church's stand on birth control and divorce; nor are all students educated in public schools or the large nonsectarian universities favorable to the democratic form of government; nor are all students educated in Southern schools favorable to the principle of equality as defined in the Bill of Rights. Investigating the effects of a course in American race problems on the race prejudices of 450 undergraduate students of the University of Pennsylvania, Young concluded that a logical presentation of facts and theories is not a very effective means of changing certain attitudes. Jones also, after studying the opinions of a large group of college students, concludes that the real opinions of these students are little affected by their college training, although he did find that seniors tended to be far more liberal than the freshmen in his study, which suggests that education did exert some influence on attitudes. Similar results are reported by

[22] See R. R. Willoughby, "A Sampling of Student Opinion," *J. Soc. Psychol.*, 1930, *1*, 164–169.

[23] The influence of education on the formation of attitudes has been defined in many sources. See, for example, B. Lasker, *Race Attitudes in Children* (New York: Holt, 1929); H. Cantril, *Gauging Public Opinion* (Princeton: Princeton University Press, 1944); F. L. Ayer and B. R. Corman, "Laboratory Practices Develop Citizenship Concepts of High-school Students," in J. M. Seidman (ed.), *op. cit.*, pp. 360–368; and Helen Peak and H. W. Morrison, "The Acceptance of Information Into Attitude Structure," *J. Abnorm. Soc. Psychol.*, 1958, 57, 127–135.

[24] C. W. Telford, "An Experimental Study of Some Factors Influencing the Social Attitudes of College Students," *J. Soc. Psychol.*, 1934, 5, 421–428, and R. R. Willoughby, "A Sampling of Student Opinion," *J. Soc. Psychol.*, 1930, *1*, 164–169.

Garrison who found that on some topics college seniors were more liberal than freshmen.[25]

These contradictory results suggest that the effect of formal education on attitudes varies in direct proportion to the object of reference, the makeup and backgrounds of the students, and the methods used in teaching. When dealing with deep-seated and long-standing prejudices, attitudes will be little affected by presentation of objective data, a fact which the writer can attest from his own experience in teaching differential psychology to college students.[26] Men do not readily accept the equality of women any more than whites accept the equality of Negroes; nor do dyed-in-the-wool communists concede the principles of democracy; nor do puritanical people easily accept the principles of sex education. Attitudes toward more objective issues like the treatment of criminals, internationalism, and prohibition may be more easily influenced by instruction if they have not become emotionalized and do not involve personal anxieties or antipathies. To influence emotionalized attitudes *one must appeal to emotion,* and here the techniques of suggestion and propaganda yield more affective results.

Referring to the influence of suggestion on the formation of children's attitudes and beliefs, Allport says, "By the time he comes of more critical age, deciding henceforth to guide his own destiny, he is already a creature of innumerable conventional forms of behavior and outlooks, acquired by suggestion, from which he can never completely escape."[27] Suggestion, of course, lies at the basis of most propaganda; and the more that formal education relies on suggestion, and appeals to emotions and needs, the more closely it resembles propaganda. Of interest in this connection is a study by Wegrocki who sampled the attitudes of a number of Catholic boys and girls from a Polish parochial school toward 56 words indicative of nationalities, races, persons, etc.[28] An attitude test was administered twice to the group, the first time without and the second time with propaganda material. Some items, such as Pope, priest, Catholic, American, Washington, and Al Smith, remained unquestioned despite the propaganda. The author concludes that it is far more difficult to change the attitudes acquired from the primary group than those derived from the secondary group. The results indicated further that children's attitudes are definitely affected by reading propaganda material, that girls tend to react more strongly to this propaganda than do boys, and that the more intelligent pupils are less likely to be influenced by propaganda than are the less intelligent.

As Hartshorne remarks,

Where propaganda is used for selfish purposes, we decry it; but we depend upon it all the time to keep the wheels of civilization going. Gossip, pull, influence, tact, personality, will oratory,

[25] D. Young, "Some Effects of a Course in American Race Problems on the Race Prejudice of 450 Undergraduates at the University of Pennsylvania," *J. Abnorm. Soc. Psychol.,* 1927, 22, 235–242; E. S. Jones, "The Opinions of College Students," *J. Appl. Psychol.,* 1926, 10, 427–436; K. C. Garrison, "A Study of Attitudes of College Students," *J. Soc. Psychol.,* 1937, 8, 490–494.

[26] See the interesting results reported by J. Walters and R. H. Ojemann, "A Study of the Components of Adolescent Attitudes Concerning the Role of Women," *J. Soc. Psychol.,* 1952, 35, 101–110.

[27] G. W. Allport, *Personality, a Psychological Interpretation* (New York: Holt, 1937), p. 166.

[28] H. J. Wegrocki, "The Effect of Prestige Suggestibility on Emotional Attitudes," *J. Soc. Psychol.,* 1934, 5, 384–394.

rhetoric, salesmanship, executive ability, getting friends and using them, getting jobs and keeping them, managing children, managing parents, running schools, homes, factories, governments — it is all a matter of propaganda, of getting people to take the attitudes which have proved most profitable or convenient to those in power. *Truth* about people or events or causes or things does not count. It is what is said about them that molds our attitudes, and the truth is helpless against convincing misrepresentation.[29]

We might add that it is not only *what* is said, but *how* it is said that makes the great difference where the molding of attitudes is concerned.

Other studies have been directed toward testing the relationship between attitude formation and suggestion. Summarizing the results of such studies, we can say that suggestion is often effective in causing a shift in attitudes; that changes in attitude may persist for long periods of time; that changes in women's attitudes are often greater than those of men, and that men are more impressed by logical arguments than are women; and that suggestibility tends to decrease with age, indicating that instruction becomes increasingly more effective than propaganda. No such studies are conclusive, but they indicate that attitudes are susceptible to the influence of instruction and propaganda, and that these techniques, skillfully used, can be exploited to produce wholesome attitudes in youth.

Personal Factors Determine Attitudes. Granted that Mary and John and the millions of other teen-agers are influenced in their attitudes by all these external factors, are we then to conclude that they

themselves have nothing to do with attitude formation? Are they so much putty in the hands of the theorists, the propagandists, the opinion makers, or the hidden persuaders? What about the personalities involved in this process of attitude formation? What about the youngster's intelligence, his needs, traits, or self-determination? These questions are not easy to answer, especially in view of the contradictory results that have been obtained by empirical studies. However, many studies do show that basic attitudes of a social, moral, and religious kind vary to some extent with intellectual level, and that higher intelligence favors the development of more acceptable attitudes. This particular relationship will be conditioned a great deal by family background, religious affiliation, and the educational process to which one has been exposed.

It is even more difficult to determine objectively the relation between motivational factors and attitudes. Needs, desires, interests, and goals certainly condition the formation of attitudes, but to establish the fact objectively is another matter. We may agree with Hartshorne that:

Tasks that are forced, barren, or unsuccessful are associated with the attitudes toward such tasks that are stimulated by coercion and defeat or by the type of success which rewards only one's desire for peace or for gain . . . activities which engage the child's whole interest and are focused on some definite, desired goal are accompanied by the concomitant learnings of happiness, love of work, joy in companionship, and the like; and these in turn become attached to the general features of the environment.[30]

This statement corresponds with Bell's observation that "attitudes are usually

[29] H. Hartshorne, "How Can Ethical Attitudes Be Taught?" in *Developing Attitudes in Children* (Chicago: University of Chicago Press, 1933), pp. 6–7.

[30] *Ibid.*, p. 15.

conditioned by self-interest. Our opinions, like our behavior, usually reflect what we fundamentally desire." Analyzing the attitudes of the youth in his study with respect to questions of government regulation of child labor and of wages and hours, he concludes that "Young people are far more interested in bread and butter than in any finespun social philosophy. It may be bread and butter for themselves or their families, or it may be for their friends and neighbors, but it is still bread and butter."[31]

From this conclusion we can certainly infer that the need for security has a direct and an important bearing on the formation of adolescent attitudes. Similarly, the dynamic needs for status, affection, independence, and self-identity seriously influence youth's attitudes toward parents, the home, friends, society, and one's self. Also, feelings, emotions and sentiments affect attitude formation. The feeling of inferiority for example, certainly affects a person's attitudes toward himself and others; and it is just as likely that sentiments of loyalty, patriotism, love, and friendship affect the formation of social, moral, and religious attitudes. The emotions and their derivatives may be expected to play a conspicuous role in attitudes toward the existence of God, the church, and other religious beliefs and practices.[32]

Finally, attitudes are often formed in line with personality traits. Introversion, aggressiveness, honesty, hyperemotionality, decisiveness, self-sufficiency, submissiveness, and sociability greatly influence the formation of different attitudes. While it is not always possible to determine which comes first, or whether, perhaps, both are formed at the same time, it is more likely that attitudes are formed in line with traits. Well-defined attitudes always depend upon a certain amount of development and maturation, even though some of them, like the traits with which they are associated, are incorporated directly from the environment of persons and events within which the youngster develops.

HOW ATTITUDES DEVELOP

Attitudes Change During Adolescence. In studying the problem of attitude *development* during adolescence we may assume (1) that attitudes do change to some extent, although the amount and character of such changes are not always known; (2) that these changes are traceable to the same factors that play a part in the original formation of attitudes; and (3) that nearly all of the other developmental alterations of the adolescent period — physical, mental, and social — will condition whatever changes in attitudes do take place.

However, the problem remains regarding the *nature* of such changes. In our

---

[31] H. M. Bell, *Youth Tell Their Story* (Washington, D. C.: Amer. Council on Education, 1938), pp. 227–228. Regarding the relationship between motivation and attitude, see the stimulating article by Helen Peak, "Attitude and Motivation," in M. R. Jones (ed.), *Nebraska Symposium on Motivation* (Lincoln: University of Nebraska Press, 1955), pp. 149–188.

[32] This relationship was clearly brought out in a study of 242 school children regarding their attitudes toward Negroes, Jews, and intolerance. The more prejudiced child tended to show more fear, veiled hostility, and insecurity than the less prejudiced child. H. G. Gough,

D. B. Harris, W. E. Martin, and Marcia Edwards, "Children's Ethnic Attitudes: I. Relationship to Certain Personality Factors," *Child Develpm.*, 1950, 21, 89–91. See also P. H. Mussen, "Some Personality and Social Factors Related to Changes in Children's Attitudes Toward Negroes," in J. M. Seidman (ed.), *op. cit.*, pp. 369–397.

study of both interests and attitudes, we saw that they are affected by experiences like movies and conversation, and can be influenced by such factors as education and propaganda. These changes, however, are fortuitous rather than systematic in character; they are not true *developmental* changes since they are extrinsically determined. A change in attitude that depends upon whether one sees a particular motion picture or not is hardly to be regarded as an integral phase of development. The question arises, therefore, whether there are true developmental shifts in attitude during the adolescent period. Are the attitudes of adolescents essentially different from those of children? Is youth more radical or more conservative than the child, more religious or more irreligious, more social or more antisocial? Do attitudes develop in the manner that intelligence and interests are said to develop?[33]

Changes in Social Attitudes. Questions like these can be answered only by careful empirical study, but the evidence now available leaves a great deal to be desired. As long as thirty years ago, Willoughby presented 20 questions dealing with political, social, and other issues to over 800 college students ranging from freshman to first-year graduate students, partly to determine differences in attitudes. He found a greater degree of con-

servatism among the freshmen than among the older students who generally were more liberal in their viewpoints. There was also a greater degree of religious skepticism among the latter group.[34] Other investigators have also found that college seniors are more liberal in their viewpoints than freshmen and that there is some shift in opinion from the first to the fourth year of college, although the changes are not always marked. Whether these findings represent a true developmental shift that is more or less universal for the particular culture, or whether the differences are nothing more than a reflection of college training, cannot be accurately determined from such data.

In the more extensive investigations of the American Youth Commission reported by Bell, certain data indicated clearly that there are real shifts in attitudes from one age level to another, changes that are not so obviously the product of extrinsic factors. For example, in sampling the opinions of these youths as to what lies at the basis of the youth problem, it was found that 53.5 per cent of the 16-year-olds thought the problem was basically economic, whereas 60.8 per cent of the 24-year-olds held to this view, indicating a small but significant shift in attitude for an entire group. On the question of government control of wages and hours there was no percentage difference whatever between these two age groups, whereas there was substantial disagreement between them on the related question of wage levels, 58.2 per cent of the 16-year-olds and 72.3 per cent of the 24-year-olds regarding wages as too low. There was also a significant age difference in attitudes toward voting, 36.7 per cent

[33] Changes in attitudes with age can be considered an actual developmental shift in many instances. See the article by Clare H. Marple, "Age as a Factor in Attitude Changes," in R. G. Kuhlen and G. G. Thompson (eds.), *Psychological Studies of Human Development* (New York: Appleton-Century-Crofts, 1952), pp. 325–331; W. H. Wilke, "Student Opinion in Relation to Age, Sex, and General Radicalism," *J. Soc. Psychol.*, 1936, 7, 244–248; V. Howard and W. Warrington, "The Inventory of Beliefs: Changes in Beliefs and Attitudes and Academic Success Prediction," *Personnel and Guid. J.*, 1958, 37, 299–302.

[34] R. R. Willoughby, "A Sampling of Student Opinion," *J. Soc. Psychol.*, 1930, 1, 164–169.

Personal contacts shape social attitudes.

of 1400 22-year-olds having voted at their last opportunity as compared with 66.9 per cent of 1544 24-year-olds.[35] Changes like these, which seem to occur more or less spontaneously, may be regarded as true developmental shifts in attitudes.

Other observers have noted the difference between racial attitudes of children and those of youths, children seldom showing the aversions to races and nationalities that typify adolescent reactions. In an investigation of the attitudes of Negro adolescents, Beckham found that while there was practically no prejudice experienced by these children during

childhood, most of them became conscious of discrimination at the age of twelve, this antagonism resulting in almost complete cleavage between the races in activities of a social nature. Moreover, it seemed to be more or less permanent in character. These aversions and antagonisms, however, are not always a permanent feature of development. Lasker cites numerous instances in which even the antagonism and aversion of white youngsters raised in southern states lessened with contact with Negroes in the more democratic school situations in the North. Watson also found that permanence of racial antagonisms is conditioned to a large extent by the amount of information and experience about the races and nationalities with which a per-

[35] H. M. Bell, *op. cit.* For other extensive data on the social attitudes of modern youth, see H. H. Remmers and D. H. Radler, *The American Teenager* (New York: Bobbs-Merrill, 1957), pp. 153–221.

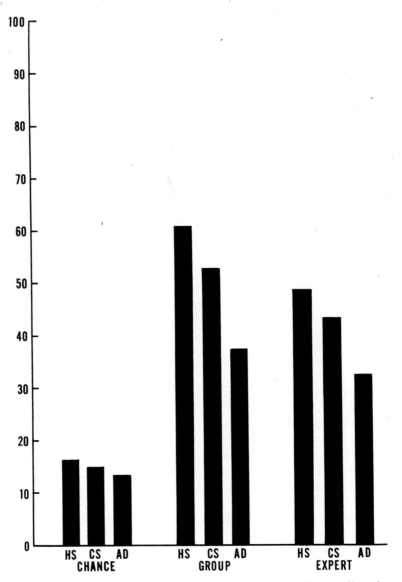

Fig. 23.   Changes in opinion due to "chance," to "group," and to "expert" opinion, for a high school group, a college group, and an adult group. In all three instances, influences decreased with age. **HS** — high school; **CS** — college; and **AD** — adult group. From Clare H. Marple. "The Comparative Susceptibility of Three Age Levels to the Suggestion of Group Versus Expert Opinion," **J. Soc. Psychol.**, 1933, **4**, 176–186.

son comes in contact. In his study of prejudice toward Orientals, he found that those individuals who knew most about oriental life and customs, and those who had fairly close contact with Orientals, had the least prejudice, whereas those with the most deep-seated antipathies knew little or nothing about Orientals.[36]

Similar results have been recorded in studies of racial attitudes of college students. Although the results indicated a high degree of racial prejudice and discrimination, there was nevertheless a noticeable decline in the percentage of prejudiced individuals from the freshman to the senior level, thus indicating a more liberal or more lenient attitude toward the Negro among the upperclassmen. All of these data may be contrasted with the results obtained by Minard in an investigation of the racial attitudes of over 1000 Iowa children in grades seven to twelve. Minard found that personal intolerance became greater with every passing year, even though there was a slow gain, in the first four grades covered, in "intellectual" tolerance.[37] Just what the reactions of these children would be in later years we do not know; but it is possible, as other evidence indicates, that both intellectual and personal tolerance increase with age (see Fig. 23).

Changes in Religious Attitudes and Personal Beliefs. In other areas, too, there are significant changes in attitude throughout adolescence. In religious attitudes particularly, studies indicate quite generally that there is a decided shift toward greater skepticism, and a turning away from the more naïve acceptance of religious values and tenets that characterizes earlier childhood. There is also a tendency for attitudes to become generalized, as has been noted for the attitudes of radicalism and conservatism. This development is of particular significance, since the motivational influence of attitudes will vary in direct proportion to the extent of their generalization.

Other studies point to a definite shift in personal beliefs during late childhood and early adolescence. In one study of unfounded beliefs among junior high school pupils, definite changes in belief between the seventh and ninth grades appeared (Table 15). In this study a list of true-false statements designed to measure belief in or attitude toward common superstitions and other related beliefs was given to 441 boys and 413 girls. From the table it can be seen that there is an appreciable difference in terms of superstitions believed between the children in the seventh and those in the ninth grades, the latter pupils having much less difficulty in determining the falsity of some of the items.[38]

TABLE 15

CHANGES IN BELIEFS AMONG SEVENTH, EIGHTH, AND NINTH GRADE PUPILS*

Grade	No. of Cases	Items marked wrong	
		Mean	SD
Seventh	252	35.01	31.46
Eighth	278	22.54	24.32
Ninth	324	20.09	19.82
Total population	854	24.47	25.97

*From O. W. Caldwell and G. E. Lundeen, "Further Study of Unfounded Beliefs Among Junior High School Pupils," *Teachers College Record*, 1934, *36*, 35–52.

[36] A. S. Beckham, "Study of Attitudes of Negro Adolescents," *J. Abnorm. Soc. Psychol.*, 1934, 29, 18–29; B. Lasker, *Race Attitudes in Children* (New York: Holt, 1929); G. B. Watson, "Orient and Occident," in *Report of the Institute of Pacific Relations*, 1927.

[37] R. D. Minard, "Race Attitudes of Iowa Children," *Univer. of Iowa Studies in Character*, 1931, 4, No. 2.

[38] In this connection, see Caroline B. Zachry, *Emotion and Conduct in Adolescence* (New York: Appleton-Century-Crofts, 1940), Chaps. 5, 6.

Changes in Vocational Attitudes. As the teen-ager moves toward adulthood there are noticeable shifts in his attitude toward different vocations. In an early study of the vocational preferences of 2026 elementary school children it was found that civil and military service became less and less attractive with age, while for boys interest in professional vocations increased. When, however, evaluative rather than preferential attitudes are studied, the changes are not always so marked.[39] In an unusual study by Anderson in 1934, 673 students were asked to rank 25 occupations in terms of social contribution, social prestige, and economic return. The results indicated that seniors differed little from freshmen in their estimation of these occupations.[40]

All such changes in attitude may be expected in view of the intellectual, emotional, social, and motivational developments that take place during the adolescent period, and in view, also, of the inescapable influence of experience, education, and suggestion. Some of these shifts are admittedly superficial, although often important; others seem to be representative of fundamental attitude changes that are more or less inevitable because of the general character of development. Other things being equal, we may expect youth, as compared with the child, to be more radical, more tolerant, less superstitious, and less naïve in his attitudes toward various issues and events. Here as always individual variation plays a sig-

nificant role, and there is no telling what to expect in a given instance; but on the whole the changes studied are fairly general and characteristic of the adolescent period.

ATTITUDES AND ADOLESCENT BEHAVIOR

Attitudes Are Important. Allport's statement that "Attitudes will determine for each individual what he will see and hear, what he will think and what he will do" is a clear expression of the significance of these tendencies for human conduct. There is hardly an area of human behavior that is not affected by them in some way.[41] Of added significance is the fact that attitudes are *closely interrelated*. In the many studies cited, it was found repeatedly that attitudes often condition each other, especially when they have a common reference. Thus, a liberal attitude is likely to influence a person's social and educational opinions as well as his religious beliefs. This is to be expected since it is the nature of an attitude to function as a generalized readiness to think and to act with respect to certain values. A person who is intolerant toward the Church will in all likelihood be intolerant in other things. A person who is indifferent toward the welfare of his children is not likely to be concerned about the welfare of society. And an adolescent who is antisocial in his attitude will not ordinarily be known for his fervent religious inclinations.

Adolescence Favors Attitude Formation. Adolescence is particularly favorable to the development of more permanent at-

[39] B. Schiller "An Analysis of the Vocational Preferences of 2026 New York City Elementary School Children," unpublished master's thesis, Columbia University, 1929.

[40] W. A. Anderson, "The Occupational Attitudes of College Men," *J. Soc. Psychol.*, 1934, 5, 435–466. See also H. D. Carter, "The Development of Vocational Attitudes," *J. Consult. Psychol.*, 1940, 5, 185–191; Caroline B. Zachry, *op. cit.*, Chap. 12.

[41] See C. M. Whitlow, "Attitudes and Behavior of High School Students," *Amer. J. Sociol.*, 1935, 40, 489–494.

titudes, since the important issues around which attitudes revolve are generally beyond the comprehension of the child. The preadolescent boy or girl knows little — and cares less — about such things as communism, atomic warfare, birth control, democracy, freedom, racial equality, the military draft, Catholicism, or the space age. But this is not true of teen-agers who show a great deal of concern about personal, social, and religious values. The average adolescent has very definite ideas about going into service, attending college, dating, and similar things that affect his life. Commenting on a study of communist leaders in Russia, Allport says, "Three quarters of the leaders began radical activities by the time they were twenty-one years of age, and virtually all of them by the age of twenty-six. This fact is an illustration of the decisive effects of the attitudes formed in youth. Most of the incomparably important attitudes not only toward politics, but toward the home, toward religion, sex, social welfare, vocation, marriage, and personal duty, are formed in adolescence, and for the most part endure throughout life. Barring unusual experiences of conversion or crisis, attitudes are likely to be confirmed and enriched rather than altered or replaced."[42] This statement adds considerable weight to the importance of using every available means to insure the development of wholesome personal, moral, religious, and social attitudes in youth, so that their efforts may be fortified and sustained by these dynamic tendencies in the crucial situations they are bound to face.

---

[42] G. W. Allport, "Attitudes," in C. Murchison (ed.), A *Handbook of Social Psychology* (Worcester, Mass.: Clark University Press, 1935), p. 806.

HOW TO DEVELOP ATTITUDES IN YOUTH

Exploiting Basic Needs and Capacities. Our study of different attitudes and their formation in adolescence should make it clear why attitudes are developed in some instances and not in others. Intelligence, for example, has a lot to do with making education and similar techniques effective or ineffective in the shaping of attitudes. Also, if the technique used manages to stimulate basic needs, feelings, and desires, or if it stimulates the functioning of a trait, then it is likely to be effective in molding the desired attitude; otherwise not. Where intelligence is concerned, we may assume that the higher and the more critical it is, the more difficult will be the task of forming or changing attitudes to conform to a desired pattern, especially where negative attitudes are concerned. While the evidence here is far from conclusive, we must remember that in the studies cited the investigators were dealing with attitudes already firmly established, which makes it more difficult to determine the exact relationship between intelligence and the formation of attitudes. It is significant that attitudes often change with age, which may mean that, as critical faculties develop, the role of intelligence in the shaping of attitudes becomes more and more prominent. The evidence with respect to the development of liberalism during college years supports this notion.

Exploiting Experiences and Education. Any program directed toward the development of favorable and dynamic attitudes in youth, or the elimination of unfavorable ones, would have to take into account all such determining factors. Youth should be provided with the kinds of experiences and activities that lead to the formation of desirable attitudes. Family influences, methods of training, and education are also of primary importance in such development. Parents have the opportunity to set the right example on the basis of which good attitudes can be formed, and teachers have the opportunity to inculcate right attitudes not only by what they teach but by the manner of teaching. Looking at the problem from a negative viewpoint, youngsters must also be protected against the possible insidious influence of group opinion, propaganda, and faulty education. Not only is it important to insure the development of healthy attitudes in youth; it is as vitally important to prevent the formation of unhealthy ones.

This statement applies particularly to moral and religious attitudes. It is an unhealthy sign when a youngster has a deep-rooted and unfavorable racial attitude, but it is much worse, both for him and society, when his attitudes on moral and religious questions are misshapen. If, for example, a teen-ager has the attitude that "anything is all right if you can get away with it," it may well be a forerunner of moral debilitation or delinquency. Right moral attitudes are extremely important for all phases of adjustment; and, as we shall see later (Chapter XV), moral adjustment is closely connected with religious adjustment. Thus, if the attitude toward religious values is one of indifference, continuous doubt, or antagonism, there are very likely to be repercussions in the moral and social spheres of conduct. This statement is supported by the close relationship between fundamental religious tenets and social attitudes. The Christian injunction, "Love thy neighbor as thyself," for example, is directly contrary to antiracial attitudes; and in some religious communions it is regarded as a moral wrong to tolerate such attitudes in oneself. The personal and social values of healthy moral and religious attitudes cannot be overestimated, and every means should be taken to insure the development of such attitudes in youth.

SELECTED READINGS

Clark, K. B., *Prejudice and Your Child* (Boston: Beacon Press, 1955).

Gruenberg, Sidonie M. (ed.), *Our Children Today* (New York: Viking, 1955), Chap. 24.

Kuhlen, R. G., and Thompson, D. G. (eds.), *Psychological Studies of Human Development* (New York: Appleton-Century-Crofts, 1952), Chap. IX.

Remmers, H. H., and Radler, D. H., *The American Teenager* (New York: Bobbs-Merrill, 1957), pp. 153–177.

Seidman, J. M. (ed.), *The Adolescent: a Book of Readings* (New York: Dryden, 1953), Chaps. 9, 11, 12.

Zachry, Caroline B., *Emotion and Conduct in Adolescence* (New York: Appleton-Century-Crofts, 1940).

Zubek, J. P., and Solberg, Patricia A., *Human Development* (New York: McGraw-Hill, 1954), Chap. 14.

CHAPTER XIV

VALUES, IDEALS, AND GOALS IN ADOLESCENCE

It is often said that youth is a period of idealism, and also that one of the more serious problems of growing up is finding the right goals. Developing ideals and finding one's goals depends a lot on one's values, and so in this chapter we want to take a look at the teen-ager's values, ideals, and goals to find out what they are, how they are related, and in what manner they develop during adolescence.

WHAT VALUES ARE

Values Are Related to Interests and Attitudes. It is not an easy task to trace the development of values in adolsecence, because here we are venturing into little explored territories of the human mind. In some respects, of course, several lines of investigation and objective results bear at least indirectly on this phase of adolescent development. Attitude, for example, has been defined as a state of mind of the individual toward a value; and if this viewpoint is correct, it means that the study of attitudes is in part a study of values.[1] This is also true to some extent of interests. That some relationship does exist among these motivations is unquestionable since both interests and attitudes are often formed in line with what is considered valuable. A vocation,

a hobby, or an extracurricular activity is interesting only to the extent that it possesses some value for the individual. Similarly, one's attitudes toward women, communism, motherhood, birth control, or democracy will be conditioned by his scale of values. Because of this relationship the study of values is very important to understanding the direction of adolescent striving, and to an adequate interpretation of the ideals and goals of young people.[2]

Values Are Motives. We do not, however, ordinarily think of values as coordinate with attitudes and interests. They seem to be more on the intellectual

---

[1] G. W. Allport, "Attitudes," in C. Murchison (ed.), *A Handbook of Social Psychology* (Worcester, Mass.: Clark University Press, 1935), p. 802.

[2] For a good discussion of the problem of values, see A. Wheelis, *The Quest for Identity* (New York: Norton, 1958), especially pp. 174–180. See also W. R. Catton, "A Theory of Value," *Amer. Sociol. Rev.*, 1959, 24, 310–317; W. A. Scott, "Empirical Assessment of Values and Ideologics," *Amer. Sociol. Rev.*, 1959, 24, 299–310; M. L. Barron, "Juvenile Delinquency and American Values," *Amer. Sociol. Rev.*, 1951, 16, 208–214.

side, and hence more closely related to ideals. A value is not a readiness to respond, nor is it a mental set; it is rather a conceptual representation of some thing in terms of its goodness, worth, or utility. A value therefore, *is a rational motive, transformed into a relatively permanent and sustaining motivational factor.* Thus for the student education is a value; for the physician healing is a value; and saving souls is a value for the priest and minister. In each case it is obvious that the value is a motive; but it is more than an ordinary motive; it is one which, through experience, reflection, or education, has been raised to the level of a permanent, pervasive, and sustaining motivational tendency. Values of this kind become integrated with other sustaining motives like attitudes, ideals, and goals, and thus become a part of the dynamic background of behavior. For this reason values, ideals, and goals cannot always be clearly distinguished one from the other.

WHERE VALUES COME FROM

Values Originate in Thinking and Deliberation. The *immediate* source of values is the process of rational deliberation or reflection. By considering the merits and demerits, the fitness or unfitness, the good or evil of any thing or act we are able to elevate it to the level of a value or to devaluate it. This process, however, *presupposes* a knowledge of what is valuable, since a person must know what is good or bad, serviceable or useless, before he can determine whether this object or this act belongs in one or the other category. For this reason very young children cannot be said to possess a scale of values. Such things as education, cleanliness, charity,

and obedience are poorly evaluated by children because of inadequate knowledge. The adolescent, because of intellectual development and the accumulation of experience, is in a much better position than the child to develop an adequate value system.

If we look for the more remote and external sources of values in adolescents, we come across the same factors that determine interests and attitudes, including cultural milieu, home environment, experience, education, school, church, and neighborhood. We should note also the influence of numerous activities like reading, television, going to movies, group activities, and conversation. Here again we see the close relationship between interests and values. Naturally, the influence of all of these factors on the formation of values in adolescence will be conditioned to an important extent by individual personality factors. Psychological needs, intelligence, and personality traits have a lot to do with the acceptance or rejection of values that are provided by experience or by the environment.

Culture, Environment, and the Value System. In a study some years ago of the ideals of Swedish children, it was found that they place intellectual and artistic qualities higher than do English, Prussian, and Armenian children, and that in selecting their ideals they do not consider money, social position, honor, and fame.[3] Here we seem to have an example of the influence of cultural milieu in the shaping of personal values, even though other factors undoubtedly played a part. Cultural influences are extremely difficult to trace, and the most

---

[3] Cited by Elizabeth B. Hurlock and C. Jansing, "The Vocational Attitudes of Boys and Girls of High School Age," *J. Genet. Psychol.*, 1934, *44*, 175–191.

that we can do is to point out a correlation between culture and values.[4] Yet there is little doubt that values often have their remote origin in group traditions, mores, and practices. Militarism, for example, held considerable attraction for the Prussian soldiers, but little for the average American male. The concept of empire may readily stir the emotions of the Briton and leave the Swiss peasant unmoved. Pragmatic values are attractive to most Americans, whereas other national groups may incline to more spiritual values. Every teacher and counselor in the American school system knows how difficult it is to arouse the interest of students in activities and goals that do not have a definite pragmatic significance. "What will it get me?" is a common inquiry of American students faced with the choice of curriculum or a career

Influences exerted by the home, school, church, and neighborhood are closely related to the cultural impact on value systems. These social units are often the wellsprings as well as the repositories of cultural values. Thus the values derived from the home are often nothing more than cultural concepts that have filtered into the minds of parents and other family members. Somewhat the same situation exists with respect to the school as a social institution, although here the relationship is complicated by the added influence of educational philosophies that are the product of tradition, experience, and experimentation. Both of these institutions, the home and the school, exert a strong and pervasive influence on the formation of values in the minds of youth, through training, formal education, and interpersonal relationships.[5]

The foregoing interpretation applies as well to the neighborhood or community, which is actually a culture in miniature, reflecting the concepts, ideals, attitudes, and values of that larger culture of which it is a part, and also altering them to conform to its own peculiar pattern. Numerous studies indicate the influence of neighborhood environments on the ideals and conduct of youth, which is to be expected in view of the close relationship between personality and environment.

The Church stands in a unique position. That it is closely related to the problem of values is suggested by the many changes in religious ideals and practices in the Protestant denominations. At one time divorce, birth control, and similar practices were regarded as inherently evil, and not to be tolerated under any circumstances. Gradually, however, values have changed, until at the present time the stand taken by many different denominations is quite different than it was formerly. A few denominations, notably the Roman Catholic Church, adhere more firmly to fundamental tenets, and have been much less influenced by cultural variations. In matters of divorce, birth control, the nature of the sacraments, etc., the church has strongly resisted basic change, although some liberalizing influences can be observed in attitudes toward rhythm, marital separation, Lenten regulations, and

---

[4] See Else Frenkel-Brunswik, "Patterns of Social and Cognitive Outlook in Children and Parents," *Amer. J. Orthopsychiat.*, 1951, 21, 543–558, and G. H. J. Pearson, *Adolescence and the Conflict of Generations* (New York: Norton, 1958), p. 85 f.

[5] In a questionnaire study of 259 students of sociology and social psychology, it was found that children often select the life patterns of their parents as models for their own behavior and ignore others. A. M. Rose, "Parental Models for Youth," *Sociol. Soc. Res.*, 1955, 40, 3–9.

the like. The unchanging character of religious values is one of the few bright spots in a world of constant flux, since the more that fundamental values change the more confused do people become. In this sense, therefore, the Church is the source rather than the repository of values, and can be one of the really great forces shaping the adolescent's value system.

Wheelis, in his penetrating analysis of the quest for identity, emphasizes the close relationship between institutional and personal values.

> Ours has become a culture of change rather than a culture of tradition. As institutions give ground the ideals upon which they have focused the aspirations of men are weakened. Some of these aspirations, which formerly were claimed by institutional absolutes, are now unattached. They form a reservoir of restless yearning and discontent. This is the source of mass movements, of the frightened retreat from reason, and of the transference manifestations of psychoanalysis.[6]

There are persons who have escaped this culture of change and the breakdown of institutional values.

> These are persons whose values have survived intact the welter of contemporary change. They know who they are and where they're going and why, and what is worth struggling for and how much. A devout Catholic and a dedicated Marxist might serve as examples. It is unusual for such persons to consult a psychoanalyst, and when they do they are not liable to the development of that intense preoccupying yearning to which people of today are so vulnerable.[7]

How Values Become Personalized. The translation of these cultural and subcultural experiences into personal values is accomplished through training, educa-

tion, experience, and imitation. The young child who is trained from the earliest years to respect authority, to control his emotions and impulses, not to lie, and so on, may certainly be expected to form values in line with this training. Discipline itself will emerge as a value from this personal experience with training. But more important perhaps is the formal and informal education to which the child is exposed. Education is in large measure the inculcation of values, especially where moral, religious, and social conduct is concerned. Mere drill and the acquisition of facts are not exercises in value formation; but instruction in the difference between right and wrong, in history, economics, or hygiene, in the existence of God, the nature of man's relationship to society — these are all lessons in values, whether taught in the process of formal education, or informally in the home. The divorce of moral instruction and religion from education in the public school system is therefore regrettable, since so much excellent opportunity for the inculcation of worthwhile values is thereby lost. The task is then left to too busy parents, or to the youngster's occasional contacts with the Church. Despite these limitations, the fact remains that education plays a leading role in value formation, if in many instances only indirectly; and for this reason the philosophy, techniques, and personnel of education require constant vigilance.

Values Are Also Dependent Upon Experience. In helping the teen-ager develop a value system, we cannot afford to overlook the influence of *experience.* Reading, conversation, travel, social activities, and amusements contribute to the youngster's concept of what is or is not valuable. This fact emerged in our

---

[6] A. Wheelis, *op. cit.,* p. 165.

[7] *Ibid.,* p. 162.

study of the effects of movies on the ideas and aspirations of youth. Let us remember that youth's scale of values is in a state of constant transition, and therefore such experiences can often cause considerable harm if they are of the wrong kind. The average teen-ager has neither the intellectual ability nor the background of experience to judge adequately regarding values. Since his value system is in the process of formation, he cannot be expected to distinguish always the real from the superficial, or the good from the bad. The inconsistency of adolescent conduct is partly explained by this fact.

Values, like interests and attitudes, are also derived from other persons through *imitation* and *introception*. In fact, the influence of experiences and activities of many kinds will always be conditioned to some extent by such processes. They are the means by which a value experience is translated into a personal affair. Young persons derive many of their value concepts from parents, friends, teachers, and others with whom they come in close personal contact. Here again, as in the case of attitudes, a certain amount of *identification* is probably necessary.[8] Thus, such experiences as reading and movies often have more influence in the shaping of values than formal education, since these experiences may involve identification, whereas the educational process may not go beyond a cold and uninteresting presentation of facts or theories. For the same reason the personal contacts of youth are of considerable importance. The old saying, "Tell me with whom

you go, and I will tell you what you are," is merely an axiomatic expression of this fact.

Personality Influences Value Formation. The formation of the adolescent's value system will be conditioned also by what he himself is like. His background of experience, attitudes, traits, capacities, and needs all determine to some extent the acceptance or rejection of particular values. Of these factors intelligence stands out prominently, since value formation is itself an intellectual process. Thus the formation of values will vary directly with *intellectual ability*. Thus one youngster may develop a fairly adequate scale of values early in adolescence, whereas another may not possess worthwhile values even at the end of the adolescent period. In both instances the background of experience of the individual will play on important part but only insofar as it is itself conditioned by intellectual ability.

The gratification of *basic needs* is also related to value formation, a point that we brought out earlier in our discussion of the relation between needs and motives. Such things as food, exercise, comfort, rest, or pleasure are readily interpreted as valuable because of this relationship. Of even greater importance is the gratification of psychological needs, particularly achievement, acceptance, social approval, independence, and self-identity. That is why social position, wealth, home and family, and marriage are almost universally regarded as valuable since they promise the gratification of these needs. In all these situations, therefore, whether we are dealing with interests, attitudes, values, or goals, the individual personality is an important determining influence.

The Selection and Organization of Values. To list and describe the internal

---

[8] W. E. Martin, "Learning Theory and Identification: III. The Development of Values in Children," *J. Genet. Psychol.*, 1954, 84, 211–217. See also Caroline M. Tryon, "Evaluation of Adolescent Personality by Adolescents," *Monogr. Soc. Res. Child Developm.*, 1939, 4, No. 23.

and external sources of values as we have done here does not carry the implication that the person himself has little to do with value formation. On the contrary, some of our most important values are the result of careful deliberation and reflection, and are thus *selected* rather than shaped by outside forces or internalized from the environment. Young Peter might start out in the early days of adolescence with only a vague notion of the value of a college education and end up in his senior year in high school with a grim determination to get a college education at all costs. This change in his value system might have come about largely through his own evaluation. One of the tasks of training and educating the adolescent is to teach him how to evaluate the realities and events of his life in a healthy and satisfactory manner, and also how to *devaluate* the trivial and transitory aspects of his life. Even interests and attitudes can be brought within the scope of self-determination and the selective process of evaluation; but it is one's personal value system that is most amenable to selection and control.

For healthy development and adjustment it is important not only that sound values are acquired or selected, but also that they are *rightly ordered to one another.* In fact, of the two aspects of value development, this one is the more important. Many of the ills of individuals and of societies spring from the failure to distinguish higher and lower values. For example, a high school graduate may consider both college training and the securing of a job as valuable, but if he subordinates the former to the latter he might be making a serious mistake. Thus one of the most fundamental tasks of all education is helping young people to

work out for themselves *an adequate scale of values.*

Some values are universally accepted and elevated to a high plane and others are not. Thus, everyone will agree that health is a greater value than the satisfaction of temporary desire, that life is more precious than inordinate drinking which tends to destroy life, that education is more to be desired than ignorance, or that heaven is preferable to hell. Just what a perfect hierarchy of values would be is not for us to say, since such a statement would constitute a claim to omnipotence. Yet it is certain that a proper hierarchy of values must be worked out if individual adjustment and happiness are to be achieved. The unhappy persons of the world are those who put last things first and first things last, and who often find out too late how totally inadequate their philosophy of life really is.[9]

> Rarely does a person whose superego strength is anchored in a genuinely firm ideology consult a psychoanalyst; and when he does, he is not so vulnerable to development of transference feelings. Such persons are becoming rare these days; they were more characteristic of the last century than of this one. . . . It is the loss of stable values and the inevitability of change that have made possible the luxuriant blossoming of psychoanalysis in the twentieth century.[10]

Values Influence Conduct.   The period of adolescence is the time when an adequate scale of values should be built into

[9] See L. D. Crow and Alice Crow, *Adolescent Development and Adjustment* (New York: McGraw-Hill, 1956), Chap. 13; C. G. Moser, *Understanding Girls* (New York: Assoc. Press, 1957), pp. 205–211; R. J. Havighurst and Hilda Taba, *Adolescent Character and Personality* (New York: Wiley, 1949), pp. 99–102.

[10] A. Wheelis, *The Quest for Identity* (New York: Norton, 1958), pp. 163–164.

the personality of the young boy or girl, and when every avenue leading to this goal should be explored. Education, moral and religious training, experience, example, and precept should be exploited in every way to help young people build for themselves worthwile value systems which will prepare them to cope successfully with the demands and responsibilities of adult living. This principle is basic to the healthy development of youth because values, like other motivations, exert considerable influence on the conduct of youth. However, even the building of a value system is not enough, since the influence of values will be determined by their dynamic quality. To be of moral worth, a scale of values *must become a dynamic part* of a person's motivational system. The ability to recognize an object or an act as valuable is unimportant in itself if the value thus stimulated fails to influence behavior. Values, therefore, must be emotionalized; they must become integrated with attiudes, ideals, and principles; and they must achieve the power to arouse strong feelings and sentiments if they are to play a significant role in conduct. In other words, if we can get Helen or David *excited* about marriage, or a career, or a college education, or any other worthwhile venture or goal in life, then we can be confident that these important values will function in a dynamic manner.

Values and Principles. Between the values that guide human conduct and the ideals that enrich it are those guidelines of behavior that we usually refer to as *principles*.[11] At times the distinction between principles and ideals becomes obscured, since an ideal may be used as a guiding principle of conduct. The two, however, are not the same. A principle, as used here, is simply *a standard of conduct*, a guiding rule according to which conduct is regulated. *Principles emerge from values and are often a starting point of ideals.* For example, a young boy or girl may arrive at the notion that it is morally valuable or good to tell the truth. This idea is elevated into a principle by the determination to act always in accordance with that value. When to such a principle are added others that are altruistic in nature, such as kindness toward the afflicted, honesty, or charity, the youngster has developed *a moral ideal.* All ideals of this kind, whether moral, religious, or social, are founded ultimately on principles of conduct. It is impossible for a person with such ideals to be unprincipled, unless the ideals are merely abstractions to which he gives lip service only. In such a case ideals have no real psychological existence and are devoid of any dynamic significance.

Principles of conduct have their sources in many factors. They can be derived from experience, inculcated by means of formal education, or emerge out of values and attitudes. *But the primary genetic source is conduct.* The idea that the principle must always genetically precede the conduct is erroneous. It is true that once the principle is formed, and begins to function as a determining tendency, the conduct flows from the principle. But in the formation of the principle conduct comes first. That is why training in childhood is so important to adolescent moral and social development. By the time the youngster reaches adolescence he should have been trained to act in ways that are morally and socially acceptable; and out of these

11 In this connection see C. M. Fleming, *Adolescence* (New York: International Universities Press, 1949), Chap. XVI.

experiences in right acting the necessary principles will gradually crystallize, under the impetus and guidance of rational deliberation. It is not inconceivable that principles can be inculcated first, but it is psychologically uneconomical. The advantage of adolescent development is that the youngster can be made to appreciate the validity and worth of the principles according to which he has been trained to act.

Principles, therefore, are the *characterological* correlates of habit patterns laid down in infancy and childhood. Made intelligible by understanding, reinforced by values, attitudes, and ideals, and made even more dynamic by emotional investment, they can become powerful, dynamic forces within the motivational system. The measure of a person's character can be taken by his ability to adhere to principles regardless of contrary influences; and a good share of the training of youth should be directed toward the formation and inculcation of such principles. Together with values and ideals of the right kind, they insure the development of a wholesome, well-integrated character and personality.

IDEALS IN ADOLESCENCE

Values and Ideals. The relationship between values and ideals is very close. An ideal, however, is more than a value. It is a value that has been converted into a *standard of excellence* through realization of its *extraordinary* merit. Thus for some persons motherhood is simply a value, something to be desired or respected because it is necessary for society. To others, however, it is a true ideal, a standard of excellence that ennobles and enriches their entire lives. Ordinarily, therefore, ideals are more dynamic than

values; they are invested with more emotional qualities, and are more pervasive in character, reaching into every corner of mental life that is in any way related to the ideal. This pervasiveness will depend upon the nature of the ideal itself, since some are restricted in their relation to conduct (such as motherhood), whereas others (such as the ideal of Christian brotherhood) tend to color and influence a great many phases of human conduct.

Objective Versus Personal Ideals. We should, therefore, distinguish carefully between types of ideals. There are those, first of all, that are *objective* in character, and that tend to influence behavior very little. One may, for example, have an ideal of what constitutes the best form of government, or the best kind of education, without the ideal ever entering into any of his decisions or actions. These are ideals in the strict sense of the term, since they are standards of excellence; but they are psychological luxuries which may never be translated into conduct. Of much greater significance are those ideals, wholly *personal* in character, that are integral parts of a person's motivational system. Youth's ideals pertaining to vocations, marriage, religion, morality, or social responsibility, are often of this kind. These are the ideals that count where personality and conduct are concerned, since they will always play some part in the making of decisions.

Pitfalls of Idealism in Youth. We may distinguish also between ideals that are *personalized* and those that are purely *conceptual*. All ideals are alike in being standards of excellence, but some of them are *personified*, which means that some *person* functions as a representative of the ideal. A boy's mother, for example, may be for him the ideal of motherhood or wifehood, the mother thus being the ideal personified. Another youngster may *abstract* the qualities of motherhood from any particular person, and also have a lofty ideal of motherhood. Personified ideals can be very important to the development of youth's idealism, but they are the source also of many real dangers.[12] Since an ideal is by definition a standard of excellence, and since no human person is excellent in the fullest sense of the term, this sort of idealism may degenerate into blind hero worship, or end in deep discouragement with the realization that the idealized person has feet of clay. This type of idealistic development is very common in adolescence and must be guarded against. Idealism that leads to blindness defeats its own purpose. The youngster whose mother is regarded as the ideal of wifehood may forever fail to find a marriageable person who measures up to that standard, having created an image that exists only in his own mind. Herein lies the principal danger of idealism. All ideals are in one sense divorced from reality; they are conceptual formulations of *what ought to be*, not what actually *is*. As such they are goals to be striven toward, *realizable but never actually realized*. A person without ideals is very poor indeed; on the other hand, a person with nothing but ideals is an impractical liability both to himself and to society. These limitations must be kept in mind in the shaping of youth's ideals.

[12] In this connection see the discussion of "Worship of Living Heroes" in G. H. J. Pearson, *Adolescence and the Conflict of Generations* (New York: Norton, 1958), pp. 77–81. See also the study of real-life measures of aspirations as compared to laboratory measures by D. P. Ausubel, H. M. Schiff, and Marjorie P. Zeleny, "Real-life Measures of Academic Vocational Aspirations in Adolescents: Relation to Laboratory Measures and to Adjustment," *Child Develpm.*, 1953, 24, 155–168.

Young people do not always realize that the "ideal" persons with whom they come in contact often have serious defects; and they must be strengthened against the disappointment and disillusion that are sure to follow upon the discovery of this fact. Or, what is even better, youth should be guided toward the selection of personalized ideals that come closest to a standard of excellence. Thus instructors of religion rightly urge that children and youth become acquainted with the lives of Christ and the saints, because they are exemplars of the great moral and religious virtues. Hero worship of Christ and others like Him is psychologically justifiable, because such persons are real heroes in every sense of the term. But it is not impossible to find among lesser persons some who are also heroic; they must be chosen carefully, and their shortcomings as well as their virtues should be known.

Teen-agers do not readily appreciate the distance between idealism and actuality. They are too often discouraged by their failures to reach a standard of excellence; they do not appreciate that ideals are never actually realized, that they are goals to strive toward rather than ends to be realized. Against such discouragement youth must be carefully guarded, for it may lead to severe emotional conflict and maladjustment. Youth must have ideals for complete development and integration, but ideals must be made to play their proper role in the dynamics of human conduct.

Ideals Can Be Dynamic Motives. Ideals are not necessarily dynamic, especially those that are purely objective; but the fact that an ideal is formed at all is indicative of an inclination to think and to act in a manner consonant with the ideal. Ideals are generally formed only after it has already been determined that a certain line of conduct is worthwhile and agreeable. The ideal of acting morally in all situations will not be adopted by a youngster who has already made up his mind that it is more advantageous to act immorally in some situations. The predisposition underlying an ideal favors its dynamic quality. If to this is added emotional and volitional reinforcement, and if the ideal is personalized so that it becomes an integral part of the motivational system, it becomes a powerful instrument for the regulation of conduct. As everyone knows, men have lived and died in the service of an ideal, and it is this dynamic quality which makes them so important to adolescent development.

WHERE IDEALS COME FROM

Many Things Determine Ideals. Since ideals are values of a particular kind, the same factors that determine the formation of values will function in the development of ideals. Ideals are thus traceable to reading, conversation, movies, and other types of experience. How often we hear the typical teen-ager remark of the newest singing sensation on television or radio: "He's my ideal." Such hero worship is not to be taken too seriously, but it does indicate the influence of different forms of experience.

Ideals are also derived from the cultural milieu, the home, the church, the community, and the school.[13] In many

instances they involve the principle of identification, as in the familiar instance of the boy for whom the father is an ideal. They are inculcated through the media of training, education, and imitation, and are importantly related to such factors as intelligence and imagination. To the extent that ideals are conceptualized standards of excellence, their formation depends upon intelligence; but they are dependent also upon imagination, since in many instances daydreaming is the source of more concrete ideals. By means of imagination the young person can project himself into future roles, and these roles often have an idealistic cast. Especially during the early phase of adolescence imaginative, concrete ideals are likely to be formed.

Ideals Change in the Course of Experience. The ideals of youth are different in both form and substance from those of younger children.[14] As we noted previously, the vocational aspirations of the child toward becoming a fireman, a policeman, cowboy, nurse, or a religious Sister are not likely to persist after pubescence. Nor are the same heroes worshiped in the one period as in the other. Whichever way we turn, we find striking differences in content between the ideals of childhood and those of adolescence. Moreover, the form of the idealism changes with greater development and maturity. As youth approaches adulthood, ideals tend to become more abstract and less immediate in character. Many new and different ideals are formed that were beyond the simpler mental range of the child. As the adolescent

---

[13] Pearson argues that the search for ego ideals outside the family is an *essential* part of growing up and occurs in the development of every individual. He then points out that this search for ego ideals creates certain adolescent problems because they are not always available, or they are inadequate and thus cause other adolescent difficulties — G. H. J. Pearson, *op. cit.*, p. 72.

[14] See C. M. Tryon, "Evaluations of Adolescent Personality by Adolescents," *Monogr. Soc. Res. Child Develpm.*, 4, No. 4, 1939; A. R. Crane, "Stereotypes of the Adult Held by Early Adolescents," *J. Educ. Res.*, 1956, 50, 227–230.

matures emotionally, socially, intellectually, and spiritually, entirely new vistas are opened to him. He may begin to form ideals relating to his future status as a husband and father; he becomes conscious of his responsibilities to society and to his fellow man; he begins to see education in its relation to his future vocational goal. In terms of these changes he formulates new ideals or revamps old ones, and his entire system of ideals may change quite noticeably.

To these changes all of the factors mentioned as sources of ideals will contribute in different ways. The youngster's intelligence and his intellectual development will condition the abstractness or immediacy of his ideals. His changing relationship to the home, measured by increasing independence, will cause parents and family to exert less influence on his ideals as he becomes more mature. Heterosexual development, and the experiences that follow in its wake, will affect his ideals concerning the opposite sex. The changing constellation of social groups of which he is a member will alter his ideals relating to friendship and loyalty. The emotional conflicts caused by moral crises, and by religious experiences and difficulties, will affect ideals of self, as well as religious and moral ideals.[15] To put the matter briefly, all of the developmental changes of this period, plus the social, cultural, and economic patterns of the youth's existence, will act to alter, condition, or enforce the development of ideals during

the transition from childhood to maturity. The pattern of ideals that finally emerges will reflect all these influences.

Objective Studies of Ideals and Their Development. The above facts concerning ideals have been verified in a number of studies in this country and in Europe. As early as 1900 Barnes conducted an inquiry among 2100 school children in England, based on the simple question: "What person of whom you have ever heard or read would you most wish to be like? Why?"[16] Barnes found that only 5 per cent of boys and 3 per cent of girls chose father and mother as ideals, and that even this small percentage decreases with age. These percentages are reversed in the choice of acquaintances as ideals, a percentage that also decreases with age. Forty-one per cent of the boys and 32 per cent of the girls chose historical and public characters, a tendency that rises perceptibly with age, especially among boys. At 8 years of age 18 per cent of boys chose such characters; at 13, this figure had risen to 69 per cent! Very few of the children chose literary characters as ideals — 2 per cent of the boys and 6 per cent of the girls. Nor were religious characters chosen by substantial numbers. Only 7 per cent of the boys and 14 per cent of the girls chose God or Christ as an ideal — this despite the fact that in the schools selected for study forty-five minutes a day was given to religious instruction. The most significant developmental feature brought out in this study was that at age 8 half the children selected their ideals from the immediate environment, but that with increase in age there was a decided tendency to reach out into other fields, indicating a lessening influ-

---

[15] As Milovan Djilas says very pointedly, "The rise of ideals, of 'ultimate goals,' does not depend, or rather depends very little, upon human will, because ideals arise out of objective exigencies, out of life and reality" — from *Anatomy of a Moral: the Political Essays of Milovan Djilas,* edited by Abraham Rothberg (New York: Frederick A. Praeger, 1959).

[16] B. Barnes, "Children's Ideals," *Ped. Sem.,* 1900, 7, 3–12.

ence of home, school, and neighborhood on the selection of ideals.

Chambers studied the evolution of ideals among 1146 boys and 1187 girls below the high school level in Pennsylvania.[17] His question was slightly different from that of Barnes: "What person of whom you have heard or read would you most like to be? Why?" He also found a constantly diminishing proportion of local characters and acquaintances chosen as ideals, and a constant increase in the number of historical and public characters chosen. While there were

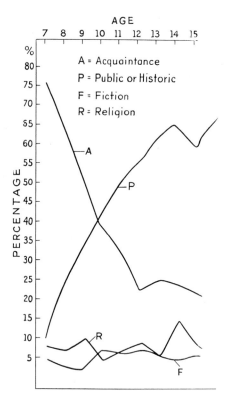

Fig. 26.   Changes in ideals with age — From D. S. Hill, "A Comparative Study of Children's Ideals," **Ped. Sem.**, 1911, **18**, 219–231.

[17] W. G. Chambers, "The Evolution of Ideals," Ped. Sem., 1903, 10, 101–143.

many sex differences, only 2⅔ per cent expressed themselves as wishing to be God or Christ, and biblical characters were named by less than one half of 1 per cent of the group. Less than 5 per cent of the girls and 2 per cent of the boys named a teacher as their exemplar; and after the age of 12, teachers were not mentioned at all. Fictional characters were named by less than 5 per cent of girls and 2 per cent of boys.

Several other significant tendencies were brought out in this study. Whereas only 3.5 per cent of the boys chose ideals from the opposite sex, 51.7 per cent of the girls did so, and this tendency increased with age for girls. Significantly, in the reason given for the choice, the moral qualities of the ideal were mentioned more often with increase in age, whereas the category "no reason" was found to decrease very decidedly. The categories "position" and "greatness" were mentioned more often by older students. Ideals that may be considered degrading were not mentioned. Historical ideals were found to be the most popular type, this popularity increasing until the age of 12 and then slowly decreasing. Compared with Barnes's study, it was found that American children were superior to the English group in their esteem for historical and contemporary ideals, but lagged behind the latter group in religious ideals. It was found also, that material possessions were not very important in determining choices of ideals.

Later investigations of children's ideals have yielded similar results. In one study of 1431 white children, ages 7 to 15, in two public schools of Nashville, Tennessee, the question was asked: "Which person among those you have seen, thought of, heard of, or read about, would you like most to resemble? Why?"

The results of this study are depicted in Figure 24. Again it was found that parental influence diminishes with age. For boys the percentage decreases from 33 at age 7 to zero at ages 14 and 15; for girls the corresponding figures are 28 per cent and zero. Girls were found to choose acquaintances as ideals much more often than boys, whereas many more boys than girls chose historical or contemporary public figures. Again, ideals from fiction were definitely in the minority, as were religious ideals. The tendency of girls to choose male ideals, while not as noticeable in this study as in others, stood out prominently.

Almost three decades later, practically the same question was asked of 8813 white children from public schools in the three largest cities of Alabama.[18] The subjects were largely native born, and of Scotch, Irish, and English descent. The results indicated that from the immediate environment father or mother, teacher or acquaintance, are the important sources of ideals, but that for boys especially parents are a diminishing influence. Girls at all ages idealize both parents and teachers more than boys do, whereas boys at every age outrank girls in idealizing American personages, especially those that are contemporary. Fiction, movies, and religion were found to be poor sources of ideals. It is significant that in this later study one third of the girls still chose to be like male characters.

The most prolific sources of ideals are historic and public characters of all kinds, and this tendency was found to increase steadily from age eight to fifteen, accounting for 64 per cent of the ideals at the latter age. At every age the boys outrank the girls in selecting ideals from the remote environment. The second largest number of ideals (34 per cent) came from the immediate environment, but the influence of this environment was again found to decline steadily within the age limits studied. At every age girls outrank boys in selecting ideals from the immediate environment.

Mencotti made a study of ideals among children to determine the relation between ideals and religious education.[19] The subjects, all of whom were Catholic and attending the seventh grade, included 100 students in Catholic schools, and 61 in public schools. The Catholic school children had received religious instruction continuously in all of their school years, whereas the children attending public schools had been receiving formal religious instruction only once or twice a week for a period of from two to five years. The method used to explore the children's ideals was substantially the same as that used by other investigators. The results indicated that children from both groups selected ideals from the same sources, including immediate environment, history, current events, literature, and religious experiences. However, the children in Catholic schools chose religious ideals much more often than children in public schools — 34 per cent as against 12 per cent. Thus there seems to be some relation between ideals and religious education, but the nature of this relation was not brought out in the study.

These various results confirm the statements made earlier with respect to the origin and development of ideals in

[18] D. S. Hill, "Personification of Ideals by Urban Children," *J. Soc. Psychol.*, 1930, *1*, 379–393.

[19] G. Mencotti, "The Relationship of Children's Ideals to the Degree of Their Formal Religious Education," unpublished master's thesis, University of Detroit, 1950.

childhood and adolescence. Worthy of special note are (1) the significant sex differences that appear in all of the studies, (2) the declining influence of the immediate environment, (3) the relatively insignificant effect of reading and movies, (4) the poor showing with respect to religious characters, and (5) the strong tendency to choose historic and public characters. Whether these tendencies would be found among all children, in every environment and in every type of school system, cannot be determined from the data. But the results obtained contain many implications for the development of ideals in youth.

Ideals and Character Formation. The emphasis that students of adolescent behavior consistently place on the formation of ideals stems from their implications for the development of character and personality. It is generally agreed that ideals are in some measure basic to moral and religious development and thus to the formation of character. The youth who cherishes worthwhile ideals relating to his own conduct, to womanhood, to his fellow man, to God, and so on, is one in whom there is likely to be formed a wholesome and strong character. As one writer says, there may be ideals without character, but there cannot be character without ideals. Ideals, like attitudes, become *determining tendencies*, strong motivational forces that tip the balance in favor of right (or wrong) conduct in a crucial moment. Ideals related to the moral life act as principles of conduct, reinforcing decisions, or excluding acts that are morally unworthy. If character is, as we will define it later, the disposition to act according to regulative principles, then certainly ideals are basic to character formation.

But more than that, ideals are *sources of integration* for both character and personality. They give direction to personal strivings, hopes, ambitions, and desires. They become the nucleus around which worthwhile aspirations revolve, and are thus powerful aids in the reduction of tension and the resolution of conflicts. Personality and character tend toward disintegration when there is no central force to hold them together, when there is lack of unity in striving, and when there is no definite direction that conduct can take. The person without ideals tends to drift aimlessly in his thinking and conduct, since he has no clear concept of what is really worth striving for. The person with ideals, on the other hand, knows what is excellent, and marshals all of his capacities and abilities to secure the achievement of his goals. This quality explains the tremendous power and energy of the great saints. With Christ and His exemplary life as their ideal, it was no great task for them to march relentlessly toward their goals, no matter what the sacrifice involved, and seldom allowing the whims and impulses of the moment to get in their way. We cannot, of course, expect youth to reach this level of idealism; but the lives of the saints are themselves exemplary ideals.

More than thirty years ago, the outstanding psychologist, William McDougall, expressed very clearly and forcibly the role of ideals in daily living, and what he said then can be quoted today without any modification whatever:

> Happy the man whose character has been formed from a well-balanced disposition under the influence of unquestioned ideals and of a definite supreme goal or master purpose. His self-respect and the ideals to which he is attached

... will supply him with dominant motives in all ordinary situations, motives strong enough to overcome all crude promptings of his instinctive nature; he is in little danger of becoming the scene of serious enduring conflicts. . . .

Comparatively few men attain such harmonious integration of character. In this modern age we no longer grow up under the influence of some well-defined moral system supported by the authority of unquestioned religion. In all the countries of western civilization, and more so perhaps in America than elsewhere, the child finds himself surrounded by odds and ends of moral and religious systems, Christian piety and pagan hedonism, Fundamentalism and Modernism, Christian Science and Mechanistic Neo-Darwinism, monogamy and polygamy, free love and birth control, the popular misrepresentations of Freud's teaching, and the cult of self-expression and the Overman. . . . Even such old anchors as patriotism begin to drag, as he is taught that love of country is an irrational prejudice, a pernicious obstacle to universal justice and to the cosmopolitan ideal. And, if he seeks to choose an ideal goal of service to which he may dedicate his life, which way shall he turn? He hears that religion is no longer intellectually respectable, nationalism is wicked, politics villainous, business corrupt, education futile, and science subversive of man's higher hopes.

In such a world crime and divorce increase alarmingly, children grow scarce, the family disintegrates, the young men ask, "Is life worth living?" . . . it is easy to understand that serious moral conflicts are frequent and neurotic disorders a common scourge. For men lack those dominant ideals and purposes which develop strong character and which alone can resolve the conflicts of motives that inevitably arise from time to time in all men.[20]

GOALS IN ADOLESCENCE

Goals, Values, and Ideals. As the teen-ager moves toward the dominant goal of all adolescent striving which is adulthood, and his values and ideals assume more definite form, particular goals also begin to crystallize and to influence his thinking and decisions. It is evident, of course, from the foregoing discussions that particular goals are intimately associated with and sometimes indistinguishable from values and ideals. The goal of becoming a research scientist is regarded as both valuable and idealistic to the college student intensely interested in science and its possibilities. The goal of the priesthood or of the religious life for the high school boy, or of the religious life for the adolescent girl would certainly be regarded in the same light. For other youngsters, anxious to assume their place in adult society, the goal of marriage and of parenthood assume the same characteristics. As we pointed out in our discussion of human motivation, goals are rational motives projected into the future, which give meaning and direction to human striving at any level of development. Goals grow out of interests and values, and are enriched and reinforced by attitudes and ideals; and thus in many instances all of the prominent sustaining motives coalesce in one dynamic urge to achieve, to succeed, and to wrest from the challenge of life a meaningful and satisfying existence.[21]

---

[20] W. McDougall, *Outline of Abnormal Psychology* (New York: Charles Scribner's Sons, 1926), pp. 216–217.

[21] Particular goals for teen-agers are described by many different writers. See, for example, C. G. Moser, *Understanding Girls* (New York: Association Press, 1957), Chaps. 8, 9; Esther Lloyd-Jones and Ruth Fedder, *Coming of Age* (New York: McGraw-Hill, 1941), Chap. VIII; L. K. Frank and Mary Frank, *Your Adolescent at Home and at School* (New York: Viking,

Goals and Adjustment. From this analysis it is easy to see why the development of worthwhile goals in late adolescence is so important to healthy adjustment. As we remarked much earlier (Chapter III), goals contribute a great deal to the direction of human striving and therefore to the integration of personality; and without integration adjustment is impossible.[22] The teen-ager

must be given all of the help and guidance possible in the selection and development of worthwhile goals. Every door that leads to enriching and worthwhile experiences should be opened to him; every idea or special interest should be exploited with a view to the development of acceptable goals. This is not an easy task because goals are elusive and fleeting. But it is a task to which parents and teachers can devote themselves with the assurance of deep personal satisfaction whenever they help a teen-ager find himself in a world of confusion and conflicting values.

1956), Chap. 5; H. B. Cobb, "Role-Wishes and General Wishes of Children and Adolescents," *Child Develpm.*, 1954, 25, 161–171; and M. E. Kirkpatrick, "The Mental Hygiene of Adolescence in the Anglo-American Culture," *Proc. 4th Int. Cong. Ment. Hlth.*, 1951, 273–280.

[22] Goals, however, do not always affect performance or achievement. See H. Witz and R. M. Colver, "The Relationship Between the

Educational Goals and the Academic Performance of Women, a Confirmation," *Educ. and Psych. Msmnts.*, 1959, 19, 373–380.

SELECTED READINGS

Frank, L. K., and Frank, Mary, *Your Adolescent at Home and in School* (New York: Viking, 1956), Chap. 5.

Gruenberg, Sidonie M. (ed.), *Our Children Today* (New York: Viking, 1955), pp. 323–333.

Pearson, G. H. J., *Adolescence and the Conflict of Generations* (New York: Norton, 1958), Chaps. IV, V.

Seidman, J. M. (ed.), *The Adolescent: a Book of Readings* (New York: Dryden, 1953), Chaps. 10, 18.

Strang, Ruth, *The Adolescent Views Himself* (New York: McGraw-Hill, 1957), Chaps. 5, 11.

Wheelis, A., *The Quest for Identity* (New York: Norton, 1958), Chap. VI.

Zachry, Caroline B., *Emotion and Conduct in Adolescence* (New York: Appleton-Century-Crofts, 1940), Chaps. 5, 6, 12, 14.

Zubek, J. T., and Solberg, Patricia A., *Human Development* (New York: McGraw-Hill, 1954), Chap. XIV.

CHAPTER XV

MORAL AND RELIGIOUS DEVELOPMENT IN ADOLESCENCE

Interests and attitudes, values and ideals touch many phases of a person's life, but none more deeply than his moral and religious conduct. If the natural goal of adolescent development is maturity, we can say with equal certainty that the goal of education is the formation of character, and without character there is no maturity. By the same rule, without morality there is no character.

MORALITY AND RELIGION

Values, Principles, and Ideals Are Important to Moral Growth. Experts in the field of adolescent development invariably link moral and religious changes and growth as though they belong together, but often without indicating the relationship between these two aspects of development.[1] There must be some reason for this practice, and it will contribute to our understanding of moral and religious development to probe the basis of this relationship. One fundamental question is this: Can youngsters be moral without being religious, or religious without being moral? The answer to this question will depend, of course, on the meaning given to the terms. If by religion is meant simply the ritualistic practice of certain forms of behavior, then there is no essential connection between morals and religion. And if morality

signifies nothing more than adherence to the accepted mores or codes of behavior established or condoned by society, then again there is no essential relationship. In other words, where moral and religious practices are purely habitual, and have *little reference to values*, the one has no bearing on the other. In such a case a person could be quite "moral" and wholly irreligious, or quite "religious" and wholly immoral.

When, however, a person's religious and moral life is determined and regulated by values, principles, and ideals, as indeed it should be, religion and morality become indissoluble.[2] The nuclear values for religion are the exist-

[1] See J. M. Wolfe, "Relation Between Religious Practices and Moral Practices," *Proceedings Nat. Cath. Educ. Assoc.*, 1930, 459–482.

[2] In her study of 526 Catholic adolescent girls on changes in moral reasoning, Sister Amadeus Dowd found that religion played an important part in determining the application of ethical principles. Sr. M. Amadeus Dowd, "Changes in Moral Reasoning Through the High School Years," *Cath. Univer. Stud. in Psychol. and Psychiat.*, 1948, VII, No. 2. See also the statement by the editors in *The Yearbook of Education, 1951* (London: Evans Brothers, 1951), pp. 19–21.

ence of God, and man's dependent relationship to God. The concept of morality embraces the regulation of conduct according to right principles (moral law) for the sake of being moral. Morality, therefore, signifies two things: a body of laws which must be obeyed, and a capability on the part of moral beings to adhere to these laws. Morality involves necessarily the principle of self-determination. From this analysis we can see that both morality and religion are rooted in a person's system of values.

Morality Is Dependent on Religion. This common basis of morality and religion establishes a connection between the two. If, for example, we ask what it is that makes moral conduct valuable, we find that the sanction for morality lies to a great extent in religious values. Although one can be moral for personal or social reasons, this sanction is likely to fail in crucial situations, human nature being what it is. If, however, one knows that by being moral he contributes something to his own future welfare or destiny, and at the same time activates his relationship to God, then moral values take on added meaning and dynamic power. We can thus see why materialistic and atheistic conceptions are destructive of morality. Obviously, if man is wholly physical or material, conduct must then be a series of physical reactions governed by physical laws, in which morality plays no part. Or, if there is no God, then so-called moral law becomes a system of conventions with no more sanction than the neighborhood prohibition regarding the noisy play of children. It would be amusing, were it not so tragic, to see writers of psychology discussing moral and religious development against a background of dogmatic materialism and agnosticism. Small wonder that representatives of these beliefs have such a difficult time reaching any certain conclusions in the matter.

Religious values make moral conduct reasonable. Religion provides a lawmaker, one whose dictates we are willing to follow, or unwilling to transgress. The certain conviction that moral laws are man-made, that they are conventions adopted for the sake of social convenience, or even to safeguard human rights, must eventually lead to distrust, and in some instances to open rebellion, especially as the doctrine of social equality becomes more widely accepted. The sanction for any law will always depend upon the character and prestige of the lawgiver. Where all men are regarded as equal, it is difficult if not impossible to develop adequate sanctions for man-made laws, and morality soon degenerates into rank subjectivism. The wholesale disregard of certain laws in this country is symptomatic of this fact; international law suffers from the same defect; and the callous attitude of many delinquent youth toward law stems partly from the same source. Morality cannot exist without adequate and proper sanction.

WHAT MORAL AND RELIGIOUS DEVELOPMENT MEANS

The Concept of Moral Development. We have referred many times in this book to the effects that developmental changes have on the morality and religion of young people. Such inferences imply that adolescents are different from children in both a moral and religious sense. In other words, some development has taken place along these lines. To understand what this means exactly we have to determine what is meant by the term "moral development." When it is said, for example, that the organism develops physically this means that there is a progression toward physical maturity, which involves the appearance or maturing of certain physical functions. On the psychological level, there is a corresponding development of intellect, memory, and similar capacities. In each instance there is an identifiable process of maturation of some faculty, capacity, or function. Mere change, therefore, cannot be identified with development, since change of itself might signify decay or degeneration.

Development, then, occurs only when there is some factor to develop: a capacity, trait, or function. Thus, to determine what the concept of moral development signifies, we must discover what factor, if any, is involved. Is there a moral instinct or need that gradually develops throughout childhood and adolescence? Is there a distinct capacity for moral experience and conduct?

Moral Development and Conscience. One factor certainly involved in moral development is *conscience*; and analysis of this concept provides a good starting point since it also sheds light on the problem of religious development.[3] The term "conscience" is etymologically related to *consciousness*, and therefore to knowledge. It may be defined simply as *intellect directed toward the moral aspects of human conduct.* It is not, therefore, a separate capacity or faculty. Thus, when a person is troubled by his conscience, it means that he understands the moral wrong of his act and is experiencing regret or remorse for having committed it. Conscience involves intellect

directly and will indirectly, since remorse is not experienced except when the person is reasonably sure that he could have done otherwise. It is worthy of note that very young children and feeble-minded persons, in whom there is little intelligence and no self-determination, are seldom troubled by conscience.

Moral development, then, really means intellectual and volitional development. It is rooted in understanding and insight, and in the acquisition of moral values, principles, and ideals; it is completed by the full development of the capacity for self-determination. Moral development requires intellectual maturation and, to a lesser extent, emotional and social maturation.[4] Where moral *conduct* is concerned, it presupposes also the development of volitional self-determination, since the capacity to choose is necessary to morality. McCarthy's description of morality is worth noting in this connection. In his view the essence of morality consists in the capacity to seek the good, *not through compulsion but for itself,* a moral nature involving the power to conceive ideals (values would be a better term), and to strive for their realization; and also to conceive of life as possessing meaning and value apart from the satisfaction of any immediate need.[5] Moral development therefore is a complex affair which does not involve a

---

[3] A very useful discussion of the development of conscience will be found in R. R. Sears, *et al.*, *Patterns of Child Rearing* (White Plains, N. Y.: Row, Peterson, 1957), Chap. 10.

[4] This point is emphasized in a symposium on the development of children's moral values published in 1957. See J. Hemming, "Symposium: The Development of Children's Moral Values. I. Some Aspects of Moral Development in a Changing Society," *Brit. J. Educ. Psychol.*, 1957, 27, 77–88. In this symposium it was urged that moral maturity is characterized by the attainment of moral autonomy and by the search for a set of transcultural values which would have universal validity.

[5] R. C. McCarthy, *Training the Adolescent* (Milwaukee: Bruce, 1934).

TABLE 16

CORRELATIONS BETWEEN CONSCIENCE, MORAL VALUES, AND OTHER FACTORS FOR 120 BOYS AND GIRLS IN "PRAIRIE CITY," BETWEEN AGES 10, 13, AND 16*

Age Levels	Conscience and Moral Values	Emotional Independence	Sex Role	Age Mates	Intellectual Skills	Average r
r 10–16	.78	.79	.42	.71	.78	.70
r 10–13	.80	.83	.61	.75	.92	.78
r 13–16	.98	.95	.84	.94	.91	.92

*From R. F. Peck and R. J. Havighurst, *The Psychology of Character Development* (New York: John Wiley and Sons, Inc., in production).

distinct and special faculty but which crystallizes out of many other changes that take place during both childhood and adolescence. Basically it revolves around intellectual development but is related also to the growth of many other factors (see Table 16).

Conscience and Superego. Earlier in this book we discussed at some length the development of the superego and its implications for adolescent behavior (Chap. IV). There is no need to repeat that interpretation at this point. However, we wish to reiterate and to emphasize here that the development of conscience and superego development are not the same thing, and have totally different implications for moral growth.[6] Conscience is essentially a moral factor that helps a person determine the rightness or wrongness of conduct, and thus to regulate it. Superego, on the other hand, is nothing more than the introception of authoritative commands and restrictions which often functions in such a way as to *impair* moral behavior. Conscience may make cowards of us all, but an overdeveloped superego will turn us into neurotics. Because of their distinctive mode of de-

velopment, and their relation to behavior, the concepts of conscience and of superego must be clearly distinguished. Conscience is ruled by the intellect whereas the superego is ruled by the emotions, and thus they have entirely different relations to morality. A healthy conscience is basic to adequate moral development, whereas the superego inhibits moral growth. Thus the moral development of the adolescent should be directed toward a gradual breakdown of the superego and a corresponding evolution of a sound, healthy conscience.[7]

Conscience and Moral Conduct. The development of conscience must also be distinguished from the development of moral conduct, because in determining the nature and extent of moral development during adolescence we may be led astray by the immorality of many adoles-

---

[6] A. A. Schneiders, "Clinical Manifestations of Guilt," paper read at the annual convention of the American Psychological Association, New York, September, 1957.

[7] Good discussions of the role of the superego in relation to morals will be found in A. Wheelis, *The Quest for Identity* (New York: Norton, 1958), Chap. IV, and G. H. J. Pearson, *Adolescence and the Conflict of Generations* (New York: Norton, 1958), Chap. III. On the basis of his data, Peck suggests the existence of two different kinds of strong superego, one of which is consistent with a fairly healthy morality, and the other more closely related to a hostility — guilt complex. See R. F. Peck, R. J. Havighurst, op. cit. See also J. Rickman, "The Development of the Moral Function," in *The Yearbook of Education, 1951* (London: Evans Bros., 1951), pp. 67–86.

cent acts. It is not a question here of whether youth *acts* more morally than the child, which he may not at all; it is rather a question of whether he is *more capable* of appreciating moral values, of developing the right attitudes and sentiments, and of accepting moral responsibilities. His conduct, good or bad, will not necessarily be a reflection of such development or lack of it, since conduct, as we have indicated repeatedly, is not determined by the *existence* of values, principles, and attitudes, but by their *dynamics*.

This fact has been brought out clearly in a number of studies. One investigator, studying the relation between Biblical information and character and conduct among 11,831 students in grades seven to twelve, found no relationship of any consequence between Biblical information and the different phases of conduct studied, including cheating, lying, loyalty, and altruism. He concluded that knowledge is not of itself sufficient to insure proper character growth.[8] There is, in other words, a clear distinction between abstract morality and practical morality, the measure of the latter being determined by the dynamic power of various motivational factors, and by the capacity to employ these various factors in the service of a goal or an ideal. Looked at in this way, we may certainly conclude that there is moral development during adolescence.

The Meaning of Religious Development in Adolescence. This interpretation of moral development applies with equal force to religious development. We cannot argue for the existence of a religious instinct or need, nor for a distinct reli-

gious capacity. However, because of his quasi-spiritual nature, it can be argued that man requires religious experiences and values for complete development. If this fact defines the existence of a need, then a religious need may be said to exist. Certainly it seems that in many instances religion affords the only possibility of a satisfactory adjustment, and adjustment is intrinsically related to the satisfaction of basic needs. Also, the fact that religious beliefs and practices are common to all cultures and societies would seem to argue that religion is founded in the basic nature of man. In speaking of religious development, however, the term desire is more appropriate than need, since true religious development depends upon the process of rational evaluation.[9] Although religious practices may be little more than senseless ritual, religious *values* and *decisions* that become an integral part of human motivation and character are dependent on man's rational nature.

It is more to the point, then, to say that there is a distinct *religious consciousness* than that there is a separate need or capacity. This means simply that, throughout the course of experience, training, and education, there is built up a system of values, attitudes, principles, and sentiments orientated toward religious realities and practices. It is this religious consciousness that undergoes development throughout childhood and adolescence. Taken in this sense it can be readily understood why some persons remain or become completely nonreligious. If we held to the view that there is a distinct religious need, we would be at a loss to explain the absence of reli-

[8] P. R. Hightower, "Biblical Information in Relation to Character and Conduct," *Univer. of Iowa Studies in Character*, 1930, III, No. 2.

[9] In this connection see E. Horan, "Religious Needs of the High School Girl," *Thought*, 1928, III, 375–395.

gious development in some persons. The concept of a religious consciousness that develops as a result of experience, training, education, or practice enables us to understand why, in the absence of such influences, there is no religious development.

MORAL DEVELOPMENT IN ADOLESCENCE

Morality in Children and in Adolescents. Children and adolescents differ in their morality to an important extent. The ordinary child is capable of moral ideals, motives, and conduct; but the adolescent has the capacity to conceive and to actively strive for truly moral goals. For the most part, the child does things or avoids doing them because he is commanded to do so, or because of rewards and punishments. The teen-ager, on the other hand, acts morally in the strictest sense of the term, that is, the requirements of moral conduct are self-imposed, and responses often reflect inner conviction rather than external constraint. In the typical high school boy and girl, concepts of right and duty are being abstracted, idealized, and formulated into regulative principles.[10] At this stage the mind is able to comprehend the meaning of moral principles as distinct from purely arbitrary rules. As concepts of right, obligation, duty, law, and morality are apprehended as objectively valid, there is a transition from external to in-

ternal morality, following which conduct flows from principles rather than from compulsion or impulse.

This transition may not occur until the end of the adolescent period, and will be affected by such factors as home environment, education, and religious instruction.[11] After studying the moral beliefs and principles of youth in a small community, Taba states:

Moral beliefs are formed by accumulating reactions to immediate situations, not by a conscious formulation of a generalized code of conduct. This reflects the fact that the teaching of what is right and wrong is done with reference to isolated, concrete acts of behavior; relatively little effort is made to help young people generalize from these situations or to help them develop a coherent moral philosophy. The development of a personal and rational code, when it does take place, grows out of the accidents of personal make-up and patterns of adjustment. Under these circumstances, maladjustment rather than adjustment tends to be the stimulating force toward reflection, criticism, and personal orientation.[12]

Findings such as these are important to understanding the development of adolescent morality; but they must be interpreted with considerable caution. First

---

[10] As an example of this development, see the "Code of Ethics for Teenagers" prepared by the united efforts of parents and youth in Grand Rapids, Mich., and published by the Diocese of Grand Rapids. This is only one of several youth codes that have been developed in recent years in different areas of the country. See, for example, the Youth Service News for December, 1958, published by the New York State Youth Commission.

[11] See A. Anderson and B. Dvorak, "Differences Between College Students and Their Elders in Standards of Conduct," J. Abnorm. Soc. Psychol., 1928, 23, 286–292; M. C. McGrath, "A Study of the Moral Development of Children," Psychol. Monogr., 1923, 32, No. 144; V. Jones, "A Comparison of Certain Measures of Honesty at Early Adolescence With Honesty in Adulthood — a Follow-up Study," Amer. Psychol., 1946, 1, 261; H. A. Grater, "Behavior Standards Held by University Females and Their Mothers," Personnel and Guid. J., 1960, 38, 369–372.

[12] Reprinted with permission from Hilda Taba, "Moral Beliefs and the Ability to Apply Them in Solving Problems of Conduct," in R. J. Havighurst and Hilda Taba, Adolescent Character and Personality (New York: John Wiley and Sons, Inc., 1949), p. 95.

of all, the quality of morality and moral conduct will vary a great deal from one individual or group to another because of the presence or absence of different influences. Second, there is the important fact that adult morality certainly differs from that of the child; and therefore some transition and development must take place. The period of youth, with its intellectual, social, and emotional developments is the time when this change is most likely to occur. As Taba remarks,

> Most of these young people seem to be eager to respond to moral values. Even those who rebel against their environment seem to cherish an inward ideal of desirable conduct. It seems, therefore, that rebellion and bad conduct are usually rooted in causes other than rejection of moral values themselves.[13]

Of interest in this connection is a study made some years ago on the attitudes of children toward law.[14] A special law attitude test was first devised and administered to 50 lawyers rated among the highest in ability and character. The reactions of these lawyers were taken as a measure with which to compare the reactions of more than 3000 grade and high school children. Intelligence and socioeconomic status were measured in order to determine the influence of these factors on attitudes toward law. The results indicated clearly that children gradually approach adult attitudes toward law as measured by the attitude test. The children in grades four, five, and six were further from adult attitudes than those in high school. Intelligence seemed to be a stronger factor in determining attitude at lower mental age levels, and

children of high school age who ranked in the highest levels of intelligence tended to draw away from the attitudes manifested by adults. Neither sex nor socioeconomic status had any significant influence on the attitudes measured. The outstanding conclusion was that, allowing for developmental changes, youth do not differ greatly from adults in their attitudes toward law.[15]

Moral Inconsistency in Youth. Because the teen-ager's system of moral values and principles is in a state of transition and development, we may expect quite a bit of inconsistency in adolescent morality. Moral turpitude and more exactitude often coexist in the same individual. Activated at times by the most ideal moral aspirations, the adolescent may at other times evidence very low lapses in conduct. There seems to be no ideal too lofty, and also no excess too repugnant. Conscience may thus appear as callous and somewhat depraved in one instance, and as morbidly scrupulous in another. Lack of experience, of an adequate value system, and of a proper perspective, plus an overdose of moral idealism, may give rise to undue sensitiveness concerning truth, honor, courage, and similar moral values. The adolescent may thus take the stand that nothing short of perfection can be countenanced, unaware that moral goals and ideals are realizable, but not often realized.[16]

---

[13] Reprinted with permission from Hilda Taba, ibid., p. 96.

[14] E. G. Lockhard, "The Attitudes of Children Toward Law," *Univer. of Iowa Studies in Char.*, 1930, III, No. 1.

[15] See also P. Crissman, "Temporal Change and Sexual Difference in Moral Judgments," *J. Soc. Psychol.*, 1940, 11, 3–10. In the latter study it was found that the two groups were remarkably similar in their moral views.

[16] On this point see Hilda Taba, op. cit., pp. 88–89; V. Jones, "Character Development in Children — an Objective Approach," in L. Carmichael (ed.), *Manual of Child Psychology*, 2 ed. (New York: Wiley, 1954), pp. 781–832, esp. pp. 822–825. See also A. A. Schneiders, "Religious Symbolism and Neurotic Disorder," *Internat. Rec. Med.* 1958, 171, 745–748.

This *perfectionism* may result in exaggerated self-scrutiny, with continuous analysis of motives, self-diagnosis, and a conviction of sinfulness that lead to intolerable feelings of guilt and inadequacy. This is the condition of *morbid scrupulosity*, or what one writer aptly called *moral hypochondria*. Scrupulosity is one of the most common neurotic disabilities that occur during adolescence, and it can be one of the most serious. The conviction of sinfulness and of chronic guilt that plagues the unhappy adolescent stems directly from an overdeveloped superego rather than from the development of conscience. The scrupulous adolescent has, it is true, a bad conscience, but this is because a too strong superego interfers with the healthy functioning of the moral intellect. The scrupulous person has a deep sense of badness or of evil which expresses itself in chronic, pervasive guilt and a craving for self-punishment. The danger of scrupulosity is not only pointed toward emotional health, but also toward the morality and religion of the unhappy person. Excessive scrupulosity becomes pathological and appears in the adult as an obsessive-compulsive neurosis. When observed in the adolescent, it is no longer a matter for the confessor but for a competent psychotherapist.

Youth and Delinquency. While guilt turned inward tends toward the development of scrupulosity, turned outward it tends toward delinquency; and thus there is always the possibility that the youngster will turn from perfectionism toward behavior that is socially and morally delinquent. In youth are found strong impulses to wrongdoing that are not often encountered in childhood, so that during the very period which witnesses decisions in favor of the noblest ideals,

and when religious experiences and conversions are quite common, the curve of delinquency reaches its apex. In contrast with the wrongs of childhood, crimes are now committed against persons and property, and youth runs the gamut from burglary and joy riding to robbery, murder, and sex attacks. According to the United States Census Bureau, for the year 1937 there were 11,591 males under 21 years of age received from courts in federal and state prisons and reformatories, of which only 39 were under 15 years of age.[17] By contrast, during 1947, there were 117,867 boys and girls under 21 years of age arrested and fingerprinted (roughly 16 per cent of all arrests). In this group the number of girls exceeded the number of arrests in 1941 by 40 per cent. It is estimated that for the year 1954 alone, 58 per cent of all auto thefts, 49 per cent of all burglaries, 15 per cent of all recorded rapes, 5 per cent of homicides, and 6 per cent of all assaults were committed by adolescents under 18 years of age. In addition, over 55 per cent of all crimes involving personal property were perpetuated by adolescents. The period 1948 to 1954 revealed an increase of 58 per cent in the number of juveniles responsible for major crimes.[18]

In addition, about 14,000 adolescents

[17] W. Healy and B. S. Alper, *Criminal Youth and the Borstal System* (New York: Commonwealth Fund, 1941), p. 6.

[18] U. S. Dept. of Health, Education, and Welfare, "Some Facts About Juvenile Delinquency" (Washington, D. C., Govt. Printing Office, 1955). More complete data can be obtained from *Statistical Abstract of the U. S.* (Washington, D. C., Govt. Printing Office, 1958), Sec. 5; M. H. Neumeyer, *Juvenile Delinquency in Modern Society* (New York: Van Nostrand, 1949), Chap. 2; H. A. Bloch and A. Niederhoffer, *The Gang: a Study in Adolescent Behavior* (New York: Philosophical Library, 1958), Chap. IX.

went through New York City's penal system last year. That is about 2000 more than the year before. Their offenses were: burglary, assault, rape, breaking and entering, car theft, armed robbery with intent to kill, and homicide. Over half the VD caseloads in public clinics throughout the country are teen-agers and young adults. In 1957, 14 states and 19 cities noted a rise in VD among the age group 11 to 19. In 1956, 11 states and 18 cities had indicated a rise in VD among teen-agers. One out of every three persons arrested for rape in 18 United States cities reporting sex offenses by age in 1956 was a teen-ager. One out of every 30 arrested for prostitution was a teen-ager. Figures such as these clearly support the notion that the problem of adolescent morality is distinct from that of childhood.

The etiology of adolescent delinquency is extremely complex, involving many factors within the individual himself, and many others that are environmental in origin. For example, sexual delinquencies are in part traceable to the ripening of the sex drive in adolescence; but, as we have already noted, these delinquencies are helped along to an appreciable extent by such influences as reading, movies, and companions. Other needs, like experience, conformity, approval, and recognition, often contribute to adolescent misconduct. But here we must face the paradoxical fact that the vast majority of youth, activated by the same needs, and having much the same experiences, do not become delinquent. This fact reminds us of the part played by the home, the school, the community, and the cultural milieu. Numerous studies have shown that broken homes, poverty, underprivileged conditions, and so on, have a definite bearing on the development of delinquent conduct; but these studies cannot solve the problem of causation either, since many morally upright youth emerge from the worst possible types of environmental setting.

The wrongdoing of youth is not usually motivated by the same factors that give rise to adult criminality, although the distinctions have broken down to some extent in recent years with the increase in gang activities in the large urban centers. In many instances of youthful delinquency there is a comparative absence of sinister motives. Conduct of this kind results not so much from moral perversity as from the craving for excitement, status, acceptance, and recognition, and often from suggestion and imitation. Delinquent behavior is perhaps determined more by peer group influences than by lack of moral principles. Motives essential to truly criminal acts, such as greed, lust, hate, and revenge do not ordinarily characterize adolescent delinquencies. The realization of this difference between youthful delinquency and adult criminality finally led to the establishment of juvenile courts, detention homes, and reformatories where the primary aims are reformation and rehabilitation rather than punishment and retribution. It is now realized that what delinquent youths need are understanding, re-education, and a willingness to help them achieve more adequate social and moral adjustments.[19]

[19] Excellent studies are available for a more thorough study of delinquency. See W. C. Kvaraceus, The Community and the Delinquent (New York: World Book, 1954); H. Bloch and A. Niederhoffer, op. cit.; Ruth Strang, The Adolescent Views Himself (New York: McGraw-Hill, 1957), Chap. 12; P. H. Landis, Adolescence and Youth, 2 ed. (New York: McGraw-Hill, 1952), Chaps. 11 and 12. See also J. J. Brennan, "Root of Our Delinquency," Soc. Order, 1957, 7, 304–310; R. H. Dresher, "Seeds

Moral Knowledge Versus Moral Conduct. The moral development of teenagers is complicated by the fact that ethical knowledge or insight of itself does not possess dynamic properties. Even where there is a clear perception of wrong, knowledge does not always act as a deterrent to immoral behavior. In a comparative study of the attitudes of teachers and prisoners toward the seriousness of criminal acts, Simpson found that their ratings of a series of 45 criminal acts in an order of seriousness correlated .95, a clear indication that the two groups did not differ in their understanding of the moral qualities of the acts rated.[20] Simpson also studied attitudes toward the Ten Commandments of a group of college students, penitentiary inmates, and boys in a state reformatory. The subjects were asked to number the Ten Commandments in the order of importance to themselves. While there were some differences, there was a marked degree of correspondence between attitudes of the college students and the penitentiary inmates, both agreeing that "Thou Shalt Not Kill" was the most important and "Keep Holy the Sabbath" was the least important commandment. Both groups tended to rate those commandments dealing with the duties of man to man higher than those that deal with the duties of man to God, which is the reverse of the Biblical order.[21]

In a similar study, Hill compared the ethical knowledge of delinquent and nondelinquent boys by means of a test dealing with social situations and offenses of various kinds. Subjects included 517 offenders in a state reformatory, and 1168 nondelinquents.[22] The general ranking of the test items did not vary much from group to group, although the delinquents were generally more liberal than the control groups on liquor law violations and sex irregularities. The high school boys especially regarded burglary in a much more serious light than did the delinquents, for whom group loyalty was very significant, "squealing" being second only to kidnaping in heinousness. Actually there were very few items that could be used to distinguish delinquents from nondelinquents, but it must be observed that tests of this kind measure opinion rather than ethical knowledge. Morality and moral conduct can be weakened a great deal by substituting opinion for ethical principles.

This lack of correspondence between moral knowledge and conduct has not been found in all studies. In her study of Paris children, Kinter-Remmlein ob-

---

of Delinquency," *Personnel and Guid. J.*, 1957, 35, 595–598, and H. Bekwin, "Causes of Juvenile Delinquency," *Amer. J. Dis. Child*, 1955, 89, 368–373.

[20] R. M. Simpson, "Attitudes of Teachers and Prisoners Toward the Seriousness of Criminal Acts," *J. Crim. Law & Criminology*, 1935, 25, 77–83.

[21] R. M. Simpson, "Attitudes Toward the Ten Commandments," *J. Soc. Psychol.*, 1933, 4, 223–230. See also T. R. Hightower, *op. cit.*;

N. K. Teeters and J. O. Reinemann, *The Challenge of Delinquency* (New York: Prentice-Hall, 1950), pp. 159–160; Sr. Mary A. Betke, "Defective Moral Reasoning in Delinquency," *Cath. Univer. Stud. in Psychol. & Psychiat.*, 1944, VI, No. 4. In this study of 50 reform school children and matched controls, both groups had an equal amount of ethical knowledge but there was a definite difference in moral reasoning. Among the delinquents emotional reasoning was present to a slightly higher degree and pragmatic reasoning in a significantly higher degree. Although the delinquent children knew right from wrong, they seemed unable to apply this knowledge in moral reasoning so that their decisions were more emotional and pragmatic than those of the controls. See also V. Jones, *op. cit.*, pp. 817–822.

[22] G. E. Hill, "The Ethical Knowledge of Delinquent and Nondelinquent Boys," *J. Soc. Psychol.*, 1935, 6, 107–114.

tained a coefficient of .58 between habits and moral knowledge, a finding that agrees with the Hartshorne and May studies of character, in which it was found that moral knowledge had a deter-ring effect on cheating.[23] However, the facts cited should serve to remind us of certain important principles regarding morality. The first is that conscience is not an all-knowing and infallible judge in matters of morality, which means that youngsters ordinarily must be taught the morality or immorality of specific forms of conduct. Both moral training and moral education are necessary for the development of a code of ethical prin-ciples and ideals.

Second, the existence of moral knowl-edge is no guarantee of moral conduct, so that principles and ideals must be made dynamic. A person must not only know what to do in a given situation, but he must want to do it. The studies we have cited, therefore, cannot lead to any generalizations about moral development in adolescence, both because of the na-ture of moral development, and because the presence or lack of moral insight and conduct in any particular experimental group is no more than a reflection of the background, training, education, and experience of that group. There can be no question that adolescents possess the capacity for adequate moral develop-ment. The fact that parents and educa-tors fail to capitalize on this capacity is no reflection on the morality of youth itself.

The Extent of Moral Development in Youth. A number of studies have been made to determine the nature and ex-tent of moral development during both childhood and adolescence. The results of the well-known Character Education Inquiry, for example, indicated that there was a great deal of specificity in reac-tions to various moral situations, sug-gesting that the responses of children are determined by the exigencies and pecu-liarities of the situation rather than by the generalization of any trait, such as honesty, virtue, or obedience, which is a process involving years of training, ex-perience, and morally correct conduct. Even at the college level insight into the morality of many actions is far below what it should be. Thus Katz and All-port, investigating the attitudes of 3515 undergraduate students on cribbing, found that even 20.2 per cent of those who admitted no cribbing regarded it as unfair but not wrong; and only 9.7 per cent of this same group characterized it as a defect of character, even though cribbing is obviously dishonest. The lack of adequate moral concepts among these students was brought out clearly by the fact that while 52.2 per cent of the non-cribbers regarded cribbing as bad as lying, only 9.7 per cent felt that it showed a defect of character, and 20.2 per cent regarded it as not wrong at all, which by implication means that many of these students must have had peculiar notions regarding the relation between lying and character. Yet the fact that noncribbers differed greatly from cribbers in their attitudes toward cribbing indicates that the extent of cribbing is to some degree conditioned by the student's ideals. Thus, those students who cheat were found for the most part to regard the practice as neither wrong nor unusual.[24]

---

[23] M. Kinter-Remmlein, "Study of a Group of Paris Children: Their Ideas of Right and Wrong; Their Reactions in Situations Involving Cooperation and Self-Sacrifice," J. Soc. Psychol., 1935, 6, 91–106.

---

[24] D. Katz and F. H. Allport, Students' Atti-tudes (New York: Craftman Press, 1931). See also the recent study by J. F. Morris, "Sympo-

This lack of insight into the wrongness of behavior carries over into actions of a more delinquent and criminal nature. One study investigated the insight of adolescents into a criminal act of such a type that the youngsters had to decide for themselves whether the act was right or wrong. The average age of the subjects was 17. The results indicated a surprising lack of ability to interpret the morality and criminality of the act.[25] Since other studies also indicate the failure of youth to generalize regarding moral principles and ideals, it may be that in many instances of delinquent conduct there is little or no knowledge of having committed a wrong. Taba reports such findings in a study of adolescents by the University of Chicago Committee on Human Development, and Fleege obtained somewhat similar results when he studied adolescent attitudes toward petting and necking.[26] All such findings should remind us that the extent of moral development during adolescence is limited by the nature of adolescence itself. We must remember that adolescents are children striving to become adults, and that in their efforts to attain maturity, whether at the intellectual,

moral, or social level, there will be many failures, many errors, and much stumbling.[27] Most adults leave a great deal to be desired on the moral plane; realizing this, we should be very patient with young people.

RELIGIOUS DEVELOPMENT IN ADOLESCENCE

Adolescents Seek a Philosophy of Life. American youth develop within a culture that is fundamentally religious in structure, and for this reason as well as others adolescence brings with it a consciousness of what is expected of a person religiously as well as socially, morally, and vocationally. Just as teen-agers develop interests in and attitudes toward recreational activities, schooling, or social practices, they gradually come to the view that some sort of religious experience or profession is necessary and correct. Moreover, the uncertainties, conflicts, and anxieties of youth stimulate a growing need for a more satisfactory philosophy of life, a set of principles and ideals that will give meaning to their experiences and strivings, in terms of which they may effectively order their existence. It is easy, therefore, to understand why many adolescents turn to the ideals and practices of religion for a more satisfactory solution to their problems.

---

sium: the Development of Moral Values in Children: II. The Development of Adolescent Value-judgments," *Brit. J. Educ. Psychol.*, 1958, 28, 1–14. In this study it was found that there are marked discrepancies between what should be done and what would be done but that with increasing age there is change in the direction of greater autonomy and equity in moral judgments.

[25] Cited by Louella Cole, *Psychology of Adolescence* (New York: Rinehart, 1936), pp. 163–164.

[26] See R. J. Havighurst and Hilda Taba, *Adolescent Character and Personality* (New York: Wiley, 1949), Chap. 8, and U. H. Fleege, *Self-Revelation of the Adolescent Boy* (Milwaukee: Bruce, 1945), pp. 286–296. See also P. H. Landis, *op. cit.*, Chap. 8, and Sr. M. Amadeus Dowd, *op. cit.*

---

[27] For additional information on the moral development of children and youth, see M. C. McGrath, "A Study of the Moral Development of Children," *Psychol. Monogr.*, 1923, 32, 144; G. S. Slavens and A. P. Brogan, "Moral Judgments of High School Students," *Inter. J. Ethics*, 1928, 38, 57–69; J. K. Johnson and K. Davis, "Attempts to Discover Changes in Moral Attitudes of High School Students," *Internat. J. Ethics*, 1934, 44, 244–251; Caroline B. Zachry, *Emotion and Conduct in Adolescence* (New York: Appleton-Century-Crofts, 1940), Chaps. 5 and 6.

During adolescence there may be striking religious changes such as conversion, but even the religious life of the average adolescent is likely to be different from what it was as a child. Part of this change is due to the nature of religion itself which affects many different aspects of personality, if not always in the same way or to the same degree. With many persons religion is a matter of sentiment or feeling; with others it is more a matter of intellectual conviction. Where attitudes play the dominant role, it may be that neither intellect nor emotion is particularly prominent. These attitudes, influenced by education and experience, may lead to a more intense need for religious experience, or conversely to rebellion against the ideas and practices of religion. Thus some teen-agers are impatient to enter the religious life as a priest or nun, whereas others go through the tragic experience of religious disintegration through which cherished values and ideals become entirely meaningless.

In the child, imagination is likely to dominate religious consciousness, since it is natural for the child to picture to himself the persons and events that constitute the framework of his religious life. At this stage of development, intellect and emotion are not very conspicuous. In youth, on the other hand, religion assumes a more precise emotional cast in which feelings, moods, and sentiments play a dominant role. This change occurs because of the affective development of the adolescent period, and because of a more pronounced tendency to interpret events in terms of their emotional significance. We must keep in mind, however, that because of the concomitant intellectual development that takes place, the adolescent is more capable than the child of understanding religious tenets and practices, so that the imaginal qualities of the simpler religious life of the child tend to be displaced by insight and rational interpretation. Religious belief, therefore, should become progressively a matter of conviction instead of authority alone; and the emotional concomitants of religious experiences and activities should be grounded in understanding.

This fact is of particular importance because of the tendency of many youngsters to question religious dogma. Religious belief should always be grounded in reason and guided by it. When young Bill or Mary demand rational explanations for the faith they are asked to embrace, they should not be turned away with short answers or authoritative mumbo jumbo. Any doubts or difficulties should be met squarely and frankly, and cleared up if possible by reasoned exposition. A faith that rests exclusively on either authority or emotion, without the conviction that evidence and reason impart, will invariably lead to difficulties, or to actual loss of religion. The goal of religious instruction should be a clear grasp of religious concepts and principles, and of their relation to the practices of religion. Results will vary to some extent with the nature of the religion to which the individual is exposed. If beliefs and practices are wholly emotional in character, then the gradual shift to intellectual interpretations is impossible, and the religious structure will retain a primitive and childish cast. Most Christian religions, however, have a generous admixture of intellectual elements, of reasoned beliefs and rational practices, so that for the majority of Christian youth there is likely to occur a shift from imaginal representation to intellectual conviction.

Religious Adjustments in Adolescence.
The manner in which adolescents react to religion will vary with the character of their religion, with the experiences, conflicts, and difficulties they encounter, and with their background of religious experience, personal contacts, and education. Thus, many Catholic youth survive the trials of adolescence without any conscious realization that their religious values were at any time threatened, or even involved in any way. There is no definite, identifiable, and separate religious experience that they can recall, no such phenomenon as conversion, and no serious doubts, scruples, or skepticism regarding religious beliefs. Their religious adjustment, if such it can be called, is gradual; and their religious life usually is an unbroken continuum, extending from the early years of childhood into maturity. The same may be true of many Protestant youth, but it is less likely because for many of them religion, at the adolescent level especially, is not an integral part of education and life; also, they are subjected much more than Catholic youth to modes of education that lead to doubt and skepticism.[28] It is partly for this reason that what Conklin calls the crisis type of conversion is found more often among Protestant than among Catholic youth. This phenomenon is to be expected, since often the only

TABLE 17

EXTENT OF TEEN-AGERS' RELIGIOUS PROBLEMS, ACCORDING TO SEX, AGE, AND DENOMINATION*

	Confused in My Religious Beliefs	Bothered by Thoughts of Heaven and Hell	Conflict Between the Bible and My School Subjects	Not Living Up to My Religion	Searching for Something to Believe in	Standards of "Right" and "Wrong"
	%	%	%	%	%	%
Total	10	12	7	22	5	19
Boys	9	11	6	22	5	16
Girls	10	14	7	21	6	21
Grade 9	8	15	6	19	4	18
Grade 10	12	11	9	23	6	18
Grade 11	10	13	6	22	6	22
Grade 12	9	10	5	23	6	17
Protestant	10	12	8	23	6	19
Catholic	7	14	4	19	4	14
Jewish	15	9	3	18	6	24
None	10	11	8	15	7	19

*Adapted from H. H. Remmers and D. H. Radler, *The American Teenager*, © 1957, p. 166, used by special permission of the publisher, The Bobbs-Merrill Co., Inc.

[28] Contrary to what one might expect from this period of confusion and stress many studies indicate that adolescents experience few religious problems. Table 17 is a typical instance of results obtained on a study of teen-ager's religious beliefs. Similar results are presented by Hollingshead, Finn, and others. See A. B. Hollingshead, *Elmtown's Youth* (New York: Wiley, 1949), Chap. 10; J. P. Finn, *A Study of the Problems of Certain Catholic High School Boys as Told by Themselves and Their Teachers* (Washington, D. C.: Catholic University of America Press, 1950), Chap. V.

alternative to a complete loss of religion is a valid and climactic return to religion through the medium of conversion.

Contrasted with this phenomenon is the decision type of religious conversion, which Conklin regards as customary and approved in the Roman Catholic, Anglican, and Lutheran communions. In this form of conversion the experience is much less intense and disturbing emotionally. It is essentially a form of religious adjustment closely resembling the gradual type mentioned earlier, but involving more or less a new orientation to life, a sense of well-being, reduction of conflict, and an integration of desires, impulses, and needs. It is a rebirth or revitalizing of religious consciousness through a realization of the true worth of religious values, their essentially rational character, and an awareness that religion offers a way of life that leads to a solution of many problems and conflicts. It is noteworthy that this type of conversion and the more gradual form of religious adjustment are replacing the crisis type in modern youth. Where once it was thought that religious conversion of the crisis type was an integral phase of adolescent development, it is now realized that religious development is like any other in that it is conditioned by cultural and environmental factors.

The Pattern of Religious Development in Adolescents. Many studies have been made to determine the pattern of religious development during adolescence. Do youth become more religious or more irreligious, more radical or more conservative, more skeptical or more credulous, as they approach adulthood? Actually, the results are so contradictory, and so much influenced by religious denomination, background, and type of educational experience, that any generalization would be extremely hazardous. Thus Carlson, studying the attitudes of under-

TABLE 18

CHANGES IN SPECIFIC RELIGIOUS BELIEFS DURING ADOLESCENCE*

Statement	"Believe" Per Cent			"Not Believe" Per Cent			"Wonder About" Per Cent		
	12 years	15 years	18 years	12 years	15 years	18 years	12 years	15 years	18 years
God is a strange power working for good, rather than a person	46	49	57	31	33	21	20	14	15
God is someone who watches you to see that you behave yourself and who punishes you if you are not good	70	49	33	18	37	48	11	13	18
I know there is a God	94	80	79	3	5	2	2	14	16
Catholics, Jews, and Protestants are equally good	67	79	86	9	9	7	24	11	7
There is a heaven	82	78	74	4	5	5	13	16	20
Only good people go to heaven	72	45	33	15	27	32	13	27	34
Hell is a place where you are punished for your sins on earth	70	49	35	16	21	30	13	27	34
Heaven is here on earth	12	13	14	69	57	52	18	28	32
People who go to church are better than people who do not go to church	46	26	15	37	53	74	17	21	11
Young people should belong to the same church as their parents	77	56	43	13	33	46	10	11	11
The main reason for going to church is to worship God	88	80	79	6	12	15	4	7	6
It is not necessary to go to church to be a Christian	42	62	67	38	23	24	18	15	8
Only our soul lives after death	72	63	61	9	11	6	18	25	31
Good people say prayers regularly	78	57	47	9	29	26	13	13	27
Prayers are answered	76	69	65	3	5	8	21	25	27
Prayers are a source of help in times of trouble	74	80	83	11	8	7	15	10	9
Prayers are to make up for something that you have done that is wrong	47	24	21	35	58	69	18	17	9
Every word in the Bible is true	79	51	34	6	16	23	15	31	43
It is sinful to doubt the Bible	62	42	27	18	31	44	20	26	28

*From R. G. Kuhlen and M. Arnold, "Age Differences in Religious Beliefs and Problems During Adolescence," J. Genet. Psychol., 1944, 65, 293.

graduate students, found that the attitude toward God was in every instance conditioned by the religious affiliation of the student, Catholic students believing most strongly in the reality of God, followed in order by Protestants and Jews.[29] The author concludes that religious affiliation is a more important factor than either sex or school training in determining attitudes on such matters as prohibition, birth control, communism, and the reality of God. He also found, as have others, that liberalism tended to be pervasive in character (see Table 18).

The bearing of liberalism on religious development has been brought out in other studies. Harris, Remmers, and Ellison, studying the relation between liberal and conservative attitudes in college students, found that the liberals tended to be less religious, especially among male students; that loss of religious faith was definitely associated with liberalism, especially in women; that those students who never attend church were much more liberal in their attitudes than those who attend regularly; and that certain types of education are important in the development of liberalism.[30] These findings suggest that the pattern of religious development is to a large extent a reflection of the educational and other experiences of youth, on the basis of which certain attitudes are formed that, in turn, condition religious beliefs.

Jones, investigating the opinions of college freshmen, upper classmen, and law students on various questions, concluded that college training had little effect on the opinions of college students. He found that conservative or reactionary opinions are influenced far more by home training and religious disposition than by the content of college courses. However, the seniors were far more liberal than freshmen in certain religious viewpoints, being skeptical on the doctrine of life after death, and tending to accept the theory of evolution, whereas freshmen were for the most part inclined to accept the first doctrine and to oppose evolution. It should be noted that the proportion of Protestant, Catholic, and Jewish students remained about the same for the two groups.[31]

Are Teen-Agers Irreligious? Many people believe that the American teen-ager is often irreligious.[32] But the empirical data do not support this conclusion. Dudycha, studying the religious beliefs of college freshmen of varying denominations, found that they firmly believe or are inclined to believe the greater part of 25 fundamental religious propositions. Thus the proposition that "The Ten Commandments should be obeyed" ranked first and was believed by 98 per

[29] H. B. Carlson, "Attitudes of Undergraduate Students," *J. Soc. Psychol.*, 1934, 5, 202–213. See also H. H. Remmers and D. H. Radler, op. cit., p. 155. P. H. Landis, op. cit., Chap. 10; Sister Mary P. Hillery, "The Religious Life of Adolescent Girls," *Cath. Univer. Center for Research in Child Development*, 1937, II, No. 1.

[30] A. J. Harris, H. H. Remmers, and C. C. Ellison, "The Relation Between Liberal and Conservative Attitudes in College Students and Other Factors," *J. Soc. Psychol.*, 1932, 3, 320–336.

[31] E. S. Jones, "The Opinions of College Students," *J. Appl. Psychol.*, 1926, 10, 427–436. See also M. C. Van Tuyle, "Patterns of Religious Thinking Among 835 College Students," *Psych. Bull.*, 1942, 39, 482–483; G. W. Allport, J. M. Gillespie, and Jacqueline Young, "The Religion of the Post-war College Student," *J. Psychol.*, 1948, 25, 3–33. In this study too it was found that a religious orientation was favored by a substantial majority of students questioned. See also E. D. Eddy, *The College Influence on Student Character* (Washington, D. C.: Amer. Coun. on Educ., 1959), Chap. 6.

[32] In this connection see Ruth Strang, "Religious Activities of Adolescent Girls," *Relig. Educ.*, 1929, 24, 313–321.

cent of the group. Belief in the existence of God was held by 96 per cent, the divinity of Christ by 93 per cent, and so on. Dudycha did find that the existence of the devil, belief in hell, immortality, present-day miracles, and the like, ranked much lower on a percentage basis, but there was not a single proposition more disbelieved than believed.[33]

In a later and more extensive study by the same investigator, 852 freshmen at six colleges and universities were presented with a similar list of 25 religious propositions and concepts at the very beginning of the school year, and 305 seniors at seven colleges were given the same list at the end of the fourth year. Five answers could be indicated: (A) implicitly believe; (B) inclined to believe, but doubt; (C) noncommittal, do not know; (D) inclined to disbelieve and doubt; (E) absolutely disbelieve. Statements included such items as "the Ten Commandments should be obeyed," "God exists," "divinity of Christ," "the soul exists," "virgin birth of Christ," and "Sunday is a holyday." The following table indicates the relative amounts of belief and disbelief among members of several denominations. Of the entire group, 92 per cent implicitly believed that the Ten Commandments should be obeyed, 88 per cent in the existence of God, 81 per cent in the existence of the soul, 82 per cent in the divinity of Christ, 75 per cent in the power of prayer, 72 per cent in the virgin birth, 69 per cent in the proposition that the Bible is the word of God, 56 per cent in immortality, 53 per cent in the resurrection of the body, 43 per cent in the existence of angels, 39 per cent in the

[33] G. J. Dudycha, "The Religious Beliefs of College Freshmen," *School and Soc.*, 1930, *31*, 206–208.

TABLE 19

PER CENT OF PROPOSITIONS BELIEVED BY FRESHMEN*

Denomination	No. of cases	A	B	C	D	E
All	852	65	13	11	04	07
United Presbyterian	72	79	11	06	02	02
Lutheran	76	78	12	05	02	03
Roman Catholic	53	79	08	08	02	03
Baptist	54	69	12	10	04	05
Presbyterian	155	67	13	11	03	06
Methodist	207	62	16	12	04	06

*From G. J. Dudycha, "The Religious Beliefs of College Students," *J. Appl. Psychol.*, 1933, *17*, 585–603. See also H. H. Remmers, M. S. Myers, and E. M. Bennett, "Some Personality Aspects and Religious Values of High School Youth," *Purdue Opin. Panel*, 1951, *10*. These findings are even more striking than those of the earlier study.

existence of the devil, and 30 per cent in present-day miracles. Again, even with this much larger group, it was found that college freshmen firmly believe, or are at least inclined to believe, the greater per cent of the 25 propositions. There were, needless to say, considerable denominational variations, but there were also some very noticeable agreements among the different denominations.

Comparing these results with those obtained from the seniors, Dudycha found a consistent drop in per cent of those believing the various propositions, but many of the statements were still believed by substantial numbers. Thus, 83 per cent of the seniors implicitly believed in the existence of God, 76 per cent in the statement concerning the commandments, 73 per cent in the divinity of Christ, 69 per cent in the existence of the soul, 62 per cent in the power of prayer, 58 per cent in immortality, 57 per cent in the virgin birth, 35 per cent in the resurrection of the body, 23 per cent in hell, 20 per cent in the devil, and 19 per cent in miracles. The entire group believed 64 per cent of the 25 propositions, and only 21 per cent were disbelieved. Seniors implicitly believed or were inclined to believe more than three times as many of the propositions as they disbelieved. Although the method of studying groups at different age levels leaves much to be desired, it may be safely assumed on the basis of these data that there are some definite losses during the college years in religious beliefs. The developmental implications of these data are clear.

Other studies dealing with changes in the content of religious beliefs lead to similar conclusions. A significant finding in some of these studies is that the trend toward belief in an impersonal God reverses itself at higher educational levels, as do other negative trends. Analysis of the changes in the concept of God indicate three trends: (1) a gradual development away from childhood beliefs; (2) an entire reconstruction following a period of doubt or disbelief; and (3) a process of reconstruction still going on in early adulthood. Such findings are directly in line with the earlier observation that the decision and gradual type of religious adjustment tend to predominate over the crisis type of conversion. As causes of these changes, and of doubts experienced, educational influences are mentioned in the majority of instances. This is particularly true where an interest in science dominates a student's thinking, this interest being negatively related to religious belief.

DETERMINANTS OF MORAL AND RELIGIOUS DEVELOPMENT

Influence of Motives and Feelings. There are few phases of development that do not bear in some way on the growth of conscience and a religious con-

sciousness during adolescence. For this reason our study of developmental changes in emotions, attitudes, values, and ideals constituted a natural prelude to a study of the religious and moral life of youth. It would be naïve to suppose that every motivational tendency has some bearing on this aspect of teen-age growth. It is certainly true that there is a close connection between dynamic factors and the gradual emergence of a moral and religious self. As Rennie and Woodward point out,

> In religious education, even more than in public secular education, there is need for attention to variations in emotional development. Many an adult has come near to developing a neurosis because as a child he was expected to behave like a grownup and felt secretly guilty when he failed to meet the standards of the adult world. Ethical standards should be presented as ultimate goals toward which one moves in progressive steps and with the hope of realizing them wholly in due time. It should be made clear to the child that improvement rather than complete achievement is the immediate aim. Honest admissions of failure on the part of instructors and other adults help the child to recognize that "to err is human" and relieve his sense of guilt, even if he has already experienced one.[34]

Influence of Intellectual Growth. Intellectual growth is one of the most important determinants of religious and moral growth, primarily because of the

[34] T. A. C. Rennie and L. E. Woodward, *Mental Health in Modern Society* (New York: Commonwealth Fund and Harvard University Fund, 1948), p. 370. See also R. J. Havighurst and Hilda Taba, op. cit., "Motivational Sources of Moral Values," pp. 92–95; R. F. Peck, "The Psychology of Moral Character," unpublished doctoral dissertation, University of Chicago, 1951; V. Jones, "Character Development in Children — an Objective Approach," in L. Carmichael (ed.), *Manual of Child Psychology*, 2 ed. (New York: Wiley, 1954), pp. 781–832, especially pp. 812–817.

influence of intellect on the formation of values, ideals, and principles. The maturing of these motives during adolescence contributes a great deal to the formation and integration of character. This maturation in turn influences the development of moral and religious characteristics and the formation of truly religious and moral values, ideals, and principles which contribute significantly to the development of other important aspects of personality. This is exactly what *integral* development means — the interrelation, interdependence, and mutual influence of *all* aspects of the human personality and character.

But it is impossible to say which of these developments comes first; whether for example, character is formed in the service of religious values, or whether it enforces their development. All such developments are co-ordinate and integral, the one contributing to and yet dependent on the other. In the area of moral and religious development, intellect certainly plays a leading role; yet even here we must guard against unwarranted generalizations. A number of studies have shown that the bare fact of intellectual growth is not enough to guarantee moral conduct and character. Results consistently indicate that there is no necessary correlation between intelligence and moral judgment.[35] Sex differences sometimes emerge but age or maturity does not seem to be a significant factor in determining moral judgment. Commenting on her own data, Taba says,

It is usually assumed that intelligence has a good deal to do with the adequacy and maturity of moral beliefs. In particular, intelligence might be expected to influence the ability to intellectualize moral problems. But this did not prove to be the case. The relation between the scores on Student Beliefs and the Binet IQ was quite low.[36]

The relation between intelligence and moral-religious development was brought out in another way by Howells who made a comparative study of students who accept as against those who reject religious authority.[37] Howells chose for intensive study those students who were most radical and those who were most conservative in their attitudes and found that these groups were clearly distinguishable as regards intellectual and cognitive characteristics. In all tests of intellectual ability, including high school content, university grades, intelligence tests, and other measures, the typical conservative always made a poor score. As a group the conservatives were also more suggestible and showed less perseverance than the radicals. This group was also inclined toward pessimism and feelings of inferiority, and was more likely to have experienced conversion or a sense of the divine presence. In general, therefore, religious attitudes and development seem to be related to intellectual level.

Environmental and Cultural Influences. Moral and religious development is significantly influenced by several external factors. The culture in which one lives, religious attitudes and practices in the home, personal experiences and activities, attitudes of church members and

---

[35] In their intensive study, Havighurst and Taba found that intelligence seemed indifferently related to the formation of moral beliefs, even though good moral character is dependent on intellectual understanding of moral principles and a conviction that these principles are worth sacrifice. R. J. Havighurst and Hilda Taba, *op. cit.*, pp. 91–92.

[36] Reprinted with permission from R. J. Havighurst and Hilda Taba, *ibid.*, p. 91.

[37] T. H. Howells, "A Comparative Study of Those Who Accept as Against Those Who Reject Religious Authority, *Univer. of Iowa Studies in Character*, 1928, II, No. 2.

authorities, moral ideals and practices of parents, teachers, and companions, and of course training and education will all exert some influence on the teen-ager's moral and religious development.[38] These factors are important because they enforce the development of attitudes, values, principles, ideals, and habits. For example, in the Maryland survey it was found that 85 per cent of youth from Catholic homes attended Church once a week regularly, whereas only 38 per cent of Protestants and 10 per cent of Jewish youth did so. Also, four fifths of youths who had some church affiliation had adopted the faith of both of their parents. Even locality of residence, sex, and marital status were found to influence religious practices.[39]

The influence of these extrinsic factors, on moral development especially, is highlighted in the many studies of the causes of delinquency. Parental attitudes, family strife, desertion, death, severe and punitive discipline, lax moral principles in the home, and underprivileged conditions have all been found to contribute to moral delinquency.[40] In the May and Hartshorne studies of character formation it was found that there is a close relationship between level of home environment and per cent of cheating done on both school tests and home tests.

That general cultural factors also affect religious development has been demonstrated empirically. In an earlier study of the ideas of right and wrong in a group of Paris children it was found that, on the moral knowledge test, 90 per cent of these children reach or excel the American average as determined in the Character Education Inquiry. There was also a higher correlation between moral knowledge and stability of personality for the French group — results that suggest at least the influence of cultural determinants.[41] Cultural influences emerge also in studies of the differences between college students and their elders in standards of conduct. In one study it was found that both parents and grandparents tended to solve problems on the basis of a right and wrong standard whereas the college youth preferred to base decisions on a standard of prudence or intelligent judgment first, the standard of right and wrong being a third choice.

---

[38] This relationship has been brought out in numerous studies. See, for example, R. J. Havighurst and Hilda Taba, op. cit., especially Chap. 4, "Community Factors in Relation to Character Formation." These investigators trace the influence of the adolescent culture, moral quality of the home life, the influence of different organizations, etc. The influence of culture change is brought out clearly in a recent article by J. Hemming, "Symposium: the Development of Children's Moral Values, I. Some Aspects of Moral Development in a Changing Society," Brit. J. Educ. Psychol., 1957, 27, 77–88. Remmers and Radler also studied the influence of culture changes by comparing student rankings of "worst practices" in 1919 and in 1954. They found that while killing, stealing, sexual misbehavior, and drinking were ranked near the top in both periods, gambling which was ranked seventh in 1919 did not appear on the list in 1954. Nor did dancing, extravagance, or being selfish. Characteristically, reckless driving, and using or selling narcotics did appear in 1954 whereas they were not included in the 1919 list, H. H. Remmers and D. H. Radler, op. cit., p. 162. See also R. F. Peck and R. J. Havighurst, Psychology of Character Development (New York: Wiley, in production).

[39] H. M. Bell, Youth Tell Their Story (Washington, D. C.: Amer. Coun. on Educ., 1938), pp. 196–198. For further evidence, see U. H. Fleege, op. cit., pp. 146–165.

[40] See the excellent discussion of "Sources of Conscience," in R. R. Sears, et al., Patterns of Child Rearing (White Plains, N. Y.: Row, Peterson, 1957), pp. 381–393. These investigators emphasize the role of identification in moral development.

[41] M. Kinter-Remmlein, op. cit.

These results indicate cultural shift.[42]

On the cultural side also, education looms large in the growth of a moral and religious consciousness, as many studies show. Searles made a study of the God experiences of a number of college students and found that educational influences were listed by 52 per cent of the group as being the first occasion of religious doubt, whereas 27 per cent of the students mentioned educational influences as being the cause for changes in their idea of God. Among these influences, science and philosophy were mentioned most often as functioning to bring about a more satisfactory conception of God.[43] This relationship between education and moral-religious development warrants a great deal of emphasis, because education is one of the most pervasive influences that youth encounters. While much of education contributes to healthy development, we must keep in mind that the religious and moral stability of far too many youth has been undermined by pernicious educational preachings.

The Influence of Religious Affiliation.

All these data and conclusions serve to emphasize the important fact that the meaning of religious and moral development must be carefully interpreted. There is little doubt that religious skepticism and moral liberalism increase with age. But, as we have seen already, what Johnny or Jane adhere to in the way of religious convictions is importantly determined, not by an intrinsic developmental pattern, but by the character of early religious training and instruction, and by the nature of the religious values acquired. Obviously, if a teenager is subjected to indoctrination that undermines religious convictions, or if the viewpoint of teachers and parents is naturalistic, agnostic, or materialistic, religious beliefs will certainly be shaken. Even more important is the fact that if the religious experiences of the youngster are not satisfying, then certainly religious development will take an unfavorable turn. Religious values and experiences have more to do with the pattern of religious development than does the kind of religious training.

In the studies cited, Catholic students almost always emerge with a firmer hold on religion than do other students. This fact can be explained by the kind of training they receive; but more important is the fact that religion plays an integral part in their lives. Religious values and practices are stressed in home, in grade school, in high school and in college; countless opportunities are afforded for wholesome religious experiences; and religious activities are as much a part of the daily routine as are play and amusement. Contrast this situation with the results obtained by Katz and Allport.[44] Of those students with no church affilia-

[42] Alice Anderson and Beatrice Dvorak, "Differences Between College Students and Their Elders in Standards of Conduct," *J. Abnorm. Soc. Psychol.*, 1928, 23, 286–292. In this connection see the article by James H. Winchester "M-bomb — World's Silent Destroyer!" in the *New York Mirror Magazine* for June 14, 1959. This article is based upon a little known UN report regarding the increase in sexual promiscuity and venereal disease around the world, particularly among teen-agers. The report emphasizes that the world has relaxed its morals and is undergoing a vast social upheaval in its sexual habits.

[43] H. L. Searles, "An Empirical Inquiry Into the God Experience of 140 College Students," *Relig. Educ.*, 1926, 21, 334–341. See also J. R. Seeley, "Education and Morals," in *The Yearbook of Education, 1951* (London: Evans Bros., 1951), pp. 386–395.

[44] D. Katz and F. H. Allport, *op. cit.*

tion, 40 per cent regarded God as an impersonal force, and 30 per cent were agnostic in their viewpoint; only 22 per cent conceived God as a personal Being, and 8 per cent adopted a mechanistic viewpoint. Generalizations on the basis of such data, therefore, are totally useless when the factor of religious affiliation is left out of account. And unfortunately, in many of the studies of moral and religious beliefs, selection of subjects has been quite inadequate. Religious affiliation is the most important single determinant of religious development.

SIGNIFICANCE OF MORAL AND RELIGIOUS DEVELOPMENT

Influence on Character Growth.   That there is a close relationship between moral and religious development and the emergence of character during adolescence is known to every observer. A truly moral person, who acts on principle rather than on impulse, habit, or expediency, is clearly a person of character. This is the very nature of character, namely, the willingness and the capacity to inhibit undesirable or destructive impulses and to act instead *according to regulative principles.* The connection between morality and character, therefore, is fundamental; without the development of the one the other cannot exist. Religious development also contributes its share to the growth of character by reinforcing and making more meaningful the moral principles and ideals that are gradually formed during childhood and adolescence, and which eventually are translated into acceptable conduct (see Chapter XVI).

Moral-Religious Development and Adjustment.   That the development of mo-

rality, religion, and character is important to the process of adjustment and to mental health is equally obvious. Maladjustment is often a sign of irreducible conflict; and it goes without saying that a person of strong character, actuated by dynamic principles and ideals, will have far less difficulty in the reduction of conflicts than the person of weak character. Both morality and religion provide the values in terms of which conflicts can be resolved, and a higher level of integration secured. In this way both aspects of development contribute not only to character formation, but to the total development of personality as well, since the surest kind of personality growth and adjustment is continuous integration.

Religious experiences and practices also contribute a great deal to the *general* development of personality. In respect to social development, for example, the emphasis laid upon religious tenets like the Ten Commandments, tends to promote thoughtfulness for the welfare of others, and to quicken the awareness of social obligations and responsibilities. The religious injunctions regarding stealing, adultery, love of one's neighbor, and the like have serious implications for social conduct and adjustment. Religious values and ideals give meaning to life and provide the individual with a satisfactory basis for working toward a philosophy of life in terms of which experiences and events can be more adequately measured or evaluated. These facts are particularly significant for the adolescent period because young people so often find themselves in need of a scale of values that will help them overcome their own inconsistencies and uncertainties. The love of God, and the feelings of inner peace and contentment provided by true religious experiences, can be of great help to the uncertain and unstable adolescent.

Religion is sometimes the only path to adjustment for the troubled person. Many psychologists and psychiatrists have noted this fact; and regardless of their own private attitudes regarding religion, they often find it a necessary instrument for restoring mental health and adjustment. Religious development, therefore, is very important to youth. It is during this period more than any other that fundamental values, enriching emotional experiences, and the right attitudes toward self, society, and God are of the greatest significance. Any system of education, therefore, that impedes such development through faulty instruction or the teaching of error is playing traitor to its basic purposes, which is the complete and wholesome development of both personality and character.

We may note also that the more that religious experiences and values contribute to the development of a life philosophy, to the solving of conflicts, and to the general processes of adjustment and integration, the less desertion of religion will there occur. Whatever a person's religious viewpoint, it is clear that unless such experiences and values prove worthwhile and satisfying, and unless they contribute materially to adjustment and happiness, they will be neither sought nor cherished. This is true of any system of values, and of any system of religious beliefs. The desertion of religion by large groups of people is in part a reflection of its failure to stand the test of worth. It certainly does not signify a natural developmental shift, even though there is a noticeable tendency for religion to become less of a sentimental and emotional affair, and more of an intellectual matter in the transition from childhood to maturity.

SELECTED READINGS

Bernard, H. W., *Adolescent Development in American Culture* (New York: World Book, 1957), Chap. 12.

Fleege, U. H., *Self-Revelation of the Adolescent Boy* (Milwaukee: Bruce, 1945), Chaps. 10, 15.

Fullam, R. B. (ed.), *The Popes on Youth* (New York: America Press, 1955).

Havighurst, R. J., and Taba, Hilda, *Adolescent Character and Personality* (New York: Wiley, 1949), Chaps. 8, 23.

Hollingshead, A. B., *Elmtown's Youth* (New York: Wiley, 1949), Chap. 10.

Landis, P. H., *Adolescence and Youth*, 2 ed. (New York: McGraw-Hill, 1952), Chaps. 8–12.

Neumeyer, M. H., *Juvenile Delinquency in Modern Society* (New York: Van Nostrand, 1949), Chap. II.

Peck, R. F., "A Psychology of Moral Character," unpublished doctoral dissertation, University of Chicago, 1951.

Piaget, J., *Moral Judgment of the Child* (New York: Harcourt, 1932).

Strang, Ruth, *The Adolescent Views Himself* (New York: McGraw-Hill, 1952), Chap. 12.

Zachry, Caroline B., *Emotion and Conduct in Adolescence* (New York: Appleton-Century-Crofts, 1940), Chaps. 5 and 6.

Zubek, J. T., and Solberg, Patricia A., *Human Development* (New York: McGraw-Hill, 1954), Chap. 14.

CHAPTER XVI

THE EMERGENCE OF CHARACTER

Discipline and values, ideals and principles, morality and religion lay the groundwork for that most precious of all commodities — character. Without character, a man is nothing; with character, there is nothing beyond his aspirations. Character is the bedrock of maturity, of control, of integration, of mental health. Let us see what it is and where it comes from.

WHAT CHARACTER IS

Character and the Development of the Adolescent. In a sense all of adolescent psychology revolves around the concept of character, because character is inseparably linked to the goals of adolescent development, which include adequate adjustment, maturity, integration, independence, and a complete personality. In order to have character, all of these things are necessary; and in order to have these things, character is necessary. Character itself is a goal of adolescent development and training; and unless the adolescent achieves a measure of character, all of the training, education, advice, precept, and example to which he is exposed will be of little worth. An adult without character is ill-equipped to deal with the hazards, conflicts, and responsibilities of mature living. These demands on the individual require courage, moral stamina, and self-discipline, all of

which are essential features of true character.[1]

If we wish to help the adolescent reach this goal, we must first determine what character is. And we must confront certain basic questions regarding the constituents of character, how it is developed, to what extent it is acquired, the manner in which it is related to personality, and its essential determinants. The all-important task of training for character depends in large measure on how such questions are answered. Moreover, if we are to employ values, ideals, and principles effectively in promoting the emergence of character, we must understand their relationship to the process of character formation. Also, to deal constructively with problems of emotion and impulse, it will be helpful to determine

[1] In this connection, see A. Wheelis, *The Quest for Identity* (New York: Norton, 1958), pp. 17–18; P. A. Blos, "Character Development in Early Adolescence," *Child Study*, 1943, 20, 105–107.

the role that such factors play in character formation. In short, if we want to help the adolescent become what he should, we must first know what he should become.[2]

Character Traits Versus Character: an Important Distinction. In defining what character is, we must be careful not to make the mistake of identifying it with certain personality traits. The idea that character can be adequately defined in terms of character traits is just as unacceptable here as it was in the case of temperament. Like temperament, character is also manifested in certain responses, on the basis of which we can infer the "structure" or make-up of a particular character as it exists in a person. There are certain human traits that belong to character, as there are others that belong to temperament; but the fact remains that these traits by themselves do not *constitute* character. To the contrary, in many instances it is character that enforces the development of traits. Because of this fact we can read backward, as it were, from traits and arrive at some notion of a person's character. But we must remember that there is a real danger in doing this. For example, a dishonest act, or even a series of dishonest acts, may be used as a basis for estimating a person's character, and the inference could be entirely erroneous. Character does not reveal itself in every act, so that inferences based on conduct must be made cautiously. However, *traits*, as distinguished from *actions*, ordinarily reveal the true character of a person, since traits are formed in line with and under the influence of character. Even here, however, we must exercise caution,

because of the fact that traits often change, whereas character remains substantially the same. Character is relatively independent of single traits, so that alteration of traits can occur without any serious character transformation.

Character Traits Are Distinct From Others. To say that 17-year-old Henry is a young man of sturdy character is to imply that Henry's personality includes a dimension of traits that is quite distinct from other factors in his make-up, such as physical prowess, emotional stability, or intellectual level. Thus the question arises — what are true character traits? What is it about a trait that sets it off as belonging to the dimension of personality that we call character? Answers to these questions are important to understanding what character is, because the identification of character traits is an essential part of the total problem.

It has often been said that there is no valid distinction between character and other personality traits. Allport, for example, suggests that character is nothing more than personality *evaluated*. In a sense, this is true since all traits of whatever kind — physical or mental, social or temperamental, moral or characterological — are expressive of and embedded in personality, and may therefore be identified as personality traits. And all of them, too, can be evaluated in one way or another by the use of different criteria. Thus, certain physical traits like beauty or grace of movement, could be regarded as *socially valuable* because they contribute to the development of social relationships. However, the implication of the statement that character is nothing more than personality evaluated is that the evaluation is extrinsic to the traits in question. This statement

---

[2] See H. Lane and Mary Beauchamp, *Understanding Human Development* (Englewood Cliffs, N. J.: Prentice-Hall, 1959), pp. 157–158.

is in error, because *the value of a character trait is intrinsic to the trait itself, and is independent of any judgment of value.* What one *thinks* of courage or honesty or virtue makes little difference; the important thing is that these traits are themselves valuable. Such characteristics are valuable because they are consonant with man's higher nature, they make for more effective living, and they enable a person to reach his goals, both spiritual and material, more easily. If we compare such traits with other personality factors, we can see that it makes little difference in a final analysis whether a person is introverted or extroverted, good-looking or homely, dominant or submissive; but it makes a great deal of difference whether he is honest or dishonest, virtuous or evil, courageous or cowardly. This is the reason why character is closely identified with the person's intrinsic worth which, incidentally, varies in direct proportion to the degree to which he expresses himself in *worthwhile* thoughts and actions.

Character traits, then, are identified as those personal tendencies and characteristics *that possess intrinsic worth.* They are traits whose intrinsic value is determined by the extent to which they conform to man's distinctively rational nature. Thus courage, honesty, sincerity, virtue, truthfulness, reliability, and determination are all character traits because they are distinctively human and expressive of man's rational nature. Negative traits, like dishonesty, undependability, and timidity have no essential relation to character; they merely indicate a lack of character.

From this analysis we must not conclude, as some persons do, that character is essentially bound up with morality. It is true that the person of good charac-

ter adheres to moral standards, and also that being moral contributes to the development of a wholesome character.[3] But morality and character are not the same thing. There are many persons who are morally above reproach, but who possess little character. These people are moral because they lack the courage to be immoral, or because their behavior is compulsively determined by anxiety, guilt, or a pathological fear of sin. Character rises above morality and embraces it. It is an aspect of personality to which morality makes an important contribution, but which is not achieved simply by following moral dictates. Morality is often developed by external pressures; character must be developed *from within.*

Habits and the Emergence of Character. It has also been argued that character is revealed in a person's habitual way of acting, that it is nothing more than the sum total of certain habits, particularly those of a moral kind.[4] Such a viewpoint is only partially true. What a person does habitually, of course, will indicate to some extent the nature of his character; but it is just as impossible to read character from habits as it is from a list of traits or moral actions. Bad habits sometimes exist within the framework of a strong and even a good character; and for this reason alone character cannot be regarded as a sum total of habits. Character is more fundamental to personality than habits, traits, or individual moral actions, even though it may be revealed

---

[3] See H. Lane and Mary Beauchamp, *op. cit.,* pp. 165–169, for a definition of the relation between character and morals. See T. H. Pear, "The Training of Character in Some English Schools," in *The Yearbook of Education, 1951,* (London: Evans Bros., 1951), pp. 313–328.

[4] R. J. Quinlan, "Conduct as the Material Component of Character," *Nat. Cath. Educ. Assoc. Proc.,* XXVI (1929), 540–545.

through them. All such factors may change considerably while character itself remains substantially unaltered, which would be impossible if character were identical with them.

Character Is Acquired. The emphasis placed on the relationship between character and habit stems from the notion that character is something acquired in the course of development; and since habits are the prototypes of acquired responses, it is natural to regard them as being the essential elements of character. Let us examine this hypothesis more closely. It is certainly true that character is acquired, and also that, in the process of character development, habit formation plays an important role. This developmental viewpoint of character, however, must not be confused with the problem of the *nature* of character. What *character is* and *how it came about* are two different problems, even though the solution of the one problem may depend upon the solution of the other.

In the formation of character in early childhood, the first step is the encouragement of certain habits which, though externally imposed, possess intrinsic worth. Such habits as promptness, truthfulness, and consideration of others, inculcated in the child in his earliest years, are of great worth and possess real character value. This process will not *guarantee* the development of character, even though it is likely to lead to its formation. Character is more than these habits; it is a quality or disposition which in the course of time *crystallizes out of these habitual ways of acting.* If this crystallization fails to occur, character is not formed; and this explains why children of good habits may develop into adolescents of poor character. This gradual emergence of character is generally completed during adolescence, and for this reason adolescence is very important to the development of character.

In this sense, then, character is acquired. But we must remember that there are several modes of acquisition, all of which are important. We shall see that character is partly what a person makes of himself; but it is also true that character is what a person is made to be. The self-discipline through which character is finally formed must be preceded by external discipline in early childhood. It is this discipline, administered by parents and others, that sets the example for and makes possible the discipline by self that occurs later in the course of development. This notion is implied in the Freudian doctrine that character is fashioned for good or ill during the first five or six years of life, which is true to an important extent. Character in adolescence will be a reflection of the character that exists in childhood, and this is where the process of forming character must begin.

To say that character is acquired does not mean that it has no basis in innate structure or disposition. On the contrary, every aspect of character is in some measure conditioned by innate capacities and dispositions, particularly intellect and temperament. This seeming paradox is the result of an unfortunate restriction of terms. Whenever it is said that a trait or tendency is acquired it is immediately assumed that it is in no sense innate, since the term "acquired" is interpreted as the contrary of "innate." This logical distinction is only partly based in fact. Considering the unity of personality, and the interrelation and interdependence of all traits, capacities, and dispositions, it is impossible that character should be wholly acquired.

True, we are not born with character; but we are born with many qualities that play a significant part in the molding of character. Factors like intellect and temperament are to a great extent innately determined, and they in turn help to determine what character will be. Character is thus acquired only in the sense that the manifest qualities of character — traits and habits — are acquired responses, whereas the fundamental, unchanging quality of character is at least partly determined by innate factors.

Character Defined. On the basis of these facts, we may define character as *an enduring and dynamic disposition within the person to think, to feel, and to act in accordance with values and principles which, crystallized out of experience, conduct, and training, govern the individual's style of life, especially in its moral, spiritual and religious aspects.* Here again, as with temperament, we see that the core of character is a *disposition* to act in a certain way, a *persistent* tendency toward one form of conduct or another. This disposition is both enduring and dynamic.[5] It is because character is an enduring disposition that it is significant. If it were to change repeatedly it would have little worth, since it would then fail to *characterize.* As we pointed out earlier, the traits and habits of character may change, but the central disposition remains the same. We cannot, therefore, determine the nature of a particular character from an act or a trait. To know the character of a person one must develop a knowledge of the fundamental disposition that underlies and conditions all traits and actions that have character value.

Character is also *dynamic.* It is a mental "powerhouse" that influences and, in many instances, determines what the individual will do. In any single instance it may fail as a dynamic factor; but if it has been developed adequately it should force the person toward a prescribed course of conduct, be it morally good or morally bad. In some persons there is no such dynamic quality worthy of the term character. They are generally referred to as persons of weak character; but actually it would be more correct to say that they have no character at all. If character is not dynamic and to some extent predetermining, it is difficult to see how we can speak of character, since in such instances the individual is the victim of every whim and impulse, and there is thus no way in which to characterize him. There are undoubtedly degrees of character, one being more dynamic or more closely integrated with conduct than another, in which case it is referred to as strong or weak. But it is more meaningful to classify character as good or bad, depending upon the kind of values and principles that regulate conduct.[6]

Character Is Pervasive in Its Influence. It is important to note that *character relates to thinking and feeling as well as*

---

[5] The enduring quality of character has been empirically verified by Peck in his study of 120 children, and reported in his chapter, "The Consistency of Moral Character Through Time." As he summarizes it, "What seems to happen is this: the entire age-group develops and changes through the years, but each individual tends to maintain about the same generalized attitudes, and also the same standing relative to the total population in terms of the quality and age-appropriate maturity of his character structure and moral behavior" — R. F. Peck, and R. J. Havighurst, *Psychology of Character Development* (New York: Wiley, in production).

[6] On the meaning of character from a different point of view, see H. Lane and Mary Beauchamp, *op. cit.,* Chap 7, "The Meaning of Character." See also E. D. Eddy, *The College Influence on Student Character* (Washington, D. C.: Amer. Coun. on Educ., 1959), Chap. 1.

to action. This quality is of particular significance because in most definitions of character emphasis is invariably laid on the action quality and little or nothing is said of its thinking and feeling aspects. But character helps to determine not only what one will do in a particular situation, but also how he will think and feel. The person with a well-developed set of principles *thinks* in a characteristic way. He makes quick and unvarying judgments with respect to things that he considers wrong or evil. His reasoning is guided also by his values and ideals, and the ideas he is willing to accept and to act on will often reflect his character structure. In other words, every mode of thinking that is related to value conduct will be conditioned by this fundamental disposition. Feelings are similarly affected.[7] The young man with principles "bristles" at the suggestion that he should cheat, or lie, or steal.

---

[7] Referring to the highest form of character, the rational-altruistic type, Peck and Havighurst state, "He reacts with emotion appropriate to the occasion. This does not mean he is unemotional, for he is enthusiastic about promoting what is good, and aroused to prevent what is bad. He knows himself, and faces his own reactions honestly. He does what is morally right because he wants to, not because it is 'the thing to do' " — R. F. Peck and R. J. Havighurst, *op. cit.*

He experiences disgust in the presence of moral weakness, either in himself or in others. His anger is easily aroused at injustice. He deplores lack of courage or moral weakness. When, therefore, character is well developed during adolescence, the whole emotional life is conditioned by what the person conceives to be good, by his system of values, and by the principles and ideals that govern his style of life (see Table 20).

HOW CHARACTER IS FORMED

Intelligence Influences Character. For parents and teachers faced with the problem of character development in children and adolescents, a question of considerable importance is the extent to which character is influenced by other personality factors. If we are to help young people form character, we must know what it is that determines character formation, and how such factors can be exploited in the training and education of the growing person. Let us examine, first of all, the relation between character and intelligence (see Table 21). Intelligence is the ability to understand, to evaluate, and to perceive relations, functions that

TABLE 20

PERSONALITY ADJUSTMENT SCORES FOR SUBJECTS OF HIGH AND LOW CHARACTER REPUTATION*

Rated on	Number		Self-Adjustment			Social Adjustment		
	High	Low	High Rates	Low Rates	Difference	High Rates	Low Rates	Difference
Honesty	40	20	70.8	63.3	7.5	74.9	65.0	9.9
Moral courage	40	25	67.3	63.4	3.9	71.5	68.2	3.3
Friendliness	33	15	70.9	59.4	11.5	72.5	65.5	7.0
Loyalty	46	19	70.2	56.8	13.4	73.6	65.7	7.9
Responsibility	46	21	69.6	63.0	6.6	74.4	65.2	9.2

*Reprinted with permission from R. J. Havighurst and Hilda Taba, *Adolescent Character and Personality* (New York: Wiley, 1949), p. 107.

TABLE 21

SCHOOL ACHIEVEMENT AND INTELLIGENCE IN
RELATION TO CHARACTER REPUTATION*

Character Reputation	School Achievement (Mean)	Binet IQ (Mean)
Above median	87.0	127.4
	84.9	117.2
	85.0	112.0
Below median	76.9	111.2
	77.7	107.0

* Adapted with permission from R. J. Havighurst and Hilda Taba, *Adolescent Character and Personality*, p. 55.

are fundamental to the development of character; and because such abilities continue to develop more completely during adolescence, character becomes more and more realizable. For the adolescent to develop a mature character he must be able to distinguish clearly good from bad, and right from wrong. He must be able to acquire a scale of values that will give meaning to his conduct and his relationships with others. He must develop a keen insight into the morality of various situations and problems, and learn to distinguish what is subjectively pleasing from that which is objectively right or wrong. Without these abilities it is impossible to develop an adequate character, and all of them depend on intellectual capacity and growth.

Young children and mentally deficient persons do not possess character to any great extent because of their inability to comprehend moral concepts and relationships, and to develop values and principles. They cannot clearly distinguish good from bad, right from wrong, what is valuable and what is worthless, because such functions require *basic concepts* that depend on adequate intellectual functioning. This is not the only reason why the development of character is difficult or impossible in some instances, since character is dependent upon many

things; but it is one of the most basic. Intelligence is the starting point of character. While the age-old aphorism "knowledge is virtue" can be accepted only with qualifications, it is suggestive of the significant relationship between character and intelligence.

Principles and Ideals Help Form Character. From our study of moral development and the growth of values and ideals in adolescence, it is clear that the intellectual acquisition of moral concepts and of moral knowledge is not enough to insure the formation of character. These concepts must be translated into values, and these values in turn must become dynamic principles, that is, rules of conduct that guide the young person toward right and away from wrong.[8] This statement does not mean that the possession of principles guarantees character either. It is not unusual to find persons with high standards of conduct whose characters are very inadequate and immature. To have character value, principles must be *dynamic*; in any given situation they should force or at least strongly incline a person to act in terms of a basic value. Thus the person with principles is said to possess character only when there is in him a dynamic disposition to act in terms of such principles.

Just as values determine the formation of principles, so principles *often function as ideals*. A boy or girl, for example, may elevate a principle of honesty or of chastity into an ideal by investing it with a great deal of emotional value. In such instances the person not only *resolves* to act according to a value or principle, but he *feels* very strongly about such ac-

---

[8] On the relation of values to character, see M. Dorr and R. J. Havighurst, "The Relation of Values to Character," in R. J. Havighurst and Hilda Taba, *op. cit.*, pp. 97–102.

tions. In a conflict situation he reacts emotionally as well as intellectually, and this quality imparts strength to his moral decisions. Ideals, of course, are not always founded in principles. Personal ideals also play an important role in the development of character; but here too it is because of the emotional value with which the ideal is invested.[9]

This relationship of principles and ideals to character development sheds considerable light on the nature and kinds of character. We suggested earlier that there are two types of character — the "good" and the "bad." However these terms are interpreted, everyone will agree, for example, that Lincoln was a man of good character, and that Hitler was a man of bad character.[10] Now the striking feature of these two men, as far as character is concerned, is that both possessed *strong* characters. The one was as resolute and determined, yes, and as principled as the other. As regards *degree* of character, it would be difficult to distinguish these two very different persons. For all we know, too, the one was as intelligent as the other. Obviously, the difference lies in the principles and ideals adhered to by each. Lincoln was a man of great and ennobling principles and ideals; Hitler a man of debasing princi-

ples. This brings us back to a statement we made earlier: that the person with character possesses principles, and that the goodness or badness of the character depends on the goodness or badness of the principles and ideals which govern character responses, this quality varying independently of the dynamic aspects of character. For this reason the development of sound principles and ideals in youth becomes a matter of the greatest importance. These factors, as we have said, will not guarantee character; but if and when character is formed, they will determine its goodness or badness, which is as important as the formation of character itself.

Attitudes and the Formation of Character. The dynamic disposition we have identified with character is of course embedded within the total psychic framework of the growing person. While such factors as ideals and principles are most directly related to character formation, attitudes and sentiments will also contribute to its gradual emergence and to its dynamic influence. The relationship between sentiments and character is exemplified in the influence of self-esteem. Important traits like honesty, courage, forthrightness, and dependability are clearly related to this sentiment. This statement means of course that such qualities must be regarded as *valuable* by the youngsters in whom character is taking shape. Here we can see the importance of the family environment in training for character.[11] Obviously, if virtue is regarded as weakness, and cour-

---

[9] The relation between motives and character has been stressed by many investigators. See H. Lane and Mary Beauchamp, op. cit., pp. 161–165; V. Jones, "Character Development in Children — an Objective Approach," in L. Carmichael (ed.), *Manual of Child Psychology*, 2 ed. (New York: Wiley, 1954), pp. 812–817; R. F. Peck, op. cit., Chap. 1.

[10] Peck and Havighurst (op. cit.), distinguish four basic types of character: the amoral-psychopathic, the conforming, the irrational-conscientious, and the rational-altruistic. It is the last type that corresponds to the concept of the good character. See also the distinction of levels of character in R. J. Havighurst and Hilda Taba, op. cit., pp. 7–8.

[11] In their study of 120 adolescents, Peck and Havighurst consistently found that family traits are the most important determinants of character formation. R. F. Peck, and R. J. Havighurst, op. cit., See also V. Jones, op. cit., pp. 800–802. These writers also stress the importance of the church, the peer group, and the out-of-home environment as determinants of character.

age as the badge of a fool, these traits are not likely to enter into the concept of self-esteem. Much the same can be said of sentiments like loyalty and patriotism. If duty toward country is regarded as nothing more than foolish sentimentalism, and a person adopts a "dog-eat-dog" attitude, neither loyalty nor patriotism will take root. In such persons character is not likely to develop, because self-seeking is the antithesis of true character. Self-seeking is next to impulsiveness, and the impulsive person cannot easily develop a mature character. (See Table 22.)

Sentiments like patriotism and loyalty help to breed courage, selflessness, determination, and other qualities that contribute to wholesome character development. This is true also of important religious and moral sentiments. To feel strongly about moral principles and conduct, to cherish religious values, or to be excited by religious concepts and practices, are firm steps toward the development of important character traits, including humility, charity, kindness, honesty, and virtue.[12] Sentiments often form the groundwork within which character traits more easily grow.

That sentiments and attitudes play an important role in the formation of charac-

TABLE 22

CORRELATIONS OF FAMILY CHARACTERISTICS WITH
THE MATURITY OF CHARACTER SCALE*

Family Vector	Child's Maturity of Character
F1 Consistency	.58
F2 Democracy-Autocracy	.26
F3 Mutual Trust and Approval	.64
F4 Leniency-Severity	— .16

    * From R. F. Peck and R. J. Havighurst, *op. cit.*

    [12] On the relation of religion to moral maturity and character, see P. H. Landis, *Adolescence and Youth*, 2 ed. (New York: McGraw-Hill, 1952), Chap. 10.

ter is exemplified clearly in the lives of many prominent persons. The extremely narrow and ignorant racial and religious attitudes of men like Hitler and Stalin are certainly reflective of a mean or debased character. On the other hand, there are the noble and tolerant attitudes of persons like Abraham Lincoln, Dorothea Dix, Jane Adams, Woodrow Wilson, and Winston Churchill whose characters are strongly reflected in their resolute stand on social, religious, and moral issues. In many such instances the attitude is as much a *product* as it is a determinant of character. Yet attitudes often influence the development of principles and ideals through which character is formed. Children often possess attitudes before they develop principles; and it is not unlikely that some principles crystallize out of basic attitudes. It is in this sense that attitudes may be regarded as determiners of character, since in such instances they precede its development.

Not all attitudes enter into the formation of character; only those that have character value play such a role; and this value, as we have noted, is determined by intrinsic worth — the degree to which any factor is in conformity with man's nature and contributes to the achievement of higher goals. Thus one's attitudes toward duly constituted authority, morality, religion, the rights of man, or personal obligations will have an important bearing on character growth. Because such attitudes constitute the matrix out of which principles and ideals often emerge, the inculcation or the development of right attitudes in children is of the utmost importance to character development. This process should be continued during adolescence, when many new attitudes develop in line with new experiences, relationships, and changed

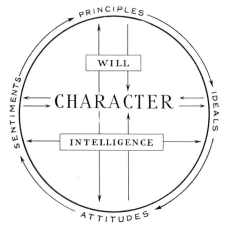

Fig. 25. Illustration of the relationships among the several determinants of character and character itself.

perspectives. The teen-ager's attitudes toward the opposite sex, moral conduct, social responsibilities, sexual behavior, and many similar realities are of considerable significance for the continued development of character.

As one might expect, attitudes have the same relationship to the kind of character that emerges that principles and ideals have. That is, bad attitudes will tend to generate bad character just as good attitudes will help form good character. The significance of this fact is doubled by the realization that principles are often generated out of attitudes. Thus the teen-ager with strong antisocial attitudes will tend to develop an antisocial character, because attitudes themselves bend the character in that direction, and also because the principles governing conduct will be formed in line with these attitudes. Wrong attitudes alone are enough to distort character, and if to them we add the force of principles character will certainly become distorted. Studies of delinquent youths bear this out, for their attitudes are characteristically amoral and antisocial.

In like manner, healthy and wholesome attitudes contribute immeasurably to the development of good character; and wise parents will insure the development of such attitudes as early as possible in their children. The earlier such training is begun, within the limits of the child's capacities, the better, because the roots of character are embedded deeply in the soil of early experience, even though the process of character formation continues into adulthood.[13] Here we are reminded again of a fact which has been emphasized repeatedly throughout this volume, namely, that between the development of childhood and adolescence there is a basic *interdependence*. As regards character particularly, the child is very much father to the man.

One of the most significant facts concerning character is the *interrelation* among the various determinants that influence its growth. In Figure 25, we have attempted to illustrate this integral relationship, so as to emphasize the connections and interdependencies that exist among all of the determinants of character, as well as those existing between the determinants and character itself.

Character and Self-Control. Unquestionably the most important element in the formation of character is self-control or self-discipline. It has often been said that character is *what a person makes of himself*, the implication being that character is formed through self-determined conduct rather than the influence of extrinsic factors. This is to an important extent true, so true in fact that without

---

[13] On the importance of early training, see V. Jones, *op. cit.*, pp. 825–826. See also M. B. Loeb, "Social Relationships and the Development of Character," in *The Yearbook of Education, 1951* (London: Evans Bros., 1951), pp. 52–66.

self-control and self-discipline *the achievement of character is impossible.* This fact must not blind us to the influence of other personality factors. After all, values, ideals, and principles have a lot to do with making self-discipline possible. As we have seen, they often function as impelling motives for the exercise of self-discipline. Moreover, we must remember that character formation begins long before ideals, principles, and attitudes are formed, and also before self-control assumes real significance for individual conduct. As we noted earlier in our discussion of discipline (Chapter XI), the groundwork for character development is the *external discipline* of the child by which he is conditioned from the earliest years to restrain impulses and to hold behavior in check. Later on, his power of self-restraint is elicited in behalf of a more thorough discipline. It is then that external discipline is replaced by the more significant and pervasive self-discipline which is basic to the continued development of character. Here again we see why discipline must begin in early childhood if the groundwork of character is to be securely laid.

Let us ask ourselves, why is self-control so basic to character formation? If we refer to the definition of character offered earlier in this chapter we can readily find an answer to this question. The disposition to think and to act according to values and principles is directly dependent upon one's *ability to do so;* that is, one must be able, if he is to develop character, to act in a manner that appeals to him as good or attractive. The person of character must *necessarily be self-determining,* possessing the ability to *select* those actions and thoughts that he considers to be of primary value. The contrary of self-disciplined action is *im-*

pulsiveness; and the impulsive person is one whose thoughts and conduct are determined, not by applying values and principles, but by the impulse of the moment. Obviously the person who acts on impulse, and is largely controlled by impulse, would find it difficult to act according to values and principles.

Impulsiveness and character are diametrically opposed. In fact, character develops in direct proportion to the extent to which *impulses are brought under control.* The person of character is always *characterized* by an ability to act and think independently of impulsive tendencies, no matter how strong they may be. Self-discipline, therefore, lies at the heart of character formation. It is the means by which the disposition to act according to values and principles is gradually forged, so that out of the many separate acts of self-control character finally crystallizes in the form of *an enduring and dynamic disposition.* Discipline, both external and internal, is the mold is which character is first formed. Values and principles, attitudes, ideals, and sentiments are the forces which give character its final form, and from which it derives much of its dynamic quality.

Because character and self-discipline are so closely related, character is often referred to the factor of will; and certainly, insofar as it is will that is directed toward values, character may be thought of as the expression of will (Fig. 25). This concept, however, should not be carried too far since will by itself is no guarantee of character. After all, there is such a thing as *willfulness,* which is only another name for impulsiveness; and the willful person is not a person of character. It is only when will is used as an instrument of self-discipline that it bears an essential relationship to character. The natural inclination toward good that is embodied in will must be converted into *separate acts of choice* before will becomes an instrument of character formation. Thus, character does not automatically flow from will; rather, it flows from will-acts, and from thoughts whose content is often determined by free choice. Only in this sense are will and character essentially related.

Our emphasis on the dependence of character upon self-discipline should not obscure the equally important fact that self-discipline is in its turn *dependent upon character*. This paradoxical situation can be understood only in terms of a developmental psychology of character. As we have pointed out, character, as a dynamic disposition, is formed partly through self-controlled conduct. But once this disposition is formed, and character achieves dynamic quality, it becomes more and more a *determining* factor. In crucial situations involving choice between equally attractive motives or courses of action, the issue is more often decided by character than by an exercise of will; and the more dynamic the character the more predetermined the result. The person of high and impelling principles, when faced with a choice between right and wrong, is not required to deliberate or to weigh alternative motives; his decision is literally made for him by the disposition to think and to act in terms of his values and principles; and this is exactly as it should be. The aim of all character training is *the formation of a dynamic disposition to do what is right and good, and to avoid conduct that is unacceptable.* Adolescents must learn that self-determination is a capacity for achieving a highly efficient moral, social, intellectual, and religious life. The extent to which they achieve this goal will be a measure of their character.

THE GROWTH OF CHARACTER

Character Formation Begins With Discipline. From the practical viewpoint of parents and teachers interested in the development of character, the all-important question is: How is character formed? Exactly what steps must be taken in order to insure the development of character? The answers to these questions are partly contained in the preceding discussion on the nature and determinants of character. Here we shall attempt to indicate more precisely what these steps are (see Fig. 26).

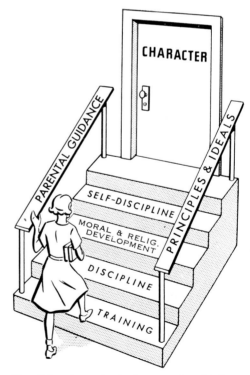

Fig. 26. Important steps and guidelines to character formation.

The formation of character begins with *external discipline* in early childhood that takes the familiar form of restrictions, punishments, and privations by which a child is conditioned to bring various impulses and actions under control. Requiring the child to control body needs, to keep himself reasonably clean, to tidy up his room, to control outbursts of temper, to stifle selfishness, and so on, marks the beginning of character. This discipline enforces the development of habits which are the first external signs of character formation; but the more significant fact is the control of impulsive tendencies which such habits reflect. This process may be characterized as the *negative phase* of character development. As the child grows older, external discipline continues, but is in time complemented and then replaced by self-discipline.[14]

With the continued development of intellectual capacity, the child begins to control tendencies and actions because of their rightness or wrongness, or because of their appropriateness to the situation. He begins to do things because he understands that he *should* do them. This attitude is based upon instruction, precept, and example on the part of parents and teachers; but it derives in large measure also from the experiences of the child himself. The negative phase of character development must be replaced in time by a *positive phase* in which there is not merely control of impulsive tendencies, but enriching experiences in the kinds of thinking and acting that have character value. The ability to hold to principles, to make

[14] See the article on character building in children by A. Drake in Sidonie M. Gruenberg, (ed.), *Our Children Today* (New York: Viking, 1955), Chap. 9.

decisions, and to exercise self-determination comes only with actual experience. The person who never progresses beyond the negative phase of character development is the timid, shy, inhibited individual whose spirit and initiative have been crushed by punitive discipline. In the more positive phase, habits of character are also formed; and the kind of habits will depend upon the nature of the examples, precepts, and instruction used with the child, and the opportunities for experience which he encounters.

Out of these persistent ways of thinking and acting the dynamic disposition underlying character crystallizes, and this disposition is already partly formed by the onset of puberty. Out of these modes of behavior, too, many of the principles and values related to character develop, so that by the beginning of adolescence the individual is already possessed of the rudiments of character. The process, however, is far from complete, so that during adolescence character must achieve a more mature form.

The Emergence of the Mature Character. Adolescence does not mark a break in the development of character; but in addition to the discipline, habit formation, and value developments of earlier years, there is added the possibility of inculcating principles, values, and ideals from outside sources. Because of greater intellectual insight, the goodness or badness, rightness or wrongness, appropriateness or inappropriateness of thoughts and actions become more clearly perceived. The adolescent is more amenable than the child to the development of ideals and principles because he can grasp their value more fully. The relationship of right conduct to human nature, to society, and to a moral order is understood clearly for the first time; and this makes possible the conversion of purely intellectual principles into dynamic tendencies. The investing of such tendencies with emotional value is a further step that is necessary; and this is one reason why the great truths of religion, as well as certain religious practices, are of fundamental importance to the development of character.[15]

The high point in the development of character, on the natural level, is reached when the individual has learned to act in terms of right values and principles. That is why these factors become dynamic. To think what is right, to feel strongly about it, to be inclined toward it — these are all of great significance in the development of character; but in the last analysis, unless one *does* what is right the development of character in its highest and most mature form is impossible.

Character, Temperament, and Personality. In our discussion of emotional development in Chapter IX, we alluded briefly to the nature and development of temperament as one of the basic components of human personality. In the final chapters of this book we shall deal more specifically with the social aspect of personality, and thus will have covered all of the essential components that together constitute the personality. It is clear, of course, that physique, character, and the social aspects of personality are not distinct and independent parts, but are instead functionally interdependent aspects of the total personality. However, this relationship is often distorted by an overemphasis on the distinctive developmental characteristics of each personality component. Thus we tend to think of temperament as being largely determined

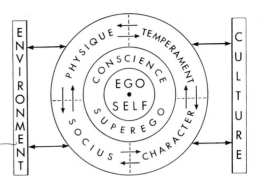

Fig. 27. Personality, its components and determinants.

genetically and as rooted in physical structure, and of character as being acquired and more closely related to the intellectual and volitional capacities of the person. Moreover, temperament is identified with affective processes, whereas character is associated with voluntary and moral responses.

These differences may lead us to think of temperament and character as being independent of each other, and to lose sight of the fact that they are *integral* components of the whole personality, so closely interwoven and interdependent that the one *cannot function independently of the other.*[16] The dispositions referred to in our study of both temperament and character are quite distinguishable, as are the traits and habits that belong to each; but it must be remembered that personality is a unity, and that any disposition or trait is conditioned by the nature of the whole, and is formed in terms of the whole to which it belongs. What character is, therefore, will depend upon what temperament is; and temperament will to an important extent reflect the character

---

[15] See the discussion of moral maturity in P. H. Landis, *op. cit.*, Chaps. 8 and 11.

[16] On the relationship between personality and character, see R. F. Peck and R. J. Havighurst, *op. cit.* See also Table 23, and Figure 27.

TABLE 23

CORRELATIONS OF PERSONALITY, CHARACTER, AND MORAL REPUTATION*

Personality Vector	Maturity of Character	Adult Reputation	Peer Reputation
Moral Stability	.84	.74	.63
Ego Strength	.77	.55	.69
Superego Strength	.68	.63	.53
Spontaneity	.24	.05	.16
Friendliness	.57	.13	.04
Hostility—Guilt	—.33	—.25	—.07

* From R. F. Peck and R. J. Havighurst, *op. cit.* Note the high correlation between moral stability, ego strength, superego strength, and friendliness on the one hand and maturity and character on the other.

of the individual. Moreover, both factors will develop in terms of the nature and structure of the total personality within which they exist as integral components.

This fact can be readily illustrated. If, for example, a child possesses a "sensitive" temperament, is easily aroused to anger, tears, and rebellion, he is much less amenable to discipline than the child who possesses greater emotional stability. For the former, the development of character may be a much more difficult task. Moreover, the character pattern finally assumed will reflect the individual's temperament to the extent that values and principles are determined by feelings and emotions. Conversely, the development of temperamental qualities will be directly in line with the character being formed. The person of well-developed character, who possesses a strong disposition to act in terms of principles, will regulate his emotional reactions in terms of this disposition. In the very definition of character the quality of feeling is included, since character involves a disposition to feel as well as to act in certain ways.

Here we have the clearest instance of the fundamental relationship between these two components of personality. As we have seen, it is by investing values and principles of character with feeling and emotion that character becomes a dynamic disposition; and this process will depend always on the structure of the temperament which a person possesses. We must learn, therefore, to think of temperament and character in terms of their interrelationships rather than in terms of their differences; and we must remember that they are integral aspects of one person who thinks, feels, and acts as a unity. By so doing we can deal much more effectively with the entire complex problem of character and personality development. As we shall see, the same principles can be applied to the development of the social aspects of personality.

SELECTED READINGS

Allers, R., *The Psychology of Character*, trans. by E. A. Strauss (New York: Sheed & Ward, 1931).

—— *Character Education in Adolescence* (New York: Wagner, 1940).

Havighurst, R. J., and Taba, Hilda, *Adolescent Character and Personality* (New York: Wiley, 1949).

Jones, V., "Character Development in Children — an Objective Approach," in L. Carmichael (ed.), *Manual of Child Psychology*, 2 ed. (New York: Wiley, 1954), pp. 781–832.

Landis, P. H., *Adolescence and Youth*, 2 ed. (New York: McGraw-Hill, 1952), Chaps. 8, 10, 11.

Lane, H., and Beauchamp, Mary, *Understanding Human Development* (Englewood Cliffs, N. J.: Prentice-Hall, 1959), Chap. 7.

Morrison, B., *Character Formation* (Milwaukee: Bruce, 1938).

Roback, A. A., *Psychology of Character* (London: Kegan, Paul, 1952).

———— "The Character Aspect in Recent Psychology and Psychiatry," in A. A. Roback (ed.), *Present-Day Psychology* (New York: Philosophical Library, 1955), pp. 239–258.

Zachry, Caroline B., *Emotion and Conduct in Adolescence* (New York: Appleton-Century-Crofts, 1940), pp. 243–259.

PART IV

The Sociology of Adolescence

The adolescent's perception of his world

The adolescent in the family

The adolescent in the community

CHAPTER XVII

THE ADOLESCENT'S PERCEPTION
OF HIS WORLD

What the adolescent does is often incomprehensible to the harried parent and the puzzled teacher. This is partly because of the changes, the confusion, the complex motivations, and the many other things that make the adolescent what he is. But equally important is the adolescent's viewpoint of the world in which he lives. To see the world as the adolescent sees it, with his psychological myopias and astigmatisms, is to take a long step toward understanding him much better.

PERCEPTION AND ADOLESCENT ADJUSTMENT

The Perceptual Process. Important as they are, it is not enough to know the basic motivations, the character structure, the personal history, or the individual characteristics of the adolescent. These things of themselves do not tell us about the relationship between the young person and reality, that is, the world of objects, institutions, people, and events in which he is trying to locate himself. How often we read with a sense of utter confusion and tragedy of the model boy who suddenly goes berserk and commits some violent crime, including murder of his parents. Such an act cannot be understood solely in terms of motivation or of personality structure, since we need to know also the peculiar manner in which the youngster perceived the people and

events around him. Thus, if Tommy perceives his parents as hating or frustrating persons, he will react in one way; if, on the other hand, he perceives them as loving, kind, and considerate, he will react in a totally different way. This perceptual process defines the distinctive relationship between the person and reality, in terms of which his responses are *individually organized.*[1]

Perception and Reality. The people and events in the adolescent's world are, of course, objectively real, but their *particular meaning* to the adolescent will be determined in large part by his individual perception of them. To a boy interested in aviation as a career, the profession of medicine or the priesthood may look very dull and unsatisfying. To the girl who craves the excitement of a career on the

---

[1] See the section "Behavior as a Function of Perception," in B. R. Sappenfield, *Personality Dynamics* (New York: Knopf, 1954), pp. 12–17.

stage, motherhood may seem equally dull. Reality, in other words, is *subjectively* perceived and evaluated, and therefore in attempting to understand the particular adjustments of adolescents we must take into account the peculiarities of their perception of reality.

> Whatever be the individual's basic attitude toward life, whether it be grounded in rational or emotional processes, he tends to perceive the world in terms of his personal outlook upon it. A maxim attributed to the French equivalent of our FBI is appropriate here: "The eye sees what it looks for, but it looks for only what is already in the mind." If a person views the world as a place in which security is to be found only through reliance upon others, through a vigorous "striking back" or through retreat into himself, he behaves accordingly. In any event, the behavior is conditioned by the way he *feels* about things; he never has learned that his feelings are relatively unimportant, that it is only what he *does* that counts. Kant has said: "We see things not as they are, but as we are."[2]

This idea that the thing perceived is determined to an important extent by the perceiver has gained wide acceptance in contemporary psychology. The well-known psychologist, Carl Rogers, states exactly the same idea when he says, "*The organism reacts to the field as it is experienced and perceived. This perceptual field is, for the individual, 'reality.'*" Rogers emphasizes that while we may be aware of this from our own experience it is a point too often overlooked, especially in trying to understand the behavior of others. "I do not react to some absolute reality, *but to my perception of this reality.* It is this perception which for me

is reality."[3] To the adolescent, therefore, his school, teachers, classmates, parents, and peer groups are somewhat different from what they are to an adult who cannot see with the eyes of an adolescent.

John was a fifteen-year-old boy who was having considerable difficulty at home. He was in almost constant conflict with his mother, whose demands and regulations irritated him to the point of rage. He rebelled at household chores, quarreled with his younger brother, and resented the father's attempts at discipline. Yet at school John was a model student. He was happy and carefree, got along well with classmates, was willing to help with extra-curricular functions, and maintained a good scholastic average. It is not difficult to understand John's adjustment problem. To him, school meant everything that his home did not. He perceived the school as a place of achievement, acceptance, security, and social equality. Actually, his home was a good one, but it was his different perception of the two situations that caused difficulties in adjustment. As John became more mature, these perceptions changed, and his adjustments changed along with them.

We can see, then, that it is not enough to know the determinants and the dynamics of human response; we must ascertain also a person's distinctive reaction to reality. This subjective reaction applies to all aspects of reality, including the individual himself; and therefore what we said earlier regarding the influence of the self-concept on adjustment and mental health becomes part of this general picture. How a person regards himself is just as important to adjustment as how he perceives objective reality.

Determiners of Perception. Granted that perception determines in part the adolescent's behavior and adjustment,

[2] Reprinted with permission from L. C. Steckle, *Problems of Human Adjustment* (New York: Harper, 1949), pp. 105–106.

[3] C. R. Rogers, *Client-Centered Therapy* (Boston: Houghton Mifflin, 1951), p. 484.

what is it within the individual or outside of him that causes him to look at things differently than do other persons? The perceptual process itself is simply a cognitive awareness of events going on within ourselves, or events in the outside world. This awareness *should* correspond to actual reality; that it does not in many instances is owing to the disturbing influences of such factors as past experiences, feelings, needs, and values.

Thus, to the starving man food, or what he perceives as food, is perceptually different than for the well-fed individual. The sexual psychopath perceives women differently than does the normal person. The overdisciplined adolescent views parental and civil authority in a light different from that of the youngster with whom discipline has been administered wisely. The man who has spent ten years in jail sees freedom in terms, of this unhappy background. Perception, then, is always organized *in terms of personal background* or *needs*, as much as in terms of external events.[4] These perceptual idiosyncrasies explain why the adolescent does not see parents as they see themselves; or why a college education may be rejected in favor of immediate financial gain; or why the prospect of getting married frightens or confuses the adolescent. Perceptually, the world is a different place for the adolescent and for the adult,

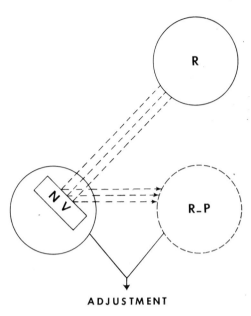

ADJUSTMENT

Fig. 28.   How needs and values influence perception and alter the process of adjustment. I — Individual; N-V — Needs and Values; R — Reality; R-P — Reality as perceived. From A. A. Schneiders, **Personal Adjustment and Mental Health** (New York: Rinehart, 1955), p. 197.

and thus they often fail to see "eye to eye" (see Fig. 28).

PERCEPTUAL DEVELOPMENT IN ADOLESCENCE

The Early Beginnings of Perceptual Response. The awareness of objects, qualities, or persons that constitutes the process of perception begins with the simpler sensory experiences of color and sound, size and shape, nearness and distance, hardness and softness. These simple experiences probably undergo very little change during the course of human development, except insofar as they become involved with the perceptual process. There is, however, a significant relationship between sensory processes

---

[4] See L. Postman, "The Experimental Analysis of Motivational Factors in Perception," in *Current Theory and Research in Motivation: a Symposium* (Lincoln: University of Nebraska Press, 1953), pp. 59–108; L. Postman, "Perception, Motivation and Behavior," *J. Pers.* 1953, 22, 17–30; R. B. Cattell and P. W. Wenig, "Dynamic and Cognitive Factors Controlling Misperception," *J. Abnorm. Soc. Psychol.*, 1952, 47, 797–809; D. Chodorkoff, "Self-perception Perceptual Defense, and Adjustment," *J. Abnorm. Soc. Psychol.*, 1954, 49, 508–512.

and motivational tendencies. These processes are the natural *psychological antecedents* of desires, impulses, body hungers, and needs; and thus they play a part in setting up a conscious inclination to or away from a perceived object or act. The more intense, then, a sensation or image is, the more intense will be the dynamic tendency aroused. Herein lies the danger to the adolescent of pornographic literature, sexy movies, exciting dance rhythms, or holding a girl too closely while dancing. The sensations and images aroused in such situations may easily touch off impulses and drives that can get the teen-ager into a lot of trouble.

In this relationship between sensory experience and motivation, the quality of pleasure plays an important role. The senses are the media *par excellence* of pleasurable experiences, and thus the pleasurable and the truly aesthetic have some common boundaries. To what extent some of these pleasurable experiences are basically sexual is hard to say; but certainly many of them derive their value from the sex drive. Some odors seem to have sexual significance, and certain tactual and thermal experiences probably have some sexual value for everyone. Even the visual experience of the human form may have definite sexual connotations, as is true of certain musical experiences. The experience of pleasure derived from gentle stroking of the skin, particularly those body zones that have erotic significance, is certainly akin to the pleasure derived directly from sexual gratification. Body contacts also have sexual significance under certain conditions, as do sensations of warmth. These connections between sexual experience and sensory stimulations lie at the basis of the pleasure derived from the wide-spread practices of necking and petting. It is significant that many youngsters who report no desire whatever for complete sexual experience nevertheless subscribe wholeheartedly to the art of petting. The fact that the sexual significance of such acts is often not realized makes petting a dangerous practice from the moral and psychological standpoints. In any event, we can see that sensory experiences are directly related to the adolescent's behavior and adjustment.

Absolute Versus Relative Sensitivity. To evaluate the significance of sensory development, it is necessary to distinguish between *absolute* and *relative* sensitivity and discrimination. As far as we know, there are no absolute changes that would make the sensory experiences of the adolescent different from those of the child; and yet, because of the fact that such experiences do not occur independently of other mental processes, some development can be noted. The relative increase in sensitivity and discrimination changes the sensory life of the adolescent as surely as if there were actual sense-organ or nervous system changes. Thus, there is a disposition in adolescence to give special attention to experiences that are peripherally aroused, plus a heightened awareness of physical contacts, unusual skin conditions, unsightly physical appearance, and the like. This is caused by *increased attention* to such experiences; but psychologically there is no clear distinction between increased awareness caused by actual sensitivity and that produced by the direction of attention to certain experiences.

There are probably a number of causes, both physical (endocrinological) and psychological for the alternating reactions; but the result of the growth in sensitivity of the perceptive system —

whether this be an actual growth of the sensory pathways or of the association tracts between the cortical centers — plays some part in it. In the latency period and before, children seem more attracted by bright colors, perhaps by the primary colors. It is only in adolescence that pastel shades seem to be differentiated clearly one from the other, and that pleasure is found in color. There is more than the verbal difference in the way a child of nine describes a sunset and the way it is described by a boy or girl of 14. It is as if the latter really sees and appreciates more shades of color — actually sees the sunset differently from the younger child. A similar difference is found in the ability to distinguish and appreciate sounds, and in the ability to distinguish and appreciate tastes and smells. . . . I do not think the difference lies in the greater ability to describe what is seen, heard, tasted, and smelled; I think it is a real difference in perception.[5]

Extent of Sensory Changes. Thus, because of physical changes or dietary indiscretions, the skin may become unattractive, or there may be overactivity of sebaceous glands, causing pimples and skin eruptions, bringing about a more acute consciousness of physical appearance. Similarly, because of sexual development, there may be a greater sensitivity to certain tactual experiences. The smoothness and softness of another person's skin may be a new kind of experience. Actual physical contacts, which heretofore were disregarded, give rise to intense sensations. Where the young boy is forced to hold the little girl's hand in playing ring-around-a-rosy and then drops it at the first opportunity, the adolescent searches for reasons to hang on to the young lady's hand. Where the young child avoids the physical contacts involved in kissing as being "mushy," the adolescent may actively seek such experiences.

It should be noted that the physical factors in these two situations are in nowise altered. The physical joining of bodies in an embrace is no different physically at one period than at another. Nor are the sensations aroused any different themselves as simple conscious experiences. Yet there is a great difference between the experience of the child and that of the adolescent in these various situations. Fondling, petting, embracing, kissing, and all the multifarious tactual experiences that are possible where two people are concerned, become different experiences under the influence of other adolescent changes. This is what we meant by relative changes in the simpler sensory functions. The experiences are more acute; they take on a different significance; some are brought from the area of dim awareness to the focal point of consciousness; some are sexualized and others are socialized. The whole pattern of sensory consciousness assumes a different coloring, not because of absolute variation in sensibility, but because of the influence of other psychic and social events.

There are changes also in smell and taste sensitivities, causing feelings of pleasantness or unpleasantness and other emotional reactions to be stimulated. Real or imagined bodily odors of self or of others become offensive, and some may even assume sexual significance. Such experiences can stimulate new and strange emotional excitements. Often, too, because of social factors or imitation, the adolescent cultivates new or strange tastes, and increased appetite causes the appearance of unusual cravings for different foods. It is during this period

[5] G. H. J. Pearson, Adolescence and the Conflict of Generations (New York: Norton, 1958), p. 33.

that the first tendencies toward smoking and the use of drugs may appear, tendencies that are fortified by the adolescent's natural craving for unusual experiences, and that must be carefully guided by vigilant parents.

The extent to which other sensory experiences or sensitivities develop during adolescence is problematical. Girls on the whole seem somewhat more sensitive to pain than do boys, but the evidence is too vague to draw any certain conclusions. Nor is there any evidence to indicate development in vision and hearing. However, these senses are subject to the same influences that condition taste, smell, and touch. Certain auditory and visual experiences of various kinds are given added significance by increased attention, or because of the influence of physiological and social factors. No one will deny that the teen-ager is unique in his capacity to tolerate for endless hours the blaring sounds and noises that emerge from rock 'n roll, bebop, and similar recordings. All in all, therefore, the sensory experiences of the adolescent are different from those of the child, which means that his perceptual world is also different.

Why Sensory Changes Occur. The question as to why these changes in sensory experiences occur is difficult to answer. One viewpoint emphasizes physiological factors, particularly the nervous system, while another suggests that they are largely due to other developments of the adolescent period. The evidence for the first hypothesis is quite meager, since investigation reveals little development in the nervous system after the first year of life. However, the changes in such a highly complicated mechanism as the nervous system may be so minute as to escape observation. It may well be that there are synaptic changes or reorganiza-tions within the nervous system that condition many psychological processes. The very fact that the organism does develop along sensory, perceptual, and intellectual lines strongly suggests that there is some development in the nervous system too.

In addition, other forms of physical maturation may affect sensory functions. Thus, functional changes associated with the sex glands exert a wide influence on some sensory experiences. Whether the sexualizing of experiences is caused by association, or involves a direction of sexual energy into sensory channels through sublimation, we cannot be sure. But we do know that some sensory experiences assume sexual significance and that this occurs principally at the time when sexual structures and functions are maturing.

> I am not sure why sensory perception increases during adolescence. The rejuvenation of the sexual impulses, which have been dormant during the latency period and which accompany puberty, certainly romanticizes and sexualizes the external world, and causes the stimuli from it to be more meaningful, more interesting, and capable of creating more intense emotional reactions. The greater awareness may also be associated with some growth in the sensory pathways themselves, and particularly in the associative pathways between the various sensory centers. I believe that both of these phenomena — an actual organic development within the central sensory nervous system and the erotization of the sensory perceptions — are two of the main reasons why perception increases.[6]

The hypothesis that psychological factors determine sensory development is more defensible. *Intellectual development,* including changes in attention,

---

[6] G. H. J. Pearson, *Adolescence and the Conflict of Generations* (New York: Norton, 1958), pp. 33–34.

judgment, or insight, certainly conditions sensory experience. Attention "intensifies" experiences and brings obscure impressions into focus; whereas understanding and insight give new meaning to many experiences. The growth of knowledge and of apperceptive background also contribute to more meaningful interpretations. In this way, the young person grows in wisdom and acquires a more adequate and better organized value system, in terms of which many experiences achieve new significance. This *integral* quality of human experience underlies all psychic development, and enables us to explain many sensory changes that occur in adolescence.

We must note also the influence of *motivational tendencies*, apart from sex. Desires for social approval, recognition, affection, status, conformity, and new experiences often condition sensory impressions. As already noted, these needs cause a reorganization of the psychological field that may alter the entire character of experience. The needs for status or acceptance, for example, may give an entirely different cast to experiences like smoking, drinking, or petting. As the adolescent approaches maturity such needs will be tempered by experience and by other personality factors, and thus exert correspondingly less influence.

Finally, the *social changes* of adolescence may affect perceptual development. Social phenomena assume new significance; attitudes and concepts may become socialized; and with this gradual socializing process, the adolescent's experiences — sensory, intellectual, and emotional — acquire a different meaning. . The attitudes and opinions of other persons, their acceptance or rejection, their remarks and glances, bring certain experiences into focus, and thus act to cause

a differential evaluation of them. As commonly expressed, the youngster becomes more *sensitive* to certain stimuli and situations; and this increased sensitivity may also be regarded as an aspect of sensory development.

Motor Development During Adolescence. External acts of behavior, or as they are called, motor processes, are the *behavioral counterparts* of sensory experience, and thus the relationship between the two is very close. Motor development during both childhood and adolescence has been widely observed, and is clearly based upon the growth and development of the muscular system.[7] Throughout adolescence there is continuous muscular growth and development, which promotes increased strength and endurance, greater co-ordination, and the development of various motor skills. This latter development results mainly from practice.

The principle of development by practice applies particularly to motor functions.[8] All necessary and useful skills, such as speech, walking, writing, dressing, or typing, are developed and perfected through repeated use. The point requires emphasis because parents are not always mindful of the need to provide youngsters with the opportunities for the development of co-ordination and skillful execution. Learning to play tennis, building model planes, working with clay, acquiring skill at the piano, or

[7] See Nancy Bayley and Anna Espenschade, "Motor Development and Decline," *Rev. Educ. Res.*, 1950, 20, 367–374; and C. E. Meyers, F. J. Estvan, and R. C. Perry, "Characteristics and Needs of Individuals," *Rev. Educ. Res.*, 1951, 21, 75–85.

[8] See F. M. Henry and G. A. Nelson, "Age Differences and Inter-Relationships Between Skills and Learning in Gross Motor Performance of Ten- and Fifteen-Year-Old Boys," *Res. Quart. Amer. Ass. Hlth. Phys. Educ.*, 1956, 27, 162–175.

learning to dance — all such acquired skills contribute importantly to the development of motor ability, the lack of which is expressed so unmistakably in persons who are clumsy, awkward, and generally unskillful.

The evidence regarding the development of *muscular strength* during adolescence is also clear. From the beginning of puberty until well into the adult years the curve for muscular power, whether measured in terms of strength or grip, or strength of back and legs, continues to rise by noticeable degrees.[9] Actually, muscular power considerably outstrips increase in muscular size owing of course to exercise and work which promote development but do not affect increase in size so noticeably.

Of greater importance than increase in strength is the development of motor skill. That such development should occur in adolescence can be argued from the general fact of maturation, particularly the gradual increase in voluntary control. It can also be argued on the principle that the more often any act or process is repeated, the greater the skill and facility with which it is executed at any succeeding stage. How can we reconcile these statements with the generally accepted view that youth is an age of awkwardness and clumsiness? No one will question that certain aspects of physical development, particularly the imbalance among growth factors, contribute to clumsy and awkward behavior on the part of the adolescent. As Schwab and Veeder point out:

> The nervous system, under the control and direction of which the whole

of the muscular system operates, has, so to speak, not yet learned the adequate and proper system of controls to handle efficiently the increased load which it is called upon to direct. Movements are therefore clumsy, overextended, and in some instances uncoordinated. The increase in strength causes often the simplest movements to be massed without control or inhibition. Conscious effort to direct or modify movement after it has once started results in awkward and jerky muscular breaks which produce the effects of clumsiness and crudeness. The nice and rhythmic flow of muscular power so characteristic of proper adjustment and training in the more mature muscular mechanism is lacking. As a result, the adolescent is apt to be noisy in his movements, clumsy in the performance of simple tasks, likely to drop things, bump into things, and disturb the orderly arrangement of a household.[10]

These inadequacies, however, are more representative of a stage in the process of physical adjustment than a true picture of the adolescent's degree of motor control. Moreover, his clumsiness and lack of physical grace are to a very large extent *social* phenomena. Under the influence of the desire for social approval, youth is extremely self-conscious, and this self-consciousness is repeatedly enhanced by the comments and attitudes of others in his immediate environment, comments that never fail to stress the very shortcomings that are the most painful to the sensitive youngster who has not yet learned to evaluate his own worth or the opinions of others. Self-consciousness, as everyone knows, is extremely detrimental to dexterity and precision of movement; for, as soon as attention is directed to what is already an automatic process, pre-

---

[9] See the article by C. E. Willgoose, "The Relationship of Muscular Strength to Motor Coordination in the Adolescent Period," *J. Educ. Res.*, 1950, 44, 318–342.

[10] S. I. Schwab and B. S. Veeder, *The Adolescent: His Conflicts and Escapes* (New York: D. Appleton and Co., 1929), p. 202. By permission of Appleton-Century-Crofts, Inc.

cision disappears and fumbling takes its place.

The adolescent, therefore, is clumsy and awkward in many situations not so much because of developmental changes, but because he wants so desperately not to appear clumsy and awkward. Acutely conscious and desirous of the favorable opinion of others, he becomes more and more conscious of himself and his actions, and thus begins to fumble what might otherwise have been a fairly graceful act. "The adolescent who is so clumsy and awkward that disaster seems to follow wherever he goes may show surprising dexterity of hand in his workshop when no one is watching him and splendid bodily control on the athletic field. His awkwardness in public is not due to lack of motor skill but is the result of embarrassment and self-consciousness."[11]

The Significance of Sensory and Motor Development. Obviously the adolescent's perception of his world is significantly affected by sensory and motor development. Vocationally, for example, there are numerous skills which, if sufficiently developed, can contribute materially to vocational adjustment. In the business world, there are many routine actions that depend upon speed, precision, and co-ordination. In the professional world such vocations as dentistry, surgery, drafting, mechanical art, and architecture indicate clearly the importance of motor control.

These developments also have psychological and social implications. Through the expressive functions like speech, writing, and play, social relationships are often established, and these functions are dependent on adequate sensory and motor development. The adolescent's expressive gestures are the externalization of his inner thoughts, feelings, and desires; they are in a measure the outer self or objective personality, and their weaknesses and limitations may be regarded as a manifestation of inner weaknesses. Awkwardness or clumsiness can easily breed distrust of self, uncertainty, and seclusiveness. It can force abandonment of social situations and experiences, particularly sports, and thus contribute to social maladjustment and the development of feelings of inferiority and insecurity. This may happen only in extreme cases; but there are many youngsters whose inadequate motor development has caused them a great deal of anguish. This deficiency is a more decisive factor in complete adjustment than is always realized.

Direction of Perceptual Change. The perceptual process itself extends beyond the data of sensory experience and is therefore more meaningful and important to the adolescent's view of the world. Perception makes us aware of total objects and situations — including persons — and therefore involves an integration of experiences that influence behavior, adjustment, and interpersonal relationships, in a more subtle and intricate manner than do the simpler sensory experiences. We must remember also that perceptual responses are closely allied to intellectual development, and therefore the act of perceiving is always influenced by the development of knowledge, understanding, meaning, and insight. Were it not for this relationship, perceptual distortion of reality might be even greater than it usually is. What does the concept of perceptual development imply? What direction does it take?

[11] Florence L. Goodenough, *Developmental Psychology*, 2 ed. (New York: Appleton-Century-Crofts, 1945), p. 475.

From a purely objective point of view, objects and persons are perceived or they are not; and this applies to any level of development. Yet experience teaches us that events are perceived more fully and more clearly as we attend more carefully to them; and in this way they become more meaningful. Qualities and relational features that may have escaped notice now become a part of the perceptual experience, and the more such factors become known the more meaningful experience becomes. This perceptual development is complemented by the growth of ideas and insights, since meanings are affected by such factors also. A child does not perceive the world of external events in exactly the same way as the adolescent. He does not grasp fully the meaning or significance of the parade that passes before him. An adolescent watching a film of the invasion of Europe or a riot in Hungary on television may see something quite different from what is seen by the child, to whom it means nothing more than a lot of men making a lot of noise. In other words, the *apperceptive backgrounds* of the two observers are different, and this causes the perceptual experience to differ.

Thus the process of perception occurs against a background of experiences, concepts, prejudices, feelings, etc., that is referred to as the "apperceptive mass." Therefore, what a person "sees" is determined by what he has experienced in the past, and by the ideas, images, attitudes, and feelings that this thing now evokes. This apperceptive reaction is not merely intellectual development superimposed on perception. The perceptual process is *actually different* at different levels of development because of the influence of such factors as apperception.

Another example of this influence is the effect produced by needs and motives, as we noted earlier. Although the object of perception is the same spacially and temporally to different observers, the fact remains that the object *is not experienced in the same way.* Perceptually it is different. The younger boy, for example, perceives a girl simply as a girl, and that is about all that she means to him. His senses reveal the blue of her eyes, the sheen of her hair, the curve of her lips, the contours of her body, the faint body odor, and so on, but all these qualities are devoid of any special significance. For the adolescent, on the other hand, these qualities possess a special meaning. Not only are the lips curved, but they are *delicately* curved, and perhaps kissable; not only is the hair blond, it is *golden;* not only are the eyes blue, but they are *inviting.* The adolescent perceives not only a girl, but a *desirable* object with features that are decidedly attractive. His perception throughout is governed and conditioned by needs and desires, and also, of course, by the experiences and feelings that the perception evokes from the past. It is easy to appreciate also the influence on perception of such factors as ideals, interests, attitudes, and sentiments, without which a person's world would not be what it is. Here again we see how important it is that the adolescent's perception of his world should not be gauged by the immature standards of childhood or by the broader and different perspectives of the adult.

Implications of Perceptual Development. In view of the integral nature of human responses, changes in perception are likely to influence the whole range of human experience in one way or another. Like other mental processes, perception functions importantly in the adjustments of the organism. Just as perception contributes to intellectual growth, it adds a great deal to the development of imagination and memory, and these two functions also play a significant role in adjustment. We have indicated earlier that reality is to an important extent perceptual, and therefore adjustment to the world of things, people, and events will be determined in large measure by a person's perception of reality. This fact alone makes the study of the adolescent's perception of his world important.

IMAGINATION IN ADOLESCENCE

Perception and Imagery.   Perception is limited to the here and now; it makes one aware of reality as apprehended by the senses and enriched by insight and meaning. But there are many situations that require a re-presentation of an object, event, or experience that is not now present to the observer; and this is where imagination comes in, because imagination enables the experiencer to deal with things even though they are absent. Without this capacity the individual would be seriously handicapped in his adjustments.

What is even more important is the fact that imagination can go beyond the recall of past experiences. In dreams, whether they occur at night or in the daytime, images often assume a pattern quite different from the original experience, in which case we imagine something not actually experienced in that form. In other words, imagination is productive as well as reproductive. At times it is even creative. To the purely imaginative content there are added intellectual elements that elevate the imagination to the plane of artistic and inventive creation. Without this ability to synthesize past experiences into something new, and to intellectualize them, all invention and all artistic, musical, and literary creation would be impossible.

Since imagery is basically the recall of previous experiences, perceptual development plays an important part in the growth of imagination. Actually, the greater the range of experience, and the more fully developed the apperceptive background of the individual, the richer will be his imagination, depending always on innate capacity. The extent to which other factors influence the growth of imagination is uncertain, but it is definitely known that drives often affect imaginal processes, as Freud has shown so clearly with respect to dreams. The behavior of children also illustrates this relationship, a fact that we will deal with in a later section.

Changes in Imagination.   Available evidence suggests that during adolescence imaginative ability undergoes considerable development. Comparison of the literary productions of children and of adolescents indicates . clearly that the imagination of the teen-ager surpasses that of children both in sweep and in richness of imagery. It is difficult to settle the issue experimentally since imagination is not too amenable to controlled observation. What we can do is study objective expressions of imagination, as in literature, art, and poetry. This leaves something to be desired in the way of scientific validity and exactness, but it does provide a partial answer to the question of development in imagery.[12]

While flights of poetic fancy, and examples of literary and artistic productions are conspicuous by their absence

---

[12] See P. M. Symonds, "Inventory of Themes in Adolescent Fantasy," Amer. J. Orthopsychiat., 1945, 15, 318–328.

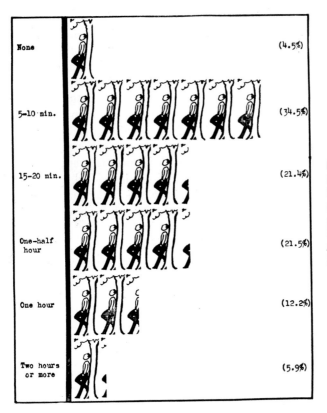

None		(4.5%)
5–10 min.		(34.5%)
15–20 min.		(21.4%)
One–half hour		(21.5%)
One hour		(12.2%)
Two hours or more		(5.9%)

Fig. 29.   Amount of time adolescent boys spend per day in daydreaming. Each symbol represents 5 per cent of the population — from U. H. Fleege, **Self-Revelation of the Adolescent Boy** (Milwaukee: Bruce, 1945), p. 227.

in childhood, we find many instances of such activities among adolescents.[13] It is not uncommon for youth to produce worthwhile poetry, fiction, and even musical and artistic creations, indicating development of the creative imagination. In some instances there is manifested considerable richness and profundity of imagery which probably reflects a wide range of experience as well as perceptual and intellectual development. Fleege, in his study of 2000 adolescent boys, found

that only 4.5 per cent of the group reported no daydreaming, the remainder indicating that they spent from five minutes to six or more hours per day in imaginative fancy (see Fig. 29). The results show that youth tends strongly toward imaginative fancy, and indicate definite developmental shifts from early to later adolescence in the things which occupied such fancy.

Imagination in Mental Life and Adjustment.   The ability to reproduce experiences imaginatively is a *sine qua non* of most of our thinking, since it is often necessary to concretize a thought in order to get a firm hold on it. Similarly, there is a significant relation between imagery and *language*. Although language is primarily the expression of thought, it is

[13] See the chapter on intellectual and creative interests in G. J. Mohr and Marian A. Despres, *The Stormy Decade: Adolescence* (New York: Random House, 1958), Chap. IX. As these authors say, "An urge toward artistic or literary creative expression, dormant during the latter years of the latency period, again emerges during adolescence" (p. 114).

often through the medium of verbal imagery that language finds expression. Moreover, to be able to recapture or to re-form previous sensory experiences into a new pattern is important in many problem-solving situations, again because of the necessity of casting certain problems in concrete form before they can be dealt with adequately. Imagination both enriches and transforms experiences, and contributes to artistic appreciation and production during adolescence.

Imagination is also related to *motivation*. A pleasant experience, for example, will motivate future behavior only in direct proportion to one's ability to recapture the original pleasurable experience. The same is true of unpleasantness. Thus, a hungry person able to imagine the appearance, odor, and flavor of food, plus the pleasantness associated with the satisfaction of hunger, is more strongly motivated than the person lacking imagination. Applying this principle to other situations involving sex, affection, status, and similar needs, the significance of imagination to the motivation of conduct emerges very clearly.

Freud has described a mode of mental functioning, motivated by needs, which tolerates no deferment of gratification. The needs constitute an imperative which reality must meet or before which reality must give way. If the need-gratifying object is not immediately at hand it will be created in fantasy or by hallucination. This mode of mental functioning is characteristic of the unconscious, is apparent in dreams, and may be observed in the behavior of infants. Freud called it the primary process. It is to a greater or lesser degree replaced in the course of growth and development by another mode of mental functioning of which rational thought is an example. This mode, too, is motivated by needs, but the needs no longer constitute an imperative. Allegiance is given to reality as well, and the needs no longer warrant the fantasied creation or destruction of fact. This mode of mental functioning is characterized by tolerance of delay, attention to reality, detour activities, and compromise solutions.[14]

Of particular significance is the relation between imagination and *adjustment*. Imagery is a substitute for reality, and sometimes this characteristic becomes an end in itself. This process is called *phantasy-thinking*, which involves a substitution of daydreaming for the kind of thinking that is tied to objectively real things, that is *reality-thinking*. It is common knowledge that anything whatever can be achieved imaginatively: fame, fortune, a trip to the moon, companions, affection, or success. However, in the pursuit of desirable things, many persons and especially teen-agers are often frustrated; and this situation constitutes the basis of phantasy-thinking. Thus the lonely, rejected adolescent will often dream of great personal success by which he becomes the center of attention and adulation. Or the youngster who fails in school dreams of coming home from the battlefield bedecked with medals and hailed as the conquering hero. Young children without playmates create them in the imagination, project these "companions" into reality, and then act as though they really exist. Daydreams are an integral part of childhood experiences, and through them a partial if inadequate adjustment to reality is often made.[15]

---

[14] A. Wheelis, *The Quest for Identity* (New York: Norton, 1958), pp. 75–76.

[15] See Lauretta Bender and F. Vogel, "Imaginary Companions of Children," *Amer. J. Orthopsychiat.*, 1941, *11*, 56–66. See also E. Walcott, "Daydreamers: a Study of Their Adjustments in Adolescence," *Smith College Stud. in Soc. Wk.*, 1932, *2*, 283–335; B. Karpman, "A Study in Adolescent Imagery," *Amer. J. Orthopsychiat.*, 1946, *16*, 1–33.

H. Armstrong Roberts

Teen-agers often dream of the future.

Daydreams are not only a typical adolescent pastime, but even the *content* of such phantasy is typical. Fleege, for example, found that of the entire group of boys who reported daydreams as a frequent activity, 28.5 per cent indicated that they were dreaming about girls, whereas only 15.9 per cent reported daydreams of future vocational plans. Moreover, a breakdown of these data revealed that, whereas 19.6 per cent of high school freshmen daydreamed about girls, *more than 35 per cent* of seniors reported girls as the most frequent object of daydreaming.[16] These data indicate that there is a strong tendency among youth to reduce frustrations through the medium of phantasy-thinking, and that these tendencies follow a developmental pattern.

This incapacity to accept reality as it is, followed by the tendency to take refuge in phantasy-thinking, is a common state of affairs at all levels of development, adulthood included. In the child it is generally not a particularly disturbing symptom for the reason that he has not had much opportunity to learn how to interpret reality and how to deal effec-

[16] U. H. Fleege, *op. cit.*, p. 231.

tively with it. In adolescence and adulthood, on the other hand, it is a disturbing symptom. The necessity for a realistic outlook on life increases in direct proportion to the achievement of maturity, which brings with it the increased responsibilities of adult living. Yet the frustrations, conflicts, and trials of adolescence are the very things that predispose to imaginal substitution. To the inexperienced vision of youth, reality often becomes intolerable, and there develops a strong tendency to achieve the satisfaction of wants, and to escape the irresolution of conflict, through imaginative flights.

Imagination and Vicarious Living. This escape can be made in several ways: through ordinary daydreaming or phantasy-thinking, and through the mechanisms of *projection* and *identification*. The child is more susceptible to the former, and youth to the latter type of imaginative substitution. The latter type of escape is characterized as *vicarious living*, which may be described as the achievement of experience and the satisfaction of needs through the medium of identification with other persons. Thus, through fiction, movies, games, and amusements, the individual can, by identifying himself with the characters involved, achieve almost any kind of experience he wishes. Depending on the thoroughness of the identification, he will experience the same events, feelings, emotions, moods, and desires that the characters themselves experience. Through them he is able to live briefly the life of a great lover, bandit, football hero, or gambler.

This mechanism of identification is *psychologically necessary* for relaxation and enjoyment. It is the basis for Aristotle's argument that the drama can be an enriching and purifying medium for human emotions, and thus a certain amount of vicarious living can be condoned. The danger lies in continuing the identity to the point where the individual becomes completely dissatisfied with his own mode of life, or confuses a fictionized portrayal with actual reality.

In the humdrum life of many adolescents (and adults) there is a great deal of room for excitement, new experiences, and emotional flights. Their imagination enables them to picture a life far more interesting and stimulating than their own. Especially is this true when there is serious conflict between the adolescent and the demands of his environment. Then he may turn to a more tolerable and pleasing unreality. If he turns to fiction, the hero or heroine dreamed about comes to life and becomes the only worthwhile reality. In the movies he witnesses life as a succession of varied, interesting, and exciting experiences. Sexual delinquencies, fly-by-night marriages, crime, divorce, gambling, war — all are portrayed in their most brilliant and alluring colors. Small wonder that some youngsters, bored with their day-to-day existence in crowded classrooms, or plagued by some insoluble conflict, go to three, four, and five movies a week! Small wonder, too, when complete identification occurs, that they often translate these two-dimensional experiences into reality, adopting or creating roles suggested by the fictional events of the silver screen. It is an easy thing for an adolescent boy to imagine himself as a gambler or criminal wanted by the police, or for a young girl to picture herself as a seductress; and this imaginative play is but one step removed from translation into conduct.

Too often this function of imagination as a medium between experience and conduct is not appreciated by parents and others charged with the care and instruction of youth. Nor do they always appreciate the inability of youth — because of lack of experience and an inadequate system of values — to differentiate between reality and unreality. Adults are too prone to regard these tendencies in the light of their own reactions. But we must remember that young people have a great deal to learn, that they do not clearly understand the purpose of life and its seriousness, and that they have not yet grasped the all-important fact that reality can be much more attractive and worthwhile than phantasy. Only experience and careful instruction can impart these things to the adolescent; and until they are learned, it is necessary to protect him from the vagaries of his own imagination. The adolescent's perception of his world must not become distorted by daydreaming, phantasy, or wishful thinking. The world is real, and he must learn to adopt a realistic attitude toward it, reserving his imagination for vicarious enjoyment, and for creative expression.

MEMORY AND LEARNING IN ADOLESCENCE

Memory, Learning, and Adjustment. The adolescent's perception of his world will be conditioned always by what he learns and remembers. To be able to retain experiences so that they may be utilized in later situations when needed is obviously necessary to the economy of human adjustment, since satisfactory adjustment to various situations is often nothing more than a measure of one's ability to apply what he has learned in such a way that the exigencies of the situation are adequately met. The acquisition of motor habits such as walking, writing, and speaking; the acquisition of useful information; the retention of concepts, principles, and beliefs; and the ability to profit through experience — these are all functions of memory and learning. Education, training, and growth in wisdom, so necessary for effective adjustment and wholesome living, would be impossible without the ability of the organism to be modified by the forces that influence it.

In evaluating the influence of memory and learning on the adolescent's perception of his world, we must not forget that learning is not always beneficial. Besides acquiring necessary skills, habits, or knowledge, the adolescent also learns how to drive a car at breakneck speeds, how to smoke marijuana cigarettes, how to neck and pet and seduce his girl friend, how to hate the people who have rejected or belittled him, how to develop neurotic symptoms and disabling mechanisms, or how to escape frustrations and conflicts by the use of alcohol. Learning is a two-edged sword that can be used to carve a wholesome world for the adolescent, or to cause gaping holes that the adoles-

cent can fall into very easily, thus causing himself serious injury.

The Extent of Memory Development. The extent of development in learning and memory will vary with the kind of learning we are referring to. The acquisition of neuromuscular responses (or motor learning) is not greatly influenced by development, nor is rote memory, which involves the learning of items of experience through ceaseless repetition. But in *logical* or *intellectual* memory, considerable development has been noted.

Memory, like intellect, may be concerned with the general and the abstract. Whereas intellect functions in the formation of concepts and inferences, and the eduction of relationships between objects or experiences, memory empowers the individual to recall these things when they are needed. For this reason all thinking is dependent upon memory to an appreciable extent. The formation of any thought structure presupposes the ability to reinstate in consciousness the concepts, judgments, and relationships that are necessary to the development of thinking. Thus, both critical and creative thinking, without which progress in human thought would be impossible, are directly dependent upon this pervasive ability. The recombination and synthesis of thought elements involved in creative thinking necessitates retention and recall as primary functions.

This fact is of particular significance for education, because education involves intellectual material, and because of the relationship between memory and association. Association is a fundamental factor in learning and remembering, and intellectual memory brings the process of association to its highest level. Learning of the highest type is dependent on an eduction of relationships between concepts, experiences, judgments, and inferences, and this is a special type of association. This process is a leading feature of logical memory, which is not simply a retention of experiences but a step toward *apperception*, a process whereby experiences, ideas, and judgments are organized into a functioning whole in which mental contents are integrally related to each other. Apperception is one of the best guarantees of later recall, and the type of association that characterizes the apperceptive process *presupposes* logical memory.

Because memory, like intelligence, can be measured easily by objective performance, evidence regarding its development during adolescence is both clear and conclusive. Every school test is a measure of memory, and the results can be expressed numerically as the individual's ability to retain and recall learned material. Recognition can be measured in a similar way, and many new-type objective tests are measures of recall or recognition.

Numerous experimental studies indicate that there are notable increases in logical memory throughout adolescence. The curve for retention rises sharply at the beginning of the adolescent period and continues its upward sweep throughout the entire span between puberty and late adolescence. Memory for words increases perceptibly during this period, which reminds us of the close relationship between language and the intellectual functions. The development of intellect of course contributes to the awareness of meanings, which explains why words are more easily learned and retained. Thus, both memory and intellect develop side by side and augment the learning process to a notable degree.

Factors Influencing the Development of Memory. The development of memory is conditioned by many of the changes that are part of the transition from childhood to maturity. Insofar as memory and learning are partly organic, their development probably involves functional, and perhaps even structural, changes in the cerebral cortex. Evidence from both clinic and laboratory indicates conclusively that these processes are strongly affected by cerebral changes. Cortical degeneration that occurs typically in senility, alcoholism, and related pathological states leaves no doubt that memory is seriously disturbed by structural changes in the brain. The work of Lashley and others on the role of the cortex in learning points to the same conclusion, namely, that the processes of memory, learning, and association are intimately dependent upon cortical conditions. This relationship reminds us that physical health and hygiene are of first importance to teen-agers, and that inadequate diet, rest, or recreation can interfere seriously with effective learning and studying.

Dynamic factors also influence the growth of learning. The desire or intention to learn is known to predispose the individual to more efficient retention of learned material. The acquisition of knowledge or experience of any kind is always conditioned by the *receptivity* of the organism; and when a need or motive is functioning at a high level, receptivity may be considerably enhanced. Where intellectual learning is concerned, the influence of needs is supplanted to some extent by the influence of rational motives. This fact is clearly exemplified by the effects of *interest*, which is one of the most important determiners of learning. The adolescent who is bored by classroom discussions, studying, or reading will find it extremely difficult to master the subjects at either the high school or the college level. This is particularly true for the learning of intellectual material. Other motives allied to interest, such as purposes, aims, goals, ambitions, and ideals also predispose the individual toward greater learning and more effective retention; and as we have noted, adolescence is characterized by the development of such motivations.

We must note here also the impact of intellectual development. The learning and retention of ideas, judgments, facts, and theories, that are important aspects of the adolescent's education, are dependent on four factors, all of which are intellectual — attention, understanding, awareness of relationships, and apperception. When these factors are diligently applied to the learning situation, retention will largely take care of itself. Each one of these processes, incidentally, is integral to the other. Attention contributes to understanding, understanding to the eduction of relationships, and all of them to apperception. Since these abilities increase during adolescence, they account for a major part of memory development.

The development of memory and learning during adolescence is important to many phases of adjustment. Normally, the first three or four years of the adolescent period, and in many instances the remaining years as well, are spent in school or college. Nearly every boy and girl is constrained by law to continue in school until the age of sixteen, so that education becomes an integral part of the adolescent economy. To this situation youngsters must make continuous adjustments, many of which are academic in character. Many of the problems of adolescents spring from conflicts or frustrations engendered by difficulty or dissatisfaction with high school subjects, problems that begin in the classroom but soon carry over into other phases of the adolescent's life. In these situations ability to learn plays a prominent role; and therefore every effort should be made to capitalize on the facts relating to memory development, particularly those bearing on the relationships between memory and the dynamic and intellectual changes that characterize the adolescent years.

DEVELOPMENT OF INTELLECTUAL FACTORS

Intellect and Learning.   In the adolescent's perception of his world, what happens to him intellectually in the transition from puberty to adulthood will make a great deal of difference. The intellect of man, when used correctly, can be a powerful instrument for good. It can help him achieve the necessary knowledge and values; it can aid in the development of principles, ideals, and goals; it can pave the way to freedom of action without which healthy adjustment and mental health are impossible. The intellect can be used as an instrument for maturity, for appreciating and laying hold of personal responsibility, and for the development of insight into one's self as well as the reality to which one must adjust. During adolescence the intellect can be sharpened by education, experience, and guidance so as to become a better instrument for realistic thinking — thinking that brings reality into better focus, and refines and improves the relationship between the individual and the world in which he lives. These are the reasons why intellectual development is important to the adolescent's perception of the world in which he lives.

An intellectual factor of primary significance in learning and adjustment is *attention* or *concentration*. As things are attended to, or concentrated on, they are apprehended more clearly and distinctly, since concentration lays bare the meaning of experience and thus contributes to better understanding. Through concentration relationships are brought out, other ideas come to mind, and the whole begins to be *apperceived*. When we recall that learning from the high school level up through college and graduate school is predominantly intellectual in character, we realize how significant the ability to concentrate is. Such learning deals primarily in abstractions, ideas, principles, laws, theorems, causes, historical movements, and the like, all of which require understanding, judgment, and reasoning. If one is to perform these functions well, he must be able to concentrate. Where this is difficult or impossible, because of immaturity, neurotic disability, or distraction, both understanding and reasoning falter, and the process of learning quickly degenerates. This formation of ideas is achieved through abstraction, and abstraction itself is a form of attention.

Concentration is the fountainhead of all critical, constructive, and creative thinking. It is by *examining* ideas, beliefs, and conclusions that we determine their conformity to truth or their falsity; and by concentrating on them, by comparing them with other items of knowledge, and by thinking about them, new ideas are often brought to light. While few adolescents will do creative thinking, they can begin the useful habit of *critical thinking*; and many of them do. The simpler beliefs of childhood do not always satisfy the more critical minds of

youth, and we often find them questioning judgments and conclusions to which they adhered for many years. What evidence there is indicates that the capacity for sustained attention or concentration continues to develop throughout the entire adolescent period. In one typical study of growth in concentration, covering the age period of six to sixteen, the scores were found to rise sharply and continuously, suggesting that the adolescent is much better equipped for work requiring concentration than is the child.[17]

Concentration is basically the organization and direction of mental functions toward some phase of experience. It is, therefore *a measure of the organism's self-control*, and a sign that the organism is tending toward higher levels of integration. Lack of will, flighty or disconnected thought, and poor attention are characteristic features of the mentally disorganized person, for whom thoughts, experiences, and events dominate consciousness. Concentration increases also in direct proportion *to the reduction of distracting influences* and *to the interest aroused by learning material*. Interest itself is complemented by other motivating factors such as *attitudes, desire to learn*, and the *goal to be achieved* by the learner. When these factors are integrated with the learning situation concentration can be raised to a much higher level. The adolescent must realize that concentration is subject to the laws of habit formation, like any other mental function, and that he will learn to concentrate only by controlling the factors that interfere with or promote concentration.

Development of Insight and Under-

---

[17] M. E. Bickersteth, "Application of Mental Tests to Children of Various Ages," *Brit. J. Psychol.*, 1917, 9, 23–73.

standing. The adolescent's perception of reality will be influenced also by insight into himself and others, and by understanding what is going on around him. The typical confusion of the adolescent means that he does not understand clearly what is happening to him or to his world; he has little insight into what is going on. Basically, insight is the ability to grasp the meaning of an experience, a total situation, or a complex event. It presupposes knowledge, and an awareness of relationships between persons, events, and objective realities. Adolescents are often confused because they do not possess the knowledge or the wisdom necessary to *interpret* reality adequately.

The evidence for development of understanding and insight during adolescence is conclusive. Results obtained, for example, with the Stanford-Binet Test, which utilizes comprehension questions of increasing difficulty, indicate a continuous growth of these abilities. The questions themselves are so constructed for various age levels that they require *increasing* intellectual comprehension, the assumption being that such an increase actually occurs. This assumption is supported by test results.

Studies more directly concerned with insight substantiate these conclusions. Cole cites several studies that reveal greater insight among adolescents. For example a test was given to 600 children and adolescents, designed to measure their ability to comprehend the sayings and parables of Jesus. As illustrations, Cole cites the results obtained with two parables, "The Sower" and "The Two Foundations," and four sayings, "What shall it profit a man if he gain the whole world but lose his own soul?"; "Judge not that ye be not judged"; "If you love God,

keep His Commandments"; and "Men love darkness rather than light because their deeds are evil." In Cole's own words:

> The gains between the mental ages of eight and eleven are gradual. Then there are large increases up to about fourteen; after fourteen the gain sometimes continues and sometimes not, depending largely on the height already reached by the curve at that time. In this investigation one finds a reflection of an increase in ability to understand allegories and double meanings. Teachers often sense this development, but proof of it is not always found in investigations using objective tests.[18]

That the ability to form judgments increases during adolescence is evidenced by the results obtained from reliable intelligence tests, since these tests invariably require the ability to educe relationships and to form inferential judgments. Thus, in the American Council on Education Psychological Examination the ability to draw correct inferences is a prominent feature. In the Stanford-Binet test, too, the items at the upper levels are based mainly on the capacity to form judgments and inferences. Only by including such items on a scale of increasing complexity can distinctions in terms of mental age be made at all. Studies other than those based on mental tests point to the same conclusion: that the abilities to judge and to reason show real gains throughout adolescence.[19]

Youth Needs Guidance. The development of intellect does not mean that the adolescent is fully equipped to comprehend every element in a total situation, or that he is no longer liable to error. His knowledge is still very limited, and

[18] Louella Cole, *Psychology of Adolescence*, 3 ed. (New York: Rinehart, 1948), p. 464.
[19] See G. Hendrickson, "Mental Development During the Preadolescent and Adolescent Periods," *Rev. Educ. Res.*, 1950, 20, 351–360.

whatever opinions he forms will be greatly influenced, as opinions always are, by non-intellectual factors. Because of limitations in his experience and knowledge, the teen-ager is particularly prone to the distorting influence of emotions, prejudices, and wishes. Furthermore, because he is just beginning to flex his intellectual biceps, he is likely to put too much faith in his capacities. The average youth is not able to determine the truth or falsity of many doctrines with which he comes in contact; and here, as elsewhere, there is need for careful guidance. Fundamental beliefs of a religious, moral, and social nature should be protected against immature thinking and inadequate knowledge. We do not entrust the responsibilities of marriage, a high-salaried job, or political office to youth; and there is no more reason for entrusting him with the care of truth. When he is intellectually mature there will be many opportunities for the exercise of his critical powers.

Determinants of Intellectual Growth. It is not an easy matter to determine the causes of intellectual development during adolescence. It may be that changes occur, which cause the nervous system to become a more efficient instrument for intellectual functioning, such as the formation of new associative patterns, but the evidence is not conclusive. As the organism matures, there is a progressive tendency toward higher integrative functioning, which is often reflected in the development of concentration. However, it is difficult to see what bearing nerve development could have on inductive inference, the eduction of relationships, or the development of abstract knowledge. Granted that a healthy and adequately developed nervous system is a *sine qua non* of mental life, the development of the nervous system by itself is incapable of furnishing the key to intellectual growth. We can be sure that the development of perception, imagination, memory, and learning influences the growth of intellect, especially in view of their integral relationships. Yet it is just as easy to say that the development of intellect influences the growth of other mental functions.

Since experience is the basic material of knowledge, it can be argued that it is an important determiner of intellectual development. Intelligence, therefore, not only develops of itself; *it must also be developed.* Comparative studies of twins, foster children, and parent-child resemblances have indicated that cultural level of the home, length of residence in foster homes, and the intelligence of foster parents have a bearing on the constancy of the IQ.[20] Intelligence, therefore, must be *nurtured;* it must be given opportunity to develop fully by providing a favorable milieu. Fortunately, during adolescence the range of intellectual experiences is appreciably broadened with obvious effects on intellectual development. This interpretation applies equally well to practical intelligence, which also develops only with experience. Unfortunately, many adolescents are deprived of this kind of experience, and when they reach adulthood they are extremely immature in the handling of practical problems, such as the selection of a career, the raising of children, or the changing of jobs. The only antidote to this immaturity is training and experience in the business of intelligent living.

Thus, if intellect is to develop to its

---

[20] R. S. Woodworth, "Heredity and Environment: a Critical Survey of Recently Published Material on Twins and Foster Children," *Soc. Sci. Res. Council, Bull.,* 1941, No. 47.

maximum, there must be provided a wide range of intellectual experiences, opportunities for its practical use, and real challenges to thinking. Just as one person becomes an expert golfer through experience, opportunity, practice, and challenge, so another grows in intellectual performance. We do not wish to minimize the limits of intellectual development imposed by the organism itself; environment, training, and experience cannot make a genius out of a moron; nevertheless, the influence of the environment should be fully exploited in the interests of sound intellectual growth.

Finally, we should note the influence of motivating factors on intellectual development. Interests, aims, ambitions, attitudes, goals, and ideals can have a direct bearing on intellectual functioning. Even certain needs, like recognition, status, and participation, can have some influence. All such factors, working in unison, give determination and goal-directedness to individual effort, and serve to bring out the best in the way of intellectual performance. Educators of youth know that a high level of motivation can spell the difference between failure and success in high school or college, and that success is often a reflection of the development of intelligence to its maximum.

Implications of Intellectual Growth. Intellectual development during adolescence has implications for many aspects of personality growth and adjustment. These implications stand out sharply in the relation between intellectual development and learning. The organism is still pliable in adolescence, and thus it is an excellent time for the growth of wholesome habits, and the incorporation of principles, attitudes, ideals, and sentiments that can contribute measurably to the formation of a well-integrated personality and a healthy character.

The growth of intellect has a direct bearing also on moral, social, and religious development because it is necessary to the understanding of basic moral and social truths, principles, and practices. Such changes are reflected in the development of important values and attitudes, which influence the growth of temperament, character, and personality. Intellectual development, therefore, paves the way to maturity, adjustment, and personal growth, and deeply affects the adolescent's perception of his world.

THE GROWTH OF INTELLIGENCE

What Intelligence Is. Intelligence is a term with many meanings. It is closely related to the term "intellect," and yet does not mean exactly the same thing. Both terms are alike in that they signify the capacity to think, as distinct, for example, from the abilities to perceive, imagine, or remember. They differ insofar as the latter term, intellect, is qualitative and serves to mark the distinction between intellectual and nonintellectual beings. In this strict sense, intellect is a capacity that is found only in rational beings. It is not something that can be measured directly since it possesses no quantitative aspects. Intellect, understood as a qualitative characteristic of man, is co-ordinate with such factors as temperament and character since they too serve as distinguishing characteristics.

Intelligence, on the other hand, is the manifestation of intellect, the operational function in which the capacity of intellect is put to use. Since such a function requires a medium through which to operate — in this case the brain — intelligence and brain power are often regarded as identical. When understood correctly, the term "brain power" is quite appropriate to designate intelligence. The brain by itself can do no thinking, but thinking becomes possible when brain and intellect function together. This process of thinking is measured by intelligence tests, the results of which can be stated in quantitative terms.

Thinking is not a single act. It involves the processes of attention, abstraction, judgment, and inference that we studied earlier. To say that a person is intelligent, therefore, implies that he is capable of doing these things in greater or lesser degree. But even this is not enough to indicate the full meaning of intelligence. The intelligent-person is able to profit by past experience, to understand and follow directions, and to solve problems in a manner to promote his own adjustment. In other words, to be intelligent one must be able not only to think, but he must be able to make good use of his thinking.

Intelligence and Adjustment.   Intelligence of this practical sort is not simply a matter of intellect. It takes more than intellect to profit by past experience, to develop foresight, or to learn how to adjust effectively to the environment.[21] Required also are experience, a dependable memory, and training in the art of acting intelligently. Intelligent behavior depends also on character, temperament, and motives. Regardless of intellectual level, it is not intelligent for a person to use medicine or drugs whose properties are unknown, or to purchase stock in a company he knows nothing about. Such crassly unintelligent conduct can be witnessed day in and day out among otherwise "intelligent" people. Obviously since

such persons are in a certain sense intelligent, their behavior is not a reflection of their ability to *think*, but rather of their abilty to *act* intelligently.

This distinction between the ability to think and the ability to act intelligently is not merely nominal. It is fundamental to the concept of intelligence. In children the disparity is especially striking. Really bright children, whose school marks reflect an unquestionable ability to understand, perceive relations, and reason, will often be remarkably unintelligent in practical matters. They often fail utterly to profit by experience, and seem at times incapable of making a sound practical judgment. In this sense, therefore, intelligence is only partly a reflection of intellect.

Determinants of Practical Intelligence. Intelligent behavior is determined by the ability to understand and to reason, and also by personality factors, and by the environment in which the organism develops. Intelligence, therefore, should be nurtured in the most favorable environment possible, one that provides experience in the application of intellectual capacities to concrete, everyday situations. It makes little difference whether an adolescent can understand the writings of Plato, Einstein, or Eddington, if he fails to solve a simple problem like staying out of debt, or if he does not know how to apply the principles he has learned in philosophy, ethics, or psychology. Can anything be more stupid than war, which involves such a criminal waste of lives, property, and spiritual values? Yet the men who make war would probably do well on an intelligence test. Whether Abraham Lincoln would have earned a high score on such a test we cannot even guess; but it is certain that he was endowed with the keenest practical intel-

---

[21] In this connection, see D. Weschsler, "Intellectual Development and Psychological Maturity," *Child Develpm.*, 1950, 21, 45–50.

ligence. On purely intellectual grounds, he should have gotten rid of General Grant when he was told that Grant was addicted to the use of liquor, since such a habit is obviously a threat to good generalship; but it was Lincoln's good fortune to subject judgment to the test of practical value.

Nor should we overlook the influence of other personality factors like will, temperament, and character. Is the teen-age drinker acting intelligently when he knows what the end result of his drinking will be? Can we say that the gambler is intelligent when he risks his earnings on a roulette table, knowing that the money is needed to support his family? Is the student acting intelligently when he knows that if he does not study he will fail in his examination, and still does not study? In such persons there is not always lack of understanding, insight, or judgment. They know better, all of them. But intellect is not enough to make them act intelligently. There must be determination (a strong will), sound character, and control of temperamental factors, impulses, and needs. Qualities such as these are not acquired by academic training in high school or college. They are acquired, if at all, in the process of growing up, and they constitute a measure of the individual's development, adjustment, and integration.

The Concept of Intellectual Development. The concept of intellectual development itself has several meanings. First of all, since intelligence embraces several functions, the concept may refer to development of any one or all of these, and we have already studied the development of these different functions. Second, intellectual development may be taken to mean the kind of growth manifested in the results of intelligence tests.

It is this aspect of intellectual development that we shall concern ourselves with in the remainder of this chapter.

There is, of course, no real difference between measuring the general factor of intelligence and the several intellectual processes, since in order to measure the former we must employ items that measure the separate functions. However, the results can be expressed differently, and usually are. The measurement of general intelligence may be expressed in terms of a raw score, mental age, intelligence quotient, percentile rank, or standard score; and the many studies attempting to determine the extent of intellectual growth and decline use such indexes in expressing their results. The measurement of a single factor like attention, however, is another matter, such concepts as mental age or intelligence quotient being inapplicable. Moreover, it may be that any single factor develops little or not at all, and is only minutely reflected in the curve of general intellectual growth. This is one good reason why the two aspects of intellectual development should be considered separately, so that we may determine on what the development of intellect more directly depends. We may expect the conclusions in each instance to coincide generally, since the measurement in both cases deals with essentially the same capacity.

Intellectual Growth in Adolescence. Intelligence seems to develop continuously throughout childhood and adolescence.[22] This fact is substantiated by the

[22] See G. J. Froehlich, "Mental Development During the Preadolescent and Adolescent Periods," *Rev. Educ. Res.*, 1944, 14, 401–412; R. L. Thorndike, "Growth of Intelligence During Adolescence," *J. Genet. Psychol.*, 1948, 72, 11–15; F. K. Shuttleworth, *The Adolescent Period: a Graphic Atlas* (Evanston, Ill.: Child Developm. Publ., 1951), Figs. 255–295. See also the articles in Chapter V in R. G. Kuhlen

results of testing of students in the elementary and secondary grades, and by the greater intellectual achievements of adolescents compared with children. It is obvious that the more difficult and abstract subjects in high school require a more highly developed intellect than grade school children possess; and the progressively higher standards of intellectual achievement used to evaluate children in high school and college indicate that intellect is expected to develop continuously throughout the adolescent period. Also, adolescents, as compared with children, have greater insight, better understanding, and perceive relationships more readily. All these facts indicate continued intellectual growth during adolescence. Just where this growth stops has never been accurately determined, but it is generally supposed that the curve of intellectual growth levels off around the end of the adolescent period. Thorndike, on the basis of a study of 1000 subjects, concluded that intelligence continues to develop until age 20 and even beyond this point.

Unfortunately, much of our thinking in this area has been determined by the use of standardized intelligence tests, and it is well known that it is impossible to separate the measurement of innate ability or intelligence from the effects of learning and development. Thus some intelligence tests measure pretty much the same factors as standard achievement tests do, and the correlations between the results obtained by the two methods of testing are correspondingly high. Most intelligence tests sample environmental background, learning, and teaching ability as much as they do innate power to think.

The language and reading skills demanded by intelligence tests are learned, and thus testing measures these skills also. Moreover, with increase in age, intellectual backgrounds and experiences become so varied that it is difficult to find a common content for tests in terms of which to measure intelligence. Thus, the kind of abilities measured by intelligence tests may reach the limits of development in later adolescence, but this may mean only that tests are inadequate to measure all aspects of intellectual growth. Certainly the standardized test is of little value for the measurement of practical intelligence, and in this area intellectual development seems to continue for some time.

Investigators in this field point to another difficulty that must be considered in evaluating test results. The norms used in interpreting these results are based on surveys of entire school populations; but every year throughout the high school period there is more and more *student elimination.* Cole states that a test used in the average high school measures only 65 per cent of that population, and that there is no such thing as an age norm based on an entire distribution of any age above twelve. Test norms, therefore, reflect both increased intelligence and increasing elimination; as more students terminate their schooling, the average score made by the remaining group will rise whether there is a real increase in intellectual ability or not.[23] In fact, when efforts are made to test the same groups over a period of years, the results obtained indicate some intellectual growth, but not nearly so much as that indicated by the usual method of testing different groups at different age levels.

and G. G. Thompson (eds.), *Psychological Studies of Human Development* (New York: Appleton-Century-Crofts, 1952).

---

[23] Louella Cole, *Psychology of Adolescence* (New York: Rinehart, 1936).

This again may mean only that the test construction is faulty; but certainly this method of testing the same groups over a period of years is much better for determining actual intellectual development.

An important fact brought out by intelligence testing is the tremendously wide distribution of abilities in high school populations. In a typical freshman class the mental age may vary from that of the average fourth grade child to that expected of college seniors. Intelligence quotients sometimes range from as low as 60 to as high as 160, with an average of 105 to 110. This variability continues throughout high school, but becomes somewhat reduced through eliminations. This wide distribution of ability is of particular importance to the teacher who must gear her instruction to meet the needs of all of her students. Unfortunately, the same teacher is plagued by the steady decrease in the average ability of entering students, and by the tremendous increase in the number of youths now attending high school. Investigations of high school populations indicate that a considerable proportion of freshman students in high school are too low in intellectual caliber to profit by the traditional academic curriculum. Knowledge of these facts is very important to the development of adequate educational procedures, and indicates how necessary intelligence testing can be in working out an acceptable program.

Growth of Special Abilities. There are several capacities besides intelligence that seem to undergo development during adolescence, some of which are allied to intelligence. *Mechanical aptitude* is such a capacity, and its development can be a matter of considerable importance in view of the large number of tasks in which this aptitude is involved. Research studies indicate that the growth of mechanical skill is especially rapid during childhood, and that this development continues throughout adolescence. This development is probably related to the physical, sensory, motor, and intellectual changes that occur, although there is a great deal of individual variation here as elsewhere. Thus where one youngster shows a high degree of mechanical ability, another may indicate very little. Such variation is to be expected since it applies to all forms of development.

There seems also to be some increase during adolescence in *mathematical* and *scientific aptitudes*. To what extent this development reflects formal training is difficult to say since children have little contact in school with mathematical and scientific learning. Whatever the reason for these changes, the important point is that the development of aptitudes is basic to many aspects of educational growth. Intellectual development is important here, because the understanding and manipulation of mathematical and scientific concepts depend to a great extent on intellectual ability. Studies of other abilities, including vocabulary, appreciation of prose, and musical ability, have produced largely negative results. In remedial reading courses given to college freshmen, the writer has often noted the extremely narrow vocabulary range of many students. This deficiency may reflect limited intelligence, or it may mean that the reading and other experiences on which the development of vocabulary largely depends are so limited throughout adolescence that vocabulary does not increase appreciably. Language is an acquired function and depends on experience and practice. This failure of vocabulary development is not true of all persons, particularly superior students.

Very often such development continues throughout adolescence and early adulthood. Not only does vocabulary increase, but the employment of language as a symbolic function becomes much more proficient.

Perhaps the same holds true of other abilities like musical and artistic appreciation. These abilities depend upon so many factors, of which intellect is only one, that the majority of individuals show little gain during the formative years of the adolescent period. Yet the greater the range of experience with phenomena of this kind, the more likely is appreciation to develop. In fact, it has been found that liking for and appreciation of classical music increases in direct proportion to experience with it, regardless of musical aptitudes or training.[24] These findings suggest that many adolescents could profit by a greater range of musical experience if given the opportunity. Other abilities, like artistic and literary appreciation and expression, could be encouraged in the same manner. Considering the important effects that these experiences can have on personality growth, every effort should be made to bring them within the range of the adolescent's exploration of his world.

THE INTELLECTUAL PROBLEM CHILD

The Problem of High School Curricula. We have seen that the variation of high school students on intelligence tests is very wide. In the typical high school one may expect that about 65 per cent will possess average intelligence, which means that they have enough ability to succeed in traditional high school subjects; about

[24] See M. Schoen, The Psychology of Music (New York: Ronald, 1940).

15 per cent will be in the dull class, those who have considerable difficulty in learning traditional high school subjects; and another 15 per cent will be bright students, those who learn more readily than the average, often complete school earlier, and whose academic work is on the whole uniformly good. The remainder of the distribution will be taken up by the intellectual defectives, who usually are quickly eliminated from the academic scene, and by the brilliant students, who constitute a special problem in the high school situation.

In view of this distribution, it is not surprising that the record of failures and eliminations throughout high school is distressingly bad. It is impossible to develop a curriculum and an educational program that will conform to the needs of such a vast hodgepodge of intellectual material. However, while elimination is excessively high, failures are not the primary cause. Actually the frequency of failures among those who drop out is smaller than among the graduates, so that failing students are eliminated with greater difficulty than nonfailures. Figures such as these bespeak discouragement, disillusionment, and sometimes despair on the part of many students who fail to "make the grade." Some of them want to graduate but lack the necessary ability to compete with others who are better endowed intellectually. They are mute testimony to the inadequacy of the high school to provide the kind of education they require. Training should be suited to their abilities, and along lines that will lead them eventually to some field of endeavor in which they can utilize their talents to the best advantage. Other factors also cause elimination, including boredom with schoolwork, desires to earn money, to get married, and so on. Even here the school could do much toward the development of curricula, subject matter, and teaching techniques that would lead to successful learning and instill in students the desire to see the educational program through to graduation from high school.

The Dull Adolescent. The youngster who is intellectually inferior to the average of the group presents a special problem. It is no longer believed that he is vocationally and educationally a loss, or that from his ranks spring the socially delinquent, the criminal, or the unemployable. Leaving aside those unfortunates with mental ages below 11 years, there is a large class of dull persons, those with mental ages between 11 and 13 years; and it is from this group that the intellectual problem children in high school spring.

These persons are characterized chiefly by inferior intellectual ability. They learn slowly, have difficulty with abstract subjects, and show little interest in books.[25] They are typically nonacademic in interests and proclivities. Their inferiority shows up clearly as the high school subjects become increasingly abstract and difficult, a situation that has important implications for their adjustment. There are no social stigmata that characterize the dull person, especially if he is not required to make unusual adjustments. He may actually exceed his brighter companions in activities that lie outside the field of his particular weakness. Given the opportunity, he can often meet very well the demands of his own social environment in such matters as co-operation, making friends, getting along with others, and so on.[26] The dull person,

like everyone else, is to a large extent a reflection of the demands of his environment. It is when such demands exceed his abilities to cope with them that undesirable traits may develop.

These persons are at a distinct disadvantage in school, and the excessive demands of formal training often cause disillusionment or rebellion, unhappiness and lack of adjustment. This situation breeds feelings of inferiority which may generate undesirable social traits that can lead to delinquency or even criminality. Dull persons have difficulty developing moral concepts and principles, and thus they may develop into social misfits when pushed intellectually beyond their capabilities. In addition, the demands of the out-of-school environment may be too heavy for them to shoulder, and certainly they are at a considerable disadvantage in the workaday world when thrown into competition with others who are intellectually normal or above average.

The dull youngster, therefore, must be trained carefully for the social and economic milieu for which he is best fitted. He needs a great deal of careful vocational guidance. He should be trained in patterns of behavior that are socially and morally acceptable, leaving as little as possible to his own judgment and decisions. This training should be instituted in the home and continued in school. These youngsters will profit little from the usual academic curriculum in high school. What they need most from school

---

[25] See the study by H. N. Hoffman, "A Study in an Aspect of Concept Formation, With Subnormal, Average, and Superior Adolescents,"

Genet. Psychol., Monogr., 1955, 52, 191–239.

[26] See Georgia F. Lightfoot, "Personality Characteristics of Bright and Dull Children," *Teach. Coll. Contr. Educ.,* 1951, No. 969; W. McGehee and W. D. Lewis, "A Comparison of Certain Personality Characteristics of Mentally Superior and Mentally Retarded Children," *J. Educ. Res.,* 1942, 35, 600–610. See also the articles in Chapter VI in R. G. Kulen and G. G. Thompson (eds.), *op. cit.*

is training in skills needed for a job they may secure later on, and skills to meet the general demands of the environment in which they live. In other words, they must be trained, within the limits of their capacities, to adjustment along vocational, social, moral, and emotional lines. We must emphasize that there are many individuals with limited intelligence who have achieved a relatively happy and contented life. Vocationally there are almost unlimited possibilities in business and industry for jobs that are especially well suited to persons with little imagination or low intelligence. In one study of 9885 such persons only 9.2 per cent were found to be delinquent. When emphasis in training is put on correct social and moral behavior, and on vocational preparation, there is no reason to regard the dull adolescent as any more of a problem than his intellectually superior brother.

The Superior Adolescent. It is now recognized that the intellectually superior individual is more than likely to be superior in many respects, including the physical. The seeming physical inferiority of such persons often results from the fact that they are thrown in with older children who are physically more mature, and thus are at a disadvantage when compared physically with them. Their greater intellectual ability manifests itself in rapid learning, ability to retain what is learned, more efficient concentration, a quick grasp of relationships, ability to manipulate concepts, and in a desire to learn.[27]

For these reasons the superior youngster is almost always an academic success, and will often be one or two years ahead of other children of his own age in school. Parents and teachers must realize that ordinary schoolwork offers little challenge to the intellectually gifted child, and that his interests can be stimulated and sustained only by work that measures up to his capacities. Considering the tendency toward lowering of standards in high school, this becomes an even greater problem. If courses are too easy, uninteresting, or boring, the superior child may react with little or no effort, developing habits of laziness and lack of initiative that carry over into later years.

Investigations of bright students indicate that they often do work in high school and college much below their real capacity. For them, training in high school should lead to mastery of those subjects and techniques that will be needed later on as a student in college, or as a citizen who most likely will assume a position of leadership. Particularly should the superior adolescent acquire habits of diligent effort, for the very reason that many tasks are performed so easily, and require so little effort on his part. In general, we may say that the curriculum and the teaching methods used with above-average students should conform as closely as possible to their abilities, that no effort should be spared in developing their superior intellectual powers to the maximum, at the same time that they are imbued with habits

---

[27] There are many excellent studies of gifted children, including the following: H. A. Carroll, "Intellectually Gifted Children, Their Characteristics and Problems," *Teach. Coll. Rec.*, 1940, 42, 212–227; Catherine C. Miles, "Gifted Children," in L. Carmichael (ed.), *Manual of Child Psychology*, 2 ed. (New York: Wiley,

1954), pp. 984–1063; Gertrude Hildreth, "Three Gifted Children: a Developmental Study," *J. Genet. Psychol.*, 1954, 85, 239–262; Ruth Strang, "Gifted Adolescents' Views of Growing Up," *Except. Child.*, 1956, 23, 10–15; Sister Josephina, "Reading Accomplishment of Gifted and Average Pupils," *Educ. & Psychol. Msmnt.*, 1958, 18, 867–871.

of diligence, discipline, and hard work.[28]

Because of his superior intellect, this type of adolescent presents different personal characteristics than do those who are either average or dull, because personal traits develop in line with innate capacities and special abilities. Such traits will be conditioned also by environmental factors, like parental attitudes and discipline; but these factors themselves will in part reflect the individual's superiority. In other words, the environment for the superior person cannot be the same as that of the average individual. For example, the superior adolescent often evidences qualities of leadership, which in turn alter the social relationships in which he becomes involved. Because he often leads others, his is a different personality and a different perspective from those who are content to be led. Consequently, others in his group treat him differently from the way they treat the average person.

Certainly the superior youngster has the capacity for developing worthwhile traits. Handled correctly, he will become a responsible, co-operative member of society, well equipped to achieve a high degree of adjustment. If, of course, his superiority is exploited, flaunted, favored, envied, or belittled, he will react correspondingly, sometimes developing very negative personality traits. He tends somewhat naturally toward introverted attitudes, which may be enhanced by insufficient social experience. Because he is superior he does not always fit in well

with the group, and there may be a tendency toward withdrawal, and a concentration on such things as academic work, which he knows he can do exceptionally well. Every effort should be made to reduce such tendencies because they are the forerunners of emotional and social maladjustment.

The superior youngster, unfortunately, belongs to two different groups at the same time. Physically, and perhaps emotionally too, he belongs with children of his own age. He is socially at ease with such children. Intellectually, however, he belongs to another group, and the method of acceleration in school often puts him there. In such a situation he is intellectually at ease, competing successfully with the best efforts of the older children in the class. But this arrangement tends to disrupt normal social development. The interests, play activities, and aspirations of older children may not be congenial to him, and he feels lost in a world of social relationships for which he is not yet equipped.

Investigations bear out these conclusions. In one study of superior adolescents entering college at the age of 16, it was found that in academic success there was little discrepancy between them and other students. But 32 per cent of the group studied reported feelings of social inadequacy in college, and 46 per cent said that they had felt socially inadequate in high school. It is noteworthy that the percentage does drop considerably as they approach the end of adolescence, where the differences in chronological age tend to be negated by the fact of a common maturity. There is a great deal of difference ordinarily between a 12-year-old and a 14-year-old boy; but there is very little difference, except chronologically, between a 24-year-old per-

---

[28] In this connection see Gertrude Hildreth, *Educating Gifted Children* (New York: Harper, 1952); Norma Cutts and N. Mosely, *Teaching the Bright and Gifted* (Englewood Cliffs, N. J.: Prentice-Hall, 1957), and W. J. Cruickshank and G. O. Johnston, *Education of Exceptional Children and Youth* (Englewood Cliffs, N. J.: Prentice-Hall, 1958).

son and a 26-year-old person. In fact, it may happen that the younger man or woman is socially and emotionally "older" than the person born two years earlier.

We may expect, therefore, that social inadequacies will tend to disappear with the achievement of maturity; but by that time the harm is often done. One cannot take chances on negative outcomes when dealing with the problems of youth. If a practice like acceleration causes social maladjustment, it were better to avoid it entirely, and to develop academic techniques that will serve the intellectual needs of the superior youngster where he is. Undoubtedly some bright children who are socially and emotionally more mature than the average of their group can be accelerated without any detrimental effects. In these cases it is perhaps just as well to accelerate them; but on the whole, this method should be used with extreme caution.

The superior child does not present as great a vocational problem ordinarily as either the average or the dull child; but there is still need for vocational guidance. There is much about the world of work that he does not know, and he must be steered into courses and toward vocations that are suited to his abilities. He should be discouraged from entering fields that are not worthy of his intellectual and other talents, because vocational adjustment depends to a great extent upon harmony between what the work requires and what one is capable of doing. In the professions, particularly, there is always room for superior individuals, and it is toward such fields that they should be directed if they are otherwise qualified. In this, as in everything else, it is necessary to take the whole person into consideration, so that by wise guidance the bright youngster may be spared the pitfalls of his own ignorance, lack of experience, or lack of perspective.

Thus we see that there are many things that influence and determine the adolescent's perception of his world. He has needs and desires and longings that sharpen or distort his perceptive acuity; he acquires sensitivities that quicken his reactions to others and to the events taking place in his environment; he possesses or develops broader intellectual perspectives that alter his system of values, his appreciation of the world in which he lives, and the people who make up his world. The adolescent lives in a world different from that of the child not only because he is growing into adult responsibilities and relationships, but because he perceives the world differently. And this perception has much to do with his reactions to the environment of family, neighborhood, community, school, and church in which he moves and has his being.

SELECTED READINGS

Cruickshank, W. M. (ed.), *Psychology of Exceptional Children and Youth* (Englewood Cliffs, N. J.: Prentice-Hall, 1955).

De Haan, R., and Havighurst, R., *Educating Gifted Children* (Chicago: University of Chicago Press, 1957).

Garrison, K. C., *The Psychology of Exceptional Children*, 3 ed. (New York: Ronald, 1950).

Goodenough, Florence L., *Developmental Psychology*, 2 ed. (New York: Appleton-Century-Crofts, 1945), Chaps. XIV, XV, XVIII.

Heiser, K. F., *Our Backward Children* (New York: Norton, 1955).

Inhelder, Barbel, and Piaget, J., *The Growth of Logical Thinking From Childhood to Adolescence*, trans. by Anne Persons and S. Milgram (New York: Basic Books, 1958).

Merry, F. K., and Merry, R. V., *The First Two Decades of Life* (New York: Harper, 1950), Chaps. 5–8.

Sherman, M., *Intelligence and Its Deviations* (New York: Ronald, 1945).

Stoddard, G. D., *The Meaning of Intelligence* (New York: Macmillan, 1943).

Symonds, P. M., *Adolescent Fantasy* (New York: Columbia University Press, 1949).

Witty, P. (ed.), *The Gifted Child* (Boston: Heath, 1951).

Zubek, J. P., and Solberg, Patricia A., *Human Development* (New York: McGraw-Hill, 1954), Chaps. 6–10.

CHAPTER XVIII

THE ADOLESCENT IN THE FAMILY

We have seen how the adolescent looks at his world, and now we shall see what the world of the adolescent is like. What is it like to be a member of a family, and what does this do for adolescent development? How does the adolescent fit into the community, and what do these experiences mean to him? There are many aspects of growing up, and this is one of the most important.

CULTURE AND PERSONALITY DEVELOPMENT

Cultural "Determinism." That the cultural milieu is a basic factor in the development of personality is a widely accepted principle. In Chapter I we indicated that adolescence is in part a social phenomenon, and referred briefly to anthropological studies which suggest that many phenomena of adolescence vary as much with the culture in which personality develops as with the physiological and psychological alterations of puberty.[1] The

studies of anthropologists like Margaret Mead and Ruth Benedict show that family structures, social traditions, and cultural taboos and mores have a great deal to do with the conflicts, frustrations, and peculiarities of the adolescent period. Discussing sexual behavior in different cultures, Bateson brings out clearly the relationship between cultural factors and behavior when he says:

At the physiological level, we can, of course, refer to the processes of sex and reproduction as universal, but when we come to use these terms as counters in psychological discussion, we find that they may mean very different things in different cultural systems. Sexual initiative may come typically either from the male or from the female (as among the Iatmul of New Guinea), and the sexual act may be conceived of as aggressive (as among the Mundugumor), or as affection (as among the Arapesh). The relation-

[1] See the interesting articles by M. W. Barnes, "The Nature and Nurture of Early Adolescents," *Teach. Coll. Rec.*, 1956, *57*, 513–521; M. E. Kirkpatrick, "The Mental Hygiene of Adolescents in the Anglo-American Culture," *Ment. Hyg.*, N. Y., 1952, *36*, 394–403; Margaret Mead, "The Impact of Culture on Personality Development in the U. S. Today," *Understanding the Child*, 1951, *201*, 17–18. Mead argues that our children are living in the most rapidly changing culture in the world, and that each generation is different from the preceding one, all of which requires the educator and parent to equip the child to meet the exacting tasks demanded of him. In this connection see P. C. Sottong, "The Dilemma of the Parent as Culture Bearer," *Soc. Casewk.*, 1955, *36*, 302–306. See also G. H. J. Pearson, *Adolescence and the Conflict of Generations* (New York: Norton, 1958).

ship between man and wife may be predominantly tinged with dominance-submission, or with succoring-dependence, or with exhibitionism-spectatorship, or with any of the many variants of composition or cooperation; and these characteristics may be relatively standardized in the most varied ways in different communities.[2]

This relationship between behavior and cultural patterns is exemplified also in the influence of more "local" determinants. Depressions, war, social conflict, migration, and racial and religious prejudices determine to some degree both the content and the pattern of behavior reactions. In 1932, Jones, studying the relation of economic depression to delinquency, crime, and drunkenness in Massachusetts, found that all adult theft crimes increased materially during the depression years beginning in 1930. Arrests for violations of liquor laws decreased, as did juvenile delinquency.[3] It is generally assumed that

the impact of World War II contributed to the rise in delinquency, and it is likely that similar social upheavals are also reflected in the moral and social behavior of individuals or of communities. The recent upsurge of interest in religion is suggestive of the same fact, in view of the widespread anxiety that has resulted from two major wars and the chronic threat of complete destruction. The exact nature of the relation between social events and different behavior patterns is not clear, but the fact remains that the relationship does exist. Numerous studies, dealing with density of population, migrations, urban versus rural influences, and the like support the concept of cultural determinism.

Culture Conflict and Behavior.   The seemingly adverse influence of Western culture on the development of personality, by causing conflict, massive anxiety, or emotional imbalance, especially during adolescence, is not so unfortunate as it may seem. The implication that adolescent development suffers from the imposition of certain taboos and social restrictions ignores the obvious fact that Western civilization — with all of its mores, taboos, and standards — has progressed further than have any primitive societies. It may be, as we suggested earlier, that conflict is actually a stepping-stone to progress and self-advancement. Or, to phrase it differently, the restrictions that are to an important extent

---

[2] G. Bateson, "Cultural Determinants of Personality," in J. McV. Hunt (ed.), *Personality and the Behavior Disorders* (New York: Ronald Press, © 1944), Vol. II, pp. 726–727. For a study of cultural deprivation, see R. M. Zingg, "Feral Man and Extreme Cases of Isolation," *Amer. J. Psychol.*, 1940, 53, 487–517. See also Erickson's study of two American Indian tribes in E. H. Erikson, *Childhood and Society* (New York: Norton, 1950), Part Two.

[3] V. Jones, "Relation of Economic Depression to Delinquency, Crime, and Drunkenness in Massachusetts," *J. Soc. Psychol.*, 1932, 3, 259–282. Similar relationships between cultural divergencies and personality development are exemplified in other studies. See, for example, Leonore Boehm, "The Development of Independence: a Comparative Study," *Child Developm.*, 1957, 28, 85–92. Boehm found that American children become more emancipated from their parents at an earlier age than do Swiss children, that they are less subjugated to adults but more dependent on peers, that they develop freedom of thought and independence of judgment earlier, and that they develop a more autonomous conscience earlier. See also J. B. Montague, "A Study of Anxiety Among English and American Boys," *Amer. Sociol. Rev.*, 1955,

20, 685–689. Confirming these cultural influences are the data on suicide for different countries and nationalities. In an article in *Time* magazine (January 26, 1959) it is pointed out that suicide among the Japanese is particularly high in the 15–24 age group, and is a leading cause of death. The rate for teen-agers and young adults is 54.8 per 100,000. Japanese psychiatrists argue that this is partly due to the rigid caste system which conflicts with conscious strivings to behave according to modern Western ways.

self-imposed in Western civilization, in line with the demands of society, morality, and religion, are the very things that make possible a more highly developed social organization. The idea that social restrictions, or the conflicts of adolescence, are necessarily evil must be evaluated in the light of results. The longer period of adolescence in modern society, if not carried to extremes, may be the means by which maturity and integration of a higher order are achieved. Learning to cope with and to resolve conflicts can be of considerable significance to the development of character, and character is basic to maturity and adjustment. A society devoid of frustrations, difficulties, or conflicts would be analogous to the family situation in which overindulgence and overprotection dominate parent-child relationships. In both instances, one might expect the emergence of weak, passive, and poorly integrated personalities.

PERSONALITY DETERMINANTS

Cultural Versus Precultural Determinants. The concept of cultural determinism as related to personality development is implied also in our definition of personality in Chapter III, where we stressed the relation between various response patterns of personality and the environment in which it develops. To determine more exactly the role of cultural determinants, it is necessary to develop this concept of personality in more detail. We may begin with a truism of modern personality theory: that at no point can we clearly separate the influence of culture or environment from that of intrinsic or innate personality determinants. We must recognize that the influence of environment is always conditioned by the intrinsic make-up of the organism. There are, in other words, certain *precultural* determinants of personality that set the stage for whatever influence environment or culture may exert. These include physical constitution, temperament, psychological make-up, motivation, and the developmental pattern peculiar to the organism. Nothing need be said about genetic determinism, since it is obvious that these precultural factors are themselves genetically conditioned.

We need not dwell on these precultural determinants here, since we have indicated their influence on personality development in many preceding chapters. We have shown repeatedly that physical development has an important bearing on the emergence of personality traits, such as aggressiveness, inferiority, and self-confidence. Similarly, intelligence, imagination, sensorimotor capacities, and physiological needs are affected by organic structure and growth. These factors are all precultural, even though they are continuously conditioned by cultural determinants. It would be a mistake, therefore, to emphasize cultural determinism at the expense of factors that exist prior to such influence. Certainly not all needs and capacities are acquired; and even granted that traits are to a large extent culturally determined, the effect of this influence is always conditioned by the nature of the personality involved. Because of this mutual interplay of intrinsic and extrinsic determinants, viewpoints which overemphasize the one or the other become one-sided, and thus give a distorted picture of how personality develops.

The Nature-Nurture Concepts of Development. Adult personality, then, is the end result of the *constant interaction* of intrinsic and extrinsic determinants; and this pattern of interaction is itself conditioned by identification, introception, and self-determination. The rule applies particularly to extrinsic determinants like education and parental guidance. The idea, therefore, that personality formation can be defined in terms of two variables — heredity and environment — is entirely inadequate, since it fails to take into account the existence of other independent variables. Actually there are five determining factors, each one of which may vary independently of the others: (1) *intrinsic structure*, including physical make-up, temperament, capacities, and innate needs; (2) *development* which, while predetermined by intrinsic make-up, is to an important extent unique and individual in character; (3) *experience*, which includes the factor of cultural and environmental determinism, since only that which is introceptively experienced can exert an effect, regardless of the structure of the culture or the environment itself; (4) *training*, including education, which is a process, and not a part of the environment as so often assumed; and (5) *self-determination*, which is the capacity of the individual person to make significant choices and decisions affecting his behavior, and thus to delimit the influence of other determinants. The significant fact here is that all these factors can vary independently of one another, and therefore one cannot be reduced to another, and each must be taken into separate account. To assume, then, that there are only two determinants of personality leads to endless misunderstanding regarding its development.

Culture and Experience. The relation between cultural milieu, environment, and experience deserves special attention, in view of the fact that we included cultural and environmental influences under the category of experience. This reduction is justified by the fact that culture itself is an abstraction whose effects can be determined only through the medium of experience. Whatever one may argue regarding the objective existence of cultural values, traditions, laws, taboos, and mores, from the standpoint of personality development these factors become real only to the extent that they are in some manner or other brought into experiential relationship with the growing organism. We may say, therefore, that intrinsic factors constitute the *mold* of personality development; experience is the *stuff* out of which traits, attitudes, values, other characteristics are formed; and training, education, introception, and self-determination are the *methods* and *processes* through which environmental and cultural influences are translated into personal characteristics.[4] In this sense personality may be conceived as *the subjective aspect of what is exteriorly identified as culture*. Habits, traits, attitudes, values, and ideals are so many introjections of the existing cultural pattern; and these take form in terms of existing needs, capacities, and physical structure, and under the guidance or influence of training, education, and self-realization.

Relational View of Personality. The idea, therefore, that personality is something possessed by the individual organism is inadequate, since it fails to take into account the dynamic relationship be-

---

[4] See the interesting discussion of experience in relation to adolescent personality by Phyllis Blanchard, "Adolescent Experience in Relation to Personality and Behavior," in J. McV. Hunt (ed.), *op. cit.*, Vol. II, pp. 690–713.

tween culture and individuality.[5] Personality cannot be a sum total of capacities, attitudes, habits, and traits for the reason that it embraces also the *relationships* that exist at any moment between the individual and the environment or culture of which he is a part. The definition of personality in terms of "stimulus value" is partly in line with this fact. In one sense these relational aspects of personality are even more significant than the relatively permanent aspects; they often determine both the content and the dynamic qualities of such stable factors as habits, traits, and attitudes. Thus, in adolescence, the relationship of identity with one or another of the parents; the relationship of love, respect, or confidence; the crush relationship and puppy love; or the relationship called discipline are all determinative of attitudes, traits, and behavior patterns in the teen-ager. This fact helps us to understand why Jane is such a "sweet" child at school and a veritable demon at home. Jane's personality, like the chameleon, takes its color from the environment.

These relationships, moreover, are essentially *dynamic* in character, and are constantly shifting under the impetus of events in the extrapersonal world as well as those occurring within the organism itself. Thus, by way of example, "friendliness" is not a trait so much as it is a relationship existing at the moment between one person and another, both of whom are influenced by cultural determinants, and undergoing constant intrinsic changes that may at any point alter or destroy the relationship. Parents

and teachers will recognize the validity of this interpretation when they recall how friendships fluctuate from day to day among teen-agers. So long as the conditions favoring a relationship exist, the relationship itself will continue; and on the basis of this quasi-static character of certain relationships the concept of permanent traits has been developed. However, to understand personality and its development we must bear in mind the relational characteristic of traits, and remember also that personality is more of a goal to be achieved than a thing possessed.

Range of Cultural Determinants. The term "culture" is very broad and embraces those extrinsic factors included under the heading of *environment*, which is in part the reflection or expression of a culture. Whereas culture is more or less an abstraction, environment is something real, composed as it is of things, persons, and events that the experiencing organism can identify and react to. Under this heading, therefore, we may include such subcultural determinants as the *home*, the *school*, and the *community*. Only by effecting a transition from abstract culture to concrete environment can the relationship between personality development and culture be successfully determined. There is no known method of determining directly the influence of culture on personality; and thus it is only by studying identifiable factors like parental attitudes, family constellation, teacher-child relationships, and community characteristics that the pattern of cultural determinism can be made to emerge. For this reason we limit our consideration in this section to the influences on adolescent development of the home, the school, and the community, three cultural determinants concerning

---

[5] On the basis of this relationship Spiro argues that the dichotomy between culture and personality is a false one. See M. E. Spiro, "Culture and Personality; the Natural History of a False Dichotomy," *Psychiat.*, 1951, *14*, 19–40.

which a great deal has been objectively determined.

THE ADOLESCENT'S HOME AND PERSONALITY DEVELOPMENT

The Adolescent's Home Is Important. In evaluating the home as a cultural determinant of personality development, we are not of course entering a new field. In many earlier chapters we had numerous occasions to note the influence of home environment on adolescent development. We reviewed a great deal of evidence indicating that interests, attitudes, ideals, principles, and values are all conditioned by home and family. We noted the important relationship between parental attitudes and such needs as independence, acceptance, and status. We saw how character, temperament, and psychosexual development can be influenced by the teen-ager's surroundings. In fact, it would have been impossible to trace the development of these many aspects of personality without considering the influence of home and family. Much the same may be said of education, the school, and the community; and it now remains to fill in the picture from the sociological rather than the psychological point of view.[6]

Some insight into the effects of home environment may be gathered from the attitudes of youths toward their homes. In the extensive Maryland survey of adolescents, in which the direct question was asked, "Would you leave your home if you could?" it was found that out of every 100 unmarried youths living at home, only three wanted to leave permanently. This finding is particularly significant in view of the fact that the median age of the youths interviewed was 20.4 years, an age at which youngsters could be expected to be pulling away from the home. Even more remarkable is the fact that of 300 married youths almost half were living with parents or relatives.[7] If this is a fair sample of youth in America, the findings are certainly an indication that most youth regard the home as satisfying their needs and desires to an appreciable extent, and that there is much less friction and conflict than is often supposed. This close affinity between youth and the home has significant implications for personality development.

Physical and Cultural Level of the Home. While it is admittedly difficult to trace the effect on personality development of the *physical character* of the home, there is little doubt that development is at least indirectly affected by such factors as squalor, lack of cleanliness, overcrowding, poverty, and inadequate facilities of one kind and another. Cole cites one study of 734 delinquent children in which it was found that 62 per cent lived in homes in which the physical conditions were distinctly poor, 25 per cent came from homes where the condition was fair,

---

[6] There are of course many references in the literature to the influence of the home on personality development. See M. E. Kirkpatrick, op. cit., especially pp. 275–278; U. H. Fleege, *Self-Revelation of the Adolescent Boy* (Milwaukee: Bruce, 1945), Chaps. 3–6; A. B. Hollingshead, *Elmtown's Youth* (New York: Wiley, 1949), pp. 441–442; R. S. Woodworth, "Heredity and Environment: a Critical Survey of Recently Published Material on Twins and Foster Children," *Soc. Sci. Res. Council*, 1941, Bull. 47.

[7] H. M. Bell, *Youth Tell Their Story* (Washington, D. C.: Amer. Council on Educ., 1938), pp. 17, 18.

and only 13 per cent from homes that were sanitary, well-equipped, and reasonably prosperous.[8] If it is true that the environment is continuously introcepted by the experiencing organism, then certainly attiudes, desires, feelings, and levels of aspiration can be affected by physical environment. What the personal reaction will be in a given case no one can determine with certainty. Cleanliness may breed the habit of cleanliness, or it may not; poverty may stimulate rebellion or an attitude of resignation. Undoubtedly, many youngsters desert their homes to escape intolerable physical conditions, while others fail to emancipate themselves from the home because of the fear that independent living would not be as desirable or as comfortable. Reactions such as these may occur only rarely, but even in more average situations development will be affected to some extent.

Of more importance to development is the *cultural level* of the home. Such factors as education of the parents, number and types of books available, occupation of the father, social status of the family, and nationality of parents can be brought under this heading. That the cultural level of the home does bear on development has been clearly set forth in the many studies dealing with the effect of environment on intellectual growth. Correlations between this development

and cultural index of the home are sufficiently high to warrant the conclusion that the home environment in its cultural aspects is significant for intellectual development. The effect on personality is more difficult to determine because personality cannot be as accurately measured; but studies like those of identical twins reared apart certainly indicate, by implication at least, that the different home environments played a significant role in determining differences in personality.[9] As one writer expresses it, "to a large extent, we are what our homes have made us."

PERSONALITY DEVELOP-MENT AND THE FAMILY

The Process of Socialization. There is no factor of greater importance to the development of personality than *the family*. Of necessity the child is born into some type of family structure toward which adjustments must be made long before the demands of the extrafamilial environment begin to have an appreciable effect. It is the family that should, though too often it does not, provide the first medium in which the *process of socialization* begins, a medium in which attitudes, habits, ideals, values, and sentiments of social significance are first acquired. As a member of a family group, the individual is provided with countless opportunities for adjustment, emotional as well as social. This, in fact, is one of the responsibilities of the family — to produce well-adjusted persons who can assume their place in society when once

[8] Louella Cole, *Psychology of Adolescence*, 3 ed. (New York: Rinehart, 1948), p. 319. See also W. C. Kvaraceus, *The Community and the Delinquent* (New York: World Book, 1954), p. 97; Elizabeth B. Hurlock and S. Sender, "The 'Negative Phase' in Relation to the Behavior of Pubescent Girls," *Child Develpm.*, 1930, 1, 325–340. These investigators found that girls from poor homes accounted for 80 per cent of the total hostility to society and 71 per cent of the loss of interest in school and friends. Various other negative characteristics were associated with girls from poor homes.

[9] Barbara S. Burks, "A Study of Identical Twins Reared Apart Under Differing Types of Family Relationships," in *Studies in Personality* (New York: McGraw-Hill, 1942), pp. 35–69.

they break away from the family circle.[10]

While there are countless situations within family life that stimulate conflict, especially where there are several children, adjustment is imperative in the early years of life. For some years the child is not in a position to exercise his own rights without regard for the wishes and rights of others; therefore, he must conform to the rules and regulations that govern the household of which he is a part. The more complex the family constellation becomes, the more does adjustment become a necessity. The needs and demands of other children in the family, not to mention those of the parents, set definite limits to what any one child can expect or hope for; and it is this situation of give-and-take that makes for both adjustment and socialization. The family is, after all, *a society in miniature*, with traditions, codes, mores, and laws that closely resemble those of the larger social

structure of which it is a part. The more, therefore, that a person learns to adjust to this situation, and the more socialized he becomes through family influences, the better equipped he will be to take his place in the environment of extrafamilial relationships. It is for this reason, among others, that the only child is at a distinct disadvantage. Partridge cites a study of 100 only children living at home with both parents, all of whom had been referred to a child-guidance clinic. He found that among the adverse factors in their background, *lack of social contacts* ranked foremost.[11] This fact serves to remind us that the social distance between parents and offspring is often very great, and that it is other children of *similar* age who can function most effectively as true socializing forces.

There is, however, an important difference that should be noted between the family and other social groups, since it bears directly on the problem of per-

---

[10] There are countless studies dealing with the relationship between family life and personality development, all of which point to the conclusion that the family is the most important element in a person's life. In their study of 400 children, ages 3 to 18, Lurie, *et al.* found that nearly all the personality disorders were due to the influence of the family, and that less than 1 per cent could be directly traced to the neighborhood. The most important disturbing conditions were immorality, lack of understanding, and alcoholism — L. A. Lurie, *et al.*, "Environmental Influences: the Relative Importance of Specific Exogenous Factors in Producing Behavior and Personality Disorders in Children," *Amer. J. Orthopsychiat.*, 1943, *13*, 150–161. See also E. D. Partridge, *Social Psychology of Adolescence* (New York: Prentice-Hall, 1938), Chap. IX; K. Davis, "The Child and the Social Structure," *J. Educ. Sociol.*, 1940, *14*, 217–229; L. A. Hattwick, "Group Life of the Young Child," *J. Educ. Sociol.*, 1940, *14*, 205–216; A. B. Hollingshead, *Elmtown's Youth* (New York: Wiley, 1949), pp. 441–447; R. J. Erickson, "The Adolescent Within the Family," *J. Child Psychiat.*, 1956, *3*, 115–136; and various items in the Selected Readings at the end of the chapter.

[11] E. D. Partridge, *op. cit.*, 219. See also Carroll Davis and Mary L. Northway, "Siblings — Rivalry or Relationship?" *Bull. Inst. Child Study* (Toronto, 1957), *19*, 10–13. These investigators found that each child used his sibling as a means of his own self-definition. Other viewpoints on sibling relationships and personality development will be found in D. M. Levy, *Studies in Sibling Rivalry* (New York: Amer. Orthopsychiat. Assoc. Res. Monogr., No. 2, 1937); J. S. Plant, *The Envelope: a Study of the Impact of the World Upon the Child* (New York: Commonwealth Fund, 1950), Chap. 20; B. S. Gottlieb, *Understanding Your Adolescent* (New York: Rinehart, 1957), Chap. 7; Mary F. Langmuir, "Discipline: Means and Ends," in Sidonie M. Gruenberg (ed.), *Our Children Today* (New York: Viking, 1955), Chap. 11. This writer says pointedly: "A certain amount of family quarreling is a valuable part of a child's growing up, of his getting along with other children in the family . . ." p. 130; and Eva D. Ferguson, "The Effect of Sibling Competition and Alliance on Level of Aspiration, Expectation, and Performance," *J. Abnorm. Soc. Psychol.*, 1958, *56*, 213–222.

sonality development. The relationships between members of the immediate family are ordinarily more intense and more emotionally charged than are those between members of nonfamily groups. From the very start it is the family, and particularly the parents, who insure *the satisfaction of basic physical and psychological needs*, on the basis of which intense and lasting ties are ordinarily established. Goldfarb emphasizes this point in his studies of psychological deprivation caused by foster home placement and other institutional care. He notes that such deprivation often results in a basic defect of the total personality.[12] In the home the individual generally derives security, affection, sympathy, and understanding; he is given food, shelter, and rest; when possible every need and

desire is gratified to a greater or less extent, and he soon learns to regard his home and family as an integral part of his life. No such ties are formed in school or society at large, and it is generally not until the individual establishes a home and family of his own that these basic ties begin to lose their hold. For all these reasons, family constellation, parent-child, and sibling relationships become extremely important factors in the development of personality.[13]

Family Constellation and Personality. Many studies have been directed toward determining the influence on personality of such factors as birth, age of parents, number of children in the family, and the breakup of the family due to death, separation, divorce, and desertion. Of these several factors, it may be supposed that family size would have an important bearing on development. Outland, investigating the home situation as a direct cause of transiency among boys, found that of 3352 boys between the ages of 16 and 20, nearly one third came from homes with six or more children. The records showed also that approximately one fourth of this group left home because of difficulties encountered in the home situation. Both of these figures indicate, if nothing else, that the behavior

---

[12] W. Goldfarb, "The Effects of Early Institutional Care on Adolescent Personality," *J. Exp. Educ.*, 1943, 12, 106–129; "Infant Rearing and Problem Behavior," *Amer. J. Orthopsychiat.*, 1943, 13, 249–265; "Psychological Privation in Infancy and Subsequent Adjustment," *Amer. J. Orthopsychiat.*, 1945, 15, 247–255. See also F. H. Allen, "Mother-Child Separation — Process or Event," in G. Caplan (ed.), *Emotional Problems of Early Childhood* (New York: Basic Books, 1955), Chap. 15; K. Glaser and L. Eisenberg, "Maternal Deprivation," *Pediatrics*, 1956, 18, 626–642; Beryl Watson, "The Deprived Child," *Med. Prac.*, 1951, No. 5828, 56–59; D. Beres and S. J. Obers, "The Effects of Extreme Deprivation in Infancy on Psychic Structure in Adolescence: a Study in Ego Development," in R. S. Eissler, *et al.*, *The Psychoanalytic Study of the Child*, Vol. V (New York: Internat. Universities Press, 1950), 212–235; N. O'Connor, "The Evidence for the Permanently Disturbing Effects of Mother-Child Separation," *Acta Psychol.*, 1956, 12, 174–191; M. Shirley and L. Poyntz, "The Influence of Separation From the Mother on Children's Emotional Responses," *J. Psychol.*, 1941, 12, 251–282; A. W. Brown, J. Morrison, and G. B. Couch, "Influence of Affectional Family Relationships on Character Development," *J. Abnorm. Soc. Psychol.*, 1947, 42, 422–428, and Catherine (Englewood Cliffs, N. J.: Prentice-Hall, 1957). D'Evelyn, *Meeting Children's Emotional Needs*

[13] Typical studies of parent-child relationships have revolved around acceptance and rejection. See, for example, L. R. Wolberg, "The Character Structure of the Rejected Child," *Nerv. Child*, 1944, 3, 74–88; A. J. Simon, "Rejection in the Etiology and Treatment of the Institutionalized Delinquent," *Nerv. Child*, 1944, 3, 119–126; and L. G. Burchinal, G. R. Hawes, and B. Gardner, "The Relationship Between Parental Acceptance and Adjustment of Children," *Child Develpm.*, 1957, 28, 65–77. In all such studies it is found consistently that parental acceptance or rejection has a direct and pervasive effect on personality development.

of youth may be seriously influenced by familial factors.[14]

In an effort to determine the relationship between size of family and personality of offspring, Maller found that family size correlates *negatively* with intelligence, moral knowledge, cultural background, and honest behavior, whereas the highest intelligence scores were made by subjects from homes of two children. This study also indicated that family size exhibits a definite curvilinear relationship with both co-operativeness and helpfulness, those children of very small families, and those of very large ones scoring lower than those of average-size families. Children of large families were found to score highest in tests of persistence. Significantly, there was a marked *negative* relationship between social status of parents and the number of children in the family.[15] These results should be com-

pared with those obtained in the studies of only-child situations, to which reference is made later on.

Other studies have also found that family size is related to development. Thus, in the Maryland Survey, while only half of the youth from white families of nine or more children were found to go beyond the eighth grade, nine out of ten youth from one-child families went beyond this level. Again, many more of the youth from single-child families felt that their school training was of considerable or even great economic value than did the children from, large families, indicating a fundamental difference in attitudes. Attitudes on the size of families also seemed to be affected by family size, those from large families wanting fewer children, and those from single-child families wanting more children than their parents had. Also, it was found that twice as large a proportion of youth from large families wanted to leave home as did youngsters from one-child families, a finding that has considerable implication for the measure of independence achieved by children from different-size families.[16]

---

[14] G. E. Outland, "The Home Situation as a Direct Cause of Boy Transiency," *J. Juven. Res.*, 1938, 22, 33–42. For other effects of family constellation, see W. C. Kvaraceus, *op. cit.*, p. 101; A. F. Fenlason and H. R. Hertz, "The College Student and Feelings of Inferiority," *Ment. Hyg.*, 1938, 22, 389–397; F. I. Nye, *Family Relationships and Delinquent Behavior* (New York: Wiley, 1958), pp. 37–38; J. H. S. Bossard, *Parent and Child: Studies in Family Behavior* (Philadelphia: University of Pennsylvania Press, 1956), Chaps. V and VI; F. H. Allen, "Dynamics of Roles as Determined in the Structure of the Family," *Amer. J. Orthopsychiat,*. 1942, 12, 127–135; J. H. S. Bossard and Eleanor S. Boll, "Personality Roles in the Large Family," *Child Develpm.*, 1955, 26, 71–78. Bossard and Boll found that specialization of role occurs whenever a number of people, such as a family, are in continuing association with each other, and the larger the group the greater the degree and diversity of specialization.

[15] J. B. Maller, "Size of Family and Personality of Offspring," *J. Soc. Psychol.*, 1931, 2, 3–27. See also Anne Anastasi, "Intelligence and Family Size," *Psychol. Bull.*, 1956, 19, 187–206. Levy found in a study of 700 children referred to a clinic that distribution of children's behavior problems seemed to have little relation

to family size — J. Levy, "A Quantitative Study of Behavior Problems in Relation to Family Constellation," *Amer. J. Psychiat.*, 1931, 10, 637–654. Bossard and Boll, however, have found a definite relationship between large family size and adjustment of siblings. See J. H. S. Bossard and Eleanor S. Boll, "Adjustment of Siblings in Large Families," *Amer. J. Psychiat.*, 1956, 112, 889–892. See also J. H. S. Bossard and Eleanor S. Boll, *The Large Family System: an Original Study in the Sociology of Family Behavior* (Philadelphia: University of Pennsylvania Press, 1956). Here the authors report that of 440 persons reared in large families, who married and were rated for happiness, 71.4 per cent were rated as happy; 15.0 per cent as of medium happiness; and only 13.6 per cent as unhappy.

[16] H. M. Bell, *op. cit.* See the interesting data regarding children's attitudes toward pregnancy of the mother in R. R. Sears, Eleanor E. Mac-

TABLE 24

FAMILY SIZE AND DELINQUENT BEHAVIOR*

Number of Children in Family	Most Delinquent		Least Delinquent		N	
	Boys	Girls	Boys	Girls	Boys	Girls
	Per Cent		Per Cent			
1 or 2	27	28	73	72	420	411
3–6	35	28	65	72	643	647
7 or more	35	28	64	72	85	94

*Reprinted with permission from: F. I. Nye, *Family Relations and Delinquent Behavior* (New York: Wiley, 1958), p. 38.

The Only-Child Situation. Studies of family constellation have been directed toward the effects on personality of the only-child situation. While the results of different studies are often contradictory, it is possible to draw several worthwhile conclusions. In general, while some researches indicate that the only-child situation is unfavorable to personality development, the majority have found the opposite to be true. Thus, Goodenough and Leahy found only children to be more aggressive, confident, gregarious, and distractible than other children, and they were fonder also of physical demonstrations of affection. Witty found only children to be superior in health, physical development, intelligence, and character to other children at the five-year level.[17] Other studies are in general agreement with these findings, although there is considerable evidence to indicate negative traits in only children. Kingsley and Reynolds, for example, found that only children show the highest mean incidence of gastro-intestinal upsets, skin disorders, feeding disorders, constipation, asthma, and allergies; whereas Ward in a much earlier study found that only children showed more restlessness, overactivity, crying, nail-biting, school difficulties, and unpopularity.[18] Ward feels that certain problems are unavoidably associated with being an only child, for example, overgratification of affection, lack of competition for parental attention, too much parental ambition, insufficient contact with other children, and excessive contact with adults which tends to lead to pathological defenses.

These findings are in contrast to Partridge's conclusion based on an extensive review of the literature, that "there was no outstanding and consistent difference between only children and those raised among brothers and sisters," although only children seemed to be more intelli-

coby, and H. Levin, *Patterns of Child Rearing* (Evanston, Ill.: Row, Peterson, 1957), p. 409. These investigators found that 74 per cent of only children were delighted when they found the mother to be pregnant, compared with 68 per cent of oldest children, and 40 per cent of youngest children. See also the article by the senior author of this study, R. R. Sears, "Ordinal Position in the Family as a Psychological Variable," *Amer. Sociol. Rev.*, 1950, 15, 397–401. For family size in relation to delinquent behavior, see Table 24.

[17] Florence Goodenough and Alice M. Leahy, "The Effect of Certain Family Relationships Upon the Development of Personality," *Ped. Sem.*, 1927, 34, 45–71. P. A. Witty, "The Only Child of Five," *Psychol. Clinic*, 1933, 22, 73–87.

[18] Alice Kingsley and Earle L. Reynolds, "The Relation of Illness Patterns in Children to Ordinal Position in the Family," *J. Pediat.*, 1949, 35, 17–24; Anna Ward, "The Only Child: a Study of 100 Cases Referred to a Child Guidance Clinic," *Smith Coll. Stud. in Soc. Wk.*, 1930, 1, 41–65. See also Norma E. Cutts and N. Moseley, *The Only Child* (New York: Putnam, 1954).

gent, healthy, and aggressive than the others.[19] These results are not in line with casual experience and popular belief concerning only children, and it must be remembered that negative results have been reported in a number of studies, and that the forces shaping personality are so numerous and complex that it is difficult to say how influential any single factor is. It is not impossible that the only children who seem to profit by this family situation did so despite the situation rather than because of it.

Birth Order and Personality. The problem of the only child is similar to that of birth order. Is ordinal position a factor in determining personality differences? Here too results obtained from empirical studies are contradictory. Steckel, investigating the relationship between intelligence and birth order of approximately 20,000 children in grades one to twelve, found that on the average later-born children have higher I.Q.'s than do early-born children and that, in general, intelligence, as measured by intelligence tests, increases fairly uniformly with cardinal numbers up to and including eighth-born children.[20] Even more to the point, from the standpoint of personality de-

velopment, is a study involving 166 children sent to the Institute for Child Guidance in New York, all of whom were characterized by the trait of jealousy. A definite relationship between frequency of jealousy and ordinal position in the family is reported, the highest percentage of jealous children being found among the oldest children, followed in order by intermediate and youngest children. There were more than twice as many jealous children among the oldest as there were among the youngest, a finding that is not unexpected, in view of the disruption of family constellation by the arrival of a brother or a sister.[21] In an earlier study it was reported also that oldest children in families of more than one child showed the greatest proportion of extreme deviations from an ideal norm.[22] (See Table 25.)

---

[19] E. D. Partridge, op. cit., p. 221.

[20] M. L. Steckel, "Intelligence and Birth Order in Family," *J. Soc. Psychol.*, 1930, 1, 329–344.

[21] B. M. Ross, "Some Traits Associated With Sibling Jealousy in Problem Children," *Smith Coll. Stud. in Soc. Wk.*, 1930, 1, 364–376. Foster also found that in 27 out of 50 cases the jealous child was the oldest in the family. S. Foster, "A Study of the Personality Make-Up and Social Setting of Fifty Jealous Children," *Ment. Hyg.*, 1927, 11, 53–77.

[22] Florence L. Goodenough and Alice Leahy, op. cit. Other studies are directed toward the personality development of later-born children. For example, McArthur found that the first child tends to be adult-oriented, sensitive, and serious, whereas the second is more peer-oriented and shows an easy-going friendliness. C. Mc-

TABLE 25

BIRTH ORDER AND DELINQUENT BEHAVIOR*

Birth Order	Most Delinquent Boys Per Cent	Most Delinquent Girls Per Cent	Least Delinquent Boys Per Cent	Least Delinquent Girls Per Cent	N Boys	N Girls
Oldest	27	24	73	75	472	474
"In between"	37	29	63	71	332	341
Youngest	37	35	63	65	251	246
Only Child	21	23	79	78	82	93

*Reprinted with permission from: F. I. Nye, op. cit., p. 37.

Whether such traits, however, are due to position in the family or to other factors like sex, intelligence, and parental attitudes is still an open question. For example, in their study of birth order, Wile and Noetzel conclude that "order of birth is not demonstrated to have any important relation to the development of maladjusted or neurotic personality," and that "ordinal position is not an especially significant factor in fixing a personality type or in establishing definite forms of difficulty in adjustment or in determining dominant attitudes and responses in human relations."[23] Buhler, on the basis of a careful study of the child in relation to the family, reaches the same conclusion.[24] Other studies of a similar nature seem to indicate that sex and *intelligence* are as important in determining certain developments. Smalley found that there was increase in jealousy as the differences in intelligence between children increased, and that the girl-girl relationship was much more productive of jealousy than the girl-boy rela-

tionship. *Parental preferences* also have been found to be more significant in some instances than was family position.[25]

Personality and Family Breakdown. Whatever the situation may be with respect to family constellation and birth order, evidence on the influence of family breakdown on personality development is conclusive (see Table 26). This inference is supported by numerous studies dealing with behavior disorders and delinquency in relation to disorganization of the family. Outland found that of 3352 boys listed as transients, 57 per cent came from broken homes. Sullenger, studying the relationship between the home and juvenile delinquency, found that in *fully half* of the cases studied, the family constellation was broken by death, desertion, divorce, or other absence of one of the parents.[26] Still other studies indicate that more working mothers are to be found in delinquent home backgrounds than in those that are non-

Arthur, "Personalities of First and Second Children," *Psychiat.*, 1956, 19, 47–54. Fischer found that in 19 of 26 families the adjustment of older siblings was disturbed, whereas Lasko found that, contrary to prediction, parents tend to baby, protect, and be more solicitous of the second child, and to give it more warmth and less control than was true of the first child — A. E. Fischer, "Sibling Relationships With Special Reference to the Problem of the Second Child," *J. Pediat.*, 1952, 40, 254–259, and J. K. Lasko, "Parent Behavior Toward First and Second Children," *Genet. Psychol. Monogr.*, 1954, 49, 97–137.

[23] I. S. Wile and E. Noetzel, "A Study of Birth Order and Behavior," *J. Soc. Psychol.*, 1931, 2, 70. However, a decade later, Wile and Davis report that first-born children form the largest group seen in child behavior clinics. I. S. Wile and R. Davis, "The Relation of Birth to Behavior," *Amer. J. Orthopsychiat.*, 1941, 11, 320–334.

[24] Charlotte Buhler, *The Child and His Family* (New York: Harper, 1939), pp. 175–176.

[25] R. E. Smalley, "Two Studies in Sibling Rivalry: II — the Influence of Differences in Age, Sex, and Intelligence in Determining Attitudes of Siblings Toward Each Other," *Smith Coll. Stud. in Soc. Wk.*, 1930, 1, 23–40. See also J. K. Lasko, op. cit., and B. M. Ross, "Sibling Jealousy in Problem Children," *Smith Coll. Stud. in Soc. Wk.*, 1931, 1, 364–376. See Table 25 for the relationship between delinquency and birth order.

[26] G. E. Outland, "The Home Situation as a Direct Cause of Boy Transiency," *J. Juven. Res.*, 1938, 22, 33–42; T. E. Sullenger, "Juvenile Delinquency, a Product of the Home." *J. Crimin. Law and Criminol.*, 1934, 24, 1088–1092. Barker reported a correlation of .79 between broken homes and delinquency. G. H. Barker, "Family Factors in the Ecology of Juvenile Delinquency," *J. Crimin. Law and Criminol.*, 1940, 30, 681–691. Salisbury says pointedly that 95 per cent of street youngsters "come from broken families or families in name only. They get neither understanding nor interest at home. Home life is apt to be a compound of neglect, curses, beatings, and drink" — H. E. Salisbury, *The Shook-Up Generation* (New York: Harper, 1958), p. 57.

TABLE 26

PER CENT OF ADOLESCENTS FROM BROKEN AND UNBROKEN HOMES
ADMITTING SPECIFIC OFFENSES*

Offense	Boys		Girls	
	Broken N = 234	Unbroken N = 941	Broken N = 241	Unbroken N = 927
Driven a car without a license	78	74	68	56
School truancy	69	49	50	38
Run away from home	18	12	18	10
Probation or expulsion from school	14	11	6	3
Defied parents to face	42	31	34	30
Reckless driving	46	46	15	17
Theft: less than $2	62	60	33	29
Theft: $2 to $50	21	14	4	4
Theft: in excess of $50	6	5	1	1
Neurotic theft	25	22	9	8
Gang fights	27	21	8	6
Auto theft or "joyride"	18	14	6	4
Bought or drank alcoholic beverages	64	56	54	42
Purposely destroyed property	47	44	15	13
Heterosexual sex relations	8	9	5	3
Homosexual sex relations	49	38	19	13

*Reprinted with permission from: F. I. Nye, *op. cit.*, p. 45.

delinquent in character, a fact partly substantiated by the rise in delinquency coincident with the rise in employment of mothers during the war years. According to a special survey conducted by the Bureau of the Census it was found that throughout the country nearly 400,000 children under 12 have to care for themselves while their mothers work. And 138,000 of this total were less than 10 years of age. During the period studied (May, 1958), 2,873,000 mothers were working full time. Of their 6,665,000 children, 5,073,000 were under 12 years of age. This situation, as Merrill and others point out, not only leaves the child alone and deserted, but creates tremendous role-conflicts for the mother herself which in turn impair her relationships with husband and family. The children feel deprived and rejected, and the husband, deprived of the companionship and need-gratification by the wife, may consider the game not worth the candle, and deserts the home for other more interesting and satisfying pursuits.[27]

This relationship is especially significant when the character of the home as a *socializing agency* is considered. While the evidence is not conclusive, studies have shown that delinquent children from broken homes are markedly deficient in such traits as self-control, self-discipline, and character generally; and that self-centeredness, depression, quick-

[27] F. E. Merrill, *Courtship and Marriage: a Study in Social Relationships* (New York: William Sloan Associates, 1949), Chap. IX. See also A. H. Clemens, *Marriage and the Family* (Englewood Cliffs, N. J.: Prentice-Hall, 1957), Chap. 5. Other aspects of this problem of the working mother are brought out in F. I. Nye, *op. cit.*, Chap. 6; "Employment Status of Mothers and Adjustment of Adolescent Children." *Marr. Fam. Liv.*, 1959, 21, 240–244; Eleanor E. Maccoby, "Children and Working Mothers, *Children*, 1958, 5, 83–89; M. Hodgkiss, "The Influence of Broken Homes and Working Mothers," *Smith Coll. Stud. in Soc. Wk.*, 1933, 3, 259–274; and R. C. Hendrickson, *Youth in Danger* (New York: Harcourt, Brace, 1956), Chap. 6.

ness to anger, lack of sensitiveness to social approval, and so on, are predominant features in such children — facts that give considerable insight into the influence on personality development of the broken-home situation. There seems to be in these youth a decided lack of socialization and a dearth of those habits which emerge from having learned to live happily with others. There can be little doubt that the threat to security, the breaking down of family relationships of affection and co-operation, and the almost complete lack of discipline that result from the broken home are bound to affect seriously many of the youth who become the victims of such circumstances.[28]

However, we must face the fact that many youngsters from broken homes do not develop personality defects or become delinquent; and also that many delinquent youths come from homes that are not disrupted in the technical sense of the term. This is another way of saying, of course, that the broken home is only one factor to be considered, however important it may be. The fact that broken homes are more likely to cause difficulties in the case of girls than of boys indicates that other elements are at work, including poverty, low moral status of the home, domestic conflict, poor recreational facilities, educational deficiencies, and "delinquent" environments. Indeed some of these factors, such as *domestic conflict*, tend to break up the family constellation as surely as

do divorce, separation, or death; and at times they have more telling negative effects on personality development.[29] It were better, therefore, to reduce the causes of inadequate development to more intrinsic factors. Whatever the environment may be, when basic physical and psychological needs are not cared for; when there are threats to security, affection, or status; when desires, ambitions, and hopes go unrealized; and when there is too little room for growth and expansion of personality — then negative personality traits and behavior patterns are likely to develop. As we have pointed out repeatedly, it is not the environment, but rather the *effect of environment* that counts where the development of personality and character is concerned. A broken home by itself may conceivably have no effect at all. But when the individual reacts positively or negatively to this situation effects begin to appear, and these effects will be determined jointly by the make-up of the individual himself and by various extrinsic factors.

PARENT-CHILD RELATION-SHIPS AND PERSONALITY

Influence of Parental Traits, Attitudes, and Behavior. The breakup of the family is closely related to another factor that bears directly on personality development — the parent-child relationship. That the attitudes of parents toward their children, their treatment of the children, their ideals, practices, and emotional reactions will be reflected to

---

[28] P. Torrance, "The Influence of the Broken Home on Adolescent Adjustment," *J. Educ. Sociol.*, 1945, 18, 359–364; G. E. Gardner, "Separation of the Parents and the Emotional Life of the Child," *Ment. Hyg. N. Y.* 1956, 40, 53–64; N. W. Ackerman, *The Psychodynamics of Family Life* (New York: Basic Books, 1958), Chap. 6.

[29] See M. H. Neumeyer, *Juvenile Delinquency in Modern Society* (New York: Van Nostrand, 1949), pp. 118–123; N. W. Ackerman, *op. cit.*, Chaps. 8, 13, 14; J. W. McFarlane, "The Relation of Environmental Pressures to the Development of the Child's Personality and Habit Patterning," *J. Pediat.*, 1939, 15, 142–154.

TABLE 27

RELATIONSHIP OF FAMILY CHARACTERISTICS TO ADOLESCENT SOCIAL ADJUSTMENT*

Family Characteristics	Peer Ratings					
	Warmth	Participation	Dominance	Impulsivity	Emotional Stability	Moral Courage
F1. Consistency	.42	.36	.42	—.08	.37	.36
F2. Democracy	.47	.49	.54	.50	.44	.51
F3. Mutual Trust and Approval	.69	.68	.68	.21	.60	.82
F4. Severity	—.35	—.44	—.32	—.29	—.28	—.49

*From: R. F. Peck and R. J. Havighurst, *The Psychology of Character Development* (New York: John Wiley and Sons, Inc., in production).

some extent in the children may be accepted without question (see Table 27). As one writer says:

Of all the important, fateful, and determining influences of childhood the relationship of a child with his parents comes first. This is his very life line, through which he establishes his relationships, for better or for worse, with the rest of the world. A child will do everything in his power to maintain this lifeline — everything from obedient submission to open, defiant, and deliberate rebellion. Few parents are wise enough to meet these rapid and necessary maneuvers of their children.[30]

―――――

[30] C. Binger, "The Concept of Maturity," in Sidonie M. Gruenberg (ed.), *Our Children Today* (New York: Viking, 1955), p. 206. This influence has been studied empirically from a number of viewpoints. See, for example, G. Hirschberg and A. R. Gilliland, "Parent-Child Relationships in Attitude," *J. Abnorm Soc. Psychol.*, 1942, 37, 125–130; A. L. Baldwin, "Socialization and the Parent-Child Relationship," *Child Develpm.*, 1948, 19, 127–136; Alice Crow, "Parental Attitudes Toward Boy-Girl Relations," *J. Educ. Sociol.*, 1955, 29, 126–133; R. F. Peck, "Family Patterns Correlated With Adolescent Personality Structure," *J. Abnorm. Soc. Psychol.*, 1958, 57, 347–350; W. Itkin, "Relationships Between Attitudes Toward Parents and Parents' Attitudes Toward Children," *J. Genet. Psychol.*, 1955, 86, 339–352; and H. H. Remmers and D. H. Radler, *The American Teenager* (New York: Bobbs-Merrill, 1957), pp. 248–250.

Thus we need to determine the extent of parental influences, as well as the developmental characteristics of the relationships that exist between parents and children.

Studies of the influence of parental behavior on children indicate that such influence is extensive but is conditioned by a variety of other factors. For example, Stott found that parental behavior, particularly that of the mother, was most significantly related to the personality development of adolescent boys in city homes, but seemed of lesser importance in the development of boys in rural and farm communities, and of girls in all three types of environment. By averaging the ratings on several personality tests, this investigator also found that low scores tended to coincide with serious criticisms of parental behavior, indicating a definite influence on the relationship in question.[31] The greater influence of the mother was brought out also in Stagner's study of the role of the parents in the development of emotional instability.[32]

―――――

[31] L. H. Stott, Adolescents' Dislikes Regarding Parental Behavior and Their Significance," *J. Genet. Psychol.*, 1940, 57, 393–414.

[32] R. Stagner, "The Role of the Parents in the Development of Emotional Instability," *Amer. J. Orthopsychiat.*, 1938, 8, 122–128. This relationship between the role of the mother

Stagner found that college freshmen who showed markedly negative attitudes toward the father and positive attitudes toward the mother were more emotional in their reactions than were average freshmen. He suggests, however, that it is not so much the attitude toward one or the other parent that determines emotionality as it is that emotionality determines the formation of the restrictive attitude, a possibility that has considerable implications for development.[33]

Sowers studied the parent-child relationship from the child's point of view by an analysis of essays written by children under eighteen years of age on the characteristics of the ideal parent, and by means of questionnaires on opinions and attitudes of college students regarding parental traits and family situations. These analyses revealed that the material aspects of the home are less important to the child than admirable parental traits and companionship with the parents; that children should never be afraid of the parents; and that family conflicts should be avoided through the use of conferences between parents and children.[34] Witmer, after studying the influence of parental attitudes on the social

and child development has received a great deal of attention during the past quarter of a century. See, for example, H. Witmer, et al., "Studies in Maternal Overprotection," Smith Coll. Stud. in Soc. Wk., 1932, 2, 281–282; H. W. Newell, "The Psychodynamics of Maternal Rejection," Amer. J. Orthopsychiat., 1934, 4, 387–401; A further study of maternal rejection, Amer. J. Orthopsychiat., 1936, 6, 576–589; D. M. Levy, Maternal Overprotection (New York: Columbia University Press, 1943); J. Bowlby, "Maternal Care and Mental Health," Bull. World Hlth. Org., 1951, 3, 335–533; J. C. Maloney, "Maternocentric Child Rearing," Merrill-Palmer Quart., 1957, 3, 54–66; L. H. Stewart, "Manifest Anxiety and Mother-Son Identification," J. Clin. Psychol., 1958, 14, 382–384; Ruth M. Butler, "Mothers' Attitudes Toward the Social Development of Their Adolescents: Part I, Soc. Casewk., 1956, 37, 219–226; "Mothers' Attitudes Toward the Social Development of Their Adolescents: Part II," Soc. Casewk., 1956, 37, 280–288; Shirley Law, "The Mother of the Happy Child," Smith Coll. Stud. Soc. Wk., 1954, 25, 1–27; Norah P. Handford, "Mothers of Adolescent Girls," Smith Coll. Stud. Soc. Wk., 1954, 24, 9–34; Helen T. Cederquist, "The 'Good Mother' and Her Children," Smith. Coll. Stud. Soc. Wk., 19, 1–26; Gladys C. Schwesinger, "The Effect of Differential Parent-Child Relations on Identical Twin Resemblance in Personality," Acta Genet. Med. Gemellolog., 1952, 1, 40–47; and C. G. Moser, Understanding Girls (New York: Association Press, 1957), Chap. 9.

[33] In recent years a great deal of attention has been directed toward the role of the father in the development of children's personalities. See Irene M. Josselyn, "Psychological Problems of the Adolescent: Part I," Soc. Casewk., 1951, 32, 183–190; Ruth J. Tasch, "Interpersonal Perceptions of Fathers and Mothers," J. Genet.

Psychol., 1955, 87, 59–65; R. E. Lane, "Fathers and Sons: the Foundations of Political Belief," Amer. Sociol. Rev., 1959, 24, 502–511; R. G. Kuhlen and G. G. Thompson (eds.), Psychological Studies of Human Development (New York: Appleton-Century-Crofts, 1952), Chap. 11. The studies of the father's influence are complemented by other studies of the effect of father's absence. See D. B. Lynn and W. L. Sawrey, "The Effects of Father-Absence on Norwegian Boys and Girls," J. Abnorm. Soc. Psychol., 1959, 59, 258–262; M. W. Barnes, "The Nature and Nurture of Early Adolescents," Teach. Coll. Rec., 1956, 57, 513–521; and Conference Report, "The Fatherless Family," Public Health Reports, 1959, 74, 779–782.

[34] A. Sowers, "Parent-Child Relationships From the Child's Point of View," J. Exper. Educ., 1937, 6, 205–231. See also T. F. Johnson, "Conceptions of Parents Held by Adolescents," J. Abnorm. Soc. Psychol., 1952, 47, 783–789; Lydia Jackson, "Emotional Attitudes Towards the Family of Normal, Neurotic and Delinquent Children, Part I," Brit. J. Psychol., 1950, 41, 35–51; "Emotional Attitudes Towards the Family of Normal, Neurotic and Delinquent Children, Part II," Brit. J. Psychol., 1950, 41, 173–185; D. B. Harris and Chu Tseng Sing, "Children's Attitudes Toward Peers and Parents as Revealed by Sentence Completion," Child Develpm., 1957, 28, 401–411; D. P. Ausubel, et al., "Perceived Parent Attitudes as Determinants of Children's Ego Structure," Child Develpm., 1954, 25, 173–183.

adjustment of individuals, advanced the viewpoint that problem children, pre-psychotics, and psychotics are much more likely to have been subjected to adverse parental attitudes than are well-adjusted persons; and that the degree of maladjust-ment in parent-child relationships is a principal factor in determining the results of social-psychiatric treatment of indi-viduals studied.[35] Buhler, in her careful study of family relationships, also re-ported that in certain cases definitely positive attitudes were a reflection of the positive relations existing between chil-dren and their parents, and that in other cases the negative attitudes of the chil-dren just as surely reflected parent-child relationships; but that emotional atti-tudes in most cases differed from those of the parents, and sometimes were even the direct opposite.[36]

Parental influence can be discerned also in the religious, vocational, and social preferences of children. In the Maryland Survey, it was found that over 80 per cent of the youth with some church affiliation had adopted the religious faith of both parents. Significantly, in those instances where there was a difference between the faith of the mother and father, there was more than twice as strong a tendency to accept the mother's faith.[37]   Various   other   studies   have

brought out just as clearly the influence of the parents in the shaping of ideals, in the choice of a vocation, and in the development of many other interests and attitudes.[38] Some of these influences have already been traced in preceding chap-ters, and there is no need for a restate-ment here. Later on we shall indicate to what extent this type of influence is con-tinued throughout the entire adolescent period.

Parental Discipline and Personality De-velopment. The significance of parent-child relationships for personality de-velopment is exemplified most clearly in the areas of discipline and punishment. We have already seen (Chapter XI) that discipline, and especially self-discipline, is one of the most important elements in the general process of development and integration, so that some discipline is not only desirable but actually necessary. Investigators have found that children themselves want discipline, *but only on certain terms*. They want it to be fair and firm, and they feel that it should be immediate, in accord with the age of the recipient, and independent of parental feelings. Such studies indicate that discipline and punishment are not unacceptable to children so long as they are administered correctly. In a discussion of the character-istics of the delinquent environment, Cole suggests the necessity of discipline when she points out that in a study of 1000 juvenile delinquents, discipline was either sadly lacking or quite unsound in 70 per cent of the homes. She found that the parents of delinquents "are evidently people who have little control

---

[35] H. L. Witmer, "The Influence of Parental Attitude on the Social Adjustment of the In-dividual," *Amer. Soc. Rev.*, 1937, 2, 756–763.

[36] Charlotte Buhler, *From Birth to Maturity: an Outline of the Psychological Development of the Child* (London: Kegan-Paul, 1937). See also Nancy Bayley, "Some Increasing Parent-Child Similarities During the Growth of Children," *J. Educ. Psychol.*, 1954, 45, 1–21; Vivian Briggs and Lois R. Schulz, "Parental Response to Concepts of Parent-Adolescent Relationships," *Child Develpm.*, 1955, 26, 279–284.

[37] H. M. Bell, *op. cit.*, p. 196.

[38] See A. M. Rose, "Parental Models for Youth," *Sociol. Soc. Res.*, 1955, 40, 3–9.

over themselves, and even less over their children."[39]

The effects of discipline or punishment on personality development will depend a great deal on the extent to which these practices are used during adolescence, and on the quality of the discipline itself.[40] In one study it was found that the number of parents who punish adolescents is far in the minority. Of 755 rural and village children and 1867 urban children, more than three-fourths reported that they had not been punished at all during the preceding week, and only about 14 per cent said that they had not been scolded. This may only mean, of course, that punishment becomes increasingly less necessary or desirable with adolescents, since parental discipline should gradually be replaced by personal self-discipline.[41]

Empirical evidence as well as clinical experience indicate clearly that the wrong kind of discipline can have decidedly negative effects on personality development. In one study of the effects of lax versus strict home training, the results indicated that those students who, as children, were subjected to severe discipline hated their parents, were quarrelsome with associates, had difficulty leading mature and independent lives, and were generally maladjusted socially. They also tended to be overconscientious, fearful, and unhappy.[42] Clinical experience with disturbed adolescents shows repeatedly that harsh or punitive discipline, and inconsistent methods of training, seriously disturb personal development. Scrupulosity, one of the most common forms of adolescent difficulties, has its roots in inadequate and inconsistent home training.

Other investigators have also found that the parent-child relationship is disturbed by punishment, there often being a clear connection between punishment and criticism of parents. Landis, for example, reported that some of the women in his study believed that the discipline in their homes had been too strict and that the parents had nagged and scolded them unnecessarily. The attitude toward severe physical discipline

[39] Louella Cole, *Psychology of Adolescence* (New York: Rinehart, 1936), p. 264. On the relationship between delinquency and discipline, see M. L. Barron, *The Juvenile in Delinquent Society* (New York: Knopf, 1954), Chap. VIII; W. C. Kvaraceus, *The Community and the Delinquent* (New York: World Book, 1954), pp. 101–106; F. I. Nye, *op. cit.*, pp. 79–91.

[40] See G. Watson, "Some Personality Differences in Children Related to Strict or Permissive Parental Discipline," *J. Psychol.*, 1957, 44, 227–249; A. F. Henry, "Sibling Structure and Perception of the Disciplinary Roles of Parents," *Sociom.*, 1957, 20, 67–74; C. W. Valentine, "Adolescence and Some Problems of Youth Training," *Brit. J. Educ. Psychol.*, 1943, 31, 57–68.

[41] E. W. Burgess (ed.), *The Adolescent in the Family* (New York: Appleton-Century-Crofts, 1934). For good discussions of parental authority in relation to adolescent behavior, see J. S. Plant, *The Envelope: a Study of the Impact of the World Upon the Child* (New York: Commonwealth Fund, 1950), Chap. 2. Plant makes a careful distinction between "authority" and "discipline," authority being a much broader concept relating to the fact that children live in a world which can make them do things whether they wish to or not. See also the ex-

cellent treatment of parental authority in P. H. Landis, *Adolescence and Youth*, 2 ed. (New York: McGraw-Hill, 1952), Chap. 9. A different slant on parental authority is presented in a recent article by M. L. Kohn, "Social Class and Parental Authority," *Amer. Sociol. Rev.*, 1959, 24, 352–366.

[42] G. B. Watson, "A Comparison of the Effects of Lax Versus Strict Home Training," *J. Soc. Psychol.*, 1934, 5, 102–105. See also Section II on methods of discipline in R. M. Wittenberg, *Adolescence and Discipline* (New York: Association Press, 1959).

was usually one of resentment. Of those who reported that they had had little or no discipline, not one believed that it should have been stricter. The most frequent complaint of these subjects against parents was lack of understanding, sympathy, and patience.[43]

Some students have found considerable evidence to indicate that lax discipline is more favorable to inducing obedience than is strict treatment. Gedeon, for example, offered evidence to show that lenient treatment was much more effective in the case of boys than was strict treatment, but that strict treatment was somewhat more effective in the case of girls. In cases where lenient treatment was relatively ineffective, strict measures were also found to be relatively ineffective.[44]

It is difficult to draw any certain conclusions from these data, because there are too many factors entering into parent-child relationships to enable us to ascribe definite aspects of personality development to one or the other of them. We may certainly assume that as the child grows older and becomes more mature the need for severe discipline grows less, and that punishment as a means of discipline should gradually be abandoned. Nevertheless, there is enough evidence to indicate that some form of discipline, whether by punishment, scolding, or deprivation, is more or less indispensable. What the outcome will be in terms of personality development will depend upon existing parent-child relationships, parental attitudes, reactions of the child to discipline, and numerous other factors.

At the present stage of our knowledge, it is impossible to assert conclusively that strict or lax discipline will negatively affect personality development, although the available evidence at present favors a reduction in the amount of strict training, especially where adolescents are concerned. This applies particularly to physical punishment.

Limits of Family Influence.   As the evidence indicates, the personality development of teen-agers is to an important degree a measure of home and family influences. However, this influence shows diminishing returns with increase in age. As youngsters approach maturity and achieve independent status, the effects of family attitudes, ideals, and practices become less and less marked. Hoffeditz, for example, studying the trait relationships among members of 100 families — including 100 fathers, 100 mothers, 111 sons, and 145 daughters — obtained coefficients of correlation which showed little agreement between the traits of one member of the family and those of others. In two of the traits, mothers and daughters showed the highest correlation, and in all three traits studied, mothers and sons showed the lowest correlation.[45]

While these results cannot be taken too seriously, in view of the limitations of personality measurement, there are other lines of evidence that support these findings. We have seen in our study of the origin and development of ideals that the parents exert a diminishing influence in the selection of the adolescent's ideals. Barnes, Chambers, Goddard, and Hill all found that parents had lessening influence in the choice of ideals as age in-

[43] C. Landis, et al., Sex and Development (New York: Harper, 1940).

[44] See Charlotte Buhler, The Child and His Family (New York: Harper, 1939), pp. 178–179.

[45] E. L. Hoffeditz, "Family Resemblances," J. Soc. Psychol., 1934, 5, 214–227.

creased.[46] These studies confirm also the findings with respect to a closer relationship between parents and girls than between parents and boys, girls at all ages idealizing both parents more than do boys. Bell reported a similar relationship, having found that girls are generally more inclined than boys to seek advice from parents. Bell also found, however, that as independence is more firmly established through marriage, a much smaller percentage of boys and girls return to parents for counsel and advice, indicating again the diminishing influence of parents and home.[47]

Studies such as these should not be interpreted to mean that parent-child or family-child relationships do not deeply influence personality development. [On the contrary, these connections with the family are often so deep-rooted as seriously to impede normal development and the achievement of independence.[48] The latter is one of the most common problems encountered by counselors and clinicians. In his work with college students the writer has found that this problem recurs more frequently than any other. Especially marked is the failure to achieve volitional independence of the parents, that is, the ability to make and assume responsibilities for one's own decisions. As Landis remarks, on the

basis of an intensive study of almost 300 women, "In general, we have found that freeing oneself from childhood family attachments constituted an acute emotional problem for most women. About 70 per cent of the individuals that we studied reported marked difficulty in breaking away from their original childish, dependent status in the home. This problem was handled adequately by the majority of cases, but it led to maladjustment in some instances."[49] These attachments were found to interfere seriously with adequate psychosexual adjustment, and no adequate love attachments outside the family were ever developed by those women who were very closely tied to their parents; at the same time autosexual excesses were found to be more frequent for this group. "In order to make a good adult adjustment in the most complete sense, it would appear that the individual must be relatively free from close emotional ties to her parents. . . . Close emotional ties to the family were more frequently found in those having poor general adjustment in marriage than in those having good adjustment."[50]

The studies, therefore, that show a diminishing influence of the home and family are merely an indication of the well-established fact that development reaches into every corner of human existence; and that as young people grow into manhood and womanhood and achieve independent status, there is gradually set up an inverse relationship between family influence and personality development. This is exactly what parents should expect, and even hope for, since it is the natural destiny of every young person to set himself up in the business

---

[46] This fact is brought out clearly in D. S. Hill, "Personification of Ideals by Urban Children," *J. Soc. Psychol.*, 1930, 1, 379–393.

[47] H. M. Bell, *op. cit.*

[48] See, for example, W. M. Cooper, "Parental Delinquency," *Phylon*, 1950, 11, 269–273; W. C. Becker, *et al.*, "Factors in Parental Behavior and Personality as Related to Problem Behavior in Children," *J. Consult. Psychol.*, 1959, 23, 107–118; Hilda Lewis, "Unsatisfactory Parents and Psychological Disorder in Their Children," *Eugen. Rev.*, 1955, 47, 153–162; Melitta Schmideberg, "Parents as Children," *Psychiat. Quart. Suppl.*, 1948, 22, 207–218.

[49] Reprinted with permission of Harper and Brothers from C. Landis, *et al.*, *op. cit.*, p. 46.

[50] *Ibid.*, pp. 48–49.

of independent living. It would be an appalling thing if the attitudes, ideals, hopes, ambitions, and traits of the parents were perpetuated unbrokenly in their offspring, since it must be granted that there is always a great deal of room for improvement.

WHAT THE HOME SHOULD PROVIDE FOR YOUTH

Negative Influences Must Be Minimized. From all that has been said in this and other chapters regarding the influence of the home on adolescent development, it should not be too difficult to isolate the more important characteristics that the ideal home should possess. One of the most adverse factors which would have to be excluded from the desirable home is *domestic conflict.* Hall made a study of the causes of such conflict in the homes of 100 preschool children referred to a habit clinic, and found the following disturbing factors to be important, in the order named: economic inefficiency, educational deficiencies, interfering relatives, separation, vices and bad habits, physical disease or defect, marked differences in temperament, neurotic traits, differences in race or nationality, mental disease, and age differences.[51] Evidently, then, the completely desirable home would be one in which such factors would be minimized or excluded as much as possible.

Other sources of conflict are to be found in the relationship between parents

and children, and between siblings themselves. Such tendencies as favoritism, jealousy, and envy are obviously inimical to adequate personality development, and would have to be excluded from the ideal home environment. Similarly, too great a "distance" between parents and children, which tends to prevent youngsters from seeking parental advice and counsel, and from forming healthy identifications, will create an unfavorable family situation. As Pearson remarks very pointedly, "Imitation of and identification with the parents, therefore, are the main methods by which the young child develops and organizes his ego in order to abolish his fears. In my opinion, it is this reaction to the conflict between his desires and his fears that is responsible for the development of the young child's ego — and not any supposed growth impulse or any striving toward maturity."[52] In terms of this identification the conflicts that arise from children's desires and activities become particularly im-

---

[51] D. E. Hall, "Domestic Conflict and Its Effect on the Children," *Mass. Dept. of Ment. Dis. Quart. Bull.,* 1929, Nos. 1 and 2, 1–16. See also F. I. Nye, *op. cit.,* pp. 48–51; F. I. Nye, "Child Adjustment in Broken and in Unhappy Unbroken Homes," *Marr. Fam. Liv.,* 1957, 19, 356–361.

[52] G. H. J. Pearson, *Adolescence and the Conflict of Generations* (New York: Norton, 1958), p. 69. There have been many studies on parent-child identification, with increasing recognition of the importance of this phase of development. See, for example, D. E. Payne and P. H. Mussen, "Parent-Child Relations and Father Identification Among Adolescent Boys," *J. Abnorm. Soc. Psychol.,* 1956, 52, 358–362; P. Mussen and L. Distler, "Masculinity, Identification, and Father-Son Relationships," *J. Abnorm. Soc. Psychol.,* 1959, 59, 350–356. G. W. Bronson, "Identity Diffusion in Late Adolescence," *J. Abnorm. Soc. Psychol.,* 1959, 59, 414–417. Esther L. Cava and H. L. Rausch, "Identification and the Adolescent Boy's Perception of His Father," *J. Abnorm. Soc. Psychol.,* 1952, 47, 855–856; L. M. Lazowick, "On the Nature of Identification," *J. Abnorm. Soc. Psychol.,* 1955, 51, 175–183; and L. Eisenberg, "The Fathers of Autistic Children," *Amer. J. Orthopsychiat.,* 1957, 27, 715–724. See also the excellent discussion of identification and the internalization of controls in A. Bandura and R. H. Walters, *Adolescent Aggression* (New York: Ronald, 1959), Chap. 6.

portant. Studies show that the choice of friends, amount of spending money, use of the family automobile, going out on school nights, school grades, and entertaining friends in the home are among the most frequent causes of conflict between parents and youth. Such conflicts can only be resolved through mutual confidence, and by conferences between parents and their children. When, therefore, there is too great a distance between the offspring and the parents, these desires and activities are certain to cause friction and to disrupt family life.[53]

Things the Home Should Provide. The satisfaction of needs and desires is always one of the primary sources of difficulty in adolescent adjustment. This statement applies with particular force to the need for independence. The ideal home, therefore, is one which allows for *gradual emancipation*, one in which the emotional ties between children and family are never so strong that the desire for independence leads to internal conflict, inadequacy, or rebellion. As Pearson remarks,

> . . . the end of the Oedipus struggle forces the child to estrange himself from his former close relationship with his parents; he must seek within himself for his own defenses and skills, and look outside his family among his peers for support. He begins to use the mechanisms of imitating, incorporating, and identifying with ideals and persons outside the family, a process which teaches the child certain realities.[54]

Therefore, as the child grows to maturity, every opportunity should be provided for independence of judgment, emotion, and decision. Too much restriction, too severe discipline, too rigid rules with respect to dating, friendships, and so on, are all inimical to the process of emancipation, and will in many instances produce friction, animosity, or open rebellion; or, which is even worse, these conditions may bring about a complete and continuing dependency upon the parents. The home should provide also for the satisfaction of other basic needs such as affection and security, and for those legitimate desires that the child acquires in the course of his experience and development.

A summary of the characteristics of the ideal home includes the following: (1) minimum amount of friction between parents, and between parents and children; (2) opportunities to utilize the home for expression of legitimate desires (as in the entertainment of friends); (3) family affection; (4) minimum amount of strict discipline; (5) opportunities for independence of thought, feelings, and action; (6) confidence in parents, and mutual respect between parents and children; (7) family conferences regarding difficulties; (8) companionship between parents and children; (9) emotional stability of parents; (10) economic adequacy; and (11) a wholesome moral and religious environment.[55] While there

---

[53] See H. H. Remmers and D. H. Radler, *op. cit.*, pp. 86–118.

[54] G. H. J. Pearson, *Adolescence and the Conflict of Generations* (New York: Norton, 1958), p. 70. Stone argues that the major task of the teen-ager is emancipation from the home — A. R. Stone, "Growth Potential During the Teen Years," *Understanding the Child*, 1956, 25, 39–41.

[55] See the excellent summary of what constitutes a good home in W. C. Kvaraceus, *op. cit.*, pp. 250–251. See also the summary of the ideal family situation in E. D. Partridge, *Social Psychology of Adolescence* (Englewood Cliffs, N. J.: Prentice-Hall, 1938), pp. 228–229; also Esther Lloyd-Jones and Ruth Fedder, *Coming of Age* (New York: McGraw-Hill, 1941), Chap. III; and J. M. Seidman (ed.), *The Adolescent: a Book of Readings* (New York: Dryden Press, 1953), pp. 547–555.

are many other factors that contribute to a favorable home environment, these are among the most important; and it is likely that if all of these criteria were fully met, other factors would take care of themselves.

SELECTED READINGS

Ackerman, N. W., *The Psychodynamics of Family Life* (New York: Basic Books, 1958).

Bandura, A., and Walters, R. H., *Adolescent Aggression* (New York: Ronald Press, 1959).

Bernert, Eleanor H., *America's Children* (New York: Social Science Research Council, 1958).

Bossard, J. H. S., *Parent and Child: Studies in Family Behavior* (Philadelphia: University of Pennsylvania Press, 1956).

Faegre, M. ᵀ., *The Adolescent in Your Family* (Washington, D. C.: Government Printing Office, 1955).

Frank, L. K., and Frank, Mary, *Your Adolescent at Home and in School* (New York: Viking, 1956).

Levy, D. M., *Maternal Overprotection* (New York: Columbia University Press, 1943).

Linton, R., *The Cultural Background of Personality* (New York: Appleton-Century-Crofts, 1945).

Miller, D. R., and Swanson, G. E., *The Changing American Parent: a Study in the Detroit Area* (New York: Wiley, 1958).

Neisser, Edith G., *Brothers and Sisters* (New York: Harper, 1951).

Nye, F. I., *Family Relationships and Delinquent Behavior* (New York: Wiley, 1958).

Parsons, T., and Bales, R. F., *Family, Socialization and Interaction Process* (Glencoe, Ill.: Free Press, 1955).

Sears, R. R., Maccoby, Eleanor E., Levin, H., *Patterns of Child Rearing* (Evanston, Ill.: Row, Peterson, 1957).

Strecker, E. A., *Their Mothers' Sons, the Psychiatrist Examines an American Problem* (Philadelphia: Lippincott, 1951).

Strecker, E. A., and Lathsbury, V. T., *Their Mothers' Daughters* (Philadelphia: Lippincott, 1956).

Symonds, P. M., *The Psychology of Parent-Child Relationships* (New York: Appleton-Crofts, 1939).

Tashman, H. F., *Today's Neurotic Family* (New York: New York University Press, 1957).

CHAPTER XIX

THE ADOLESCENT IN THE COMMUNITY

The business of socialization begun in the home in early childhood is carried on and completed by the community. Just as the child steps into another world when he crosses the threshold of adolescence, so he steps into another world when he leaves the home — a world of people, events, and changes that we call the neighborhood, the Church, the school, and the community. Each in its turn contributes something to the molding of the adolescent personality.

COMMUNITY INFLUENCES AND PERSONALITY DEVELOPMENT

Community, Home, and Family. In the preceding chapter we emphasized the point that the human organism is of necessity born into a social organization, the home and family, and that this fact is basic to its social development. Without this framework of interpersonal relationships, among other things that characterize family life, there would be little or no socialization, unless of course some other agency took over the functions of the home. This is exactly what happens in the case of neglected and dependent children; and it is widely recognized, on the basis of both casual observation and empirical evidence, that no such agency is capable of substituting entirely for the natural home and family. In the rare cases on record of feral children, where social influences of any kind are absent, the organism not only fails to develop socially, but is handicapped in many other ways as well.

In much the same manner that the child develops socially within the family, he also develops within the larger social framework, the community. In a relatively few instances this relationship is not prominent, as when the child is reared on a farm or in an extremely small rural community, and social contacts are greatly limited; but for the great majority of youngsters it is as inevitable to grow up within a community as it is within a home. If, therefore, as we indicated in the preceding chapter, personality can be partly defined in terms of the relations that exist between the individual organism and the persons and events that come within the range of his experiences, the conclusion is inescapable that the community in all of its aspects will figure prominently in the development of personality. This fact is of particular significance for adolescent development, since in the nature of things the teen-ager becomes increasingly independent of the home and family, and more and more dependent on the peer group and other nonfamily contacts for his ideas, experiences, goals, and ideals. Quite often a teacher is more important to an adolescent than his father or mother; and too often adolescents substitute the unwise judgments and decisions of companions for the wisdom and counsel of parent and teacher. Be that as it may, the neighborhood and the school, the Church and the community are important determiners of personal and social development, and it is this relationship we wish to explore in the present chapter.

The Different Phases of the Community. We begin our study of this relationship by noting the structure and essential characteristics of the community, since the measure of its influence will be determined by these factors. Moreover, communities differ among themselves, and these differences are reflected in varying personality effects. As Partridge points out,

> No two communities furnish exactly the same kind of social field for young people; hence the attitudes and abilities of young people who grew up in different communities are apt to vary widely. Indeed, there is apt to be a wide disparity in the behavior of young people coming from different neighborhoods in the same community, because of the disparity in what is demanded or expected of them.[1]

Facts such as these, therefore, suggest a careful study of what the term "community" signifies. As many writers have indicated, a community is not simply a political or a geographical unit; it is an organismic whole that emerges from the

relationships that exist among the members of the community, and among the various subunits within the community. These relationships, more than factors like size or geographical location, determine the effects of the community on personality growth. The concept of the community as an organismic totality makes it clear that we are not dealing with a static entity, but with an organic thing whose characteristics strongly resemble those of living organisms. Like living things, communities are structured; they grow or decay, they are healthy or diseased, and they possess individuating characteristics. The community is thus the larger social expression of 'the individuals of which it is composed, and of the relationships that bind them together and influence their dealings with each other and with the members of other communities. While less easily defined than features like size and composition, these aspects of the community have the more direct bearing on personality development.

Within the larger framework of the community may be distinguished smaller social organizations that are integral parts of the community, but which exercise their influence *in terms of their own structure and characteristics*. In some instances these smaller units become institutionalized, as is true for example of the Church and the school; in others, the exact boundaries are not so clearly marked, as is true of the neighborhood. All these organizations are essential parts of the community, but it should be noted that the internal structure of the institutional organization is considerably different from those less definitely structured. The implications of this fact are sharpened by the realization that the neighborhood is a *primary outgrowth of com-*

---

[1] E. D. Partridge, *Social Psychology of Adolescence* (Englewood Cliffs, N. J.: Prentice-Hall, 1939), p. 255.

munal organization, whereas the school, the church, and similar organizations are *secondary* derivations.[2] This is not always true since in some instances communities have developed out of church organizations. Thus, in some localities political units are still referred to as "parishes," and there are quite a few communities in America whose social cohesion is determined by religious convictions, as in the case of the Amish. Normally, however, to live in a community one must of necessity live in a neighborhood, but he does not have to have membership in a school or church. Only when every member of the community is also a member of the social institution do the sharp distinctions fade. This condition exists to a degree in small communities where the children in the neighborhood are all classmates, or where all the members of the community belong to the same religious group.

In larger communities, even the children in the same neighborhood (still less those in the entire community) do not attend the same school or church; and many individuals do not "belong" to either one. Most communities, therefore, may be thought of as organizations of neighborhoods, certain elements of which are further organized into institutional subgroups. Out of such organizations many relationships emerge. Any two persons within the community may be neighbors but hold membership in different churches or schools; or they may attend the same school, but belong to different churches, and so on. This complex situation is, of course, found most often in the large urban communities;

and the more complex a community becomes, the greater are the implications for personality development.

How the Community Influences Personality Growth. The effects of community characteristics on personality development are apparent largely because of the differential influences of different community organizations. Thus, the city youth differs in some important respects from his counterpart in the smaller community; and the youngster raised in the slum areas of a large city is ordinarily different from one brought up in suburbia. What the situation would be if everyone grew up in the same type of community we cannot even guess, but under such circumstances it would be very difficult to define the relationships between these influences and personality growth.

Because of these differential effects on personality, psychologists and sociologists today are keenly interested in community influences. As Partridge expresses it:

> To the young person growing into maturity, the community and the neighborhood furnish a stage for his activities, and the people in the community an audience to interpret his actions. Just what those in the neighborhood applaud or hiss has a great deal to do with the kind of behavior patterns that the young person develops. In his own neighborhood, the adolescent is on speaking terms with those who live about him. He is conscious of the fact that his actions are the subject of conversation and that various kinds of social pressure can be brought to bear upon him if his behavior is too much outside the pale of acceptability. Thus the process of growing up is to a great extent concerned with the matter of tempering one's behavior until it fits into the community relationship.[3]

[2] For a more complete discussion of this notion, see E. D. Partridge, *op. cit.*, pp. 256–259; A. B. Hollingshead, *Elmtown's Youth* (New York: Wiley, 1949), especially Part II.

[3] E. D. Partridge, *Social Psychology of Adolescence* (Englewood Cliffs, N. J.: Prentice-Hall,

In evaluating the differential effects of community organization on personality development, there are several features of particular importance, just as size, make-up, attitudes, practices, and relationships are important in determining the influence of the family. Where community is concerned, there are three factors of primary significance: (1) the *physical make-up* of the community, including size, physical condition, disorganization, stability or mobility of population, and composition; (2) the *psychological make-up*, including such elements as attitudes, taboos, mores, customs, and relationships with other communities; and (3) the *cultural make-up, which* embraces cultural and recreational facilities, historical background, and similar qualities.

COMMUNITY CHARAC-TERISTICS AND PER-SONALITY DEVELOPMENT

City and Country Youth Compared. Two types of communities that differ in all three respects, and which have been widely studied for their effects on human personality, are the urban and rural communities.[4] The differential effects of these two communities have been recog-

nized for a long time, and from time to time they were reflected in a clearly identifying terminology. Not too long ago the boy from the city was generally referred to as a "slicker," and the youngster from the rural areas was a "farmer" or "hick." Nowadays the unsophisticated boy or girl would simply be referred to as a "square." Some of these terms are not as current now as formerly, but their usage indicates clearly a conviction of difference between classes of people from different areas. These differences are not merely literary — they really exist; and they exist for the simple reason that the two kinds of community in which these young persons grow up are physically, psychologically, and culturally different. However, with increased transportation facilities, the frequent migration of rural youth to the larger cities, and the general spread of cultural influences that has characterized the twentieth century, these differences are daily being minimized, so that the old identifying terms are no longer used because they are inappropriate. Nevertheless, there are still marked differences between urban and rural communities, and so long as these differences exist we can expect differential effects on personality development.

A number of these effects have already been noted in preceding chapters. For instance, in our discussion of the characteristics of physical development in Chapter V, we saw that the onset of puberty varied to an appreciable extent with locality. Many studies point to other significant differences. Furfey found that urban boys were more mature than country boys as measured by developmental tests. In the Maryland Youth Survey, it was found repeatedly that there were striking differences between rural and urban youth in such important areas as

1939), p. 261. See also W. H. Brueckner, "The Adolescent and the Community: Symposium," *Amer. J. Orthopsychiat.*, 1956, 26, 471–496; R. J. Havighurst and Hilda Taba, *Adolescent Character and Personality* (New York: Wiley, 1949), Chap. 4.

[4] See L. J. Elias, *Farm Youths' Appraisal of Their Adjustments Compared With Other Youth* (State College of Washington, Institute of Agricultural Sciences, 1949), Bull. No. 513; E. D. Partridge, *op. cit.*, pp. 271–274. In his study of factors determining delinquency, Nye found a clear-cut relationship between delinquency and urban ecology — F. I. Nye, *Family Relationships and Delinquent Behavior* (New York: Wiley, 1958), p. 39.

interests, recreational activities, and attitudes.[5]

These differences are not surprising in view of the different structures of the two communities. Because of its compactness, in the small rural community much more social pressure can be brought to bear in the formation of basic attitudes and values; also, we may expect that interests will vary as opportunities and activities vary. Thus we may suppose that the rural youth's attitude toward the "guardians of the law," who happen to be next-door neighbors, will be quite different from that of the city youth to whom a policeman is just a man in uniform, who may be regarded as an enemy rather than a protector because of his interference with freedom of action and expression. Similarly, a youth's attitudes toward the home, the school, the Church, and the neighborhood will be conditioned by the structure of the community. In a community where every classmate is practically a neighbor, the school becomes a more integral part of one's existence, and this compactness conditions many aspects of behavior. In such a community freedom of movement, of thought, and of expression is greatly reduced by the fact that there is *little chance for anonymity*. What one does or thinks or says is almost certain to become common property; and there is, as a result, less likelihood of antisocial attitudes and conduct being developed. These observations regarding the influence of community structure should be applied to the new phenomenon of Suburbia, since Suburbia in many respects resembles the rural community. There can be no doubt that growing up in Suburbia has an effect on personality development different from that of growing up in the densely populated areas of Metropolis.

Communities differ to a considerable extent, also, in the matter of avocational and vocational interests. The simpler pleasures, like picnics, outdoor amusements, and church festivals, are more likely to find a following in the smaller community, because of tradition, lack of other amusements, or a more pervasive spirit of neighborliness; and these interests and activities serve to weld the community into a still more compact and integrated unit. This, in turn, contributes to the development of similar attitudes, values, and other personal characteristics. Hollingshead made a thorough study of structural influences on adolescent behavior in a small community. He found behavior varied considerably with the social class to which the adolescent belonged, and that each of five different classes affected behavior differentially. Through the medium of such activities and experiences, community traditions, customs, and mores are gradually evolved; and out of this residue of crystallized human experience are formed many of the attitudes, beliefs, and values of the individual.[6] Phrased in another way, we may say that the perspective of people in different communities differs in certain important respects; and this different outlook on life is reflected in many phases of personality development. This fact, too, has been brought out in numerous studies. In an investigation of home punishments of adolescents, Stott found

[5] P. H. Furfey, "A Note on Relative Developmental Age Scores of Urban and Rural Boys," *Child Develpm.*, 1935, 6, 88–90; H. M. Bell, *Youth Tell Their Story* (Washington, D. C.: Amer. Coun. on Educ., 1938).

[6] A. B. Hollingshead, *Elmtown's Youth* (New York: Wiley, 1949).

that rural children seemed to reach adolescence trained to accept parental control more often than urban children, a fact that suggests a basic difference in attitudes.[7]

Still other effects are determined by the *physical condition* of the community. In the underprivileged areas of large cities, with their narrow streets, inadequate housing facilities, poor if any recreational facilities, and a general atmosphere of squalor and decay, one could not expect to find the same activities, interests, attitudes, and values that obtain in a more favored environment. Such conditions easily provoke rebellion, insecurity, discouragement, and asocial viewpoints. A trip through such areas is all that is needed to convince the observer of this possibility. The physical condition of the community, like that of the home, is sure to leave its mark on the growing personality. Even so stable a factor as intelligence seems to vary with community characteristics. Thus Lichtenstein and Brown, studying the intelligence and achievement of children in an area of low economic status, found that only 43.6 per cent fell within the I.Q. range of 90–109 as compared with 60 per cent in an unselected school population, and that those in the fourth, fifth, and sixth grades were considerably retarded in every subject tested. One characteristic of the area mentioned was *physical deterioration.*[8]

Community Composition and Stability Influences Personality. Of importance also are the composition of the community and its stability or instability. In

[7] L. H. Stott, "Home Punishments of Adolescents," *J. Genet. Psychol.*, 1940, 57, 415–428.

[8] M. Lichtenstein and A. W. Brown, "Intelligence and Achievement of Children in a Delinquency Area," *J. Juven. Res.*, 1938, 22, 1–24.

an area characterized by a medley of different racial and national traditions, mores, practices, and sentiments, there is not the homogeneity of thought and attitude that contributes to the stabilization of the more homogeneous community. This situation is most likely to result when, in addition to racial mixture, there is added the factor of *migration*, through which community stability and integration are made even more difficult, or impossible. Faris believes that migration is among the most important factors contributing to behavior abnormalities. He says:

Migration of the type under consideration here has characteristic effects on the behavior of persons; effects which for the most part are in the direction of abnormality. It achieves these by interfering with some of the essential elements of cooperation. One of the essentials to normal and conventional behavior is full membership in primary groups in communities of stability. The migrant is separated from such membership and therefore becomes increasingly individuated as the length of separation increases. . . . In addition to this individuating effect, migration also has a secularizing effect. The resident of a stable community who knows of no other way of life takes for granted the customs of his community, and regards as outlandish and abnormal the deviations he hears of only occasionally and distantly. But the migrant sees people living quite naturally in other systems, apparently as contentedly as his own people in their culture. When these alternative ways are seen to be successful his own ways become less sacred and less inevitable, and begin to lose their hold on him. . . .

The effect on a nonmigrant of residence in an area of high mobility is similar. He has no stable community life, and is exposed to the secularizing influence of a variety of ways of living.

The ecology of behavior abnormality, then, is largely a matter of the consequences of migration. The aspects significant to behavior are not the migration itself, but the individuation and the secularization that are the consequences of it. . . .[9]

Characteristics such as these are most often found in the highly industrialized urban communities rather than in smaller towns and villages, where populations are considerably more stable. For this reason the majority of studies on this problem have been directed toward determining the relationships between urban and industrial existence on the one hand, and a variety of behavior patterns on the other, including suicide, mental disorder, delinquency, and crime. Most writers are quick to note that in some simple, nonindustrial societies, particularly those of preliterate peoples, certain behavior patterns such as suicide and crime are virtually unknown; and there are even a few societies in which functional mental disorders are rare or absent. These findings clearly suggest that behavior and mentality are to an important extent *a function of community organization.*

Community Organization, Crime, and Delinquency. This fact is emphasized in a more positive manner in the studies on the causes of crime and delinquency. While the picture is changing somewhat in more recent years, the rates for both crime and delinquency are generally much higher in the cities than in rural areas, although such comparisons must take into account that cities are not

uniform in composition, nor are they clearly defined in terms of actual boundaries. Even in the industrial cities with a high rate of social disorganization, it is only a part of the city that is affected by disorganization, and that is involved in the relationship to delinquency and crime. As Partridge points out, a city is really a number of communities, joined together by industrial and political ties; and the mores, standards, practices, and sociopsychological characteristics of these different communities may vary considerably from one to another.

These facts and their implications for urban ecology have been studied intensely by several investigators. One of the most prominent facts noted is that delinquency varies markedly according to the section of the city. Thus the slum areas, characterized by density of population, physical deterioration, high rates of dependency, and with a high incidence of foreign and Negro populations, have relatively high delinquency rates; whereas in the outlying residential areas, inhabited largely by native-born business and professional groups, the rates are lower.[10] Correspondingly, in the areas be-

---

[9] R. E. L. Faris, "Ecological Factors in Human Behavior," in J. McV. Hunt (ed.), *Personality and the Behavior Disorders* (New York: Ronald, 1944), Vol. II, p. 738. See also F. I. Nye, *op. cit.,* Chap. 7, "Spatial Mobility and Delinquent Behavior"; and R. L. Stubblefield, "Children's Emotional Problems Aggravated by Family Moves," *Amer. J. Orthopsychiat.,* 1955, 25, 120–126.

[10] This interpretation is not accepted by all investigators. Some authors argue that delinquency is a characteristic of all adolescent youth. Referring to the idea of a progressively declining rate of delinquency from the center to the periphery of large urban areas, Bloch and Niederhoffer state, "Despite the popularity of this view since the 1920's, it has been consistently demonstrated that such concentrations of rates of delinquency and gang behavior do not apply to most American cities" — H. Bloch and A. Niederhoffer, *The Gang: a Study in Adolescent Behavior* (New York: Philosophical Library, 1958), p. 4. Similarly, Salisbury: "If you sample the upper-income suburbs of any eastern metropolis you quickly find tell-tale indications of gang mores among 'respectable children' "; "Poverty increases the pressures which drive young people in blind revolt against the world. But it is not the cause of the revolt. Delinquency is a

tween these two extremes, delinquency rates vary in terms of proximity to the debilitated areas. It is significant that these findings indicate also that it is *disorganization* more than community composition that regulates incidence of delinquency, since the rates for many national and racial groups decline as they leave the disorganized areas and move out toward the more stable residential areas.

On the basis of these and similar data, a sociological explanation of the persistence of high delinquency rates is offered in place of psychological and moral hypotheses. The hypotheses that delinquency is due to innate characteristics, low mentality, neurosis, psychopathic inferiority, moral defect, or mental conflict are rejected in favor of an environmental interpretation. This viewpoint is at least partly substantiated by the findings that members of delinquent gangs are on the whole quite normal and sociable. It stands to reason, however, that a purely sociological interpretation is as unpalatable as a purely psychological one, since such a hypothesis cannot account for the large number of nondelinquents in delinquent areas, or the delinquents who occasionally emerge in a nondelinquent area, a paradox which continues to plague the theorists who try to simplify the problem of crime and delinquency. These findings should not be taken to mean that psychopathic tendencies, intellectual deficiency, and other abnormalities are rarely found in delinquents, since there is considerable evidence to the contrary. Nor should we assume that all forms of delinquency are dependent on the socioeconomic milieu. Crime and delinquency are forms of maladjustive behavior, often influenced by ecological factors, but reflecting also considerable disorder within the personality of the individual involved.[11]

In many aspects of delinquent and criminal behavior the differences between urban and rural ecology stand out clearly. Seldom is there evidence in the rural community of the processes of disorganization that characterize some aspects of urban life; and nowhere in certain areas of city life are there available the social pressures that operate to stabilize existence in the rural community and keep behavior patterns in line with traditional concepts and viewpoints that are socially acceptable. The injunction, "What will the neighbors think?" for example, has little influence in a highly mobile or disintegrating urban community where the term "neighbor" is a mere euphemism. Even the family organization is not enough in many instances to prevent the development of delinquency, sometimes because this organization is itself weak and unstable, sometimes because

symptomatic disease, and disease knows no geographical and no social boundaries" — H. E. Salisbury, *The Shook-Up Generation* (New York: Harper, 1958), pp. 15, 17. In this connection, see the discussion of the delinquent culture of American society and ecological factors in delinquency in M. L. Barron, *The Juvenile in Delinquent Society* (New York: Knopf, 1954), Chaps. XII, XIII; also W. C. Kvaraceus, et al., *Delinquent Behavior: Culture and the Individual* (Washington, D. C.: Nat. Educ. Assoc., 1959), and S. Glueck and Eleanor Glueck, *Predicting Delinquency and Crime* (Cambridge, Mass.: Harvard University Press, 1949).

[11] For a study of delinquent behavior as a mode of adjustment, see W. C. Kvaraceus, *The Community and the Delinquent* (New York: World Book, 1954), Chap. 4, and A. A. Schneiders, *Personal Adjustment and Mental Health* (New York: Rinehart, 1955), Chap. 12. See also D. R. Peterson, H. C. Quay, and G. R. Cameron, "Personality and Background Factors in Juvenile Delinquency as Inferred From Questionnaire Responses," *J. Consult. Psychol.*, 1959, 23, 395–399, and M. L. Barron, op. cit., Chap. VII.

the delinquency is overlooked¹ or condoned by family members, but mostly because *ecological influences are stronger than the family*. Even in those instances where there is complete family disorganization due to death, divorce, separation, or desertion, it has been found that community disorganization is often the more significant factor.¹²

If we inquire why many children in both delinquent homes and neighborhoods do not manifest or develop delinquent behavior, the answer is to be found partly in the fact that these negative "causes" are supplemented by more positive factors, to which some individuals react and others do not. The various studies of delinquency seem to indicate that delinquency is an integral feature of certain areas, and that the concepts, traditions, and practices involved in such behavior are learned and passed on in much the same manner that other cultural patterns are transmitted. Questions of right and wrong, or of social approval and disapproval, are passed over as not applying to group behavior of this type.

There still remains the question, of course, as to why some youngsters react "favorably" to these group pressures and others do not; and here we face again the inescapable conclusion that in the last analysis the problem is a psychological one, to be understood to a large extent in terms of the needs, feelings, desires, and experiences of the youth to whom delinquent behavior exerts an appeal.¹³ Naturally, what these experiences are, and how needs are expressed, will be determined by the environmental milieu in which the individual lives. Thus Jameson, in her careful study of psychological factors contributing to the delinquency of girls, found that delinquencies were not isolated incidents, but were aspects of a whole series of problems and experiences. In the families of these girls there was a conspicuous lack of close and satisfactory emotional relationships. In many cases the girls had slept with fathers or brothers in late childhood, leading at times to early sex experiences. Twenty per cent had observed sex relations between members of the family. There was also a conspicuous absence in the family of constructive discipline and training necessary for the establishment of socially approved habits and attitudes. And the satisfaction derived from sexual experience was greater than that associated with other forms of

---

¹² However, the relationship between broken homes and delinquency has been found by different investigators to be very close. In an early study, Sullenger found that 54.1 per cent of delinquent boys, and 64.1 per cent of delinquent girls came from broken homes. Kvaraceus, summarizing data from various prominent studies, cites 51 per cent, 33 per cent, and 60 per cent of delinquents as coming from broken homes. The figures for a control sample were 27 per cent, 25 per cent, and 34 per cent respectively. These figures should be compared with those of Shaw and McKay who report that the incidence of broken homes among a delinquent group of 1675 boys was only 42.5 per cent as compared with 36.1 per cent for a control group — T. E. Sullenger, *Social Determinants in Juvenile Delinquency* (New York: Wiley, 1936), pp. 23, 24; W. C. Kvaraceus, *op. cit.*, 102; C. R. Shaw and H. D. McKay, *Social Factors in Juvenile Delinquency*, Vol. II of *Report on the Causes of Crime*, Nat. Comm. on Law Observance and Enforcement, Report No. 13 (Washington, D. C.: Government Printing Office, 1931), p. 283.

¹³ Numerous studies have consistently shown that psychological factors and personality characteristics are closely related to delinquent behavior. See, for example, A. J. Reiss, "Delinquency as the Failure of Personal and Social Controls," *Amer. Soc. Rev.*, 1951, 16, 196–207. See also A. A. Schneiders, *op. cit.*, p. 356, Table VI; W. C. Kvaraceus, *op. cit.*, pp. 88–93, Table 3, and Chap. 5; Bernice M. Moore, *Juvenile Delinquency: Research, Theory, and Comment* (Washington, D. C.: Nat. Educ. Assn., 1958), Chap. 3.

social activity.[14] All such factors coalesce to form the psychological background of the individual delinquent; and it is where such a background exists that environmental forces exert a decisive influence.[15]

The Community and Mental Disorder. In much the same manner that community characteristics have been related to delinquent behavior, it has been determined also that disorders of a more distinctly psychological kind vary with the environmental setting in which they occur. One might expect this, since the neuroses and psychoses are nothing more than abortive attempts to adjust to the demands of the environment. As this environment varies, as it becomes more complex, more disorganized, or more threatening to individual security, mental and behavioral patterns will also vary. In some simpler societies mental disorders that are very common in our own are practically unknown; whereas in our highly organized, complex, and competitive culture the number of neurotics and psychotics increases day by day. Taking a cue from Freudian psychology, we may suggest that this results from a heightened conflict between the demands of the individual and those of a reality that becomes increasingly complex and threatening, thus giving rise to greater repression, conflict, and symptom formation.

It cannot be said, of course that there is a one-to-one relationship between mental disorder and community make-up, since mental difficulties occur in the simplest and most benign settings; yet various studies show clearly that the incidence of many disorders is proportionately greater in urban than in rural areas, and in certain urban areas than in others; and that the incidence varies also with different cultures. In urban areas, the pattern of distribution is quite similar to that which obtains for delinquency, the incidence of mental disorder decreasing as one leaves the central business district and moves out to the residential areas. This distribution, admittedly, will be affected by many factors besides the ecological; nevertheless the hypothesis that there is a clear relationship between community organization and mental disorder still stands. This fact is of considerable significance to the study of adolescent behavior phenomena, since there are many behavior difficulties and disorders that have their beginnings in the conflicts of youth.[16]

Psychological and Cultural Factors in the Community. No less important than

---

[14] A. Jameson, "Psychological Factors Contributing to the Delinquency of Girls," *J. Juven. Res.*, 1938, 22, 25–32. Bloch and Niederhoffer argue that because of the prevalence in the youth culture of middle-class America of sexual misbehavior "it almost seems fitting to consider such practices as distorted phases of the normal behavior patterns of teen-age dating and courtship practice" — H. Bloch and A. Niederhoffer, *op. cit.*, p. 9.

[15] It is obvious of course that delinquency has many facets, causes, and ramifications. For various interpretations of delinquent behavior, see Bernice M. Moore, *op. cit.*, Chap. 4; A. L. Church, "Adolescence and Juvenile Delinquency," *The Nerv. Child*, 1944–45, 4, 142–146; and W. H. Sheldon, *Varieties of Delinquent Youth* (New York: Harper, 1949). An excellent statement of basic principles regarding delinquency will be found in W. C. Kvaraceus, *op. cit.*, pp. 52–55. For a thorough study of the etiology of delinquency, see M. L. Barron, *op. cit.*, Part II.

[16] See A. J. Bruecker and H. H. Remmers, "Environmental Determinants of Basic Difficulty Problems," *J. Abnorm. Soc. Psychol.*, 1952, 47, 379–381; J. W. McFarlane, "The Relationship of Environmental Pressures to the Development of a Child's Personality and Habit Patterns," *J. Pediat.*, 1939, 15, 142–154; C. Landis and J. E. Page, *Modern Society and Mental Disease* (New York: Rinehart, 1938), Chap. V; J. McV. Hunt (ed.), *Personality and the Behavior Disorders* (New York: Ronald, 1944), Vol. II, Part V.

the factors so far considered is the psychological and cultural status of the community. We realize, of course, that these aspects are to an important extent determined by or significantly related to community organization; but it would be incorrect to suppose that the psychological make-up of the community is simply a reflection of its physical or social make-up. This is evident from the fact that crime and delinquency rates and suicides vary from one city or culture to another, even though they are quite similar in structure. It is evident also in the fact that behavior patterns of various kinds vary from one locality to another within the same community. It may be safely assumed that — whatever the size, physical condition, or composition of any community — if the right attitudes prevailed, if values were sound, if moral and legal standards were of a lofty character, if there existed healthy relationships with other communities, and so on, the community itself would be socially healthy. Shaw and McKay recognize this fact in their discussion of the "spirit" of delinquency areas. "More important than the external realities of the area are the traditions, standards and moral sentiments which characterize the neighborhood life. While these more intangible factors are difficult to ascertain and do not readily lend themselves to objective analysis, they are nevertheless important aspects of the moral world to which the growing child must make an adjustment."[17]

While such psychological characteristics are always to a degree intrapersonal in character, it is nevertheless true that they gradually become "communized," and emerge as the "spirit" of the community. They are the cultural residue of communal living, of the sharing of common experiences, hardships, attitudes, values, and interests. Through these media the community gradually assumes a psychological character, and one begins to speak of community attitudes, desires, hopes, and feelings. Naturally, the repository of such factors are the individual minds of the members of the community; but their quasi-independent character is evidenced by the fact that these characteristics persist even though there are noticeable shifts in population. It is not improbable that the negative effects of community disorganization stem from the lack of well-defined or integrated psychological frameworks.

This community psychology, in the final analysis, is more important for the development of personality than its peculiar structure; for behavior, good or bad, is to an important extent a direct result of the introception by the individual of community characteristics. If, for example, the neighborhood adopts a lenient or laissez-faire attitude toward delinquency, crime, vice, and other behavior patterns, the chances are that these patterns will flourish among its young men and women; if, on the other hand, its attitude toward such transgressions is severe, if its social and moral standards are high, if by example it encourages religious practices, respect for authority, and so on, the effect on personality development will be much more beneficial. This fact more than any other makes the sociological approach to the study of behavior important.[18]

---

[17] C. R. Shaw and H. D. McKay, op. cit., p. 109. See also the study by the same authors, Juvenile Delinquency in Urban Areas (Chicago: University of Chicago Press, 1942), Chap. 7, and M. L. Barron, op. cit., Chap. XII.

[18] In this connection, see A. B. Hollingshead, Elmtown's Youth (New York: Wiley, 1949),

Of significance also to adolescent personality development is the presence or absence in the community of certain cultural influences. The presence of good libraries, of modern and well-equipped schools, of museums, theaters, clubs, youth organizations, and recreational facilities (not to mention the positive group influences that stem from them), is an important factor in the development of attitudes, interests, and values, in the wholesome use of leisure time, and in the satisfaction of basic needs and desires. Conversely, the presence in the community of negative influences, like the traditional poolroom, houses of prostitution, gambling dives, and similar "institutions" is very likely to impair the healthy development of many youth. Here again we may note the significant differences between urban and rural life. On the negative side is the fact that many rural communities boast very few of the outstanding cultural institutions of the large city; but by the same token it is rare to find in the small community any of the undesirable influences mentioned above. In all communities, adequate cultural and recreational facilities are necessary for the complete development of the adolescent. Whenever these are at hand, the more negative pastimes lose much of their attractiveness.

Adolescent Development and the Community. All these facts taken together lead the sociologist and social psychologist to conclude that the understanding of behavior and development lies more in the social order than in the characteristics of the organism, or in the changes that occur throughout its life

Chap. 7, especially pp. 149–152; and J. R. Seeley, R. A. Sim, and Elizabeth W. Loosely, *Crestwood Heights* (New York: Basic Books, 1956), pp. 106–109.

history. Thus Reuter, in his interesting and provocative article on the sociology of adolescence, criticizes the notion that adolescence is a period of storm and stress, preferring to ascribe the erratic behavior of youth to the expectations and assumptions regarding the adolescent period that characterizes people with whom the adolescent comes in contact. In similar vein he criticizes the view that disordered adolescent behavior is a social expression of maturational changes.

Comparative studies seem to show the behavior phenomena in these years to be a function of the culture. There is apparently little evidence that the period is one of mental or social disorder in the so-called primitive groups where life and social organization are relatively simple and where a simple set of culture patterns provides at most limited opportunities for diverse activities.

The character of youth behavior is socially defined in each group, and more or less each class and level of society defines it in a somewhat distinctive way. Certain adjustments are expected, certain behavior is enjoined; the degree of license or restraint considered appropriate depends upon the group. These social definitions and group expectations seem to determine the behavior that manifests itself at this as at other age periods. The group patterns set the standards of behavior; the growing child is coerced into the group mold and acquires incidentally or by inculcation the set of attitudes and standards of behavior that bring him into line with the required behavior norms. The degree and type of mental distress and social disorder that accompanies the process are matters of local incidence. . . . The time of appearance, the nature, and the extent of maladjustment in the adolescent period vary with the group and culture and with the social class or economic stratum to which the individual belongs. . . . Apparently, the social behavior characteristic of adolescents in the modern urban culture is a function of the peculiar social situation — an expression of a given time and place, rather than a function of physical development.

In the culturally homogeneous group, the problem of adjustment is relatively simple. The accepted group norms define the good life; the patterns of behavior in every situation are explicitly defined . . . transition from the child to the adult status seems to be made with ease and completeness.[19]

A similar viewpoint is expressed by Furfey who stresses the factor of learning in the determination of social behavior, at the same time that he plays down the contributions of instinctive elements. Admitting the importance of instincts in animals, he says:

But instinctive behavior is minimal among human beings. Learning is so important in human behavior that it plays a dominant part in all but the simplest reflex and impulsive behavior. Today certainly no reputable psychologist would dare to explain behavior as complicated as adolescent group life in terms of instinct.

If group life is learned and not instinctive, then we must turn for our explanation to the study of the conditions under which this behavior is learned and the emphasis shifts from the purely psychological study of the individual adolescent to the more sociological study of the circumambient conditions.

The inner psychological characteristics of the individual may indeed explain his capacity for group life; but the particular forms which this group life takes are learned; they are part of the cultural heritage which the adolescent receives from the society in which he lives.[20]

---

[19] E. B. Reuter, "The Sociology of Adolescence," Amer. J. Sociol., 1937, 43, 417–419; © 1937 by the University of Chicago.

[20] P. H. Furfey, "The Group Life of the Adolescent," J. Educ. Soc., 1940, 14, 198, 199.

Thus, we return to the idea advanced in the first chapter of this book, that adolescence is to an important extent a social phenomenon, a function of the culture in which youth develops. In this we are not ascribing to the viewpoint that the physical, mental, and motivational changes of the adolescent period are relatively unimportant. Indeed, it could be argued that these changes have a part in shaping the cultural milieu of youth, and that it is impossible to understand the adolescent personality without a thorough knowledge of such changes. What we have been attempting throughout this entire book is to bring into line the two complementary viewpoints — the psychological and the sociological — since it is only by recognizing the contributions of both the organism and the environment in which it develops that the phenomena of adolescence can be fully understood.

THE TEEN-AGER AND THE COMMUNITY

The Neighborhood and Adolescent Growth. The psychological and cultural characteristics of the community are transmitted to the growing child through his membership and activity in a primary social entity, the *neighborhood*. It is as a member of play groups, gangs, neighborhood clubs, and the like that he first comes in contact with social realities that exist outside the family. As Sullenger remarks:

All the arrangements for human living in the neighborhood are such as to favor the transmission of custom and tradition. The family, the playgroup, and the neighborhood become the first school for the child. He acquires here the social traditions, social attitudes, and social values of his group. They make him what he is, socially, and in order to understand him we must study him in this setting. . . . The ideals of freedom, justice, and good citizenship originate largely in the experience of neighborhood life. Culture patterns are formed, diffused, and transmitted through direct association.[21]

This process of socialization, occurring independently of family relationships, and often in conflict with them, begins early in life as the child associates with children outside of the family and engages in various social activities, including play, group membership, gang formation, and the like. Through participation in these activities intimate relationships with companions, play groups, and gangs are formed, and the child begins to seek his gratifications, values, and experiences outside of the family circle. It is then that the peer group comes into prominence. As Pearson points out, the adolescent turns to his peers partly to solve his conflicting feelings toward his parents:

He begins to recognize that he and adults belong to two separate generations, and that these two generations can never mix. He becomes suspicious and wary of adults, and no longer trusts them with any vital confidences; although he continues to regard them with tender feelings, he more and more separates himself and his life from them.[22]

Through membership in peer groups, the young person is able to free himself from his family and secure the emotional support necessary for him to function independently. His search for identity involves the adolescent's finding his relationship not only to himself and to his family, but to the larger social group. This often involves a repudiation of the group as well as of the family. Ordinarily, group membership helps to gratify basic needs, promotes interests of various types, and helps the adolescent to define his own role and his relationship to the opposite sex. Group membership stimulates the influence of an increasing number and variety of personalities, social activities, and moral norms; and studies of the life histories of both delinquent and nondelinquent children indicate clearly that these experiences are important factors in determining behavior traits.[23] (See Fig. 30.)

The influence of the neighborhood, and the relative effects of neighborhood

---

However, teen-agers are not entirely responsive to peer group influences. See H. H. Remmers and D. H. Radler, *The American Teenager* (New York: Bobbs-Merrill, 1957), pp. 222–237.

[23] See G. J. Mohr and Marian A. Despres, *The Stormy Decade: Adolescence* (New York: Random House, 1958), Chap. X. There are numerous studies of peer-group relationships. See L. A. Hattwick, "Group Life of the Young Child," *J. Educ. Sociol.*, 1940, 14, 205–216; C. Tryon, "The Adolescent Peer Culture," in the forty-third *Yearbook* of the National Society for the Study of Education, Part I, *Adolescence* (Chicago: University of Chicago, 1949); Irene M. Josselyn, "Psychological Problems of the Adolescent: II," *Soc. Casewk.*, 1951, 32, 250–254; R. M. Wittenberg and Janice Berg, "The Stranger in the Group," *Amer. J. Orthopsychiat.*, 1952, 22, 89–97; J. R. Christiansen and Therel R. Black, "Group Participation and Personality Adjustment," *Rur. Sociol.*, 1954, 19, 183–185; W. B. Barbe, "Peer Relationships of Children of Different Intelligence Levels," *Sch. & Soc.*, 1954, 80, 60–62; Juanita M. Luck, "A Study of Peer Relationships," *Group*, 1955, 17, 13–20.

---

[21] Reprinted with permission from T. E. Sullenger, *Social Determinants in Juvenile Delinquency* (New York: John Wiley and Sons, Inc., 1936), p. 74.

[22] G. H. J. Pearson, *Adolescence and the Conflict of Generations* (New York: Norton, 1958), p. 86. See also W. L. Wilkins, "Social Peers and Parents," *Education*, 1952, 73, 234–237; B. C. Rosen, "Conflicting Group Membership: a Study of Parent-Peer Group Cross-Pressures," *Amer. Sociol. Rev.*, 1955, 20, 155–161; M. C. Jones, "Guiding the Adolescent," *Progressive Educ.*, 1938, 15, 605–609; J. R. Seeley, R. A. Sim, and Elizabeth W. Loosley, *op. cit.*, pp. 112–117; M. L. Barron, *op. cit.*, Chap. IX.

Ages 15–16–17 years
About 10–11–12 grades

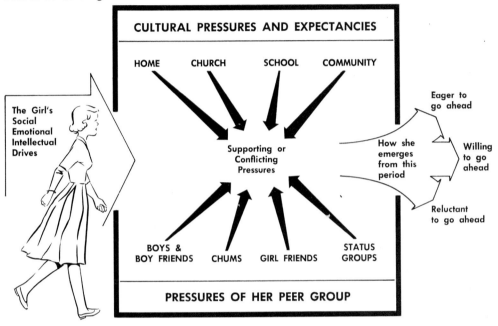

Fig. 30.   How the adolescent is influenced by group pressures.
By permission from C. S. Moser, **Understanding Girls** (New York:
Association Press, 1957), p. 184.

and family life are brought out sharply by Hollingshead. On the basis of his careful study of adolescents in a small community, he states that

> . . . children's behavior patterns are established primarily by their early experiences in the family and secondarily in the neighborhood . . . similar experiences in family and neighborhood mold children into similar social types because their learning in both areas tends to be strongly associated with class. The great majority of these adolescents have had most of their childhood experiences in the intimate, limited area of family and neighborhood. In this world of close, interpersonal relationships they have learned how their families are regarded in the larger non-family area of society. In the neighborhood they also come in contact with persons, both children and adults, from other classes and neighborhoods. It is here that they first become aware that there are people socially different from themselves.

> Thus we infer that the family and neighborhood sub-cultures not only set the stage upon which the child acts, but they also provide him with ways of acting and definitions of action.[24]

The tendency of youngsters to organize themselves into some form of social group is characteristic of every type of community, and stems from such basic tendencies as the need for experience, belonging, and participation described

[24] Reprinted with permission of John Wiley and Sons, Inc., from A. B. Hollingshead, op. cit., pp. 444–445. See also C. M. Fleming, Adolescence (New York: International Universities Press, 1949), pp. 164–172.

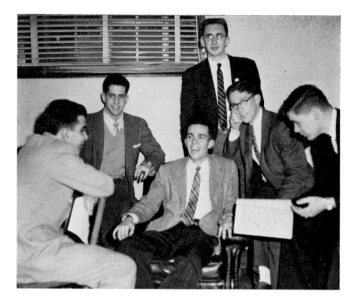

Peer-group membership has a strong influence on adolescent development.

Fordham University *Maroon*

earlier in this book. As Salisbury says, in referring to the shook-up generation, the gang serves

> as a substitute for many things which are lacking in the lives of its members. It may provide a reason for existence, a source of personal satisfaction, a pseudo-purpose for a life which lacks any purpose.[25]

In the following statement we see the close relationship between group membership and the gratification of important individual needs.

> In the gang the street boy feels himself important. Nowhere else does he seem to matter. Not at home (if he has what can be called a home). Not at school, where he can barely read, where there is nothing he can do well enough to give him even a faint glow of achievement. Not on the job, where the boss makes him feel inadequate and inferior.
>
> But with his comrades and with his gang he is important. He is needed. He is wanted. He has a place. His gang is his life. As it grows in rep, so he grows in rep. He stands taller on the streets.

[25] Reprinted with permission from H. E. Salisbury, *The Shook-Up Generation* (New York: Harper, 1958), p. 37.

He shows his heart with more reckless abandon. He becomes a Big Man.[26]

This viewpoint is substantiated by the findings of many investigators of delinquent and nondelinquent groups.

[26] *Ibid.*, pp. 37–38. See also H. Bloch and A. Niederhoffer, *The Gang: a Study in Adolescent Behavior* (New York: Philosophical Library, 1958), especially Chap. I. These authors express the same idea when they state that "observation of male adolescent behavior suggests strongly that this wish to be a man cuts across class lines and can be considered the cultural imperative of gang behavior" (p. 144). Chapters XI and XII of this book are especially important for the understanding of gang dynamics. Much the same idea is developed by G. H. J. Pearson, *op. cit.*, in his discussion in Chapter V of "Adolescent Strengthening of the Ego Through the Use of Group Ideals." Other viewpoints on gang formation and dynamics will be found in A. R. Crane, "A note on preadolescent gangs," *Aust. J. Psychol.*, 1951, 3, 43–46, and "Preadolescent Gangs: a Topological Interpretation," *J. Genet. Psychol.*, 1952, 81, 113–123; Ruth Strang, *The Adolescent Views Himself* (New York: McGraw-Hill, 1957), Chap. 12; Department of Health, Education and Welfare, *Youth Groups in Conflict*, a *Report of a Conference* (Washington, D. C.: Government Printing Office, 1958). All of these sources indicate clearly the pervasive influence of gang life on the formation of the adolescent personality and the shaping of the ego.

Such groupings are usually spontaneous in origin and constitute a form of primary group relationship. While these groups are more or less universal in all sections of the city and possess many common characteristics with respect to the mechanisms of control within the group, they differ widely in regard to cultural traditions, moral standards, and social activities. In certain areas of the city the practices and social values of many of these groups are chiefly of a delinquent character. Frequently these groups develop persistent delinquent patterns and traditional codes and standards which are very important in determining the behavior of the members. Some of these groups are highly organized and become so powerful in their hold on members that the delinquent traditions and patterns of behavior persist and tend to dominate the social life throughout the area.[27]

The influence of peer group membership on the development of behavior and personality traits has been exemplified in many different studies. Early studies of juvenile delinquency pointed out that delinquencies are typically committed by groups of two or more boys, and that even in instances of solitary delinquency the influence of companions was often apparent. It is now recognized by sociologists and social psychologists that peer group influences, particularly in adolescence, are among the strongest factors determining behavior. In one study, it was found that in 62 per cent of 3000 cases of delinquency, companionship could be regarded as a contributing factor. In another, it was found that from about 75 to 89 per cent of the boys studied committed their delinquencies in groups.[28]

The findings of this study indicate quite conclusively that most juvenile of-

[27] C. R. Shaw and H. D. McKay, op. cit., pp. 191–192.
[28] Ibid., pp. 193–196.

fenses . . . are committed by groups of boys; few by individuals singly. It is obvious that not all such group delinquencies are committed by well-organized gangs. While many of the delinquents may be members of such gangs, they usually commit their offenses in the company of only one or two other boys.[29]

Studies such as these, while concerned almost exclusively with the influence of group life on the development of delinquent behavior patterns, throw considerable light on the whole problem of the relationship between personality development and social experience as derived from group membership. There is every reason to suppose that if delinquent behavior is seriously conditioned by group membership of one kind or another, nondelinquent behavior is similarly affected. It may be that among the delinquents group life is more highly organized, and thus more seriously affects the development of individual characteristics of the members involved; but it is unquestionable that group life of any kind will leave its mark on the growing personalities of children and youth.

The Adolescent in the School. We are well aware by now that personality development is affected by all the social institutions and memberships in which the adolescent participates; but to determine the exact nature and degree of this influence is an extremely difficult task. We may assume that the experiences of teen-agers while in school, including intellectual stimulation, gratification of needs and interests, achievement, discouragement, or frustration, will all have important effects on development (Fig. 30). We may assume, too, that personal development will be favorably or

[29] Ibid., p. 199.

unfavorably conditioned by the various social activities and experiences that are a part of school life. Empirical studies as well as the observations of teachers and counselors clearly indicate the validity of these assumptions.[30] Knowledge such as this, however, leaves unanswered the question of the part played by the school *as a social institution* in the development of personality. Is school membership itself important, regardless of intellectual, social, or athletic activities? Are boys and girls who leave school early different from those who graduate? Is it better to send a child to a coeducational school rather than to an all-boys' or all-girls' school? Are youngsters affected by school traditions, policies, and special practices?[31]

These issues are implied in a recent report on delinquent behavior published by the National Education Association. Under the heading, "The school as a social institution," the authors state,

> It is important to keep in mind that although the public school is more recent than such time-honored institutions as family, church, state, and army, it has become a highly organized and pervasive societal institution. Because of this high degree of organization as well as the principle of compulsory attendance, the school can be an extremely powerful instrument for influencing the behavior of young people during a crucial age period. At present, changes in many aspects of American society make it necessary for the individual to continually adapt to new and increasingly complex conditions. The school, therefore, must constantly apprise itself of social realities and the nature of changing social conditions, and must devise programs which will enable each individual to adapt effectively to the complex circumstances of modern life.[32]

And again,

> Despite the fact that the fundamental objectives of the school still center around intellectual training and communication skills, its adoption of a wide range of objectives relatively peripheral

---

[30] See, for example, D. L. Farnsworth, *Mental Health in College and University* (Cambridge, Mass.: Harvard University Press, 1957), especially Chaps. 2, 4, 8; R. W. Edgar, "Discipline and Purpose," *Teach. Coll. Rec.*, 1955, 57, 8–14; A. T. Jersild, *In Search of Self* (New York: Teachers College, Columbia University, 1952), Sidonie M. Gruenberg (ed.), *Our Children Today* (New York: Viking, 1955), Part V.

[31] Some of these questions have been raised and studied empirically by different investigators. See, for example, W. C. Trow, *et al.*, "The Class as a Group: Conclusions From Research in Group Dynamics," in J. M. Seidman (ed.), *The Adolescent: a Book of Readings* (New York: Dryden, 1953), pp. 599–603; D. H. Jenkins and R. Lippitt, "Interpersonal Perceptions in the Classroom," in J. M. Seidman (ed.), *op. cit.*, pp. 583–599; E. D. Eddy, *College Influence on Student Character* (Washington, D. C.: Amer. Coun. on Educ., 1959), Chap. 7; Camille Low, "The Adolescent and Education. Symposium," *Amer. J. Orthopsychiat.*, 1956, 26, 471–496; Barbara Biber, "Schooling as an Influence in Developing Healthy Personality," in Ruth Kotinsky and Helen L. Witmer (eds.), *Community Programs for Mental Health* (Cambridge, Mass.: Harvard University Press, 1955), pp. 158–221; N. Sanford, "Personality Development During the College Years," *Personnel Guid. J.*, 1956, 35, 74–80; M. W. Barnes, "The Nature and Nurture of Early Adolescents," *Teach. Coll. Rec.*, 1956, 57, 513–521. Other studies of a related kind also point up the relationship between school attendance and personality development. See A. T. Jersild and M. D. Fite, "The Influence of Nursery School Experience on Children's Social Adjustment," *Child Develpm. Monographs*, No. 25, 1939; B. W. Hattwick, "The Influence of Nursery School Attendance Upon the Behavior and Personality of the Preschool Child," *J. Exper. Educ.*, 1936, 5, 180–190. Numerous investigators have also drawn a relationship between school attendance and delinquency. See Bernice M. Moore, *op. cit.*, Chap. 5; W. C. Kvaraceus, *op. cit.*, Chap. 10; and L. M. Miller, "Schools — Our Nation's First Line of Defense Against Juvenile Delinquency," *School Life*, 1954, 37, 21–22.

[32] W. C. Kvaraceus, *et al.*, *Delinquent Behavior: Culture and the Individual* (Washington, D. C.: Nat. Educ. Assoc., 1959), p. 142.

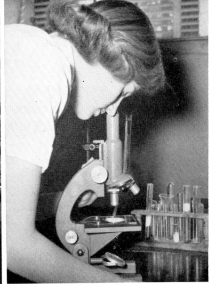

St. Gabriel's High School, New Rochelle, N. Y.

Adolescents derive valuable experiences from school activities.

to academic training in its strict sense has forced it to become directly involved in the area of values, and the system of values incorporated by the schools directly reflects official middle-class ideology.[33]

The questions raised by this viewpoint are of considerable practical importance, not only because of the amount of time spent in school by most adolescents, but also because there are so many different types of schools, whose size, teaching staff, composition, and traditions differ as markedly as do the homes from which the students come. If factors such as these are important to development in the home and community, they are certainly as important in the school, where the adolescent spends from six to eight hours a day for a period ranging from one to eight years. There are rural schools with only a few hundred pupils, and urban schools that have several thousand. There are public schools with student bodies representing numerous races, nationalities, and creeds; and there are parochial schools that admit members of only one religious denomination. There are private institutions in which the teaching staff is made up of lay personnel, and others in which the staff is predominantly or exclusively clerical or religious. Some schools boast a history extending back several centuries, and are loaded with hoary traditions; others are newly founded and can boast of no traditions. Some are coeducational (the public schools particularly), and others are restricted to members of the same sex. There are in addition the boarding schools, the military academies, and the "finishing schools," all of which differ in important ways. It is characteristics such as these that we have in mind in referring to the school as a socializing influence, which unquestionably has a direct and important bearing on personality development.

That the attitudes, interests, habits,

[33] *Ibid.*, p. 143.

Teachers are an important influence on youth.

and social development of youth attending these different types of schools will be differentially affected by their experiences while at school may be assumed without fear of error. It is extremely unlikely that a youngster attending, let us say, a boys' boarding school for four years should develop in the same direction as one who attends a coeducational public high school. In matters of discipline, social attitudes, psychosexual development, interests and values, we may expect considerable differential development. Unfortunately, the exact character and extent of such influences can only be surmised at present, since there are few systematic studies that shed any real light on such problems as the following: "What are the merits or limitations of coeducation?" "What is the effect on students of teacher attitudes?" "To what extent does the boarding-school situation influence psychosexual development?" "What effect on development ensues from the type of teaching personnel?" Questions such as these call for serious investigation; and until we have the answers to them, we can only guess what influence the school as a social

institution has on the development of personality.[34]

Church Membership and Adolescent Development. Even less is known concerning the influence of church membership on personal development. Here again factors such as type of church, size, composition, and tradition loom large. But the problem is not so complex as is that of the school, because much smaller numbers of adolescents actually belong to a church; because the church is not as complex an institution as the

[34] A number of investigators have turned their attention to such problems as the influence of teachers' attitudes, identification with teachers, the influence of school administration, and the like. See D. B. Ellis and L. W. Miller, "The Relationship of Teachers' Attitudes to Children's Problem Behavior," *J. Educ. Psychol.*, 1946, 37, 501–510; U. H. Fleege, *Self-Revelation of the Adolescent Boy* (Milwaukee: Bruce, 1945), pp. 107–122; J. Gabriel, *An Analysis of the Emotional Problems of the Teacher in the Classroom* (Melbourne: F. W. Cheschire, 1957); T. A. C. Rennie and L. E. Woodward, *Mental Health in Modern Society* (New York: Commonwealth Fund, 1948), Chap. XIII; D. L. Farnsworth, *op. cit.*, pp. 189–207; J. R. Gallagher and H. I. Harris, *Emotional Problems of Adolescence* (New York: Oxford University Press, 1958), pp. 13–25; C. M. Fleming, *Adolescence* (New York: International Universities Press, 1949), Part II.

school; and because even among those who attend church regularly attendance is generally limited to a weekly one-hour visit. It is to be understood that we are distinguishing here between the church as a social institution and religious experiences and practices. We have already dealt with the latter problem in Chapter XV.

When we consider the relatively small number of youth who claim active church membership as compared with the number who attend school, it would seem that the church as an institution exerts little influence on personality development. The degree to which it does influence personal growth will vary of course with the nature of the membership. If church membership is accepted as an *integral* part of one's life, if attendance is regular and often, if participation in church activities is part and parcel of one's experiences, then it may be that development would be affected to an appreciable extent.[35] There are un-

doubtedly many youth who have been influenced by membership in different church organizations, but this number is comparatively small. In one study of this relationship, the author concluded, "This study leads to the conclusion that church membership itself is not an independently powerful influence in the development of character, but that church membership is often associated with other factors or constellations of factors that tend to produce good or bad character reputations."[36]

---

early adolescence on the Church gives a great many children a sense of belongingness which has greater continuity and certainty for the individual than anything provided by his parents. This is true whether the individual looks to a personal God interested in him as one of His children, or finds in his religious experience an orientation to basic and everlasting 'values' " — J. S. Plant, *The Envelope: a Study of the Impact of the World Upon the Child* (New York: Commonwealth Fund, 1950), p. 26.

[36] Dorothy Neubauer, "The Relation of the Church to Character Formation," in R. J. Havighurst and Hilda Taba, *Adolescent Character and Personality* (New York: Wiley, 1949), p. 68. A different aspect of church membership is described by J. Stapel, "Gauging People's Personalities," *Publ. Opin. Quart.*, 1949, 13, 320–324, who found a relationship between political and religious views and personality traits.

[35] See, for example, P. H. Furfey, "The Group Life of the Adolescent," *J. Educ. Sociol.*, 1940, 14, 195–204. Furfey makes pointed reference to the importance of church membership to certain Negro groups. As Plant states, "From

TABLE 28

RELATION BETWEEN RELIGIOUS OBSERVANCE AND CHARACTER REPUTATION*

	Quartile Standing on Character Scores (Honesty and Responsibility)			
	I	II	III	IV
	(Lower-middle class)			
High religious observance	2	5	4	12
Low religious observance	3	1	4	. .
Non-church	3	2	1	2
	(Upper-lower class)			
High religious observance	2	4	2	6
Low religious observance	6	3	4	1
Non-church	10	6	2	2

*Reprinted with permission from: R. J. Havighurst and Hilda Taba, *op. cit.*, p. 65.

TABLE 29

ADOLESCENT CHURCH ATTENDANCE AND DELINQUENT BEHAVIOR*

Frequency	Most Delinquent		Least Delinquent		N	
	Boys	Girls	Boys	Girls	Boys	Girls
	Per Cent		Per Cent			
Never	38	38	65	62	174	69
1–2 year	43	32	58	68	155	96
Once a month	32	37	68	63	140	114
2–3 month	33	34	67	66	232	247
Regularly	25	22	75	78	452	631

*Reprinted with permission from: F. I. Nye, *Family Relationships and Delinquent Behavior* (New York: John Wiley and Sons, Inc., 1958), p. 36.

While more investigations and data are needed before any certain generalizations can be made concerning the relationship between church membership and personality development, the evidence available does indicate a positive relationship (Table 28). In his thorough study of the relationship between various background factors and delinquent behavior, Nye found a definite relationship between church affiliation and adolescent behavior. He says, "Both attendance by parents and attendance by adolescents are related to delinquent behavior. For adolescents, there appear to be only two meaningful patterns of attendance: namely, regular and non-regular attendance. Delinquent behavior is no less among those who attend irregularly than among those who never attend. . . . The adolescent who attends irregularly may have some knowledge of Church teaching, but he probably gets little from the group in terms of meeting his sociopsychological needs, and, therefore is unresponsive to its controls. The reverse may also be true: that those who attend infrequently do so because of lack of need fulfillment in the church group."[37]

[37] Reprinted with permission from F. I. Nye, *Family Relationships and Delinquent Behavior* (New York: John Wiley and Sons, Inc., 1958), p. 35.

Table 29 indicates these relationships.

The Sociology of Adolescence Restated. In these two chapters on the adolescent in the family and in the community, we have marshaled considerable evidence and opinion to indicate that adolescent personality is significantly conditioned by the social and cultural milieu in which development takes place. While this does not mean, as some writers contend, that all development can be explained as a reflection of existing cultural patterns, it does signify that human development cannot be completely understood if cultural impacts are left out of consideration. From the practical standpoint, therefore, the approach to a solution of the youth problem must be sociological as well as psychological. Until we effectively tackle the problems of the broken home, inadequate parent-child relationships, ineffective parental discipline, and the delinquent neighborhood, the disorganized community, poor recreational facilities, and so on, we will remain at a loss to cope with adolescent difficulties, even though, from the purely psychological standpoint, they are completely understood.

As one noted sociologist remarks:

Culture traits are subject to modification, but only if they are treated as cul-

H. Armstrong Roberts

Participation in group activities is important to the development of social traits.

ture traits. If we study a delinquent adolescent and decide that his delinquency is a learned reaction, then it can be changed; but it cannot be changed merely by psychiatric prestidigitation. It can only be changed by changing the culture in which the delinquent remains.[38]

This is a lesson that all who deal with the problems of modern youth need to learn. The school psychologist, the psychological clinic, the psychiatrist — all are important to the business of ironing out youth's difficulties (see Chapter XX). But to the extent that traits and behavior patterns are culturally determined, to that extent must the existing culture be

[38] P. H. Furfey, "The Group Life of the Adolescent," *J. Educ. Sociol.*, 1940, 14, 204.

changed whenever it interferes with normal and healthy development.

SOCIAL GROWTH IN ADOLESCENCE

The Emergence of Social Personality. This study of the adolescent in the family and in the community brings us to a final phase of personality development — *the adolescent's social growth.* Throughout this book we have studied many things that contribute to or play some part in converting the child into an adult, including physical changes and their implications, basic motivations, discipline, and the family, the church, and the community. And we have studied closely the emergence of different aspects of the adolescent's personality — his physical make-up, his growth to sexual manhood or womanhood, his emotional make-up or temperament, his moral and spiritual growth and character formation, and his distinctive relationship to his environment. Many of these determinants, and the emergents to which they give rise, have a great deal to do with the youngster's social growth. Physical development has many social implications; sexual development necessarily includes heterosexual orientation; moral development helps to shape social values, attitudes, and ideals; and emotional growth touches social relationships at a thousand different points. Similarly, such factors as needs, perceptions, discipline, and family relationships exert the most profound influence on social growth. These facts are easily recognized; but in order to complete the picture of adolescent development, we need to go one step further and trace specifically the emergence of social personality, just as we have previously traced the emergence of physical make-up, temperament, character, and the moral aspects of personality.

The Meaning of Social Development. The social aspect of personality, like temperament and character, assumes to itself and embraces distinctive personality characteristics that are not ordinarily thought of as belonging to other components of personality. Just as moral traits are distinctive of character, and emotional traits are related to temperament, so other traits "belong" to the social component of personality — the "socius." Thus, integrity is clearly a character trait, optimism is a feature of temperament, and friendliness a trait of socius. We need hardly point out that these traits, although assigned to differ-

ent categories, are not independent of one another. Moral and emotional traits have a great deal to do with the development of social values and attitudes, and social development exerts considerable influence on the emergence of temperament and character. Thus the moral teen-ager will avoid lying, cheating, and stealing, all of which have distinctive social implications; and the truly social adolescent, by reason of his attitudes and values regarding his fellow man, will emerge with a stronger character and a more adequate personality. These are important relationships that point up the necessity of understanding and constantly emphasizing the integral nature of human personality. To distinguish different personality traits, or even different categories of traits, will lead to no harm as long as their interrelationships and mutual dependencies are fully appreciated.

Social growth, or the emergence of socius, refers to the development of those habits and skills, mannerisms and mores, values and ideals, interests and attitudes that influence and channel the relationships that exist among individuals, and that bind people together into groups. Thus many racial and religious attitudes, humanitarian values and ideals, political beliefs and prejudices, social graces and mannerisms, such as politeness and poise, set the pattern for and become a part of an individual's social personality. We have many terms to describe these traits: good manners, breeding, polish, poise, social grace, politeness, charm, friendliness, loyalty, and the like. It is all such traits taken together that constitute the socius of the personality, and that help to create a disposition to think, feel, and act in a manner that conforms to the rules and standards of society. In instances where such conformity does not develop, as in the delinquent, the eccentric, or the rugged individualist, social growth has taken a wrong turn with the result that the socius is likely to become warped and distorted. Normal social development, which begins in childhood and is completed in adolescence, promotes the *socialization* of the individual human being. Particularly in adolescence, the egocentrism and the impulsiveness of the child should be gradually modified by the growth of a sociocentric awareness and attitude that will help the youngster find his place and fit into the society to which he belongs.[39]

---

[39] There are many good sources which describe the social development of the adolescent. See, for example, Margaret E. Tresselt, "The Adolescent Becomes a Social Person," *J. Soc. Hyg.*, 1954, *40*, 130–134; C. W. Meredith, "Personality and Social Development During Childhood and Adolescence," *Rev. Educ. Res.*, 1955, *25*, 469–476; E. G. Parameswaran, "Social Adjustment of a Group of Early Adolescent Boys," *J. Psychol. Res.*, 1957, *1*, 29–45; J. P. Zubek and Patricia A. Solberg, *Human Development* (New York: McGraw-Hill, 1954), Chap. 12; Caroline Tryon and W. E. Henry, "How Children Learn Personal and Social Adjust-

Social Growth, Maturity, and Adjustment. The emergence of a truly social personality, along with the process of socialization, are fundamental to both maturity and adjustment. The adolescent needs to become socially mature, just as he needs to become physically, intellectually, emotionally, and morally mature; and, as we have noted many times in this volume, maturity is essential to healthy adjustment. Without social maturity, and therefore social responsibility, adequate adjustment is impossible, and without maturity and adjustment combined, mental health is impossible. The growth of the human personality must be total, and no aspect can be ignored.

---

ment," in N. B. Henry (ed.), *The Forty-Ninth Yearbook for the National Society for the Study of Education*, Part I, *Learning and Instruction* (Chicago: University of Chicago Press, 1950), pp. 156–182; R. Centers, "Social Class Identification of American Youth," *J. Pers.*, 1950, *18*, 290–302; H. T. Himmelweit, A. H. Halsey, and A. N. Oppenheim, "The View of Adolescents on Some Aspects of the Social Class Structure," *Brit. J. Sociol.*, 1952, *3*, 148–172.

SELECTED READINGS

Bloch, H. A., and Niederhoffer, A., *The Gang: a Study in Adolescent Behavior* (New York: Philosophical Library, 1958).

Cohen, A. K., *Delinquent Boys: the Culture of the Gang* (Glencoe, Ill.: Free Press, 1955).

Erikson, E. H., *Childhood and Society* (New York: Norton, 1950).

Farnsworth, D. L., *Mental Health in College and University* (Cambridge, Mass.: Harvard University Press, 1957).

Fleming, C. M., *Adolescence* (New York: International Universities Press, 1949), Chaps. 11–13.

Frank, L. K., and Frank, Mary, *Your Adolescent at Home and in School* (New York: Viking, 1956).

Havighurst, R. J., and Taba, Hilda, *Adolescent Character and Personality* (New York: Wiley, 1949), Chaps. 2, 4, 5, 6, 7, 22, 25.

Hollingshead, A. B., *Elmtown's Youth: the Impact of Social Classes on Adolescents* (New York: Wiley, 1949).

Kvaraceus, W. C., *The Community and the Delinquent* (New York: World Book, 1954).

Landis, P. H., *Adolescence and Youth*, 2 ed. (New York: McGraw-Hill, 1952), Chaps. 4, 6, 7, 11, 12, 21–25.

Linton, R., *The Cultural Background of Personality* (New York: Appleton-Century-Crofts, 1945).

Neumeyer, M. H., *Juvenile Delinquency in Modern Society* (New York: Van Nostrand, 1949).

Nye, F. I., *Family Relationships and Delinquent Behavior* (New York: Wiley, 1958).

Partridge, E. D., *Social Psychology of Adolescence* (Englewood Cliffs, N. J.: Prentice-Hall, 1939).

Pearson, G. H. J., *Adolescence and the Conflict of Generations* (New York: Norton, 1958).

Plant, J. S., *The Envelope: a Study of the Impact of the World Upon the Child* (New York: Commonwealth Fund, 1950).

Salisbury, H. E., *The Shook-up Generation* (New York: Harper, 1958).

Seeley, J. R., Sim, R. A., and Loosley, Elizabeth W., *Crestwood Heights: a Study of the Culture of Suburban Life* (New York: Basic Books, 1956).

Seidman, J. M. (ed.), *The Adolescent: a Book of Readings* (New York: Dryden, 1953), Chap. 17.

Strang, Ruth, *The Adolescent Views Himself* (New York: McGraw-Hill, 1957), Chaps. 8, 12.

Zachry, Caroline B., *Emotion and Conduct in Adolescence* (New York: Appleton-Century-Crofts, 1940), Chaps. 5, 7, 8, 9, 10, 11, 14.

PART V

Principles and Practices

Counseling the adolescent

CHAPTER XX

COUNSELING THE ADOLESCENT

> To know what the adolescent is like, how he develops, or how he perceives and fits into his world, are important steps in helping him to grow up and to achieve maturity. But understanding is not always enough. There are times when we must put this understanding actively to work in the arts of guidance and counseling. In this final chapter, let us examine the basic principles underlying these important processes.

BASIC PRINCIPLES OF ADOLESCENT DEVELOPMENT

Guidance, Counseling, and Human Development. Intelligent and effective guidance and counseling of the adolescent depend a great deal on how much one knows about human development. This knowledge has been our principal concern in the preceding chapters of this book. At times we have described practical procedures that should be used in helping the adolescent cope with the complex business of growing up; but for the most part we have concerned ourselves with the facts and characteristics of development, and their bearing on the problems of adolescent adjustment. Here, then, we wish to direct attention to the principles and procedures involved in dealing with the problems of youth in a guidance or counseling situation. In the handling of human problems *knowledge* always comes first; but it is equally im-portant to become thoroughly acquainted with the *practices* that underlie the skillful solution of such problems.[1]

This practical approach to the handling of adolescent problems can be augmented to an important degree by pulling together the basic principles of adolescent development that are contained in the preceding pages. This will enable us to summarize the more basic facts concerning the adolescent's push toward maturity, and at the same time it provides a suitable bridge between the knowledge *about* the adolescent and working *with* him in a concrete problem situation.

---

[1] See E. G. Williamson and M. E. Hahn, *Introduction to High School Counseling* (New York: McGraw-Hill, 1940); C. A. Curran, "Guidance and Counseling in Education," *Educ.*, 1952, 73, 223–228; M. D. Hardee, "Counseling as an Integrating Factor in General Education," in M. D. Hardee (ed.), *Counseling and Guidance in General Education* (New York: World Book, 1955); H. T. Morse, "General Education and Individual Guidance," in M. D. Hardee (ed.), *op. cit.*, pp. 3–25.

1. *Adolescence is characterized by constant change and transition.* In working with the teen-ager, it is important to realize that he or she is undergoing constant change in all of the different areas of personality. Many of the problems of adolescence arise from the fact that it is essentially a period of transition.

2. *Development is gradual and continuous.* Although there are occasional sporadic bursts in human growth, development is a process that moves by imperceptible degrees toward the goal of maturity, and it does so ineluctably. The young person is not a child today and an adolescent tomorrow, nor is he an adult the day after. Development must be given a chance to realize its own intrinsic aims, and nurtured in a favorable environment.

3. *Development is pervasive and interlocking.* The processes of growth by which the organism strives toward full maturity reach into every nook and corner of the human personality, and are inextricably interwoven one with the other. Whatever goes on in one area of development is likely to reflect on or be reflected by many other areas. For this reason, adolescent problems are often complex and difficult to solve.

4. *The adolescent personality is formed by heredity and environment, culture, and self-determination.* There are many forces that help to mold the personality and channel the behavior of the teen-age boy or girl. It is a mistake to overemphasize one to the disparagement of the other. Heredity and environment are important, but the adolescent must sooner or later accept responsibility for himself.

5. *Most teen-agers are "normal," and it is normal to have problems, frustrations, and conflicts.* Because of these facts we distinguished carefully among the adolescent problem, the adolescent with problems, and the problem adolescent. There is a problem inherent in the adolescent thrust toward maturity, and all adolescents have problems; but this is very different from saying that the majority of adolescents are problem children. The delinquents, the truants, the sexual deviates, the neurotics, and prepsychotics are problem adolescents, but the rest of the teen-agers are merely adolescents with problems.

6. *The majority of adolescent problems resolve with maturity.* As the goal of maturity is more fully realized, and the adolescent learns gradually to accept adult responsibility, the problems that loomed so large during the "storm and stress" of adolescence begin to dissipate and eventually disappear. These are of course replaced by problems of adulthood, but the conflicts and frustrations peculiar to the adolescent period gradually fade into the background and are soon forgotten.

7. *All adolescents want to be normal, mature, and adult.* Just as there is an intrinsic thrust toward maturity and adulthood, there is a deep and pervasive tendency toward normality in all adolescents. The problem children whom we encounter among the delinquents and neurotics are those who could not exploit these natural, healthy tendencies because of acquired limitations within their own personality structure, or because of limitations imposed by a harsh and restricting environment. Parents and counselors should exploit these healthy tendencies to the utmost whenever opportunity provides.

8. *A healthy body-image and self-concept are basic to wholesome growth, self-identity, and self-realization.* The

adolescent's perception of his physical make-up, and his idea of himself, enter into all of his adjustments, relationships, and goal-seeking. It is recognized today that an adequate self-concept is basic to mental health and adjustment.

9. *The physical changes of adolescence underlie and support the growth of a mature personality.* It is important for parents and teachers to realize the significant role which physical development plays in the total development of the adolescent personality. The conviction of growing up, the feeling of being adult, and identity with the mature person are supported to an important extent by physical growth and maturation. Moreover, adequate physical growth requires physical health and therefore the application of principles of hygiene. *Mens sana in corpore sano* is still, after two thousand years, a sound principle for the guidance of adolescents as well as adults.

10. *Psychosexual development during adolescence conditions social, moral, emotional, and religious growth.* Here we have a special instance of Principle 3 which emphasized that development is pervasive and interlocking. But the influence of psychosexual development is so important that it requires special emphasis. The whole character of the adolescent's interpersonal relationships and strivings toward adulthood is affected by the changes that take place in the psychosexual area, and this fact must be considered always in guiding the adolescent toward a more secure viewpoint and a more efficient attack on his own problems.

11. *Adequate sex instruction is basic to healthy sexual development.* As we saw in Chapter VI, the sex instruction of youth is on the whole very inadequate, even though empirical evidence clearly supports the hypothesis that good sex instruction is closely correlated with good sex adjustment. Parents particularly should become aware of this important relationship, and should assume the responsibility that is properly theirs.

12. *Adolescents are strongly influenced by certain basic needs, particularly love, belonging, status, security, self-identity, achievement, participation, and conformity.* Counselors of youth must pay heed to the existence of these basic needs in human personality. These needs, and the desires that grow out of them, are more important to the understanding of adolescent behavior than any other group of factors. Goals and ideals, motives and interests can be denied; but basic human needs cannot, unless we are willing to risk personality distortion, maladjustment, and ill-health.

13. *Needs, motives, goals, and ideals constitute an interlocking motivational system.* In trying to understand and to cope with human behavior and adjustment problems, the counselor of youth must recognize that the dynamic factors underlying the adolescent's efforts to cope with reality and to establish secure relationships are woven into an interlocking directorate. Motives grow out of or are conditioned by needs; goals have their starting point in motives; and ideals are goals of a special kind. The counselor, therefore, cannot be satisfied with a purely rational interpretation of behavior when he is dealing with moral lapses, religious reorientation, or vocational selection. At every point rational decisions will be influenced by many other factors in the personality, particularly basic needs.

14. *During adolescence the motivational pattern shifts to an important degree at different levels of behavior.*

Apart from other characteristics of motivation, from the standpoint of guidance and counseling it is necessary to recognize that there are significant shifts during adolescence from sensory to rational motivation, from impulse control to decision making, from egocentric to sociocentric motivation, from an asexual to a sexual orientation, and from a relatively blind determination to a more insightful one. These are all important changes in the dynamic picture, and will bear directly on counseling approaches and techniques.

15. *Both external and internal (self) discipline are necessary to healthy growth and maturity.* In our discussion of discipline, we emphasized the point that discipline is essentially the proper ordering of a person's life and behavior. Without this order, the adolescent's psychic life and behavior are likely to become confused and disjointed, with a resulting impairment of interpersonal relations. Of particular significance is the steady growth of self-discipline, because self-discipline involves accepting responsibility for one's self; and without this important development, maturity is impossible.

16. *Feelings and emotions, out of which temperament emerges, undergo considerable change during adolescence.* The teen-ager, often for the first time, encounters sexual feelings, aggressive tendencies, hostility, guilt, shame, and anxiety, feelings that often confuse and frighten him. In counseling, therefore, such feelings and their effects on the self-concept, behavior, and adjustment must be thoroughly understood and skillfully manipulated. In addition, there are structural changes in the affective life, particularly in the behavioral aspects of emotions. All such changes condition the emergence of the adolescent temperament.

17. *During adolescence there are significant and profound changes in interests and attitudes.* While some interests and attitudes may carry over from childhood, empirical evidence indicates pervasive changes in these areas that are of deep significance for the adolescent's leisure time activities, vocational orientation, moral development, and social adjustments. These developments enter into the guidance and counseling process at many points.

18. *Values, ideals, and goals tend to crystallize during adolescence, and thus play an increasingly larger role in the dynamics of behavior.* In the thrust toward maturity and the adult roles he will be expected to assume later on, the adolescent is deeply affected by the values which he learns to accept, by the ideals which he fashions for himself, and by the goals toward which he orients his striving. All of these factors are basic to an adequate philosophy of life, and in their formation the adolescent needs a great deal of thoughtful guidance.

19. *There are significant moral and religious changes which deeply affect character development during adolescence.* In view of the changes in attitudes, values, ideals, and principles, it is to be expected that there would be corresponding changes in the moral and religious life of the young person. We can suppose that individual conscience will be sharpened, that the moral and religious consciousness of the adolescent will be broadened and deepened, that some concepts and beliefs will drop out or be greatly altered, and that moral and religious perspectives will assume more mature characteristics. There will also be changes in the structure and

function of the superego depending on the other aspects of moral development. All of these changes will condition the emergence of character because of the close relationship between moral values and character growth.

20. *The adolescent's perception of his world is conditioned by personal experiences, basic needs, feelings, failures, and successes.* In counseling adolescents, it is important to keep in mind that their perception of the world in which they live is not the same as that of the child or of the adult. The failure to recognize this fact leads to many failures in counseling. It also distorts the relationship between parents and teen-agers. If the adolescent is frightened, cynical, or pessimistic, it is because he has not yet acquired the perspective or the wisdom necessary to interpret reality in an adequate or wholesome manner. His perceptions are often distorted by needs, his fund of learning is limited, and he may resort to daydreams as a substitute for the real thing. Thus, in the perception of his world, the adolescent's developing intellect will play a most important part.

21. *The adolescent's family is the most important single determinant of his growth pattern, his mental health, and his adjustment.* Empirical evidence demonstrates conclusively that family constellation, stability, and relationships play a major role in shaping the conduct and personality of youth. The feeling of acceptance, a sense of belonging, security, self-identity, and a rewarding sense of being worthwhile are all affected for good or ill by family experience. Thus the family broken by divorce, death, separation, or a working mother; and the family torn apart by internal strife and conflict is bound to sow the seeds

of insecurity, rebellion, maladjustment, and delinquency.

22. *The emerging personality is conditioned throughout adolescence by cultural factors, community influences, and the environment.* As the child moves out from the protective surroundings of the home and family, the emerging personality begins to be influenced by group memberships, neighborhood mores and traditions, ethnic influences, and the like. In adolescence particularly, the emerging personality is most strongly influenced by peer group membership which often supplies the adolescent with values, ideals, acceptance, a sense of belonging, and other satisfactions that were formerly provided by the family.

These twenty-two statements comprise some of the most basic principles of adolescent development. Together, they constitute a workable framework for the application of guidance and counseling procedures. To this problem, then, we now turn our attention.

SOME BASIC PRINCIPLES OF GUIDANCE AND COUNSELING

The Continuum of Factors Influencing Personality Growth. Before outlining and defining the procedures involved in guidance and counseling, it would be helpful to bring these procedures into line with other factors affecting the growth process. There are certainly countless adolescents who never experience formal counseling, and there are even more who never come into contact with psychotherapy. But certainly the great majority of young people will receive some guidance during the adolescent period, and almost all of them without exception will be influenced by

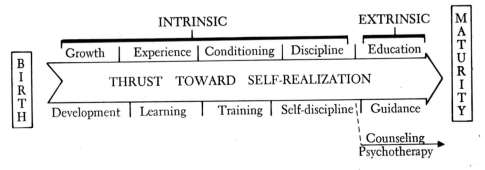

Fig. 31.   Factors affecting the growth process from birth to maturity.

the educational process. Thus the question arises: Why are guidance, counseling, or even psychotherapy necessary at times to promote the growth process or to solve problems? Since it is obvious that these special processes are not available to everyone, they cannot be intrinsic to the achievement of maturity. In fact, even formal education — and particularly education at the higher levels — is not absolutely necessary for full growth.

In Figure 31, therefore, we have diagramed the continuum of factors that influence the growth process from birth to maturity. Each factor is a member of a pair, one of which complements the other, either in the natural process of growing up, or in situations where special procedures become necessary. The first four pairs of factors are *intrinsic* to the growth process, whereas the last two are in themselves *extrinsic* and therefore not absolutely necessary to the achievement of maturity. It should be emphasized that, with the exception of the last pair of factors, counseling and psychotherapy, all of these determinants exist on an unbroken continuum that begins with physical growth and development in the earliest stages of life and continues in a time sequence until the termination

of formal education and the use of guidance procedures. Because counseling and psychotherapy are very *special adjuncts* to education, guidance, and the other elements of growth, they are set off by themselves with a broken line.[2]

This arrangement of factors affecting the growth toward maturity enables us to answer the question why special procedures sometimes become necessary. In any single case of personality development, it is clear that if all of the pairs of factors on the straight line were completely adequate and wholesome, there

[2] In this connection see E. G. Williamson and J. D. Foley, *Counseling and Discipline* (McGraw-Hill, 1949); F. McKinney, "Basic Similarities in Counseling and Extra-Curricular Activities," *Educ.*, 1952, 73, 241–244; E. G. Williamson, *Counseling Adolescents* (New York: McGraw-Hill, 1950), Chap. 1.

The close relationships between education, guidance, and counseling should not be used as argument for their identity, as too many writers are prone to do. As Jacques Barzun remarks somewhat scathingly of this tendency: "Thus the school is not to teach but to cure; body and mind are not to use for self-forgetful ends but to dwell on with Narcissus' adoring anxiety; the arts are not to give joy and light but to be scanned for a 'diagnosis' of some trouble, a solution of some 'problem,' or else exploited for the common good in occupational therapy . . ." — reprinted with permission from J. Barzun, *The House of Intellect* (New York: Harper, 1959), pp. 23–24.

would never be any need for counseling and psychotherapy. It is because af failure or impairment in development, damaging experiences, inadequate learning, faulty conditioning or training, disciplinary failures, and weaknesses in the educational process that some people find it impossible to cope successfully with reality and to resolve their own problems. In such instances counseling or psychotherapy often becomes necessary. The need for guidance generally reflects nothing more than a lack of experience or wisdom on the part of young people, and therefore does not of itself indicate a failure in the growth process.

Adolescent Problems in Relation to the Continuum of Growth Factors. Where the adolescent is concerned, we have seen that problems of one kind or another are likely to arise because of the nature of adolescence itself and its complex relationship with the environment. While the basic aims of development, learning, discipline, education, and similar growth factors are directed toward adequate, healthy adjustment, and thus the avoidance of problems — which is exactly what happens in many instances — in our complex and frustrating society these aims are not easily realized. In the ordinary course of growing up youngsters do learn how to tackle and to solve many problems that arise, but almost invariably situations develop which require more knowledge, skill, or coping ability than they possess. It is then that special procedures, such as guidance and counseling, become necessary.

In order to simplify this situation, we have organized problems encountered by

LEVEL	PROBLEMS	TYPES	PROCEDURES
I	Everyday problems	Friendships Family School, etc.	Experience Education (Guidance)
II	Special problems	Educational Vocational Premarital Personal, etc.	Guidance (Counseling)
III	Adjustment problems	Emotional Sexual Social Religious Moral	Counseling (Psychotherapy)
IV	Mental health and personality problems	Neuroses Homosexuality Alcoholism Drug Addiction Psychoses Psychopathy, etc.	Psychotherapy (Medical Treatment)
V	Medical problems	Injury Disease, etc.	Medical treatment

Fig. 32.   Kinds of problems.

adolescents into different levels, and have indicated how these problems are or can be resolved. These relationships are pictured in Figure 32. It will be noted that the problems extend from the relatively simple everyday problems encountered by everyone to the most complex problems of mental ill-health and disease. For each level, we have indicated the kind of problem included in that category, and have indicated also the approach that can be made to the problem. Because education, guidance, counseling, and psychotherapy exist on a continuum, so that one readily passes over into the other, at each level the next step is put in parentheses.

From this diagram we can see that problems have a way of determining the procedures or treatment to be used. In many instances, the problem is simply one of utilizing experience or knowledge in order to figure out the answer, or of adjustment to a local condition which does not involve deep-seated emotional difficulties or mental symptoms. Such, for example, are the problems that arise in ordinary friendships, at home, or in school.[3] In other instances the problems are of such a magnitude that they require the special techniques of guidance; and in still others counseling or psychotherapy is indicated.[4] If, of course, a simple problem leads to anxiety, rebellion, or

isolation, more intensive treatment may become necessary.

It is important for counselors and parents to recognize that some problems

> can be effectively resolved by information, advice, suggestion, or counsel. Many school problems and many difficulties that arise in marriage are of this kind. For example, a youngster may get into academic difficulties because he does not know how to evaluate a curriculum properly in terms of his ultimate aims, or he may need advice regarding the choice of the right vocation. Similarly, married couples often get out of difficulties by learning what they should have known regarding sex in marriage, or by learning how to work out a satisfactory budget. There are countless problems in human adjustment that require nothing more than good sound advice, and any treatment that goes beyond this is predicated on the doubtful assumption that every human problem is at bottom an emotional one.[5]

Thus, where adolescents are concerned, it is quite important for the parent, teacher, or counselor to make a preliminary evaluation of the problem presented so that the right kind of help can be sought.

The Aims of Guidance and Counseling. Basic principles of guidance and counseling will be influenced to an important extent by the aims or goals the counselor has in mind when working with the adolescent. And these aims will of course vary to some extent with the nature of the problem brought to the counselor and the procedure that seems to be indicated. In some instances, the goal of the counselor may be to provide necessary information in order to resolve an immediate problem. In others it may be

---

[3] See the article by Frances M. Wilson, "The Best in Life at Every Age," *Ment. Hyg.*, N. Y., 1955, 39, 483–488.

[4] See G. Goldberg, and N. Shoobs, "Guiding the Adolescent Boy," *Nerv. Child*, 1944–45, 4, 159–166; M. E. Hahn and M. S. MacLean, *General Clinical Counseling in Educational Institutions* (New York: McGraw-Hill, 1950); E. G. Williamson, "The Clinical Method of Guidance," *Rev. Educ. Res.*, 1939, 9, 214–217; Florence Powdermaker, "Psychotherapy of Adolescents," *Amer. J. Psychiatr.*, 1936, 92, 1205–1212.

[5] A. A. Schneiders, *Personal Adjustment and Mental Health* (New York: Rinehart, 1955), p. 535.

the *relief of symptoms;* in still others it may be *personality growth.* Certainly the aims of guidance are different from those of counseling, and by the same rule the aims of counseling are different from those of psychotherapy. The main purpose of guidance is to help the youngster *chart a steady course toward a particular goal.* Thus the guidance officer, in a typical school situation, helps the student in the development of efficient study habits so that he may eventually achieve his goal of a high school education. He will help the youngster learn how to read or to take notes more effectively. He will discuss with him possible educational and vocational goals. He will give information and advice as to the choice of a curriculum. He may instruct the young person in matters of psychosexual development. In all such instances, his principal tools are information, knowledge, and advice imparted in such a manner that the client can arrive at his own reasonable decision.

The aims of counseling are quite different from those of guidance, even though both processes are closely related. Counseling as it is understood today takes a long step beyond guidance into the realm of personality growth and dynamics. As Bordin points out,

We have said that psychological counseling is directly connected with personality development. The implications of this reach farther than is at first evident. They mean, for one thing, that when a troubled person comes to the psychological counselor, as he often does, with concrete decisions to be made, specific problems to be solved, or particular situations to be clarified, the *primary goal* for the psychological counselor is not to contribute to the resolution of these immediate situations. That major goal lies farther ahead. The *primary goal* requires understanding of the obstacles

to further personality growth and development that are typified by this person's rather specific and, for the time being, limited difficulty. The counselor aims to contribute to the removal of these deeper-lying personal obstacles and to bring about the reactivation of the psychological growth processes in that person. Thus, the solution of the immediate problem is one desired outcome, of course, but it alone is not a sufficient measure of the psychological counselor's usefulness to his client.[6]

* * *

Psychological counseling has as its aim influencing the individual's maturation and integration at the profoundest level possible. How general and how far reaching will be the effect of a particular counseling relationship will depend, assuming fully competent counseling, upon the particular needs of the client and his readiness for growth.[7]

This viewpoint is echoed in many places, and the emphasis is always the same — on the removal of barriers to personal growth and self-realization. Thus Curran, building on the concepts supplied by Carl Rogers, says:

The purpose of counseling, therefore, is to facilitate this research and deliberation of reason. Its aim is related to the immediate circumstances of a man's life. Even though he may know in general what he should do, the problems of a particular situation can be so wrapped up with intense emotion that, sometimes, even to try to work them out without help seems only to encourage precipitation and cause him to rush violently into a series of actions more unreasonable and sometimes even more tragic than before. People in such personal difficulties need a means by which they can bring to light the fundamental

---

[6] E. S. Bordin, *Psychological Counseling* (New York: Appleton-Century-Crofts, © 1955), p. 9. For a similar statement applied to the guidance and counseling of students, see T. A. C. Rennie and L. E. Woodward, *Mental Health in Modern Society* (New York: Commonwealth Fund, 1948), pp. 282–383.

[7] E. S. Bordin, *ibid.*, p. 13.

motives behind their confused and disordered urges so they can understand the hidden values and goals of their lives. Because they are failing to move toward these, they are in conflict.[8]

This idea is directly in line with that of Rogers who points out that counseling

aims directly toward the greater independence and integration of the individual rather than hoping that such results will accrue if the counselor assists in solving the problem. The individual and not the problem is the focus. The aim is not to solve this problem, but to assist the individual to grow, so that he can cope with the present problem and with later problems in a better-integrated fashion. If he can gain enough integration so that he can handle this problem in more independent, more responsible, less confused, better organized ways, then he will also handle new problems in that manner.[9]

From these quotations, then, it is clear that whereas guidance is oriented toward the solution of the immediate problem, counseling is specifically directed toward *personality growth and integration*.

While our primary aim here is to define the processes of guidance and counseling, we may mention briefly that the aims of psychotherapy go one step beyond those of guidance and counseling. Psychotherapy is also interested in personality growth, but it is directed also toward readjustment and mental health. It strives for increased integration, dissipation of unhealthy personality traits, increased self-esteem, greater efficiency, desensitization, increase in resistance, and emotional stability. It seeks to promote insight and self-knowledge, a whole-some orientation to reality, adequate need-gratification, and increased ego strength and security. In the process of psychotherapy, the patient will experience release of pent-up feelings (catharsis), reduction of frustration, conflict, and threat, adjustment and integration of bodily functions, and reduction of disabling symptoms. Psychotherapy, as distinct from counseling, reaches into the deeper recesses of personality and works toward a more complete reconstruction of the personality. This brief statement should not be construed as a complete account of the aims of psychotherapy, but it does convey an idea of how the aims of psychotherapy differ from those of guidance and counseling.[10]

Definitions. In general, therefore, guidance is a process by which one person strives to help others toward the solving of an immediate problem, or toward a better orientation to some life area. Counseling is a process by which a person (the counselor) strives to help another person (the client) rid himself of negative and inhibiting personality factors and thus promote self-realization and personality growth. Psychotherapy is essentially a *clinical* process by which a person (the therapist) strives to promote better adjustment, mental health, and personality integration in another person (the patient) by a reduction of symptomatic or pathological behavior, inadequate personality traits, or developmental failures through analysis and reduction of dynamic factors or conditions that have caused the personality disorder. Ordinarily, these processes are carried on in

[8] Reprinted with permission from C. A. Curran, *Counseling in Catholic Life and Education* (New York: Macmillan, 1952), p. 36.

[9] C. R. Rogers, *Counseling and Psychotherapy* (New York: Houghton Mifflin, 1942), pp. 28–29.

[10] See E. G. Williamson, *Counseling Adolescents*, pp. 6–9; and A. A. Schneiders, *op. cit.*, pp. 547–553. See also S. Berman, "Psychotherapeutic Techniques With Adolescents," *Amer. J. Orthopsychiat.*, 1954, 24, 238–245.

a person-to-person situation, in which the interview technique plays a leading role. However, in recent years, we have witnessed the growth of *group approaches* to guidance, counseling, and psychotherapy, and in some instances with considerable success. While the same set of principles will characterize both group and individual approaches, it must be remembered that group situations involve dynamic factors that are not present in the ordinary interview situation.[11]

Conditions of Guidance and Counseling. Every counselor, if he is to be effective in his work, must keep in mind certain conditions that influence and determine good counseling. First of all, every counselor should learn *to adapt treatment procedures* to the demands and characteristics of the treatment situation, and *to make necessary changes* during the course of guidance or counseling. As Wolberg says in another connection:

> Rigidity in the therapist is a destructive force in psychotherapy. Unfortunately it is a common occurrence whenever there is tenacious adherence to any one "system" of psychotherapy. Rigidity prevents the therapist from coordinating his approach with the exigencies of the therapeutic situation. Too zealous regard for the sanctity of any system must of necessity reduce his therapeutic effectiveness; for, the requirements of the therapeutic interpersonal relationship call forth promptings that defy methodologic bounds. Flexibility is not only essential in the execution of technical procedures, but in other aspects of therapy; such as, the defining of goals and the setting of standards. Flexibility is also necessary in interpreting the value system of the culture, in order to permit of the relaxation

of certain austere demands in the face of which a change in the patient's severity of conscience may be thwarted.[12]

Second, it is important to adjust counseling *to the nature of the problem*.[13] It is foolhardy and sometimes even dangerous to give advice to a person whose basic problem is personality disintegration. To advise a psychotic to "pull yourself together" or an alcoholic to "be a man" or to "show a little will power," or an adolescent to "stop feeling guilty," is not worth the time it takes to utter such advice. Similarly, a problem in vocational orientation may respond very well to a guidance approach in one instance, and very poorly in another, because of the different "setting" of problems as they occur in different people.[14] It is for this reason that some kind of a diagnosis must be made in the initial stages of contact if one is to follow the proper procedures. It could be a serious mistake to undertake guidance or counseling of a student when actually he should be referred as quickly as possible to a psychiatrist for psychotherapy. The organization of problems in terms of treatment indicated in Figure 32, therefore, should be of help to the counselor in determining what path to follow.

A third factor of considerable magnitude to consider in determining

---

[11] See R. Hoppock, *Group Guidance* (New York: McGraw-Hill, 1949). A more informal method of group guidance is discussed in H. Geist, "Adolescents and Parents Talk It Over," *Understanding the Child*, 1955, 24, 98–102.

[12] By permission from L. R. Wolberg, *The Technique of Psychotherapy* (New York: Grune & Stratton, 1954), p. 143. See also E. G. Williamson, *Counseling Adolescents*, p. 102, for an expression of the same viewpoint.

[13] See A. A. Schneiders, *op. cit.*, pp. 534–535.

[14] Williamson emphasizes the same fact and points out that vocational guidance practices have been considerably broadened because of a deeper appreciation of the influence of personality factors on job aptitude. E. G. Williamson, *Counseling Adolescents*, p. 5. See also A. S. Thompson, "Personality Dynamics and Vocational Counseling," *Personnel Guid. J.*, 1960, 38, 350–357.

procedures is the *client's personality*, including such things as age, sex, intelligence, education, maturity level, emotional make-up, personality organization, dependence on symptomatology, and degree of resistance. Sex and age differences are quite real, as we know, and therefore the counseling approach must be adapted to these two conditions. Similarly, intelligence and education will alter the course of guidance and counseling, because the response of the client to counseling procedures is always affected by knowledge, insight, and perceptive ability. Also, the client will respond to counseling or fail to respond in terms of his level of maturity. This is the reason why guidance is sometimes very effective with some teen-agers and very ineffective with others. In point of fact, it may well be that immaturity is the client's central problem, in which case counseling rather than guidance would be indicated. In still other instances, the personality is so poorly organized, or the dependence on symptomatology is so deep and long standing, that nothing short of intensive psychotherapy would work. All such personal factors play a part in determining the procedures to be used in any given case. Not only that, but they will also influence the specific type of counseling or therapy in each case. For example, in one instance it might be very helpful to use a *nondirective* or *client-centered* approach, whereas in another it might be better to use a very direct approach. Similarly, psychoanalysis is particularly well adapted to some problems, whereas interview therapy is better adapted to others.

It is equally obvious that *characteristics of the counselor* will determine the procedures to be used. Some counselors work very well in the area of guidance, others with nondirective counseling, and still others with the directive approach. Such choices will depend upon the personality of the counselor, his theoretical orientation, and particularly his experience and training in the field of counseling or psychotherapy. Ordinarily, the person who is trained in professional education is oriented toward formal guidance procedures and possibly nondirective counseling, whereas the person trained in the field of clinical psychology will tend toward psychological counseling and psychotherapy. In any event, the important rule to follow is that the counselor should use procedures with which he works most effectively.

On this point it should be further emphasized that the effective counselor *must possess the personal characteristics that are essential to good counseling.*[15] Above all, he must be able to inspire confidence, have a deep and abiding interest in people, be able to listen, possess clearly defined objectives in counseling, and have respect for the dignity and value of the human person. In addition, he himself must be emotionally stable and well adjusted, which means freedom from damaging feelings, crippling defensive mechanisms, and symptomatology. The good counselor possesses self-esteem, self-respect, security, sensitivity, objectivity, flexibility, warmth, and ability to establish empathic relationships. Finally, the counselor must possess integrity based upon sound ethical principles and right attitudes. While he himself possesses a sound philosophy of counseling, and a well-defined system of values, he never exploits the client to his own advantage, nor does he ruthlessly impose his own

---

[15] For a thorough discussion of traits essential to counseling, see E. G. Williamson, *Counseling Adolescents*, Chap. 10.

ideas and value system on those who come to him for help. At all times, he must convince the client of his personal interest in him, and assure him of the complete confidentiality that characterizes all such relationships.

One other factor to consider in dealing with the conditions that determine good counseling is the *person-environment relationship*. Skilled counselors are acutely aware of the fact that human personality, behavior, and problems reflect the environment within which the client develops and of which he is a part. As Gardner Murphy points out,

> It is becoming recognized more and more clearly that what individual therapy can accomplish is limited by the nature of the polarity of the situation between physician and patient. The therapeutic interview is only one kind of situation, and it does not necessarily prevent the patient's subsequent failure when he confronts the other situations of which his life is comprised. For this reason psychiatry is making more and more use of situational therapy, is placing the patient in a world which will bring out what is wanted, a world like the one he has to face.[16]

Therefore, where high school and college students particularly are concerned, it may be necessary to work with the parents or guardians of the student as well as the student himself. This is particularly true when the client's problem revolves around conflicts at home, as they so often do in the adolescent period. Counseling, no matter how expert or efficient, may not be able to offset the limitations of damaging family relationships.

By the same rule, good counseling requires a *proper setting*. A counseling situation should always insure complete confidentiality, the exclusion of distractions as much as possible, the promotion of the client's comfort, and whatever facilities that are necessary to bring counseling to a successful conclusion. The idea that counseling can be done in any circumstances as long as there is a good relationship between counselor and client is indefensible. The counseling situation is as important in its own way as the relationship between the client and his environment.

GUIDANCE AND COUNSELING PROCEDURES

Accumulation of Evidence. In both guidance and counseling, it is important to have as much information about the client as possible. Whether we are dealing with a problem in vocational guidance, choice of curriculum, parent-child relationships, interpersonal relationships, disabling neurotic symptoms, or fits of depression, we need to know a great deal about the background of the client, past performance, intellectual level, history of emotional disturbance, and similar factors. In most circumstances, this process of accumulating evidence can be best initiated by a *personal history*, which can be used to secure certain vital statistics that are necessary to initiate the process of counseling. These background facts can then serve as a basis for the *initial interview*, which is one of the most important steps in guidance and counseling. This interview is important in setting up a good relationship between client and counselor, in defining the problem that requires attention, and in laying the groundwork for subsequent counseling. Failure to exploit the initial interview to advantage may disrupt the counseling relationship at the very start with the

---

[16] Reprinted with permission from G. Murphy, *Personality* (New York: Harper, 1947), p. 885.

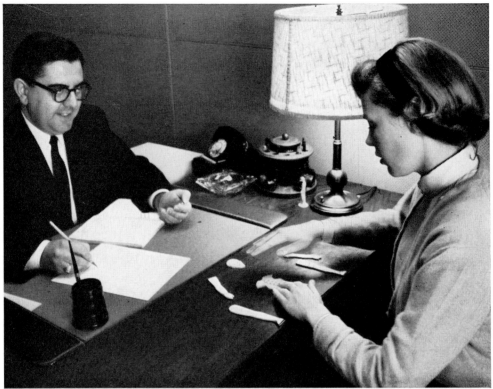

Testing is one way to find out important things about adolescents.

result that the client never returns for subsequent interviews.

Depending on the nature of the problem, local circumstances, time available, and the like, it may be desirable or necessary to supplement the personal history and initial interview with other data that shed light on the problem. In some instances, a *physical examination* may be indicated because of the possibility that the presenting problem is directly related to an underlying physical condition. This procedure is particularly advisable whenever there is the possibility of incorrect diagnosis because of failure to take into account the physical health or make-up of the individual. Similarly, in problems of vocational orientation, educational fail-

ure, and the like, it may be worthwhile to utilize tests and inventories that will shed light on the client's intellectual potential, reading proficiency, patterns of interest, special aptitudes, and basic personality characteristics. This evaluation of the client's abilities and potentialities is part of the *psychological examination* which is used extensively in guidance and counseling situations. When a problem takes a turn in the direction of emotional disorder, neurotic disturbance, or psychotic symptomatology, the psychological examination may be extended to include other testing procedures such as individual mental examination, and projective tests like the Rorschach and the Sentence Completion Blank. Here again we see why it is important in the initial evaluation of the problem to determine as precisely as possible the exact nature of the difficulty.

Evaluation and Diagnosis. The several steps involved in gathering information are pointed toward an understanding of the problem, evaluation of the client's adjustment, and diagnosis. Evaluation and diagnosis, in turn, are antecedent to treatment procedures. While formal diagnosis should be reserved to the clinical psychologist or psychiatrist in their approach to problems of psychological disorder, the guidance counselor must also attempt to identify and classify the problems brought to his attention, and to determine the underlying causes and conditions that contributed to the development of the problem.[17] The counselor is failing in his responsibility if he confuses a vocational problem with a personality difficulty, or a moral problem with one that is basically psychological in nature. He also fails to meet the demands of good counseling if he does not recognize the existence of neurotic trends, psychological mechanisms, or personality disorganization. In any case, no matter how simple the problem may seem on the surface, there is always the possibility that emotional and psychological factors are at work, and that to understand and to resolve the difficulty a careful evaluation must be made. It must always be remembered that any problem *is embedded in the personality of the client* and will therefore be influenced and conditioned by the client's distinctive characteristics.

The Interview Process. Of the various procedures that can be used to help young people solve their problems and to de-

velop a more adequate personality, the face-to-face interview technique is certainly the one most widely used. And, depending on how it is used, it can become a very effective instrument for guidance and counseling. All that we have said, of course, about the conditions of effective counseling apply to the interview situation. And with these conditions in mind, the counselor must skillfully employ the interview to elicit necessary information, provide an outlet for important feelings, and steer the counseling process to a successful conclusion.

> At the very heart of the counseling process is the interview. Whether it is 15 or 90 minutes long, whether the participants explore feelings or discuss facts and schedules, whether or not it is supplemented by test scores and information from the files — whatever changes counseling brings are related most closely to the way this time is spent. The would-be counselor should direct his attention first to this most indispensable skill.[18]

In view of this crucial role of the interview, what objectives should the counselor keep in mind, and what rules should he follow?[19] Naturally, the primary objective of the interview is *to help the client*; and all other aims are subsidiary to this one. The counselor, therefore, must always focus his attention and skills on eliciting that information, and those feelings, conflicts, frustrations, and problems that will help him to understand his client, and that will lead eventually to the achievement of specific counseling aims. These aims — whether to solve an

---

[17] See E. G. Williamson, *Counseling Adolescents*, Chaps. 8, 9; A. A. Schneiders, *op. cit.,* p. 541.

[18] Leona E. Tyler, *The Work of the Counselor* (New York: Appleton-Century-Crofts, © 1953), p. 23.

[19] See R. L. Kahn and C. F. Cannell, *The Dynamics of Interviewing* (New York: Wiley, 1957), Chap. 4. See also C. E. Erickson, *The Counseling Interview* (Englewood Cliffs, N. J.: Prentice-Hall, 1950), pp. 155–157.

Counseling is important to teen-agers.

Fordham University

immediate problem, relieve pent-up feelings, tension, or anxiety, or to remove barriers to personality development — should be clearly formulated in the initial stages of counseling, and then reformulated as counseling progresses. At all times, the interview should be directed toward the achievement of these aims. Therefore, the counselor should be wary of digressions into irrelevant material, especially when such digressions are used as defensive tactics against the uncovering of important information.

By the same rule, the interview should always be organized in terms of *proper time limits*. Generally, the interview should not last more than 45 minutes to one hour, and should be scheduled in such a way that it is convenient to both the counselor and the counselee. Anxiety about time limits, particularly on the part of the counselee, can disrupt the work of the counselor. Depending always on the nature of the problem, the frequency of interviews should ordinarily be limited to one period a week, so that the counseling process can proceed in an unhurried, orderly fashion. The number of interviews is determined by the complexity of the problem, and the success

with which the counselor achieves his aims. Interviews should never be continued when it becomes clear that the aims of counseling are not being realized.

In the interview situation, a correct relationship between counselor and counselee must be maintained at all times. While the counselor should do everything possible to put the counselee at ease, and to create a warm, friendly, accepting atmosphere, the interview must not be put on a personal-friendly basis, nor must it be allowed to degenerate into a "bull session." The counselor must clearly identify his role as a professional person engaged in the business of helping people to solve their problems, and must always maintain this professional atmosphere. A too-close relationship with the client will quickly destroy the counseling process. If these few rules are followed carefully, supplemented of course by the conditions of effective counseling described earlier, the interview will become a very efficient counseling tool.

The Process of Referral. Whenever careful evaluation or diagnosis indicates the existence of pathological processes or prepsychotic trends, the guidance counselor should consider the possibility of referral to another person or agency for therapeutic treatment. Similarly, it is necessary at times to refer clients for reading difficulties, moral and religious problems, economic difficulties and the like.[20] This rule should be applied whenever the problem reaches beyond the competence of the counselor. Like counseling, the process of referral demands a great deal of skillful handling. It can be accomplished successfully only when there is a good relationship between the counselor and client, and when the most careful consideration is given to the selection of the person to whom the referral is made. The client must be provided with clear insight into the reasons for the referral, and every effort should be made to instill full confidence in the person to whom referral is made. When these principles are followed closely, referral becomes an important adjunct to the counseling process.

Evaluation of Guidance and Counseling. There are many criteria which we could use to evaluate the processes of guidance

and counseling.[21] Obviously, if the problem presented to the counselor is effectively resolved and the client subsequently makes a better adjustment to his environment, it can be assumed that the counseling process has been brought to a successful conclusion. Similarly, if counseling leads to the reduction of anxiety, the dissipation of hostility, weakening of defensive mechanisms, or a greater degree of happiness and contentment, then it has served a useful purpose. Also, if through counseling the client is in a better position to achieve more clearly defined goals, or to realize his own potentialities, the aims of counseling are clearly realized. In all instances, counseling can be regarded as successful when it promotes the healthy adjustment of the client, and helps him to develop more effective relationships at all levels of human striving.

[20] L. T. Benezet, "Guidance in Moral and Spiritual Values," in M. D. Hardee (ed.), Counseling and Guidance in General Education (New York: World Book, 1955), pp. 73–99.

[21] See C. P. Froehlich, Evaluating Guidance Procedures (Washington, D. C.: Office of Education, Misc., 3310, 1949); Leona Tyler, op. cit., Chap. XII; E. G. Williamson, Counseling Adolescents, pp. 111–125; J. D. O'Dea and F. Zeran, "Evaluating Effects of Counseling," Personnel Guid. J., 1953, 31, 241–244; Ruth Strang, "Criteria of Progress in Counseling and Psychotherapy," J. Clin. Psychol., 1946, 3, 180–183.

SELECTED READINGS

Balser, B. H. (ed.), Psychotherapy of the Adolescent (New York: International Universities Press, 1957).

Blum, M. L., and Balinsky, B., Counseling and Psychology (Englewood Cliffs, N. J.: Prentice-Hall, 1951).

Brayfield, A. H. (ed.), Readings in Modern Methods of Counseling (New York: Appleton-Century-Crofts, 1950).

Burton, A., Case Studies in Counseling and Psychotherapy (Englewood Cliffs, N. J.: Prentice-Hall, 1959).

Curran, C. A., Counseling in Catholic Life and Education (New York: Macmillan, 1952).

Erickson, C. E., The Counseling Interview (Englewood Cliffs, N. J.: Prentice-Hall, 1950).

Hadley, J. M., Clinical and Counseling Psychology (New York: Knopf, 1958).

Hall, R. K., and Lauwerys, J. A. (eds.), The Yearbook of Education, 1955 (New York: World Book, 1955).

Hardee, M. D. (ed.), *Counseling and Guidance in Education* (New York: World Book, 1955).

Jones, A. J., *Principles of Guidance and Pupil Personnel Work*, 4 ed. (New York: McGraw-Hill, 1951).

Kahn, R. L., and Cannell, C. F., *The Dynamics of Interviewing* (New York: Wiley, 1957).

McKinney, F., *Counseling for Personal Adjustment in Schools and Colleges* (Boston: Houghton Mifflin, 1958).

Pepinsky, H. R., and Pepinsky, P. N., *Counseling: Theory and Practice* (New York: Ronald, 1954).

Rogers, C. R., *Client-Centered Therapy* (Boston: Houghton Mifflin, 1951).

Traxler, A. E., *Techniques of Guidance* (New York: Harper, 1945).

Tyler, L. E., *The Work of the Counselor* (New York: Appleton-Century-Crofts, 1953).

Williamson, E. G., *Counseling Adolescents* (New York: McGraw-Hill, 1950).

GLOSSARY

Abnormal — Deviating from the usual, average, or normal, in a quantitative as well as a qualitative sense; sometimes used to mean pathological.

Adjustment — The process of coping with internal and external demands, stresses, conflicts, frustrations, and problem situations by means of personal response, and by which the organism strives to become more adequately and efficiently related to itself and its environment.

Adolescence — The developmental period between childhood and adulthood, beginning with pubescence and marked by gradual and continuous maturation of organic, psychological, and social factors in personality.

Adrenal Glands — A pair of endocrine or ductless glands, located over the kidneys, which have an important relation to emotional responses.

Affective Processes — Psychological functions, including feelings and emotions, marked by affect or hedonic tone.

Anxiety — Fearfulness or apprehension regarding one's self or some external event. It is usually intense and disturbing. When no real danger or threat exists, it is called neurotic anxiety.

Apathy — Emotional indifference; marked absence of feeling or emotion in situations that normally evoke such responses. Often observed in adolescents faced with serious personal problems that they cannot cope with.

Apperception — A process of integrating new knowledge with knowledge already in the learner's possession.

Aptitude — An interest in and special capacity for certain forms of response or achievement.

Asexual — Nonsexual; generally refers to a period of development which precedes the maturation of sexual structures and functions.

Atrophy — Gradual reduction in structure and functional efficiency of an organ, e.g., muscular atrophy resulting from paralysis.

Attitude — A relatively permanent determining tendency to think or act in a characteristic manner with reference to some object or value.

Autistic — Inordinately subjective or self-centered; directed toward self.

Autonomic Nervous System — That part of the nervous system which regulates involuntary responses, such as digestion, glandular secretion, etc.

Autosexuality — A phase of sexual development or response in which desire, interest, or behavior is directed toward self.

Behavior — The whole complex of observable and measurable activities of a living organism, including muscular movements, language, motor habits, and interpersonal responses.

Behaviorism — A system of psychological thought which emphasizes the study of behavior rather than mental life, and tends to exclude concepts developed within the framework of traditional introspective psychology.

Behavior Pattern — A set of responses organized in time, and manifesting some degree of sameness or stereotypy in the sequence in which they occur.

Biosocial — A term used to refer to processes or traits that are determined jointly by the biological nature of the organism and the social environment of which it is a part.

Catharsis — The process of release of disturbing ideas, conflicts, tensions, and anxiety, by emotionally reliving incidents

453

of the past and developing insight into the causes of the difficulty.

Central Nervous System — That part of the nervous system that includes the brain and spinal cord.

Character — A dynamic disposition within the total personality to feel, think, or act in terms of regulative principles; the organized totality of the moral responses of a person.

Chronic — Pertaining to a condition or disorder that progresses slowly and is long continued.

Coefficient of Correlation — The numerical expression of the degree of relationship between paired values.

Cognitive — Of or pertaining to cognition or knowledge; knowing processes as distinct from affective or striving processes.

Compensation — A mechanism by which personal inadequacies or deficiencies are obscured by direct or vicarious achievement.

Compulsion — A strong and sometimes irresistible impulse to perform some act or ritual even though it is conceived to be unreasonable.

Conative — Pertaining to purposive or goal-directed activity; appetitive tendencies or acts resulting from desire, impulse, etc.

Conditioning — A process of learning or behavior change by which originally ineffective stimuli become effective in producing a response.

Conflict — A state of mind, sometimes prolonged, that occurs when two drives or motives associated with incompatible behavior patterns occur simultaneously and are equally strong. Conflict can also be extrapersonal when it involves incompatible motives of two or more persons.

Congenital — Present at or before birth, but not hereditary.

Correlation — A relation between two variables of such a nature that changes in the one are accompanied by definite changes in the other.

Cultural Determinism — The viewpoint that personality and behavior are wholly or in large part determined by cultural factors.

Culture — The pattern of customs, mores, beliefs, traditions, and practices that characterize a large social group.

Defense Mechanisms — Adjustive reactions, usually unconscious, designed to protect the individual from personal limitations or from external stresses and frustrations.

Delinquency — Socially nonconforming behavior committed by persons not legally of age.

Depression — A mental condition involving emotional dejection, unpleasant feelings, and a sense of foreboding.

Development — Progressive, internal changes in the functions and capacities of a living organism which begin at conception and are directed toward complete maturation.

Developmental Psychology — That branch of psychology which studies the human organism in transition from birth to adulthood. It emphasizes the investigation of physical, mental, and social changes that characterize different levels of development.

Disorientation — A state of confusion about place, time, or personal identity.

Drive — A dynamic tendency, based on or related to need, which impels the organism toward some form of goal-seeking behavior.

Dynamic Psychology — That branch of psychology which studies the entire range of human motivation, including needs, drives, desires, emotions, attitudes, and the like.

Dysfunction — Disturbance, impairment, or abnormality in the functioning of an organ.

Ecology — A branch of biology which investigates the relationships between organisms and their environment.

Ego — The whole person signified by the pronoun I; that part of the person that mediates conscious experiences; in psychoanalysis, that part of the psyche that mediates between the Id and reality.

Egocentrism — A mechanism used to force recognition and obscure inadequacy by boastfulness and self-aggrandizement.

Emotion — A complex affective response

characterized by feeling, excitement, and bodily changes.

Endocrine Glands — A group of organs that secrete internally and pour their secretions directly into the blood or lymph.

Endocrinology — A branch of biology that investigates the structures and functions of the endocrine glands.

Erotic — Of or pertaining to sex, or sexual love.

Euphoria — Exaggerated feelings of well-being, often unfounded.

Feeling — The experience of pleasantness or unpleasantness; affective states or tendencies, like hostility, inferiority, etc., that grow out of other emotional experiences.

Fetus — The embryo in its more advanced stages of development.

Fixation — The arrest of emotional and other development at the child or adolescent level.

Frustration — The blocking of motivational tendencies or behavior; hindrance in effecting adequate adjustments.

Functional Disorder — A disability without known alteration or damage to underlying structure. Thus a *functional psychosis* is a mental disease without known organic cause.

Genetic Psychology — A branch of psychology that studies mentality and behavior in terms of their origin and background in the individual or in the organic species.

Gestalt Theory — A viewpoint in psychology that emphasizes the unitary nature of mental processes and behavior as opposed to the elementarism of behavioristic or structural theory.

Gonads — The male or female sex glands, in which germ cells develop.

Guilt, Sense of — The feeling or conviction of having contravened some principle, rule, or law. When unconscious and morbid, it is referred to as pathological guilt.

Hedonism — The theory or viewpoint that the primary aim or goal of all human conduct is pleasure.

Heterosexual — Pertaining to the other sex, or to relations between the sexes.

Homoerotic (Homosexual) — Of or pertaining to sexual or libidinous tendencies and acts directed toward members of the same sex.

Hormone — A specific chemical substance, secreted by an endocrine gland, that includes functional changes in other organs.

Hostility — A feeling or attitude, often unconscious, involving behavior detrimental to individuals or groups against whom the hostility is directed.

Hyperthyroidism — A pathological condition, generally accompanied by hyperexcitability, caused by excessive secretion of the thyroids. The opposite condition is *hypothyroidism*, which is characterized by general sluggishness of reaction.

Hypochondria — Morbid concern about one's health.

Hysteria — A psychoneurotic disorder characterized by a wide variety of functional symptoms normally caused by organic disease, these symptoms being utilized for adjustive purposes in the reduction of conflict.

Ideals — Concepts converted into standards of excellence because of their extraordinary merit. Ideals may be abstract or personal in nature.

Identification — The unconscious assumption of identity with another person or group for the enhancement of prestige or personal worth.

Inferiority, Attitude of — An attitude or complex, usually unconscious, engendered by feelings of inadequacy, lack of self-confidence, failure, etc., and leading to unfavorable comparison with others.

Innate — Inborn, natural; existing from conception or birth.

Insight — In mental hygiene and psychotherapy, the understanding and evaluation of one's own characteristics, weaknesses, motivations, etc., by which mental health and adjustment are enhanced.

Integration — A process (or condition) whereby diverse elements in any structure or system are organized into a harmonious, co-ordinated whole. It is basic to mental health and adjustment.

Intellect — The capacity to generalize, perceive relationships, judge and reason; also, a factor that distinguishes human from subhuman organisms.

Intelligence — The ability of an organism to perceive relationships, solve problems, and adapt itself efficiently to personal or environmental demands; briefly, the capacity to carry on abstract thinking; the measurable aspects of intellect.

Introception — A process whereby a conscious organism accepts and incorporates within itself qualities, characteristics, etc., of objective reality.

Introjection — A psychological mechanism by which external qualities (especially of other persons) are adopted into the self.

Introspection — Subjective observation of mental phenomena; an examination by the subject himself of his own experiences and mental processes; conscious reflection.

Level of Aspiration — A subjective standard by which one judges his own performance; the degree of an individual's striving, especially as it compares with the strivings of others in the group.

Maladjustment — Inability to meet personal and environmental demands and to resolve conflicts and frustrations in a wholesome or efficient manner.

Maturation — The process whereby organisms, processes, or functions reach a stage of complete growth or development. The state of full development is called maturity.

Mechanism — In psychology, an acquired response by which self-respect, ego integrity, etc., are maintained without the use of choice or deliberation.

Mental Hygiene — The development and use of principles and practices relating to the preservation of mental health and adjustment, and the prevention of mental and personality disorders.

Mentality — A term used to refer to mental processes, both conscious and unconscious, taken as a whole.

Migraine — A psychosomatic disorder characterized predominantly by severe headaches on one side and also by nausea and sensory disturbances.

Mood — A pervasive and relatively persistent affective state which often results from strong emotional response; also an internal state of readiness to respond behaviorally in certain ways.

Mores — Customs which characterize a social group and which are considered right and necessary to the welfare of the group.

Motive — Technically, any factor, intellectually evaluated, which stimulates volition or rational conduct. In psychology, the term is often used for any factor, such as need, drive, or instinct, that stimulates a response.

Narcissism — Self-love; a psychoanalytic term to denote libidinal interest in one's own body; admiration or love of self.

Need — A tension aroused in the organism by the absence or deprivation of some object, quality, or experience required for its well-being.

Negative Identification — The unconscious rejection of traits, attitudes, values, etc., of another person or group with whom one is ordinarily closely related.

Nervousness — A chronic emotional state marked by tenseness, restlessness, and irritability, and often manifested in behavioral symptoms like nail biting.

Neurasthenia — A neurosis marked by chronic fatigue, headache, chronic irritability, and vague aches and pains.

Neurosis — A relatively mild psychological disorder, the cause of which is psychogenic rather than organic; hence the term "psychoneurosis."

Neurotic — Pertaining to neurosis; a person suffering from a neurosis.

Obsession — Any idea or idea complex with a strong emotional quality (usually disagreeable) that forces itself into and disturbs the normal processes of thought.

Oedipus Complex — A psychoanalytic term to designate an excessive love relation between son and mother, which is accompanied by hostility toward the father.

Ontogenetic — Of or pertaining to the development of the individual organism.

Organic Psychosis — A mental disorder or disease caused by injury to or pathology of the nervous system.

Organismic — Of or pertaining to organisms considered as functional totalities.

Paranoia — A psychosis characterized by systematized fixed delusions, usually of a grandiose and persecutory nature.

Personality — The organized, emergent totality of a human organism's individual characteristics, dispositions, mannerisms, and values that regulate his adjustments to self and environment.

Phantasy-thinking — Daydreaming; thinking that is determined by needs, desires, or frustrations.

Phobia — A strong, morbid, persistent fear, usually of unknown origin.

Precocious — Premature or advanced development of physical or mental functions in childhood.

Prognosis — A prediction, based on diagnosis, of the probable outcome of a disease or disorder.

Projection — A mechanism by which one's own weaknesses, failures, or undesirable traits are attributed to external sources.

Projective Techniques — Specialized instruments, such as the Rorschach inkblot test, for the investigation of personal traits and characteristics.

Psychiatry — A branch of medicine concerned with the diagnosis, treatment, and care of persons suffering from mental or personality disorders.

Psychoanalysis — A theory and method of treatment, originated by Sigmund Freud, relating to mental and personality disorders.

Psychogenic — Pertaining to causes or conditions that are psychological in nature.

Psychological Determinism — The viewpoint that all human conduct results from such factors as needs, emotions, and habits, rather than from self-determined choices.

Psychological Field — A term used to denote all those factors or variables which, at any given moment, affect or determine an individual's reactions.

Psychological Freedom — Free will or free choice; the ability of a person, when conditions are appropriate, to regulate or control his own responses.

Psychoneurosis — See NEUROSIS.

Psychopathic Personality — A term used to designate persons who are extremely egocentric, asocial, and impulsive, but who manifest no derangement of the cognitive functions.

Psychosexual — Pertaining to sexual functions and development involving psychological processes and conditions.

Psychosis — A severe mental or personality disorder, characterized by disorganization of personality and a progresive deterioration of mental functions.

Psychosocial — A term used to refer to processes or traits that are determined jointly by psychological and social conditions.

Psychosomatic — Of or pertaining to mind and body taken as a unit; also, a specialized field of medical investigation that emphasizes the fundamental unity of mind and body, pertaining to physical disorders, such as peptic ulcer, that are determined by emotional or psychogenic causes.

Psychotherapy — Any clinical process involving psychological methods, such as psychoanalysis or hypnosis, used to treat mental disorders by the reduction of symptoms and underlying causes.

Puberty — The period of life during which the reproductive functions become operative; the beginning of sexual maturation.

Pubescent — Pertaining to the period of puberty; an individual who has just reached the period of puberty.

Rationalization — A mechanism by which an individual justifies doubtful attitudes, beliefs, or actions by giving spurious or inadequate reasons, and thus safeguards his own ego.

Regression — A reversion to an earlier and usually less adjusted pattern of response for purposes of preserving ego integrity or security.

Repression — In psychoanalysis, a mechanism by which emotionally toned experiences, wishes, etc., are unconsciously forced out of or prevented from coming into consciousness because of their undesirable or threatening quality.

Sadism, Sadistic — Sexual abnormality in which sexual gratification is derived from infliction of punishment or cruelty on another person.

Saltation — An abrupt transition or development.

Schizophrenia — A functional psychosis characterized by loss of contact with reality, disorganized thinking, and emotional apathy.

Self-Concept — An individual's personal idea of himself, including his attitudes, ideals, principles, values, and so on; the self-ideal.

Self-Insight (see INSIGHT) — Knowledge of self, of one's own motivations, feelings, prejudices, attitudes, deficiencies, and strengths.

Sentiment — A complex affective disposition organized around some object, person, or event.

Sibling — One of several offspring of the same or different sexes, produced by the same parents.

Social Facilitation — The enhancement of a response by the influence of social stimuli which are in some way related to the response.

Somatic — Organic or bodily as distinguished from mental or psychological.

Sublimation — A mechanism by which the energy of a drive or motive is redirected into other channels of activity.

Superego — In psychoanalysis, that part of the psychic structure that resembles the conscience. It is based upon the introjection of parental restrictions, demands, etc.

Syndrome — A more or less organized group of symptoms occurring together and characteristic of a certain disorder.

Temperament — The affective quality or disposition of a person which regulates his emotional responses.

Therapeutic — Pertaining to the act of healing, or therapy.

Trauma; Traumatic — Of or pertaining to any wound or injury; whether physical or psychological.

Unconscious — Total absence of awareness. In Freudian psychology especially, the mental processes that are inaccessible to the subject but still exert a dynamic influence on mental life and behavior.

Value — A conceptual representation of some aspect of reality in terms of its goodness, worth, or utility; a rational motive.

Volition — A general term applied to all will acts, such as choice, resolution, and intention.

Worry — Persistent nonadjustive thinking about personal problems, characterized by a strong, unpleasant emotional tone.

GUIDEBOOKS AND PAMPHLETS

SELECTED GUIDEBOOKS FOR PARENTS, TEACHERS, AND COUNSELORS

Britton, E. C., and Winans. J. M., *Growing From Infancy to Adulthood* (New York: Appleton-Century-Crofts, 1958).

Catty, Nancy, *Social Training From Childhood to Maturity* (London: Methuen, 1951).

Connell, W. A., and McGannon, J. B., *The Adolescent Boy* (Chicago: Fides, 1958).

Daly, Maureen (ed.), *Profile of Youth* (Philadelphia: Lippincott, 1951).

Gallagher, J. R., *On Adolescence* (Boston: Atlantic, Little, Brown, 1951).

Gilmer, B. von H., *How to Help Your Child Develop Successfully* (Englewood Cliffs, N. J.: Prentice-Hall, 1951).

Gottlieb, B. S., *Understanding Your Adolescent* (New York: Rinehart, 1957).

Government Printing Office, *Counseling Handicapped Adolescents* (Washington, D. C.: Government Printing Office, 1958).

Gran, J. M., *How to Understand and Teach Teenagers* (Minneapolis, Minn.: T. S. Denison, 1958).

Jenkins, Gladys G., Bauer, W. W., and

Schachter, Helen S., *Guidebook for Teenagers* (Chicago: Scott, Foresman, 1955).

Josselyn, Irene M., *The Adolescent and His World* (New York: Family Service Assoc. of America, 1952).

Letton, Mildred C., *Your Child's Leisure Time* (New York: Bur. Publ., Teachers Coll., Columbia University, 1949).

Moser, C. G., *Understanding Girls* (New York: Association Press, 1957).

Overton, Grace S., *Living With Teeners* (Nashville, Tenn.: Broadman Press, 1950).

——— *Living With Parents* (Nashville, Tenn.: Broadman Press, 1954).

Roberts, Dorothy M., *Leadership of Teen-Age Groups* (New York: Association Press, 1950).

Torelle, Ellen, *Your Child's Growth. Health and Happiness* (New York: Knopf, 1951).

Wilkes, E. T., *Family Guide to Teenage Health* (New York: Ronald, 1958).

Wittenberg, R. M., *On Call for Youth; How to Understand and Help Young People* (New York: Association Press, 1955).

SELECTED PAMPHLETS

Escalona, Sibylle, *Understanding Hostility in Children* (Chicago, Ill.: Science Res. Assoc., 1954).

Kirkendall, L. A., *Helping Children Understand Sex* (Chicago, Ill.: Science Res. Assoc., 1952).

Menninger, W. C., *Enjoying Leisure Time* (Chicago, Ill.: Science Res. Assoc., 1950).

Remmers, H. H., and Hackett, C. G., *What Are Your Problems?* (Chicago, Ill.: Science Res. Assoc., 1951).

Ridenour, Nina, *Building Self-Confidence in Children* (Chicago, Ill.: Science Res. Assoc., 1954).

Seashore, R. H., and Van Dusen, A. C., *How to Solve Your Problems* (Chicago: Science Res. Assoc., 1950).

459

Ullman, Frances, *Getting Along With Brothers and Sisters* (Chicago: Science Res. Assoc., 1950).

——— *Life With Brothers and Sisters* Chicago: Science Res. Assoc., 1952).

Witty, P., and Bricker, H, *Your Child and Radio, TV, Comics, and Movies* (Chicago: Science Res. Assoc., 1952).

Wolf, Anna W. M., *What Makes a Good Home? The Beginnings of Emotional Health* (New York: Child Study Assoc. of America, 1951).

FILM BIBLIOGRAPHY

I. GENERAL SOURCES

Fattu, N. A., and Blain, B. B., *Selected Films for Teacher Education: a Bibliography* (Bloomington, Ind.: Indiana University, 1950).

Lekkerkerker, E. C., "Films and Mental Health," *Bull. World Fed. Ment. Hlth.*, 1953, 5, 230–235.

Nichtenhauser, A., Comeman, M. L., and Ruhe, D. S., *Films in Psychiatry, Psychology, and Mental Health* (New York: Health Education Council, 1953).

UNESCO and WHO, *Child Welfare Films; an International Index of Films and Film Strips on the Health and Welfare of Children* (Paris and Geneva).

U. S. Dept. Health, Education and Welfare, 3660 *16mm Film Libraries* (Washington, D. C.: Government Printing Office, 1958).

U. S. National Institute of Mental Health, *Mental Health Motion Pictures, 1952: a Selective Guide* (Washington, D. C.: Government Printing Office, 1952).

II. FILM SOURCES AND AGENCIES

CIF — Coronet Instructional Films, 65 East South Water, Chicago, Ill.

CMC — Communications Materials Center (Columbia University), 413 West 117th Street, New York, N. Y.

EBF — Encyclopaedia Britannica Films, 342 Madison Ave., New York, N. Y.

IFB — International Film Bureau, 57 East Jackson Blvd., Chicago, Ill.

McGH — McGraw-Hill Films, 330 West 42nd Street, New York, N. Y.

MOT — March of Time, 369 Lexington Ave., New York, N. Y.

NFB — National Film Board of Canada, 1270 Avenue of the Americas, New York, N. Y.

NYU — New York University Film Library, 20 Washington Place, New York, N. Y.

PCR — Psychological Cinema Register, Pennsylvania State University, State College, Pa.

III. SELECTED FILMS FOR ADOLESCENT PSYCHOLOGY AND DEVELOPMENT

All films listed are sixteen millimeter, sound films, unless otherwise indicated.

Act Your Age (CIF). 14 min.
Angry Boy (IFB). 33 min.
Are You Ready for Marriage (CIF). 16 min.
Better Reading (PCR). 13 min.

Children Growing Up With Other People (PCR). 23 min.
Children on Trial (CMC). 62 min.
Conflict (PCR). 18 min.
Confront Your Emotions (CIF). 14 min.
Emotional Health (McGH). 18 min.
Facing Reality (CMC). 12 min.
Families First (PCR). 17 min.

Farewell to Childhood (MHFB). 23 min.
Fears of Children (IFB). 29 min.
Feeling of Depression (NFB). 30 min.
Feeling of Hostility (NFB). 27 min.
Feeling of Rejection (NFB). 23 min.
Getting Along With Parents (PCR). 14 min.
Good Loser (PCR). 14 min.
Head of the House (PCR). 37 min.
Homer Starts to Work (PCR). 10 min.
Learning to Study (PCR). 14 min.
Meaning of Adolescence (PCR). 16 min.
Meeting the Needs of Adolescents (McGH). 19 min.
Meeting Emotional Needs in Childhood (NYU). 33 min.
The Outsider (PCR). 10 min.
Overcoming Fear (PCR). 13 min.
Overdependency (NFB). 32 min.
Physical Aspects of Puberty (PCR). 19 min.

Planning for Success (PCR). 10 min.
Planning Your Career (PCR). 16 min.
Problem Children (NYU). 20 min.
Promoting Pupil Adjustment (PCR). 20 min.
Psychology for Living (McGH). (5 films on emotional maturity, facing reality, etc.). 9–15 min. each.
Self-conscious Guy (CIF). 10 min.
Shy Guy (CIF). 13 min.
Sibling Relations and Personality (McGH). 22 min.
Social Development (McGH). 16 min.
Social-Sex Attitudes in Adolescence (McGH). 21 min.
Unconscious Motivation (NYU). 38 min.
Understanding Your Emotions (CIF). 13 min.
Understanding Your Ideals (CIF). 13 min.

INDEX